CW01646900

MASTER of DEATH

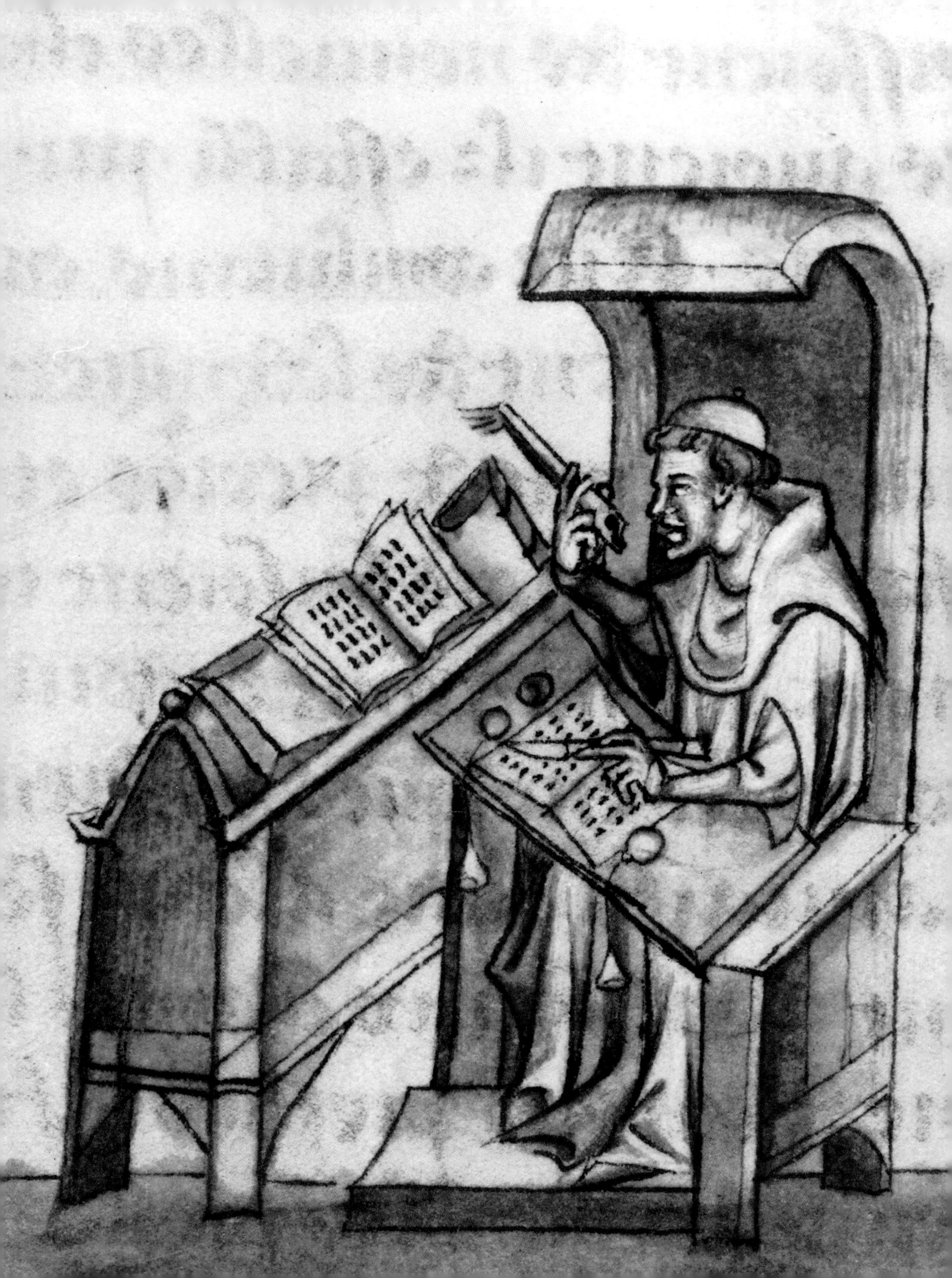

Michael Camille

MASTER of DEATH

The Lifeless Art of **PIERRE REMIET** Illuminator

YALE UNIVERSITY PRESS
New Haven & London 1996

For Stuart

Frontispiece: Remiet. London, British Library, MS Lansdowne 1179, fol. 34v. *Miroir historial*. Seneca and his books.

Copyright © 1996 by Yale University

All rights reserved. This book may not be reproduced, in whole or in part, in any form (beyond that copying permitted by Sections 107 and 108 of the U.S. Copyright Law and except by reviewers for the public press), without written permission from the publishers.

Designed by Faith Brabenec Hart
Set in Linotron Bembo by Best-set Typesetter Ltd., Hong Kong
Printed in Hong Kong through World Print Ltd.

Library of Congress Cataloging-in-Publication Data

Camille, Michael.
Master of death: the lifeless art of Pierre Remiet, illuminator
Michael Camille.
p. cm.
Includes bibliographical references and index.
ISBN 0-300-06457-8
1. Remiet, Pierre–Criticism and interpretation. 2. Illumination of books and manuscripts, Medieval–France–Paris. 3. Illumination of books and manuscripts, French–France–Paris. 4. Death in art. I. Title.
ND3146.R45C35 1996
745.6′7′092–dc20 95-9088
CIP

A catalogue record for this book is available from the British Library.

Contents

Preface vii

Introduction: DEATH IN MINIATURE 1

1. A GAP IN THE TEXT 11
2. THE BIRTH OF DEATH 57
3. THE LIFE OF DEATH 97
4. THE FACE OF DEATH 131
5. THE BODY OF DEATH 169
6. THE DEATH OF DEATH 214

Appendix: MANUSCRIPTS CONTAINING MINIATURES BY PIERRE REMIET 249

Abbreviations 255

Notes to the Text 257

Index 281

Preface

Since the demise of the roll in late antique culture until the arrival of the scrolling computer screen in our own time, the turning page has helped construct our notions of witness and identity, not only in recording past voices but in transmitting the visual traces, the smudges, erasures and tears of material lived existence. As you stand browsing at the library or bookstore, or in a more private space where you might even have begun to read this book, it has already, even after a sentence and a half, become bound up in the narrative of your own opening and closing. Its sturdy white paper alone will outlive your frail flesh by a hundred years. Such a statement sits less well in our minds than it used to. Perhaps you are already repelled by the morbid subject matter announced by the title page and you will read no further. Death does not sell well, my publisher has cautioned me. By contrast, medieval readers, for whom every tome was a tomb, every inscription a *memento mori*, who looked to the authority of dead writers and ultimately to that volume fastened with seven seals to be opened at the end of time, there could never be enough death. This book attempts to understand this morbid appetite in a series of images made by one fourteenth-century illuminator in books that no one looks at any more. Or so it seemed, when I opened an enormous volume of the *Bible historiale* in the municipal library nestling in the shadow of the cathedral at Soissons, as clouds of dust rose from its thick crackling parchment pages revealing sheer sheets of gold leaf and sparkling miniatures that seemed to have been shut within its boards, totally undisturbed, for centuries. The study of manuscripts is a kind of necrophilia. Writing about a dead person whose only remains are held in these sepulchral volumes and whose miniature theatre of action was not in the world, nor even the word, but in the empty spaces between lines written on parchment, I have sought throughout to retain a tension between dead and living flesh, between the book and the body.

My own previous books, *The Gothic Idol: Ideology and Image-Making in Medieval Art* (1989) and *Image on the Edge: The Margins of Medieval Art* (1992), were both large overviews, synthetic studies of what I argued were key thematic issues structuring late medieval art as a regime of signs. I was responding, no doubt, to the spectacularly manipulative image-world of my own late twentieth-century situation. In this book, however, I am interested less in the medieval society of the spectacle and more with how an individual subject was projected within it. I am increasingly aware that, in order to have a greater vision, one has to be somewhere in particular and that the eye and the 'I' must meet in a body if history is not to float aimlessly above those persons and those objects that it scrutinizes. Focusing not upon an object but upon a single historical subject in the past has, in fact, made me all the more aware of my own subjectivity in the present and, although it has been at times disconcerting during the writing of this book, I have not avoided those moments of sudden illumination when the shimmering screen, not of electronic impulses, but of the golden surfaces constructed by the fourteenth-century illuminator, suddenly seemed to reflect back at me my own face peering over the manuscript page.

I first became aware of the artist who forms the subject of this study nearly fifteen years ago when working on my Cambridge dissertation, 'The Illustrated Manuscripts of Deguileville's "Pèlerinages", 1330–1420'. Of the more than seventy illuminated copies of this popular late medieval allegorical poem that I examined in libraries throughout Europe and North America, the copy that he illuminated in 1393 was one of the most intriguing. I still remember the morning in the magnificent manuscript room at the Bibliothèque Nationale in Paris when I first opened MS fr. 823, which records what I shall argue was his name – Remiet. I can recall being struck by how much it felt like an encounter with more than just another 'hand', or even a name, that I had somehow come face to face with a person who was somewhere in the paint. Yet how could that be? How can an individual be transmitted by a few marks and colours on a parchment surface? How can a series of images in a few dozen old books suggest something of the flesh and blood of an individual body?

These questions strike me as especially relevant to current concerns about the role of the subject in the construction of meaning and recent notions like 'the death of the author' upon a field like Art History, so much defined by the study of a series of 'old masters'. More generally, they also lead me to ask about the relationship between history, or history-writing, and image-making. These issues are addressed in the Introduction, which also lays out for the reader why I have written about this artist in the way that I have, laying out a corpse rather than a life. The problematic evidence for the identity of this man who might have been called Remiet is the subject of Chapter 1, which also seeks to place him not only on a particular street and working situation in fourteenth-century Paris but also, from the very beginning, in relation to his own death. The following five chapters each deal with Remiet's mastery and manipulation of various aspects of that indefinable and endless finality he would have called 'la mort'. Chapter 2 treats the important female-focused foundational myth of death's origins at the Fall and the associations that attended its similarly gendered opposite – birth. Chapter 3 deals with Remiet's numerous depictions of violent ends in human history as they were shaped by contemporary concerns. That final grim face gazing upon the individual is the subject of the next chapter, along with the problem of visualizing the exact moment when a person ceases to be alive – a debate that is still very much with us today. Chapter 5 takes us *post mortem* to the inevitable and usually hidden decay of the flesh – Remiet's repeated representations of the rotting corpse which was, in medieval terms, still neither officially nor properly dead. In the sixth and final chapter, I shall exhume what were, for this artist and his patrons, the most dreaded and disturbing images of all – those depicting rebirth into the ambiguous afterlife, afterdeath.

ACKNOWLEDGEMENTS

In thanking friends and colleagues for their help in illuminating the life of Pierre Remiet, I am struck by how much making a book today is as much a group effort as was making a manuscript in medieval Paris. For filling in numerous gaps, I must thank my fellow makers of *histoires*, art historians Sandra Hindman, Anne D. Hedeman, Claire Sherman and Brigitte Buettner and historians Richard and Mary Rouse and Elizabeth R. Brown. Three more professors working in the shadows not of Remiet's university but of that in New York were indispensable correctors and rubricators: Pamela Sheingorn, Nancy Regalado and Jonathan Alexander. One of Remiet's *libraires*, Regnault du Montet, went on trial for selling books to the English, whereas my *libraire*, John Nicoll of Yale University Press, surveys a world market in illustrated books from his London office. The crucial job of editing the text and then deciding where to place images in it belonged to Faith Hart, whose vigilance and energy seemed endless.

In the many libraries and manuscript collections visited in the course of this research, I must mention Roger Wieck at the Pierpont Morgan Library, New York; Martin Kauffmann at the Bodleian Library, Oxford; and Glenise Mathieson, at the John Rylands Library, Manchester, for their invaluable assistance. Most of all, however, I am indebted to François Avril, director of the Department of Manuscripts at the Bibliothèque Nationale, Paris, who generously provided me with details of his own research on Remiet and pointed me to a number of manuscripts I had not known. Many of the ideas explored here were first discussed in my seminars and lecture courses at the University of Chicago, and I want to thank those present for their stimulating ideas: Kim Brooker, Sarah Hanrahan, Anne Harris, Martha MacFarlane, Maureen Kupstas, Karen Matthews, Mitchell Merback, Lori Simons, Jennifer Spreitzer, Ben Withers, Laura Weigert, and Athene Reiss. My research was also supported by a fellowship from the National Endowment for the Humanities and the Wissenschaftskolleg zu Berlin, where I spent a very productive and enjoyable period.

Another site implicated for obvious reasons in this study is the *quartier latin* in Paris, where Remiet lived and worked and where, during a number of visits in recent years, I have enjoyed the hospitality of medievalists Jean-Claude Schmitt, Jean-Claude Bonne, Jerome Baschet and Georges Didi-Huberman at the École des Hautes Études en Sciences Sociales. However, on my last visit and during the final stages of the research for this book, I deliberately avoided my usual contacts on the Left Bank and instead spent a strange and solitary week at the Hôtel Parc Saint Séverin, which overlooks the corner of the Rue Boutebrie and the Rue de la Parcheminerie. With its teeming multi-ethnic 'fast-food' stalls, students and travellers streaming through its narrow streets from all over the world, this remains as 'central' and simultaneously 'marginal' an area of Paris today as it was when Remiet lived there. Every night as I climbed into bed, my head swimming with Remiet's corpses, skulls and crypts, I hoped for a visitation from the dead, for a ghost that never came.

A rather worn cliché propounded by most twentieth-century historians of the endless subject of death is that, today, compared to our medieval and early-modern ancestors, we have lost the ability to face it as an experience. This seems to me to be no longer really the case, especially in light of the recent AIDS crisis, which has so radically changed the landscape of mortality. Tragic because it also revealed how much levels of fear, intolerance and ignorance still exist in our supposedly 'post-medieval' culture, this 'plague', as it has sometimes been ominously termed, with direct reference to the fourteenth century, has, at the same time, produced multi-coloured quilts, theatrical masterpieces, powerful cultural actions and projects of protest. There are people everywhere, some of them artists, but most of them, like Remiet, just ordinary makers, in whose everyday life and work, fear is being faced and resistance celebrated in ever more indomitable ways. This book has been inspired by them and by many friends whose going on living positively continues to show me why death is not such a depressing subject for a book after all.

Photographic Acknowledgements

Acknowledgement is made for permission to reproduce photographs to:

Bayeux, Bibliothèque Municipale, 73, 165
Baltimore, Walters Art Gallery, 135, 190
Besançon, Bibliothèque Municipale, 101
Bloomington, The Lilly Library, Indiana University, 52, 155
Bordeaux, Bibliothèque de Bordeaux, 20, 21, 22
Brussels, Bibliothèque Royale Albert I[e], 5, 37, 102, 103, 104, 105, 106, 124
Cambridge, Fitzwilliam Museum, 184
Chantilly, Musée Condé (Photographie Giraudon), 96, 111
Douai, Bibliothèque Municipale, 90
The Hague, Museo Mermanno-Westreenianum, 95
Laon, Musée, 123
Leiden, University Library, 163, 191
London, British Library, 11, 13, 16, 55, 72, 74, 75, 76, 78, 83, 88, 93, 128, 174, 182
London, Courtauld Institute of Art, Conway Library, 129, 183
Lyons, Bibliothèque Municipale, 3
Manchester, John Rylands University Library, 14, 109, 110, 153, 154, 156, 171
New York, Metropolitan Museum of Art, 28, 187
New York, Pierpont Morgan Library, 41, 61, 92, 108, 114, 136, 137, 140, 141, 159
Oxford, Bodleian Library, 143, 189
Oxford, President and Fellows of St John's College, 44
Paris, Bibliothèque de l'Arsenal, 42, 57
Paris, Bibliothèque Nationale 1, 2, 4, 6, 7, 8, 12, 15, 18, 19, 23, 24, 25, 26, 27, 30, 32, 34, 35, 36, 38, 39, 40, 45, 46, 47, 48, 49, 50, 53, 54, 58, 59, 60, 62, 63, 64, 65, 66, 67, 68, 69, 71, 77, 79, 80, 84, 85, 86, 89, 94, 97, 98, 99, 100, 107, 112, 115, 116, 117, 118, 119, 120, 121, 122, 126, 127, 130, 131, 134, 138, 139, 142, 144, 147, 148, 149, 150, 151, 152, 157, 158, 160, 161, 162, 164, 166, 169, 170, 172, 175, 176, 177, 178, 179, 180, 181, 186, 188, 192, frontispiece
Paris, Bibliothèque Sainte-Geneviève, 167, 168, 173
Paris, Musée de Cluny, 125
Paris, Phototèque des musées de la ville de Paris, 10
Rome, Biblioteca Apostolica Vaticana, 33, 43
Soissons, Bibliothèque Municipale, 17, 29, 56, 81
Troyes, Bibliothèque Municipale, 70, 82, 132, 133, 145, 146
Vienna, Österreichisches Nationalbibliothek, 51, 87

Introduction
DEATH IN MINIATURE

Now, our perception of former times, our historical organ, so to say, is becoming more and more visual. Most educated people today owe their conception of Egypt, Greece, or the Middle Ages, much more to the sight of their monuments, either in the original or by reproductions, than to reading. The change in our ideas about the Middle Ages is due less to a weakening of the romantic sense than to the substitution of artistic for intellectual appreciation. Johan Huizinga[1]

The Dutch historian Johan Huizinga's *The Waning of the Middle Ages: A Study of the Forms of Life, Thought, and Art in France and the Netherlands in the Fourteenth and Fifteenth Centuries*, many times reprinted since its first publication in 1919, when its title meant 'Autumn of the Middle Ages', has provided our century with the major paradigms for understanding late medieval culture – decadence, decline and death.[2] The author states that he wrote the book 'to arrive at a genuine understanding of the art of the brothers Van Eyck . . . by seeing it in connection with the entire life of their times', but he produced a much more expansive and gloomy canvas, full of brilliant detail but anachronistic value judgements about a culture that clearly both fascinated and repelled him. Describing a 'violent and high-strung' era, during which 'living emotion stiffens amid the abused imagery of skeletons and worms' and in which thought becomes increasingly 'crystallized into images', Huizinga was not so much responding to the early fifteenth century as to the early twentieth, revealing his own anxious relation to a modern world in which images were increasingly taking the place of words and the Freudian 'death-wish' was making pleasure and death inseparable.[3] The 'superfluity' and repetition of forms 'hardening' into images, which for Huizinga reflected the relapse of civilized society into anarchic barbarism, means something quite different to a historian like myself, writing at the end rather than the beginning of this century. Not only has the idea of history as a path of human 'progress' been eroded, but the empirical 'God's-eye' view of the intellectual historian has itself been shown to be a chimera, challenged by a history viewed 'from the bottom up', bringing the very notion of any historical knowledge of the past into question. Whereas Huizinga saw the proliferation of images in the late fourteenth and fifteenth centuries as evidence of the autumnal atrophy of 'civilization' – as a vast visual and cultural 'death-wish' – I see this frenzied imaging of the end as a powerful deconstructive challenge and as a reversal of the seasonal metaphor, as the carrying back of death into life.

If Huizinga's argument that pictures are not 'intellectual' and that they exist somehow in a separate 'artistic' sphere outside language seems today a misguided distinction, it is none the less one that continues to separate 'art' from 'history' in our understanding of the past. The great period of popularity for the picture-history book was exactly when Huizinga was writing, when new reproductive technologies made photographic images part of every historian's arsenal. After a cooling-off period when the fashion for lavishly illustrated history texts seemed past and both the French Annales School and the 'New Historians' laid increasing emphasis upon the archives, demographics and written sources, recent years have seen a return to the large-scale use of visual material, especially in France, in works like Braudel's *Civilization matérielle* and series like *Bibliothèque illustrée des histoires*, which utilize numerous illustrations.[4] For example, the second volume of the lavish five-volume work produced under the direction of Georges Duby and Philippe Ariès and recently translated as *The History of Private Life* utilizes manuscript images and photographs of architecture to 'illustrate' medieval social history, without, however, any questioning of their problematic mediating status as documents.[5] 'Illustration' is a nineteenth-century notion and has little to do with how texts and images functioned during the Middle Ages when such images in books were called, ironically enough, *histoires*. Miniatures made by the illuminator who is the subject of this book have been reproduced in exactly this fashion, cut out of their textual site by historians who relabel them, for example as representations of 'the diversity of men and their functions'.[6] Historians of literature have also been eager to utilize images made by our artist as representations against which their poetic texts can be read.[7] These 'mirrors' of history, 'reflecting' the solider social realities of feudalism or medieval marriage laws or poetic 'mentalities', remain mere secondary, supplemental surfaces separated from the still-textbound vision of the past as something that can only be understood through language. Yet it is precisely the gaps between history and its images, places where the visual distorts and erases the words rather than holds them up for analysis, that can tell us most about historical processes. Because medieval miniatures exist in an ambiguous space, not entirely free of the tyranny of the text but not yet views through a window on to the visible world outside the book, their opening, closing, always partial and constantly unfolding optics have to be carefully negotiated. Images, so often used by historians to evoke a *zeitgeist*, a *mentalité*, a 'period eye', are, in most cases, deposits of much more local experience constructed in a particular place. This study aims not to return images to the texts from which they are so often severed, nor even to put them into some broader historical 'context' which is necessarily constructed from these very same images, but rather to put them back into an embodied life. Challenging Huizinga's vision of the period as one of superficial excess and cultural decline, I shall adopt an altogether different strategy, utilizing as many disparate fragments of texts and images as did the great Dutch cultural historian; but instead of shaping them into a seamless narrative 'picture' of an era, I shall try to understand them in terms of the quotidian tactics of the man who made multiple pictures of a world but never put them together to see what sort of world he had created.

The book as an embodiment of a single person – as biography – was, like the visual genre of portraiture, nascent during the period focused on in this study. This saw the writing of *The Life of Bertrand du Guesclin* (during the reign of Charles V), *The Book of Deeds of the Good Lord Jehan le Maingre, known as Boucicaut, Marshal of France* (1409) and Christine de Pizan's *The Book of the Deeds and Good Morals of the Sage King, Charles V* (1404), which describe famous princes and kings as exemplars of morality, in the tradition of *De viris illustribus*.[8] The unillustrious 'little people' in history have only recently been treated with the same depth. This was owing to scholars working within or influenced by the Annales School who in recent decades have redirected its economic, demographic and socio-historical concerns more towards the individual life narrative. These historians have explored the mentality of 'ordinary' folk, the inhabitants of the fourteenth-century southern French village of Montaillou or the sixteenth-century peasant Martin Guerre – people forgotten in the traditional story of great events – who seem to speak to us directly across the silence of centuries.[9] Most of the evidence used in these justly renowned studies, however, is the verbal record of their subjects' forced legal confessions, their abberrant, heretical voices when put to the question. This is history 'born out of the archives', the fragments of 'inglorious lives put to rest in a few brief lines that brought them down'.[10] It is as though we are able to grasp the past only through the tortured testimony of the inscribed exception. But what of other kinds of archives, those that are retained in scraps not of words but of images, and those which represent not the unique but the ordinary, the repeatable. The question is whether we can explore a past life not through the things someone has said or written but rather through the images that person has made?

What is most important about that person who forms the subject of this book is the fact that he is not important – at least in terms of the History of Art. His name does not appear in general surveys nor even in Charles Sterling's recent survey of medieval painting in Paris. In Millard Meiss's monumental three-volume study of book illuminators of this period, his works are listed not even under the rubric of an anonymous 'master' but only as a 'trend' – 'Late Boqueteaux'. Even when named and singled out by Patrick de Winter, he is described as never transcending the status of a 'mere illustrator'.[11] This scholarly disdain is reflected in the archives. Of the fifteen manuscripts he illuminated that are now kept in the Bibliothèque Nationale in Paris, only one is in the difficult-to-access 'Grand Réserve' (fr. 20029, Deschamps's *Lay de la fragilité humaine*), and that is more because of its unique text than because of its pictures. The rest are all in the general storage and not counted among the institution's 'treasures'. The director of the library's Department of Manuscripts and a leading scholar of this period of French manuscript illumination, François Avril, described Remiet's work when displayed in a recent exhibition as 'monotonous'.[12] Though I agree with this judgement, I do not take it as negative and, indeed, want to argue that repetition is the crucial performative dynamic, not only for this artist but for late medieval culture in general, which saw no self-contained and entirely original referent – except in God. Art history tends to focus on historical ruptures and new breakthroughs, the individual innovator whose images transcend their time and space, whereas this book concerns the ordinary maker precisely because he is rooted in a world he can never transcend.

It was at this century's first great exhibition of medieval art held in Paris in 1904, the *Exposition des primitifs français*, that the artist Remiet was first brought to public attention, although without being named. In a review of the exhibition, it was none other than

Émile Mâle, the great compiler of cathedral iconography, who remarked on the artist's lugubrious interests and prematurely old physiognomies and characterized him as a 'maître original'.[13] In the intervening years, knowledge of the working practices of medieval manuscript illuminators has changed considerably, and their originality has been called into question in a number of painstaking and scholarly studies which have shown how pictorial conventions were shared by numerous artists who we assume were, for the most part, copiers rather than creators.[14] Here is a talent that was by no means as innovative as Jean Pucelle had been in the 1320s or the Limbourg brothers were to be after 1400. Yet for me this is an advantage, since my goal is not to 'discover' a long-forgotten genius in the line of great anonymous medieval masters, but rather to imagine the working world of an ordinary artisan making run-of-the-mill products in the proto-industry of the fourteenth-century Parisian book trade. Interest in the everyday and popular that has deeply affected how history is researched and taught has not yet had much impact upon the hierarchies of 'greatness' that structure art history, especially at the level of production, despite the fact that most art being made today is coming not from above but from below, to use the infamous and unyielding 'high–low' category. Of course there is a continuum from the 'great masters' to any artist for whom an oeuvre can be assembled, and the truly anonymous devalued artists of the Middle Ages are those countless men and women who made bone rosary beads, lead pilgrims' badges and clay pottery, which sometimes share museum *vitrines* with those works to which we can ascribe the all-important name. It simply did not matter to patrons and readers of illuminated manuscripts whether there were four or five 'hands' in their books, much less what names those hands bore. Yet the value of the exceptional artist, so crucial to our modern notion of what constitutes 'art', was on the ascendent in exactly this period, especially in the fashionable matrix of the court. But unlike the extraordinary Limbourg brothers, clearly sought after by eminent patrons of the day, our illuminator was just one among many ordinary, anonymous picture-makers, one whose name has come down to us purely by chance. Today such names matter more than ever before. A single folio cut from a manuscript of Livy's *Histoire romaine* attributed to Remiet was recently sold at Sotheby's for 4,830 pounds.[15] What was mundane then is, in its sadly torn-out state, strangely wondrous, collectable, and of course investable as a fragment now.

Although I would question many of the presumptions and categories by which historians of medieval manuscript illumination have constructed artistic agency in individual identity ('the hand'), group identity ('the workshop'), and even a kind of era identity ('the trend'), my task has, of course, involved attributing miniatures to Remiet. But rather than describe Remiet's *style*, a word which suggests a static code, I want to detect Remiet's *performance*, which suggests the arc of the arm and the pressure of a tensed hand grasping the pen or brush. Miniscule mark-making motions can be discerned, such as the way he made little tufts of grass with five short pen strokes or highlighted the bridge of a figure's nose, or the cheek and chin with a few swift smears. I believe that I can recognize his peculiar graphic acts among the thousands of miniatures produced in Paris around the years 1400, just as I can recognize the jaunty walk of an old friend in a crowd. But, as always, such an analysis is rooted in subjectivity, and there is always a tension between the shared and conventional pictorial language of a period that can be articulated over and over again by numerous individuals and the distinct voice. To give just one example: I do not reproduce here, but have included in the handlist of manuscripts in the Appendix, the miniatures in a little volume of the *Dit du lion* in Berlin, which was first attributed to Remiet in 1892 by the great nineteenth-century bibliophile Paul Durrieu.[16] I have seen this manuscript twice. The first time I looked at its nine miniatures, over ten years ago, I wrote in my notes, 'these are definitely not by Remiet'. But last year, when I looked at the same manuscript once again, I felt sure that some of them were his youthful work. Perhaps never making up one's mind is the best way to view these medieval works, as objects in a culture that did not need constantly to name the self as the site of production, as we do today.

In addition to this problem of defining the physical marks of labour left by an individual, treating these as moments of self-reference as well as representation, there is the difficulty of following those patterns over time. I have always been suspicious of the way art monographs, in their sequential catalogue of attributed 'works', tend to isolate representations from human history as 'hands', as though the whole body and mind were not involved in the process, and then go on to categorize hundreds of images into a hermetic sequence of 'early', 'middle' and 'late' production as though artefact and artist are synonymous. When the average life expectancy for men was twenty-four (as it was in 1400), life surely meant something entirely different, especially a long life of making pictures like Remiet's, which ended, not with the glorious flowering of a free 'late' style (such as with 'old masters' like Titian) but with the feeble scribbles of someone whose style was by then redundant and whose very techniques were superceded by younger and more up-to-date professionals. It was only in the very last stages of writing this book that I came across the last, sad vestiges of Remiet's career in the book trade, in two Brussels volumes which show that the old man ended up in the margins, just as he had begun his career there. Thus, this is partly the story not of the ascendency, but of the decline that at the end of decades of hard labour was the fate of most pre-modern image-makers before the triumph of the age of art.

Although I have tried to locate all extant manuscripts illuminated by Remiet (which are listed in the Appendix) and to examine them for myself, I have avoided creating a chronological sequence of stylistic development of works. Of course there are complex changes over time that one can discern; more often, though, stylistic changes are in relation to the type of text being illuminated or the patron for whom it is being produced. Viewing this artist not as a mere formalist 'hand' but as the practitioner and performer of a visual repertoire which was, initially at least, inherited and not entirely 'his', will allow us to register, perhaps more carefully than has previously been possible, the intersection of the image and pressures external to it. The 'hand' should, in this respect, be viewed as more than a passive label to which we assign various images. Images register the activity of a whole body – a body tense, weak, fatigued or frail – visible in the strength of the line, the viscosity of the paint. The flux of bodily fluids that fourteenth-century people thought controlled their humoral dispositions, the bile that darkened and the blood that brightened, were also constitutive of the fluids that were brushed on to the surface of the parchment. Avoiding the urge to label this artist physically, psychologically and symptomatically from his morbid subject matter, say, for example, as a skinny melancholic, we can still see his art somatically, as the imprint of flesh upon flesh. With a series of repeated gestures and dextrous moves (although Remiet may, for all we know, have been left-handed), Remiet signed off on the world he had created not with the flourish of a signature but with his compulsion to make death visible.

Fastening upon death as my theme, rather than trying to cover all aspects of the many images that Remiet produced during his long career, has its obvious advantages. It is also highly relevant to my theoretical exercise of exploring a life that I should choose its opposite as the means to do it. One of the arguments of Philippe Ariès's enormously influential 1977 study, *L'Homme devant la mort*, published in English as *The Hour of Our Death*, is that people in the late twentieth century have tended to ostracize and marginalize an experience that had previously been central – an observation no longer borne out by recent scholarly fascination with the subject.[17] For today, as another French historian of death puts it, 'la mort est à la mode'.[18] But as against the many massive compilations of documents and local data published in recent years, charting the demographic minutiae of death in different periods, regions and contexts, its enormous scale and its force as the motor of history, I aim to produce a far less monumental history of the subject, even in art-historical terms.[19] What follows is a history of death in miniature. It unfolds in the hundreds of tiny but sharply delineated pictures produced by one person in the gap he found between words.

For late twentieth-century Parisian philosophers and poets like Maurice Blanchot, Georges Bataille and Jacques Derrida, just as for their late fourteenth-century counterparts Eustache Deschamps, Jean Le Fèvre and Pierre d'Ailly, the artwork is an emblem of death, and artistic production takes place in the crypt, both for the creator and for the viewer mourning the lost object of desire. It is important to place Remiet's art within this still vital necrophilic poetics which recent French philosophers have especially cultivated and to which I allude in epigraphs. The latter can also be read as contemporary *epitaphs* at the head of each section, to the buried text below, and it is hoped they help emphasize how Remiet's work is relevant to current debates about the relationship between artistic identity and human mortality. On the one hand, these words should be read against the grain of the sections that follow, since they posit a post-Freudian and Heideggerian view of death as 'a limit beyond all limits'. This resistant, starkly existential battle-cry of modern life *against* death was negotiated quite differently during the Middle Ages, when the end was more likely to rest unopposed, as a *transitus* rather than a *terminus*. Yet on the other hand, they echo many of the pronouncements made by medieval authors of the *ars moriendi*. Continental philosophers have similarly sought to face rather than flee the end and see death as ecstacy rather than limit (Bataille), as poetry rather than silence (Blanchot), and as identity rather than absence (Derrida). Indeed, Jacques Derrida's recent analysis of how nothing is closer to individual consciousness, closer to the idea of 'me' and more properly mine than 'my death' has helped shape my attempt to communicate with the dead, along with his contention that it is not enough to show that in historical cultures 'death changes face, meaning, language, or even body', but that 'culture itself, culture in general, is essentially, before anything, even a priori, the culture of death'.[20] If nineteenth and early twentieth-century historians of the Middle Ages feared the dead and kept the corpses in their graves by treating the past as 'passed', holding down the lids on the coffins with the heavy weight of documentation, and frantically reinscribing tombstones and markers, boundaries between periods, epochs and ages, the philological mausoleums they so carefully erected are now themselves in ruin. Recent history-writing has tried instead to bring the dead to life, to resurrect the realities of past experience and to dig in its constantly re-enriched soil for the bones of a less textual, more material past in the body itself. Rather than attempt to conjure up Huizinga's 'spirit of the age', today 'it is necessary to learn spirits', to use Derrida's phrase, to commune with more particular phantoms of our political and social memory. In this scenario of history as a spectacular seance, images play an obviously crucial role. They are not merely echoes but actual apparitions, blurring the line between the past and the present, emphasizing not the chasm that separates the living from the dead but the shared space where the gazes of both can meet.

Yet in all these displacements there is something in the design of this book which not only reproduces but at the same time remembers Remiet in the same way that a monument is always a living absence, an empty memory to a dead person. In describing how 'death cannot be eliminated from the historian's field of attention if history is not to lose its historical quality', Paul Ricoeur has underlined the importance of 'the trace', the vestige of a mark left by a thing. 'On the one hand, the trace is visible here and now, as a vestige, a mark. On the other hand, there is a trace (or track) because 'earlier' a human being or an animal passed this way. Something did something.'[21] In my examination of the traces left by Remiet in his wiry acts of depiction, wavering lines of ink and spreadings of liquid colour, all hardening on the carefully scraped parchment, I have often been struck by certain salient continuities with my own experience as a maker of marks. The trace made by human hands is, to mix corporeal metaphors, on its last legs. In the fifteen years that I have been seeing and reading illuminated manuscripts in libraries throughout Europe and the United States, I have always jotted down the folio numbers and contents of the pages, transcribed pieces of text and carefully described the details of each miniature with a pencil on lined paper (the latter reminding me perhaps of ruled parchment). It was as if the pages were speaking to me, since I often felt the urge to read aloud as I did my own seeing and reading, to perform the text as I believed it was performed by the non-silent spectators of the Middle Ages. I also made little sketches to remind me of the hundreds of miniatures in their ruled boxes that I could not afford to have photographed. In these performative practices, I was making my own miniatures from and within Remiet's own However, in recent months I have begun to use, for the same purposes, a portable computer, which calls itself a 'book'. An unbridgeable gulf has now opened up between the objects I am describing and the shimmering pixels that constitute their transcription, not just in the murmurless click of fingers on a keyboard but even in their 'printed-out' form, because whereas before my own body used to register the imprint of another body's mark-making with identical physical movements and similar tools, this is now done by a machine. I should add that I am not one of those medievalists who is wary of new hyper-text and imaging technologies; indeed, I look forward to the day when the thousands of manuscript pages and the millions of miniatures from uncatalogued collections that I have never been able to travel to see are made available to me on my screen at home. Huizinga's fear that history as a collection of texts is being increasingly engulfed by a proliferation of images is now a fact with which we must interface and welcome if we are to revitalize the past on the screens of our students, who will do far more looking than reading in the future.[22] But at the same time, I am gratified by the fact that my tracking down a dead man through the spoor left on parchment pages is not a film, a video, or an interactive computer program, but, even in its machine-produced and printed form, is a book – very much the type of thing Remiet would not only have recognized but might very well have had a hand in making himself. And of course he did.

Another aspect of computer technology, which is altering our ability to perceive the past, is its ability to reduce or enlarge scale, miniaturizing images to infinitely small size, or expanding them to enormous proportions. One of the problems with producing a book about manuscript illumination is that, without going to the expense of producing a facsimile, which would attempt to reproduce the exact dimensions and colours of the original, one is usually enlarging things or making them smaller. My editor and I have tried to keep a sense of relative scale, but occasionally Remiet's work has had to be enlarged to allow the reader to see his minute mark-making at close-quarters. Remiet was clearly acutely conscious of scale. His series of small pen and ink miniatures have a very different effect from his larger, fully illuminated frontispieces. Some of his work appears in tiny Books of Hours while much of it illuminates vast volumes, almost too large and heavy to carry to the desk. The images might in fact be the same size, but their matrix is vastly different. The full measurements of each manuscript are given in the Appendix. Reproduction also tends to equalize things, and although we are used to thinking of these problems when reproducing paintings, the fact that Remiet's work appears in books makes it more difficult for us to be conscious of the differences, limits and possibilities of his medium. Miniatures too easily turn into what we call illustrations. Modern art criticism has tended to denigrate illustration and see it as a second-class art form, closer to design, but perhaps that is changing. Earlier I distinguished Remiet's art from our modern concept of illustration, yet there is one salient point of comparison – the status of the image-maker in relation to the author of the text and its readers. How often do you notice the name of the illustrator, always in tiny print, that runs vertically alongside a particularly witty drawing or a beautiful full-page illustration in your Sunday newspaper or glossy magazine?

One final aspect of the text that follows requires some introductory explanation, if only because I sense that it might put off some readers who do not like to see the certainty they think resides in 'history' and the fantasy that creates 'fiction' co-habiting between the same covers. The only certainty that can be known about the person, whatever his name was, who made many of the images reproduced here, is that he was born and that he died. But both of these moments are, like those experienced by the majority of people in the distant past, lost and unrecorded. As Remiet spent his career filling in the spaces in texts with vividly imagined *histoires*, it seemed only fair that I should try to complete his own last *histoire* for myself – to, as it were, fill in the last gap. Each chapter thus begins with a kind of testament – my account of Remiet's last day, utilizing, in a very different way, some of the images reproduced in that chapter. If his last gasp went unheard in history, it shall be pictured in my words here. These words are fragments of an experiment, the first draft of this book, in which I tried to recreate Remiet's life chronologically from his images. This project faltered, perhaps because words *are* different from images and the pressure of the latter towards the real was so strong that I could not sustain imagining Remiet any longer without asking historical questions about him from outside his own experience – from the viewpoint of the late twentieth-century art historian rather than the fourteenth-century manuscript illuminator. Consequently, there is a tension in my two narratives: between what can be learned from the more traditional conventions of an objective, distanced and descriptive account of the artist's work and what can be drawn out of a more subjective, embodied and imagined account of his life. I intend for these two very different viewpoints to converge around the images made by Remiet himself. In my own text, the reproductions of these images are called 'figures' – a word used in Remiet's day to refer to diagrams or explicatory images in texts as distinct from the painted pictures or *histoires*. Thus Remiet's *histoires* become my 'figures', distorted by new and different interpretative strategies than those which first positioned them in the matrix of the manuscript. Rather than refer to the tired opposition or interaction of 'text and image', I am, throughout this book, struggling to interpose a third term – somewhere in between, something closer to sensation. To call this third term life itself would sound too sentimental. Perhaps I should call it death itself. No, I should instead call this third term – between text and image – story, as Walter Benjamin defined it, in relating how the inevitable fact of mortality constructs all of humanity's historical narratives.

> Just as a sequence of images is set in motion inside a man as his life comes to an end – unfolding the views of himself under which he has encountered himself without being aware of it – suddenly in his expression and looks the unforgettable emerges and imparts to everything that concerned him that authority which even the poorest wretch in dying possesses for the living around him. This authority is at the very source of the story.[23]

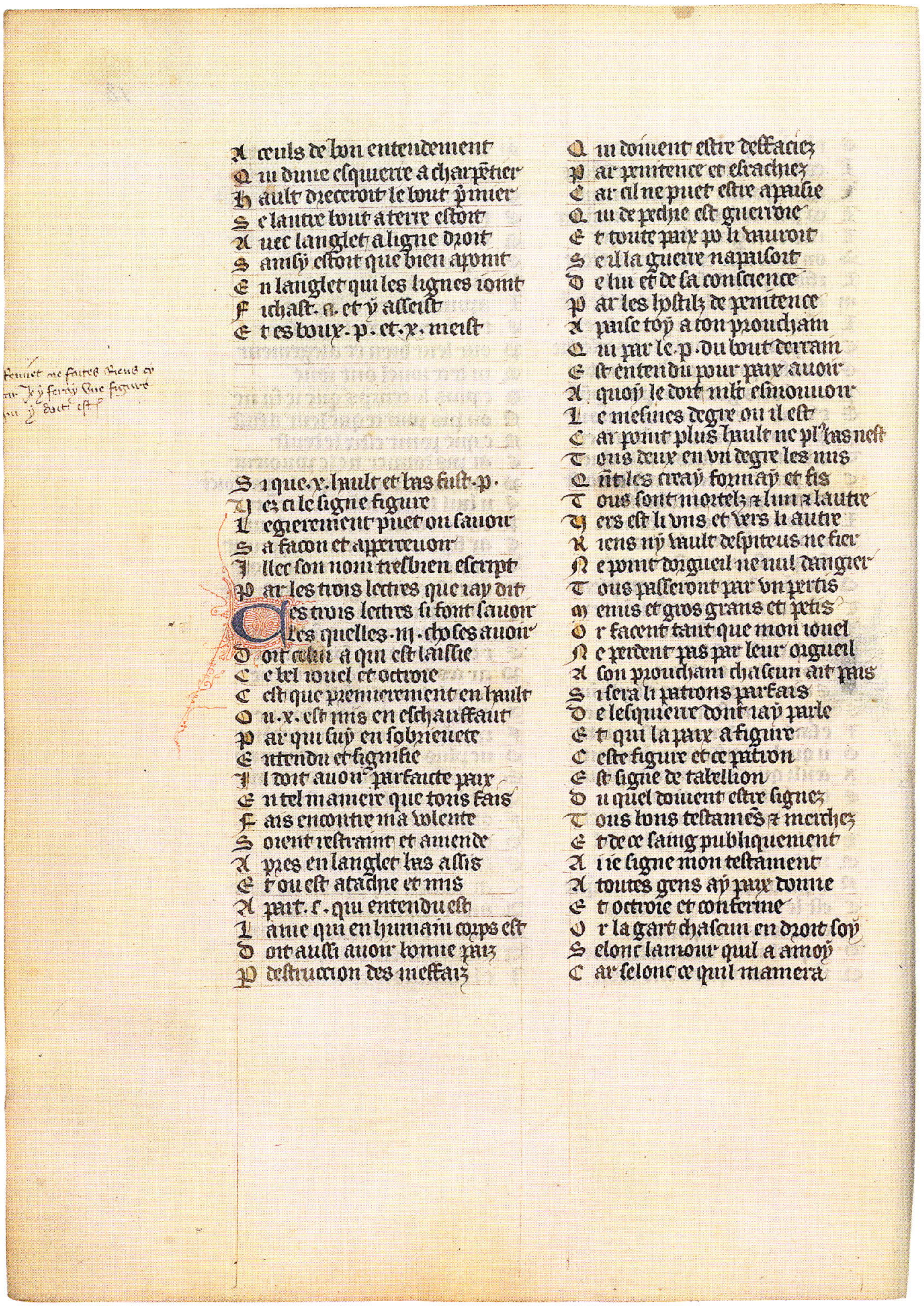

1. Paris, Bibliothèque Nationale, fr. 823, fol. 18v. Guillaume de Deguileville, *Pèlerinage de vie humaine*. A gap in the text and the marginal message 'Remiet, make nothing here'.

1. A GAP IN THE TEXT

A creak on the wooden staircase that led from the downstairs shop to the cramped living quarters above announced her coming. The slow deliberate step was audible to the old man even above the creakings and wheezings of that 'minor mundus' of his own body and other clattering sounds that came through the open window from the bustling streets of the 'major mundus' outside. Both worlds had for so long now been in decay and decline and, as the preachers never tired of screeching from their pulpits, 'the end is nigh'. They had been saying that for as long as he could remember. But perhaps now at last, this day, for Remiet it was. He had forgotten how long he had lain here, 'usque ad mortem' – 'sick unto death'. He no longer had the strength to get up and sit by the second-storey window, which looked out on to the narrow Rue des Enlumineurs. He had lived here for many years on the corner where it met the wider Rue de la Parcheminerie only a short step from Notre Dame. Only memories now of the sights but also the smells and sounds of the vibrant and ever-changing life of his beloved city that had been called a paradise, 'Parisius paradisus', but which, around where he lived, partly because of the foul stench from the shops of the parchment-makers, partly because of the refuse of too many squalid human lives squeezed between its alleys and passageways, stank like the foulest pits of Hell.

Certainly Paris was a paradise for some, heaven indeed for those who loved books. All the streets around the parish church of Saint Séverin, with its wicked gargoyles jutting insolently out above the rooftops and whose fine new western portal he could see from his window, were associated with the book trade. In his declining years, he had often watched from here the comings and goings of the various métiers that had supported him all his working life. The traffic of the parchment-makers was the noisiest. He often heard them coming back from the butcheries and tanneries on the Right Bank, their carts loaded with 'boites' of foul-smelling skins in still-discernible shapes of calves, goats, kids, coneys, hares and even cats. Others carried flesh transformed, after much time and labour, into pearly parchment as large as white winding-sheets, neatly stacked on their shoulders on their way to the Halle aux Parchemins at the nearby Convent of the Mathurins where it would be taxed and inspected for quality by the university officials. But it was not for the 'parcheminiers' like his old friends Agnes d'Orliens and Jehan de Beauvais that this congested intersection of narrow little alleyways was known throughout the realm and beyond. For in these small two-storey hovels had lived countless 'escriptvains', 'reliures de livres' and at least a dozen 'enlumineurs' like himself. It was these men and women who worked upon that flesh, to make wonders, weapons, treasures, talismans, storehouses and reliquaries of writ. Bound between boards, the truths of the priest, the laws of the jurist and the desires of the lover all looked the same. Only after opening them would one see the glorious variety of God's great illuminated world, written and painted in gold and azure.

Someone had told him that there were sixty thousand scribes in the city, a number he could not imagine, though certainly counting those on the Rue Neuve Notre Dame in front of the cathedral of Our Lady and the concentration in his own poorer university neighbourhood on the Left Bank it had seemed at times that the life-blood of the capital flowed not with the filthy sewage that often ran darkly down the middle of the streets but with streams of the purest, blackest ink. Neighbours like the scribe Jean Cauchon had been professionals who, like himself, had made an oath before the members of the university to follow its rules and serve its masters, but these days most writers were part-timers, bachelors of law or would-be masters of arts copying for cash between lectures, mere student scribblers. The illuminators were in decline too, having to make their livings as innkeepers and worse. There were not the family businesses there used to be. Most women were as ill-suited to books as his own wife had been. Better give them a needle and thread than a quill and ink, he had always said. Yet he remembered the fame of the lady 'libraire' Jeanne de Montbaston, who was better at babooning books than her husband had ever been and after he died of the plague still served the university from her shop near the cathedral. Then there was Jean le Noir's daughter Bourgot and of course Anastasie, whose beautiful vine borders and glittering patterned backgrounds had more recently tantalized the courtiers at the other end of the Île de la Cité. Anyway, nowadays many scribes were often clerics – men who had taken first tonsure, though they were still better at ploughing fields of female flesh than the page. Some of the official booksellers, the 'libraires jurés' of the university, were themselves men of learning, as were those who were also 'stationnaires', whose shops regulated the production of accurate copies of texts for scholars. Yes, times had changed since his youth when the 'libraires' were always breathless from running 'back and forth down alleyways and streets, night and day', as the scribe Raoulet d'Orléans he had known in his youth wrote at the end of a Bible he had copied.

Those were the times when there seemed not enough hours of sunlight in a working day, so many gatherings of parchment leaves, their edges already curling inwards while their hair-sides contracted as if around the bodies of beasts they once were, lay stacked on his worktable. All were to be 'enluminé d'or et d'azur et à ymages' or to be historiated with the black and white 'portraits d'encre' as stipulated. Although the bachelors of the university constantly demanded books for their own use and for the great library at the Sorbonne, just down the lane, nowadays they were more interested that the text be copied from an uncorrupted exemplar than in the shape of its opening letters or the golden vines, the lovely 'vignettes' in its borders. Besides, illuminated books had become too expensive. Who could afford them with all the sufferings Paris had felt in recent years, when during some winters, it was said, people in this very 'quartier' had boiled parchment to feed their starving bellies? The great libraries of King Charles V and those of his brothers, the dukes of Berry and Burgundy, which had once kept these streets alive with commissions of the finest and most beautiful volumes, were now all dispersed or destroyed. It was said that all the books in the magnificent royal library in the great white tower of the Louvre collected by the wise king before the accession of the mad one, and in which many of his finest miniatures were contained, had been confiscated by the English regent, the Duke of Bedford, and taken as booty across the sea.

He had also heard tell of the looting of castles and even churches throughout the kingdom in the recent civil wars between Armagnacs and Burgundians and the invasion of the English. In his fevered imagination, he saw piles of stacked volumes, in numbers such as he had never seen, even at the great Lendit fair or in the libraries of schools, come crashing down like the stones of a great cathedral. As they hit the hard ground their precious contents unfolded and broke apart, into loose leaves – the very form in which he had received them in his shop in order to make them beautiful. Amidst the swords and screams, he imagined some of his finest images being snipped out and torn away by childen to make their folded toys. How those poor books suffered, their satin chemise clothes stolen, their oak-board covers ripped away for firewood, their pearl-encrusted bookmarks long since looted by the vulgar crowd who cared neither to read nor to preserve such treasures. Did no one realize how valuable they were, how much expensive gold leaf and precious pigments were contained on each page? He imagined an old man bending down to the gutter to save a single sheet whipped by the wind, but when he lifted it close enough to his almost sightless eyes, rain and time had done their work and there was nothing there.

A Name and Nothing

Because to copy is *to do* nothing; it is *to be* the books being copied. Michel Foucault[1]

You can do nothing of yourself. Theophilus[2]

Although we know the names of a small number of medieval artists from works they signed, Remiet's name is known to posterity not because of something that he painted but because of something he did not paint. This nothing is a gap on folio 18 verso (Fig. 1) of an otherwise fully illuminated manuscript of Guillaume de Deguileville's *Pèlerinages* (Paris BN fr. 823). The two columns of elegant script have already had the first stage of rubrication and decoration added: a blue two-line-high 'C' initial with elaborate red pen flourishes has been inserted into the space left by the scribe, and a delicate yellow wash highlights the capital letter at the beginning of each line. Yet there is not even a frame in the empty space left in the first column. But alongside, nearly cut off by subsequent trimming of the yellowed outer edge, is a scribbled note written in the same scrawling cursive that puts a small guide letter 'c' before the initial on this page as an indication to the rubricator. These three lines read: 'Remiet ne faites rien cy car je y feray une figure qui y doit estre (Remiet, make nothing here because I will make a figure which should be there)'.[3]

This 'I' belongs to the scribe and *libraire* Oudin de Cavarnay, who informs us of his name in a rhymed acrostic poem at the very end of the book and writes on fol. 168v that he completed the text on 29 April 1393.[4] The *libraire* was under the control of the university and could be a scribe, or sometimes even an illuminator, who co-ordinated the various stages of production. These included, after first gaining the commission from the patron, procuring the parchment and finding craftsmen who would do the ruling, writing, rubricating, illuminating and sometimes even the binding of the finished manuscript.[5] In this period, books were illuminated before they were bound, while they were still in loose single sheets folded down the middle, in this case, in gatherings of eight leaves or four bifolia, folded loosely in double sheets like a modern Sunday newspaper. The page with Remiet's name, the verso of the second sheet of the third gathering, represents what would have greeted the illuminator every morning as he laid the first sheet on his desk to begin work. Empty spaces like this are often to be found in medieval manuscripts, mostly in cases where the money for miniatures ran out or where practitioners were never found to fill in the gaps. What makes this example more interesting is that the 137 other spaces in the book have all been filled with lavish miniatures and the fact that the scribe addresses the illuminator directly by name – Remiet.

Remiet certainly took notice of these instructions on the day he came to paint this third gathering of eight leaves, since he followed them to the letter: 'ne faites rien cy' – 'make nothing here'. This injunction *not* to paint tells us that the image-maker, known in this period as the *enlumineur* or *historieur*, was still at this time under the direction of the scribe/*libraire*. These directives took various forms. They could be oral orders, shouts across the street that of course go unrecorded – 'paint such and such!' They could be roughly sketched drawings, made by a *libraire* with some facility at copying from a model, or sometimes by the more adept hand of a master illuminator as a guide to an assistant. They could be written instructions placed in the margins, indicating the subject of each miniature.[6] Sometimes these vernacular directives were not necessary, since the *libraire* provided the illuminator with an already illustrated exemplar from which the complete picture cycle could be copied. Remiet probably had such an illustrated exemplar to hand, since these instructions occur only here, where the directive is *not* to follow it.

Why did Oudin de Cavarnay write a message to Remiet telling him to paint nothing? What was actually meant to go here? This six-line space, half the size of the usual twelve lines that were left for the other miniatures, should be occupied by a line-drawn *figure*, more text than image – the PAX or carpenter's 'L-square', a didactic mnemonic image carefully described in the text of the *Pèlerinage de vie humaine* below. Referred to as a *signe figure*, this tool helps the pilgrim in Deguileville's narrative to memorize the proper relationship that the soul or *l'âme* at the centre has to negotiate between its love towards Christ above (X) and its love towards its adjacent neighbour, or *prochain* (P). From the many other illustrated copies of Deguileville's poem, we know that this image was often part of the miniature cycle. It may be set in a pictorial space, even sometimes a landscape (Fig. 2). Significantly, this mnemonic device occurs as the only visual sign in otherwise totally unillustrated manuscripts. Thus what has been described as the most intrinsic of all the illustrations in Deguileville's poem is strangely the only one missing in this manuscript.[7] It is also still a mystery as to why Oudin did not insert the simple L-square right away while he was copying the text or why for that matter he wanted to reserve its delineation for himself. Perhaps it was missing from the exemplar from which Remiet was copying the cycle of pictures and thus Oudin needed to read the text in order to create it.

We have seen that these curt negative instructions were an index of the superior social position of the *libraire*, who enjoyed closer links to the university and the clerical privileges that went along with it compared to the lower-status lay illuminator. Oudin was indeed among a group of artisans whom King Charles V ennobled in a document of 1371.[8] Although the *libraires* had to make an oath of allegiance to the university and were the only persons allowed to keep a shop and sell books for more than ten sous, according to letters patent of Charles VI in 1411, this did not affect their lucrative outside dealings with other patrons. It was the *libraire*, not the illuminator, who met with the official intermediaries who procured books for aristocratic and royal book buyers. The Valois 'vellomaniacs' Charles VI and his uncles Philippe le Hardi, Duke of Burgundy, and Jean, Duke of Berry, along with his younger brother Louis, Duke of Orléans, all depended on court retainers, or sometimes wealthy merchants like the Italian Jacques Rapondi, to seek out books and gain commissions from local *libraires*. With the exception of a few artists like the Limbourg brothers, who were famous in their own time and elevated to the rank of court retainers by the Duke of Berry, most illuminators waited to receive their orders from this middleman in their small urban workshops where they laboured, sheet by sheet and piece by piece, filling the gaps in what came to them as fragmented sections of Latin and vernacular texts. The distance between their shabby small world on the Paris street and the luminous luxury of the court was not geographically wide, but mentally it was vast. It was these *petits gens* who could provide the nobility with bountiful luxury in miniature. This ability of the lower orders, not only illuminators but seamstresses, armourers and other Parisian tradespeople, to provide their superiors with the very symbols of distinction and status from which they were themselves excluded is one of the fascinating sub-topics of this book. Maintaining the continuity of this rigidly hierarchical upward system of exchange depended to some extent on maintaining the system of traditional models used and re-used in the illuminator's workshop, which not only precluded change but encoded human action in signs that were always old.

What did Remiet think when he read 'make nothing here'? Nothing ('rien') had none of the numerical associations of zero, a sign that was a novelty at this time and still distrusted by many merchants as a devilish invention of the Saracen.[9] This nothing is a square rather than a circle – a space of emptiness that went unsignified. An anxiety about vacant spaces in this period, which is evidenced in everything from scholastic discussions of nature's abhorrence of the vacuum to decoration of housewares, goes some way to

2. Paris, Bibliothèque Nationale, fr. 376, fol. 17. Guillaume de Deguileville, *Pèlerinage de vie humaine*. The missing image of the carpenter's square.

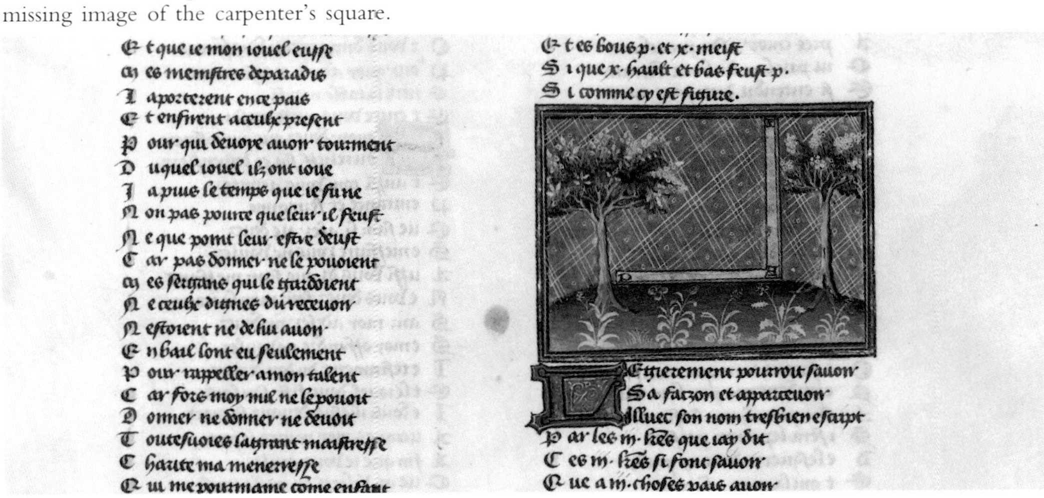

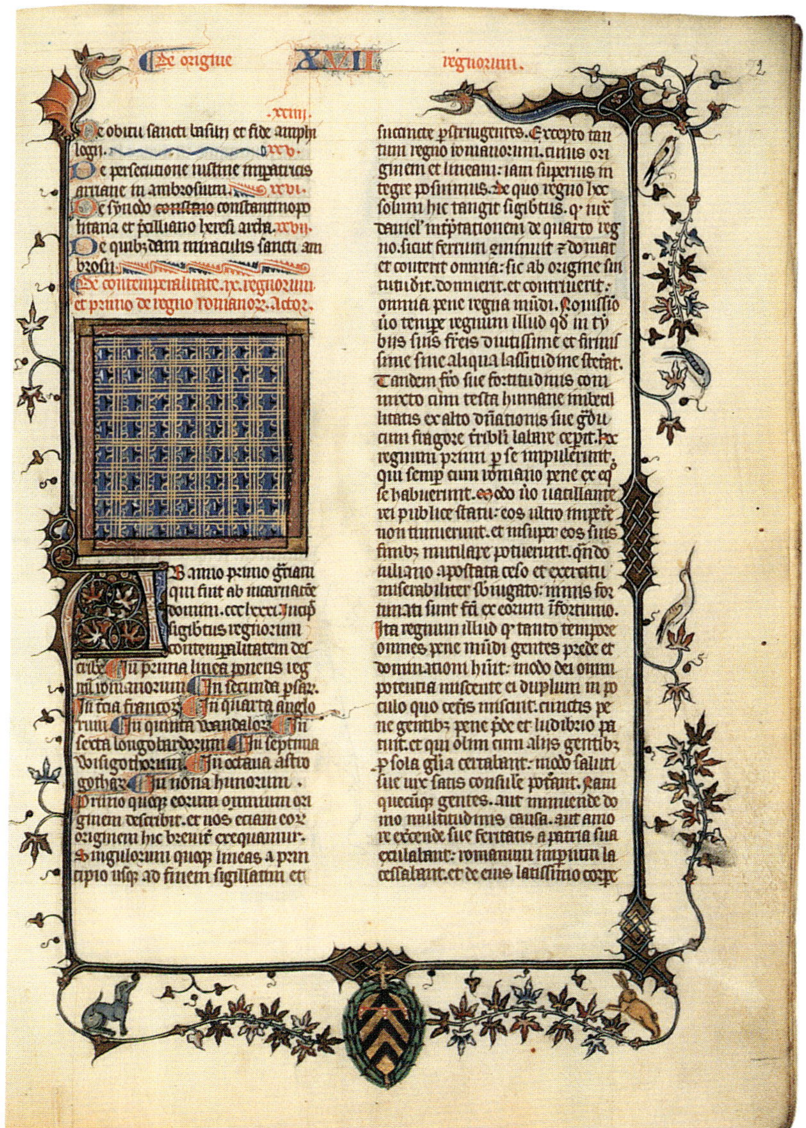

3. Lyons, Bibliothèque Municipale, MS 180, fol. 22. *Miroir historial*. The frame and nothing.

explaining the importance and popularity of manuscript illumination as a way of filling the text to the brim. Within the framework of reading, every part of the page, from running-title at the top to the *bas de page* in the bottom margin, filled a void to excess in the form of vines, curling scrolls and snapping dragons, completing the book's appearance as a luxury object. In medieval discourse a complete thing automatically ranked above an incomplete one. 'Nothing' could even be lavishly completed and painted in gold and colours, as occurs in a volume of the *Miroir historial* in Lyons (Fig. 3). Here an artisan trained in the very same visual vocabulary as Remiet, perhaps even the young illuminator himself, produced a series of richly decorated vine-scroll borders with dragon terminals, marginal monsters and full-blown frames complete with delicately painted blue and gold reticulated backgrounds. Most disturbing to our iconography-hungry modern eyes, however, he made all this without picturing any subjects inside them! This empty encyclopaedia is an example of the pitfalls in the Parisian workshop's dependence upon models. When a model was not available, as probably was the case here, it was just too much time and bother to devise a new one from scratch – that is, from reading the text. But the gaps had been left and still had to be 'painted'. Pattern had priority over pertinence, making it possible to have all the rich surface effects of illuminations and carefully painted miniatures, quite literally 'signifying nothing'.

That the unfinished folio of the *Pèlerinages* manuscript seems dead is not so much that it has a gaping hole where a miniature should go, but that it is lacking the blue, red and gold bar-border and spiky leaves, known as *vignettes* from the word for vine, that brought the simulation of living nature within the culture of the page. Documents reveal that these borders were sometimes produced by specialist illuminators who were highly regarded in their day and not viewed as either 'secondary' or mere 'decorative' artists, which they so often become in our modern classification. Such was the famous Anastasie mentioned by Christine de Pizan, 'who is so learned and skilled in painting manuscript borders and miniature backgrounds that one cannot find an artisan in all the city of Paris – where the best in the world are found – who can surpass her, nor who can paint flowers and details as delicately as she does, nor whose work is as highly esteemed, no matter how rich or precious the book is'.[10] One very distinctive specialist of this kind worked in close co-operation with Remiet in producing the elaborate curling borders for a lavish missal in Bayeux which was made for Étienne de Loypeau, Bishop of Luçon.[11] While we tend to take these winding vines for granted as part of the 'look' of late fourteenth-century illuminated manuscripts, contemporaries held them as important, if not more so, as the miniatures. Enclosing and sometimes dividing the text columns with their upward-shooting tendrils and leaves, sometimes of specific types of leaf, these forms most likely had their origins in traditional metaphors that described the page as a vineyard. Pliny had derived the word *pagina* from the trellis that joins together rows of vines, and for centuries Christian writers had used organic metaphors to describe the divine words of scripture, urging readers to see their books as open gardens, whose flowers, fruits and fragrances stimulated the senses. The fourteenth-century English bishop Richard de Bury, delighting in the 'green pleasure-gardens of all kinds of volumes' that he found in the libraries and bookshops of Paris, censured the 'greasy scullion' for spoiling 'the lilies of the book'.[12] Nearly every miniature that Remiet ever made is framed by such growths. His own border speciality, however, was not the robust and round flowering bud seen in some of his contemporaries, but the sharp, almost arrow-like ivy or vine leaf atop a curling spine. Whether or not he always painted these prickly and attenuated borders himself, as I tend to think was most often the case, they are an important and too often neglected field for Remiet's art, not so much a framework (which implies a seeing through) as a ground and trellis from which, and intertwined with which, text and miniatures are grown. The only unfinished image I have come across by this illuminator occurs in a copy of the *Cité de Dieu* of 1396 in which the lower bar-border terminates with a sketch of the head of a bishop sticking out his tongue, which was never painted (Fig. 4). This is important evidence that the whole page and not just the miniature cycle was pre-planned by one person.

Remiet painted a different kind of nothing in the margins of another encyclopaedia, a copy of the French translation of Bartholomeus Anglicus's *Livre des propriétés des choses*, or 'Book on the Properties of Things', which was commissioned by Philippe le Hardi from the *libraire* Jacques Rapondi, an Italian merchant based in Paris, who was paid 400 ecus on 3 January 1402 for delivering this manuscript 'newly written and illustrated (tout neuf, escript et ystorie)'.[13] Some of this money must have gone to Remiet for painting the fabulous four-part frontispiece showing God laying the circular table of the cosmos with the golden sun, moon and stars, setting birds to fly against the blue sky and filling the dark green forest with a menagerie of beasts (Fig. 5). One of his most magnificent pages, it is still, however, far from being *his* 'creation'. Donal Byrne has shown that this frontispiece, and other copies, like one in the Bibliothèque Sainte Geneviève which was bought by Louis d'Orléans in 1396, were based on that in the copy, now lost, which had been presented to the duke's brother, Charles V. It is the typical story of fraternal competition and keeping up with the king that stimulated so much visual art in the period. Remiet's copy, however, does retain something special: most probably the only vestige we have of his writing hand (not his handwriting) in the letters inscribed on the curling scrolls held by God in the first three scenes and by the translator, Jean Corbechon, in the fourth.[14] The first scroll reads: 'J'ay fait le ciel et la lumiere / Pour estre a homme chamberiere (I made the sky and the light to be man's dwelling)'. The 'I' here is God and the *vous* or 'you' addressed by the kneeling translator in the last scene on the page is the original royal patron. Remiet's subjectivity, as I/eye and the actual maker of the light in this marvellous miniature universe of creatures, is subsumed by both other lords, the earthly and heavenly ones. The medieval artist is still unable to create 'nothing' from himself, not only because of the traditional attribution of the art object that is the universe to God, but also because of the royal extension of that divine power in the ruler, whose directives create new texts and their images.

Remiet's 'signature' in fact appears not in the copied words and images of the frontispiece but at its limits. In this case we know that Remiet also painted the elaborately

4. Remiet. Paris, Bibliothèque Nationale, fr. 170, fol. 47v. Augustine, *La Cité de Dieu*. Unfinished marginal drollery.

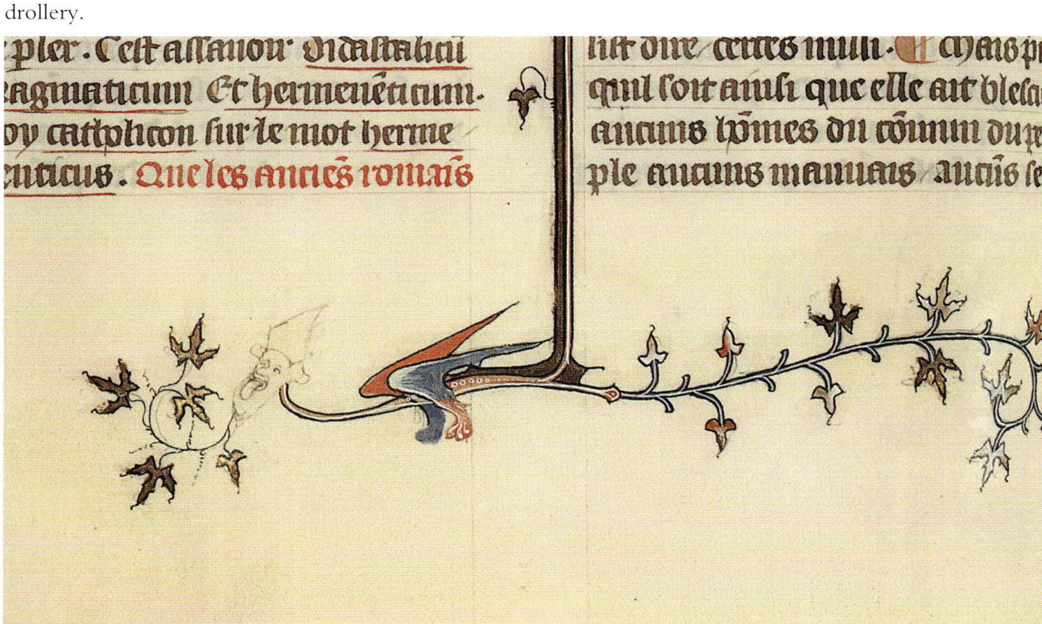

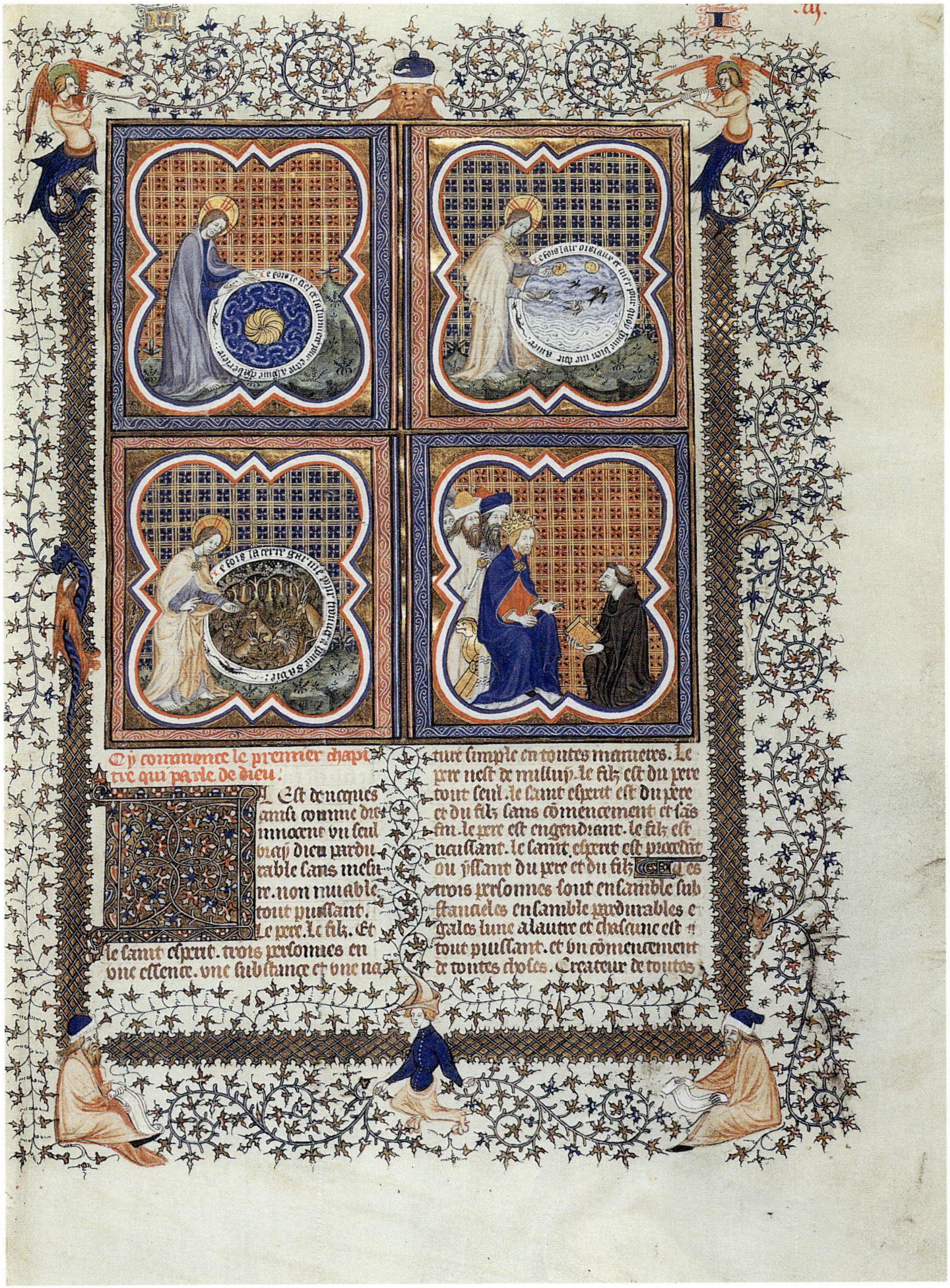

5. Remiet. Brussels, Bibliothèque Royale, MS 9094, fol. 12. *Livre des propriétés des choses.* Frontispiece: God's Creation, the translator's presentation, and some 'thing' in the top margin.

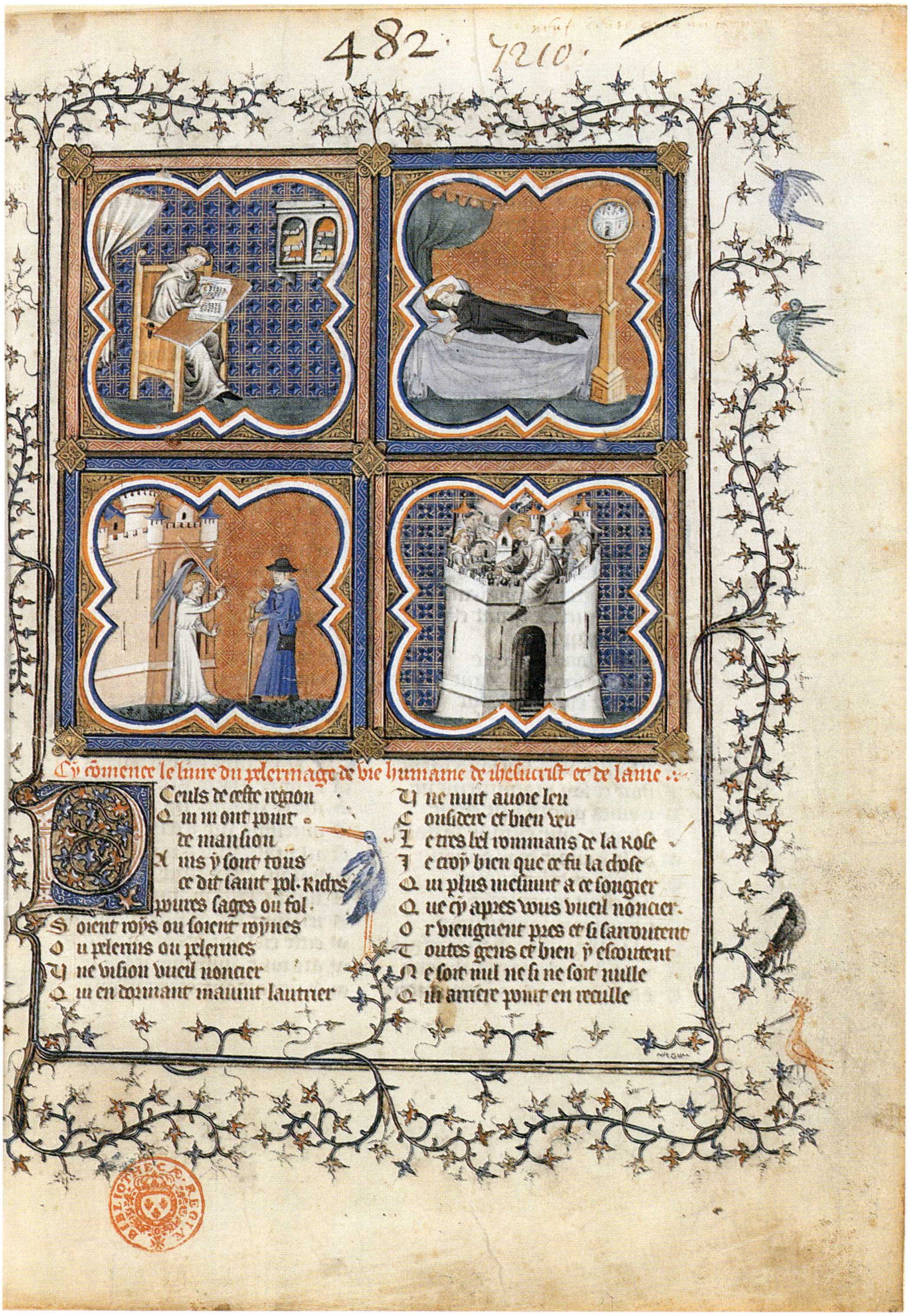

6. Remiet. Paris, Bibliothèque Nationale, fr. 823, fol. 1. Guillaume de Deguileville, *Pèlerinage de vie humaine.* Frontispiece: the author reading, dreaming his vision of the Heavenly Jerusalem in a mirror, as a pilgrim having his way barred by an angel with the flaming sword, and seeing the religious orders scale the walls.

winding border vines himself, because at the top, one of his painted figures is literally joined to them (Fig. 5). This preposterous creature, some thing outside the 'properties of things', has a gap between its body which is a grimacing face or mask, and which is surmounted by a hat-like object. Perhaps this is a playful allusion to the 'darkness upon the face of the deep' in the second verse of Genesis – the chaos of *nihil* or nothing out of which the universe is created in the miniatures below. Placing a human face in the middle of a blob of primal chaotic matter out of which nature is unfurling, Remiet has literally made a person out of a vacuum, nobody out of nothing, *nemo* out of *nihil*. This anti-person projected on to a void, was in many respects emblematic of the illuminator himself, whose purpose was to fill in the gaps not only between texts but between things, at the same time remaining hidden. Grammatical games were played with *nemo* throughout the Middle Ages. Because in the scriptures 'nemo deum vidit (Nobody has seen God)', the fact that 'Nemo saw God' makes everything impossible, inadmissable and inaccessible quite possible for *Nemo*. This individualized anonymity is perhaps also, in its human characteristics, an early example of a picture of nobody – literally a face without a body – whose portrait was to become popular in subsequent centuries.[15] I have never seen anything comparable in manuscript borders of this period. That this is one of the few indefinite, vague things that Remiet ever painted, is perhaps because he did not copy it but, like God the divine artificer below, produced it *ex nihilo*.

The order to paint nothing in the *Pèlerinages* manuscript is unusual in that it distinguishes an illuminator by name, drawing his particular attention rather than someone else's to the gap. If only one illuminator had been involved, the direction need not have named Remiet. Since manuscripts were not illuminated as complete books but were farmed out as separate gatherings for speedy decoration and only later bound together, they often contain the work of more than one artist, and BN fr. 823 is no exception. The first poem in BN fr. 823, the twelve gatherings that form the *Pèlerinage de vie humaine* (including the gap on fol. 18v), contains miniatures solely by the illuminator I shall call Remiet, especially his splendid four-part full-page frontispiece, which is always the most prestigious image in a book (Fig. 6). Rather like the cover of a modern paperback, the opening frontispiece aroused expectations of what lay further within. But there are three such 'covers' within this volume, each announcing a different poem in the trilogy. The frontispiece to the third poem, the *Pèlerinage de Jésus-Christ*, was also completed by Remiet along with all the miniatures to this poem (see Fig. 34). The frontispiece to the second, the *Pèlerinage de l'âme*, is, however, by an illuminator sometimes associated with the name Jean de Nizières, whose miniatures are so close to Remiet's as to suggest he had been apprenticed under him (see Fig. 162). Eight of the nine miniatures illustrating this second poem are by yet another hand and represent the earliest dated work of another prolific illuminator of the period, whose fleshier faces can be seen in manuscripts produced well into the second decade of the fifteenth century and whom Millard Meiss has dubbed 'the Virgil Master' (Fig. 7).[16] His miniature on fol. 105v is a confused amalgam of elements in the text for which no standard programme had yet been devised. In the corner we see how, during the trial of the soul after death, Satan acts as a 'court reporter', writing the accusation. But this post-mortem experience has been oddly combined with the figure in bed on the left, who illustrates part of Justice's speech about the sick body being comforted by a letter from Grace Dieu. The flatness of this miniature, emphasized by the grid-like background and square frame, contrasts with Remiet's much more intense handling of such themes, as we shall see. The blander work of this younger practitioner can be found alongside Remiet's in a number of books, including the Duke of Burgundy's *Livre des propriétés des choses*, the frontispiece of which we have just described and which was produced nearly a decade later, and the three-volume Soissons *Bible historiale*, suggesting a long period of professional association.

Was there a Remiet workshop? I prefer to think of him as working alone, like the writer Deguileville he painted in the first frontispiece, revealed by a drawn curtain, his ink-pot fixed to his desk (Fig. 6). Most images of scribes and illuminators at work show isolated figures, never the 'workshops' that some scholars have hypothesized must have existed in order to create such composite and stylistically diverse miniatures within single manuscripts. So when we see miniatures by Remiet next to those of other artists in the same volume, this does not mean they were necessarily working together under one roof, but that the *libraire* was wearing out his shoe leather carrying gatherings between them. The fact that the three 'hands' found in the 1393 manuscript are also found together in other manuscripts suggests that they are neighbours and perhaps loose associates but not partners. In the rush to get all three poems that comprise this elegant volume completely illuminated in the three shops to which he had delivered them, then to the binder and finally to the important patron who had ordered them, the *libraire*, Oudin, forgot to fill in this important memory image as he had promised. Moreover, he did not remember to take his pumice-stone and erase his scribbled instructions from the parchment.

But the note in the Paris *Pèlerinages* allows us to do more than build up a picture of a system. It refers to a person whose name we might otherwise never have known. The modern obsession with finding a name to fit an artistic oeuvre was not one shared by the fourteenth-century patrons of illuminated manuscripts, however. Even the Limbourg brothers were indistinguishable as individual 'hands', never signed their works and were still referred to as a team of workers in documents. Sometimes an individual scribe, like Oudin de Cavarnay in this case, felt it appropriate to add his own name in an acrostic, yet most illuminators, like the parchment-makers and the binders, go unrecorded. This scribe is recorded not only by the words of this manuscript but also by those written on a monument. His tomb, next to his wife Jeanne's in the choir of the little church of Saint Merry in Paris, bore the inscription: 'Here lies Oudart de Cavarnai, merchant and bourgeois of Paris, who passed away the year of Our Lord 1412 on 26th August'.[17] Remiet has only a book for a tomb. The only verbally inscribed place of his memory is, ironically, this empty space in a text. That the scribe, the transcriber of another's words, should be so self-conscious when the (to our eyes) more individualistic image-maker is veiled in anonymity, is an indication of the still superior value of writing over painting. Even an English law student paying his way through the schools by working as a scribe was able to leave his name and his testimony at the end of a manuscript of the *Arbre des batailles*, which he tells us he finished copying on Sunday, 28 October 1397, in his house before the door of the church of Saint André des Arts on the Left Bank.[18] This ego, who writes 'Ego Johannes Cachelart' in Latin, even within the context of a vernacular text, suggests that the ranking order in the Latin Quarter was still predicated on learning that language. But of course the main reason why Remiet cannot proclaim his place and station in the same way is because his medium is not writing in any

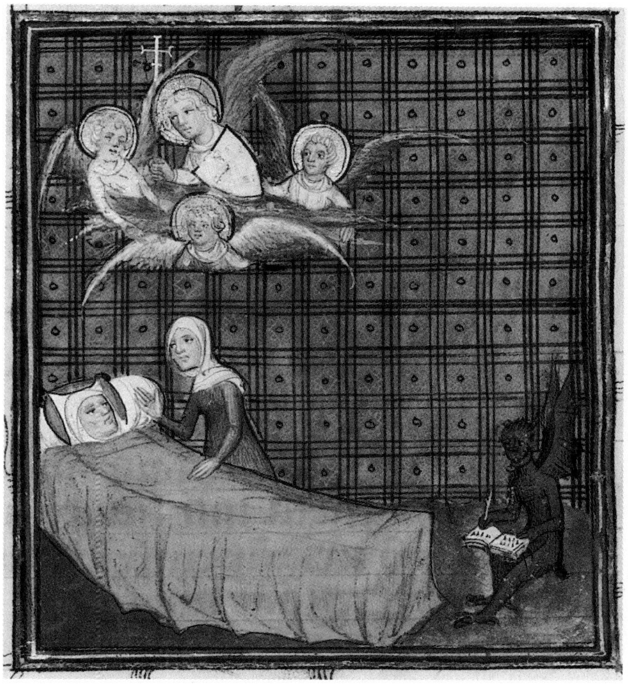

7. The Virgil Master. Paris, Bibliothèque Nationale, fr. 823, fol. 105v. Guillaume de Deguileville, *Pèlerinage de l'âme*. The devil writes the accusation against the sick soul who is nursed by Grace Dieu.

language but painting, which calls for more mediated and hidden forms of self-projection.

Remiet might thus seem to exemplify Émile Mâle's notion of the medieval artist as 'the passive interpreter of great ideas'.[19] But this is to rely on the standards of modern art-making with its emphasis upon primacy of conception and originality. Medieval writers also saw themselves as interpreters, as pygmies on the shoulders of giants, authors of texts whose authority always lay elsewhere, and which they only re-presented. Remiet's frontispiece to the *Pèlerinage de vie humaine*, for example, depicts the author Guillaume de Deguileville not so much writing a new text as perusing an old one in his library (Fig. 6). In the opening lines of the work, reference is made to the famous secular dream poem the *Roman de la Rose*, which the monk was reading before he went to bed and which then inspired his own vision of the Heavenly Jerusalem in a mirror. Even the dream is not a psychologically original experience but a copy. Just as the author is at pains here to legitimate his own poem by founding it in the framework of another, images were also seen as effective only if they were couched in terms of the already-known. Remiet's four-part frontispiece is itself modelled on the visual authority of similar four-part 'dreamer' frontispieces to the *Roman de la Rose*, which show the dreamer asleep and the beginning of the dream narrative he experiences, except that Remiet's protagonist is a pilgrim rather than a lover. Of course there are differences. Whereas in the earlier poem the goal is penetration of a woman's body, in this pilgrimage the climactic and longed-for experience is more final. In the third scene of the frontispiece the pilgrim's way into the Heavenly Jerusalem is barred by the angel with a flaming sword, the angel of death from Genesis 3:24. Death thus opens the pilgrimage of human life, just as we shall see, in a later chapter, it will eventually close it, again with a figure brandishing a sharp instrument.

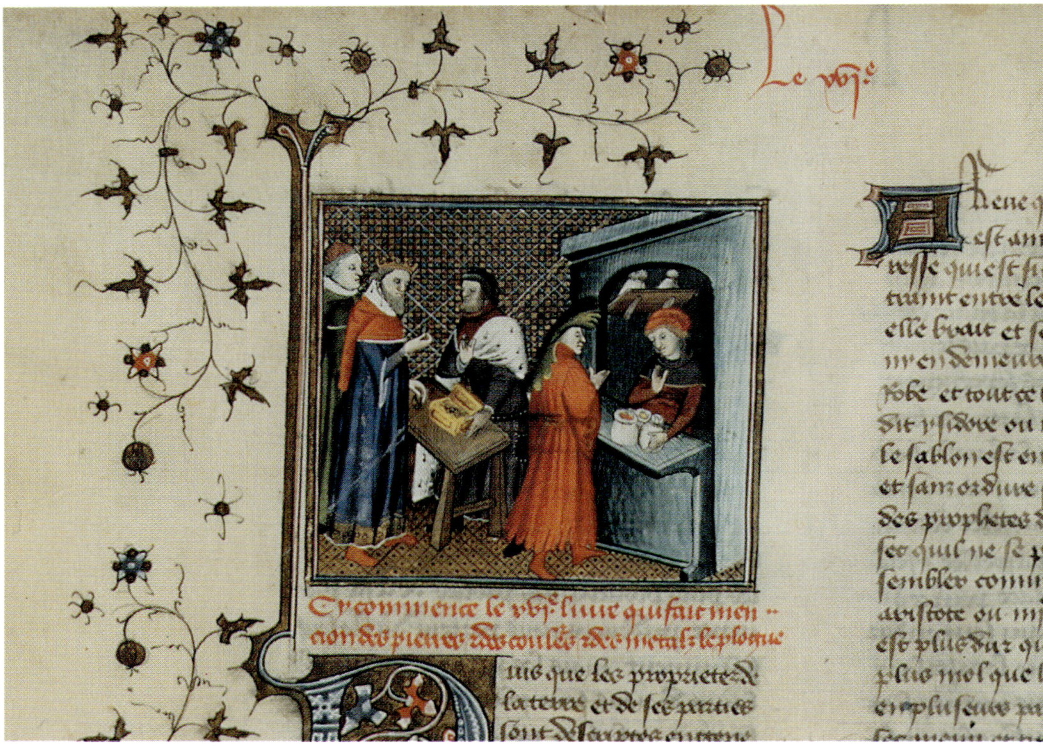

8. The Boethius Master. Paris, Bibliothèque Nationale, fr. 22531, fol. 257v. *Livre des propriétés des choses*, Book XVI, 'on stones and colours'. A king buys gems and a noble buys ground colours at a shop.

The name and nothing visible on fol. 18v of this manuscript become emblems of the gap in history itself, if history is seen only as that which can be written down. Although he left no monument, no tomb, as did the scribe Oudin de Cavarnay or his royal patrons whose carved effigies crowd the choir of the abbey church of Saint Denis, Remiet left countless documents of a painted life, or rather a life in painting. These are in numerous texts, or rather in the gaps between them. We tend to think of images as monuments rather than as documents of the past. Monuments, with their imposing finality and commemoration, always seem more transparent to interpretation, since they were not simply inherited but were constructed specifically for the purposes of collective memory. By contrast, a document is not an end but part of a flow, and can often be an unintentional trace or vestige that is left in the place where someone passed. Yet documents are, for the most part, not expressively unique but more often formulaic, fitting experience within inherited and repeated formulae.[20] Must a document be in writing, like that pseudo-legal script penned by the devil in the open book in order to damn the dying man in the *Pèlerinage de l'âme* miniature (Fig. 7)? For Remiet's contemporaries, this official or legal construction of a self was a new but increasingly powerful notion. The recording demon in this miniature exemplifies how written records were coming to shape how people defined not only their lives but also their deaths and afterlives, as stories and scripts that could be recorded and used against them. If the devil took notes at Remiet's deathbed, that book is not available to us, nor is any contemporary scripted story of his life. Even if a detailed account were extant, it would be less useful for my purposes than those things that Remiet made for himself. This deathbed miniature by his younger associate can be taken as a certain type of record, neutral in its objectivity, telling us about attitudes to 'death' in the Late Middle Ages but not about a particular death. By contrast, the images made by Remiet's hand, I shall argue, are a different kind of evidence, when viewed as articulations of a subject. Not only do I see his frontispiece to the *Pèlerinage de vie humaine* (Fig. 6) as a copy of an earlier allegorical model, I interpret it as an embodiment, a re-membering of a man whose members have long since disintegrated. It resurrects the possible life journeys and sites of projection available to the body that made it. Thus we shall remember Remiet not in the finality of a monument but through the constantly unfolding, unwritten documents of his own artistic practice. In this sense we are witnesses to his own illuminated Last Will and Testament in the spaces he filled between texts. But before we can begin to track the lines of that painted trajectory that lead from his birth to his death, we have to locate him in a space, not on the page, but in the place where he made his living.

A Shop on the Street of Illuminators

The skin of the servant is the parchment on which the master's hand writes . . . Books are only metaphors of the body. Michel de Certeau[21]

Man's flesh is viler than the skin of a sheep.
When sheep are dead, their skin still has some use,
For it is pulled and writ upon, both sides.
But with man's death, both flesh and bones are dead.
Mortuary Roll[22]

We often associate medieval artists with the monastery and cloister, the cathedral and especially the court, but we forget that their new and pre-eminent location in the fourteenth century was actually the street. Parisian artisans like goldsmiths were required by ordinance of the city's guilds to work 'on the street, their window or door ajar', and most manufacturing, whether it was pewter-beating or paternoster-bead production, took place in this semi-public space as set down in the famous *Livre des métiers* in the previous century.[23] What the artisan/artist did was not the private and secret 'creation' later associated with the Romantic genius. If the artisan's work was not to be viewed with suspicion, as trickery, it had to be seen to be performed. Monopolies were strictly enforced, it being forbidden by a royal decree of 1391 to sell anything in the city that was 'made outside Paris, in Germany or elsewhere, because these works were often false and of bad quality'. Most shops in fourteenth-century Paris had shutters that opened outwards to create horizontal tables on which wares could be displayed, as in the apothecary's shop depicted in a miniature from the chapter on colours in the *Livre des propriétés des choses*, illuminated by one of Remiet's younger contemporaries (Fig. 8). It was from such a shop that Remiet would have bought ready-ground pigments, like the bright vermillion here used to paint the cloak worn by the gentleman before the counter on which are displayed the ground colours in bags. Although one of the distinct features of much of Remiet's work is its rejection of the bright saturated colour of his contemporaries, pigments and their function and meaning are, as we shall see, crucial to understanding the decoration of books in this period.[24] In 1323 the *libraires* working for the university vowed to keep clearly visible in the windows of their *boutiques* 'a parchment list of works for sale', and by 1342 it was stipulated that prices had to be clearly marked on the books themselves.[25] The books referred to here were copies of those common school texts that would attract students and not the lavish manuscripts that Remiet illuminated which, like custom-built cars today, were commissioned long in advance and destined for particular patrons. Since the illumination of manuscripts was a bespoke trade and the artisan did not usually sell finished work directly to customers, but usually through a *libraire*, it is unlikely that Remiet's shop had such a front. None the less, we should think of him at work in a sphere less private than that of the modern artist, his shutters open to let in the daylight for working by as well as the gaze of passers-by.

With the royal and ecclesiastical government on the Île de la Cité, markets and merchants on the Right Bank and the university on the Left, Paris was a city with clear spatial demarcations of power. Each trade had its quarter, for example the apothecaries on the Île de la Cité, the money-changers and goldsmiths on the Grand Pont, and the butchers on the Right Bank near the Grand Châtelet. The *libraires*, booksellers, parchment-makers, binders, scribes and illuminators were no exception. They were located in two specific areas, the earlier one centred on the Rue Neuve Notre Dame on the Île de la Cité, which ran right up to the cathedral. Since the thirteenth century, this area had been the site of a book trade that catered not only to the ecclesiastical needs of the canons but to a growing clientele seeking luxurious illuminated volumes.[26] By the mid-fourteenth century a second area had developed on the Left Bank in the parish of Saint Séverin, a major mercantile crossroads in the city and the heart of the university district, and this is where we shall find Remiet. But, no longer limited to these locales, books had begun to permeate the whole metropolis.[27] When Dante described in the *Divine Comedy* 'the art which in Paris they call illumination', he was referring to the pre-eminence already in the thirteenth century of the French capital as a centre of book painting.[28] Linked to its establishment as a political and administrative centre under the Capetian and Valois kings, the fame and expansion of its university and the lucrative trade in luxury goods via the Seine, Paris became the first 'art' city in Europe, the first 'city of books'. When Eustache Deschamps wrote a *ballade* with the refrain 'nothing can compare to Paris', he was echoing a long tradition of encomia that included John of Jandun's description of 'Parisius paradisus'.[29] Formal liturgical books for the mass and divine office were required by the many religious institutions that ringed the city, such as Saint Martin des Champs, Saint Germain des Prés and Saint Victor, as well as the vast new convents of the Franciscans and Dominicans on the Left Bank where the new portable breviaries and pocket Bibles were so popular. The university institutions also required properly copied textbooks for study, as well as tomes of the Church Fathers and pagan philosophers for college libraries, like the Sorbonne's. Increasingly, students wanted to own their own books, filled with marginal 'baboonery', as did the masters and high-ranking Churchmen of the Latin Quarter who were also setting up private libraries. On the Right Bank, where much of the mercantile activity was focused around Les Halles and the Châtelet, the seat of the provost of Paris, who represented the king in the city, many noble families had their *hôtels*, complete with books for pleasure and prestige, illuminated romances and histories, written in French rather than Latin. Here too was the new Louvre palace with its great tower library in the Tour de la Faconnerie built to hold over nine hundred volumes collected by Charles V. From here the wise ruler could lift his eyes from one of the tomes on his *roues* or 'wheel' reading desk and look out over the Île de la Cité, where at one end stood the great cathedral of Notre Dame with its constant need for service-books and at the other, the Palais Royale, where, in addition to ledgers and account books of the administrative Chambre des Comptes and the Parlement, were living quarters for the royal family. Here were the most prestigious patrons of luxury illuminated manuscripts of all, setting the tastes of the rest of the city but no longer focused only on the palace but spreading, in addition to the new Louvre, to other splendid stations throughout the city, like the favoured royal residence the Hôtel Saint Pol, at the other end of the Right Bank. Here were other fashionable *hôtels* where the newest private libraries of the city were begun, like that of Remiet's greatest patron, the Duke of Orléans, who had another *séjour* near the Bucy gate on the Left Bank. In this network of sites of making, buying and displaying books, Remiet was well situated.

The Paris *taille*, or property tax registers, for 1428 list a 'Pierre Remyet' as having a 'maison' on the 'Rue de la Parcheminerie' that is described as 'looking on to' the 'Rue Erembourth de Brie'.[30] The latter street, made up of old houses built *c.*1250 and named

9. Map of Paris by Truschet and Hoyeau of 1552 (detail) with the university quarter of the Left Bank showing Remiet's corner, the intersection of the Rue Boutebrie and the Rue de la Parcheminerie, both labelled.

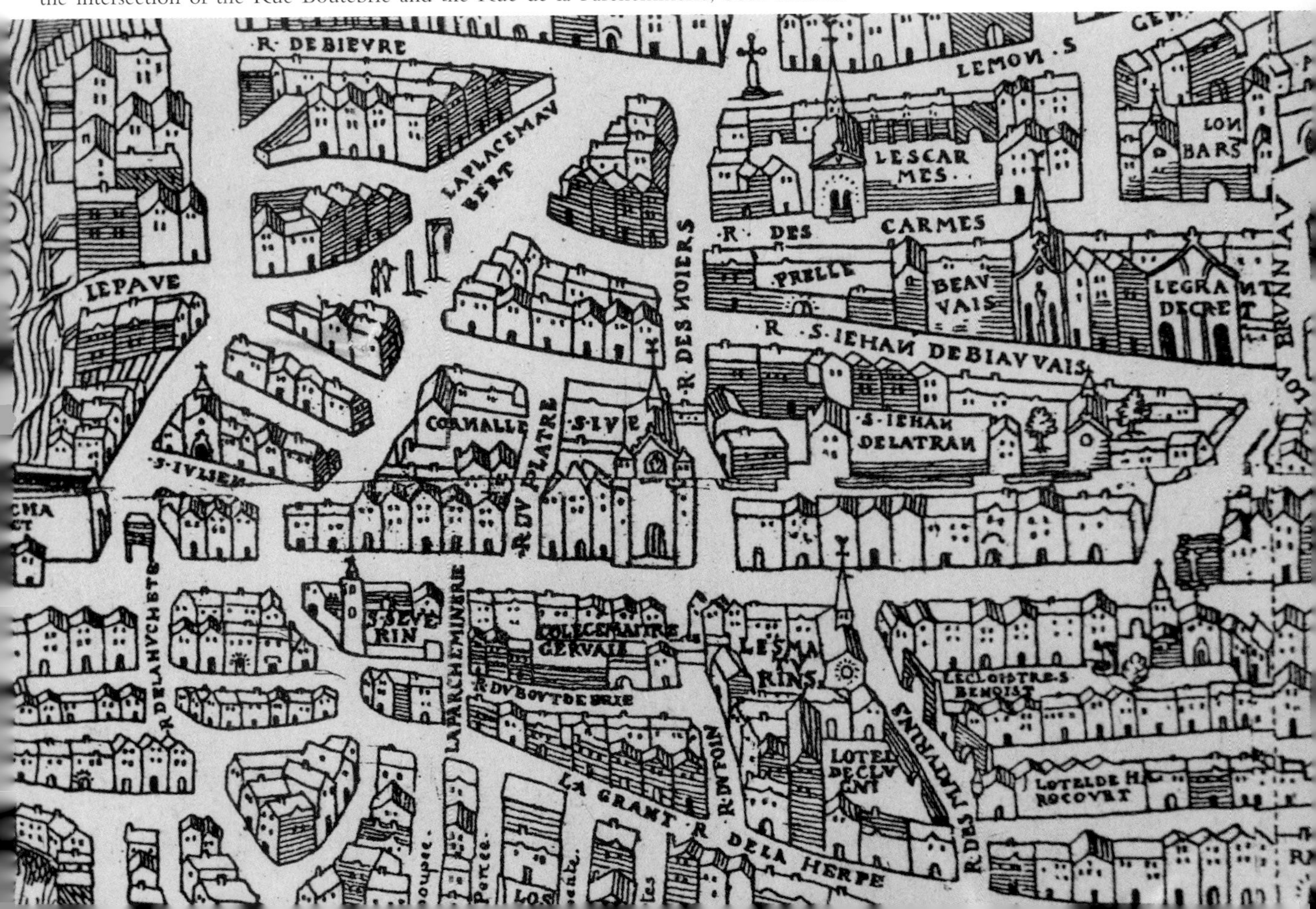

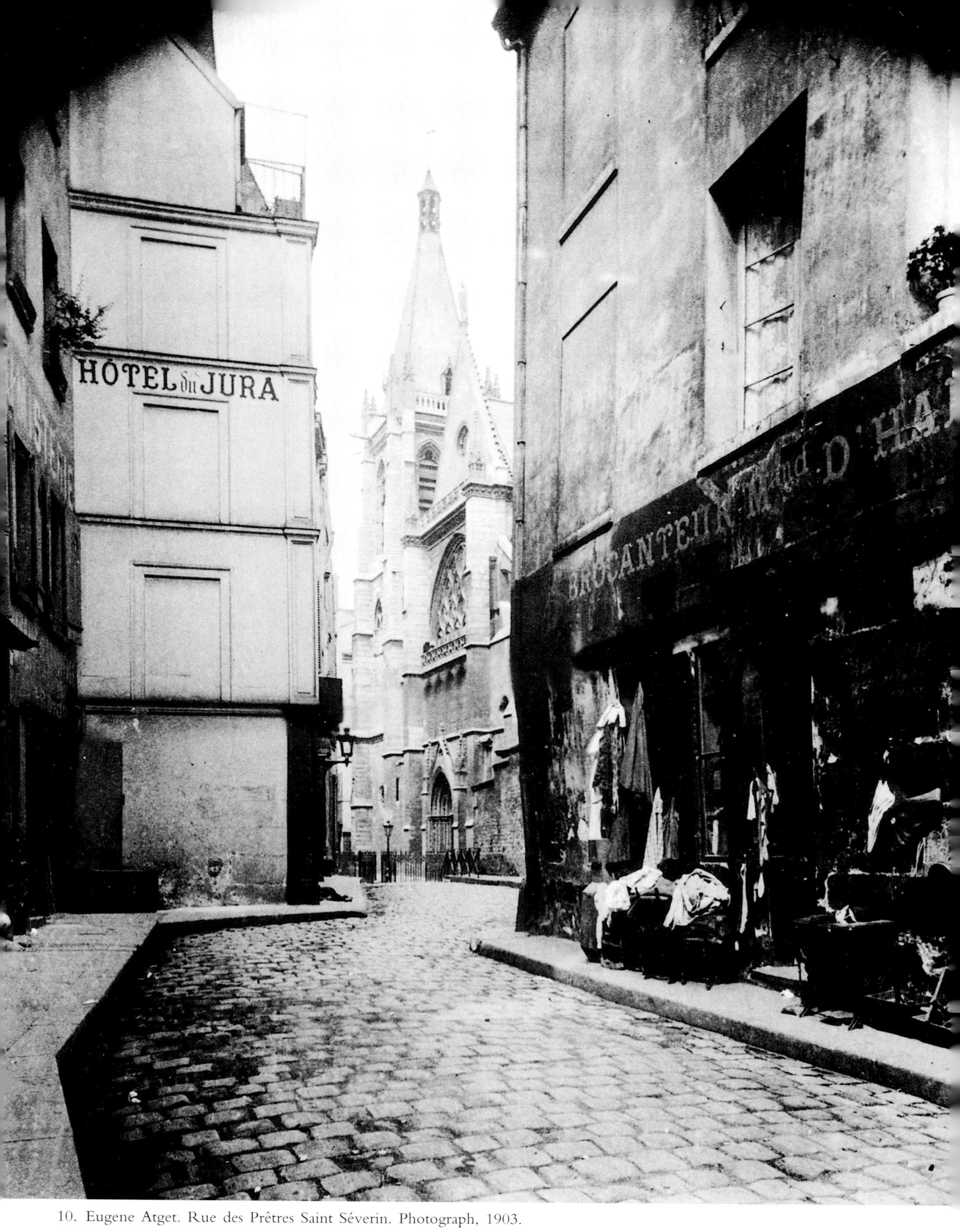

10. Eugene Atget. Rue des Prêtres Saint Séverin. Photograph, 1903.

after a lady resident, was popularly known in the fourteenth century as the 'Rue des Enlumineurs', or Illuminators' Street. The *taille* records of 1292 list no fewer than eight illuminators living and working there.[31] The Rue de la Parcheminerie, which runs parallel to the river, refers to the word 'parchemin' (derived from the name of the Greek city Pergamum), which is a term found in documents more often than the term 'vellum' (calfskin). Here parchment-makers, who did the washing, de-hairing, scraping and stretching-out of animal skins that formed the material base for Remiet's work, had lived for generations.[32] Later it was known for a time as the 'Rue aux Écrivains', suggesting an elevation in the area's status. This corner where the two small streets met is visible in sixteenth-century maps of the city (Fig. 9), which show a clutter of small two-storey houses a few blocks from the Seine. Remiet's corner was in the heart of the busy Latin Quarter and faced, to the north, the imposing parish church of Saint Séverin, which had been recently enlarged, and to the south the Convent of the Mathurins, which was a major university institution and the site where all prepared parchment had to be inspected before it could be made into books. You can stand on this corner today, where the Rue Boutebrie leads down to the Boulevard Saint Germain (formerly the Rue du Foin), and there are even tiny bookshops on the Rue de la Parcheminerie, about the size of that of Remiet's neighbour, the *libraire* and bookseller Regnault du Montet. But now the street names are inscribed in white on the ubiquitous blue plaques of the city; addresses in medieval Paris were signalled by visual images, brightly painted boards or carved objects, which hung above the doorways or were inserted high on the exterior walls. These gave the houses their names, like the 'Maison des Coquilles' and the 'Maison d'Étoile', even the 'Maison des Trois Morts et des Trois Vifs'. Medieval urban dwellers defined where they lived not by a number and a name but by an image and a sign. The house that belonged to Remiet is later listed, in 1506, as at the 'enseigne de Sainte Catherine', but we do not know whether it already went under the sign of that saint – a wheel – in the fourteenth century.[33]

In 1903 the great Parisian photographer Eugène Atget made a view of the same corner, looking up to the western porch of the church from the top of Rue Boutebrie along the Rue des Prêtres Saint Séverin (Fig. 10). The run-down rag-and-bone shop, or *brocante*, its written sign above, stands on the site of Remiet's long-gone shop, but the scale of building is the same, as are the dark shadows created by squeezing two- and three-storey tenements so close together. I am using this image as a 'document', which was one of its intended functions. Atget took it as part of his *Topographie* series of over seventeen hundred pictures in order to provide antiquarians with inexpensive records of the city's urban fabric that had changed little over the centuries but which was, in his day, facing demolition or modernization. But Atget was also an 'author', and, for those who later collected his prints, also a great artist. The same split, between the image as a neutral historical record and the image as a work of artistic self-expression, will confront us when dealing with Remiet, linking the early twentieth-century Parisian photographer and his fourteenth-century predecessor. Both were, in their own times, the patient producers of multiple standardized images, made in their modest, commercially located shops for a varied clientele of collectors and official bodies. Both produced, not unique single images, but serial sequences of documents which are repositories of memory. Both submerged their authorial identity in the apparent practicality of what they made, and both created, in the course of long lifetimes, a vast archive of images that have subsequently been reconstructed and recirculated as 'art'. More importantly, the half-empty and melancholy images that they both produced are as much about death and absence as the life and presence they seemingly sought to record. The difference is that, while the photographer's enormous oeuvre not only serves to document Old Paris but was also capable of slipping away to be used in other discourses, popularized, sanitized and even, by the surrealists, fetishized, Remiet's multiple parchment albums, hidden between the covers of a more distant past, have not been reanimated in the same way. They are more thoroughly dead.[34] One could also argue that another major difference between the two image-masters of Parisian memory is that Remiet was not, like a photographer, aiming to make an accurate pictorial record of his time and place. But this is exactly what he managed to do, not by fixing things through a chemical process working on light-sensitive material but by copying things by more manual illumination. For both masters, what was most often revealed in their meticulous labour of light and darkness was neglect, decay and death.

Remiet and his heirs are described as paying a tax of four Parisian *livres* a year on this corner property well into the fifteenth century. Then in 1440 it is listed as empty and ruined along with most of the declining neighbourhood during the years of Parisian depopulation following the English occupation, when many illuminators fled the capital.[35] This sum is not inconsiderable and, although it does not show that Remiet was rich, it places him, as a property-owner, in the category of the *gros* rather than the *menus*, the big rather than the little people, as Parisians were defined in tax documents.[36] Like most artisans, Remiet would have had a working space on the ground floor with a window to the street and would have either used the upper floors for his own family's accommodation or rented them out.[37] That there are no rent-payers listed in the 1428 tax records suggests the house was the family home. Not only does this document pinpoint a habitation for our name, it locates it right in the centre of the university district and at the heart of the Parisian book trade. Illuminators like Remiet were thus placed in close proximity to those who could provide them with work as well as to the suppliers of materials.[38] The Convent of the Mathurins where parchment was inspected was at the bottom of Remiet's side street, and colours could be bought at the many apothecary shops in this area, many of which were linked to the medical schools of the university. Here too were concentrated those who might commission manuscripts. Just down the narrow passage from Remiet's place was the courtyard of one of the newly founded university institutions, the College of Maître Gervais, founded by one of Charles V's physicians for the study of astrology and astrological medicine. Here, in six houses converted into a library, chapel and living quarters, were housed twenty-six scholars from the region of Bayeux.[39]

Remiet's close ties to the university are indicated by another, much earlier document. The name 'Perrin Remy' appears among the 15 illuminators, 14 *libraires*, 11 scribes, 6 bookbinders and 18 parchment-makers who were all made exempt, as 'servants of the university of Paris', from the onerous civic responsibility of city guard duty in a letter patent issued by Charles V on 5 November 1368.[40] Names are spelled in multiple ways in documents from this period, but Perrin is an affectionate diminutive of Pierre, and the surname Remy (from St Remigius) can also appear as Remiot/Remiet.[41] Little Pierre appears along with some of the most well known and established artists of the previous generation, like Jean le Noir, who had also worked as an official court artist for Charles V, suggesting a measure of success at an early age. The young illuminator would have finished his apprenticeship and was already working as an independent master at the time of this document. Since most apprentices began as children of eight or nine and worked for an average of ten years before they became masters in their own right, Remiet would have to have been at least twenty years old in 1368. This would push back the date of his birth to 1348 – the year the Black Death first struck Paris.

Remiet displays an intimate knowledge of the university and its containment of knowledge in books, in a miniature in one of the few Latin manuscripts he ever illuminated, a copy of Nicolas de Lyra's *Postilla litteralis super Biblia* (Fig. 12). Remiet represents how this text was used in the schools, showing a group of students seated on a bench listening to a master lecture from the open book on his lectern. One of the tonsured students, who sports fancy pointed shoes in contrast to the austere sandals of the Franciscan teacher, also has a volume opened on his knees. But this is not an image that Remiet 'sketched' from attending such lectures at the nearby Sorbonne or the Convent of the Cordeliers. It is an image of the idea of the Word, as it comes from God, who in the golden-curtained upper room of heaven is tentatively opening his own volume. This opening, painted with blobs representing writing, is pointed at the scholar below who in turn must interpret it for his audience. In this hierarchy of reading, the open book, not writing itself, signals varying degrees of access to the Word, according to whose hands are holding it.

The words that Remiet had to read were far more mundane. Rather than an interpreter of the text, like these scholars, he was, as we have seen, mostly following the instructions of the *libraire*. In addition to the directions in the Paris *Pèlerinages* discussed above, there is in a second manuscript a marginal note recording his name which provides more clues to workshop practice, although it complicates rather than clarifies matters and, for one scholar at least, has called the whole issue of 'who is Remiet?' into question. It appears in the bottom margin of fol. 8v of a richly illustrated *Histoire ancienne jusqu'à César* (London BL MS Royal 20.D.i) (Fig. 11). Written below the catchword, which keyed the text at the end of this first gathering to the beginning of the next, it reads: 'Ci faut le secont cayer que maistre Renaut doit avoir, qui fu baillié à Perrin Remiet pour faire l'enlumineure de l'autre cayer (Here should be the second gathering which master

11. London, British Library, MS Royal 20.D.i, fol. 8v. *Histoire ancienne* (detail). Another message scribbled at the lower margin for Remiet.

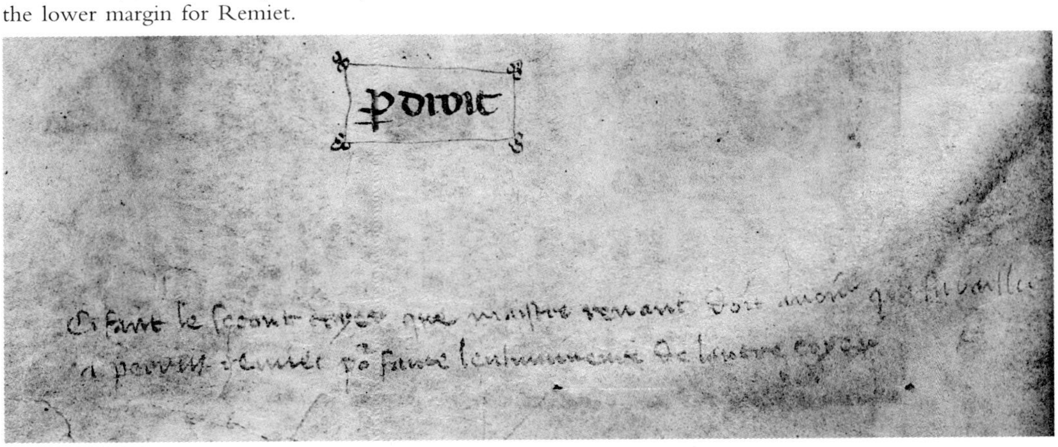

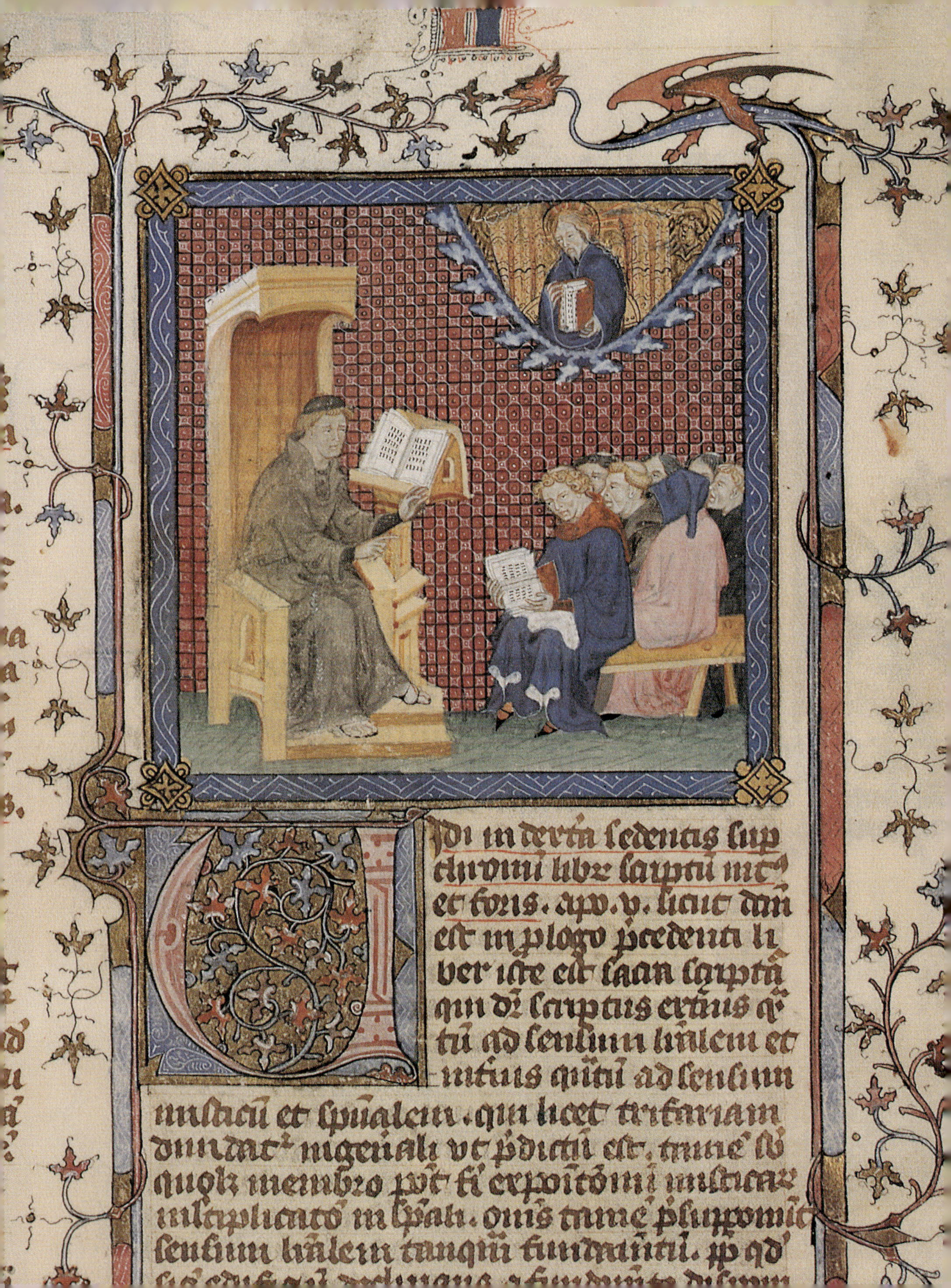

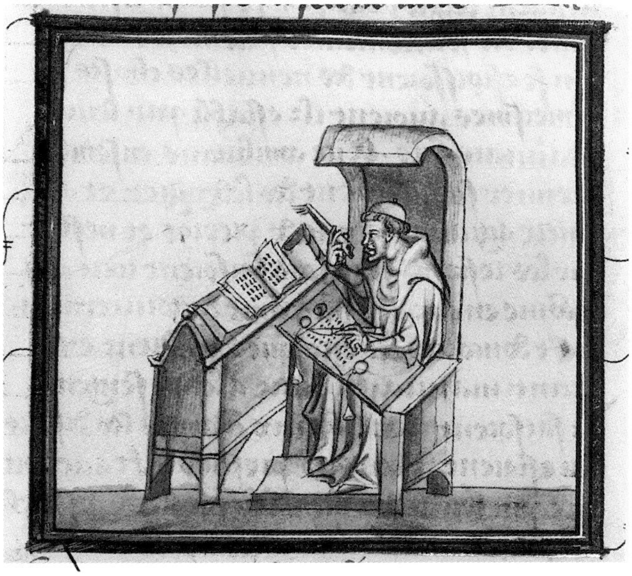

13. Remiet. London, British Library, MS Lansdowne 1179, fol. 34v. *Miroir historial.* Seneca and his books.

Regnault should have given to Perrin Remiet to do the illumination of the other gathering)'.[42] The name Renaut here refers to another Parisian *libraire*, Regnault du Montet, one of the four *grands libraires* to the university who regulated prices, and who was in fact Remiet's next door neighbour on the Rue de la Parcheminerie in the difficult years after the turn of the century when courtly patronage of the book trade was in decline. In 1416 Regnault was tried by the Parlement of Paris for the treasonable act of selling books to the English.[43] He was dealing internationally long before this scandal, since this manuscript of the *Histoire ancienne* is not in fact a Parisian product at all but was written and illuminated in Angevin Naples earlier in the fourteenth century. One can hypothesize that this volume had come into Regnault's hands and that the note mentioning Remiet's name was added, perhaps by the scribe, when it was being disbound to be sent quire by quire to be copied. As Remiet is mentioned specifically as doing the illumination, one would expect to see his hand in a Parisian copy of the Angevin *Histoire ancienne* (Paris BN fr. 301) that was bought by Jean de Berry in April 1402. But it contains no illuminations by the artist I am calling Remiet. Most of its lavish miniatures and frontispieces are by the Orosius Master and the second hand in the 1393 *Pèlerinages*, which I have identified as Jean de Nizières.[44] This indicates that a number of copies of the London *Histoire ancienne* were probably produced and that Remiet's was lost, or, that he was serving as a *libraire* in organizing the work of other illuminators.[45]

The process of copying directly from another book is visualized by Remiet himself in an image of 'Seneca et ses livres' in the *Miroir historial* (Fig. 13). This miniature also shows us some of the furniture and the tools that would have been found in the illuminator's shop. The tall curved-top 'chair' was more an attribute of the scholar and teacher and not for the humbler likes of a worker like Remiet. Such a piece of furniture is listed by the Parisian teacher of grammar Jean of Garland as 'among the instruments needed by clerks'. In other aspects, however, Jean's list could almost describe Remiet's little scene: 'books,

12. Remiet. Paris, Bibliothèque Nationale, lat. 14247, fol. 2. Nicolas de Lyra, *Postilla litteralis super Biblia.* Second prologue: a university teaching scene.

a desk, an evening lamp with tallow and candle holder, a lantern and an inkwell with ink, a pen, a plumb-bob and ruler for ruling lines, a table, and a ferule, a chair, a blackboard, a pumice-stone along with an erasing knife, and chalk. The desk (*pulpitum*) is called a lectern (*letrum*): we must note that the desk is equipped with a notched device which enables it to be raised up to the height at which one reads, for one places the book upon the lectern.'[46] The sloped desk with the open pages of a complete book serving as a model and the single bifolio sheet that is held down on Seneca's own *letrum* by two circular cloth-covered weights held on strings, much like those still used in many library manuscript rooms today, are objects from Remiet's familiar world. Most striking too is the feather quill, clearly distinguished from a reed pen, whose broad ink-holding nib is brought up for inspection by the writer, his knife in the other hand having just sharpened or recut it. This occurred many dozens of times in the course of a scribal day. What can be described as Remiet's self-inscription in this image draws attention to the instrument that holds the ink and makes the lines and to the repetitious labour of his body in the act of transcription from one site into another.

How long did it take Remiet to complete the various stages of illuminating a page? Longer than we might think. The image of Seneca was made with the ink-holding pen in the technique known as 'portraits d'encre', a technique not that different from the strokes used by the scribe writing the text (Fig. 13). Unlike illuminators and more like fresco painters with their 'day's work' visible in the plaster, scribes sometimes numbered each writing session. From these, codicologists have estimated that the average number of folios that a scribe could complete in a day was between three and three and a half; that is, about seven pages.[47] Does this mean that Remiet could expect to complete seven miniatures with their borders at a sitting? If this was the case, in a large commission like the Duke of Orleans's *Miroir historial*, which with the missing fourth volume would have had over seven hundred illustrations, the number of days would make up half the working year. A fully illuminated page on the other hand, like the teaching scene in the Nicolas de Lyra manuscript with its transparent layers of colour, reticulated field of pink and darker red squares and four golden cornerpieces, not to mention its elaborate initial letter and border, could easily have taken up at least a working day, especially considering the complex preparation of the parchment and allowing time for glues to dry and gold leaf to be fixed (Fig. 12).

But what was a day for Remiet, and how was it measured? The question of Remiet's time is as crucial as his space, but how it structured the production of illuminated books has been little studied. Solar rather than clock time was the ordering principle of urban as well as agricultural life in the fourteenth century. An ordinance of the provost of Paris of 1395 reminded workers in all crafts that 'the working day is fixed from the hour of sunrise until the hour of sunset, with meals to be taken at reasonable times'.[48] However, there was enormous variety of conditions concerning work time depending upon the regulations of the different craft guilds and religious institutions, each of which was governed by different bells in the city. These rang the major temporal divisions of the liturgical 'hours', starting with matins at midnight. At the beginning of a household guide, *Le Menagier de Paris*, written for his fifteen-year-old wife, the goodman, who was a contemporary of Remiet's, admits that the matins bell is rung for monks 'and not because I mean that you, dear sister, nor married women should rise at this hour', but he urges that his wife, on hearing the bell in her bed, should whisper a prayer.[49] This emphasizes the extent to which time was experienced bodily in the pre-modern period, sensed through vibrations felt in the air, as sound, and through its changing luminosity as light. A fourteenth-century poem actually refers to God as 'our master illuminator' bringing light to the world with his hands.[50]

Remiet probably rose, like most craftspeople who depended on the master illuminator's sun, very early, his major time reckoner being the bells of Saint Séverin, not far from his bed, which rang its first mass bell at prime, or six o'clock, and then tierce in the mid-morning, sext at noon, and nones at three. He might also have heard during the early morning hours, the time for most intensive labour in field, classroom and workshop, the hours and quarter hours tolled by the first clock in Paris, set up by order of Charles V in 1370 in the Palais Royale on the Île de la Cité in a tower still known as the Tour de l'Horloge. But this royal attempt to centralize time in the city was undermined by the multiplicity of local micro-temporalities that structured the days of persons quite differently, according to their site and *métier*. Dinner, the main meal of the day, was taken at mid-morning, although delayed until early afternoon on fast-days, and was followed by a long afternoon of work punctuated much less by audible reminders of time's passage. I like to think that I can see in some of Remiet's miniatures this 'break for lunch', in the lassitude of a line or the forgotten termination of a tendril. The end of the Paris working day was regulated at seven o'clock in winter and eight in summer, church bells and the *crieurs du soir* announcing the curfew, or *couvre-feu*, which was strictly enforced in the city and was when the city gates were shut. Saint Séverin also rang the 'macé bell' which announced the end of the day for the scribes and students of the Latin Quarter and to which Remiet most likely took heed as a sometime employee of the university. During the winter he had probably already long put aside his colours when he heard the *cor de guet*, or the horn, sounded at the Châtelet calling those Parisians on the nightwatch to their duties. Hearing it, Remiet must have felt relieved that his working for the university spared him from sharing in this wearisome nocturnal burden of guarding the city gates that most of his neighbours undertook once every three weeks.

The 'hours' of a medieval workday were not of equal duration but varied according to the time of year, shortening in the dark of winter. But this affected artisans in the building trades more than scribes and illuminators, the former being paid according to time, the latter according to the job undertaken. The Parisian friar Michael de Massa urged that it was better to pay workers according to the job, for 'those who are paid according to the measure of time work more deceitfully . . . But those who are paid according to the job receive only what they earn and no more.'[51] Remiet's working day was thus a long one, in summer lasting up to twelve hours. But then there were numerous holidays, or 'holy days'. Besides governing working hours, statutes also stipulated the *chômages*, or days when work was prohibited. These numbered no fewer than ninety per year in the late fourteenth century. 'No one of the guild ought to work on holy days which the people of the city keep, nor on Saturdays during *charnage* (the time it was permitted to eat meat) after Vespers, nor after Compline on Saturdays during Lent, nor at night at any time of the year.' Nightwork was allowed for bakers and wine-sellers, but expressly forbidden for goldsmiths, sheath-makers, weavers and other artisanal crafts, 'for the light at night does not suffice for the trades aforesaid'.[52] Smaller units of time were measured not only by the

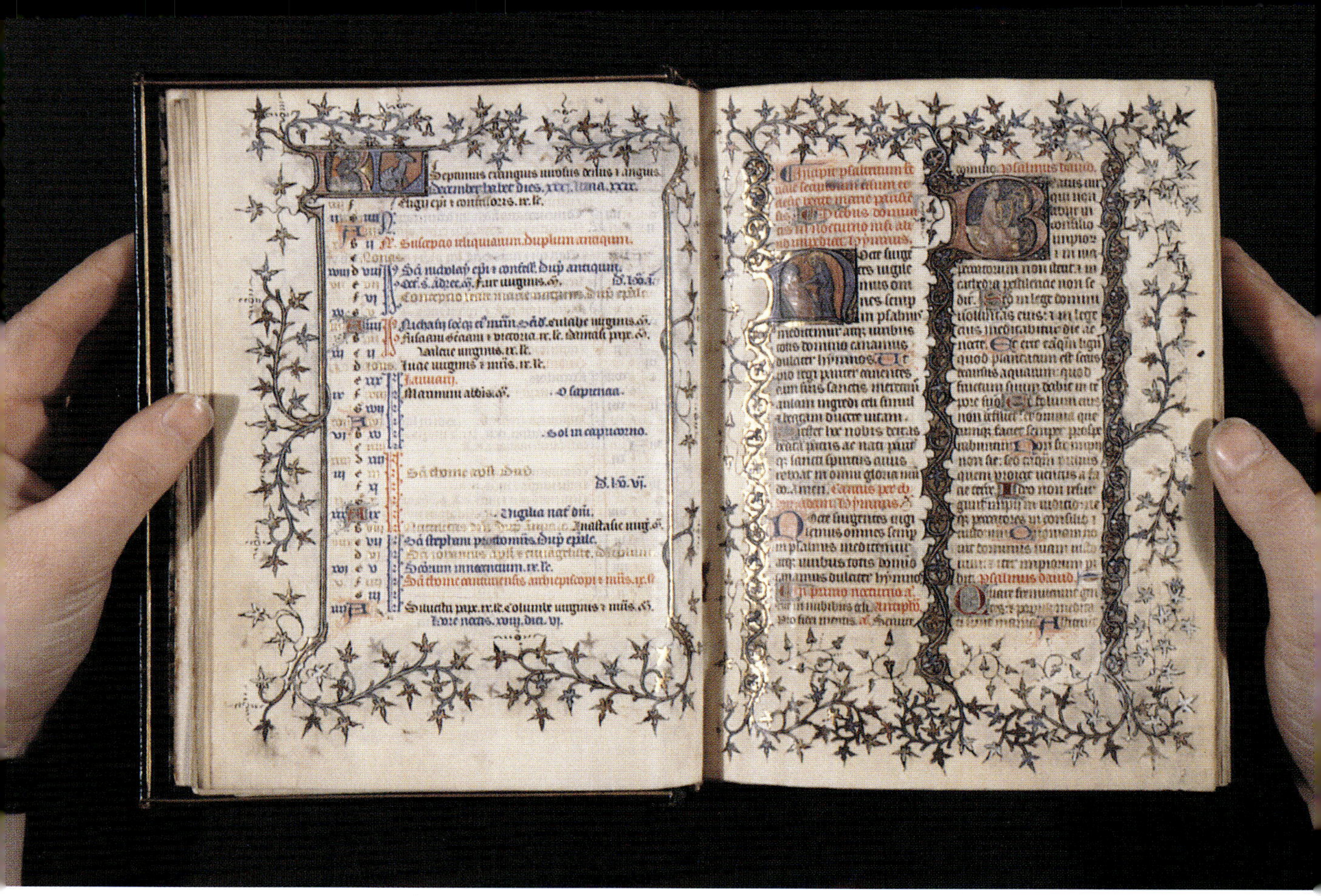

14. Remiet. Manchester, John Rylands University Library, lat. 136, fols. 6v–7r. Breviary for use of Paris, Notre Dame. Last folio of the calendar with the month of December; first folio of the Psalter.

new mechanical clocks kept in the art collections of the king and his brothers along with their manuscripts and other curiosities, but by the dwindling decay of matter in graduated wax candles and, more commonly, by the ebbing away of sand in the hourglass. Thus the very way in which Remiet measured time stressed diminution, a falling away of things. As the sand in the hourglass emptied, the spaces of the pages filled up.

A year's space was measured first according to church-time, the annual cycle of anniversaries known as the *temporale*, along with the corresponding saints' days of the *sanctorale*. But, in addition, there were the changing cycles of the seasons and of agricultural time as well as the movements of the heavenly bodies, or the zodiac of astrological time. Remiet illuminated time as it was ordered in all of these modes in the twelve calendar pages that preface both volumes of a breviary, made for Louis d'Orléans. The breviary was a more complex indicator of time than the more popular Book of Hours, which had unvarying lessons for use every hour of the day. By contrast, the breviary allowed laymen to follow the clergy in reciting the canonical office with all its changes of prayers, psalms and lessons throughout the year. Too long to fit into a single volume, it was divided into a summer and a winter portion. The volume now in Manchester contains the summer portion, from Easter to November, the office for the rest of the year resides in Paris (Fig. 14). These pages recall the lines of Guillaume de Deguileville that

Chaucer translated as 'Kalenderes enlumyned ben thei / That in this world ben lighted with thi name'.[53] In the 'KL' at the top of each month page, standing for *Kalends*, Remiet painted two minute images – the labour for that month, from January feasting to December pig-killing, and the zodiacal sign, from the two-headed Janus to the goat Capricorn in its strange shell. The scribe wrote out each day below, making distinctions between ordinary days in blue, 'red-letter days', like St Stephen's, and the important feasts, written in gold. The feast of the Virgin's conception early in the month and Christ's Nativity at the end made December the most glittering of all. On this type of page, though perhaps a less ornamented one, Remiet could chart each day of rest and labour.

Perhaps since he was paid not by the day like masons but by the piece, the illuminator was less conscious of time than the modern worker, although Remiet's evolving a rapid technique of illustration for the hundreds of miniatures required in some commissions suggests an awareness of speedy production. Some of his art was made very quickly, as can be seen in the slashes of paint and rapid lines that delineate these miniscule signs and labours of the months, images that were so common they could be knocked off rapidly without much ado, even prepared ahead of any particular commission. Once again the dragon terminals and minute marks that made up the vine borders must have taken up most of the hours of labour. Especially since he was working to deadlines set by the *libraire*, it is likely that the regulations against working at night and on holy days were broken. The opening of the breviary opposite the December page of the calendar shows a figure being urged to wake from his slumber not to work but to perform the night offices (Fig. 14). However, restrictions against non-devotional nightwork did not apply to that done for the household of the king, the queen, princes of the blood, the Bishop of Paris and other great lords. These account for most of Remiet's extant production, including this breviary, which was made for the king's brother. Perhaps on holy days and Sundays too, Remiet lifted his pen to the page because he could argue, as did the preacher Jean Gerson, that his labour as a scribe was a form of praise to the Lord. The contemporary Parisian theologian Henry of Langestein had also argued that the aspiration of any labourer should be meritorious 'of eternal life'.[54] Thus Remiet's labour was framed partly by church-time and partly by the new merchant's time, and unlike the work of the monastic illuminator, for whom the elaboration of the Word of God, like a meditative prayer, could be revealed in infinitely elaborated artifice, his was constricted by the numbers, counted not by the hourglass but by the piece, and every single miniature mattered. When the *libraire* Oudin de Cavarnay told Remiet to 'make nothing here' in 1393 so that he could add a diagram himself, was he perhaps trying to cut costs?

Those costs were certainly high, the price of an illuminated manuscript amounting to as much as the best horse. However, it would be a mistake to associate this expense lavished on books by royal and courtly bibliophiles with sums spent at the level of illumination alone. In 1382 the *libraire* Thevenin de l'Angevin, who was to provide Remiet with much work in the following decade, received a commission for the production of a missal which gives some idea of the relative costs involved in producing a single luxury book.[55] From first procuring the parchment to finally paying 'une bonne dame' to make an embroidered binding, this book cost a total of about 55 livres. The parchment in this case was provided by the College of Dormans-Beauvais, whose foundation stone had been laid on the Left Bank by Charles V in 1374, and who had commissioned the missal. The copyist received 24 livres, which means that only about half the expense was incurred by writing the text itself. It is also significant that 32 sous were paid in this case for the location of an *exemplaire*, or model. One *enlumineur* was paid 5 livres 4 sous for having executed the enormous number of 2,305 *grosses lettres* at 4 sous per hundred and 2,214 *versets* (line-endings) at 12 derniers per hundred. Even if he made three hundred of these each day, this artisan was making less than the master masons and carpenters of the time, whose fixed wages varied from between 30 and 45 derniers per day. The masons of the College of Dormans-Beauvais had been paid a total of 895 livres and the master architect, Raymond du Temple, 40 livres.[56]

For making his hundred line-endings, the horizontal pen flourishes or sometimes fully illuminated horizontal bars that probably took more than a few minutes each, what could this anonymous book-worker buy at the Paris market? – a chicken or a rabbit to roast for dinner, according to the *Menagier de Paris*, written in the same decade.[57] In contrast to the latter, the illuminator who made the miniatures and the large decorated gold and blue letters is named in the Dormans-Beauvais document as one Joachim Troislivres, who appears alongside Remiet in the 1368 letter patent as among those working for the university. Troislivres received two livres more than his name suggests – 5 livres 12 sous – hardly more than the previous illuminator, although unlike the latter's careful accounting of hundreds or thousands of letters, it is not stipulated how many miniatures or larger letters he produced.[58] Missals did not have the vast pictorial programmes of historical works, so clearly each miniature, with its outlay of gold and colours, was seen as being worth a good deal more than a border or line-ending.

Here is important evidence that the maker of *histoires* like Remiet also often provided the large burnished initials 'grans lettres d'or et d'azur' and their linked borders, called 'vignettes à baston' in inventories. Another document of 1401, however, also listing manuscripts made for the same college, shows that the borders of a manuscript could be made by an individual different from the painter of *histoires*. For his work in an antiphonary, one Robin Guelin, 'faiseur des vignettes', was paid 3 livres for painting thirty-six *vignettes*, at 20 derniers each.[59] The sums mentioned in these various documents give us some idea of the relative worth of the various aspects of the *mise en page*. The same expensive colours of blue and gold were used both inside and outside the framed image; indeed one could argue that the borders were more resplendent in terms of cost. This was obviously because these various elements were valued in terms of the time and materials it took to make them – much less for a single pen flourish than for a large illuminated letter – rather than in our ineffable terms of individualistic 'art'.

Accounts like these are couched in terms of money of account, 'livres d'or' or 'francs d'or', but most people in the fifteenth century never handled gold coins at all. They were paid in and spent the black money of everyday use, the silver 'blanc', which first issued in 1385 and was worth 8 'deniers parisis'. When Eustache Deschamps, the poet and 'conseillier et maistre d'ostel' to Louis d'Orléans, procured a copy of the three *Pèlerinages* in 1398, he received from his master 24 'ecus d'or en blans'.[60] This small coin, made of slightly less than half silver, was also what the *libraires* would have used to pay Remiet for his labours and with which he would have bought at the Paris *espicier* his yellow saffron, which cost 3 sous, or 4 blancs, per ounce. The price of pigments and parchment was often included in the first payments, but some contracts stipulate that the patron provide the materials. As the documents also reveal, payment was not always quick in coming, even from the royal household. When Louis d'Orléans ordered five vast illustrated volumes, including the *Cité de Dieu* and a *Miroir historial*, Thevenin de l'Angevin received between February 1395 and September 1396 various payments of between 40 and 300 francs d'or from Godefroy le Fèvre, the duke's treasurer, in order 'to buy parchment' and to 'pay the scribes and illuminators' for their labour. Clearly Remiet was being paid in installments as he produced the hundreds of *histoires* in these volumes. But this period also coincided with the defeat of the French crusaders at Nicopolis, which resulted in the near doubling of the price of silver, the debasement of currency and enormous price rises the following year. It was those, like Remiet, who received payment from debtors fixed in nominal money of account that suffered most, since between gaining a commission and finally being paid for its completion, economic conditions could change quite drastically.[61] Precisely because of the fluctuations in prices that occurred in Remiet's lifetime through multiple debasements of coinage and economic crises, it is difficult to calculate exactly how much he would have needed to work, how many *histoires* and *vignettes* he would have needed to complete per week, in order to feed himself and his family. What is certain is that the job of illuminator was no less precarious and hand-to-mouth than any other trade in the city, which explains why many in the book trade had other jobs on the side, like innkeeping. Remiet never depicted an illuminator at work, though he pictured many scribes and numerous artisans in other Parisian trades.

Along with the 'peintres imagiers, brodeurs, émailleurs and graveurs de sceaux', scribes and illuminators came under the justice of the Bishop of Paris, partly because they traditionally worked for the Church.[62] But another document reveals Remiet's association with the most prominent secular lords of the day. A quittance dated 22 June 1396, made by 'Pierre Remiot, enlumineur', requests payment of one hundred 'sols parisis' for work he had done not in a manuscript but in Louis d'Orléans's private chapel at the Paris Célestins. Built as the head of the French province of the Order in 1370 on the Right Bank, the splendour of this lavishly patronized church was so famous that it was later likened to a museum.[63] The document records work undertaken for Remiet's most important patron, Louis, Duke of Orléans, the younger brother of King Charles VI. Remiet is paid for having 'illuminated and gilded images with gold and fine colours, on a panel' on which a papal indulgence was inscribed.[64] This shows how an illuminator was not confined to parchment books, but could also be called upon to decorate more public images like that displayed in the duke's chapel. However, being distinct from a 'painter' proper and confined to book-production networks, Remiet's name is not among those 'maistres' listed in the first statutes of the 'Tailleurs d'Images, Sculpteurs, Peintres et Enlumineurs de la ville de Paris' drawn up in 1391. However, the same Colart de Laon who was mentioned working with Remiet in the 1396 quittance occurs on this list as 'painter and valet de chambre' of the duke. Louis also had a private library built in his *hôtel* on the Rue de la Poterne with decorations completed by a number of painters, including this same Colart de Laon who had worked with Remiet the previous June. Here another mysterious name occurs, that of 'Peirin de Dijon', documented as being paid another hundred 'sols parisis' for work on 'la librairie neuve' in March 1397 and who some scholars have suggested may have been identical with the man who decorated so many of the books that went into it. However, the name Peirin was extremely common in this period and nowhere else is our Remiet linked with the Burgundian capital.[65]

Remiet's major patrons were examples of a new type of social agent – the 'art collector' – embodied in Louis d'Orléans, who had modelled himself on his uncles, the Valois brothers Charles V, Philippe le Hardi, Louis I d'Anjou and Jean de Berry. These men embarked on the first 'cultural policy' in French history, using their vast landed wealth and political power to secure the finest works of architecture, sculpture, goldsmithswork, painting and book illumination. While ownership of illuminated manuscripts was expanding to include royal secretaries and advocates like Robert Le Coq, and clerics of the Parlement and chancery like Nicolas de Baye, as well as members of the university, Remiet's commissions all seem to have been directed towards the upper stratum of the aristocracy. He illuminated books that belonged to Charles VI (Paris BN fr. 20029, *Lay de la fragilité humaine*) and to the king's three brothers, Jean (BN fr. 176, *Rational des divins offices*), Philippe (Brussels MS 9094, *Propriétés des choses*), and Louis (at least half a dozen manuscripts including BN fr. 171–2, *La Cité de Dieu*, and BN fr. 312–14, *Miroir historial*). In addition there were important lords like Jean I de Foix (Troyes MS 261, *Faits et dits mémorables*) and Nicolas Rolin, Chancellor of Burgundy (London BL, Yates Thompson MS 45, *Book of Hours*), and of course prominent ecclesiastics like Étienne de Loypeau, Bishop of Luçon (Bayeux MS 61, Missal-Pontifical). Although female patrons form an increasingly important group in this period, they are conspicuously absent from this list.[66] This may be because Remiet seems to have specialized in illustrating encyclopaedic and historical compilations rather than the types of texts popular with the ladies of the court: courtly romances and pious devotional treatises. This gendered viewpoint, from both the maker and his intended audience, will be significant in understanding his peculiarly violent and misogynistic fantasies of death and dismemberment.

Of all these documentary references to Pierre or Perrin Remiet, the most problematic is the first one that I cited but which is chronologically the latest. This is the tax document listing his habitation in the parish of Saint Séverin in 1428. If this refers to the same Remiet who was already working for the university sixty years before, and not to a son of his, Remiet must have lived to be nearly eighty years of age at a time when life expectancy was at best half that. Yet it has recently been argued that our conception of the Middle Ages as a society dominated by youths is misguided and that once a person reached the age of twenty, life expectancy was good, with many persons living to be over sixty.[67] There are in fact miniatures in manuscripts dating from the second decade of the new century which show that Remiet, already an old man in medieval terms, was still hard at work, though by now his pictures have, like his own body, degenerated and have lost all their earlier delicacy and suppleness. But that is to speak of ends before we have even discussed beginnings.

An Apprentice and a Father's Corpse

History or historical science, which puts to death or treats the dead, which deals or negotiates with the dead, is the science of the father. To be sure, the master, even the good master, is also a father. Jacques Derrida[68]

Now my teacher had a harsh love for me, for he showed excessive severity in his unjust floggings, and yet the great care with which he guarded me was evident in his acts. Clearly I did not deserve to be beaten, for if he had the skill in teaching which he professed, it is certain that I, though a boy, would have been well able to grasp anything he taught. Guibert of Nogent[69]

In the copy of the French translation of Aristotle's *Politics* made for Louis d'Orléans in 1397, Remiet represents a fundamental trope of the medieval transmission of knowledge – the dictator or author of the text and the scribe who records it, in this case Socrates, whose words we know only through their being written down by his pupil Plato (Fig. 15).[70] Remiet's Socrates – his master – also remains a shadow about whom we can only hypothesize, since medieval artists, unlike medieval writers, did not proclaim their intellectual paternity so directly. The genealogies of many fourteenth-century artists have had to be carefully worked out, not along bloodlines, but along paintlines. Art historians have never concerned themselves with biological mothers and fathers in the formation of an individual identity, but rather with artistic masters and teachers in the formation of an individual style. This may in fact be closer to conveying medieval notions of the continuity of pictorial as well as literary tradition, since medieval painters and sculptors

15. Remiet. Paris, Bibliothèque Nationale, fr. 9106, fol. 31. Aristotle, *Politiques*. Socrates lays down the law.

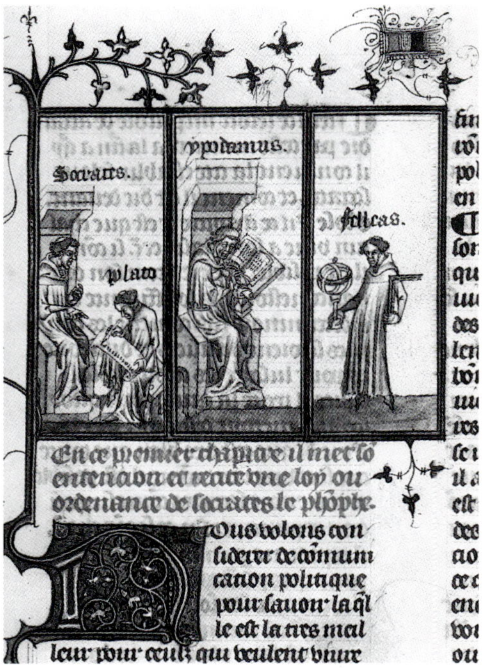

16. Boqueteaux Master (Master of the Bible of Jean de Sy). London, British Library, MS Royal 17.E.vii, fol. 1. *Bible historiale*. Shooting at the father's corpse as one of the Judgements of Solomon.

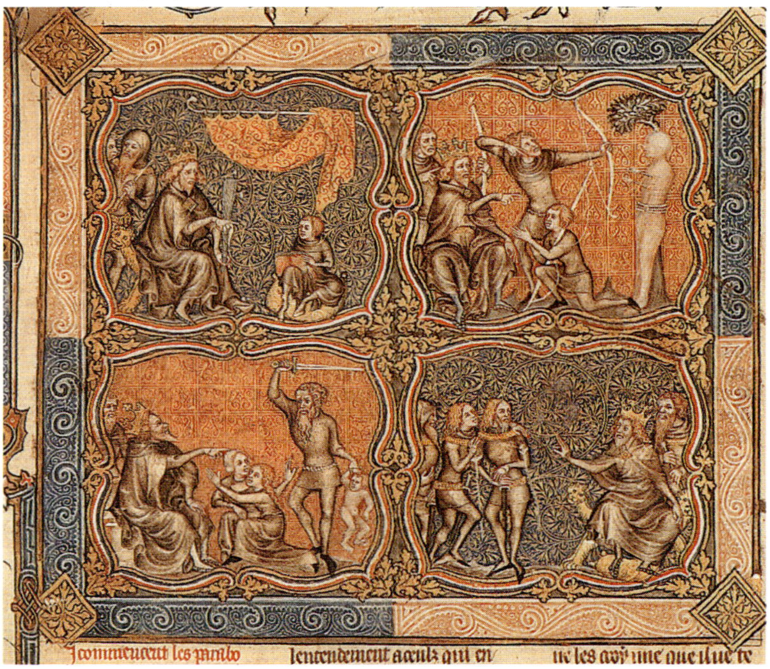

were for the most part formed in a master–apprentice relationship quite as painful and traumatic as the familial one. Just as the aristocratic model of agnatic lineage, an organized fellowship of males stretching backwards and forwards in time, became the norm in France and served to exclude women, so too did artistic genealogy. When Remiet was an infant, Jeanne de Montbaston, 'libraria et illuminatrix', took over running her husband's shop after his death from the plague, but this trend seems to have diminished later in the century. Bourgot, the daughter of Jean le Noir, who we know was also an illuminator, does not appear on the 1368 university list of book*men*, the only woman mentioned being the nameless 'mother of Pierre Davy, binder'. The single famous female illuminator Remiet might have known is the mysterious Anastasie, whose speciality, according to Christine de Pisan, was borders and backgrounds.[71] The only women who could become involved in the trade were either mothers, wives or daughters of the various artisans. Many sons also followed their fathers, although we do not know if this was the case with Remiet. Even a son would have had to learn his trade, as an apprentice, from his artisanal father.

The career of an illuminator was not that different from those variously outlined for the hundred and one craft guilds of Paris listed in the thirteenth-century *Livre des métiers* of Étienne Boileau. Here apprenticeship is described as commencing at an age between eight and eleven years. The term varied, but for high-status goldsmiths, for example, it was ten years, and the number of apprentices was usually restricted to one unless the wife of a master knew the trade, in which case most guilds allowed two. Special privileges were granted to sons of masters, who could rise 'to the mastery' without any fixed term, which must also have encouraged a number of artist families, generations of whom can be followed through the fourteenth century. The master's obligations consisted in lodging, feeding and clothing the apprentice and of course teaching him the trade. Apprentices could be sold in some circumstances and not all could rise to the dignity of master; some remained as valets, or hired men. Girls were apprenticed in crafts traditionally associated with women, such as bead-work, lacemaking and embroidery. In many of the higher status artisanal guilds like the goldsmiths, the transition from apprentice to master was dependent upon the production of a 'masterpiece' or *chef-d'oeuvre*, as it is described in the statutes of the painter's company approved in 1391. It was goldsmiths and tapestry weavers, 'to whose handiwork we would readily ascribe an "artistic" quality or intention', that saw this practice institutionalized; there are no records of illuminators having to produce such a work displaying their skill in order to work independently.[72] At the time Remiet was apprenticed, the book trade was booming, with the young dauphin Charles commissioning lavish manuscripts for his new library and the thriving university providing special privileges for its workers, so quality control was paramount. However, Remiet's was the plague generation, and, without hypothesizing about the psychological trauma of being born into a world inhabited by a third fewer fathers and mothers, the economic effects of the pestilence were felt for decades. Prices may have been much lower initially, but the decimation of the urban artisanal population, including many of its leaders like Richard de Montbaston, resulted in a reduction of the number of skilled craftsmen. If there was 'a decrease in skill levels among survivors, since long training was necessary for the transmission of semi-artistic craftsmanship', this might explain the stagnant styles of the plague generation of illuminators working in the eighties and nineties, who seem to have stopped dead in their tracks.[73] Only around the year 1400 would the next generation of Paris-trained illuminators, among them the Boucicaut Master and the Master of the Épître d'Othéa, present new and startling techniques of miniature-making.

The image of the tonsured Plato seated as the humble scribe at the feet of the tonsured Socrates, in his university chair, presents an intellectual version of the master and apprentice relationship. Looking at the intent boy-scribe as he struggles to take the dictation of his master raises the issue of Remiet's labours in the fourteenth-century hierarchy of knowledge. Painting was a mechanical not a liberal art, and thus the work of an illuminator, though it might be found in the very same Latin textbook used by a doctor in the schools, was removed from the arena of philosophy. Unlike the scribes who wrote the texts, Remiet the man who painted the pictures was not educated. However, one has to assume at least some basic literacy, to grammar school level if not more, for most book painters. At the very least, they were required to read the instructions provided for them in the vernacular, if not make out some of the letters of the Latin texts they illustrated. There were a number of small schools on the Left Bank organized by the chancellor of the university, partly to prepare students to attend the university at the age of fourteen but also to provide basic education. These were run by *maîtres* or *maîtresses* who were licensed by the university, according to a document of 1357.[74] Many craftsmen and craftswomen were probably illiterate, as is attested by their having copied instructions along with the proper inscriptions on metalwork objects, like 'Inscribe, workman, with your file', but those active in the book trade would have needed to read at least in the vernacular and have basic numeracy just to undertake transactions.[75] In the Aristotelian miniature, the instruments of astronomy and geometry, the armillary sphere and the carpenter's square, the latter the very thing he had been told *not* to paint five years before and here held by 'Felleas', are given equal footing with the books of "Ypodamus' in his doctoral chair. This expansion of the idea of practical knowledge into the realm of things will have enormous repercussions in the century that follows. But for Remiet the worlds of word and image were separate. He was a representative not of the *artes liberales* but of the *artes mechanicae*, which are practised by 'the ignoble sons of men', according to Hugh of Saint Victor.[76]

The ways of the world of image-making could be hard indeed for the tender young apprentice, as a decree from the Court of the Châtelet dated 3 September 1399 attests. A goldsmith is here enjoined to treat his apprentice, the son of a *prud'homme*, as stipulated in the contract 'without having him beaten by his wife but that he should beat him himself if he misbehaved'.[77] In the same year a father broke his son's contract because his master had hit the apprentice with a bunch of keys and 'made a hole in his head', and there are cases of female apprentices being abused and forced to become prostitutes. Just as scholars learned their Latin under the rod of the schoolmaster, so too many apprentices learned their skills in fear and trembling. It was not the case, as today, that an aptitude for drawing was seen in a child who was then encouraged to develop it and even to go to school to study it. Just as they talked of 'correcting' faulty texts, secular legislators, guild statutes and teachers talked of their right and duty to 'correct' children. Most medieval artists were not child geniuses like Giotto, whom, according to the often-repeated legend, Cimabue 'discovered' as a shepherd sketching sheep on a rock. In this scenario the apprenticeship is 'more symbolic than real since it can invariably be reduced to the singular and unequal confrontation between the master and his disciple' in which the master is turned into the disciple and 'suffers a symbolic death' by seeing his powers usurped and overtaken by the manifestation of genius.[78] For most apprentices it was a struggle to grasp the rudiments of picture-making, and for some it may never have worked. This may explain why some illuminated manuscripts of the period, in the words of Millard Meiss, look as if 'the Master must have gone into the street and thrust a brush into the hand of the first person he encountered' or some fall under the category he used occasionally without irony of the 'would-be-illuminator'.[79] These labels distort the medieval artist's productions by association with modernist notions of the 'gifted' artist and forget that artistic practices had to be learned. An exemplum of the period tells of an artist who, when asked why his images are so beautiful when his children are so ugly, replies that the former he engenders in daylight, the latter in the dark. Notions of creation current in this period were far more likely to be linked to metaphors of generation and corruption than to genius and creativity.[80]

Art might be the product not only of forced labour but also of pain. At the end of writing 1,500 pages of the first volume of a *Bible historiale* which Remiet helped illuminate, the exhausted scribe added a colophon expressing relief.[81] Scribes traditionally described their agonized hours of inscription, back bent over the desk, fingers numb with cold, eyes bleary and tired. Such discomfort must also have been endured by illuminators who, unlike writers, had no way of expressing relief at the end of the job. They often worked just as repetitively. In 1401 an illuminator called Jean des Champs was paid 16 livres for having painted 1,025 *grands lettres* and 5,142 *petite lettres* in an antiphonary.[82] Servants who produced feasts for the eyes just as cooks provided feasts for the flesh, it is all too easy to romanticize their labour. The pain that is pictured in so many fourteenth-century manuscripts, the flagellations, beatings, rippings, tearings and disembowelments of bodies, was felt too, though perhaps less spectacularly, by their producers. The violence that we see depicted on the parchment page could erupt in the very process of representation itself, and was no doubt inscribed on the bodies of many recalcitrant apprentices.

Philippe Ariès, the most influential of the French historians of death, wrote an earlier book which argued for the non-existence of childhood in the pre-modern period, a view that has been challenged by more recent studies.[83] Remiet's childhood years of apprenticeship starting in the late 1350s are so deeply embedded as to be almost invisible in the borders and backgrounds of a number of manuscripts produced for the court of King Jean le Bon and, after his death in 1364, for his son Charles V. Many of these manuscripts have been attributed to an artist known as the Boqueteaux Master, or 'Master of the Little Trees', after the mushroom-like bushes that constitute his hallmark, although it has become clear recently that a number of individuals were working in this mode.[84] The word 'master' is worth considering for a moment in this context of surrogate labels given by modern art historians to anonymous artists of the past according to some trait or motif in their work, or sometimes, as in the case of the Boucicaut Master, after an important patron. In the fourteenth century, the word *magister* signified 'one who possesses authority over others' and was used by artists, for example a 'Magister Alexander' who takes credit for illuminating a thirteenth-century Parisian Bible. This master was among the first lay illuminators to set up a workshop in the city and suggests a parallel with the early freelance teachers of the liberal arts, who were also known as 'masters'.[85] Having little to do with the way art historians have used the concept in connoisseurship, the term 'master' suggested professional competence rather than distinction and primarily defined social and legal status. In 1421, 195 out of the 1,394 household heads in Paris bore the title *maistre* without specifying profession or trade.[86] While the illuminator Master Honoré had lived on Remiet's street at the opening of the century, it is significant that by its close artists were referred to less by this status title and more by their full names.

Mastery as a verb, however, is a useful way of understanding the practice of the illuminator's workshop, where control and manipulation of traditional techniques, understanding of effects of various pigments and movements of the hand, were all part of the master's teaching of the craft. Learning to become an illuminator was an effort to ape, as painstakingly and exactly as one could, the practices of one's master, starting from the grinding and mixing of colours and advancing through the laying of patterned grounds or *champs* to the articulation of whole figures. Few modelbooks survive from Paris in this period, suggesting that training was done on the job, as it were, apprentices actually taking a hand in the minor decoration of a page. Sameness, not difference, was the rule. Remiet's earliest efforts with the quill pen and colour-filled brush would have been quite indistinguishable from his master's and indeed merged to become part of it. Who knows how many frames and reticulated grounds he laid down in the years of learning while he watched figures form within them over the shoulders of others.

An oversize two-volume *Bible historiale* dated 1357 with delicate grisaille figures by the Boqueteaux Master would have been among the first luxurious commissions that Remiet would have seen painted page by page in this master's shop in the first months of his apprenticeship, if he began at the usual age. The incredibly dense surfaces of its miniatures filled with filigree-like gold and undulating curves of foamy white highlight laid over a rich vermillion utilize many of the showy effects that Remiet would later reject and yet also many of the traits that he would adapt for very different purposes (Fig. 16). At this stage, however, the boy probably hardly touched the parchment, but he might have helped mix the gesso that fixed the corner pendants of gold leaf on to the frontispiece, between the more mundane duties of sweeping the floor and running errands. Here he may have learned to make the simple and repetitive curling patterns that fill so many of his later frames. He would have struggled to grasp the grammar of colour, to decline the basic properties of pigments, understanding that the main colours were blue and red and that these, and never yellow, were to be used on the robes of saints and important figures. These associations of colours with positive and negative attitudes were not only socially constructed. They were bound up in the techniques of picture-making itself, yellows being highly unstable pigments; lapis-lazuli blue, being the most permanent, was the most highly prized of all. He studied how the world of things and the world on the page were not the same, how texture was applied only to things like grass and water and how the illuminator's greatest art lay in the suggestion of sheen of silk and shine of the costliest jewels. There was very little mixing of colours, purity of saturation was sought above all, and what the boy Remiet poured into shell palettes were little pools of purity. Miniatures were not necessarily worked on one at a time but in sequences throughout the quires available. First the blues would be done and the backgrounds, using up the mixed colour for that day until the shells ran dry. It was not that different from a child's 'colouring-in' of today, except for its intensity, and the fact that everything, from the paint itself to its support, had also to be prepared with painstaking care. A thousand tricks were to be

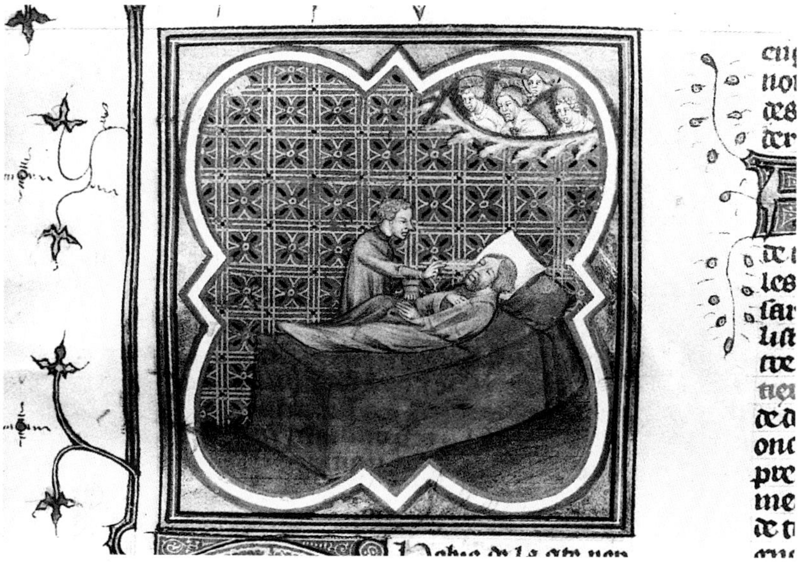

17. Remiet. Soissons, Bibliothèque Municipale, MS 211, fol. xxxviii. *Bible historiale*. Tobias heals his blind father with a fish's gall.

remembered by heart involving everything from twists of the wrist to complicated recipes for certain rare hues. He learned how much of himself went into the paint, in not only back-breaking grind but spittle and even urine, which was preferable to water for the concoction of some colours.

What he probably did more than anything else was watch as the delicate curtain revealing King Solomon was itself unveiled under his master's brush. The wonderment of such making must have taken the child's breath away, as, almost by magic, the empty space of parchment was filled with minute men and beasts that danced before his eyes. This learning process was a matter not only of acquiring technical expertise but also of incorporating the messages of the images themselves, becoming conversant with a repertoire of themes, an ideology of motifs. Just because these artists were copying does not mean that they were indifferent to what they copied; indeed copying involves an acting out or reinscription of what is being copied. It insinuates the maker, even more radically than inventing something new, within the gestures and rhythms of the performing self. In the case of the *Bible historiale*, the messages inscribed upon the child's learning body emphasized following rules and not transgressing the law of the Father.

The second volume of the 1357 manuscript opens with the Book of Proverbs, which occurs only in Guyart Desmoulins's vernacular translation and not in the *Historia scholastica* by Petrus Comestor on which it was based. Here are images of the wisdom of Solomon, exemplars for the young which would have stood too as exemplars of practice, both material and moral, for little Remiet (Fig. 16). The first scene is a biblical scene of instruction parallel to that of the ancients Socrates and Plato, with the wise King Solomon instructing the boy Roboam seated before him. Solomon holds the proverbial rod just as Lady Grammar would in a contemporary teaching scene. Opposite is a scene where violence against the body is more explicit, depicting Solomon's testing the filial piety of two sons who are ordered to shoot arrows at their father's corpse, as an illustration of

Proverbs 19:26, condemning him 'who maltreats his father'.[87] In medieval culture, reverence for one's elders was absolute. It was the duty of the young to shape themselves according to paternal authority and to respect the memory of their ancestors through mimetic emulation and not reject them as did the wicked son here. In this image the good son kneels and pleads before the wise king to be exempt from such an unnatural exhibition of filial ingratitude. The father's corpse is tied to one of the little trees that we have seen are synonymous with this master's style, its shroud-wrapped anonymity identical to those that Remiet will paint in the decades to come. Rather than desecrate the dead father, the son, in this case Remiet, was bound to respect him, to copy him.

The vernacular reformulations of the *Bible historiale* provided the story of shooting at the father's corpse, but the *Bible* also provided an image of the new generation opening the father's eyes. Years later when Remiet was working on the illuminations of a vast three-volume copy of the same text along with at least four other much younger Parisian illuminators, he pictured the opening of the Book of Tobit, choosing not the traditional scene of the blinding by dung from a swallow's nest falling in the eyes of the old man as he lay in bed, but the moment where his son Tobias heals him by anointing his eyes with a fish's gall (Fig. 17). Tobit who, like Job, was an example of faith tested by God, is here attended by a son who, like an artist with a pot of ointment/pigment, brushes the paternal eyes open so that the old man can see 'the light of heaven'. It is the nearest Remiet ever came to depicting a painter at work; he depicted a son making his father's vision possible in a reversal of the traditional patrilinear genealogy of the book painter. This outstretched arm also suggests the broad bodily sweep of the wall or panel painter. By contrast, Remiet's was an art of the wrist and hand rather than the whole body; feather strokes no longer than a finger filled the tiny frame. The cramped position of the medieval illuminator, his back bent over, his gaze penetrating, was like that of the myopic scribe, intense and concentrated. Its perimeters were identical to those of writing, except that the illuminator wrote in gold and colours and the flowers of his rhetoric were counted at so many pence per hundred.

Another lavishly illustrated Bible translation associated with the Boqueteaux style, this time a more literal one of the Vulgate itself, translated by Jean de Sy for King Jean le Bon, was, at the king's death in 1364, left unfinished (Fig. 18). Because of this half-completed state, it reveals more clearly the nature of these minute movements and meticulous

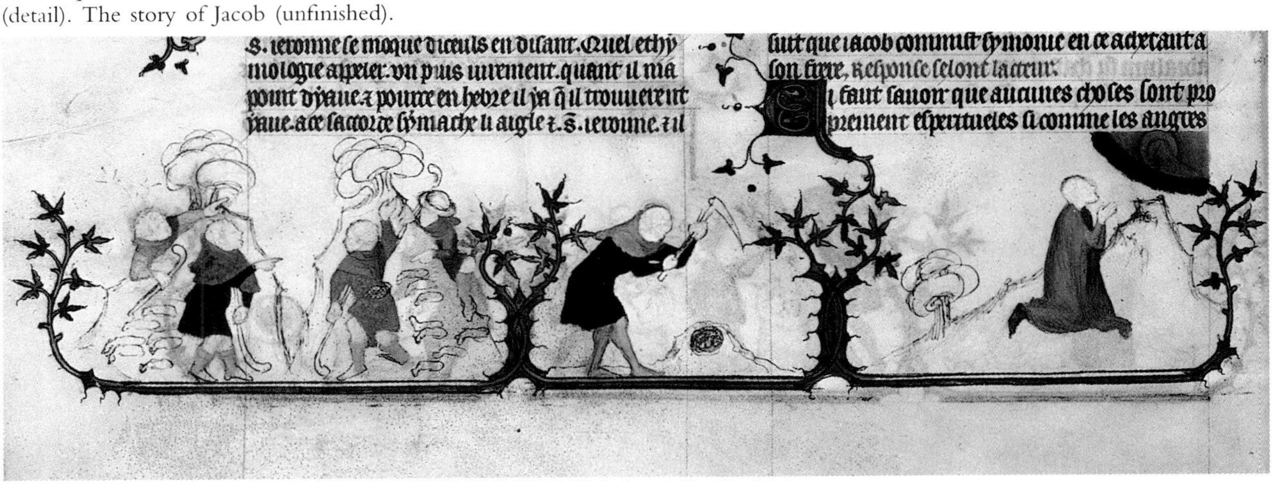

18. Boqueteaux Master (Master of the Bible of Jean de Sy). Paris, Bibliothèque Nationale, fr. 15379, fol. 47v. *Bible of Jean de Sy* (detail). The story of Jacob (unfinished).

procedures that the boy Remiet learned by copying his master. But it also shows what elements from the father's work the son selected and what he rejected. In the lower margins of many folios, the *vignette* borders with sharp spiky ends have all been carefully painted, but only the sketches in pen remain of the master's soft and rounded little trees and animated figures, filled in here and there throughout with blocks of the same colour. This gives us some idea of the stages involved in illumination, with all the gold leaf being laid down first and then the flat areas of paler colour being laid in and, only in the final stages, crisped up with outlines in black (Fig. 18).[88] Body was suggested by colour, but Remiet would for the most part avoid the corporeality of bright clothing in his later work. Making the linear skeleton of his master's work the basis of his own painterly practice, Remiet often allowed the sketchy pen lines of his drawing to remain visible. The scale and fullness of these squat little figures is also thinned out so that Remiet's characters are far more emaciated and incorporeal presences. Unlike all his contemporaries, he was not afraid of emptiness. The problem with tracing a stylistic genealogy in this way is deciding which pictorial features are more generally fashionable, to be associated with the sharper and attenuated excesses of court fashions in dress and deportment as they changed in the *fin de siècle*, for example, and which can be seen as personal traits of an individual as he diverges from his master's tropes. Remiet's master had painted some of the most ravishing grisaille manuscripts in the generation after Jean Pucelle, and shared with the latter a wry, sensuous humour and a tendency to delicate, almost fairy-tale, sweetness that make even his lions seem as docile as toy dogs, furry little animals frolicking amidst his cottoncandy trees. If the 'master of the little trees' was the master of the master of death, the latter went on to create a very different visual world from these elements. He would also live through a different world as well, one in which the green tree gave way to the dry, its darker tones casting shadows on its boughs, and where sin and death shook all trees at their roots, inverting them and making them into monstrous men. The corpse and the tree, which Remiet first saw combined in the *Bible historiale* image of filial desecration (Fig. 16), are also recombined in Remiet's later work in which trees grow out of bodies and bodies drop out of trees.

The only images that evoke the workshop situation in which Remiet began are those miniatures that depict not image but text producers. The earliest datable miniature we can securely associate with Remiet is a small one-column-wide portrait of the fourteenth-century scientist Nicole Oresme, writing his translation on a strange, cramped desk, two weights holding down the parchment sheet which unfurls like a scroll. This appears at the beginning of a pocket-sized two-volume copy of his translation of Aristotle's *Politics* and the pseudo-Aristotelian *Economics* made in 1375 for Charles V with an elaborate series of miniatures by the Master of the Livre du Sacre and the Boqueteaux Master. This manuscript, now in a private collection in Paris, was the only volume known to me containing miniatures by Remiet that I was unable to consult.[89] Remiet, as the youngest and least-experienced illuminator of the group, was given the task of providing the image not of the writer as author, but as translator. This focus on the writer as mediator will continue throughout his work. Here Remiet was, like his subject, not creating something new but translating it from the idiom of his master into his own.

Another image of writer as mediator is the first frontispiece to Nicolas de Lyra's *Postilla litteralis super Biblia*, which comes before the first prologue, the *Commendatio sacre scriptura*

19. Remiet. Paris, Bibliothèque Nationale, lat. 14247, fol. 1. Nicolas de Lyra, *Postilla litteralis super Biblia*. First prologue: Jerome passing on the sublimity of scripture to the author.

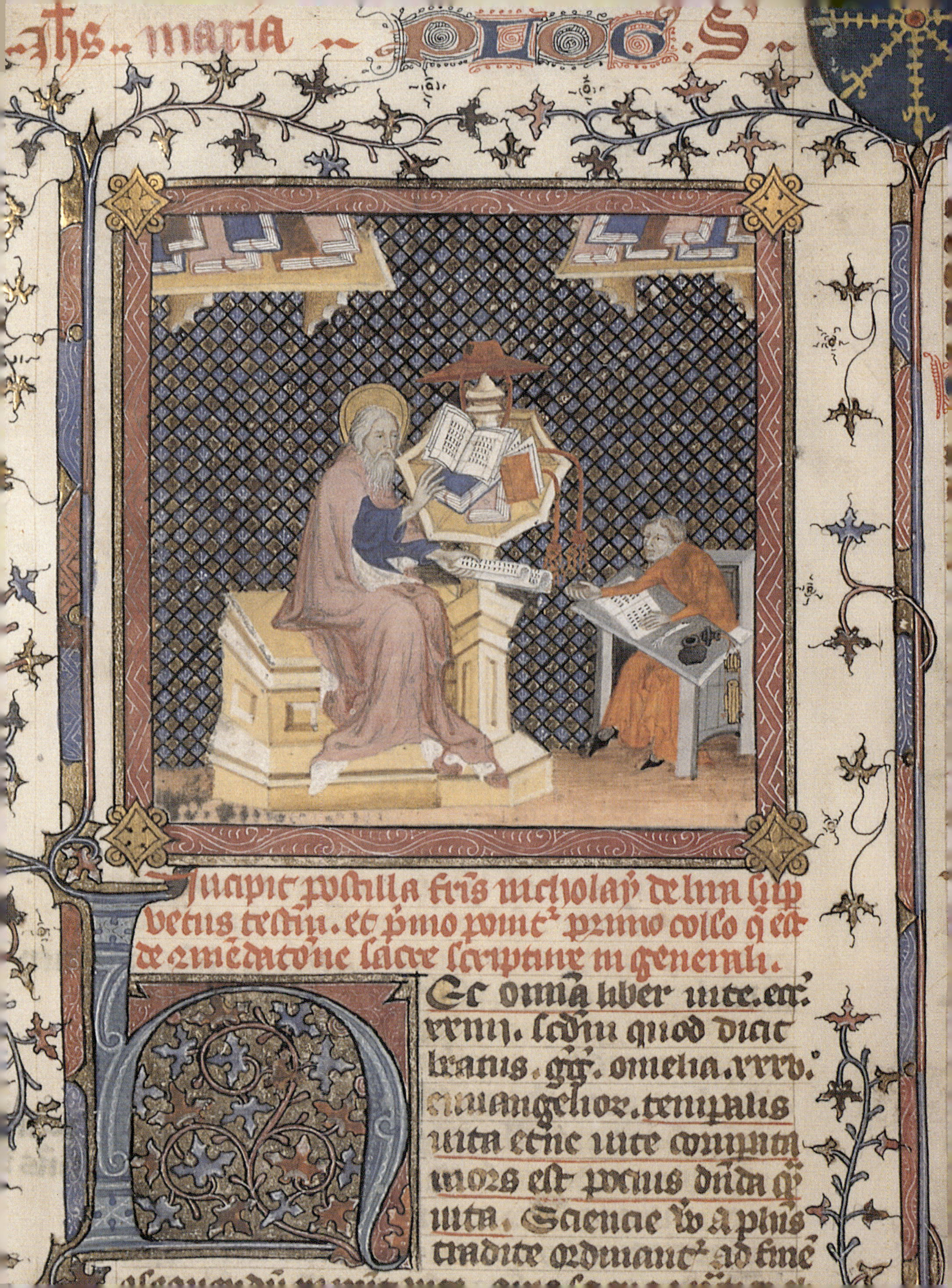
Ihs. maria — Prolog. S.
Incipit postilla fris nicholai de lira sup vetus testm. et pmo ponit' pmo collo q est de comedatone sacre scripture in generali.
Hec omnia liber vite. ecc. xxiiii. secdm quod dicit beatus. gg. omelia. xxxv. in euangelior. temporalis vita eterne vite comparata mors est pocius dicenda q vita. Sciencie vo a plus tradite ordinant' ad fine

in generali and shows the Church Father St Jerome, translator of the Vulgate, leafing though books on his large octagonal book wheel (Fig. 19). Many more volumes lie on shelves above him with their back covers uppermost, like literal building blocks of the Church, indicating how books were arranged before they were stacked spine-outwards. The only part of the scene that has any spatial complexity or attempts at creating perspective are these piles of books, the architecture that Remiet knew best. The Father leans out to the smaller author and scribe seated at his writing desk on the right. This figure in red is about to take from him not a book or a scroll but a single curling sheet of parchment. This is what this red-robed figure is to copy, using his black ink pot and a quill from the gold case that hangs on his belt. Remiet emphasizes the gap and the relation between past and present, between the near-biblical robes of the saint and the contemporary fashions and pointed shoes of the writer. This underlines the exegetical argument of Lyra's text, which favours literal rather than allegorical interpretations of scripture and the superiority of the past words of scripture over the new books of philosophy, which are called here, just below the miniature, 'books of death' compared to the eternal book of life – the Gospels. The second prefatory miniature, which we have already seen, shows the university as a place for biblical exegesis of these inherited texts and was probably painted soon after the first, having identical pale woody yellow, soft pink and bright blue colours, which had been mixed in the same pots or shells throughout (Fig. 11). This first image grounds the Word in the writings of Fathers of the Church. Nicolas de Lyra saw himself as a small *compilator* not a giant *auctor*. As Alistair Minnis has shown in his study of medieval theories of authorship, de Lyra was mainly concerned with the *auctores humani* who worked *sub deo* and who could collect God's words into an accessible format for dissemination. Significantly, this emphasized the work of individual human mediators, like the Fathers and the Evangelists, allowing literates to read of the personal life of their *auctor*, relating his experiences to their own.[90] Would Remiet have considered himself a visual compiler in the same way, as taking cues from his visual 'Father' just as de Lyra takes authority from the Church Father? Being an *auctor* was far more prestigious than being a mere *actor*, which meant being a mimer or performer of another's language. Most scribes were considered just *actors*, performing the text each time they wrote it out. Illuminators are described in much of today's scholarship as though they were commentators of the texts they decorated, which according to Bonaventure was an activity of higher status, closer to the author and superior to the mere scribe. But, more likely, they were closer to the next lowest category, the compiler who, like the artist, brought disparate things together, especially since much of Remiet's work appeared within vernacular versions of the great Latin compilers of the previous century, Peter Lombard and Vincent of Beauvais as well as Nicolas de Lyra.[91]

These are writing corpses in the sense that all were long since dead. Inscribed within the workshop structures of master and pupil, father and son, model and copy, was a paradigm of continuity and tradition which not only respected but resurrected the dead on a daily basis. This copying process might at first appear to allow little room for what we today call self-expression. Yet in Remiet's images of authors at work, be they of Socrates, Nicolas de Lyra or Nicole Oresme, the idea of copying is not equated with anything secondary or debased but with an animated performance of the self in an act of communication with subsequent generations. Likewise the inherited image was a venerated model rather than an empty simulacrum. In the fourteenth century, the relationship between writers living and dead was not barred by the angel with the flaming sword, for if there was one place in which the dead communed with the living and those who breathed articulated the voices of those long since turned to dust, it was within the pages of a book. Just as Richard de Bury described how 'in books I find the dead as if they were alive', Remiet's art partakes of this revivification through parchment, not only the words but also the forms and figures of these corpse authors, once again fleshed out in paint.

A Sign and a Self

The writing subject cancels out the signs of his particular individuality. As a result, the mark of the writer is reduced to nothing more than the singularity of his absence: he must assume the role of the dead man in the game of writing. Michel Foucault[92]

Some learn to write with styluses on wax tablets. Others follow the custom that consists in forming letters with the pen and they paint on the flesh of sheep and calves, learning to colour. They paint flowers. They make illuminations. Jean Le Fèvre, *Le Respit de la Mort*[93]

Soon after recovering from a life-threatening illness, Remiet's contemporary, the jurist and poet Jean Le Fèvre wrote of the equivalence of painting and writing in the poem *Le Respit de la mort.* In this long reflection on human generation and mortality, not only is death itself 'bought off' by an official document of reprieve (a *respit*), but *escritures* and *paintures* are described as being the only way of deferring the inevitable. As another fourteenth-century figure obsessed by the genealogy of his own celibate body in relation to engendering knowledge, the English bishop Richard de Bury repeated the classical topos in his erotic epistle to necrophilic/bibliophilic pleasure, the *Philobiblon*, or 'Love of Books': 'A book once made, renders its author this return, that, so long as it shall endure, the author remaining *athanatos*, or immortal, cannot perish.'[94] Poems and paintings also leave behind monuments of individual memory and models of social action for subsequent generations, but for medieval culture they carried the weight of a more literal, even biological, genealogy. In a similarly anxious pause on the possible posterity of fame, the court poet Eustache Deschamps, in his misogynist *Miroir de la mariage*, reminds his male readers that only by producing a lineage in the form of human offspring or, significantly, in the form of 'writings *or paintings*' can they strive 'to represent your form, you and your name, after death (Pour ta forme representer / Toi et ton nom apres la mort)'.[95] This obsession with the name as the crucial sign of artistic identity was still only nascent in the fourteenth century, when people were still mostly designated according to rank, profession or place of origin, but it became increasingly important as the individual's self was embodied more and more in external signs. It was the nobility, with its long trees of genealogies and colourful heraldries that brought individual names into prominence. The designated appellations in manuscripts illuminated by Remiet are those signalled by elaborate heraldry and coats of arms, which emphasize the bodily inscription of the family and continuity of the owner and reader of the book rather than its mere isolated and

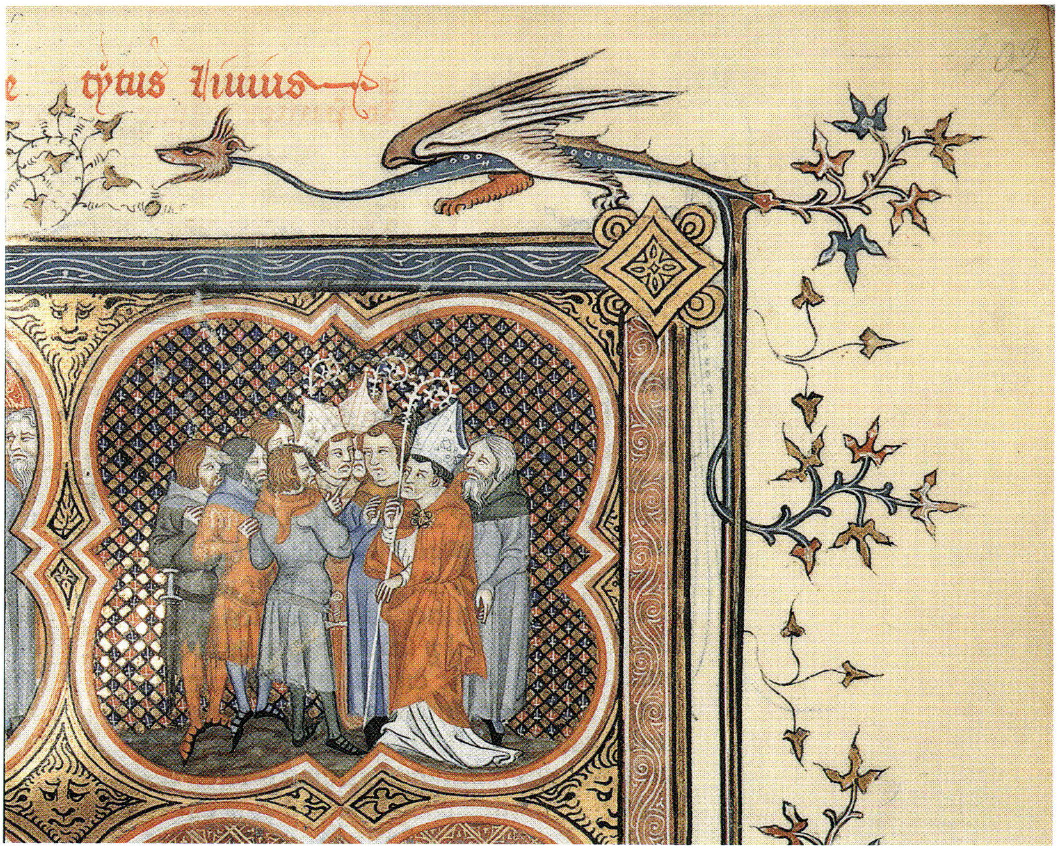

20. Remiet. Bordeaux, Bibliothèque de Bordeaux, MS 730, fol. 192 (detail). Livy, *Histoire romaine*. Frontispiece to the second decade: deliberations on peace or war, and a dragon in the upper margin.

21. Remiet. Bordeaux, Bibliothèque de Bordeaux, MS 730, fol. 192 (detail). Livy, *Histoire romaine*. Frontispiece to the second decade: an ape and a bird in the lower margin.

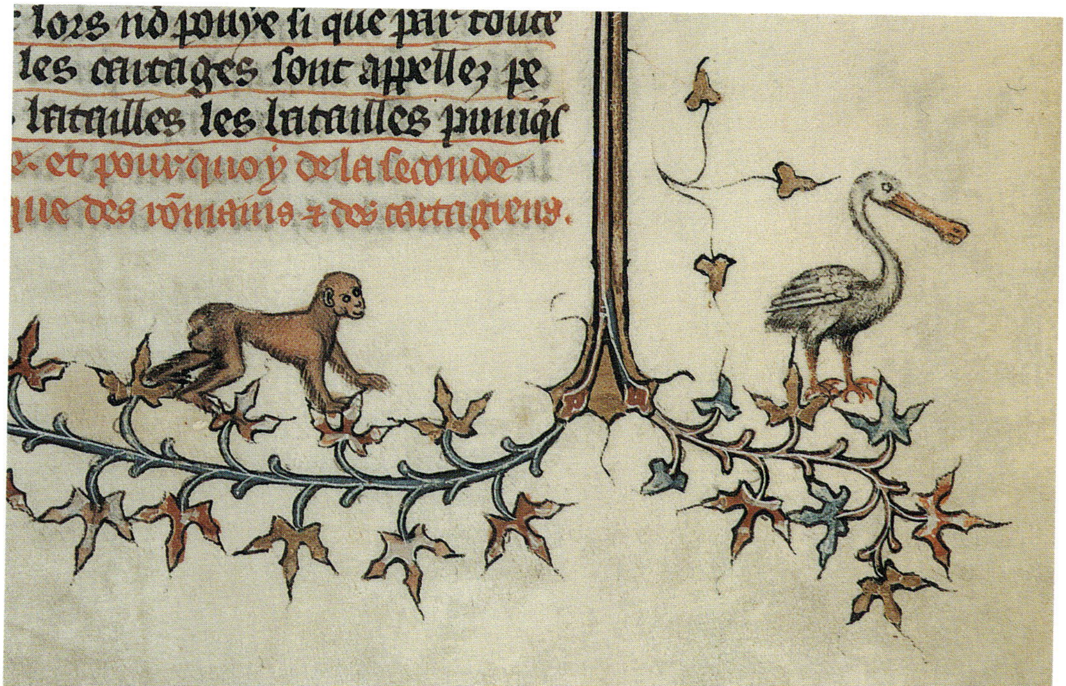

individual maker. Books, like blood, were passed from generation to generation, and art was too, in the patrilineal descent of the medieval workshop.

The two parts of a person's name in the fourteenth century served different functions, one articulating a civic and the other a spiritual identity. The given baptismal name, in this case Pierre, or Perrin, proclaimed the individual's beginning in the world and his relation to God. It was after all what we still refer to as his 'Christian' name and was part of a sacramental nomination that carried on through marriage ('I, Pierre, take thee, Agnes') as well as at confession. For boys this was often the name of the father, the literal continuity of patrilineal power in the formal replica of the son. The 'patron' was both the template or visual model and the father. In the *taille* records from early fourteenth-century Paris,

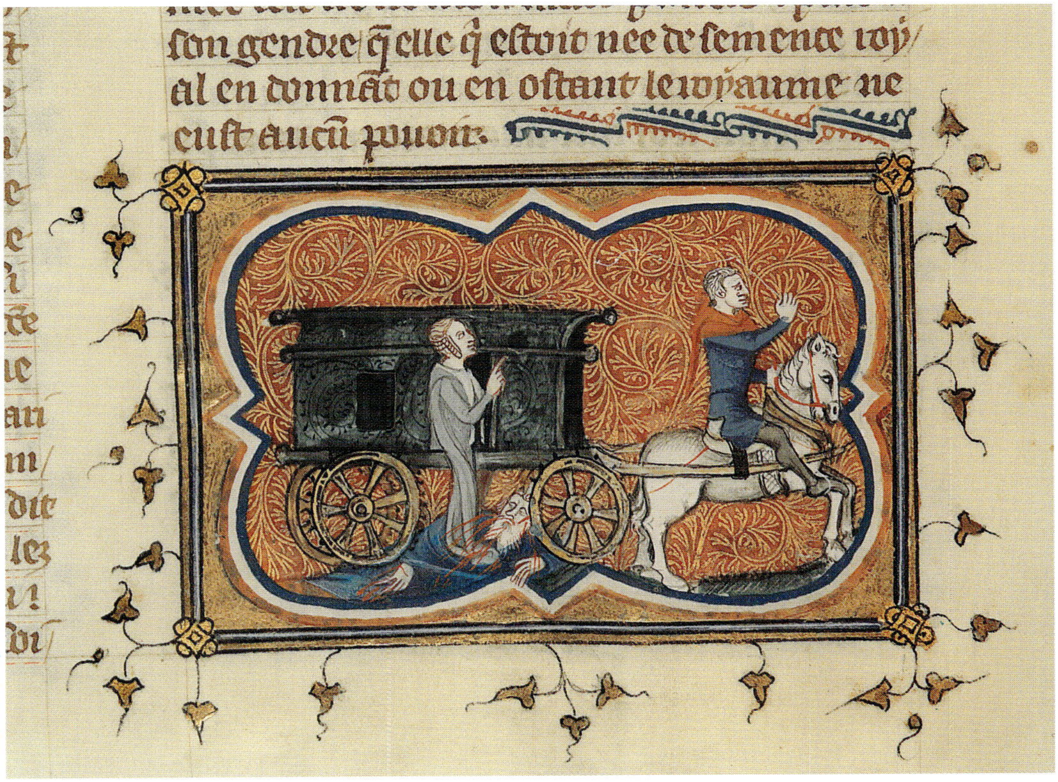

22. Remiet and others. Bordeaux, Bibliothèque de Bordeaux, MS 730, fol. 22v. Livy, *Histoire romaine*. Tullie passes her coach over the corpse of her father.

Pierre was the third most popular male name, after Jehan and Guillaume. If the given name signalled the beginning, the surname, the family name, signalled the end – it became the sign for one's elective relations, for naming one's progenitor specified the disposition of personal property in wills, for example.[96] Commonly it also designated profession – the smith, the carpenter, even the painter – defining the individual within a non-familial social group. It is in this more public, legal form that our illuminator appears in the tax records and significantly in the trace of him at his site of work, in Oudin de Cavarnay's scribbled instructions. By calling him Remiet throughout this book, I am assuming reference to this official, public persona, his death-name rather than his birth-name.

Léopold Delisle made the intriguing suggestion that 'the signatures of copyists are so common and those of illuminators so rare, that one might well suppose that the first were authorized by *libraires* to sign their works, while it was forbidden that the second should add even the least notes to the books they were charged to decorate'.[97] Sometimes one finds names surreptitiously inserted into illuminations, but this is easier to do for those artists who specialized in border decoration, like the individual who inserted 'Petrus Gilberti me fecit' in numerous line-endings in a Brussels *Bible historiale* in which Remiet also worked as one of a large team of anonymous painters.[98] Ironically it is at the margins where identity is most easily revealed. The ways in which an artist like Remiet could make himself known to his contemporaries by this last, public name, might not only be through writing. In another poem by Jean Le Fèvre, his translation of a well-known pseudo-classical Latin poem supposedly found in Ovid's tomb, called *La Veille*, there is a list of the many birds that are found in France:

> Par faucons ou autre mal art.
> Pies, jaiz, merles et plouviers
> Grues, mauviez, coulons, *ramiers*.[99]

In the margins of a manuscript of Livy in Bordeaux, Remiet painted two large four-part frontispieces that can count among his earliest independent works. In the margins of the first, he pictured a row of little trees in the style of his master, although in the right margin is a large stork-like bird of a type that his master never painted. In the second frontispiece, he did away with little trees altogether and made at the top a snapping red dragon that will become part of his parchment personality (Fig. 20). It appears as a protective snarling force in many of his full-page pictures, but it is not this beast that is most significant. Nor is it the marginal ape, emblematic of the artist's own situation as a copier 'aping nature' rather than as a producer of things. Balancing on a vine next to this anus-exposing simian is another tall bird with a fat bill (Fig. 21). Is this passerine fowl a 'ramier', homonymically the same and identical to the young illuminator's name given the fluidity of spelling in this period? Has Remiet depicted and used the 'ramier' as a self-signalling pun? Naturalistic representation of birds had been common in the margins of Parisian manuscripts since Jean Pucelle in the twenties, but rather than being used as signs of verisimilitude to some exterior 'nature', their vague, never very ornithological detail points rather inward to a self.[100] The same bird type also occurs in the border of the frontispiece to the poem where we find written witness to this name (see Fig. 6). For illuminators to make marginal devices or visual emblems punning on their names was not uncommon in this period. Some Parisian artists, like Remiet's associate Colart du Laon, had their own seals which often used animal rebuses.[101] Colart's was a cock. Remiet, whether or not he owned a seal, may be referring to his own proper name in the margins here in the Bordeaux manuscript, just as though he were putting his seal on parchment. The word 'remiet/ramiet/ramier' had associations with woods and forests; perhaps it emerged as a nickname related to the type of images he was known to produce, initially the 'little trees', just as Jean Pucelle (*pucelle* can mean little bird, girl or virgin) probably hints at the softly delicate things made by, or perhaps even to the physical appearance of his Parisian predecessor. In a number of his writings, Jacques Derrida has shown that the proper name ought to have no meaning outside its reference, but is none the less constantly being contaminated by sense and nonsense so that it begins to signify, especially in the realm of concealed or fragmented names. In his manuscript-like and much-glossed *Glas*, Derrida describes how 'the great stake of literary discourse – is the patient, stealthy, quasi animal or vegetable, tireless, monumental, derisory transformation of one's name, a rebus, into a thing or name of a thing'.[102] This very transformation of the hidden name into an organic thing occurs in Remiet's frontispiece as he seeks to mark something as his own.

The Livy manuscript has been described as emerging from the atelier of the Boqueteaux Master.[103] But by the 1370s, that great master was probably already dead, leaving his professional offspring squabbling over their inheritance and struggling to replicate and at the same time reinvent a style which had been so popular with the court. This clash is enacted in the confused illumination of the Livy manuscript and its painted procession of murderous battles, horrific punishments and laid-out corpses. There is a darker, more violent streak in the gash-like appearance of the paint, which throughout avoids the delicate scumbled surfaces of the master. We can see Remiet positioning himself against his colleagues/brothers, responding to inherited models even to the extent of finishing or colouring-in designs that had been devised by the father. One can discern two or three individuals pushing one another out of the miniature space, overpainting previously painted scenes and erasing the other's work, pens replacing swords in a squabble not of blood but of vermillion. But this is a quarrel about blood in the sense that this manuscript stages the problem of inheritance. Who will take the father's place?

An answer to this can be inferred from the fact that the most fundamental violence depicted in the manuscript is that perpetrated against the father and that it is undertaken by Remiet himself, in the two frontispieces and in the miniatures where he buries the father's corpse in his own paint, an effacement of old lines with new orders of colour. Once again there is a congruence between what is painted and how it is painted, the pictorial patricide enacted both in form and in content. Scenes throughout the book show the bloody sacrifices of sons and daughters, murders of fathers and mothers, and general violence against one's progenitors that are among the archetypal tropes of all history. Such is the 'act of bestial inhumanity' when the daughter of Servius drives a carriage over the already mutilated body of her white-haired father, staining her clothes and spattering her carriage with blood, which curses her family forever (Fig. 22). Here Remiet was still following the underdrawing provided by his master. The father's corpse is still in the father's style. Although this old, dead body might well be made by Remiet's hand, it is not yet really *in* 'his' hand. The dead king is represented in a twisted semi-frontal pose, unlike all Remiet's subsequent depictions of the defunct person, which are in profile. The young illuminator merely repeats gestures he has been taught, practices he has had drummed into him over the years. But ultimately the father's corpse has to be erased, overturned and reinscribed, not just run over, so that it may be buried and something made to replace it.

The Bordeaux Livy may indeed be Remiet's 'masterpiece' (in the craft sense of the word), since it marks his emergence as the most important independent illuminator to come out of the Boqueteaux shop in the 1370s. Yet what it evidences most poignantly is that Remiet was not able to forget the name of the father and replace it with his own. It was not in the framed miniatures but only in the borders that Remiet could inscribe himself purposefully for posterity in the bird-rebus. Only here was the illuminator free to depart from the tradition and show off his skill. However, whereas Parisian illuminators a hundred years before had been able to create rampant anti-texts of phallic and often obscene resistance that showed their participation in a popular culture and the ability of their patrons to 'get the joke', by the time Remiet was making images on the edge, these too had become somewhat standardized.[104] Besides, it was an age of increasing prudery and censorship, not just on the part of churchmen like Pierre d'Ailly, but even at court. These autodefinitional marginal themes are thus no longer manic and monstrous manifestations of the medieval imagination (what we would call the unconscious) but more superficial signs. Often they are not monstrous at all but natural beasts and birds that exhibit the illuminator skilfully aping nature and following the latest Lombard fashions, rather than rivalling her in the creation of hybrid fantasies. Whereas Otto Pächt saw naturalistic bird depictions by fourteenth-century illuminators as the artist's 'seeing for himself', here the bird ironically allows the reader to see him.[105] Later, in the fifteenth century, illuminators in Bruges would use tiny geometric signs, registered by the guild, like labels, not to identify a self but to protect their monopoly over the trade.[106] Signs such as these, like modern company logos, are hardly revealing of personal identity. If we accept the unconscious as an agent in history, it is precisely that which is not self-consciously displayed but that which is rather displaced, in lapses, errors, and dreams, or repeated in manic repetition, where a self emerges. Just as a signature on a will represents the testamentary force, the still-present voice of the deceased, Remiet is most vital in those images where life is most absent – in the sign of the corpse.

The rest of this book will trace the history of this sign in Remiet's work, a sign we have not yet seen. Redolent not of formation but of decay, constantly recurring as a focus of his fascination and as a force of mourning and mediation for both artist and observer, the corpse is Remiet's site of self-inscription. Far more important and suggestive than a single name, which is meaningless to us because we have no body, no face, to pin it to, this sign was not invented by Remiet but only appropriated by him. Perhaps, like a name, it was given to him and he incorporated it, repeating it again and again just as instrumentally as though he were writing his signature. A sign of a thing that is simultaneously both present and absent, an actual corpse is always its own double. The cadaver, as Maurice Blanchot describes, is a strangely empty sign. It bears no resemblance except as an image, no likeness to anything except itself and in that sense it evacuates any individuality or identity the deceased might have had. If this is the semiotics of the corpse itself, what of the image of the corpse, the double of the double that Remiet spent his life duplicating? How can we find identity in its blank space? If this chapter started with nothing, in the form of the gap in the text that first revealed Remiet to us, it ends with a similar blank, waiting to be filled in.

> The corpse is a reflection becoming master of the life it reflects – absorbing it, identifying substantively with it by moving it from its use value and from its truth value to something incredible – something neutral which there is no getting used to. And if the cadaver is so similar, it is because it is, at a certain moment, similarity par excellence: altogether similarity, and also nothing more. It is the likeness, like to an absolute degree, overwhelming and marvellous. But what is it like? Nothing.[107]

2. THE BIRTH OF DEATH

He had lost all sense of time. Had the curfew bell yet tolled, announcing the beginning of enforced darkness, his last night? He could still hear mingled voices in the street outside, the cry of a small infant – probably a beggar's – and the sweet strains of a lovely lullaby that seemed to sooth it. As he twisted and shivered in his own sweat-sodden sheets, listening to the song, he felt that here at his end, there was something of his beginning. At his birth, the first face he had seen was not the midwife's or his poor mother's but hers, hovering over the bed of parturition as though she had mistaken it for a deathbed. How often had he heard his uncle relate to astonished friends and neighbours the way his nephew had come into the world that terrible dry summer when so many were taken from it. Born during the time of the first great pestilence, his first breath inhaled that fatal perfume, the stench of a new kind of death that came with sudden signs – spitting blood, painful swellings under the armpits and a burning fever so terrible that it cured its victims of life sometimes between matins and vespers. Five hundred corpses a day were carried in carts from the hospital at the Hôtel Dieu to the Holy Innocents for solemn burial, and the prices charged for a good service by priests doubled as the months of morbidity passed and as their own numbers dwindled.

Remiet reflected on her whose suffering had allowed him life, of her terrible pain, much worse than his own racking agony at this moment. He remembered the preacher ranting, 'there is no pain like that of a woman in labour: thus Rachel died from the excessive pain of childbirth, and, dying, 'called her son's name Benoni, that is son of pain'. His own mother had lived long enough to call him Pierre, like countless others.

Naked he had come forth and naked he was now to return. Poor he came and poor he would go back. That waxy white flesh that he had worn like a gleaming mantle at his birth was now all wrinkled, torn and tattered like a shirt worn ragged. Why was it not possible to remember such an important moment? He had drawn it once, the agony of that terrible passage, in the dour booklet he had illuminated in 'portraits d'encre' for the poor mad king, recently mercifully taken from us. How different was that ink-black nativity to those he had often illuminated in the little Books of Hours made for the quiet contemplation of pious priests and nuns in their cloisters and courtiers in their glittering private chapels. The crystal-clean and painless coming of the Lord who slipped out of the Virgin's womb like a fruit dropping from a tree, which, of course, one never pictured – how could it even be imagined – no, for as his good master had taught him, the bodies of the saints are only of the purest colours. Our Lady always held the already swathed child to be adored in the stable with the ox and the ass. Death was not meant to cast its shadow there. But in his finest Hours he had wanted to add a melancholy note to the wonder of that special birth, a premonition of His future death, and had placed something like an open tomb-slab between the mother and the beasts, a black box, like the coffin carried on to the pilgrim's deathbed. He wanted to show how this wonderful birth conquered death by death. It was a brilliant touch, but who would notice? Yet, not to sound blasphemous, must not his own appearance upon the earth have seemed just as miraculous, even though tainted with the sin of Adam and Eve, since it also took place long ago amidst the first terrible visitation of that other mother?

The Little Book of Human Frailty

What then is the essential meaning of our horror of nature? Not wanting to depend on anything, abandoning the place of our carnal birth, revolting intimately against the fact of dying, generally mistrusting the body, that is, having a deep mistrust of what is accidental, natural, perishable. Georges Bataille[1]

Of all earthly things the most frail is our human nature. Filthy, vile and full of misery, conceived in sin, born in pain, nourished in the foulness of the belly of birth, such, certainly, is man. Eustache Deschamps, *Lay de la fragilité humaine*[2]

Death had not always loomed over humanity but had itself been born with the Fall of Adam and Eve. The image of this founding moment which Remiet made in 1383, is a crucial beginning for him in another sense, since it is the earliest extant appearance in his work of the laid-out corpse whose horizontal form haunts so many of his later products (Fig. 23). Beneath the Tree of Good and Evil and between the feet of Adam and Eve as they commit the primal sin, lies the corpse in question, a stretched-out body ambiguously neither a personification nor a person, not even a symbol – just a fact of what has been born at this moment. Its unsexed status, neither male nor female, is crucial to the curse it carries. For this thing, simultaneously an absent and a present body, will come to all the descendants of Adam and Eve, whose transgression sets in motion the span of human life, beginning with the agonies of childbirth and ending with the throes of the deathbed. The modernist nihilism of Samuel Becket's famous phrase about giving birth 'astride a grave' is quite different from such medieval juxtapositions of life's start and finish, which were framed by the larger confines of eternity. Indeed contemplating this brief flicker of human existence was central to the medieval *contemptus mundi* tradition, a 'contempt for the world' which underwent something of a revival in the late fourteenth century.[3] This is in fact the context for this scene of Adam and Eve, which appears in Remiet's earliest surviving royal commission, the *Lay de la fragilité humaine*. Now preserved along with so many manuscripts containing miniatures by this illuminator in the Bibliothèque Nationale in Paris, this volume is described in the opening table of contents as a 'petit livret'.[4] Its small size and mere twenty-four folios belie its importance in the late fourteenth-century renaissance of repugnance. As an illustrated book it deserves to be ranked alongside more famous contemporary productions like the *Grandes Heures* made for the Duke of Berry and the *Grandes Chroniques* made for Charles V. Compared

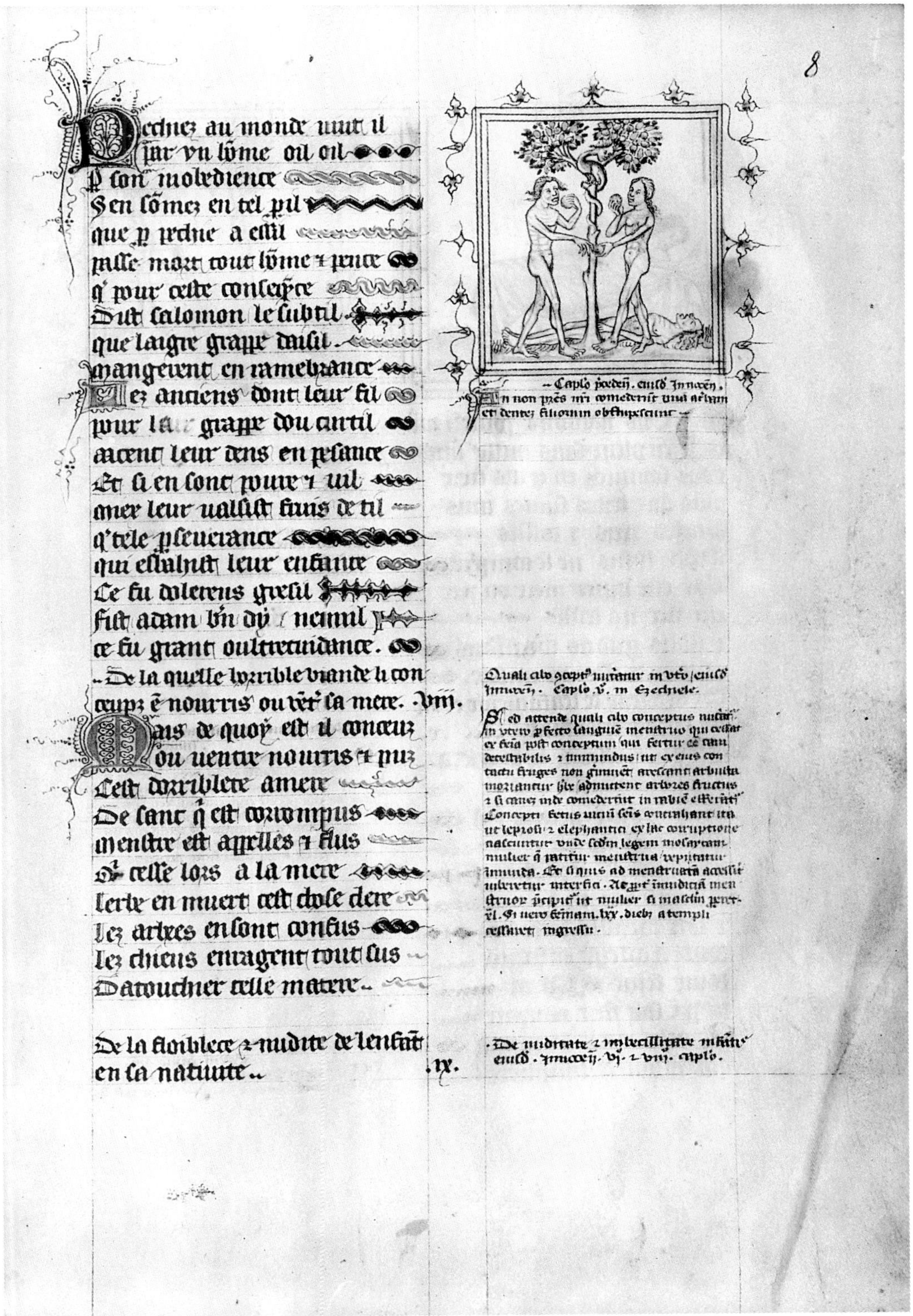

23. Remiet. Paris, Bibliothèque Nationale, fr. 20029, fol. 8. *Lay de la fragilité humaine.* How death entered the world through Adam and Eve.

to the sunlit blue skies of divine visitations and the golden backgrounds of lavish royal rituals painted in these famous books, its half-empty horror and near-colourless devotion to the darker realms perhaps explains why it has been almost totally overlooked by art historians.

The *Lay de la fragilité humaine* was the poetic work of the courtier poet Eustache Deschamps, who in addition to many satirical and political *ballades*, composed no fewer than 105 poems on the themes of old age and death. The loss of his young wife while giving birth to their fourth child combined with frequent financial troubles are thought to have spurred many of Deschamps's acerbic meditations, as did the sudden demise of his patron Charles V in 1380, which saw him still scrambling for preferment in an age when poets, like artists, sought advancement through court appointments as *valets de chambres* and the like. He eventually found a secure position in the retinue of the king's younger son, Louis d'Orléans (the same prince for whom Remiet illustrated so many volumes), whose *écuyer* and then *maître d'hôtel* he became in 1392. Perhaps Deschamps himself saw in Remiet's art something fitting his own sombre vision of the massive deterioration of the world, a world grown old, and what he referred to in one of his *ballades* as 'the fragility of our age'.[5] Just as Christine de Pizan, one of the most illustrious poets at the court of Charles VI, has been shown to have been intimately involved in the design of the richly illuminated presentation copies of her works, so too Deschamps must have supervised the planning, layout and design of the little booklet of death.[6]

The work is in fact a translation of one of the most influential products of the venerable *contemptus mundi* tradition, a Latin tract entitled *De miseria condicionis humane* (On the Misery of the Human Condition), written in the late twelfth century by Lotario dei Segni (later Pope Innocent III) and extant in many manuscripts. Deschamps's vernacular version with its scholarly-looking Latin gloss had probably been planned as a prestigious royal gift to help him advance at court, as its subject matter perfectly suited the dour devotional tastes of Charles V, who had previously commissioned so many translations into French from Latin. The king actually already owned a French prose translation of the work, in a lavish 'Mirror of Princes' compilation completed in 1372 now in Besançon and in which Remiet may have assisted.[7] But this earlier version, apart from a frontispiece, does not illustrate the horror, and its prose text is a literal translation of the original. By contrast, Deschamps's *Lay* constitutes a far more intense and, because of its vernacular poetic structure, visceral meditation on themes in the original treatise.

The completion of Deschamps's new and far more elaborately visualized as well as poetically more emotive verse translation was interrupted by the sudden death of the king in 1380. Called 'the Wise' because of his love of books, Charles had always been congenitally weak; partially paralysed owing to a sickness contracted in his youth and constantly attended by doctors, he obsessed around one of his royal bodies – the earthly fleshly one. In this respect he would have enjoyed every worm and empty eye-socket in Deschamps's and Remiet's work. He seems to have spent most of his final years as a morbid hypochondriac, fearing poison, lavishing money on a retinue of quack doctors, on magical gem stones, on eastern elixirs and mandragora to cure the terrible toothaches, forever mumbling over a rag-bag of expensive saints' relics to alleviate rheumatism. But in August 1380, according to the minute particulars recorded by his physicians, the protracted and painful weeks of his final torment began when his throat became

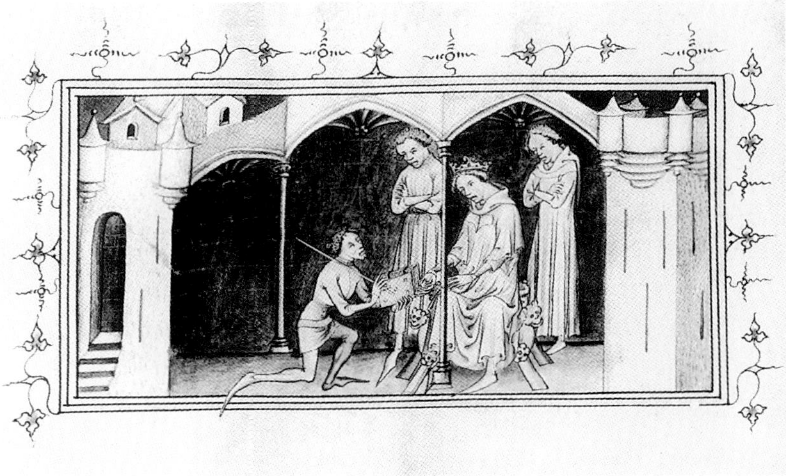

24. Remiet. Paris, Bibliothèque Nationale, fr. 20029, fol. 4v (detail). *Lay de la fragilité humaine.* Deschamps presents his work to the young Charles VI.

obstructed by sputum, and by the middle of September the first signs of oncoming death were noted – the retraction of his eyes and teeth into his head.[8] He finally expired in apoplectic agony during a solemn reading of the Passion of St John. Ironically, all the while Remiet was carefully delineating every possible shrivelling and lingering death agony in the *Lay de la fragilité humaine*, the patron for whom it was intended was actually living them.

So what happened to the presentation copy of the poem? In the colophon at the end of the work, Deschamps refers to himself as 'eustace morel de vertus escuier darmes du roy charles le (quint) chastelain de fymes' and gives the date of presentation to the king as 18 April 1383. The number after 'King Charles' was originally left blank and later the number 'q-nt' or 'quint' was added in darker ink. But since Charles V had been dead for three years in 1393, it is clear that the word 'fifth' is a much later addition and, as the presentation frontispiece shows, the book was eventually presented to his son Charles VI (Fig. 24). Book presentation in the fourteenth century amounted to what we think of as the publication of a work, and it was usually depicted in a large frontispiece to the volume, directly linked to the subsequent text and showing the ritual delivery from poet or translator to prince. Remiet's measly miniature is very different from the splendid full-page presentation scenes found in manuscripts made for Charles's father. It occurs on fol. 4v at the top of an otherwise blank folio and was obviously added as an afterthought in order to make it 'fit' its new patron, Charles VI. Remiet sets the scene in a draughty-looking darkly vaulted brick interior, perhaps representing the royal residence of the Hôtel Saint Pol in Paris. The kneeling Deschamps is shown wearing a crown of roses, a sign of the poet, and bearing the tall staff of a *huissier d'armes* on his shoulder, the position he had held under Charles's father. He hands over the closed volume, much thicker than the *livret* itself (which is wafer-thin), to the enthroned monarch, whose mouth gawps open and who sits isolated on his throne, his ungainly body partly obliterated by a column and flanked by two cross-armed attendants looking more like mental-ward heavies than courtiers. Is this the dark and lonely cell of Charles's madness? I doubt it. One nineteenth-century commentator noted of this picture that 'the physiognomy of the king seems to indicate that he was at this moment suffering from one of the bouts of melancholy that reading the *Lay de la fragilité humaine* was certainly not produced to dissipate', and more recently another scholar has seen this miniature as a depiction of the 'mental illness that unbalanced him and demonstrated so dramatically the frailty of the human condition'.[9] But neither Remiet nor any other artist of this period thought of putting madness in a face. It was too terrible a thing to be a mere matter of expression. It was rendered through signs of extremity, physical deformity or going on all fours, animal-like, as had Nebuchadnezzar, the biblical prototype of the mad king. Moreover, the poem and its cycle of illustrations were finished ten years before Charles VI's first attack of insanity in 1393, and Remiet gives much the same uniformly glum gaze to the two men attending the fourteen-year-old monarch and even to the poet himself. The illuminator had probably hardly set eyes on the boy king, whose gawky figure in this image bears no relation to contemporary descriptions of him as robust, rosy-cheeked and athletic, fond of hunting and women, very different from his scholarly father but also from the uncontrollable fool he was to become during his forty-three bouts of insanity, a living death that was to last from 1393 until 1422. One can still wonder, however, if the boy king ever opened Deschamps's little book and saw its pictorial premonitions of things to come.

Remiet's picture of the origins of death (Fig. 23) embodies the words of the foregoing rubric: 'How sin entered into this world by one man (par un homme) and how death (la mort) through sin came among all men.' His small double-framed miniature is placed in the right-hand column of the page, which also contains the text of the original Latin treatise. In devising his poem in the form of a 'double lay', Deschamps called for his French version to be placed in the main column of every page and the Latin text, in smaller script, almost like a gloss, adjacent to it, thus monumentalizing his own importance as a vernacular author while keeping a strategic balance among textual, visual and vernacular authorities. At first glance, the miniature offers the standard image of the Fall. On either side of the tree of good and evil stand the mother and father of mankind, each holding a circular fruit to his/her lips. This is not to suggest that there was more than one apple, but is an old convention whereby Eve first bites and then hands to Adam the forbidden fruit, which appears a third time at the centre of the picture held by the two of them together. The visual symmetry of the complicity of man and woman in the first sin is offset by what is another standard element in this scene from the thirteenth century onwards, the dragon-like female-headed serpent coiled around the tree, whose gaze mirrors that of Eve below.[10] Associating women with visual temptation and death, the serpent's female disguise is not described in the text but is one of Remiet's own 'additions'. In fact both Latin and French texts on the page emphasize that sin and death entered the world 'par un homme'; it is only Remiet's image that makes woman more culpable.

Another element in this drawing not usually found in the archetypal scene of the Fall, however, is the supine corpse lying under the tree, almost trodden on by the naked couple. This is Remiet's trademark. The French verse here is not based on the Latin text of Innocent III but is one of the fourteenth-century poet's own inventions. It asks a question that is answered by this image. 'Pechiez au monde vint il / Par un homme?' – 'Did sin come into the world because of a man? Yes, Yes. By his disobedience all were put into such peril that . . . by the sin of exile death passed to all men.' The corpse is drawn lying on the earth, the tree hiding its loins and gender, yet in other respects the

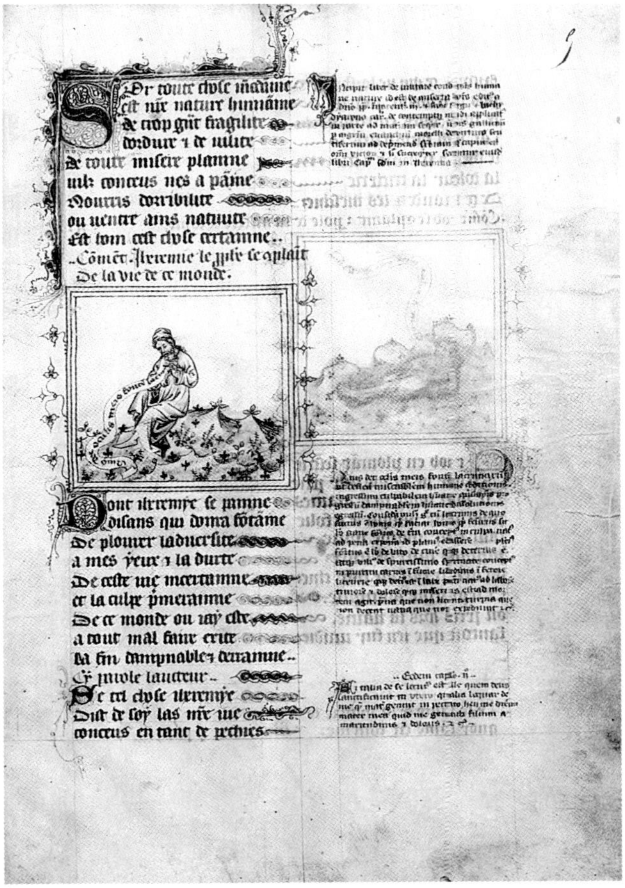

25. Remiet. Paris, Bibliothèque Nationale, fr. 20029, fol. 5. *Lay de la fragilité humaine*. Jeremiah's lament.

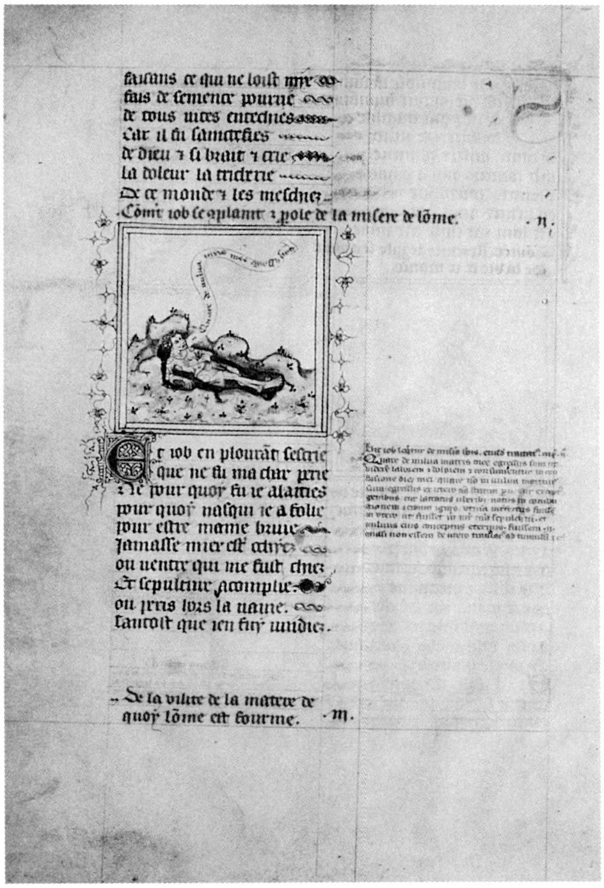

26. Remiet. Paris, Bibliothèque Nationale, fr. 20029, fol. 5v. *Lay de la fragilité humaine*. Job's curse.

composition is comparable to the traditional Gothic image of the Tree of Jesse. However, from the loins of the corpse sprout not new generations of life but the empty inheritance of sin and death. The tree, which for Remiet's teacher – the 'Master of the Little Trees' – had been merely a pretty punctuation in the *bas de page*, here takes on an ominious aspect, and will, like the cadaver beneath it, reappear again and again in Remiet's later work. The tree, like the corpse, is rooted to the earth, another of the very few props in Remiet's minimal pictorial universe. There are frail human figures. There are knobbled, ragged and dry trees. And there are the ubiquitous clumps of earth, little mounds sprouting shoots, like that in the very first miniature in the book showing the lament of Jeremiah (Fig. 25).

The prophet of gloom is also shown seated on the earth. As humanity's witness, he holds a scroll that reads 'Quis det oculis meis fontem lacrimarum', crying that his eyes are fountains of tears that 'bewail the beginning of the miserable human condition'. From the very first page of the treatise, the emphasis in the Latin text, the vernacular version and the image is upon visualizing the 'filth and vileness' of the earth, which metaphorically represents the womb. In the soil of the mother, according to the text here, man is 'nourished in horribleness'. Just visible through the very fine, thin, perhaps uterine, vellum of this first page, and thus itself formed on womb-skin, is the uterine image painted on

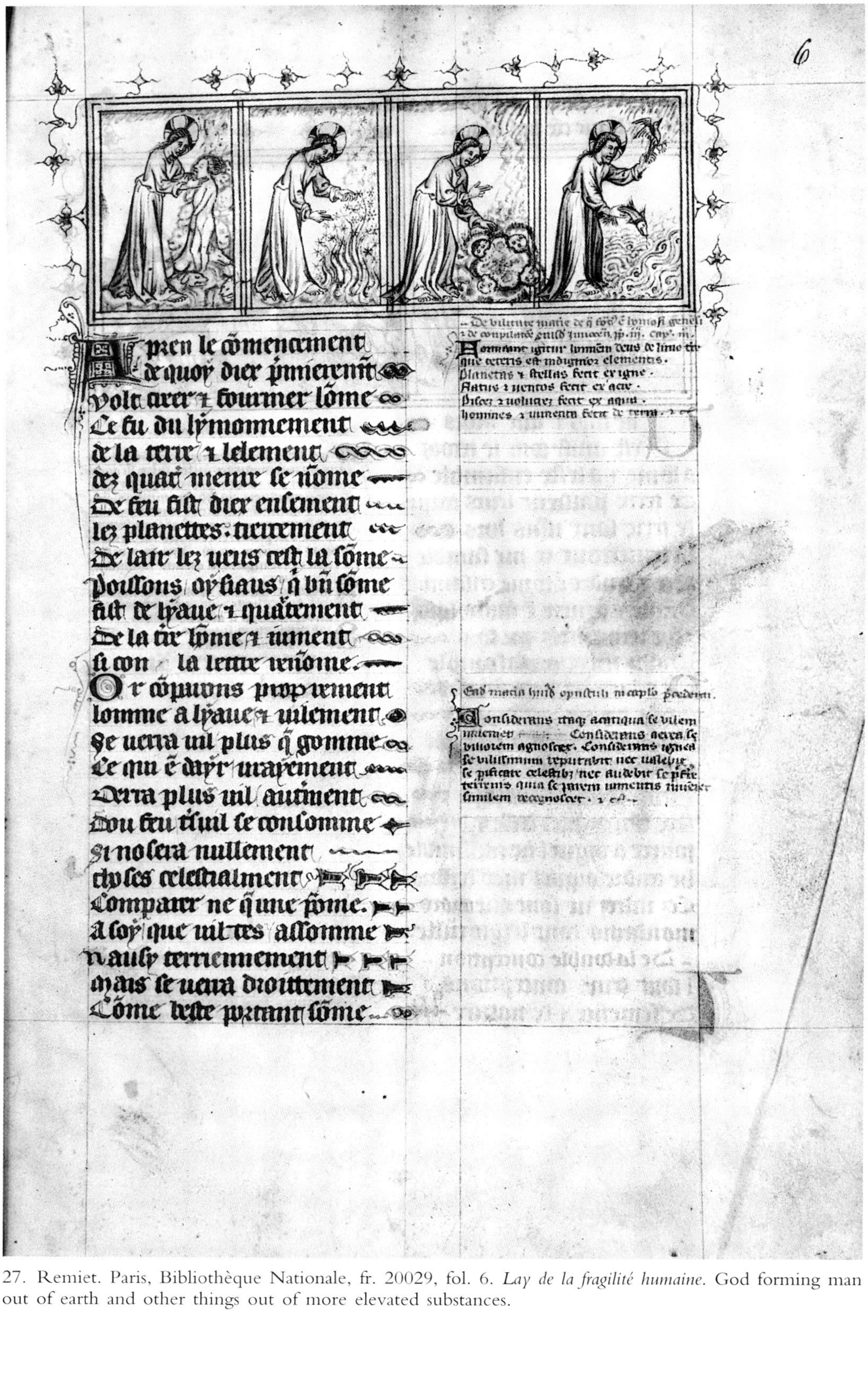

27. Remiet. Paris, Bibliothèque Nationale, fr. 20029, fol. 6. *Lay de la fragilité humaine*. God forming man out of earth and other things out of more elevated substances.

the verso of the page (see Fig. 25). It shows Job not lying on the dungheap, as he traditionally appears in biblical contexts, but actually inside the womb-like belly of the earth, like a ghostly foetus grown old (Fig. 26). This page is typical of Remiet's work in the manuscript, probably his most refined and subtle ever, in a perverse way since, although it represents his most painstaking drawing efforts, its miniatures are intentionally drab, using watery washes touched-up with dribbles of dull yellows and greens, the vile colours of the earth, dirty with human excrement and the dust of generations. These were thought of at the time as 'ugly' colours compared to the bright reds and blues that saturated other royal manuscripts. In this sense the manuscript was carefully constructed to appear as dead and sickly as its subject matter, as a brilliant anti-aesthetic object, the sophisticated style today we call 'grunge' of a lavishly profligate elite who could afford to luxuriate in the ugly as well as the beautiful.

In the French verse, Job's complaint links the 'ventre' or belly of conception with the 'sepulture' or tomb of death (what Innocent III's Latin described in the phrase 'de utero translatus ad tumulum'), eliding the moments of death and birth. Parallels are made in earlier medieval texts between the Virgin Mary's producing Christ and the virgin earth producing Adam. Before being tilled by man, soaked by rain, made to swallow Abel's blood and penetrated by the first corpse, the earth had been virginal.[11] The newly tainted earth, the place of rot, is another of Remiet's trademarks, its surface blistered by pock-like shoots and suppurating mounds that remind one of Job's own flaming flesh. Job's bitter lament towards his tainted mother is most eloquent in the Latin text on this page:

> Why came I out of my mother's womb to see labour and sorrow and that my days should be spent in confusion? If he whom God sanctified in the womb spoke such things about himself, what things shall I say of myself, whom my mother brought forth in sin? Ah me, that I might say, my mother, why did you bear me, the son of bitterness and sorrow? Why did I not die in the womb? . . . If only I had been destroyed in the womb and, so that my mother might have been my grave and her womb an everlasting conception.[12]

Nearly twenty years later, Remiet depicted another Job under the earth in a manuscript of Guyart Desmoulin's *Bible historiale*, this time totally naked and curled up like a foetus, being molested there by a demon as his friends look on (Fig. 29). This dark image, rubbed away by later readers out of fear, is a more literal one of the dark death of the body which returns to the filthy earth of its conception. It simultaneously illuminates and obfuscates an addition made by the translator to Comestor's text that became known as the 'petit Job' because it was an abridged version, deliberately avoiding exegesis of Job's curse, a curse so horrible that Desmoulins cannot bring himself to translate it:

> Job opened his mouth, and he cursed the day that he was born and said many things that no one should translate, and his friends spoke to him at length. And these words that they said to each other are in such difficult Latin and full of such great mystery that no one can understand the mystery of them if he is not a very great scholar of theology. And for this reason I shall pass over them here. For no one should dare to translate them. Since lay people could go astray here, I will be silent about it henceforth and will proceed to the end of the Book of Job.[13]

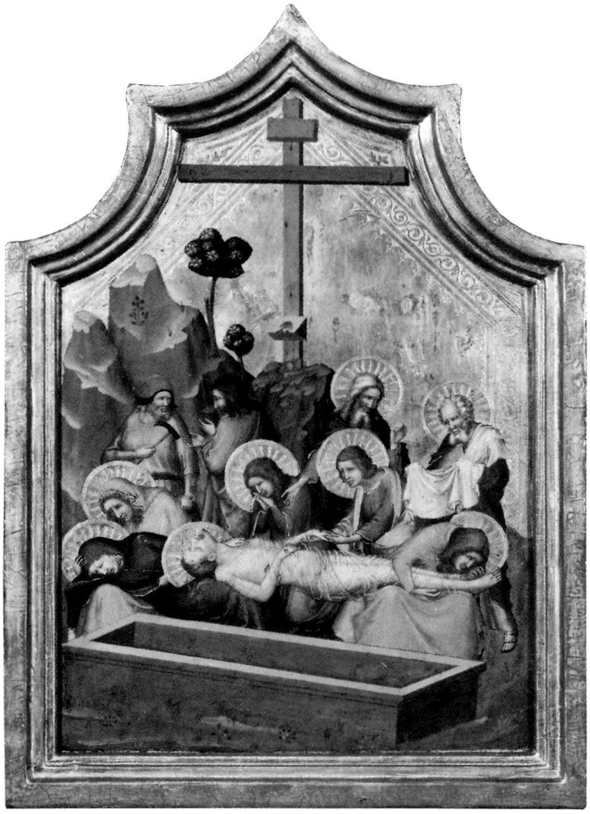

28. Master of the St George Codex, *Lamentation*, 1340–50, tempera on wood. New York, Metropolitan Museum of Art.

29. Remiet. Soissons, Bibliothèque Municipale, MS 211, fol. cxxvi. *Bible historiale*. Job in the earth.

30. Remiet. Paris, Bibliothèque Nationale, fr. 171, fol. 45. Augustine, *La Cité de Dieu*. The fall from the Tree of Life.

This censoring of Job's curse is significant in that we shall see how the illuminator, faced with similar controversial subject matter in the *Lay de la fragilité humaine* can similarly pass over material in his translation from text into image.

Remiet made an image depicting God forming the first man out of the earth, before this virgin mother is 'soiled' by death at the Fall in the *Lay* (Fig. 27). Here we read that God made the planets and stars from fire, the breezes and winds from air, the fish and birds from water, but he made men and beasts from the basest of all the elements – earth. The four parts of the miniature represent the four elemental media used by the Deity. Remiet's own medium is stretched to its limits here, but he manages to deploy transparent washes of grey and blue and to model in white body-colour over his delicate pen lines in order to evoke the immaterial becoming material under the hands of the Divine man-manufacturer. Both the Deschamps verse text and the Latin original at this point emphasize that if man compares himself to the rest of creation he sees he is vile and of inferior workmanship. Remiet actually pictures God the Creator as a sculptor moulding his human creation from soft clay amidst the unformed and half-finished mess of bits of animals, fish and dog-heads heaped on mounds of matter that lay about in the cosmological workshop. For an artisan like Remiet, the association with his own trade could not be more suggestive. Most of the artist's pigments, not only the greys and browns and carbon-based charcoal blacks, but even the crystal-derived blues, came from the earth, if they did not, like white, come from bones.

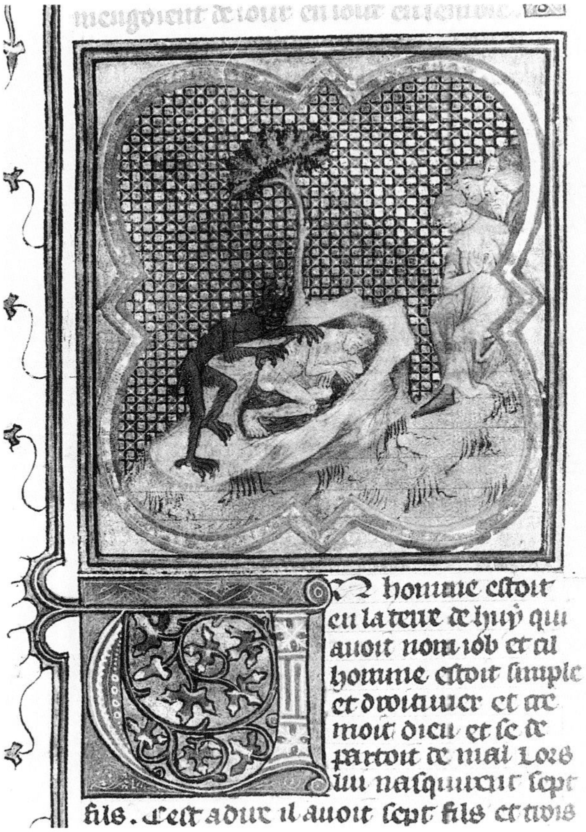

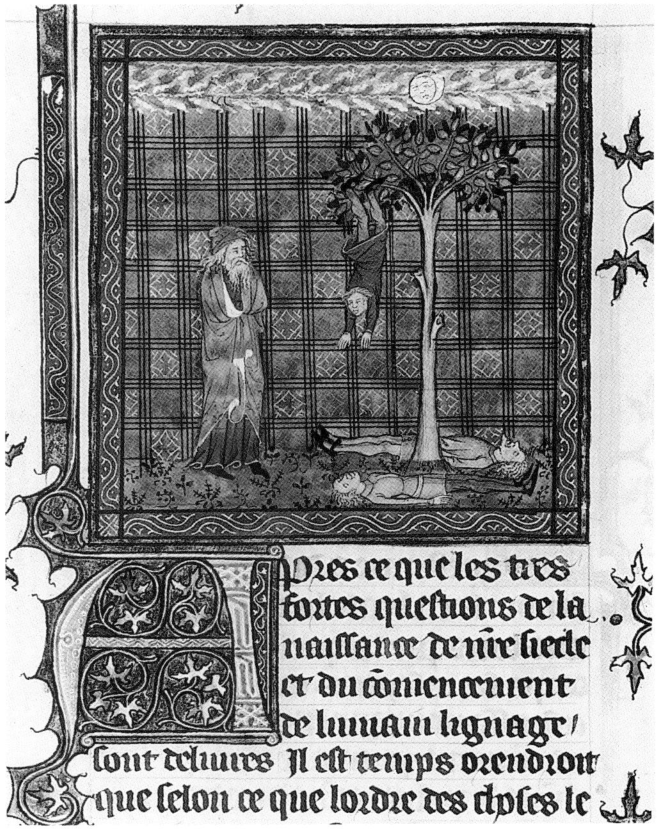

Teeming with fecundity, this is matter that in the divine artificer's hands is living form, not yet tainted by death, which will transform all matter and all creation into a lesser substance and cause man's flesh to rot and distintegrate, the opposite of its forming here. The little Adam of the creation scene stands upright, although we know from other examples of images of artisans and sculptors at work that carving was usually done on the figure as it lay horizontally. For Remiet to portray God's making man in this fashion, however, would be to introduce the idea of death, already so clearly associated with the horizontal, into the founding moment of its opposite. So Adam stands, as he does a few pages later, when, beside the tree, God's creation turns against his creator (see Fig. 23).

The motif of the corpse under the tree, seen for the first time in the 1383 manuscript, was a motif to which Remiet would often return. But it would be wrong to talk of his 'inventing' it at this moment. There are countless places in earlier Italian panel paintings that the Parisian illuminator could have seen the laid out body, notably that of Christ, as a powerful way of constructing death. Notably there was the example painted by an Italian master working at Avignon earlier in the century, which may have been transmitted through modelbooks (Fig. 28). Painters like Simone Martini and the Master of the St George Codex made Christ's body the focus of horizontal death. But more interesting than these sources or any hypothetical moment of its origins are the multiple ways in which Remiet repositions and resurrects this motif in numerous contexts throughout his career.

The Fallen Body and the Morbid Prince

Never did sexuality enjoy a more immediately natural understanding and never did it know a greater 'felicity of expression' than in the Christian world of fallen bodies and of sin. Michel Foucault[14]

Now it may be asked what sort of death God threatened to the first human beings if they broke the commandment He had given them. Was it the death of the soul? Or of the body? Or of the whole person? Or was it what is called the second death? The answer is 'All of these deaths.' St Augustine[15]

An opportunity to revivify the image of death as a point of origin came when Remiet illuminated for Louis d'Orléans a two-volume copy of Augustine's *Cité de Dieu* (BN fr. 170–1), which contains a highly idiosyncratic image of the fall of man as a literal fall from the Tree of Life (Fig. 30). Before focusing on this fascinating image, it is worth emphasizing that it is part of the single largest commission of Remiet's career, which was supplied to him by one of the leading Parisian *libraires* of the period, Thevenin de l'Angevin, a clerk of the diocese of Sens, *stationnaire*, *escrivain* and *libraire juré* to the university. Thevenin received forty francs d'or from the Duke of Orléans on 19 April 1396 to buy parchment and to engage scribes to write for 'le dedit seigneur', four books, 'le livre de la Cité de Dieu, les livres des Éthiques et Politiques, le livre du ciel et du monde, et la grant Bible', and a series of subsequent documents traces the long path to completion of these volumes.[16] The first two, the Augustine and the Aristotle, both illuminated by Remiet, are still extant, along with three volumes of a four-volume *Miroir historial* that was commissioned during the same hectic period. The two-volume translation of Augustine's great work was one of the most expensive manuscripts, in its lavish rubrication and gilding, that Remiet had a hand in. That it may not originally have been intended to go to his shop for illumination is suggested by the fact that the first miniature in the first volume, a splendid portrait of the enthroned author St Augustine (fr. 170, fol. 1r), is by a leading Parisian illuminator of the period, Pseudo-Jacquemart, who worked for the Duke of Berry and who was perhaps unable to complete the rest of the miniatures. That there were indeed problems with production is suggested by the length of time it took to write and illuminate these books: two years later the *Cité de Dieu* was still not finished. In 1398 Louis is documented as finally paying the ten francs to the Parisian Collège de Presles for the loan of a copy of the same work, 'pour y étudier et faire sa volontier'.[17] This had probably supplied Thevenin with a model of the text, but the price of the loan suggests that this model can hardly have been a luxurious illustrated copy. This is important, for while it had provided the scribes with a textual exemplar it did not provide Remiet with a set of visual models. The twenty-one miniatures in the two volumes of Remiet's *Cité de Dieu*, as a consequence, differ in all respects from the traditional cycle that had been devised to illustrate this text when it was first translated by Raoul de Presles for Charles V in 1371–5. Remiet, without access to the lavishly illuminated copies in the libraries of the Louvre or the copy later made from the same model for Jean, Duke of Berry, fell back on his own prototypes.[18] This is one of the very few places where we can be sure that he was not copying but struggling to illustrate the vernacular text before him.

The lugubrious interpretations that Remiet gives to Augustine's work might also be seen as a direct appeal to the tastes of his young patron. A strange mixture of piety and perversity, Louis, Duke of Touraine and later Orléans, the younger son of Charles V, was still in his twenties when he ordered Thevenin to supply him with the *Cité de Dieu*. He stands as a young and pudgy-faced pupil, clerical looking among the life-size royal family carved at Amiens cathedral (1375–8) in a scheme paid for by his tutor, Jean de la Grange, Bishop of Amiens, his keen and penetrating gaze already apparent (Fig. 31). Did his broken-off hand hold a book? Louis certainly shared his father's love of parchment and yet was notorious throughout Paris as being a lover of other kinds of flesh. Married at the age of sixteen to Valentina Visconti, daughter of the Duke of Milan, Louis was always plotting to take power from his uncles, the dukes of Berry and Burgundy. While he had been crucial in restoring to power his father's old advisors, men of humble birth, nicknamed the 'Marmousets' – the same word used to describe the crouching Atlases that seem to carry the weight of stones in Gothic buildings, like the bearded prophet that lifts up his own statue at Amiens as well as those painted in miniscule form in manuscripts – his own hold on power was similarly simulacral rather than real. His fortunes took a downturn in 1392 with his brother's first attack of insanity and the ascendancy of his uncle Philippe, Duke of Burgundy, as regent. This same year Louis was granted the rich appanage of Orléans in return for surrendering that of Touraine, and although his real power was eroded, he seems to have plunged into its spectacular simulation in artifice. Christine de Pizan described him as a gabbling pseudo-intellectual, a 'grand parleur, haranguer les compaignies de sages docteurs en sciences et les clercs sollonels', and he probably read some Latin, which was unusual for a prince.[19] At the same time that he kept a private cell in the austere common dormitory of the Convent of the Célestins, whose evangelical eremetic order was much patronized by the royal family and where he heard up to six masses a day, he is recorded as buying twelve barrels of Damascus rosewater from a Parisian merchant. In the year he paid Remiet one hun-

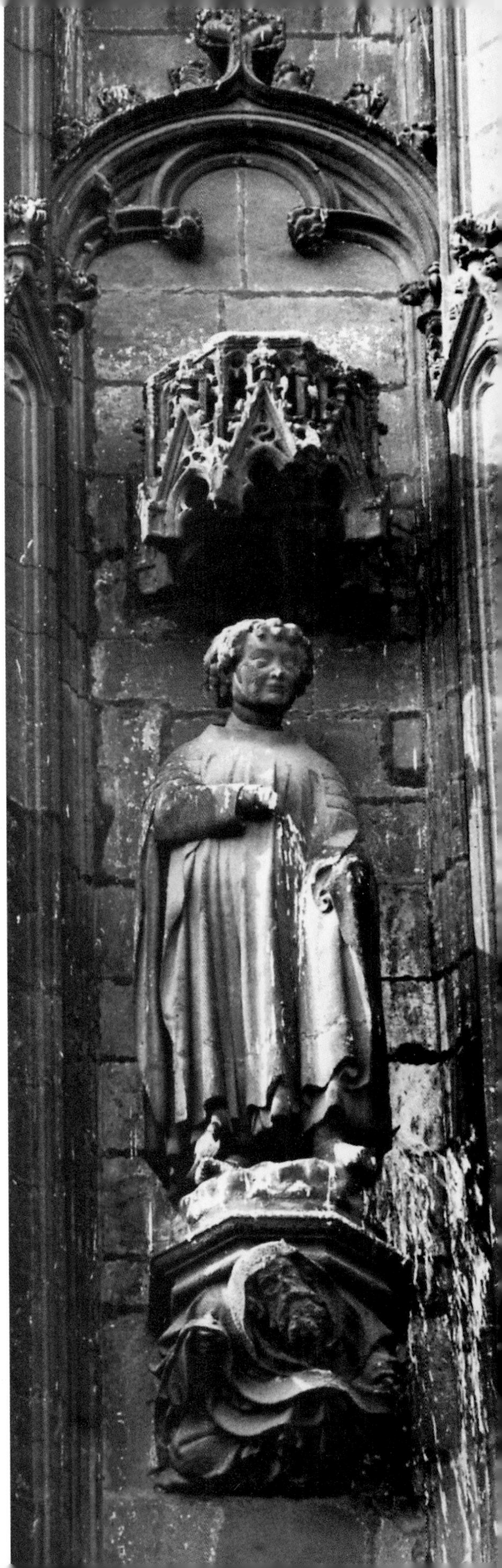

31. Jean de Launay. Amiens cathedral, north side buttress statue of Louis, Duke of Touraine (later Orléans), *c.*1378.

dred *sols* for gilding done in his royal chapel at the Célestins he paid a fool, 'master Pierre d'Aragon', the far greater sum of ten gold crowns merely for 'pulling faces'. His collection of jewels outshone even that of his uncle the Duke of Berry, but according to his enemies this included magical rings that were used to fascinate (which means to bewitch with a look) the unsuspecting victims of his lust, and gossip had it that he practised necromancy, dallying with the dead. In 1401 the cost of jewellery alone, as supplied to him by a single Parisian merchant, was 4,600 francs d'or, far more than he ever spent on books.[20]

His founding and decorating a private chapel at the Célestins was partly in expiation for his involvement in one of the most infamous incidents of this medieval *fin de siècle*, a masquerade gone wrong that had occurred in 1394 at the Hôtel Saint Pol, the king's Right Bank residence, during which Charles VI himself had nearly been burned to death. Later known as the Bal des Ardents, the escapade involved the king and six young nobles who disguised themselves as wildmen 'so that they appeared shaggy and hairy from head to foot'. A spark from Louis's torch, as he sought a closer look at the identity of these men, set ablaze the pitch and wax costumes. The room filled with screams as four of the six were burned alive before the eyes of the whole court; the king was saved only by the Duchess of Berry's throwing her skirt over him to protect him from the flames.[21] Parisians continued to blame Louis for the mishap, despite his act of penance in walking barefoot behind the king's horse in a special solemn procession to Notre Dame. It was probably the papal bull that Louis had sought absolving him in this affair that Remiet illuminated for his private chapel in the church of the Célestins in 1396, and where a similar contrast between austerity and excess was made visible. Death stalked Louis in other ways too, taking two of his small children in the same decade; their tombs too were at the Célestins.[22]

In the elaborate frontispiece that Remiet painted to open the second volume of Louis's *Cité de Dieu*, the third frame shows the young duke, dressed in blue, kneeling before a crucifix, which bridges the gulf between earth and heaven (Fig. 32). His pious pose contrasts with that of the proud king of the earthly city surrounded by his whispering courtiers arranged in a strange symmetry in the next scene. This is meant to contrast with the Heavenly King placed above, but it also hints at the intrigue and duplicities that shook the throne of France during these years when Louis's ambitions to usurp his elder brother's role were more than rumours. However, until his brutal murder in 1407, this flamboyant prince was Remiet's most consistent and important patron. Moreover, the *Cité de Dieu* was produced during the very period when Louis was building a private library to match those of his three bibliophilic uncles, and in addition to illuminating a number of manuscripts for this collection, Remiet may also have been involved in decorating this space.[23] In December 1397 Louis had acquired a *hôtel* on the Rue de la Poterne from Chancellor Pierre de Giac and charged the architect Raymond du Temple and the painter Colart de Laon with refitting and decorating it.[24] Louis also obtained the services of Gilles Mallet, who had been in charge of his father's great library at the Louvre. This library was to become the kernel of the great royal library at the château of Blois in the next century and when Charles d'Orléans had an inventory made in 1417, ten years after the death of his father, it contained liturgical books, commentaries on the Bible, romances and historical works. Of ninety-one volumes, only sixteen were in Latin.[25] Unlike in the shelving system in a modern library, books were not stacked upright, spine outwards, but

32. Remiet. Paris, Bibliothèque Nationale, fr. 171, fol. 2. Augustine, *La Cité de Dieu*, Frontispiece: the translator and the Earthly City; the Virgin and Christ enthroned in the Heavenly City; Louis, Duke of Orléans, kneeling before the crucified Christ; an Earthly King and his court.

XI

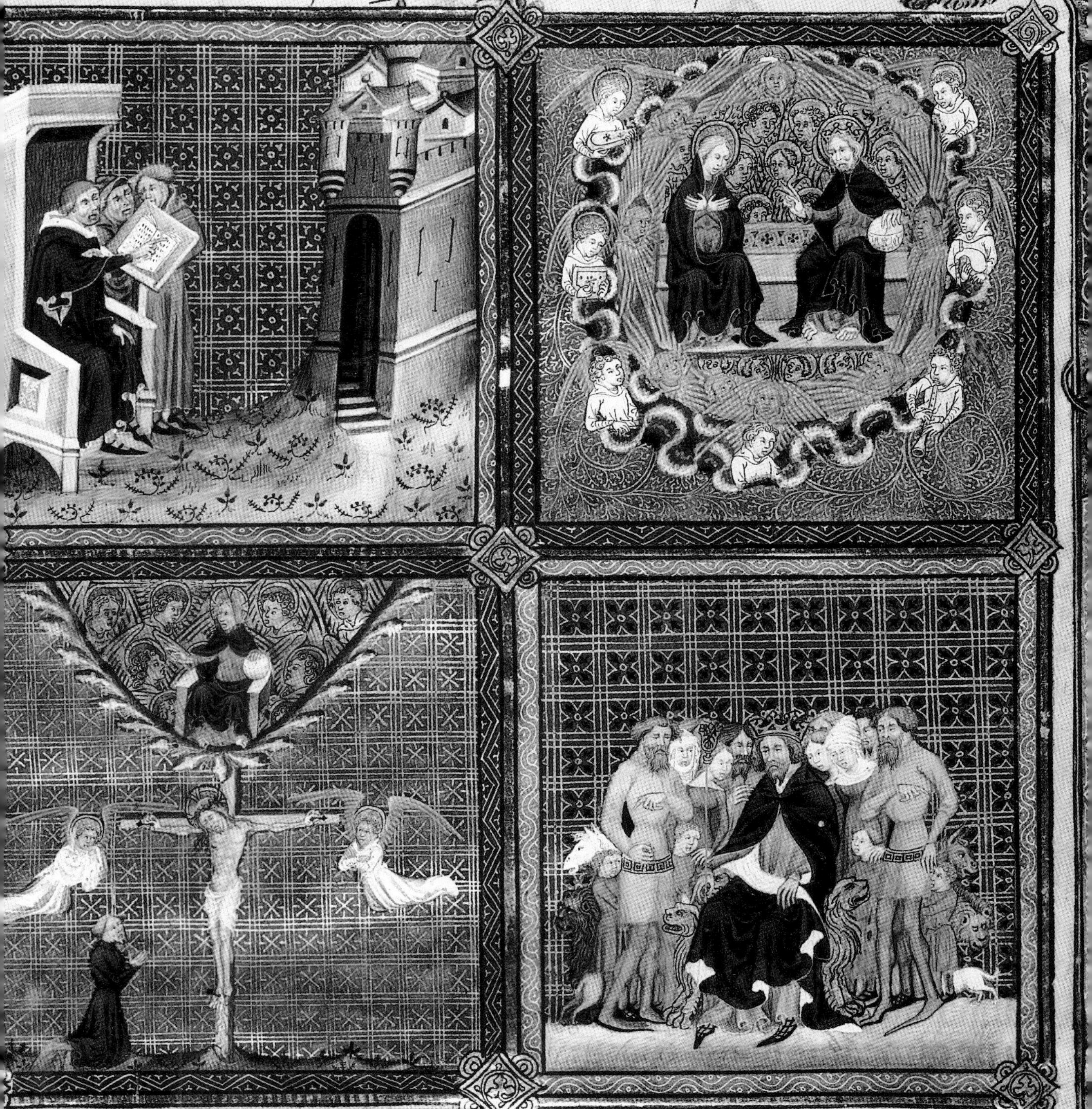

Com- prologue du
biē translateur:
que au cōmence
ment de ceste trās
lacion et exposici

de toucher a ce qui regarde la the
ologie. Car telz choses ne cheent
pas en nr̄e exposicion quāt a no9.
mais cheent a desputer et arguer
en la chaiere. et a determiner a

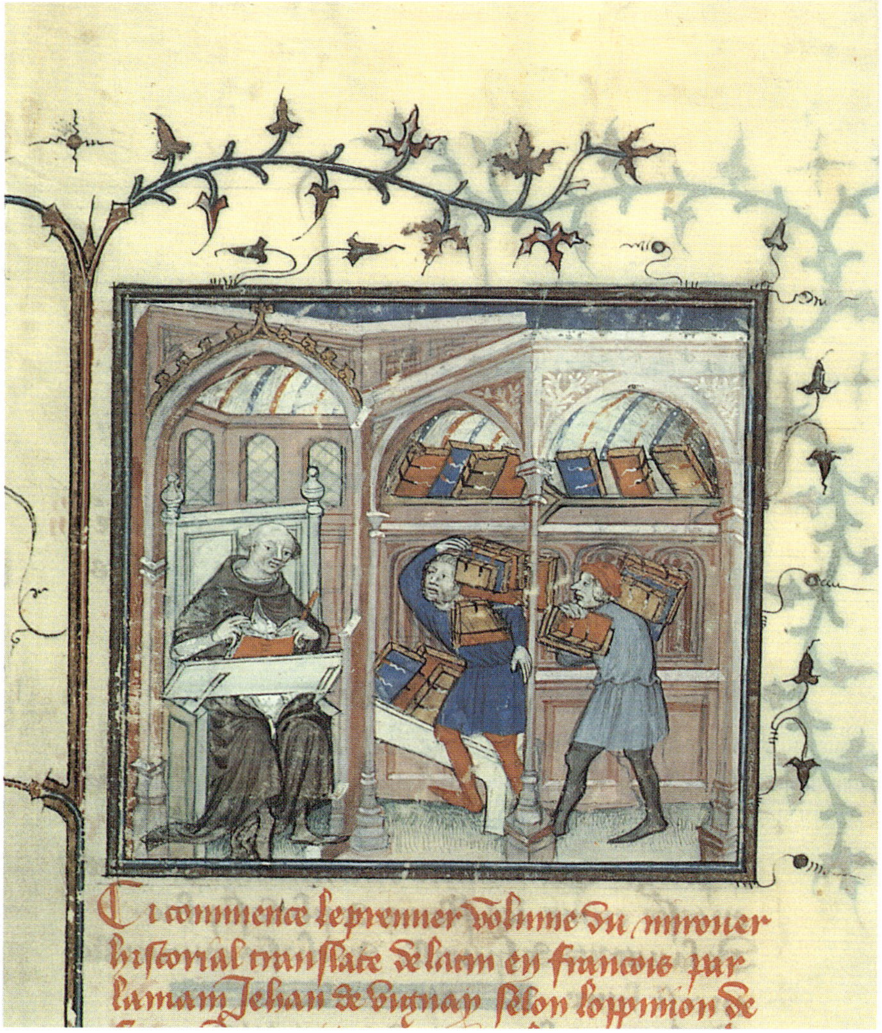

33. Jean de Nizières. Rome, Biblioteca Apostolica Vaticana, Reg. lat. 538, fol. 1. *Miroir historial.* Vincent of Beauvais compiles his encylopaedia from books brought to his desk.

were stored in wooden chests, or arranged in elaborate wooden cages, as were the books in the Louvre, or, when in use, placed flat on reading desks, reading stands and wheels, which displayed their closed surfaces as objects of luxury. Most of the volumes listed in the 1417 inventory were bound in black velvet, for which Guillaume de Villars, 'relieur de livres', had been paid eleven francs in 1397. This was true of the three volumes of Remiet's *Miroir historial*, but some were more lavishly adorned with jewels and even pictures. The exterior appearance of a book was as important as its interior, which explains why the duke's consort, Valentina, had the copy of *Guiron le courtois* 'renewed' by having it covered in red leather and supplied with four clasps. In 1393 Florence la Boutonne, 'broderesse', was commissioned to cover seven books kept in Louis d'Orléans's private chapel, one of which was a two-volume breviary illuminated by Remiet, which was also decorated with an enamel scene of the Annunciation and a sapphire bookmark in the shape of a heart.[26] This obsession with exterior adornment reached its apogee in the Christmas gift given to the Duke of Berry by the Limbourg brothers in 1411, a simulacral volume made of wood but enshrouded in real velour and locked by two enamelled clasps.[27] The use of locks on books is interesting, since this approximates the bound volume to the treasure chest, its contents kept closed and safe by clasps made of the finest enamel and gold. Opening a book illuminated by Remiet and his contemporaries was like unlocking and slowly prying into a wonderful chest full of half-hidden and glistening gems; one couldn't just flick through its contents.

The effects sought by Louis in his new library were also those of the magic and wonder of secret compartments, openings and sumptuous illusionistic surfaces, and although we have little evidence of its interior, a description of another *hôtel* of the same period provides an idea of the setting for so much of Remiet's art. In the description of Paris written between 1407 and 1420 by Guillibert de Metz, who served as a *libraire* to the dukes of Burgundy, there is an account of the *hôtel* of Jacques Duchie on the Rue des Prouvelles: 'Item: a beautiful chapel where he had lecterns upon which were placed marvellously artificed books, one could come to these from various benches, near and far, to the right or left. Item: a study where the walls were covered with precious stones and sweet smelling spices.'[28] Remiet's associate Jean de Nizières, who illuminated the third volume of the *Miroir historial* which belonged to Pregent de Coëtivy, shows a well-stocked library stacked under pink eaves and two straining servants carrying large volumes (of the same hefty size as this book itself) to the desk of the great compiler Vincent of Beauvais (Fig. 33). Certainly scholars and eminences like Louis would not have carried or lifted such large books themselves and probably even paid others to turn their pages. The private library was thought of as a 'garden' and a 'treasure chest', mingling metaphors of nature and culture in a way that framed the experience of reading as one of sensuous and social synaesthesia, delightful discovery rather than individual studious enquiry. Louis, seated in his newly built library contemplating Augustine's austere moral vision of the body and soul in his just-finished copy of the *Cité de Dieu*, was a new kind of reader. Despite all this excessive expenditure on exterior show and display, he was concerned not only with his public image out in the world but with the construction of a private realm for his own senses.

What would this prince have made of the mysterious miniature of the invention of death (Fig. 30)? Certainly he had the intellectual and poetic ability to explore an image with as much care and thought as a text. That he owned manuscripts with highly convoluted images that had to be explained by written commentaries, like the *Livre de Sallust* by Jean le Begue, and the *Épître d'Othéa* by Christine de Pizan, makes it clear that Louis had a sophisticated visual sensibility, not in the superficial sense usually derived from Huizinga's vision of later medieval decadence, but what scholars have described as a 'proto-humanist' interest in images as complex systems of thought.[29] The image opening Book XIII of the *Cité de Dieu* shows a representation of the Fall that is not described as such in the text (Fig. 30). A white-bearded old man stands at the left, his arms folded. He looks at a tree from the branches of which a young man is falling; below are two male corpses, both similar in appearance to that in the Adam and Eve scene in the *Lay de la fragilité humaine*, except that they are both clothed. The tree, whose lifespan is several times that of man, stands as a sign in Remiet's work of the imperishability of the book itself,

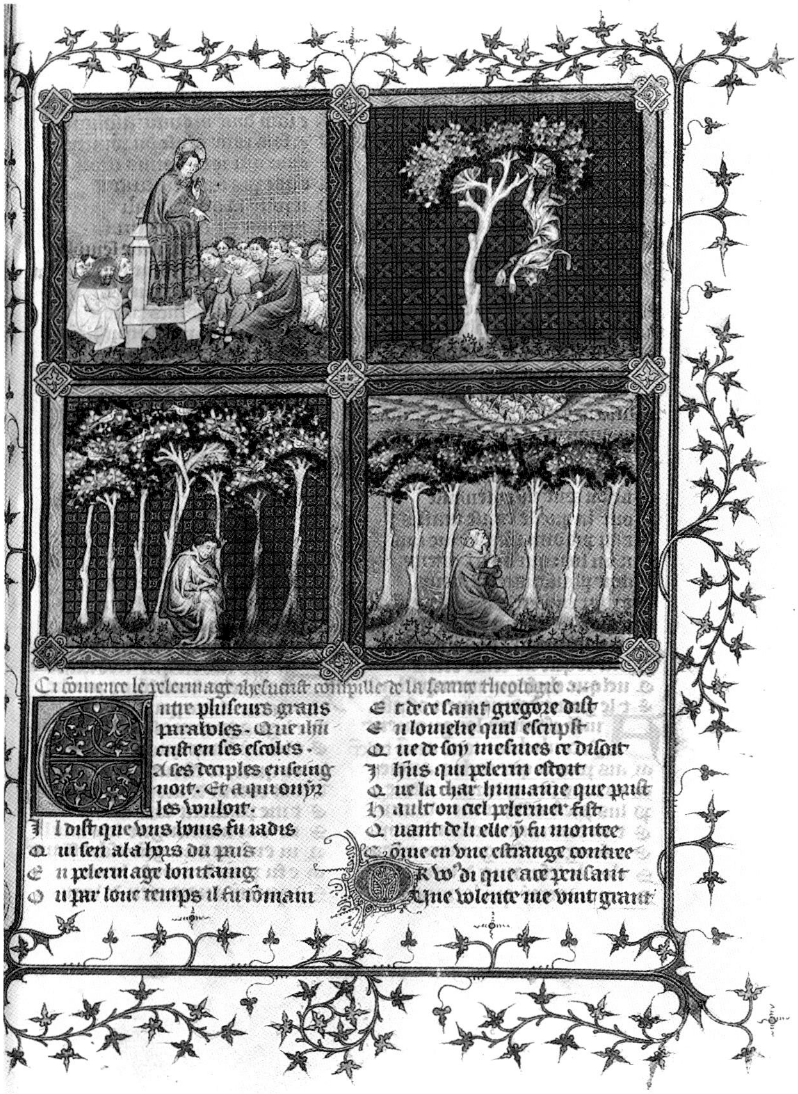

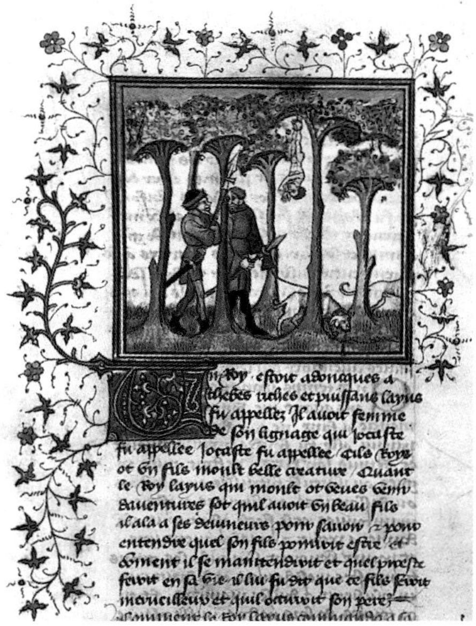

35. Remiet. Paris, Bibliothèque Nationale, fr. 250, fol. 60v. *Histoire ancienne*. The discovery of Oedipus hanging from a tree in the woods.

34. Remiet. Paris, Biblionthèque Nationale, fr. 823, fol. 169. Frontispiece to the *Pèlerinage de Jésus-Christ*. Christ preaching; the fall from the tree; the dreamer in the garden.

since the Latin word *liber* and the French *livre* refer to the layer between the sapwood and the bark of a tree, and *bouquin* (slang for book) and the English word 'book' are both derived from *boscus*, or forest in Latin, adding more dimensions to the metaphorics of nature and the trellis of the text we have already seen articulated in the flowering borders of manuscripts.[30] In the miniature the moving sky and sun and moon above suggest the turning time of the heavens and elements that cause the things of nature to decay. There is nothing akin to this scene in the long tradition of illustrating Augustine's great work, in either the Latin or the vernacular tradition. Its peculiarities suggest either that Remiet was following some oral or lost written instructions by the *libraire* Thevenin or that he read the French text himself, especially the extensive commentaries supplied by the translator, Raoul de Presles, who introduces this chapter as 'monseigneur saint Augustin here treats the fall (trebuchement) of the first man and the birth of death (et de la naissance de la mort)'.[31]

Book XIII of Augustine's work giving death a central place in the schema of salvation was the most widely read meditation on the subject throughout the Middle Ages.[32] But there is no mention in the text or commentary of the fall from the tree or of the old man in the miniature. This peculiar image in the *Cité de Dieu* is actually paralleled in a text that Remiet had illustrated five years earlier and which he probably drew upon in conceiving this one. This is the second sequel to the pilgrimage of man's life by Guillaume de Dèguileville, the *Pèlerinage de Jésus-Christ*, in the manuscript dated 1393 that records Remiet's name (Fig. 34). The second scene in the four-part frontispiece shows a man tumbling headlong from a tree, just as in the *Cité de Dieu* scene (Fig. 30), illustrating the poet's vision at the beginning of the poem where, having fallen asleep in a beautiful tree-filled garden with singing birds, the poet sees an old man climb an apple tree filled with fruit and then fall from its branches into a hole that opens up in the earth below it. This is Adam who falls into Hell and who will be redeemed in the poem that follows only by Christ's pilgrimage.[33] In the Augustine miniature it is not the 'old Adam' who falls into Hell but three young men, who have fallen or are falling to their death. The old man is present but he stands as an observer on the left, reminiscent of the figure of Elde in Chaucer's Pardoner's Tale, an eternal witness of recurrent death which he himself longs for but is tragically unable to experience. In both the *Pèlerinage* and the *Cité de Dieu*, Remiet has constructed an image of the Fall as spectacle, as something which happens to other people rather than to the subject, something witnessed.

But to see this as an image in which Remiet has projected himself as the endlessly undying observer would be exaggerating. The limited repertoire of elements to hand constrained the illuminator and confined his created world to a re-combination of stock elements. This can be seen in another odd coincidence between the figure falling from the tree in the Augustine miniature and an illustration in a very different kind of text that Remiet illustrated during the same period. This is the ancient narrative in the *Histoire ancienne* (also probably from the Duke of Orléans's library) of the baby Oedipus hanging upside down from a tree being discovered by the hunters of Polybus (Fig. 35). The rubric explains how 'Laius, the King of Thebes, had a child named Oedipus whom astrologers told him would be a marvellous man and murder him'. The baby is therefore abandoned in the woods by slaves who take pity on the infant and refuse to kill him, but this suspension upside down from a tree is an invention of the medieval tradition and points to the curse of death that cannot be avoided.[34] Our urge as historians is always to 'read' iconography in terms of historical events, as though they happened against a 'background' that stimulated their production. At this date in Paris, newborn children were still being abandoned in less flamboyant ways. There were rumours rife in the capital of a variety of Oedipal secrets at the French court; for instance whispers that Louis was in fact the lover of his elder brother's wife and actual father to the dauphin Charles. It is clearly easier to posit a point of view for Remiet's patron, Louis d'Orléans, than for the illuminator of his books. Partly because the historical and visual record of Louis as an 'important' character in the constructed drama of history, carved, painted and represented in numerous effigies, there is so much more to imagine him doing with his books and images, whereas Remiet remains, like the scene-painter or the set-designer of history, somewhere offstage. I am more interested in how and why Remiet put such images together and allowed them to resonate, not only with the world outside the book but with other books, other images.

An image then can have very different meanings for a patron than it might have for its maker and rather than always seeking to place 'iconography' as an intentional blueprint on meaning in the mind of the artist, which is then conveyed to the viewer/patron, as though by some direct relay, we should see many more circumlocutions in the circuits between conception, construction and reception. Remiet was making death out of pieces of his modelbook vocabulary, pieces that no patron could know in their isolated position as fragments and yet which can be combined to form a pictorial universe. The *Cité de Dieu* miniature thus appears not as Remiet's unique exegetical 'reading' of the text but as something far less original and thus much more interesting. Rather than a new interpretation, it is more an amalgam of current visual ideas and associations stimulated by the numbing repetitions practised in the illuminator's workshop, the tracings and copyings, modelbooks and pricked-pounced pages, that allowed trees and falling figures and the like to be reconstituted and combined in different contexts. But these models were not just neutral units that could be borrowed and passed on without charge. Increasingly they were being seen as the property of those who devised them, a nascent notion of copyright that is evidenced in a lawsuit brought against Remiet's contemporary, the royal painter Jacquemart de Hesdin, by another painter, John of Holland. The latter alleged that

36. Remiet. Paris, Bibliothèque Nationale, lat. 14247, fol. 3v. Nicolas de Lyra, *Postilla litteralis super Biblia*. God makes Eve from Adam's rib.

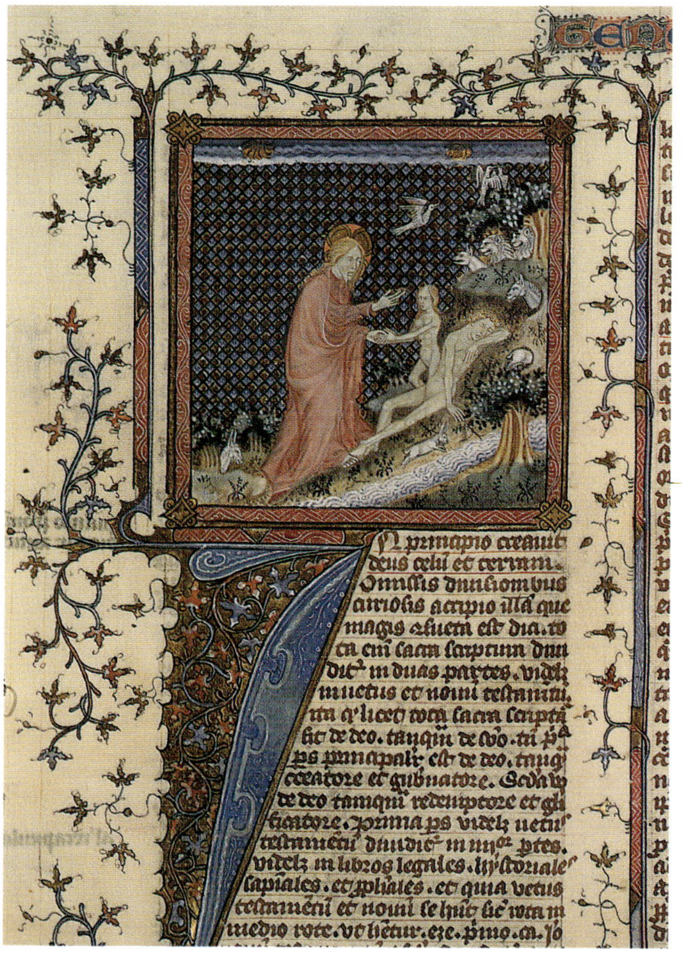

37. Remiet. Brussels, Bibliothèque Royale, MS 9094, fol. 30v. *Livre des propriétés des choses*. God makes Eve from Adam's rib.

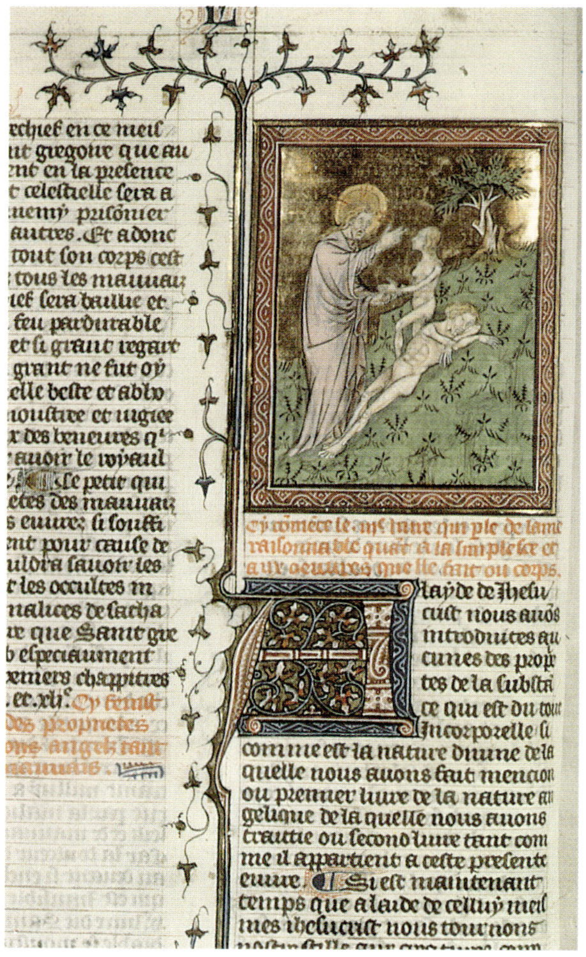

Jacquemart had stolen certain of his patterns to use in his own work.[35] Both this evidence of litigation against copying and Remiet's reconstructions of new images out of the old suggest not the originality of the individual artist but, by contrast, a dearth of pictorial resources that could be called into play at any one moment. This lack results in the continual reabsorbtion of the standard pictorial types, sometimes echoing their earlier meaning but often not, in cycle after cycle. This is the stereotype that Remiet adheres to even when he is not copying directly from a model, as in the *Cité de Dieu*. Instead of invention, he plays at endless repetition. Because he has emerged out of that matrix, just as from the womb itself, images make him more than he makes them. Precisely because 'Remiet' constitutes his artistic identity out of the narrow range of motifs at his disposal, these form not so much a 'background' or context to some real historical world in which he must be placed as actual pieces of the jigsaw. These recycled images and texts all associate death with the Fall and Adam and Eve, with the physical body, horizontally or invertedly dead, falling and fallen. For many contemporaries of Remiet, however, especially the clerics, masters and doctors of theology and their students in the Latin Quarter, St Jerome's admonition that 'death comes in through the windows of the eyes' appeared in the form of a particular coded and gendered body – that of woman.

38. Remiet. Paris, Bibliothèque Nationale fr. 312, fol. 36. *Miroir historial*. God makes Eve from Adam's rib.

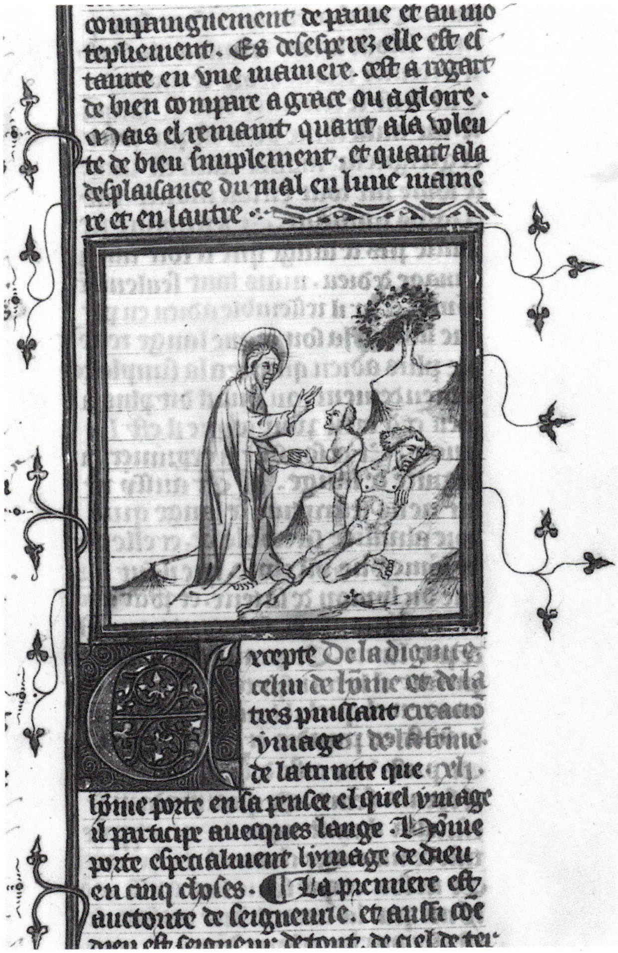

39. Remiet. Paris, Bibliothèque Nationale, fr. 338, fol. 39v. *Guiron le courtois*. Adam's pose used for a sleeping knight.

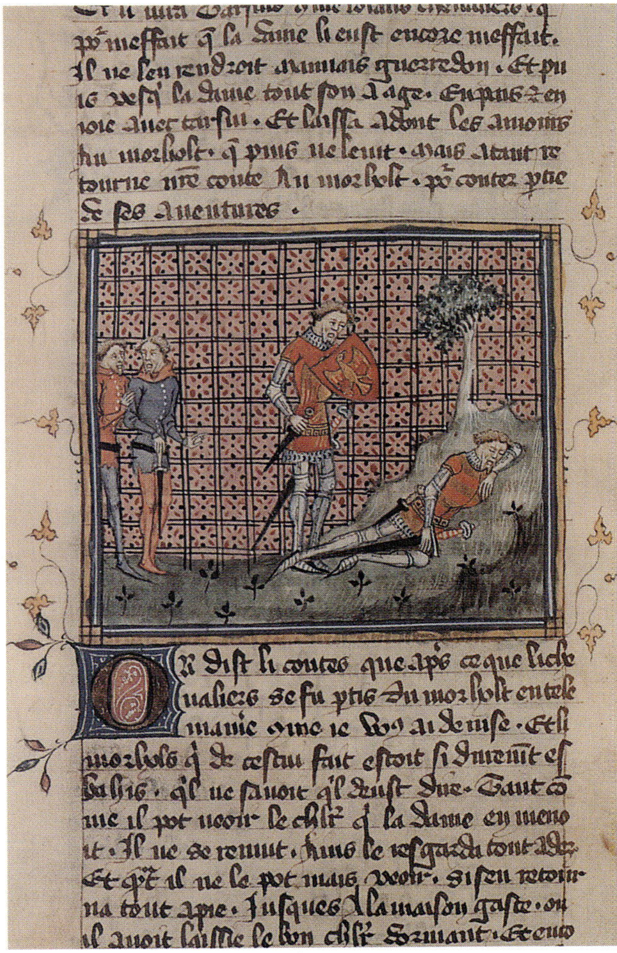

THE CREATIONS OF EVE AND THE GAP IN SEX

Woman is the guardian of the blood. But as both she and it have had to use their substance to nourish the universal consciousness of self, it is in the form of *bloodless shadows* – of unconscious fantasies – that they maintain an underground existence . . . This enables us to understand why femininity consists essentially in laying the dead man back in the womb of the earth, and giving him eternal life. Luce Irigaray[36]

Woman, created from the rib of man, is not made in the image of God. Vincent of Beauvais[37]

Louis d'Orléans, who joined Queen Isabeau in the 'Court of Love' and who was criticized by his enemies as an adulterer and profligate womanizer, owned a number of semi-scholarly accounts of the origin of the objects of his desire in texts by Vincent of Beauvais, Petrus Comestor and Nicolas de Lyra, all illuminated by Remiet. One of Remiet's most magnificent images is the Creation of Eve that opens the text of Nicolas de Lyra's *Postilla litteralis super Biblia* from the library of Louis d'Orléans (Fig. 36).[38] The artist here plays off warm and cold colours, balancing the chromatic pairs of blue and rose with gold and green, placing a shocking pink God against a densely reticulated gold and blue ground. White is used as froth of water and edge of cloud, the literal 'frills' of a nature that is totally artificial, having been made by God the divine artificer. But this scintillating scene of creation and fecundity, teeming with flowing rivers, running rabbits and flying birds, also illustrates an anxious exegetical moment in the Latin text and for the male gaze. The Franciscan author takes up the difficulty of the plural creation in Genesis 1:27: 'And God created man in His own image . . . male and female created He them.' In order to elucidate this problematic reference to a double-gendered genesis, which the midrashic tradition interpreted as God creating a hermaphrodite, Lyra mentions a medical case of his own day, the birth of 'Siamese twins', or what he calls a 'monster'. Such a birth, he argues, occurs in nature *per accidens* and thus cannot be compared to the prototype of God, the supreme artist's work.[39] In opposition to the polymorphous gender of the first couple discussed in Jewish tradition, Lyra concludes that human nature had to have been created in one individual, in the male or 'virile sex' only – making man the origin of all individuals, just as God is the origin of the universe. Moreover, he states that a man will adhere more closely to his wife precisely because he recognizes her as a product of his own body. This astonishing interpretation, in which woman is born out of man's body, built from a rib, is visualized as the first and primary theological image in the whole manuscript (Fig. 36). The Creation of Eve, which logically should be secondary – pictured after the creation of Adam – is here placed at the very beginning, as a birth that displaces woman from her biological position as mother.

The same replacement of the original creation by this secondary birth occurs in a number of other texts illuminated by Remiet. In Philippe le Hardi's copy of the *Propriétés des choses*, Remiet pictured the creation of woman to illustrate the opening of the third book, which actually describes God's creating the body as a receptacle for *man's* soul (Fig. 37). Almost identical to the previous example, God takes Eve by the hand and beckons her forth like a parent teaching a child to walk, although her brisk step hides her genitals in this case. The correspondence between the human body and 'properties of things' in nature is playfully realized by Remiet in the twisted copulation of two trees in the background, or is this a splitting or grafting that represents pre-lapsarian 'natural' reproduction, like that of Eve from Adam's rib? Only serpents were thought to generate themselves thus in the fourteenth century. This tree also points forward to the Fall and is the only prop in this staging of the primal scene of creation. Likewise in another encyclopaedic text, the copy of Vincent of Beauvais's *Miroir historial* made for Louis d'Orléans again, a smaller version of the same composition, this time in pen and with a celibate tree in the background, is used to depict the five ways in which 'man especially is made in God's image' (Fig. 38). Here Vincent describes also how God is a divine *artifex* and how 'the artistry of the omnipotent, this very same artistry, works through human craftsmen in order that they make beautiful and harmonious things'. But the Deity here is not creating new shapes *ex nihilo* but taking one out of part of another. In many respects the Creation of Eve is a perfect image of Remiet's art, building new forms from reconstituted fragments of earlier prototypes, all representation being associated with female secondariness.

In all three of these creation images, the unusually muscular form of Adam replicates itself in the form of Eve, who steps out of his body at God's magician-like command. In each of these texts, the emphasis is upon the male as origin, yet the image displays the bifurcation, an articulation of difference, in the relation between male and female. In all three the image and text are ultimately used to justify the gender roles within contemporary marriage. Yet it is a strange reversal, in that it is the created woman who is the focus of attention and movement, while Adam lies still and passive. In the later *Biblia pauperum* the text explains that 'the sleeping Adam signifies Christ dead on the cross from whose sides the sacraments flowed for us when the soldier opened the side of Christ with his lance'.[40] In all of these images, however, Adam does not lie stretched out, as if dead. Rather, his body is given a muscular, classical pose with the head resting on the bent shoulder and a diagonal body that was associated more with sleep. The image of God creating Eve out of Adam's side while he lies against the earth in a semi-upright position is more suggestive of a tranquil nap than eternal rest, yet it might, because of the common association between sleep and death, also have evoked its mortal outcome for mankind. That death might creep upon one in sleep was illustrated by Remiet in one of the few images he made for an Arthurian Romance very late in his career, *Guiron le courtois*, in which a knight, recumbent in exactly the position of Adam and with the same tree behind him is approached by another with a sword (Fig. 39).[41] What these repetitions suggest is not only that the same visual types were reproduced in workshop practice with very different meanings according to the context, but also that they were circulating among a small group of patrons like Louis d'Orléans and his uncle Philippe le Hardi, thus significantly also forming part of the semiotic structure of the audience's reactions and expectations.

As an image of birth and the emergence of one body from another, this myth of Eve's secondary creation from the rib of Adam was also fundamental to then current medical and theological positioning of woman as inferior, adjacent and secondary to man. The emphasis in all three of Remiet's creation of Eve images, each with its slightly different exegetical point to make, is the same, however. It is that woman is taken from man and that it is his body, in its tranquil heroic sleep, that is the ideal one imaged on and in God. She, by contrast, is made, and is in Nicolas de Lyra's terms 'architecture', manufactured, literally being made out of man and built on his model as a mere re-arrangement of matter, just as an artist like Remiet copies his schema from one place to another.[42] A French treatise on cosmetics reports that 'when God made Eve from the rib of Adam he gave her an imperishable beauty, but because of Eve's fault' it was lost and now can be regained through artificial treatment of 'hair, face, eyes, eyebows'.[43] That Remiet nowhere depicts the primal or initial creation of man in these encyclopaedic contexts is interesting, suggesting not just a theological but also a creative anxiety around depicting God making the 'original'.

In Chapters VI and VII of Deschamps's 1383 *Lay de la fragilité humaine*, death is also seen as originating in the woman's body in what is called 'la double conception'. However, in the Paris manuscript it is presented only in verbal form, because the two framed miniatures that should illustrate the text at this point in the manuscript have been left mysteriously blank (Fig. 40). These voids are not explained by Remiet's predeliction for emptiness. Double-lined frames have been carefully drawn in as though miniatures were intended for these spaces which were, at the last minute, left empty. These are the words that Remiet could not, would not or, more probably, was told not to visualize.

> There is, however, a double conception, one of seeds and the other of natures. The first is in the commission, the second is in the fulfillment. In the first the parents commit, in the second the offspring fulfill. Who does not know that copulation, even conjugal, is never performed entirely without the heat of desire, without the fervour of the flesh, without the stench of lust. Because of this conceived seeds are made filthy, defiled and spoiled, from which seeds the soul ultimately imparted contracts the blemish of sin, the stain of guilt, the filth of iniquity, just as an infused liquid is spoiled by a tainted vessel, and, touching the polluted item, is polluted by the contact.[44]

Whether Remiet was unable to bring himself to depict the conception of man in 'the stench of lust' or was following orders from Deschamps is difficult to know. These gaps have no tell-tale instructions in the margins alongside them, nor do they seem accidentally empty as in the *Pèlerinages* manuscript produced ten years later. It is more probable that they were left blank because both planner and artist thought that conception was not a proper subject to picture in a manuscript made for a king and eventually presented to a fourteen-year-old boy. This lurid text was explicit enough in its double Latin and French exposition and did not require visualization, although models for miniature copulation were readily available to Remiet from manuscript cycles of Latin texts of Aristotle's *De generatione et corruptione* and the vernacular *Roman de la Rose*, with Nature's lusty sermon ordering celibate clerics to 'plough' with their penises as much as they do with their pens (Fig. 41)! Such images enforced the notion that, in the words of Bartholomeus Anglicus, 'the father is the origin of conception. He produces a child similar to himself in species and appearance, especially when the virtue in the seed of the father overcomes the virtue in the seed of the mother.' This obsession with resemblance and continuity between father and son continues so that the son is loved most by his father 'when he bears a close resemblance to him'.[45] Conception as a founding moment of human representation is

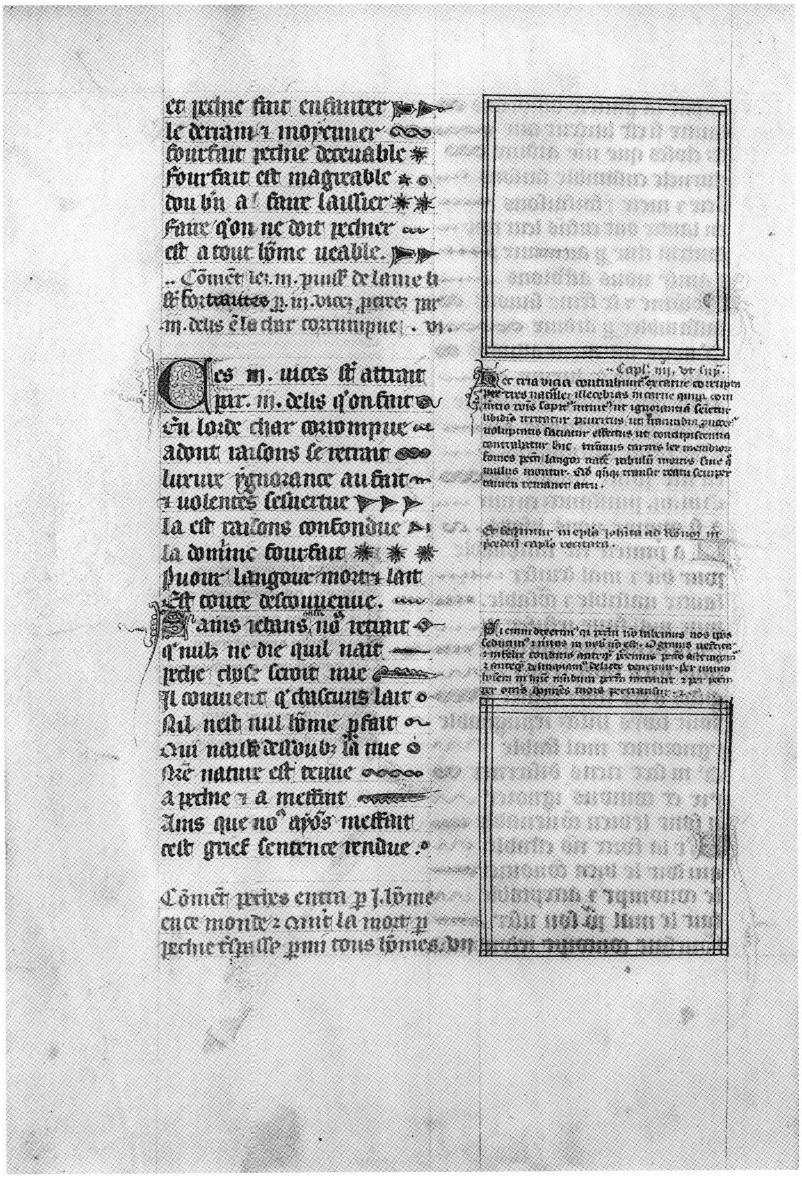

40. Paris, Bibliothèque Nationale, fr. 20029, fol. 7v. *Lay de la fragilité humaine*, Sin, death and sex illustrated by nobody.

avoided, however, in the Deschamps treatise. Unlike with the space Remiet is told not to fill in the *Pèlerinages* ten years later, here he perhaps made up his own mind, suggested by the fact that frames have been created as if to hold nothing. In many respects this non-illustration is a more individual and creative act than many of his miniatures because it registers disturbance and even shock. The link made in the text between sex and death is an analogy that Remiet perhaps thought about more than he did with most miniatures, precisely because he did *not* illustrate it. Innocent III's text and Deschamps's paraphrase discuss the three natural powers of the soul that are perverted by three vices:

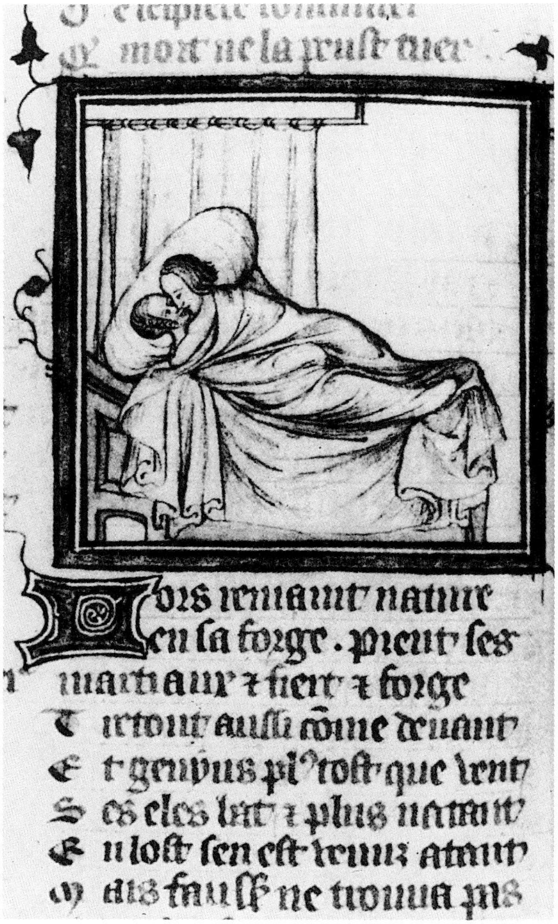

41. French illuminator, late fourteenth century. New York, Pierpont Morgan Library, M.132, fol. 137v. *Roman de la Rose.* Nature urges the clerks to coitus.

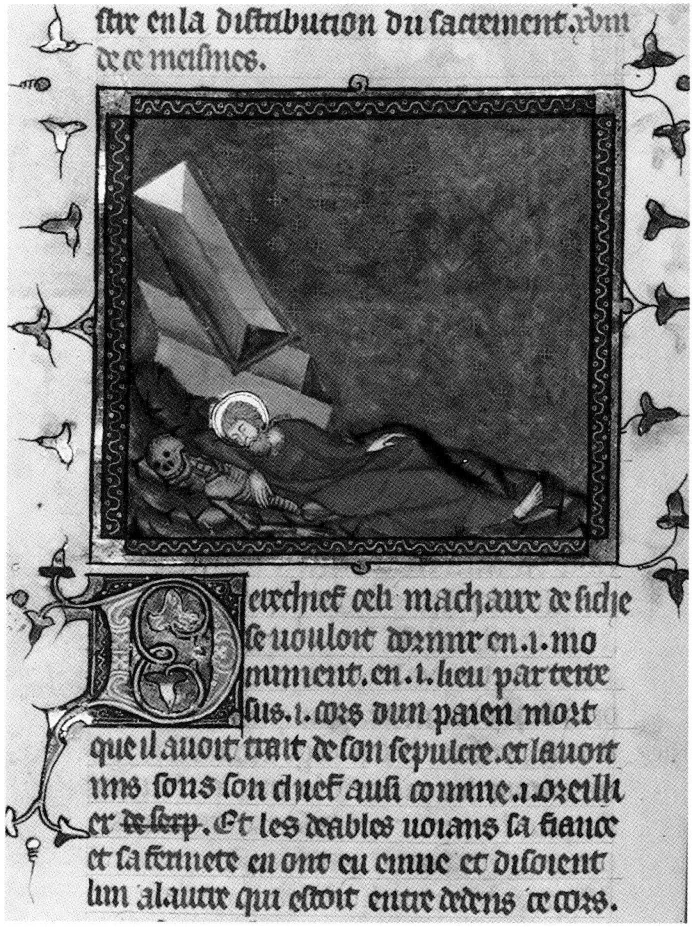

42. French illuminator, early fourteenth century. Paris, Bibliothèque de l'Arsenal, MS 5080, fol. 328v. *Miroir historial.* St Macarius sleeping with skeletons.

> These three vices are contracted from the corrupt flesh through three fleshly enticements. For in fleshly intercourse the clarity of reason is lulled to sleep, so that ignorance is begotten; the heat of desire is stimulated so that anger is propagated; the desire for pleasure is satiated, so that lust is produced. This is the tyrant of the flesh, the law of the bodily members, the kindling wood of sin, the weakness of nature, the nourishment of death, without which no one is born, without which no one dies.[46]

Death and sexual intercourse were linked in more ways still. In Aristotle's *Problemata*, translated into French for Louis d'Orléans in 1399 by Jean Doche, Master of Arts at the university, we read how 'a person having sexual intercourse and also one who is dying casts his eyes upwards, while a sleeper casts them downwards, because the heat going out in an upward direction in both makes the eyes turn in that way, whereas in sleep the heat collects in the lower part of the body'.[47] The *petit mort*, as the French still call it, was a dangerous moment for the male constitution, according to medical thinking of the time, because it entailed a loss of the vital heat and moisture that sustained life. Too much copulation, it was believed, like eating too many onions, made men more susceptible to the plague. But for some churchmen like Innocent III, the vileness and stench of man's lust for the female body in the sexual act meant it was always already the equivalent of death. For saints like Macarius, pictured in an earlier *Miroir historial* that Remiet knew as a partial model for his own versions, to lie in a tomb full of pagan bones inhabited by evil spirits who entice him with the voices of women (Fig. 42) was the same sort of renunciatory act of self-control seen in those saints who tested their spiritual mettle by sleeping in the same bed as, but not succumbing to, prostitutes.

The increasing belief in and power of astrology in all circles, from the court of Charles VI down to the barber surgeons who bled the Parisian populace according to their charts of the stars, meant that people often counted their beginning not from the day of their birth but, like the self-obsessive compulsive clerical illuminator Opicinis de Canistris of Pavia, born in 1296, from the time of conception – the very moment that Remiet did not picture.[48] Besides designing a diagram with the moment of his conception, the mad Italian miniaturist produced a powerful image of the simultaneous and adjacent births of prince and pauper, their unequal lives and totally identical ends (Fig. 43). It is not coincidental that the position of the babies and the corpses is the same inverted one of the fallen body. Opicinus's diagrammatic and unbalanced mentality placed death upside-down, as a literal semiotic negation, whereas for Remiet it was always horizontal, placed in the world as though somehow still living within it.

43. Opicinus de Canistris. Rome, Biblioteca Apostolica Vaticana, Vat. lat. 6435, fol. 48v. The birth, life and death of prince and pauper.

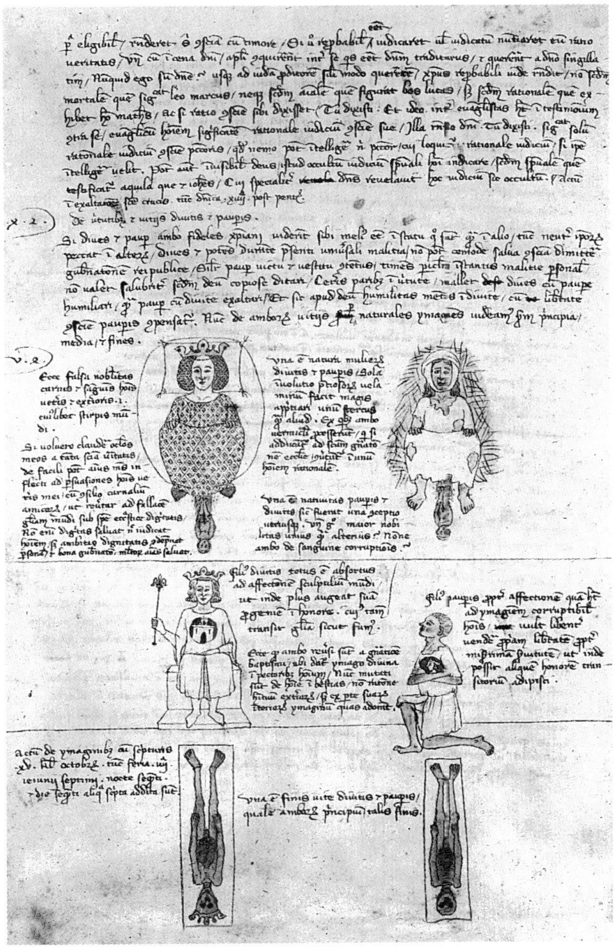

44. Oxford, St John's College, MS 164, fol. 160. Astrological treatises made for Charles V. The horoscope of Louis, Duke of Orléans.

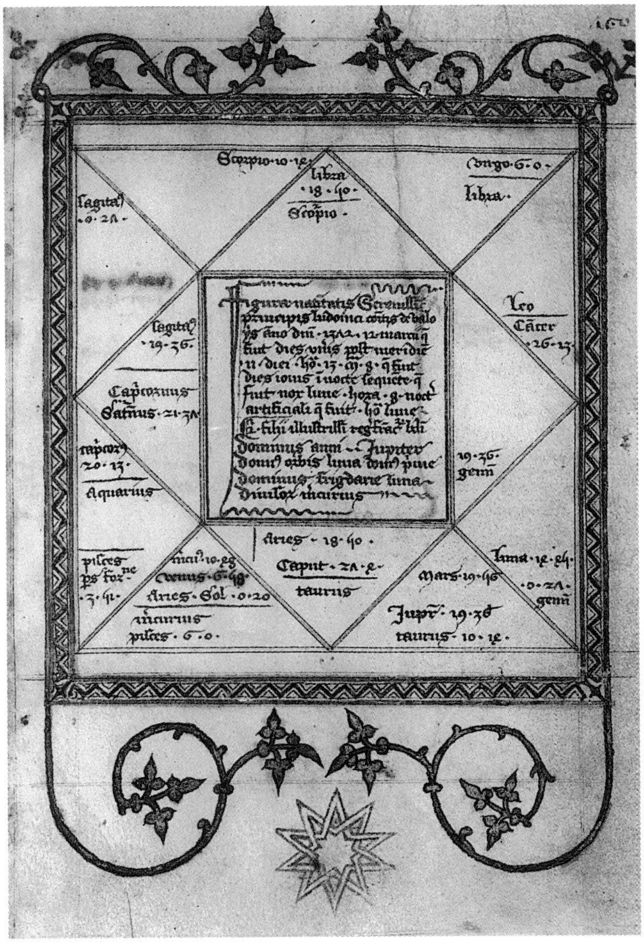

Remiet and his audience never sought to lay out birth like death in this way. But birth was the most dangerous juncture, the moment met with fearful anticipation not only by the mother but also by the family who were concerned to have the happiest conjunction of the stars for their offspring. A manuscript now at St John's College, Oxford, is a richly illuminated series of astrological tracts by a close associate of Remiet's who had worked with him on books made for the royal family early in his career. It contains the five full-page framed horoscope charts of Charles V and the four of his children who were living between 1373 and 1377, including the chart of the future Charles VI and the fateful one of Louis d'Orléans (Fig. 44). Constructed like a miniature with a frame and rule, this diagram defines the position of the cosmos at the moment of birth, written in the square at the centre: 'Wednesday, 12 March 1372, at eight minutes past one in the morning, which is an hour of the moon.'[49] Three infants previously born to the royal couple had died in infancy, and the birth of a daughter in 1378 resulted in the death of Queen Jeanne de Bourbon. Such high infant mortality statistics among even the wealthiest in society explain something of the desperation that caused most people to look to the stars for signs of their future life and death. A person's life was seen to be exhibited more clearly in these horoscopes, in which a whole future set of circumstances could be read, than in anything resembling what we think of as biography. One might argue that the growing obsession with astrology in this period actually helped foster an increased sense of individual identity, linking each person's destiny to a unique trajectory unlike any other and guided by the arrangement of the zodiac. For royalty especially, the heavenly bodies ruled over those who ruled over earthly bodies. For the royal recipient of the *Lay de la fragilité humaine*, conceiving heirs at the right conjunction of the heavens was essential and, despite his periods of madness, Charles VI would father no fewer than eleven children with his consort Isabeau of Bavaria, who was thought to have lost her sanity under the strain of royal mass production.

The truly abhorred corpse in Innocent III's treatise and its courtly reworking was that of the woman whose intervagination in conception and labour is endlessly re-enacted in rhetorically sensuous passages of luridly fascinating but entirely misogynistic repulsion. This helps explain why Innocent's original text was always among the most popular works enjoyed by male clerics throughout the Middle Ages. The most monstrous aspect of this 'other' body was its liquid breaking boundaries during menstruation, a passage that Deschamps translates almost word for word from the original: 'the bitter horror of putrefied blood. It is called menstrual blood and flux, which ceases in the mother after conception so that with it the fetus is fed inside the woman. Grass is killed by it, this is clear; trees are destroyed by it; dogs go completely mad from touching this matter.'[50] This is the double horror concealed in the two blank spaces on the previous page: not only that the child is conceived in the slimy liquid of lust but that, in the womb, putrefaction corrupts the infant soul just as 'a bucket of filth attracts infections'. Fed and formed out of putrid and poisonous menstrual blood, humans carry the taint of original sin.

Of course both male and female contribute to conception, and a more general misanthropy vitiates Innocent's treatise to be translated into Deschamps's lines and Remiet's outlines. A telling transformation occurs from its original Latin monastic and mendicant context to that of the palace with its very different corporeal codes. Obsessive concern with human ordure is something that Remiet and his audience could enjoy only

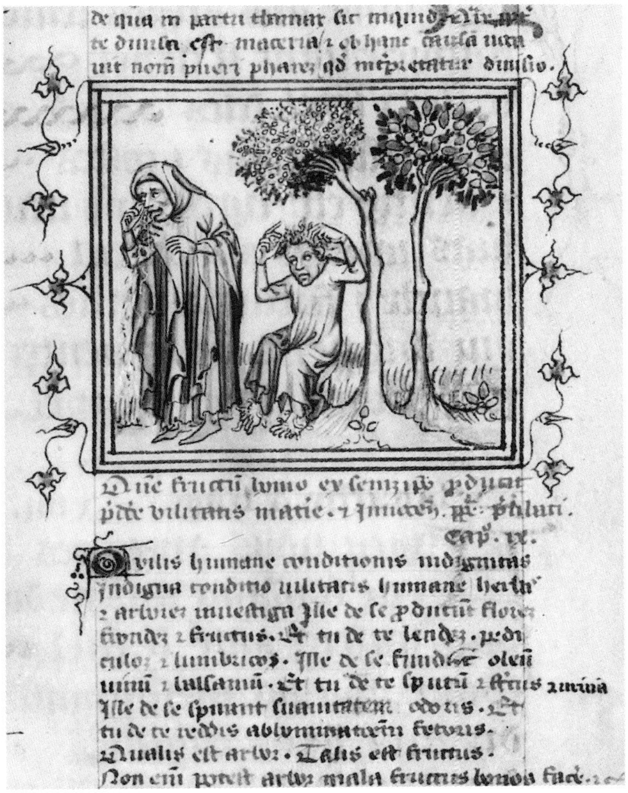

45. Remiet. Paris, Bibliothèque Nationale, fr. 20029, fol. 9. *Lay de la fragilité humaine.* The vile products of the human body.

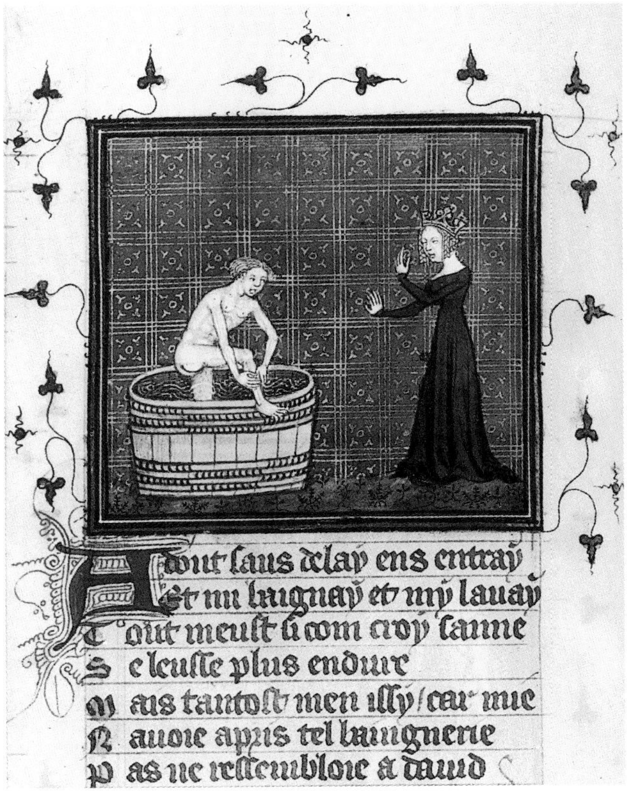

46. Remiet. Paris, Bibliothèque Nationale, fr. 823, fol. 78v. *Pèlerinage de vie humaine.* The pilgrim bathes in the tears of penitence.

at some distance. While for an ascetic Benedictine monk, the foetid filth of his body had been something that he learned to endure, even delight in, as a sign of his humility, for a fastidious fourteenth-century courtier, dirt became something more of a social stain. To stink was not as delectable in the court as in the cloister. One of Remiet's most powerful miniatures in the *Lay de la fragilité humaine* is devoted to exactly these stinking and ignoble fruits of the body (Fig. 45).

> O vile unworthiness of the human condition, unworthy condition of human vileness! Investigate the plants and the trees: they produce flowers, and fruits from themselves, and you, nits and lice and worms from yourself. They bring forth oil, wine and balsam from themselves; you, spittle, urine and excrement from yourself. They emit a sweetness of smell from themselves and you give out an abomination of stench from yourself.[51]

Alongside two elegant 'little trees' with their luscious fruits are Remiet's grubby little men with their mucilaginous equivalents. The one on the left, dressed in long robes like a cleric, blows his nose on to the ground – the earliest representation of 'snot' that I know of, suggesting that already at this date there existed courtly taboos about making bodily acts into such a visible performance. Remiet worked hard to make this picture disgusting, and evocative of Deschamps's rich vernacular vocabulary of piss and spit ('pyssat et cracherre') in the text. In addition to the nose-blowing, standing figure, a seated man ruffles the lice in his hair while fat, white maggot-like creatures stream down his legs. If this image seems extreme to our over-sanitized modern Western sensibilities, we shouldn't forget that this filthy creature, while representing something distasteful to Remiet's royal audience, actually might not have been so strange to an urban-dweller like Remiet himself. His contemporary, the author, scribe and illuminator Jean le Begue gives a recipe in one of his manuscripts, after those for blue pigments and gold leaf, for 'how to make maggots and lice fall from your head. Anoint your head with the juice of rue.'[52] Nor were such filth and lice solely the prerogative of the poor. According to chroniclers, in 1405 after five months of a bout of his insanity during which he refused to wash or be attended by doctors, the king's body was described as oozing with 'suers fetides' and pustules, fleas and vermin having gnawed into his skin to such an extent that his vestments had gelled with his flesh and could not be torn from him.[53]

Such vermin were seen as quite natural. They were thought to be produced by the body itself, which, when the flesh cannot sweat, engendered skin furfurs, freckles, leprosy and, if the heat was strong enough, fleas and other imperfect animals.[54] But it would be wrong to think of fourteenth-century people as universally foul-smelling and permanently rancid. Remiet, like many ordinary Parisians, probably frequented the *estuves*, or public baths, which were numerous in the university quarter, but we do not know how often.[55] The nobility, beneath their rose-water-soaked silks and Arabic-spiced pomanders, were in fact probably less washed than the urban populace. A new attitude to the body as a site of cleanliness, and the association between external filth and a person's dirty internal moral state, can be seen in Remiet's magnificent miniature in the *Pèlerinage de vie humaine* showing the sprightly, youthful body of the pilgrim who, at the orders of Grace Dieu, washes himself clean of his sins in a tub filled with the tears of penitence (Fig. 46).

Another thing to bear in mind is that while certain kinds of human effluvia, especially excrement, were not linked to death and horror as directly as they are today but were more visibly integrated into culture, in jokes and carnivalesque imagery, there was a growing problem in the fourteenth century with dirt. This was exacerbated by the vast growth of cities like Paris. We know that Charles VI used a *chaise percée*, or a chair with a hole in it, as a personal toilet, that the Duke of Berry besides ordering many expensive books, ordered vast amounts of toilet paper ('quatre livre d'étoupes') in 1398 and that Louis d'Orléans's *chaière nécessaire* was decorated with embroidery as fine as spider's webs. Most Parisians, however, used the river, which was where Louis's luxurious latrine probably also emptied. The polluted state of the main artery of the city became such a problem that the king issued a royal ordinance in 1404 urging people not to treat it as a dumping ground. The river was described as being polluted with 'ordures, putrefactions et immondices' which are a 'great horror and abomination to see', making it a 'miracle de nostre Seigneur' that those who use the river for their drinking and cooking water have not incurred 'mort et maladies incurables'.[56] This filthy urban world was impossible to keep pure and clean and was yet another instance of the decay of things that Remiet's art so lovingly delineated.

The *Lay de la fragilité humaine* goes on to compare the body of a man with a 'tree turned upside down', the latter reversed on the left of the picture, its protuding and shaggy tubers paralleling the dangling genitals of the stretched-out man on the right (Fig. 47). 'Its roots

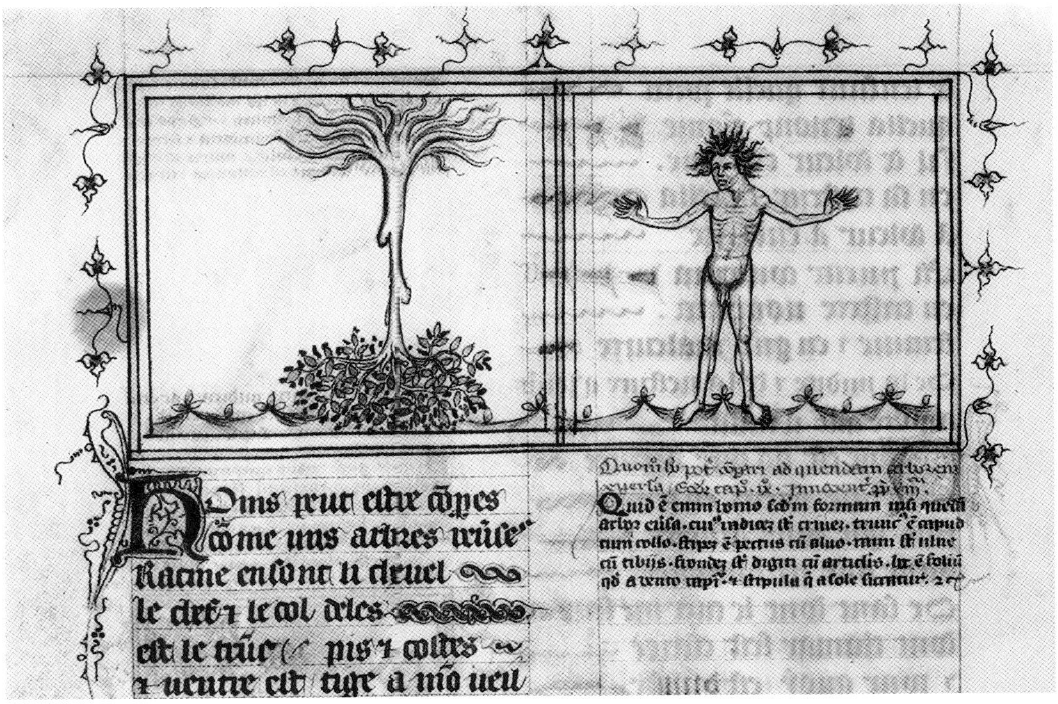

47. Remiet. Paris, Bibliothèque Nationale, fr. 20029, fol. 9v. *Lay de la fragilité humaine.* Man's body is like an inverted tree.

are the hair, its base is the head along with the neck, its trunk is the chest along with the belly, its branches are the arms along with the legs, its foliage is the fingers and toes along with the joints. This is the leaf that is carried away by the wind and the straw that is dried by the sun.'[57] Whereas such a frontal, naked figure with outstretched arms had represented man's elemental unity with the cosmos in earlier twelfth-century manuscripts, this figure is literally rooted in the ground, the macrocosmic Neo-Platonic possibilities shattered by the mundane microcosmic prison of the flesh.[58] This is Remiet's 'everyman', an ideal like that of the macrocosm man and zodiac man so popular in the Later Middle Ages, but one that has been inverted, the head, which was usually seen as the noblest region of the body and the site of reason, at the opposite end of the organism from the site of flowering and budding. That this is a body with which Remiet might have identified is suggested by its gender, for, although it is meant to stand for all bodies, male and female, it is only one of these. This male body, in contrast to the lurid metaphors and images of the dark, dead female body in the same treatise, none the less stands phallocentrically for organic growth. A triple reiteration of the ignobility of the body is at work here, first in Latin prose, then in the ten lines of rhyming French and finally – or perhaps from the viewpoint of the reader looking at the layout of the page, we should say initially – in the double image. The tree man is ultimately based on the metaphor in Matthew's Gospel that 'an evil tree cannot bring forth good fruit', quite different from the metaphor as it appears in contemporary medical discourse where it is used to describe the veins and heart as the root and trunk of the many-branching organism of man.[59] This is not the tree of Good and Evil from which man falls and under which he dies because of his curiosity and concupiscence. Nor is it the tree full of singing birds, setting the scene for love-poetry, the *locus amoenus*. This is the tree that, according to the text, will dry up and die, its arms/branches terminating in dry, twig-like fingers. This is, finally, far from an evocation of that other arborial image common in the fourteenth century, a family tree, which is also inverted so that the family line descends from its patrilineal roots down to the present fruits.[60] Yet the species, or the family line, can only continue outside this fruitless autumnal male body. It bears only one sign of having been grafted or grown elsewhere, in the prominent point of the navel, which simultaneously locates his centre and provides his only link to the effaced womb of the mother.

The Dead Mother

There is the birth of the child – and the threat of death weighing down upon it. But above all death weighs on the painter as a father whom the coming generation would one day displace. Julia Kristeva[61]

A woman, like a person shipwrecked, when she is in labour indeed hath sorrow: but when she hath brought forth the male child, she remembereth no more the anguish for joy that a man is born into the world. Lotario dei Segni (Innocent III) quoting the Gospel of St John[62]

For the medieval artist, life's beginning was actually a far more controversial subject for representation than its end. Whereas death was often a public event witnessed by crowds of onlookers and, even for the poor, an eminently social experience, birth was, by contrast, the secret of the midwives, forbidden to the male gaze and a breach in nature much more disturbing and dangerous for all the living.[63] Both events, birth and death, took place on what constituted for most people in this period, the most valuable moveable good that they owned – the bed. This was the central object of domestic life and of course death, since it is described in great detail in wills and in post-mortem inventories. The *lit*, whether it be the straw-filled, lice-infested pallet of the poor or the vast, wooden-framed and profusely curtained couch of the wealthy, was where individuals were conceived, born, died and spent half their lives in between. Representing up to twenty-five per cent of the value of household furniture, the bed was an inner sanctuary in the home, a cradle of the maternal universe at the heart of private life.[64] One of the few objects of domestic daily experience that Remiet included in his sparse universe of things, the bed was also, however, an important social space where great ruptures and border-crossings took place, beginning of course with birth.

Remiet's illustration of the pain of the child's arrival into the world in the *Lay de la fragilité humaine* is headed by the rubric 'De la foiblesse et nudité de l'enfant en sa nativité' and is another dual icon of human helplessness. The treatise again makes the analogy with the baser world of animals and shows an ass birthing and suckling its young alongside a scene of 'How all are born crying to express the misery of nature' (Fig. 48). Remiet has depicted the moments after the event, not the drawn-out agony of labour itself as described in the text. The bed is large, lavish even, with embroidery-covered pillows, a

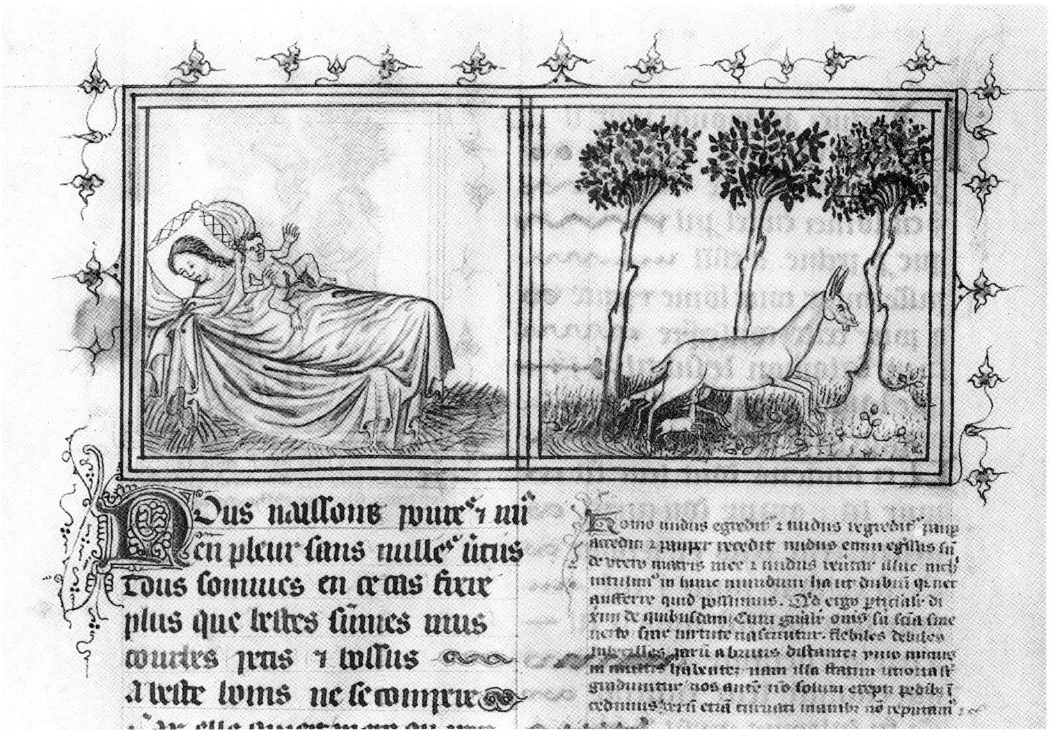

48. Remiet. Paris, Bibliothèque Nationale, fr. 20029, fol. 8v. *Lay de la fragilité humaine.* The wretched birth of man compared to that of beast.

pallet and a voluminous cloth. The mother is strangely alone and there is no midwife, otherwise ubiquitous in scenes of birth.[65] The naked infant squirms on its mother's belly, as if just left there, the twisted newly cut umbilical cord a livid red streak breaking its bond with the maternal source. Naked our flesh arrives and naked it shall return 'en terre', clothed only in the tainted coat of blood, the 'pel diffamée de sang'. The mother's head looks away from her child, bowed in sleep, exhaustion, perhaps even death. There is melancholy here in both the image and the French verse that is totally lacking in the Latin original, the plight of the fragile individual who emerges poor and naked, in tears and without any virtue: 'povre et nus, / En plour, sans nuls vertus'. The baby's outstretched arms express its anguished cries, the 'braie de l'enfant', according to the text, paralleling the braying ass in the facing scene of 'nature'. One baby ass is suckling already, but for the bereft human new-born opposite there is no succour. A gender distinction is made in the text between female babies, whose first sound is to cry 'E' for 'Eva', and male babies, who cry 'A' for Adam. That this baby is wailing 'A' is evident from its clearly visible penis. The large space of empty parchment which opens up before the newborn is like an awaiting chasm of the future.[66] Even the infant's pre-linguistic stage communication is an instinctual memory of the sin of its first parents. That tainted inheritance is communicated visually here by the stiff form of the mother rather than by the child.

After the delivery, in many areas of medieval France, a woman was considered unclean and not allowed to make bread or fetch water until she had been 'purified by the efforts of her priest' and by a churching which, forty days after the event, readmitted her to the altar and the sacrament of the mass.[67] According to Bartholomeus Anglicus's encyclopaedia, translated into French by Jean Corbechon and illuminated by Remiet for the Duke of Burgundy, 'when the child is born the midwife or wisewoman cuts the umbilical cord the length of four fingers and knots it' and washes the infant in salt and honey to cleanse it of filthy blood, taking care to rub the limbs of male children even more since they must be stronger than females 'pour le labeur'. This pre-baptismal cleansing washed the physical stain that could be fully removed only at baptism. The baby was then put in a dark place, for it was feared that too much light would turn its weak eyes blind.[68] Other rigorous means of moulding the body mentioned by Bartholomeus, which emphasize the different bodily types of male and female offspring, were common in both noble and peasant households, like massaging the limbs and wrapping the infant in layers of tight swaddling bands.[69] These tight bonds were pictured by Remiet in his depiction of the male and female spheres of labour in Louis d'Orléans's copy of Oresme's translation of the Pseudo-Aristotelian *Livre d'économiques* (Fig. 49) and were meant to shape the limbs of girls to soft contours and to strengthen the bodies of baby boys. In this image the ploughman represents external male work while the mother stands for the inner domestic sphere of female labour. In the interior of the home, hers is literally a dual dolour. Holding the swaddled infant between her legs refers back to birth, while she balances the traditional attribute of women's work, the distaff. It is worth noting that just as women were the ones who, present at birth, wrapped the newborn infant in its first cloth, they were also associated with washing and wrapping the corpse in its final winding-sheet. A number of fifteenth-century Books of Hours show the wrapping of the corpse as an exclusively female occupation.[70]

At Baptism, the ritual cleansing of the child, the priest referred to the ability of the

49. Remiet. Paris, Bibliothèque Nationale, fr. 9106, fol. 358. Aristotle, *Économiques*. The different labours of men and women.

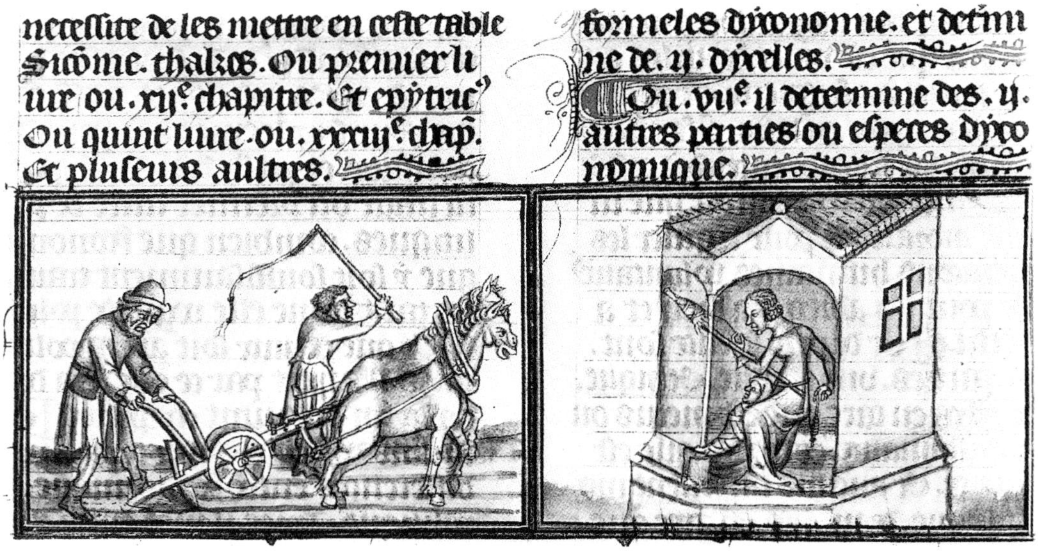

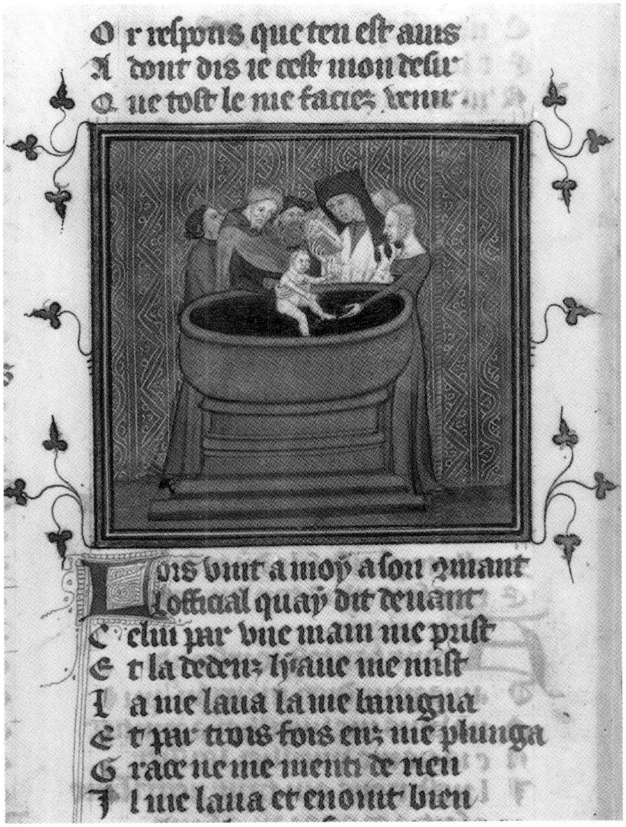

50. Remiet. Paris, Bibliothèque Nationale, fr. 823, fol. 4v. *Pèlerinage de vie humaine*. Baptism.

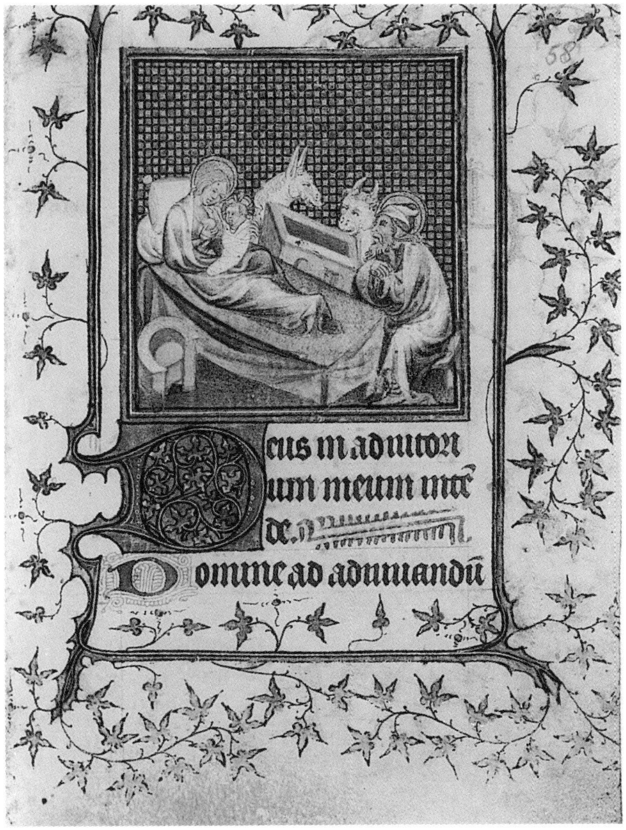

51. Remiet. Vienna, Österreichiche Nationalbibliothek, cod. 1969, fol. 58. Book of Hours. The Nativity with empty chair and empty tomb/manger.

purifying holy water to remove the stain of birth and asked the Lord to 'delay his death and prolong his days' before putting salt into the infant's mouth. In the *Pèlerinage de vie humaine* this moment is illustrated by Remiet with his usual ambiguities and vacant spaces. The baptismal font looms like an ominous black chasm into which the baby is dropped (Fig. 50). This sacramental anointing, publically announcing the individual's entry into the Christian community, paralleled the last sacraments administered at the individual's departure. Moreover, infants who died before this rite, and stillbirths, were refused Christian burial. The new-born infant was thus viewed, not with our sentimental satisfaction in the creation of new life, but with an anxiety at its vulnerability, its blind, helpless but above all tainted origins which required radical scrubbing, binding in its first winding-sheet and most of all the cleansing rites of the Church. In the words of one of Deschamps's poems: 'Happy is he who has no children, for babies mean nothing but crying and stench; they give only trouble and anxiety; they have to be clothed, shod, fed; they are always in danger of falling or hurting themselves; they contract some illness and die.'[71]

Birth was only glorious when the taint of death was supplemented by the possibility of salvation. Remiet would often have been called upon to depict the births of divine persons in ubiquitous subjects like the birth of the Virgin, as he pictured it in a single leaf cut from a large missal illustrating the feast of her birth 'Hodie nata est beata virgo maria' (Fig. 52). The high social status of the mother of God is attested by the tall bed-head

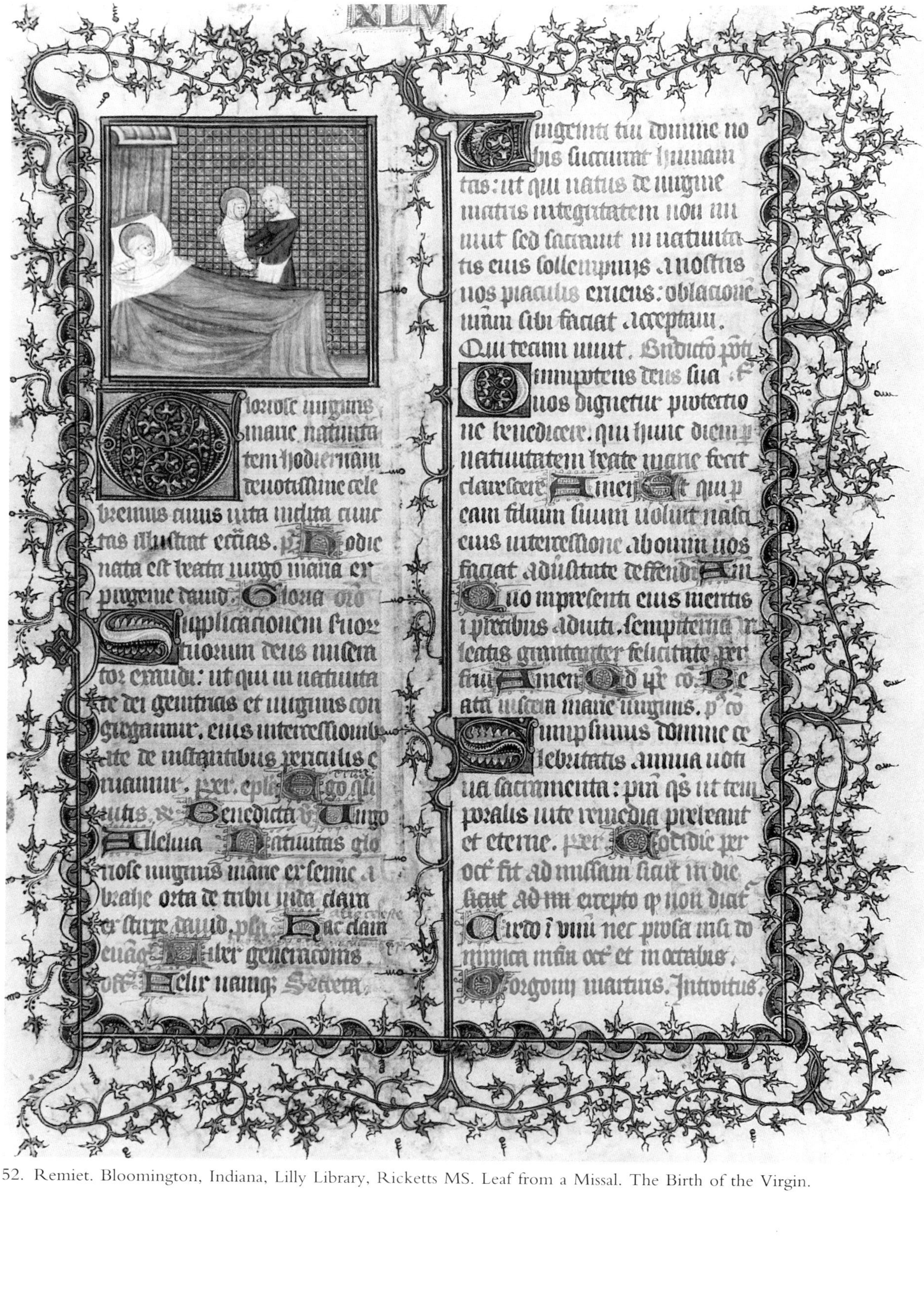

52. Remiet. Bloomington, Indiana, Lilly Library, Ricketts MS. Leaf from a Missal. The Birth of the Virgin.

which rises up on the left. The Virgin's conception and birth were matters of intense theological as well as popular debate in Paris during the 1380s when the *Lay de la fragilité humaine* was written and illustrated. Many of the faithful celebrated the conception of the Virgin Mary on 8 December, nine months before her birth on 8 September. The saying that 'Eve was conceived without sin, but she conceived in sin; Mary was conceived in sin but she conceived without sin' was hotly debated at this time. A Dominican named Juan of Monzon had denied the immaculate conception and was condemned by the Pope and the University of Paris.[72] No pain or squirming offspring is visible at the Virgin's birth in this missal image, made for a prominent bishop, Étienne de Loypeau, who would have sided with the immaculatist orthodox position. This is the dematerialized arrival of the one who will herself transcend the need for physical conception. Was it possible that she who is 'without stain' (*sine macula*) could herself have been in that foul place?

Mary's productive body could be shown, however, in one crucial role of maternal construction, and that is breast feeding. This was something that Remiet would have seen every day on the streets of Paris and in chapels and churches, not only in real nursing mothers but in the realm of simulacra, where the image of the lactating Virgin was more popular than ever before.[73] A startling image even of post-mortem breast feeding occurs in a story that Remiet illustrated in the *Miroir historial*, in which a duke comes to an island where he had lost his wife and new-born son in a shipwreck two years before (Fig. 53). Miraculously, the duke finds the baby alive and suckling at the dead mother's breast! Such miracles emphasize the ways in which women could be like Mary, able to perform the maternal function in ways that are sometimes supernatural. At the same time as the maternal body was focused upon in these ways, it was anathema to the male gaze. The great negative exemplum of this forbidden territory was Nero, who, according to the *Golden Legend*, 'spurred by a shameful zeal, had his mother killed and cut in half to see how he had been nurtured in her womb'. Illuminators were often called upon to depict this obscene scene of gynaecological voyeurism, which takes place on an anatomist's table (Fig. 54). They did not depict the later part of the story where the emperor actually demands to conceive a child in order to experience 'what pain my mother suffered', eventually giving birth to a frog.[74] Instead they focused upon Nero's perverse desire for the spectacle of origins in the body of his own dead mother.

The death that the maternal body contained was usually of a different order. In many fourteenth-century works of devotional art, the onlooker was meant to contemplate the innocence and sweetness of the Christ-child in his mother's arms and his future suffering on the cross, looking forward to death rather than backward to the rupture of birth. In a little Book of Hours now in Vienna, Remiet juxtaposed birth and death more subtly in the scene of the Nativity by making the empty manger in the middle of the minature not so much the altar of the eucharistic sacrifice, which was a traditional allusion, but the hollow, rectangular tomb-slab (Fig. 51). Its diagonal form even echoes the Virgin's own childbed. If the dark hole of origins, outside the very specialized genre of medical illustration, was unrepresentable, that at the other end of life was not. Ironically then, conception and birth were much more dangerous subjects for the medieval artist to approach than death. This is clearly indicated in the two gaps in the otherwise richly illustrated *Lay de la fragilité humaine* and the ways in which this same work can describe human emergence from the female body, but cannot present it in pictures. The painless

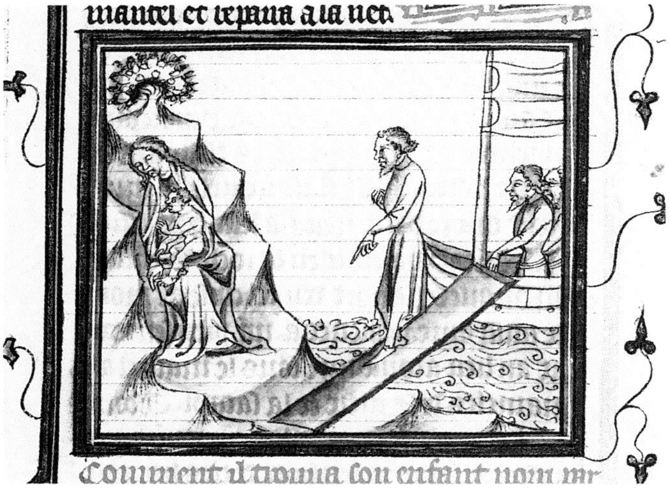

53. Remiet. Paris, Bibliothèque Nationale, fr. 313, fol. 96. *Miroir historial.* How a duke found his son nourished at the breast of its dead mother.

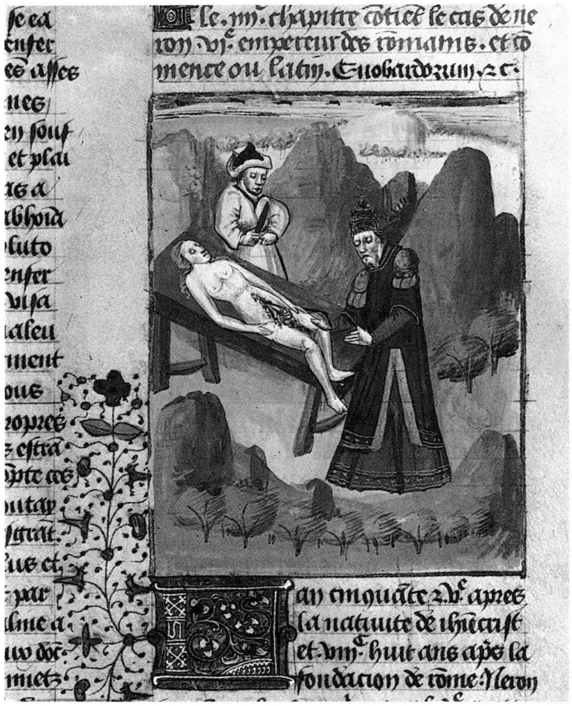

54. French illuminator, c.1450. Paris, Bibliothèque Nationale, fr. 232, fol. 249. *Golden Legend.* The Emperor Nero has his mother opened to see whence he came.

parturitions that Remiet usually depicted were distinct from the filth and suffering of ordinary human labour and usually showed the divine child already swathed in his mother's arms. For the ordinary human child at this moment, death begins. According to Giles of Rome, who followed basic Aristotelian and medical sources, 'Pure flesh is only generated from food when this takes place in the womb of the mother. When the child is outside the womb, the food that it eats is no longer turned into pure flesh. As a result, the flesh becomes more and more impure . . . in the end so impure that it cannot function as flesh any longer. This means that the soul can no longer remain in that body, and therefore man must die.'[75]

But before we leave the theme of birth juxtaposed to death, it is perhaps worth looking back at Remiet's own birth not as a human being but as an artist. Though he never pictured the child actually being born from between its mother's legs, he pictured it *not* being born in one startling instance. The miniature of the birth of Julius Caesar, torn from his mother's corpse and thus, according to medieval beliefs, not really born at all, is one of the earliest miniatures that I would attribute to Remiet.[76] It occurs in a copy of the *Faits des romains* produced in the 1360s before he became an independent master and when he was still working in the Boqueteaux shop as an assistant, painting some of the backgrounds and borders. Certain aspects, such as the tricolour frame, the striped parti-coloured bed-curtain pulled to one side, and the dense gold scrollwork background, will later become his trademarks. But it is in the scene of the birth of Caesar where Remiet emerges, and goes beyond the rote copying of an apprentice, producing 'like out of like', according to Aristotelian doctrines of generation (Fig. 55).

Remiet's art, as outlined in the previous chapter, was born out of that of an earlier generation of illuminators, like the little figure of the baby Caesar here, growing out of

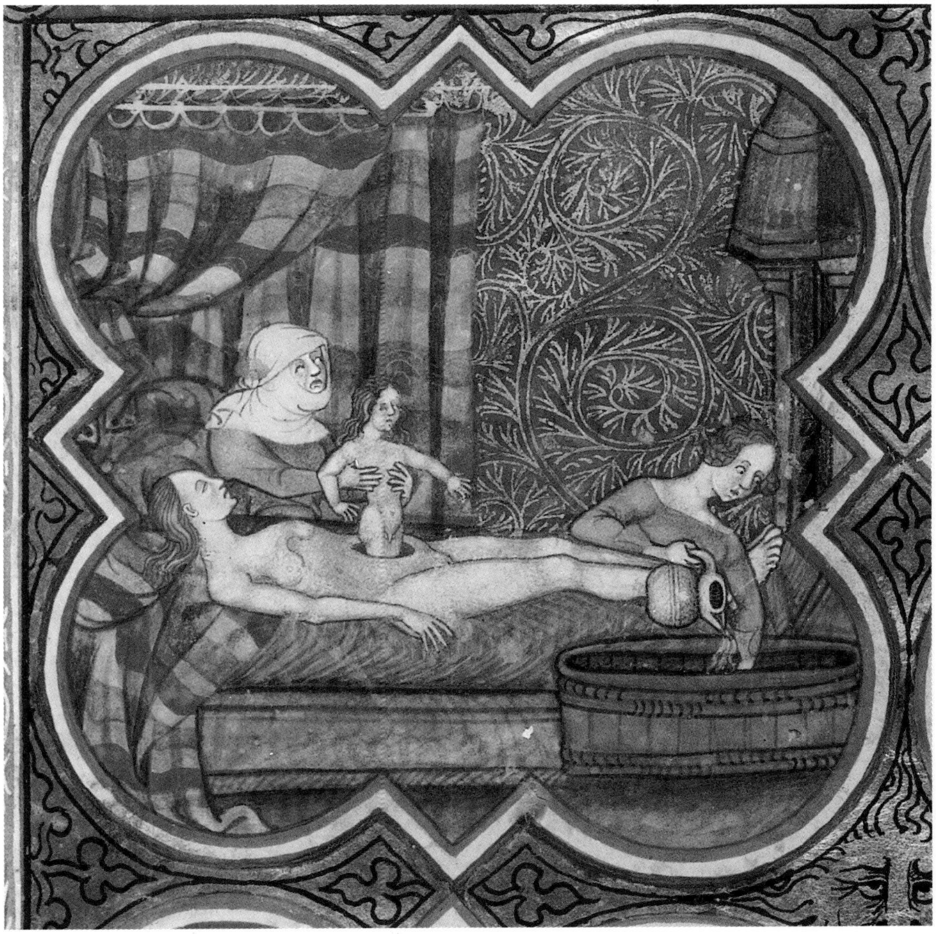

55. Remiet and others. London. British Library, MS Royal 16.G.vii, fol. 219. *Faits des romains*. The birth of Julius Caesar.

the same segmented structures whence he had come. It was not, however, this curly-headed little creature, something meant to be alive, that fascinated the artist and provided him with a pattern for the future. It was instead what was left behind and what he had so laboured upon – the body emptied by labour, whose long limbs and thrust back face present what might be the first body that Remiet ever painted. This posture would have struck viewers as odd, for parturition was usually experienced squatting in what was the 'natural' position for giving birth. This horizontal cadaverous mother comes to stand for the basic unfigurability and unrepresentability of origin. Here both art and death are brought together, albeit unconsciously, in the extravaginal but no less bloody birth of a replica which embodies the birth of all images. Here then, years before its appearance in the presentation copy of Deschamps's *Lay* or Louis d'Orléans's *Cité de Dieu*, is the prototype for the horizontal cadaver, not in the sexless corpse beneath the Tree of Life but in the corpse of that lost, dead mother, the *mater* who gives form to *materia* and who must ultimately have given birth to Remiet and to his pictorial idea of death.

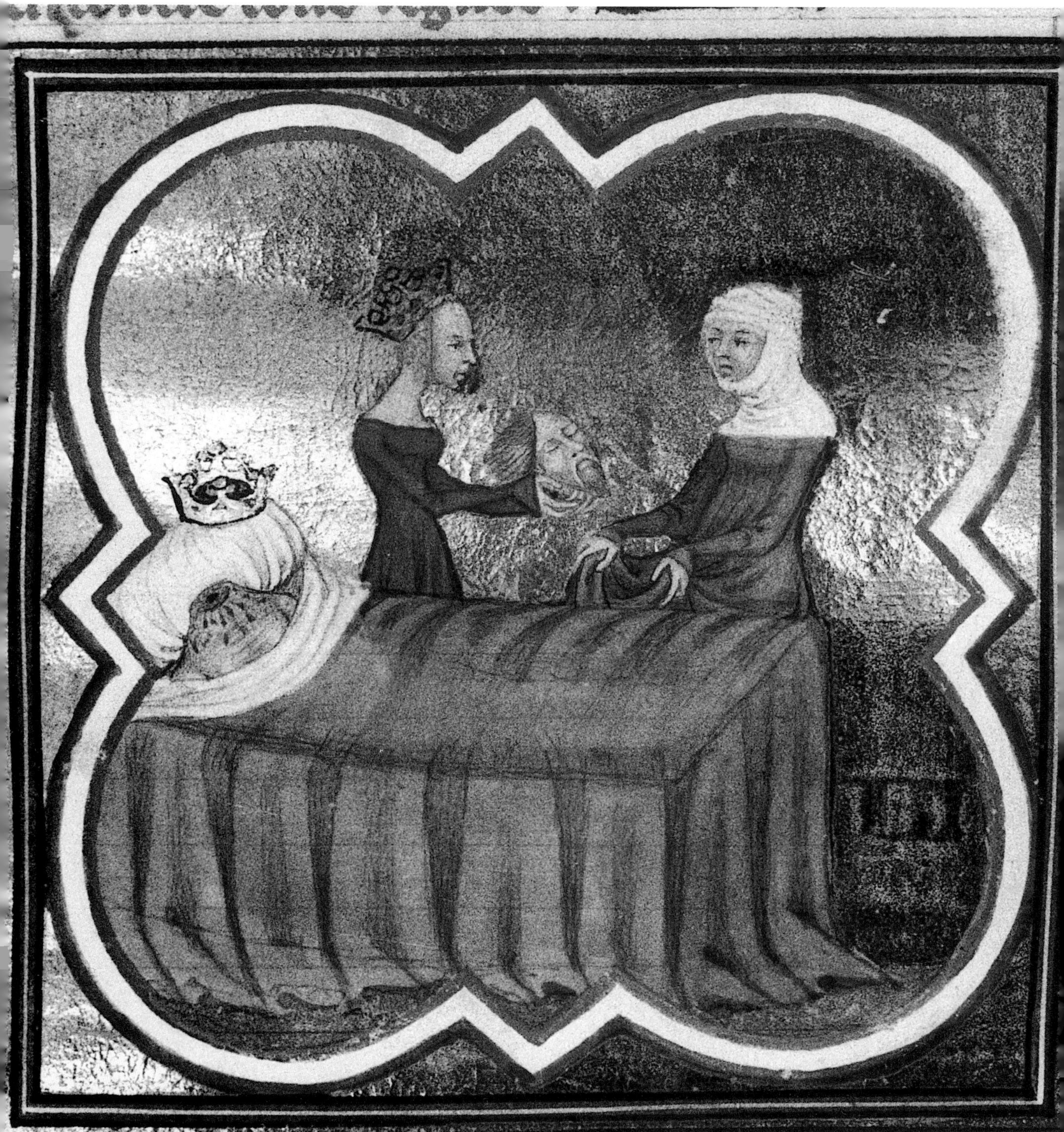

56. Remiet and another. Soissons, Bibliothèque Municipale, MS 211, fol. cxiii. *Bible historiale*. Judith and Holofernes.

3. THE LIFE OF DEATH

A sharp noise made him start. Was she still there, waiting, rustling the rushes on the floor with her skirts? Or was it just the snorting and scratching of hogs on their way to the slaughter that he could hear, scurrying down the narrow alley outside. Perhaps he even smelled them, or was it his own sweat-filled covering that reeked so. In his long illness Remiet had become expert in the clatter of different cartwheels in the dirt, and he liked to guess what they carried and to what Parisian market they were going. He could also discern the high-pitched laughter and curses of the boy bachelors from the droning and incomprehensible Latin gossip of the doctors of theology making their way to and from the college down the street. He heard too the call for alms of the blind beggar who sat on the porch of Saint Séverin, a wretch to whom he had always given a penny but whose affliction had now also come to visit Remiet himself. The irony was that he, of all people, should go sightless into the darkness, he who had illuminated the world with his 'histoires' and who had presented mirrors of great deeds to princes. Now the mirror was dark. He had heard it argued among the masters of arts that some of the ancients held that a man sees by a beam or rather cone of light that comes out of the eyes like a beacon, or the lamp of a night-watchman in the dark streets of Paris. He believed it, since many had died of the plague because of the aerial spirit in the look of a sick person. Now his illuminator's fiery eyes had been extinguished, put out by a fever that hit him on All Saints' – the day of the dead – last November when all his vital spirits and not just those of his visual ray were diminished by a terrible fire that swept through his body. He had been waiting ever since.

He contemplated the good times when he worked for the masters of the university. The scholars of the Collège de Sorbonne and the devout doctors in the time of the Wise Charles with their ascetic ways had loved his pithy 'portraits d'encre'. Although the colours that are natural and necessary for illuminating are eight – black, white, red, yellow, blue, violet, rose and green – his favourite had always been the first, made of lamp-black and refined with his own secret recipe. His greatest skill was not illuminating at all but outlining with the quill from that one pitch-dark pot and just touching the draperies of his figures with a subtle wash of rose or green, suggesting the smooth surface of ivory carvings or the expensive shimmer of cameos. It was an art that Queen Jeanne's favourite illuminator, the delicate little Jean Pucelle, had taught Paris to admire over seventy years before – yes, a long lifetime ago. He himself while still a child had watched as his master filled in the outlines with a sure swift touch as though he were like God illuminating the world with colour, making copses and clouds that floated on the pages like dreams. But tastes had changed today and the craze was all for brash colour and flowery surfeit, for pictures filled with fat fleshy folk dancing with heavy clod-hopping feet on chequerboard floors. It was all measured like the geometers of the schools. Either that or it was gardens galore, flower-filled and thick with gold leaf rather than the beauty of green. Only occasionally did Death come to spoil the garden party. The young no longer wanted to see even her shadow in their books. They wanted to gaze only on those light-filled meadows and the blue skies trailing golden clouds and melting into white on the horizon, mere sublunary illusions that competed with nature. These were new tricks of the painters, like those the famous brothers from the North started but never finished in the Hours they made for the good King Charles's brother, the fat and bibliolatrous Jean, Duke of Berry. They were not true illuminators, indeed their images diminished the texts they sought to illustrate, not lighting them but casting shadows over the Word of God.

The only books he had loved to try to read as they crossed his desk and whose stories were still fresh in his mind were those written in his own tongue that narrated the deeds of great men. The bright banners and the sharp metallic surfaces of helms and pikes, the black-faced heathens and the glorious banners of the Christians – he had a whole book of models for them all. How he had pored over those tales of ancient times when the great war-lords Hannibal and Caesar ruled mighty armies and had conquered half the earth. If only France had men of such valour today, she might have escaped the ignominious defeat at the hands of the English! All the suffering and pain he could hear in the streets outside, all could have been avoided had not the princes of the realm been so greedy for power and riches and the Parisians so fickle in their allegiances. Had they taken heed of the wonderful teaching of those histories that he had illuminated, like the great Chronicles of the kings of France in which he and his master had painted pictures for the king himself long ago or even the vast mirror of history by Friar Vincent that told the whole history of the world that the Duke of Orléans himself had ordered. If these great lords had only read of those wars and famines and seen pictured the lamentable and marvellous sufferings of bygone ages, then they might not have been so headstrong and vain in making so many wars themselves. But these people never seemed to learn from books. Like him, they just looked at the pictures and found in them confirmation of what they knew already.

MASTER OF HIS/STORIES

The dead aren't dead until the living have recorded their deaths in narratives. Death is a matter of archives. You are dead when stories are told about you, and when only stories are told about you. Jean-François Lyotard[1]

For when one sees a painted history ('estoire') of Troy or something else one sees the actions of men who have gone before as if they were present. Richard de Fournival[2]

Another violent rupture which, like birth, occurs in the context of a bed appears in one of Remiet's illustrations to Guyart Desmoulin's *Bible historiale*, except here the Old Testament heroine Judith acts not as a midwife to the horizontal Holofernes but as his murderer (Fig. 56). What is rent and borne away from this source is not a squirming bundle of new life but a dead head. The tyrant's crown still sits on the pillow, drawing attention to the gap where the head, the centre of life, should be. Judith plays the role of 'la mort' here and hands the severed head into the skirts of a waiting servant. Remiet also handed over responsibility for this attendent figure, which was painted by someone else. The face is more open, the flesh tones lighter and the figure fuller and more rounded. Why did Remiet not paint this single figure? Was he called away on an errand? Was it left unfinished to be completed by one of the four or five other illuminators whose work appears in this vast three-volume *Bible historiale*? Was Remiet testing the skill of an apprentice to match his own style? Although the story behind this *histoire* is irrecoverable, this moment of vernacularized biblical history had its place in shaping the histories of those who made it.

Despite the fact that the story of Judith is one of triumphant female virtue overcoming debased male vice, this is still history as his rather than her story. Remiet and his assistant were illuminating the French version of one of the most widely read Latin school texts of the Middle Ages, originally written over two hundred years before by Petrus Comestor, who was known as 'the Master of Histories' (*Magister historiarum*).[3] The framed narrative miniatures in manuscripts, as distinct from the red, blue and gold illuminated letters, called *lettres enluminées* or *petites lettres* in inventories, and the ivy-leaf borders called *vignettes*, were often referred to in fourteenth-century accounts as *histoires* and those who made them were known as *historieurs*.[4] Remiet was such a *historieur* but he was also a historian in our sense of the term. Copying, and adapting the vast picture cycles that had been devised to illustrate the various current genres of historical writing, he was at the same time interpreting the past for the present. History deals with the deeds of the dead, but the stains of Remiet's own turbulent times bleed through his tinted drawings of deeds and deaths long gone, especially since there there is no visible difference in these illustrations between the death of a fourteenth-century king and that of a Roman emperor. These images did not appear anachronistic as they would to us. They reinforced a specific theory of history whereby past events were seen as continuous with contemporary ones and thus by extension with the world of the reader.[5] The past was not 'other' because, in Christian eschatology, the dead were not cut off from the world of the living. The dead and the living were united in their waiting for history, for time itself, to end.

Historical writing popular in the vernacular among Remiet's princely patrons at this period told the stories of three distinct cultures, Frankish, Roman and Jewish, but all in terms of an evolving notion of nation and self-identity. First were the Chronicles of the kings of France themselves, second, ancient narratives like Livy's, and third, Christian compilations like the *Bible historiale*. During his long career Remiet was involved with the illustration of no fewer than seven copies of the *Grandes Chroniques de France*. This was a vernacular version of the official Latin Chronicles of the French kings prepared by the monks of Saint Denis, which told the story of the Franks from their ancient Trojan origins, through 'the long succession of French kings' that was continued up to the reign of King Charles himself.[6] Stimulated by that ruler's lively interest in the Latin classics in translation, the second genre of historical narrative dealing with the deeds of the ancients, *la matière ancienne*, also became fashionable. Remiet illustrated three copies of Livy's *Histoire romain*, which had been translated earlier for King Jean le Bon by Pierre Bersuire, as well as a lavish *Histoire ancienne* (BN fr. 250), which includes the *Histoire universelle* by Orosius and an older compilation, the *Faits des romains*. A splendid copy of the 1375 translation of Valerius Maximus's *Faits et dits mémorables* by Simon de Hesdin with seven miniatures by Remiet is now in the library in Troyes.[7] Sacred history, which often overlapped and contained elements of the other two genres, was contained in the French version of the Dominican Vincent of Beauvais's *Miroir historial*, which Remiet illustrated in two vast four-volume sets. Jean de Vignay of the Hospitallers of Saint Jacques on the Left Bank had translated it into French before 1332 for Jeanne de Bourgogne, wife of Philippe VI of Valois. This enormous encyclopaedia provided a chronology of the world beginning with Adam and Eve, interweaving pagan and biblical events, and including stories of the saints and fathers of the Church, and going even further than the present to include signs of the Last Judgement yet to come.[8] The story of God and his chosen people took priority in Remiet's oeuvre, for in addition there was Guyart Desmoulins's version of Petrus Comestor's *Historia scholastica*, known in its vernacular version as the *Bible historiale*, already mentioned. The professed aim of its translator was to allow lay people to understand the stories of scripture ('les hystoires de l'escripture'). Two copies survive in which Remiet completed a few of the numerous miniatures.[9] He produced all 233 illustrations, and there were originally even more for a much rarer paraphrase of scripture, by Hermann de Valenciennes, known as the *Histoire de la Bible* and now in the Pierpont Morgan Library, New York.[10] Whereas a Parisian illuminator one hundred years before would have spent most of his career illuminating the sacred archetypes in Bibles and psalters, the bulk of Remiet's output narrated in far more mundane detail the stories of those who had lived and died in time. The increase in the number of vernacular manuscripts that deal with this temporal trajectory, either political, pagan or sacred, as evidenced in the inventories and libraries not just of the royal family but of royal administrators of the period, like Arnaud de Corbie and Jean de Montaigu, suggests a growing need to control the past, the ideological imperative of constructing not just national but also personal identity in a period of profound crisis.[11]

All of these historical works follow a similar large folio format with fully painted *vignettes*, or borders, placed at the various chapter headings of the two-column text along with framed column-wide rectangular miniatures with tendril-sprouting vines. They are all illuminated in a technique Remiet knew as *portraits d'encre*, or 'histoires de blancs et de noir' as they are sometimes referred to in inventories. Quite distinct from the rich grisaille technique of the earlier fourteenth century, this was not the refined application of opaque pigments in greys and off-white tones to produce the shimmering effects of mother-of-pearl and ivory that was used to great effect by Jean Pucelle and his followers in devotional manuscripts, especially Books of Hours. Remiet's was a much more rapid and less costly technique, which was really a form of drawing directly with the pen, allowing the white of the parchment to provide the common light tone and then adding darker washes of grey.[12] In many ways Remiet's miniatures are the pictorial equivalent of *lettre bâtarde*, a hybrid cursive script that scribes increasingly used in copying these enormously long narratives (see Fig. 67) and which did not require the pressure, frequent changes of direction and liftings of the pen that the earlier, more formal Gothic scripts had. This fluid momentum and scribal ease, visible in Remiet's own calligraphic production, worked in the process of reception too, for people looked at these pictures much faster than did their monastic predecessors. The intimacy and privacy fostered by cursive scripts may also have encouraged silent reading, which also favours speed.[13]

Remiet's *histoires* are repetitive because people viewed history itself as repetition. This is especially evident in the *Miroir historial* and the *Grandes Chroniques* where set subjects like battles and martyrdoms occur over and over again. Remiet would have made each miniature following a standard procedure, beginning by drawing his frame with a rule, usually consisting of four lines in the already ruled and written text. Unlike the miniature worlds of the Boucicaut Master and the Limbourg brothers, who often used the horizontal ruling of the text in laying out their depth and geometric space, Remiet's is a curving and ad hoc universe without straight lines and planes.[14] A usually uneven ground-line is stretched across the frame, about an eighth of the way up, coloured in green and sprinkled with little trilobed shoots, similar to those outside the picture in the offshoots of the frame itself. The figures come up to about two-thirds of the height of the miniature. All action takes place laterally along this planar axis. There is no zooming in for close-ups and no distant vistas or aerial views. We are not watching an unfolding multi-viewpoint film but rather a series of boxes in which Remiet's actors can move only on the shallowest of ledges. This restriction of movement and viewpoint should not be seen as a deficiency. It actually provides history with a strategic uniformity and narrative cohesiveness that is at once satisfying and compelling. Any one moment can be superimposed on any other, providing a sense of human continuity in which Adam and Eve use identical gestures and walk in the same direction as Mary and Joseph. Christian typology, with its matching of Old and New Testament events and characters, is thus literally inscribed on the bodies of these uniform historical homunculi.

There is very little sense of place in these narrative images and few things. Most notable are the trees, which we have seen have a special resonance in his work, although they are often just pictorial punctuation marks. Apart from these, History is a vast horizontal green plain with a few shrubs upon which saints are beheaded, women commit suicide and battles are fought. Austerity was in fashion. Colour was mixed in big batches of cheap and watery green and yellow and probably applied all at once through the finished quires of drawings when they were complete. One can trace various shellfuls of colour through a few quires and then see a darker green where a new batch of colour had to be mixed or was filled in on a different day. The props of history, writing desks, thrones and the verticals of banners and spears, provide the only other things in Remiet's inventory of the world, and these too have an instrumental sharpness to them. The uniformity of presentation across all three genres of history – political, pagan and religious – is also part of this ideological use of repetition in order to create not only boundaries across space, such as the nascent notion of the nation France, but also across time, which is shaped into one great transparent ritual in which bodies die and are buried only to be reborn in identical moduli in miniature after miniature. The very place where we expect an intersection of 'reality' with representation – history – is not where we find it, for as Nancy Regalado has observed of the force of history upon medieval poetic texts, 'representational realism is . . . weakest in those fifteenth-century works most strongly tied to history, strongest in works whose themes are literary commonplaces, of love, death and trickery'.[15] Whereas Remiet's illustrations to Deschamps's poetic *Lay* register the impact of pain upon the body, his historical representations are strangely asomatic and neutral, as if referring not to events but to archetypes. History was far too important a trajectory to be a mere record of the real.

Political Histories

To postulate that there is prior to religious or artistic repetition, a real violence, a true murder, a 'cruelty' . . . does not change a thing. No matter how much one invokes the suffering, the injury, the wounds and death, all the thing's *physicality* . . . there is never any factuality that is not from the 'start' hollowed out and eroded by representation. Philippe Lacoue-Labarthe[16]

The effort and application of historians have endeavoured to commit to literary tradition, as an example, the most memorable deeds of kings and princes who reigned in ancient times, lest we see them slip from human memory and be destroyed by devouring time. Guillaume de Nangis[17]

In 1397 a 'belle chronique de France' was offered to Philippe le Hardi by Guillaume Malet, 'maistre ostel du roy', in return for a golden vessel valued at 200 francs d'or and was given by the duke to Queen Isabeau the following year.[18] This manuscript, now in the Bibliothèque de l'Arsenal, Paris, has a four-part frontispiece by Remiet that presents the Trojan myth of French national origins so crucial to French national identity in the fourteenth century (Fig. 57). The rubric that opens the text reads: 'comment francois descendirent des troyens de troye la grant et de la genealogie des roys'.[19] In the first framed scene, history is being told rather than written as a monk of Saint Denis reads the text to an assembled group of monks, who were the official maintainers of the genealogy of French kings. In the frame to the right, the Frankish exiles from Troy build the city of Sicambria. In the most violent of the four episodes, the armoured Franks are shown expelling the invading Romans back across the sea at the point of their swords, an image which would have resounded with the then current territorial ambitions of the French in the Hundred Years War. The last scene returns to the present with the presentation by the monks of Saint Denis of the book to a seated monarch, a figure who could stand for France's present ruler, Charles VI, and evoke the continuity of kings.

The three dynasties of French kings described in the *Grandes Chroniques* – the Merovingian, Carolingian and Capetian – are shown as equally bloody in the 175 miniatures that illustrate the most famous copy of the work. This was written by the scribes Henri de Trevou and Raoulet d'Orléans with numerous illustrations by the Master of the Bible of Jean de Sy and other major illuminators, and was completed in three distinct stages for Charles V between 1370 and 1380.[20] The Merovingian age is replete with executions, murders, battles and scenes of eyes being gouged out, wives being strangled and queens being tortured, but so is the most recent continuation, which illustrates the murder of the advisors of Charles V by the partisans of Étienne Marcel. One of at least seven artists involved in this prestigious project has been identified as Remiet (Figs. 58 and 59).[21] The miniatures associated with Remiet reveal the pressures to conform to a visual style that was not his own when dominated by more prestigious and established artists. While certain traits, like the pugnacious profiles and the bony extremities, are ubiquitous, it is the way in which this illuminator treats the subject matter and in fact the

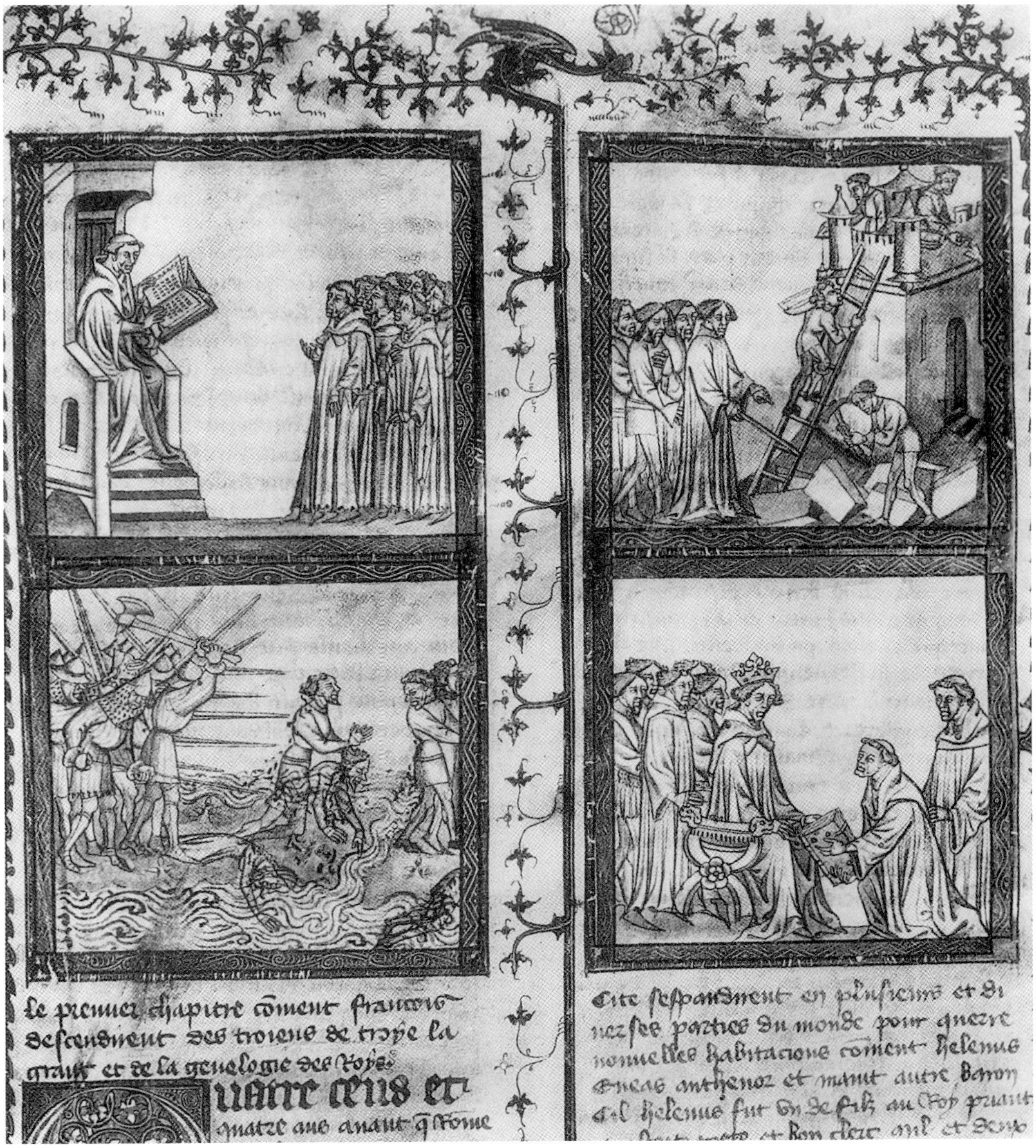

57. Remiet. Paris, Bibliothèque de l'Arsenal, MS 5223, fol. 2. *Grandes Chroniques de France*, Frontispiece: how the French are descended from the Trojans.

kind of subject matter he is delegated to produce, which, if anything, gives away his identity. One of these subjects occurs on fol. 194r and depicts a lord being murdered in his castle (Fig. 58). Although this actually illustrates an episode during the much earlier reign of King Louis VI, the associations with current civil insurrection against the nobility could not have gone unnoticed. The scene takes place not in his castle, as the text indicates, but in a chapel, as though the victim were a saint like Thomas Becket. The miniatures ascribed to Remiet appear only in certain gatherings of this two-volume copy of the *Grandes Chroniques*, towards the middle, from fols. 149 to 230, but significantly he gets more than his fair share of death depictions. A few scenes later Remiet provides a picture of a traitor being hanged, in which his delineation of the taut, pendulous body is a powerful first example of an interest in the muscular tension of rigor mortis (Fig. 59).

More than twenty years later, Remiet repeated this same subject, but to illustrate a later chapter of French history in another copy of the *Grandes Chroniques* (Fig. 60). The similarities and differences between the two exemplify just how much Remiet's art is not static, despite its adherence to repeated models. Although the horse at the left with its one raised leg is identical to that in his earlier rendition, and could almost have been traced from the same modelbook, a technique we know illuminators utilized, the gibbet is no longer planimetrically set against the swirling decorated ground but against empty vellum, and the hangman works behind the gibbet to present the dangling corpse isolated as in a frame. This is another aspect of Remiet's ink technique – it emphasizes empty space, a vacuum that most medieval artists abhorred. In the later miniature this draws out a desolation in the scene of death by introducing the intractable solidity of the vast mound of earth, to which the criminal's body, as it is cut down, will return. This criminal, moreover, who represents a rebel who rose up against Philippe IV, has none of the heroic musculature of the earlier corpse; his exposed genitals display his bodily shame and his punishment for treason. Books could point to the gallows even more directly. In one contemporary manuscript the anathema, meant to protect the volume from theft, proclaims, 'Whoever steals this book, will hang from the Paris gibbet!'[22]

The hill upon which this hanging takes place provides a clear view for the royal party on horseback below, but there is no audience as such. Although there is a more tangible sense of a site and place for public death in this miniature, there is no suggestion of the increasing visibility of public executions in Paris during Remiet's early life. In March 1382 a new royal tax caused insurrection when people armed themselves with leaden mallets stored in the town hall (giving their name to the uprising as that of the Maillotins), killing Jews and tax-collectors. The ringleaders were eventually arrested and put to death. Several hundred of those involved in the rioting as well as innocent men who had tried to intervene as mediators, like Jean des Mares, were publically executed; according to chroniclers, every day 'they cut off heads, three or four at a time'. Between 1389 and 1392 there were fifty-one public hangings, thirteen dragging and hangings, four burnings at the stake and three burials alive, meted out as proper punishment for crimes as varied as sorcery and petty robbery by the justices at the Châtelet.[23] Although by law, treason was punishable by a 'cumulation of deaths' inflicted upon the body of the criminal, public executions were not yet the theatrical urban spectacles they were to become in the Paris of later, more 'enlightened' eras. They were none the less crucial forms of public negotiation in which the social body redefined its unity by tearing apart the bodies of those who threatened it. The king in Remiet's scene pointing to and ordering the hanging is displaying his power and control over life and death.

Corpses were, as a matter of course, and except for those buried alive, hung out in public as grim warnings against revolt. For two years, between 1411 and 1413, the dismembered limbs of Colinet de Puiseux dangled from the main gates of the city and his torso remained on the gallows, for in the words of the *Bourgeois de Paris*, 'he deserved to be burned and thrown to the dogs rather than to be laid in hallowed ground'.[24] Remiet would have seen many a corpse hanging in this fashion in the troubled city during the

1380s and 1390s at the famous gibbet of Montjoie or, nearer to his home, in the Place Maubert. But of course he never would have thought of going and drawing the decaying subject directly into his sketchbook as artists were doing in Italy.[25] The hanged man, with his bulging eyes, blackened face, swollen protuding tongue, who always befouled himself in his death agonies, according to contemporary accounts, did not merit the delineation of naturalistic portrayal. The body of the traitor hanging from the gibbet in these two images in the *Grandes Chroniques* was a thing to be reviled, eviscerated and eaten away before the eyes of the public, signalling disintegration without hope, for no traitor was allowed to be buried in consecrated ground. Refusing confession and extreme unction to the condemned criminal was one of the most terrifying aspects of the sentence of death, since it denied the victim any hope of salvation in the next world. The Council of Vienne had ordered that the condemned be given at least the sacrament of Penance, but Charles V, remembering the Parisian rebellions that had scarred his youth, had sought no change in the law. It was in the time of Charles VI that the issue surfaced once again. The chancellor of the University of Paris, Jean Gerson, and councillor Philippe de Mezières urged the king to leniency, and finally a royal decree of 12 February 1397 ordered that confession be accorded to the condemned.[26] The shame of public death without hope was seen as a deterrent to crime. Even when the Parisian courts moved more toward lesser penalties like banishment, the verdict was still meant to instil in the guilty person the idea of his 'civil' death in being hounded out of the community and his scrape with physical death, when, with a halter round his neck, his head was rubbed against the gallows. Noble criminals of course were meant to lose their heads more spectacularly, as did the king's financier and collector of illuminated history manuscripts, Jean de Montaigu, who was publicly beheaded in Paris in 1409 and whose books went to the Louvre.[27]

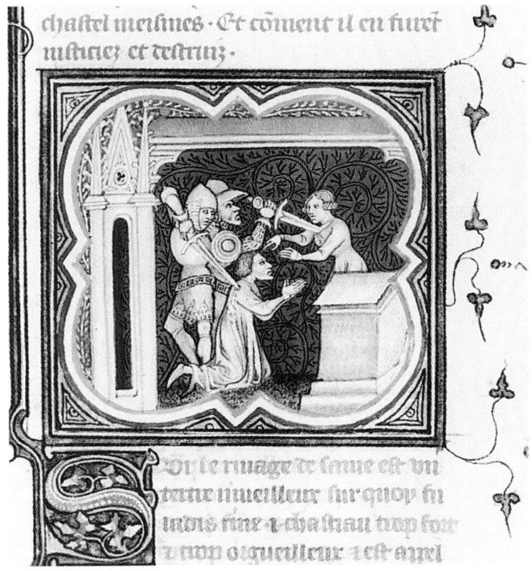

58. Remiet. Paris, Bibliothèque Nationale, fr. 2813, fol. 193. *Grandes Chroniques de France.* A lord is murdered in his castle.

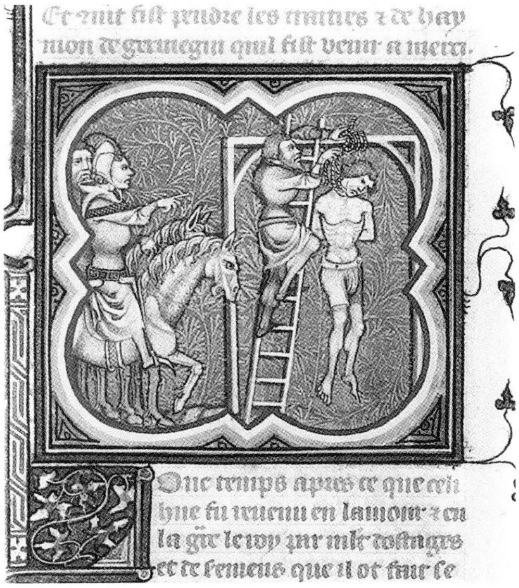

59. Remiet. Paris, Bibliothèque Nationale, fr. 2813, fol. 200. *Grandes Chroniques de France.* A traitor is hanged.

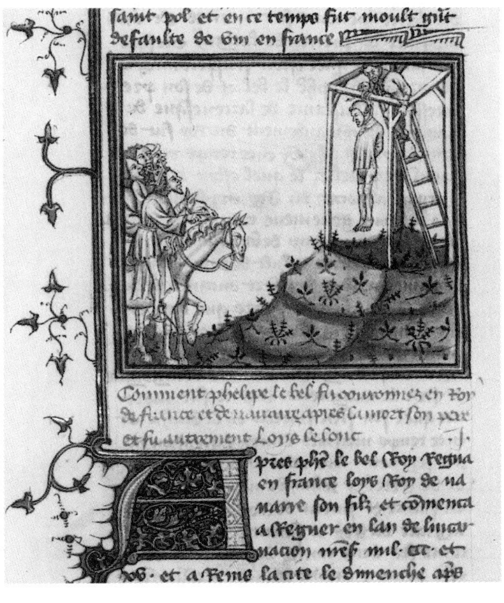

60. Remiet. Paris, Bibliothèque Nationale, fr. 2606, fol. 361v. *Grandes Chroniques de France.* A traitor is hanged.

The history of France depicted in the *Grandes Chroniques* is represented not only in images showing the ruler's strict justice over the bodies of his subjects, but also in those showing the various wars that had enlarged the territories of France, beginning with the Trojan War. History was indeed the story of never-ending conflict, which continued its bloody trail well into Remiet's lifetime. The French had been at war with the English for at least a decade before he was born, and civil wars would rip the country apart in his old age and bring his own city to its knees soon after his death. It was in the very last years of the war-weary century that Remiet illustrated the most important medieval treatise on the art of war, Honoré Bouvet's *Arbre des batailles* (Fig. 61). Dedicated to Charles VI between 1386 and 1389, it describes the tribulations of the Church and the destruction of four ancient kingdoms (Babylon, Carthage, Macedonia and Rome) through war. The Benedictine author also added an interpolation that chronicled recent European history between 1139 and 1354, citing as inspiration the 'recent glosses' on the ancient prophecies which claim that through 'a member of the high lineage of France healing will be given to an age which is in such travail and disease'.[28] It has to be seen in the context of the millenarian fears that swept the country in the *fin de siècle*. The manuscripts of this treatise of fruitless prophetic hope at the beginning of the reign of Charles VI open with a visual analysis of war, a diagram of despair which the author called his 'tree of mourning', or 'l'arbre de douleur' (Fig. 61).

> I make a tree of mourning at the beginning of my book, on which you may see, first, at the head, the governors of Holy Church in such tribulation as never was before. . . . Next you may see the great dissension which is today among Christian princes and kings and afterwards you may see the great grief and discord which exist among the communities; then, so that the Tree and its meaning are better understood, I will ask certain questions. I ask first: 'What is war?'[29]

Remiet's version of the sad tree was created soon after the text was written and has two main branches, between which are placed 'many great discords and great war against the Holy Papacy in Rome'.[30] For the fourteenth-century illuminator, trees were not only resonant signs of nature, Romance and death (in the case of the Tree of Life) but were pre-eminently a scholarly means of dividing knowledge into its various branches in the *arbores* of scholastic concepts. In the centre at the top stands Fortune with her wheel, whose revolution is the cause of all sublunary conflict in the world, according to Bouvet. On the highest fork of the tree spreading across the whole of its two uppermost branches is the conflict that overshadowed all in these years – the great Western schism which lasted from 1378 to 1417, resulting from the double election of Pope Urban VI in Rome in April 1378 and Pope Clement VII at Fondi in September of the same year. When Remiet made this image, the popes had changed, but the scandalous division that brought into question the sacred authority of the Church to christen and moreover absolve its members continued. The French favourite of the moment, the antipope Pedro de Lune (his flag is a white crescent on a red ground), known as Benedict XIII, had been elected in 1394 and stands with his cardinals behind his army on Fortune's right. His papal cross is upright whereas that of Boniface IX opposite points downwards, giving this image a particular ideological thrust, which Remiet can only have completed after 1394 and before 1404 when the papacy changed yet again.

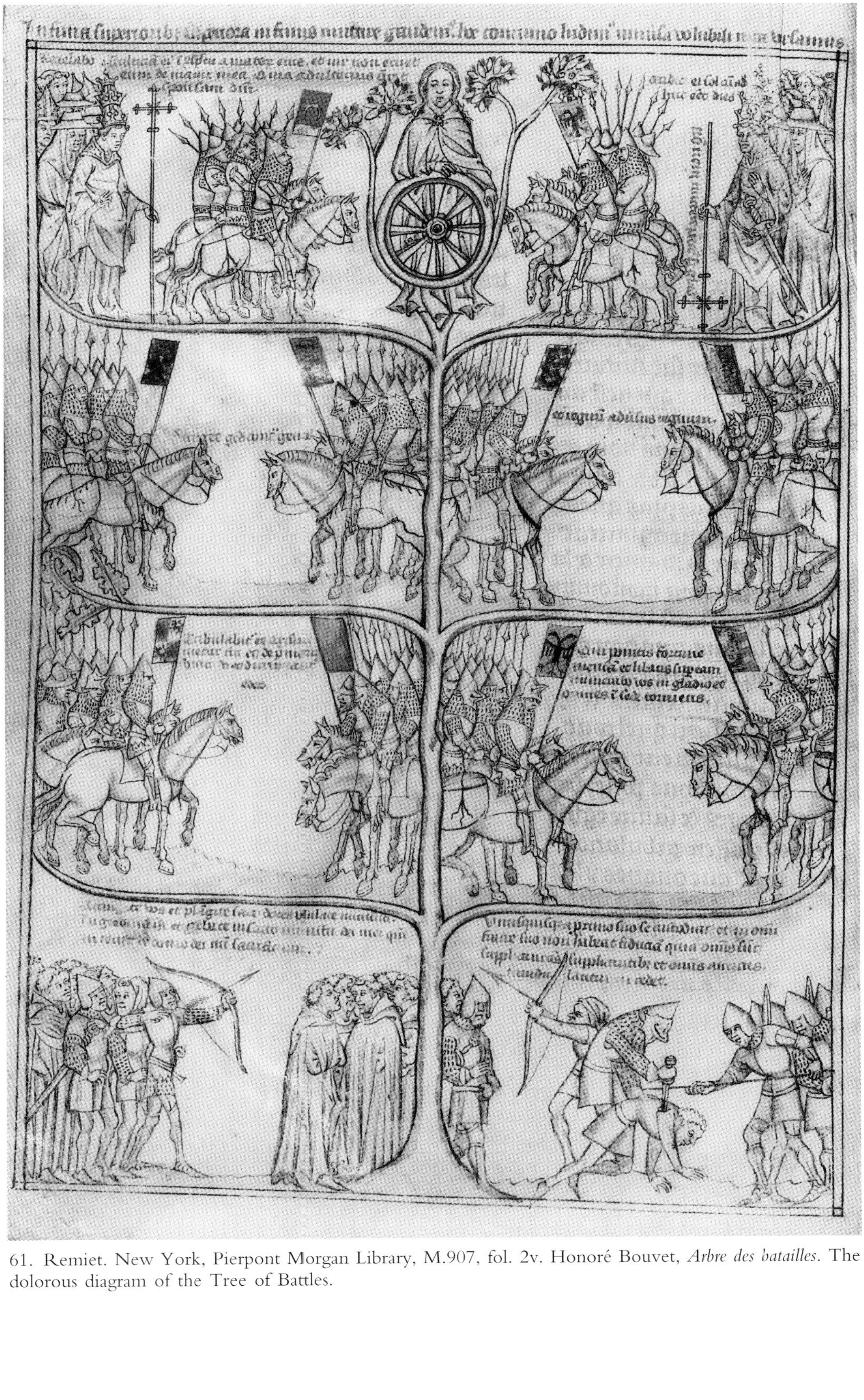

61. Remiet. New York, Pierpont Morgan Library, M.907, fol. 2v. Honoré Bouvet, *Arbre des batailles.* The dolorous diagram of the Tree of Battles.

On the next level, the conflicts multiply with two armies on each side of the tree. On the left, heraldic flags identify the armies of France and England in their hundred year battle, across from the armies of Louis d'Anjou and Philippe le Hardi, a conflict over the regency of Charles VI that had errupted between 1380 and 1383. To the left on the next level, the army of the King of Castile and Leon faces the army of the King of Portugal, a conflict between two half-brothers for the throne of Portugal. On the right the iron-clad armies of the Emperor Charles VI and Lewis the Great, King of Hungary, face off before battle. All these conflicts are depicted by the uniform massed anonymity of armies on horseback, indistinguishable except for their heraldry. But on the lowest level, underneath rather than on the tree, the skirmishes of those who are not knights and who go on foot are depicted. On the left stand a group of tonsured men, their arms folded under their long robes signalling their inaction, because, as the author states, 'the clerical estate and office is separate from all war, for the service of God, to which clerks belong, makes them unfit to carry the arms and harness of temporal battles'. Archers and foot-soldiers face these unarmed clerics on the lower left while on the right an unarmed man is stabbed in the back. These are the battles of the small that Bouvet also describes as part of the scheme of things, making this tree into a hierarchical model of society as well as a map of the world at war in the late fourteenth century.

War was on a world scale: another major crisis of these years was the defeat of the Western crusaders at Nicopolis by the Turks on 25 September 1396, which was followed by a bloody massacre and the holding to ransom of thousands of French prisoners. When news reached Paris at Christmas, 'affliction reigned in all hearts' and the poet Deschamps wrote of 'funerals from morn to eve', a sorrow made more intense because the sons of so many leading families had died in foreign lands without proper Christian burial. Such cataclysmic events, not from the past but contemporary, were too painful for representation. They would have to become history before they could be delineated by illuminators in later fifteenth-century copies of Froissart's Chronicles. However, Remiet depicts earlier confrontations between the holy warriors of the Christian Church and the 'sarrasins' of Satan throughout the *Grandes Chroniques* and in the *Miroir historial* (Fig. 62). These are conflicts visualized by Remiet, literally in black and white, between the cross and the dragon, the two signs carried as banners by the two sides in the miniature – the white armies of the Church on the miniature's right side and the black, turbanned armies of the 'other' on the 'sinister' side. By contrast to Bouvet's exclusion of clerics from the battlefield, Remiet places prominent ecclesiastics in the forefront of his crusader images, as valiant leaders in the Holy War, as the forces of life against the forces of death.

The apocalyptic misgivings about human conflicts in the late fourteenth century revealed in Bouvet's 'tree of mourning' should not, especially in the light of the ongoing Holy War, be mistaken as equivalents of modern pacifism. War is described as in the nature of things, according to the rest of the treatise, which was to become the key text in theories of the 'just war' for the next two centuries. Bouvet saw legitimate conflict affecting the whole of nature, animate and inanimate, because 'everything is inclined by its nature to contradict its evil form'.[31] Moreover, war accords with the Law of God, who ordered and encouraged it, and it is only as a result of misconduct and human evil that abuses like rape, torture and pillage of church property tarnish war's impeccable image in

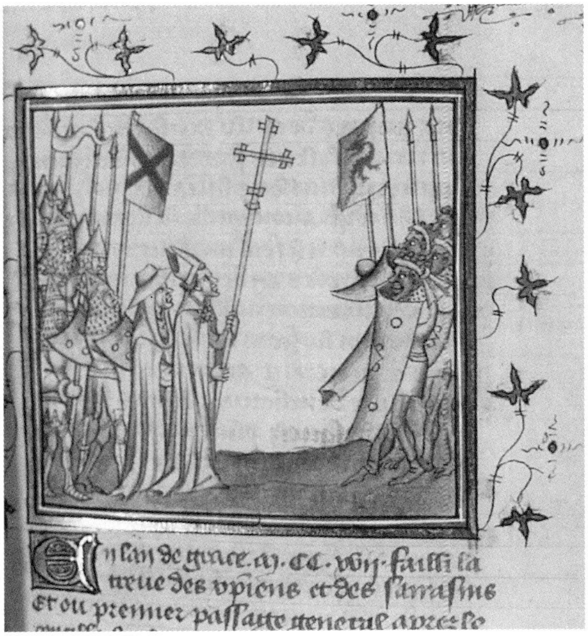

62. Remiet. Paris, Bibliothèque Nationale, fr. 52, fol. 312. *Miroir historial.* Christians face Saracens in the Holy War.

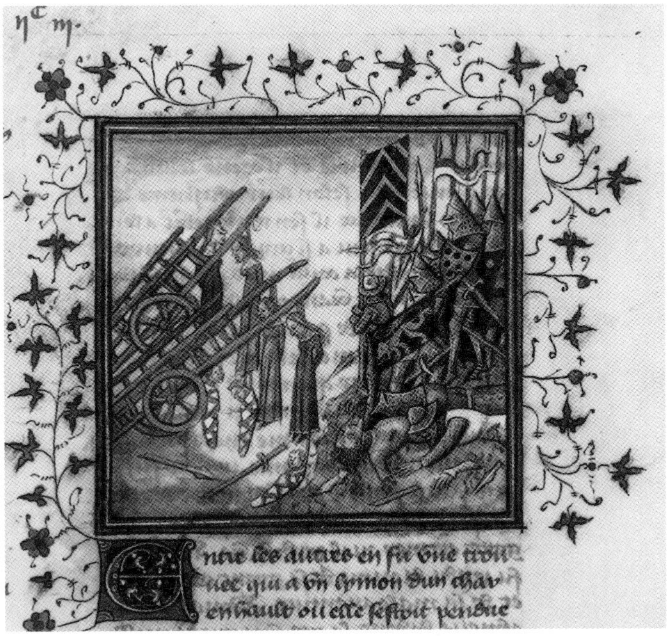

63. Remiet. Paris, Bibliothèque Nationale, fr. 250, fol. 219. *Histoire ancienne.* Women and children as victims of war.

the Divine scheme of things. 'If in war many evil things are done,' he writes, 'they never come from the nature of war but from false usage; as when a man-at-arms takes a woman and does her shame and injury, or sets fire to a church.'[32]

The history of France during Remiet's lifetime is filled with massacres, civil strife and famine – the atrocious repression in Flanders after the victory of the Duke of Burgundy at the Battle of Roosebeke in 1382 for example. Despite the truce in the Hundred Years War, which began in 1396, the civil war that erupted after the murder of Louis d'Orléans in 1407 escalated into a thirty year conflict between the Orléanists, or Armagnacs, and the Burgundians. The Cabochian revolt of 1413, named after the skinner Simon Caboche, was partly successful, although promised reforms never came. In the summer of 1418 bands of wild men led by the butchers and the hangman Capeluche brought to Paris the worst massacres the city had ever seen, with 1,600 men, women and children killed.[33] Reading the history of the period, it seems as though human lives were mere pieces in a game being played by the ambitious dukes of Burgundy and the new Duke of Orléans and that images like this tree which were made for these powerful men were somehow a means of abstracting and keeping at arm's length the actual cost in human suffering resulting from these conflicts. Remiet's image of the tree is a diagram of political death. In its organic aestheticization and objectification of countless expendable casualties, this is the ancestor of the geometric, computer-enhanced images that directed pilots to their targets during the Persian Gulf War and that similarly helped distance television audiences from the actual blood and guts of bodies being blown up before them.

There are no women in Bouvet's 'tree of mourning' since war is here theoretically conceived of as a totally male concern. Of course it never is. Today's spectacular theatre of war emphasizes, especially in newspapers and television images, the suffering of innocent women and children, a category of victims also visible in Remiet's simulations of annihilation. The deaths of women and infants still in their swaddling clothes are depicted by Remiet in his rich and glossy *Histoire ancienne* (Fig. 63). This, however, is a scene not of the innocent victims of war but of what the text calls a 'marvellous' event that happened during Rome's war against the Cimbrians, whose womenfolk strangled their own babies and then killed themselves rather than face capture and humiliation by the enemy.

It is significant that the only actual death depicted on the 'tree of mourning', that of the foot-soldier, occurs on the very lowest level, raising the issue of the relationship between death and social distinction. While the popular iconography of this period, such as the Dance of the Dead, plays on the sweeping equality of death's inevitability for all estates from king to beggar, the clear social demarcation between the various orders of society in this period meant that death as a historical force was different for each. Remiet had made a scheme of the different types of men in the world, when illustrating Nicole Oresme's translation of Aristotle's *Politics* for Louis d'Orléans in 1396, which expands the traditional three orders of society, those who plough, fight and pray, into six separate types of *gens* deemed necessary for civil society (Figs. 64 and 65).[34] In Remiet's version, however, the two groups that come first are literally twice the size of the other four and separated from them at the bottom of the previous page, whereas all six compartments had been equal in earlier versions of the scheme made for Charles V.[35] These two taller and pre-eminent

64. Remiet. Paris, Bibliothèque Nationale, fr. 9106, fol. 243v. Aristotle, *Politiques*. Different types of men: soldiers and councillors.

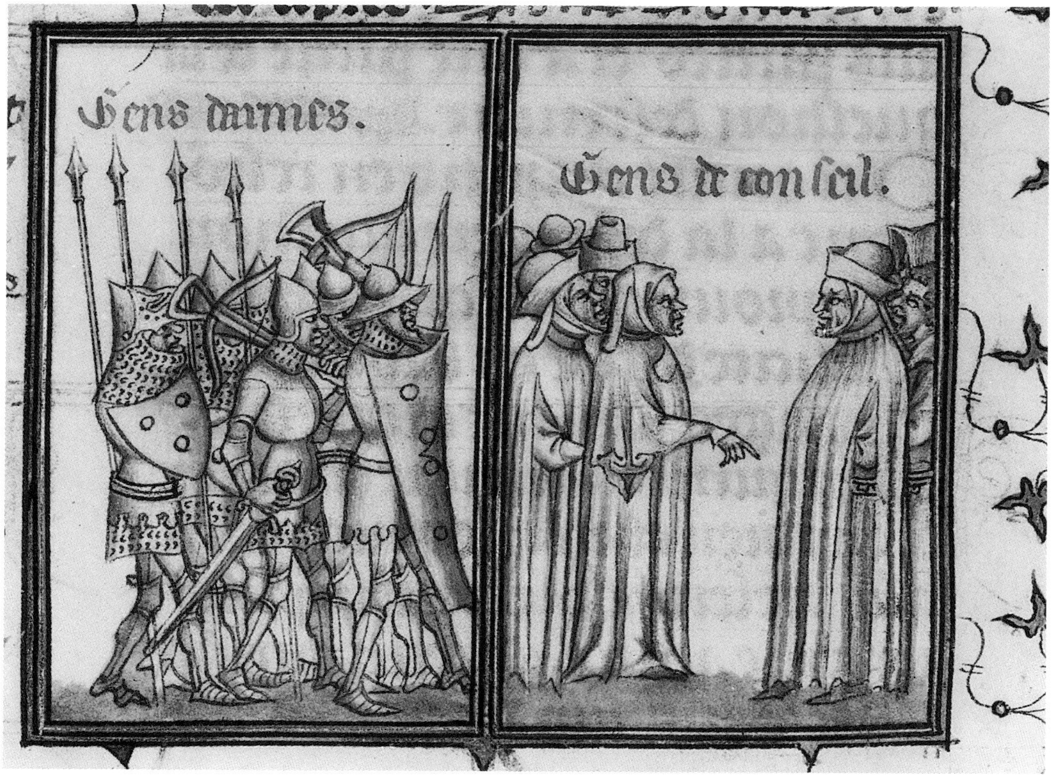

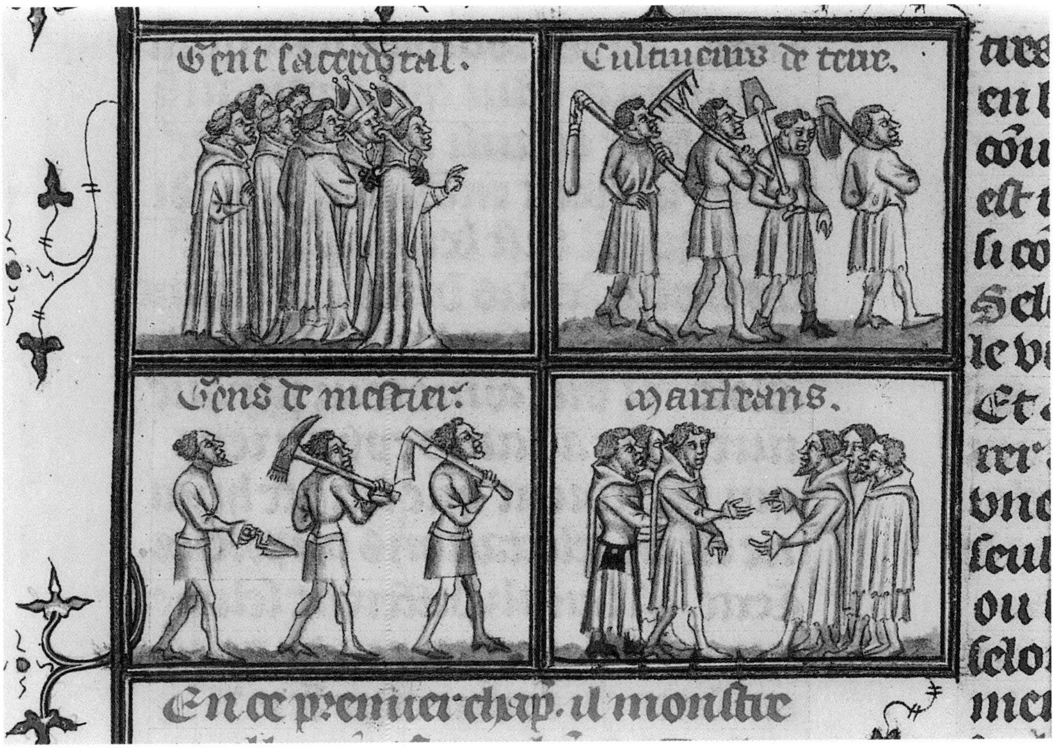

65. Remiet. Paris, Bibliothèque Nationale, fr. 9106, fol. 244. Aristotle, *Politiques*. Different types of men continued: priests, peasants, craftsmen and merchants.

social groups are the soldiers ('gens darmes') and the men of government ('gens de conseils') (Fig. 64). It was among these groups that the patron of this copy, Louis d'Orléans, as a seasoned knight and as an advisor to his brother, probably counted himself. On the next page are four smaller compartments where Remiet pictures the four other groups: priests ('gent sacerdotal'), peasants ('cultiveurs de terre'), craftsmen ('gens de mestier') and merchants ('marchands') (Fig. 65). Nothing much distinguishes the peasants from the urban craftsmen holding their tools. All these squat little men are equal except for their costume, which distinguishes the clergy in their long robes and the bourgois merchants in their longish robes and hoods hanging down their backs from the labourers and craftsmen in their short tunics. They all move to the right, in the direction of reading, except the two groups whose role is to exchange words and things, councillors and merchants, both classes of mediators.

Did Remiet think of himself as a craftsman or as a merchant? Whereas the *libraire* Thevenin de l'Angevin, who organized the production of this manuscript, was a clerk of the diocese of Sens, Remiet's social demarcation is more ambiguous. While his pen and brush constitute the equivalent of the pick and shovel, the 'tools of his trade', he might also have thought of himself as part of the merchant class, involved in exchange. On these pages Remiet has created an ideal co-existence of clearly demarcated social groups, who were in reality in the late fourteenth century scrambling to take possession of each other's spaces, rights and privileges. The craftsmen of Paris, for example, had risen up not long before under Étienne Marcel against Charles V. In Louis d'Orléans's miniature microcosm of Parisian society as distinct from all other copies of this text, Aristotle's equally balanced *polis* of six groups is clearly distorted and, just as was the case in the world beyond the book, two groups, the soldiers and the statesmen, seem to be in control of things. The king is nowhere to be found in this scheme. But then the king, being mad, was literally 'out of it' anyway. Aristotle's political theories were everywhere being appropriated by political authorities, secular as well as papal in this perod, but it is significant that in this particularly princely presentation of social distinction, Remiet made clerics and peasants equally diminutive in relation to the powerful knights and noble advisors of the realm who seem to have been the very groups who formed the major audience for historical works in vernacular translation.

Pagan History

We should be attentive to those things that happened in a thousand instances, dispersed on every side: fulgurating battles, assassinated generals, burning tiremes, queens poisoning themselves, victories that invariably led to further upheavals, the endless exemplary Actium, the eternal event. Michel Foucault[36]

The Roman people above all others by virtue of their constancy, intelligence and chivalric power carried their arms to strange lands and conquered empires and countries for themselves . . . and of their marvellous feats, all princes should take notable example. For this reason you have commanded me, most excellent lord, to translate the three decades of Titus Livius which contains 'les hystoires romaines' from Latin into French. Pierre Bersuire[37]

The classical past was a contradictory space for the late fourteenth-century French rulers, knights and courtly officers who sought to have lavish illuminated copies of ancient texts describing the exploits of their Trojan ancestors. The popularity of pagan authors had been established by the French kings themselves. Jean le Bon and his son Charles V had commissioned a number of translations of classical texts and by the end of the century the private libraries of men like Nicolas de Baye, councillor of the Parlement of Paris and the ill-fated Jean de Montaigu, also contained a number of 'Histoires des Troyes'.[38] These provided fourteenth-century readers with a number of moral and political exemplars, but also with a problem not so much related to the lascivious lives of the ancients but to their deaths. The deaths of pagans were different from those of Christians, as the many retellings of ancient histories of the time were at pains to prove and Remiet often was called upon to delineate. In his magnificent frontispiece to a multi-volume copy of Livy made for the king's daughter, Jeanne de Navarre, Remiet pictured in the first quadrant, the clerical Christian translator, Pierre Bersuire, not as a scribe or author but as the sad contemplator of history (Fig. 66). Seated at his scholar's book wheel, his hand goes to his chin in a gesture of sadness as he points to the unfolding horrors in the open book before him.

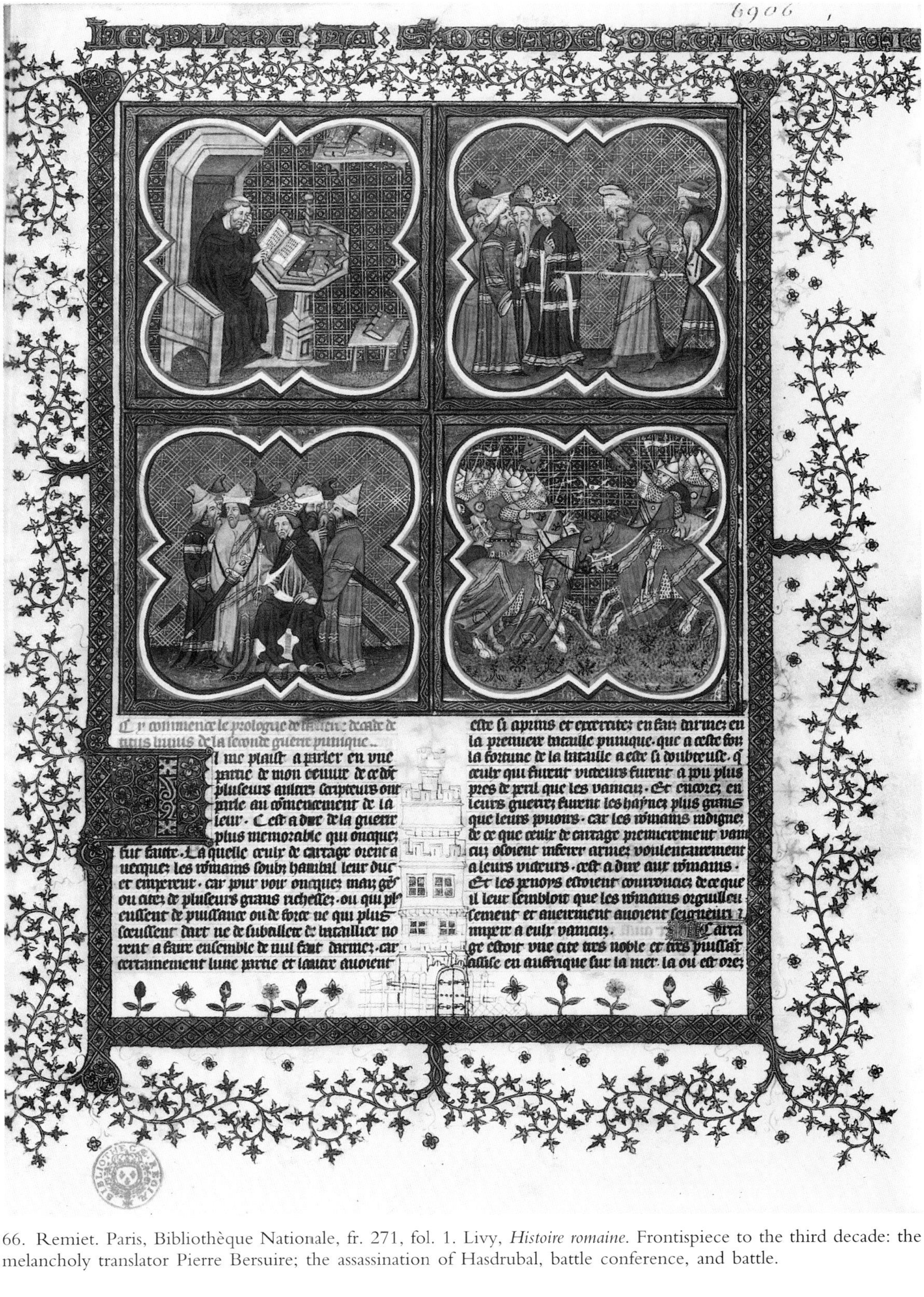

66. Remiet. Paris, Bibliothèque Nationale, fr. 271, fol. 1. Livy, *Histoire romaine*. Frontispiece to the third decade: the melancholy translator Pierre Bersuire; the assassination of Hasdrubal, battle conference, and battle.

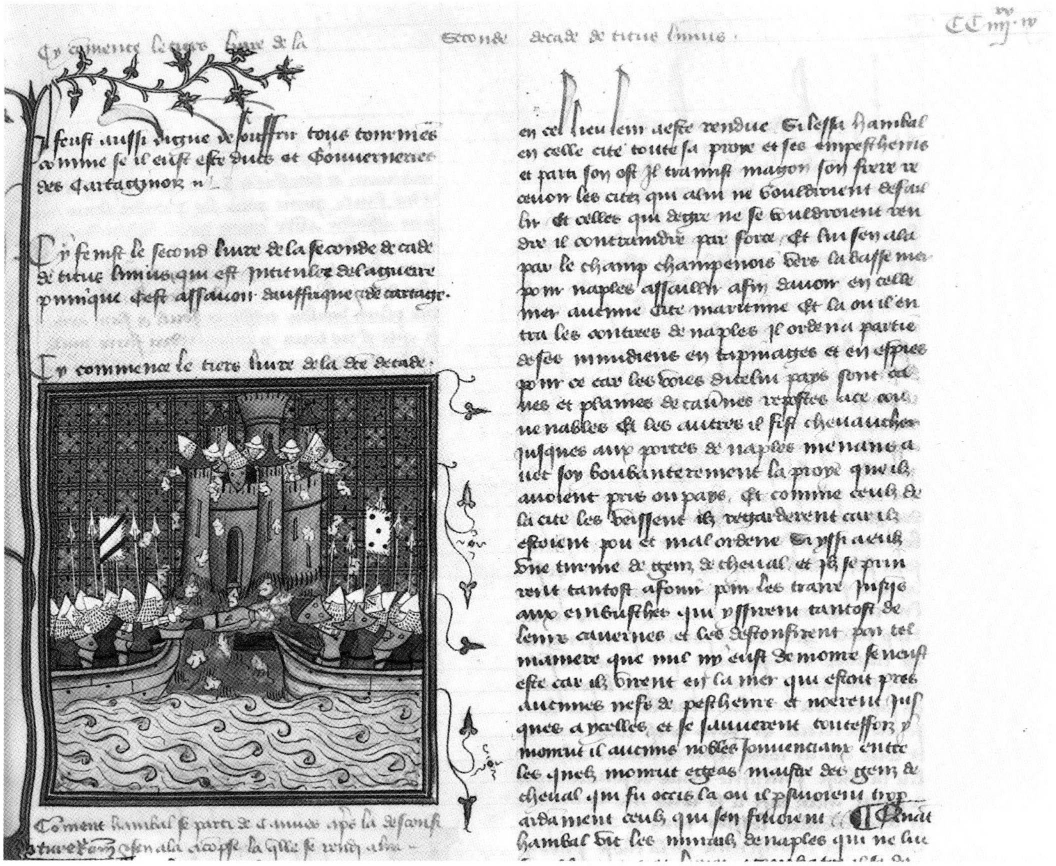

67. Remiet. Paris, Bibliothèque Nationale, fr. 268, fol. 289. Livy, *Histoire romaine*. Sea battle before a castle with corpse.

These horrors begin in the next scene with the violent assassination of Hasdrubal. While the visual similarity in costumes and settings between these ancient potentates and their fourteenth-century counterparts provided their readers with a shared social identity, the one thing that separated the lives and deeds of the Caesars and Hannibals from them was their ignominious ends. The library of Nicolas de Baye contained a copy of Valerius Maximus listed under the title 'The History of Human Calamities', which had been transformed into a moralistic dirge by the doctor of theology Simon de Hesdin in 1372, as evidenced by its opening phrase 'La brefté et fragilité de ceste doleureuse vie temporelle (The shortness and fragility of temporal life)'.[39] When Remiet illuminated the beautiful Troyes manuscript of this text he was thus illuminating not pagan history so much as another *vanitas mundi*-like lament. Perhaps it was only because the idea of the senility of the world was so strong and argued by preacher and politician alike, that the ancients in their childish pagan innocence could be viewed as inhabiting a certain type of gloriously tainted Golden Age.

A later copy of Livy's *Histoire romaine* illuminated by Remiet towards the end of his career belonged to Jacques, grandson of Louis de Bourbon, Comte de la Marche, King of Hungary, Sicily and Jerusalem, who died in 1438.[40] On one of the 579 folios of this large tome is a confused and crowded miniature of a naval battle before a castle, in which the artist is struggling to use the newer opaque colours and pastel pigments of his younger contemporaries (Fig. 67). Remiet adds in the dead centre of the picture the cadaver, with a glaring wound in its side, its body literally bloated with too much paint. This is the motor of history in all the various genres of historical writing to which Remiet turned his hand and was especially significant in pagan histories where these bodies are well and truly 'dead' – having no hope in Christian resurrection.

There were, however, a small number of pagans who were deemed 'virtuous' and whose position in history was more ambiguous, such as the Emperor Trajan, who earned his place in heaven from some medieval commentators, most notably Dante. The tale most often repeated concerned a widow who came before Trajan begging that he bring justice to those who had murdered her innocent son.[41] Remiet followed Vincent of Beauvais's version, where the woman implores the emperor, already mounted on his horse and about to go off to war, by showing him the corpse of her son (Fig. 68). This image of the emperor/warrior listening to the weak and lowly earned Trajan reprieve from the fires of Hell (but not, for most commentators, a place in Paradise), and yet this should not be viewed as a picture of Christian clemency. The corpse, Remiet's usual corpse, halts the emperor in his tracks, and cries out for vengeance, reinforced by the mother's pleas for revenge against those who have killed her son. It is a sign of 'an eye for an eye'. The dead body is the trigger that leads to violence, the object of retribution that is the foundation of holy and not just pagan war. This image also displays a major pictorial and performative trope that occurs again and again in Remiet's historical images, which identifies women with the work of mourning. Just as women in many traditional societies, because of their association with birth, are made to stand in mor-

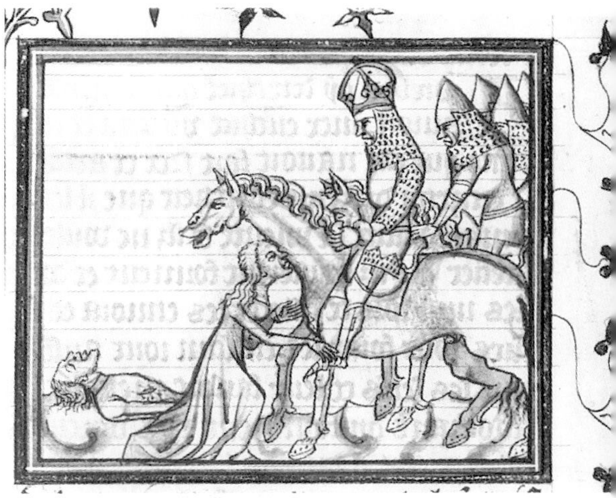

68. Remiet. Paris, Bibliothèque Nationale, fr. 313, fol. 126. *Miroir historial.* A mother implores the Emperor Trajan to avenge the death of her son.

69. Remiet. Paris, Bibliothèque Nationale, fr. 312, fol. 255v. *Miroir historial.* The suicides of Anthony and Cleopatra.

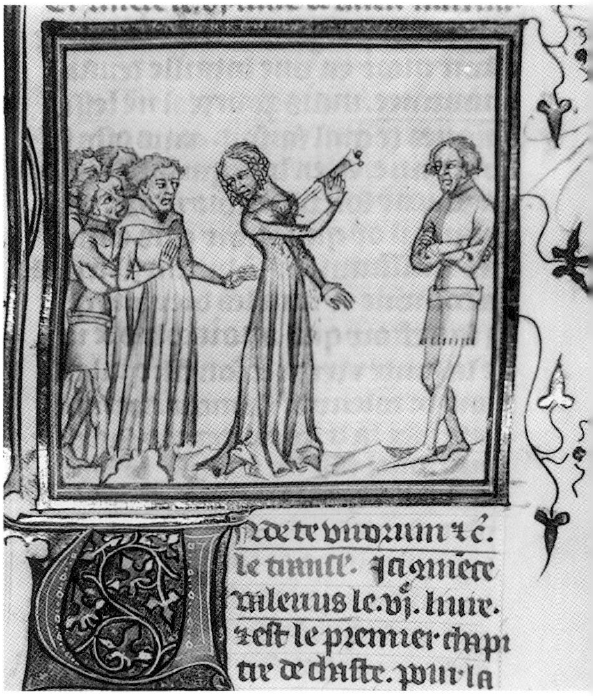

70. Remiet. Troyes, Bibliothèque Municipale, MS 261, fol. 205v. Valerius Maximus, *Faits et dits mémorables.* The suicide of Lucretia.

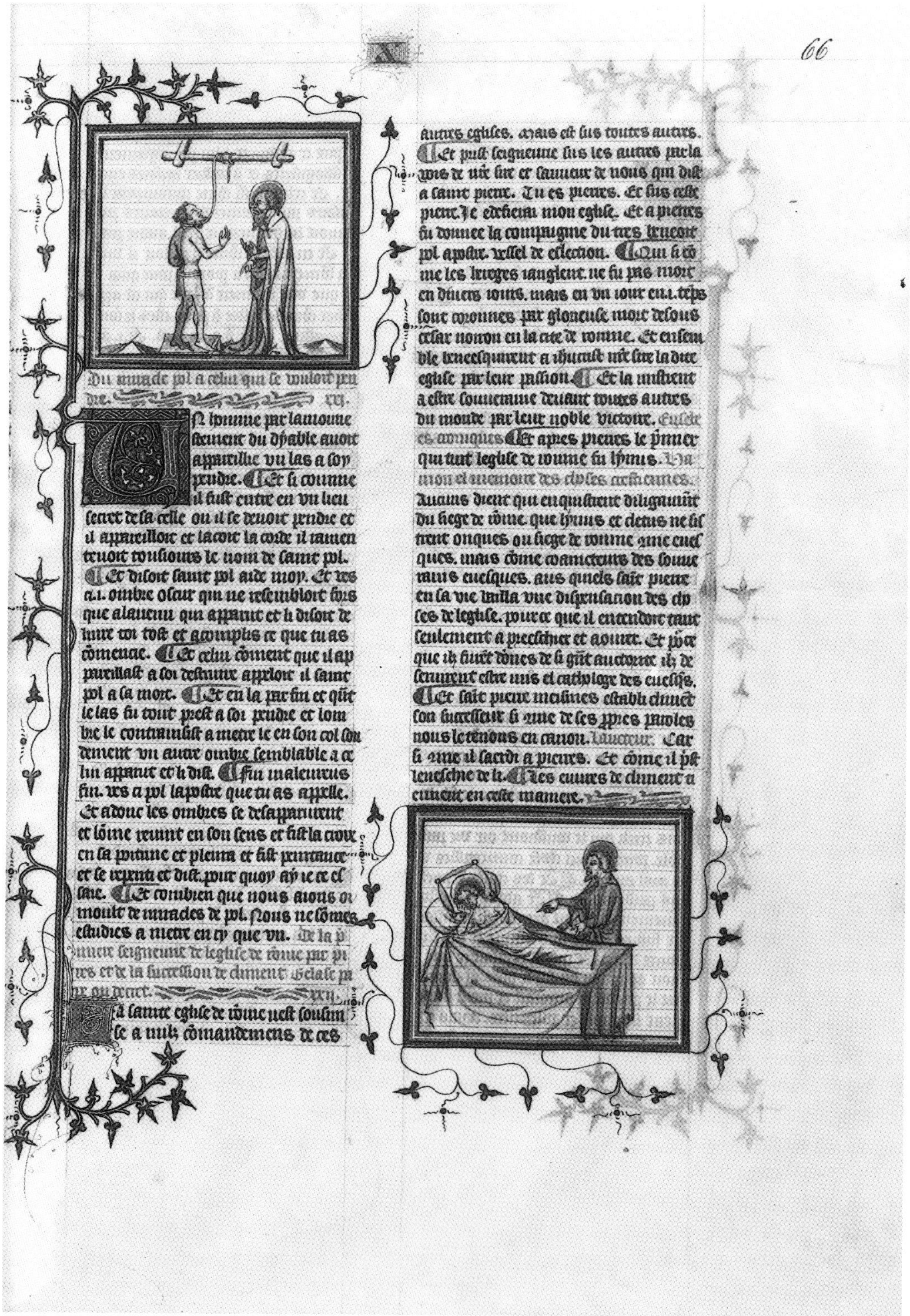

71. Remiet. Paris, Bibliothèque Nationale, fr. 313, fol. 66. *Miroir historial.* St Paul prevents a man from hanging himself; St Peter at a sickbed.

tuary rituals for 'division, death and sorrow', they often stand or kneel over the deceased in these ancient narratives. In fact in fourteenth-century funerary rites, official mourning was predominantly the work of male ecclesiastics and only in remote villages was there a continuation of ancient wailing traditions.[42] Remiet and his audiences were thus tapping into a much more deep-rooted tradition in which women wailed the deaths of their fathers, brothers and sons.

In Vincent's *Miroir* the more problematic pagan deaths from the Christian point of view are the suicides. What was considered a noble end for the ancients, Augustine had decried as a cowardly act against the creator. The simultaneous suicides of Mark Anthony and Cleopatra are described and depicted as sinful and corrupt, like the body of Cleopatra itself, which Remiet paints at the very bottom of the miniature, covered in worms and dragons, signalling not only the method that she used to greet death but the eternal damnation of her soul (Fig. 69).[43] In Valerius Maximus's *Faits et dits mémorables*, the translator Simon de Hesdin often glosses the pagan narrative with his own Christian morality, making ancient narrative histories into examples of vice and virtue. So there is none of the pathos of pagan death, even in the battles of ancient heroes. The death of Lucretia, for example, had another dimension besides that of the stoic virtue of constancy overcoming the evil of force, because suicide in Remiet's time was the sin of self-murder and excluded the perpetrator from a proper Christian burial (Fig. 70).[44] His scene has a power for us today because of the contrast he evokes between the gawping male onlookers, voyeurs of Lucretia's self-conscious act and towards whom she turns, and the strangely nonchalant rapist Tarquin, his arms folded, who stands on the right. Another image in the *Miroir historial* shows St Paul talking a man out of committing the sinful act of self-annihilation (Fig. 71). We have already seen Remiet's haunting image of the mass suicide of mothers and their children in the *Histoire ancienne*, which is described as 'marvellous'.[45] The vast distance between ancient and medieval conceptions of death can best be measured in these fourteenth-century Christian incarnations of the bodies of the ancients who, like Seneca, are shown choosing death only under condemnation of tyrants like Nero and only because they have some premonition of a Christian God to whom they can return. Yet this begs the question of what separates suicide from the self-destructive acts of the most violent of all deaths depicted by Remiet, those of Christian martyrs, who go happily to their ends appropriating some of the pathos of their classical predecessors.[46]

Sacred History

Perhaps Christianity is even fundamentally the pressing demand for crime, the demand for the horror that in a sense it needs in order to forgive. Georges Bataille[47]

The precious death of the saints, for whom the death of Christ had already merited so much grace that they hastened to lose their own lives in order to find Him, proves that the right use of death, which was originally intended as the punishment of sin, may bring forth abundant fruits and holiness. St Augustine[48]

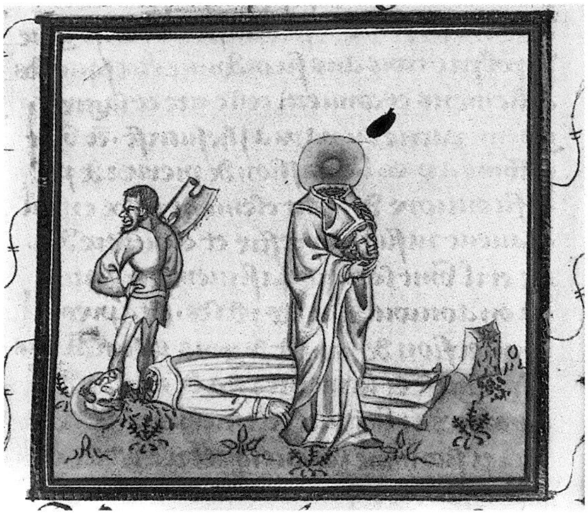

72. Remiet. London, British Library, MS Lansdowne 1179, fol. 95. *Miroir historial.* The martyrdom of St Denis.

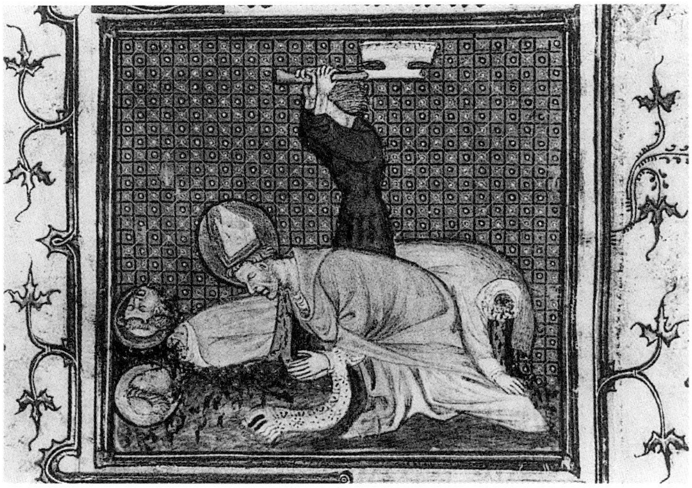

73. Remiet. Bayeux, Bibliothèque du Chapitre, MS 61, fol. 50v. Missal-Pontifical. The martyrdom of St Denis.

The only heroes in the history of death are the saints. Augustine, in his *Cité de Dieu*, gives the most succinct account of their triumph over mortality in 'the right use of death'. The most horrific and violent deaths in Remiet's art occur not in political or even in pagan history but in his depiction of sacred time in the *Miroir historial*, such as the most important Parisian foundation myth – the martyrdom of St Denis (Fig. 72). The saint's disciple is decapitated by a grinning executioner on the left, and in front centre stands the saintly bishop, his halo still hanging like a sunrise over an oval red sea where his head should be. He calmly holds the mitred head, its eyes closed – a dead head – in his living hands. It is perhaps a joke on Remiet's part to emphasize the head's absence through the blank nimbus, although it is of course this very sign that elevates Denis to the status of a saint. This small circle is what saves him, in his termination, from the fate of the ordinary victim. The head of the patron saint of Paris was in fact a highly controversial object in this period and the subject of a dispute, brewing since the 1390s between the monks of the Abbey of Saint Denis and the cathedral chapter of Notre Dame, which culminated in a trial held at the Parlement of Paris on 3 April 1410. Both religious bodies claimed to have the saint's head, only the monks believed that they had more of it. They often paraded the entire head surmounted by a golden mitre on feast days, as when Louis d'Orléans visited the abbey in 1406 before an important battle to beg protection from the saint and was able to take the whole head 'quite naked' out of its reliquary and kiss what the chronicle describes as its already eroded forehead. The canons of Notre Dame boasted nothing as fleshy as a forehead, only the sliced-off cranium. When in January 1406 the Duke of Berry, as insatiable a collector of holy body bits as of illuminated books, sought a small piece of this skull fragment in exchange for an entire head of St Philip the apostle, having earlier been refused a piece of the other whole head belonging to the monks, the race was on as to who could prove the authenticity of what Jean Gerson called 'these two contradictory relics'.[49]

Representation itself was on trial here, in an argument over whether the saint had been only partially decapitated or whether his whole head had been removed by the executioner's axe. It was the monks who were on the defensive, having to prove the authenticity of what they claimed was the head of their patron saint. To this end they presented evidence in old documents, citing the historical truths of the *Grandes Chroniques de France* and charters; but more important for our concerns, they brought before the Parlement what they called 'very old paintings' in 'old books'. They argued that these 'images anciennes', earlier thirteenth and fourteenth-century illustrated lives of the saint, had 'the most truth and authority'. The 'new' manner of depicting St Denis with only a sliced-off cranium, as he appeared in stone at Rheims cathedral, for example, was a hagiographical confusion and erroneous in their eyes. They claimed that 'without following the truth in paintings (sans y ensuir la vérité des ystoires)', false novelties were being introduced. For the monks of Saint Denis, history could indeed be verified by *ystoires* – images. This was probably the first use of illuminated manuscripts as evidence at a trial, but the monks were adept at propaganda, having already hung a painting in their church denigrating the relic preserved at the cathedral as an 'error' of the Parisians. But the Parisian court did not buy their pictorial arguments so easily, stating that many of the monks' illuminated books were in fact 'nouvel', not dating from the time of the saint's actual decapitation and that, moreover, there was an important difference between miniature paintings and public icons of the saint in reliquary, statuary and even street signs. They argued that in book painting ('portraitures ou enlumineures de livres') 'each could have his book illuminated in any manner that he so wished (chacun puent faire en son livre tele enlumineure comme il lui plait)' in contrast to public images, which were 'the books of the laity' and therefore had to be subject to stricter rules. Images in books, by contrast, are shown secretly ('expose clandestinement') as opposed to those which are in the public gaze in stone and glass and cannot be used in evidence in this way.[50] This notion of manuscript images as the site of a more personal vision, even fantasy, has interesting implications for the production and reception of Remiet's art, as a different kind of 'history', more closed within the secret gaze of particular groups and individuals than in the public eye. Although the trial court recommended legislating images, stating that 'if error is intolerable in words (*in dictis*) it is the same in pictures (*in pictis*)', this was in reference to public imagery. The system thus allowed Remiet, the book illuminator, his jokes.

Some manuscripts, however, are more public than others. While the *Miroir* made for the privacy of a ducal library could take certain liberties with these saintly bodies and even, as we shall see, make them into objects of desire, the illumination of a service book was a different matter. In the missal-pontifical made for the Bishop of Luçon and now at Bayeux, Remiet illuminated a more majestic version of the same subject with the saint's head still in place, suggesting that only in the more informal and intimate *paintre bâtarde* of the historical genre could he take the liberty of decapitating his city's saintly father (Fig. 73). But it might also have been a way of avoiding the controversy, since this bishop would probably have sided with his Parisian peer against the monks. Remiet avoided the controversy and portrayed the preceding moment when the executioner raised his axe. In both images, however, severed heads lie about on the ground, suggestive of their multiplication and market value in the flourishing relic trade of the city.

The missal image preserves a historical moment of bodily fragmentation. Whereas the relic preserved the saint's power through his actual bodily presence, such a small narrative image was merely his *memoria*. Generally Remiet worked on very few books for liturgical

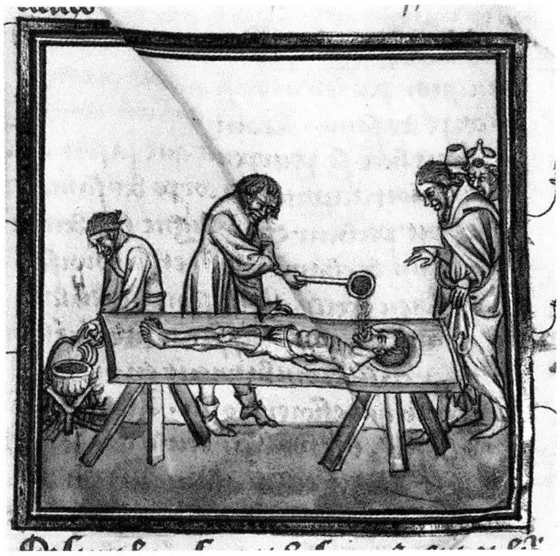

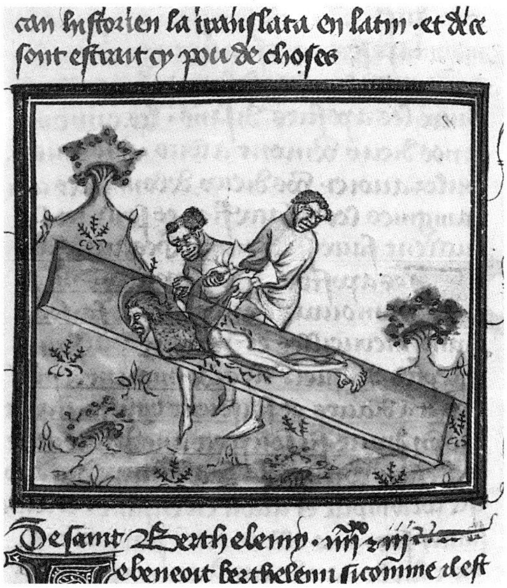

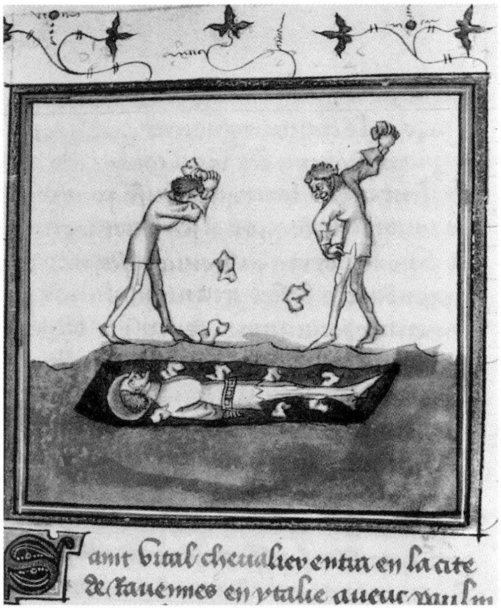

use, to judge by what remains today. This was partly because pontificals and psalters were required texts for the clergy, used over long periods and often available in the thriving second-hand market. Most of the manuscripts illuminated by Remiet were the newer vernacular works that had only been available for a generation or two. Liturgical books like this one made for more public use or the private devotional *memoriae* of the saints in Books of Hours formed part of a calendar of torment inscribed upon time as well as space, in that each saint was commemorated on his or her day, often with specific prayers, antiphons and masses. What the text of the missal calls the *supplices* or tortures of the saints were recited aloud as part of a performative structure of death very different from the silently scanned simulacra of torment that fill the vernacular *Miroir*. Yet both the public and the private, the spiritual and sensational, function of the saints was still grounded on the idea of their deaths.

If the *Grandes Chroniques* are a visual chronicle of the deaths of great men in battle, the *Histoire ancienne* a catalogue of the finite, decadent deaths of the pagans, and the Bayeux missal a memorial of the publicly celebrated and endlessly recalled deaths of the saints, the *Miroir historial* is a private, almost voyeuristic, journey through the saint's repertoire of self-suffering in which 'the only body that speaks is the dead body'.[51] Remiet produced the illustrations in two vast four-volume versions of this massive text. The first set was begun for Louis d'Orléans in 1396, three volumes of which are extant in Paris and contain the enormous number of 552 miniatures, all by Remiet. The text of the first volume, finished on 2 June 1396, was written by the most famous and sought-after of all Parisian scribes of the period, Raoulet d'Orléans, as he records in a rhyming colophon, so Remiet probably began his own labours on the project soon after. The second set, also lacking a volume and which Remiet only

74. Remiet. London, British Library, MS Lansdowne 1179, fol. 191. *Miroir historial*. The martyrdom of St Boniface.

75. Remiet. London, British Library, MS Lansdowne 1179, fol. 73v. *Miroir historial*. The martyrdom of St Bartholomew.

76. Remiet. London, British Library, MS Lansdowne 1179, fol. 64. *Miroir historial*. The martyrdom of St Vital.

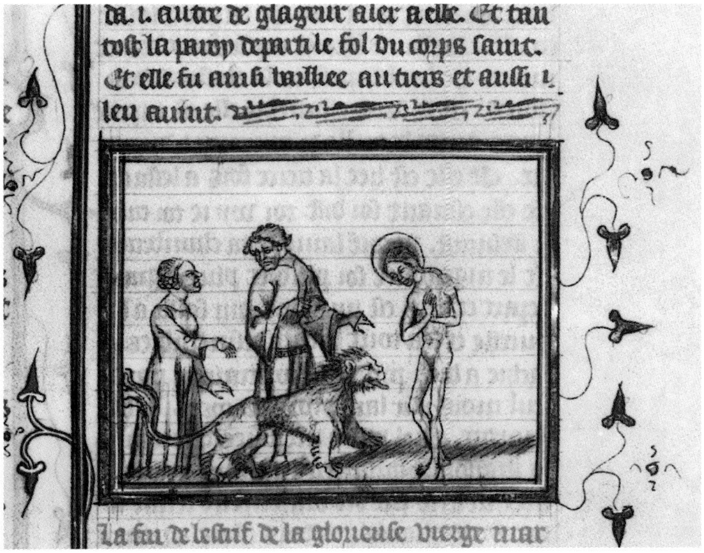

77. Remiet. Paris, Bibliothèque Nationale, fr. 313, fol. 276. *Miroir historial.* The martyrdom of St Marcienne.

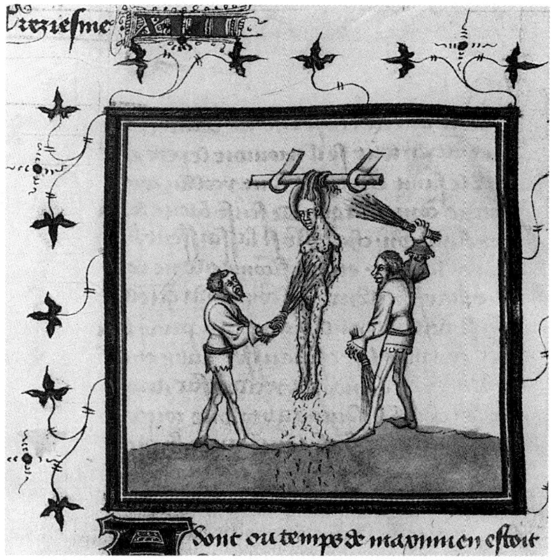

78. Remiet. London, British Library, MS Lansdowne 1179, fol. 192. *Miroir historial.* The martyrdom of St Julien.

partly illuminated, is divided between London, Paris and the Vatican and belonged to the great bibliophile and royal councillor Prigent de Coëtivy.[52] Ironically there are more scenes of gory dismemberment and sadistic theatre in this encyclopaedia of religious history than in the pagan and political histories of the *Histoire ancienne* or the *Grandes Chroniques* put together. Those who complain today of our bombardment with violent images of indiscriminate death on film and television forget that audiences in the past were just as entranced by such scenes and that what we witness only on screens, they often experienced at first hand in the sanguinary public squares of cities. But whereas in our media the heroes tend to avoid bodily dismemberment and instead inflict pain and death on others, medieval Christians revelled in the passive acceptance of bodily fragmentation as a means of spiritual fulfilment and saw in the horrific death of the martyrs, models for life everlasting. For Louis, who was a relic collector, they also provided pictures of the historical events that created his much-loved body-parts.

The very awkwardness of Remiet's figures helps convey the stubborn flesh under torment, de-eroticized and passive. While other illuminators of the same generation were deploying the new fleshy fashion for colour and volume not only to eroticize the female body but also to provide naked boys frolicking in the line-endings of manuscripts like the *Grandes Heures*, made for the infamous Duke of Berry's polymorphous tastes, Remiet's tormented saints seem at first to have gender-neutral, sexless bodies.[53] However, there are differences between the tormented bodies of the male saints compared to the more exposed, often totally naked, bodies of their female counterparts. St Boniface's scrawny frame wears drawers as molten oil is poured down his gullet (Fig. 74). The Apostle St Bartholomew is indeed naked on a diagonal table but has his red raw skin peeled off like clothing and displayed like an expensive vair lining by two straining tormentors (Fig. 75). St Vital, dressed as an elegant Parisian noble, is buried beneath a pile of stones while wearing his pointed shoes and golden belt in one of Remiet's very few dressed cadaver types (Fig. 76). Among the female saints, by contrast, the totally naked St Marcienne is eyed by an eager lion whose tongue already extends towards her genitals (Fig. 77). Even more startling is St Julien hanging naked by her hair from a rail that Remiet failed to attach to anything, so interested was he in suspending her exposed and mutilated body spattered lovingly with droplets of red, blood-like paint (Fig. 78). The tormenters of her resilient body wear out three sharp birches.

This ambiguously eroticized sadism has to be seen in terms of the viewers as well as the artist, patrons for whom spectacles subjecting bodies to molten oil and being burnt alive were far more than early Christian history. Coëtivy, the admiral of France who later owned the London manuscript of the *Miroir* until felled by a harquebus shot to the head at the siege of Cherbourg in 1450, was certainly in a position of power to have enabled him to carry out some of these very torments on real flesh, and his own daughter married the most notorious child-murderer of the fifteenth century, Gilles de Rais. In accounts of Gille's trial, we can see some of the same juxtapositions of fragmented bodies, child-like sexlessness and bloody evisceration that remind us of Remiet's representations of saintly sacrifice. Familiar with such images in monumental as well as miniature scale, Gilles, like a latter-day Nero, had them recreated in perverse pseudo-sacred tableaux vivants 'contemplating those who had the most beautiful heads and members, and he had their bodies cruelly opened up and delighted at the sight of their internal organs'.[54] We should also not forget that throughout Remiet's lifetime, torture was used in the notorious Châtelet prison as part of the normal legal means of extracting the truth from suspects. Being buried alive like St Vital (Fig. 76) or burnt alive, like many saints pictured in the *Miroir*, was still a common sentence which drew large crowds in Paris. But these were the bodies of miscreants without haloes and the viewer would hardly have sought identification with them. Where such images of the suffering saints would have served as points of self-projection was in their protection and cure of bodily illness. In this respect the countless droplets of blood and marks of pain are not so much celebrations of violence as signals to those who were themselves in bodily discomfort. For example, St Bartholomew was called upon to aid those suffering from skin diseases, and St Lawrence, from burning fever. That the saints had endured terrible torment in their quests for bodily purity and immortality encouraged people to pray to them from within their own dire somatic situations.

Remiet's art embodies contemporary dying as well as deaths of the distant past. He is concerned with the suffering of famous saints and sinners, but equally concerned with the everyday anonymous agonies of those who longed for death and who were skeletal not through fasting but through poverty. One of Remiet's specialities was the ragged emaciation, the bandaged sores, the torn body of the vagrant, which he portrayed in minute detail in many different texts. The poor were viewed in a dual perspective at this time. On the one hand, Christ had preached that it was easier for the man with nothing to enter heaven than it was for the rich miser. Large spiritual institutions like the Franciscans were totally based on mendicancy. However, social and civil strife had created insurmountable numbers of homeless who flocked to cities like Paris and who were viewed with increasing alarm.[55]

Two pages of Deschamps's *Lay de la fragilité humaine* are concerned with 'la misere du povre home et de la douleur de riche home'. The first (Fig. 79) imagines the 'riche au monde' whose insatiable desire for more money Remiet depicts in the traditional guise of

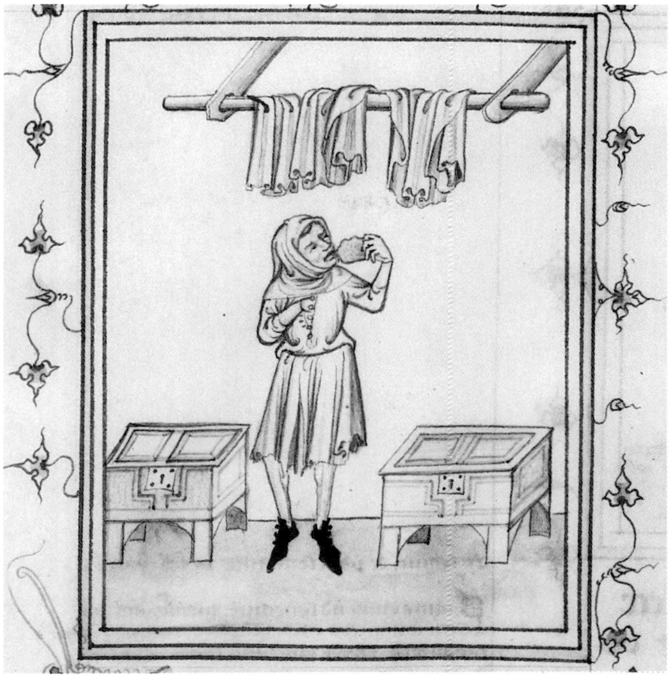

79. Remiet. Paris, Bibliothèque Nationale, fr. 20029, fol. 10v. *Lay de la fragilité humaine*. The sadness of the rich.

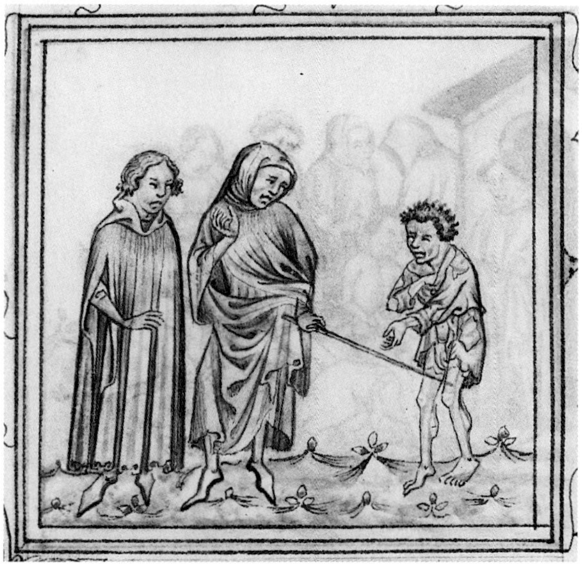

80. Remiet. Paris, Bibliothèque Nationale, fr. 20029, fol. 11. *Lay de la fragilité humaine*. The misery of the poor.

Avarice, a man standing between two locked chests and below a rail. The rail is a favourite 'prop', but there is no tortured body here, only hanging clothes. This scowling, unhappy figure bites on a piece of bread to express the never-satisfied hunger for more riches, while his other hand is tucked under his vest. These gestures, not mentioned in either Innocent III's Latin or Deschamps's French text, were probably devised by the artist, though as a pictorial type for idleness they are based on Proverbs 26:15: 'The slothful hideth his arm under his armpit, and it grieveth him to turn it to his mouth'.[56] On the facing page, a pendant picture shows the barefoot vagrant not rooted to his prison of geometric riches but wandering the clumpy earth, his bony legs cruelly prodded by one of two well-dressed gentlemen with a stick, as though he were a piece of carrion or an animal (Fig. 80). It is hard to guess whether Remiet's sympathy is any more for this figure than for the rich miser opposite, for if one arm reaches out to beg the other mimics the same laziness, the hand in the shirt. Thus both the rich and the poor are seen as inherently idle and deserving all the scorn they receive. However, Remiet's art is never so straightforward. The image-type he used to depict the poverty-stricken man reoccurs in a Job illustration in the Soissons *Bible historiale*, where the same ragged holes and gestures are used, but this time for the great exemplar of human suffering and patience in adversity (Fig. 81). Such visual associations with sacred prototypes make the beggar a sympathetic figure, one of God's chosen, and again show Remiet working against the text in the case of the *Lay* illustration. The text of the *Lay* here makes clear that the existence of the beggar is no more than a living death.

> The poor are indeed oppressed by starvation, tortured by need, hunger, thirst, cold, nakedness; they become worthless and waste away, are despised and confounded. O

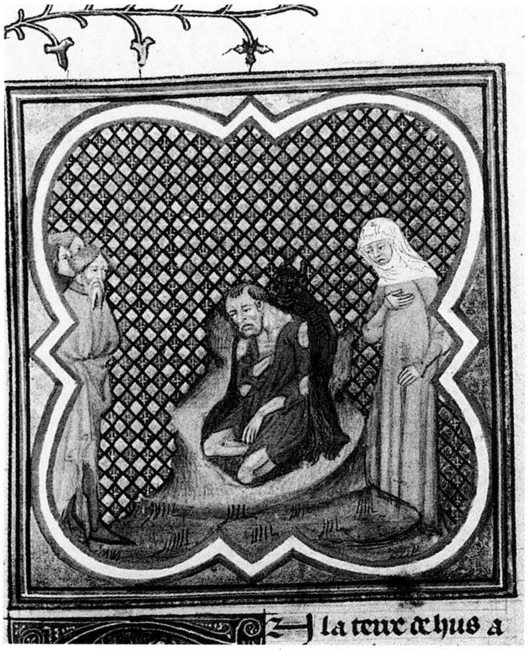

81. Remiet. Soissons, Bibliothèque Municipale, MS 211, fol. cxxxvi. *Bible historiale*. Job on the dung-heap.

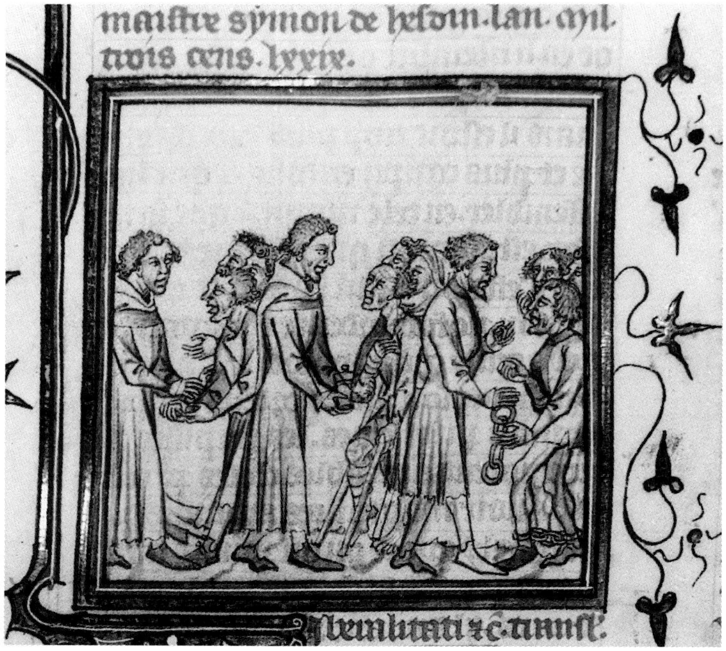

82. Remiet. Troyes, Bibliothèque Municipale, MS 261, fol. 205v. Valerius Maximus, *Faits et dits mémorables*. Liberality towards the poor.

> miserable condition of a beggar! If he begs he is confounded with shame, and if he does not beg he is consumed with want, and indeed is compelled by necessity to beg. He maintains that God is unjust because he does not dispense properly; he accuses his neighbour of being evil because he does not help fully; he is offended, he complains, he curses. Consider the opinion of the wise man on this subject: 'It is better to die than to want.'[57]

Animosity towards the vagrant was especially widespread in the plague years when they were accused of spreading the disease from one town to another and even, like the Jews, of poisoning wells. Yet many, seeking perhaps to sneak into heaven, wanted to be buried as paupers, like those who in their wills registered at the Parlement of Paris between 1392 and 1421 wished to be thrown into the paupers' grave at the Cemetery of the Holy Innocents, including a dealer in skins from the Rue Saint Denis and Elie de Tourette, a former president of the Parlement himself.[58]

In his careful illustrations to Valerius Maximus's history, Remiet depicts the virtue of liberality, in which the poor, the lame and prisoners are given alms (Fig. 82). Charity was a crucial Christian virtue and social bonding mechanism in the Middle Ages, providing a safety net for those in need and literally earning good marks in heaven for those who gave to the needy. Thinking of their deaths, folk gave to the living dead who huddled outside every church. But this was different from the classical virtue of 'liberality' represented in this miniature, which was ancient history. In Remiet's time fewer folk seemed to have followed this ideal than ever before, and beggars were demonized and treated like vermin rather than supported as living signs of humility.

Some of the worst famines of the century occurred in Remiet's lifetime. Although Paris was often spared more than the countryside, where the ravages of civil wars wrought worse havoc, in 1417, following the civil war, famine reached the suburbs of the city. The most horrific but often-repeated story of hunger that Remiet illustrated appears in both extant manuscripts of the *Miroir historial.* Vincent of Beauvais took it from Josephus and it was cited in Innocent's *Miseria* treatise; it was a terrible tale that caught Remiet's visual imagination perhaps because it juxtaposed the body of maternal generation with that of death, returning the flesh to the body that had produced it via that other vagina, the mouth (Fig. 83). It describes a woman whom war had reduced to starvation.

> Having adopted the worst counsel, she herself was now armed against the laws of nature. For there was at her breasts a baby boy, holding whom before her eyes she said, 'Oh more unhappy son of an unhappy mother, in war, and famine and the plundering of robbers, for whom shall I save you? For though your life could be hoped for, we would be oppressed by the yoke of Roman slavery. Come now therefore, O my son, be food for your mother, madness for the robbers, a tale for the ages of what alone was lacking in the defeats of the Jews.' And when she had said this she immediately killed her son. Thereupon she roasted him, superposed over the fire, and she ate half and kept half concealed. And behold, the robbers immediately rushed in, having recognized the aroma of burned flesh; they threatened death unless she would without delay produce the food that they assumed had been prepared. Then she: 'I have saved the best part for you,' and she immediately revealed the members that remained of the child. But suddenly a great horror seized them, and frozen though their monstrous souls were, their voice was cut off in their throats. But she with a fierce look and more savage now than the robbers themselves: 'My son,' she said, 'he is my offspring and it is my crime.'[59]

Significantly, the tiny baby is pictured as a miniature *transi*, a shrunken version of Remiet's cadaver type, though frying on a griddle rather than lying on a cold tomb slab, food not for worms but for his own flesh and blood. In the copy of the *Miroir* that belonged to Coëtivy, Remiet went even further than the cooking of the children in duplicating this scene of maternal mastication to show a crowd of ravenous, monstrous

83. Remiet. London, British Library, MS Lansdowne 1179, fol. 96v. *Miroir historial.* The woman who ate her own child.

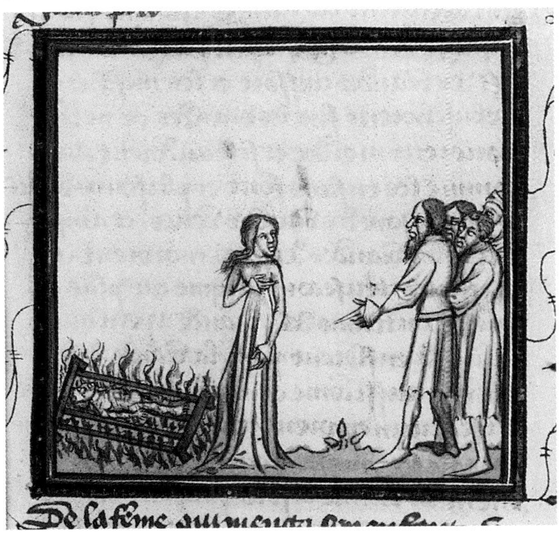

84. Remiet. Paris, Bibliothèque Nationale, fr. 313, fol. 110v. *Miroir historial.* Women devour their own children.

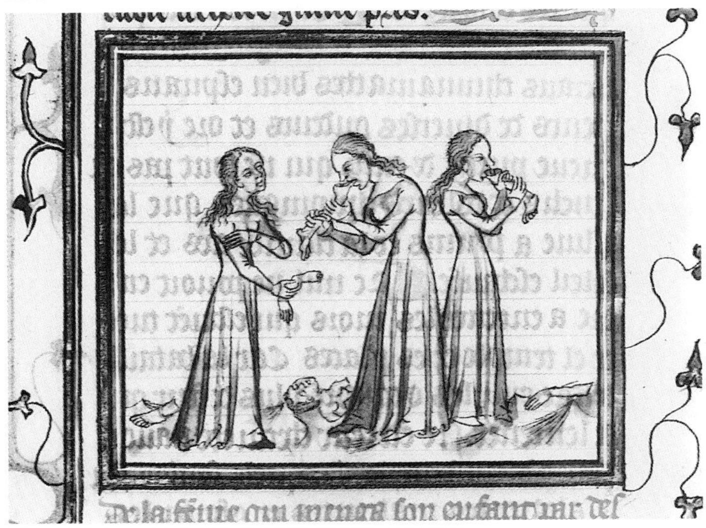

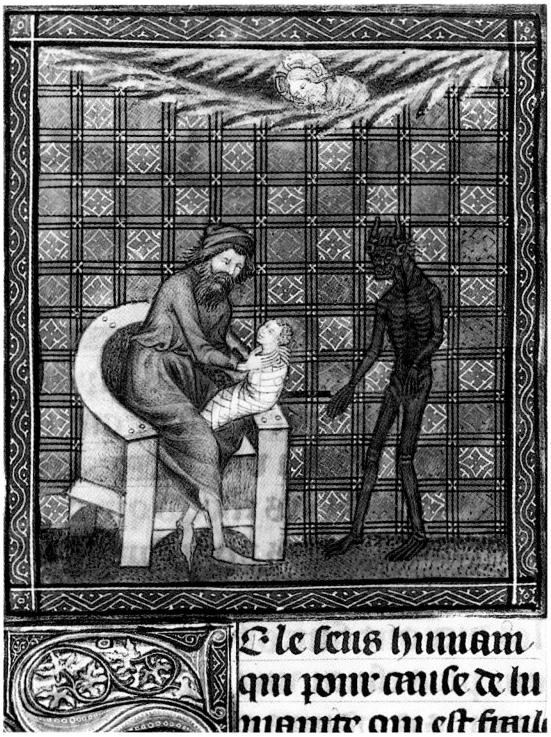

85. Remiet. Paris, Bibliothèque Nationale, fr. 170, fol. 38v. Augustine, *Le Cité de Dieu*. A pagan strangles a baby as a sacrifice to the gods.

mothers devouring their infants (Fig. 84). Opposites of the mothers in the Massacre of the Innocents, in which maternal sorrow at the death of children was ritually performed and which Remiet repeated in a number of contexts, these women are seen as unnatural. Rather than see depictions like this as somehow reflecting a reality and despite the fact that the chronicler Monstrelet reported the arrest, near Paris in 1439, of a woman accused of killing little children 'whom she had dismembered and salted down secretly in her house', we should recognize that these are all representations of a mass anxiety surrounding cannibalism in a society weighed down by hunger.[60]

Remiet seems to have had a penchant for sensational images of infanticide. Among the illustrations to the *Cité de Dieu*, for which no model was available, he chose to portray Augustine's discussion in Book II of 'the ugly and horrible things' that the pagans performed to honour their gods, a strangely domestic scene of baby strangulation, this time by a man seated in a chair, watched over by a black rubbery-looking demon (Fig. 85). This horrifying scene, which has no parallel or place in Augustine's text, convinces me that Remiet rather than an advisor or *libraire* made the decisions about what to depict in this prestigious two-volume copy of Augustine's work and that Remiet chose to emphasize the history of death at every turn.

The suffering and death caused by political conflict and abuses of law and order are described in the twenty-third chapter of the *Lay de la fragilité humaine*, where Remiet depicts some of the violent ends that were possible, accidental falling into the river, mortal duelling and imprisonment (Fig. 86). The fourth scene shows two hungry dogs and

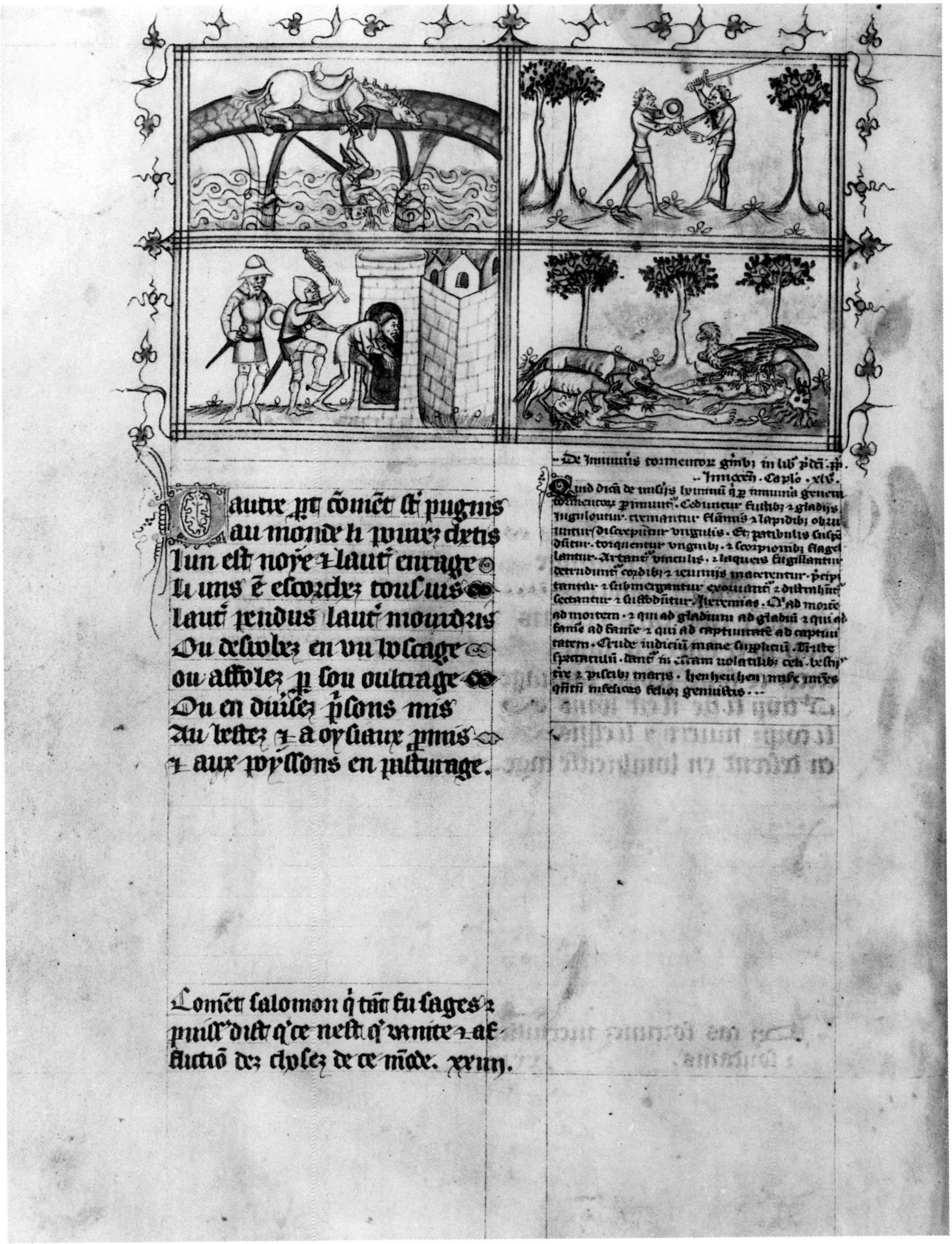

86. Remiet. Paris, Bibliothèque National, fr. 20029, fol. 13v. *Lay de la fragilité humaine.* The sudden accidents of fortune.

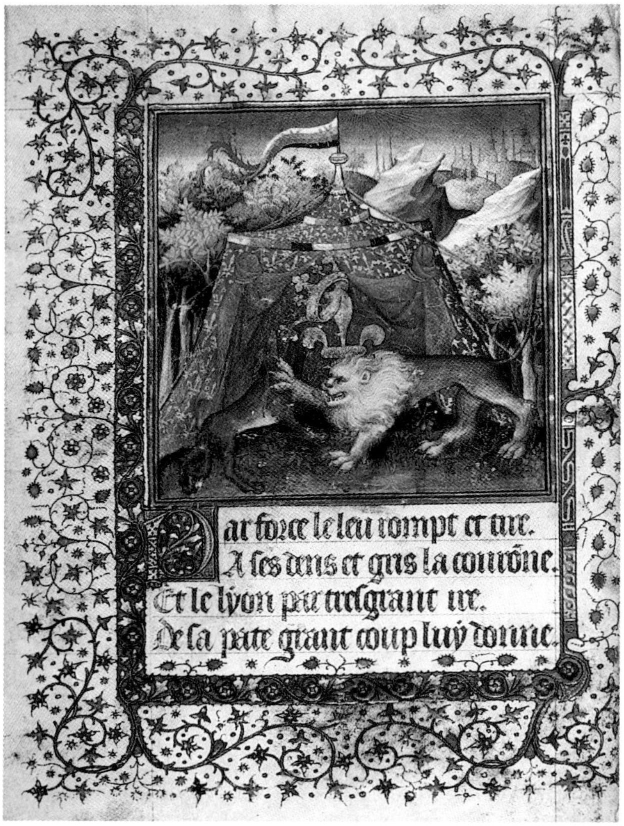

87. French illuminator, after 1407. Vienna, Österreichisches Nationalbibliothek, MS 2657, fol. 1v. *Allegory of the Assassination of Louis d'Orléans.*

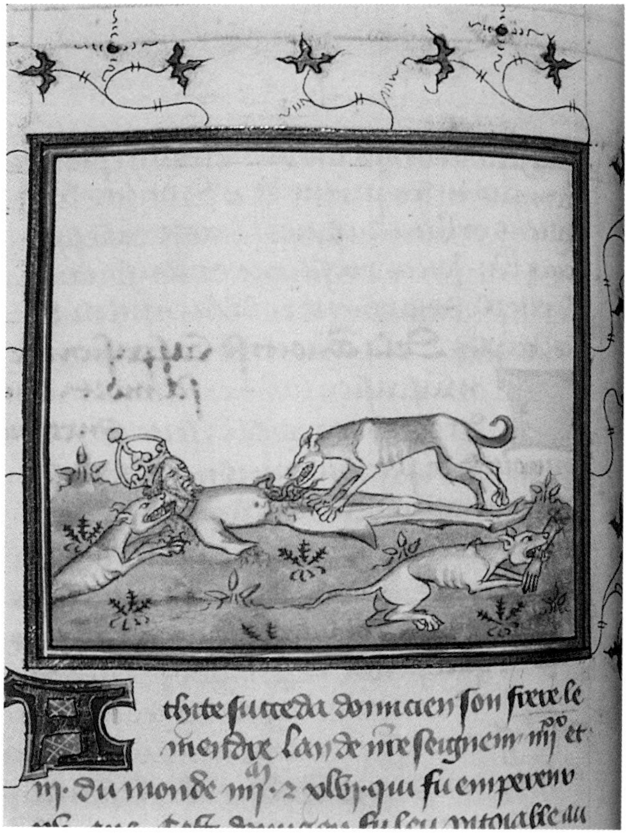

88. Remiet. London, British Library, MS Lansdowne 1179, fol. 93v. *Miroir historial.* The corpse of a Roman emperor eaten by dogs.

ravenous vultures devouring two corpses, one with its eye-sockets already eaten away. Before three 'little trees' a far more horrifying nature reveals itself, against which humanity is helpless:

> What may I say about the miserable people who are destroyed by countless kinds of torments? They are beaten with clubs and slain with swords, burned with flames and overwhelmed with stones, torn to pieces with claws and suspended with yokes, tortured with nails and whipped with scorpions, restrained with chains and bruised by fetters, subdued by prisons and made thin by fastings, thrown down and submerged, flayed and torn apart, cut up and pierced through. 'Such as are for death, to death.' Jeremiah XV:2[61]

Such horrors affected even artists. This is suggested by the interesting case of one of Remiet's contemporaries, the well-known illuminator and highly successful court artist Jacquemart de Hesdin, who was involved in the murder of another artist in 1399. While he was working at the Duke of Berry's castle at Poitiers, a painter called John of Holland accused Jacquemart and Jacquemart's brother-in-law and valet of having broken into a box and stolen 'certaines couleurs et patrons'. When walking in the city soon after, the three accused met the wife and brother-in-law of John of Holland, who was stabbed in the stomach in the ensuing fight. The illuminator is recorded as saying something to the equivalent of 'Now we've had it!' and the three fled for asylum to the abbey of Montierneuf, where they were eventually pardoned for their complicity in the murder by a royal decree which spoke of Jacquemart's previously blameless character.[62] Squabbles like this one between professionals erupting into violence were even more common in the city and are attested by litigation between craftsmen, who were always a violent and volatile group, protective of their rights and duties.

But such individual acts were nothing compared to the mass slaughter that erupted in the streets during the last quarter of the fourteenth century, which threatened the whole body politic. Historical images are to be seen in terms not only of the past, or even of a present. They can have a future or portentious aspect too. As we have seen, Remiet made a number of stunning images of death in books of history destined for the library of Louis d'Orléans, especially the countless dismemberments and deaths in the *Miroir historial*. One of the horrors Remiet pictured in the mirror of history was also a mirror of things yet to come. It shows the desecrated corpse of the assassinated Roman emperor Domitian, gutted on the ground, its innards gnawed by dogs and its severed arm carried off by another (Fig. 88). Remiet could not have known when he made this *histoire* that such a scene would take place on the streets of Paris and the victim be none other than the duke himself.

On 23 November 1407 at seven o'clock in the evening, Louis was enjoying dinner with the queen in the Hôtel Barbette on the Rue Veille du Temple in Paris when he received a false summons to visit the king. On leaving the residence of the queen, he was preceded on the street by a torch-bearer and accompanied by two pages when he was suddenly set upon by a band of men, agents of his cousin and rival Jean sans Peur, Duke of Burgundy. Armed with hatchets, these men came out of a dark doorway, dragged him from his mule, and struck him four times, also killing the page who tried to protect his master. A contemporary chronicler described how the mutilated remains of the duke were found all over the street by the provost of Paris, his head bleeding from two gashes in the skull that went from ear to ear, 'wounds so enormous that the head was split up, the brain protruding . . . the left hand severed from the arm . . . the right arm broken so that the master-bone stood out to right of the elbow'. His severed hand lay in the gutter.[63] During the political reverberations that followed, Parisian illuminators were hired to delineate allegorical propaganda images excusing the Duke of Burgundy's act as a patriotic one. They produced an allegory of two animals, the lion of Burgundy protecting the tent of the kingdom of France from the ravening wolf, or *loup*, which of course stood for Louis (Fig. 87).[64] These allegorical depictions deflect violence into the abstract realms of the heraldic and symbolic, justifying the violent murder by effacing its grim reality. The horrendous murder that was to cause decades of civil strife in France was later depicted in historical chronicles, but there is no contemporary depiction, apart from these propogandistic pictures put out by the perpetrator himself. But then there is Remiet's mirror of violent deaths and dismemberments in the *Miroir* made for the victim himself. No miracles, like that of St Denis who can pick up his head and walk with it, could bring together the pieces of this violated princely body from its fragmentation on the Parisian street. Remiet's greatest patron and the period's finest connoisseur of cadavers had himself become a sign of the times and of the future, symbolizing, in his broken body, decades of dismemberment yet to come.

Une faux en sa main tenoit
Et un sarqueu de fust portoit
Et avoit ja un des piez mis
Pour moy estaindre sur le pis

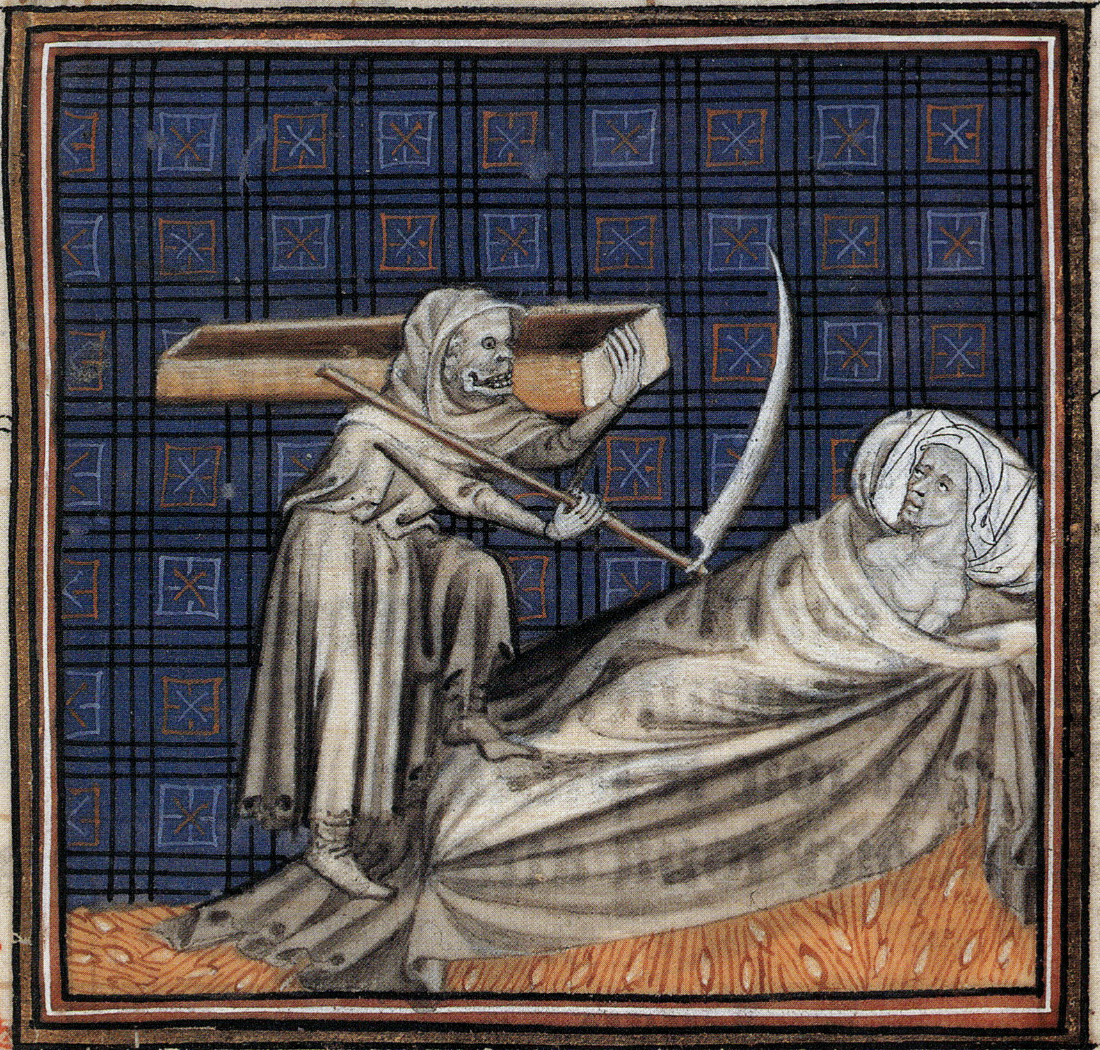

Ho ly advint dist grace dieu
Qui nestoit pas loing de ce lieu
Actenz un po je li diray

4. THE FACE OF DEATH

He began to imagine what she looked like, to remember her from an image he had made, somewhere, years ago. It was at the end of the pilgrimage, the poem by the monk of Chaalis which told the story of man's life from birth to death. Over thirty years ago, that must have been, the year the king first lost his mind – 1392 – and when his friend Colart de Laon, the panel painter, had begun the Guild of 'Tailleurs d'images peintres et enlumineurs'. What a good year it had been for painters on parchment as well as panel. With the 'libraire's' advance he had been able to buy all the fresh ground colours he wanted, 'terra rubea', cinnabar and azurite, more gold leaf than he had ever seen before in light-thin sheets, transparent almost. He had even been paid on time. The 'champaignes d'histoires', or chequered backgrounds, which he had laboured on for as long as a day, had been exquisite. No two were identical. It was against such a rich red, or was it blue, ground that he had painted her stout figure (strange to think now that death should be so substantial, so fleshy) stepping up on to the pilgrim's bed, carrying an empty open coffin on one shoulder and swinging a great scythe on the other.

He was alone now, just as the pilgrim had been in that miniature. The doctor had long gone, having given him up for gone, after months of fruitless purgations and bleedings that had cost him his last derniers. He had said special prayers to the saints and had had himself laid out for measurement with a thread which had then been incorporated into a candle that his son had offered in the cathedral of Notre Dame, but to no avail. The boy must have gone to fetch the priest. What was taking him so long? If he did not hurry . . . He hoped he had time to repent, unlike some poor wretches, like the brother of the king, Duke Louis, who fell himself in the streets of Paris, not under the divine arrow of the pestilence but under the worldly knife of the murderer, unshriven and carried off by black devils some had said. It was rumoured that he was a whoring wastrel, but all the books that Remiet had made for him were love songs to that dark lady, not revelling in life but rather preparing for its proper end. Sometimes it was indeed possible to die well, as had his wife, of good memory, surrounded by friends and family, warmth and respect, knowing that her unblemished life of giving to others would reap its eternal rewards and that the many folk who prayed for her soul would ease the flames of Purgatory. He was still working then too and had money which helped pay for a few thousand years' remission, and the beautiful funeral mass and the distribution of bread to the poor of the parish. More than Agnes's end, the departure that still could bring tears to his eyes was that of the boy from Provins who could paint such beautiful little flowers – his last apprentice. He had worked in his shop only one spring, had grasped merely the way to make the little gold buds at the ends of vignettes before

89. Remiet. Paris, Bibliothèque Nationale, fr. 823, fol. 94. *Pèlerinage de vie humaine.* Death and the pilgrim.

withering away himself in the autumn. That had been his only hope of having someone to take over his shop. But it was too late. That was in 1414, the summer of the cough they called the 'coqueluche', when no one could hear the priest's Sunday sermons above the hacking. Only four years later the pestilence returned to Paris to reap an even richer harvest, worse than any time before, even in the memories of old men like him. Fifty thousand people died in the city in less than five weeks, it was said, and most were the young, like his boy painter, and tiny children. It was like a vengeance, like the Old Testament angel of death smiting the first-born of Egypt he had drawn once. The doctors of astrology at the university as usual came out with their pronouncement that the pestilence was caused by a malign conjunction of planets in the sign of Aquarius. It was easy to blame the stars, but there were always people to accuse as well, and many shook their fists at the corrupt clergy, complained of the lax morals of the court, chased out the poor deformed and crippled from their towns, or looked for the few Jews left in the city whom they always blamed for poisoning the world. But no one invited her. She just came when she was ready.

Remiet had not yet succumbed to her just as he had not in all the lady's terrible revisitations of the city, after her inaugural triumph at his birth, not in 1360, nor in 1374 or 1403 or 1419. He was immune to her darts, it seemed, and he felt guilty, like the immortal 'Elde' in the story who never finds that peace but watches others fall again and again. Perhaps it was because he had been her offspring, born into her care. But now at last she was coming, not to strike down swathes of folk with one swish of her scythe, taking entire streets and whole communities of the cloistered as she had in the past, but for him and him alone she was making a special journey. In his life he had just been one of many, part of the crowd of book-makers flocking for commissions, but now, at his end, he almost felt special, honoured by her visitation.

He felt her cold shadow coming nearer and nearer to his bedside, making his whole frame shiver and shake so that he could almost feel his bones, the skeleton within. He remembered the skeletons of the 'Danse macabre', at the Holy Innocents cemetery. When he first saw the great painted frieze showing all the states of society, each led by a grinning dancing corpse, a work lauded by all of Paris and new and magnificent, he had felt bitter, for here was nothing new to him. Here were the very skeletons he had himself pictured on a smaller scale forty years before, just enlarged and with captions to make the message easily understandable to the simple folk. 'O mortal man and reasonable being! If, after death, you do not wish to be damned you must, at least once a day, think of your loathsome end so that you may have a long life and die well.' Fifteen pairs of persons, emperor and pope, monk and peasant, usurer and doctor, lover and lawyer, were each led in the dance by a corpse, the living stiff, mortified with fear, as they beheld the sensuous dance of the rot they must follow. The painting was well executed with good colours he had had to admit, but there had been an error. There was every trade, métier and station in life, but no painter. No artist was led in the dance, which he had thought was an oversight on the part of the painter. For who else but the image-maker knows death when he sees her.

The Skull

The face is not in front of me but above me; it is the other before death, looking through and exposing death. Emmanuel Levinas[1]

Suddenly and without warning I saw a tall old woman climbing upon my bed, which greatly shocked me. She so terrified me that I could neither speak nor ask anything of her. In her hand she bore a scythe and she carried a wooden coffin and then she put one of her feet on my chest to restrain me. Deguileville, *Pèlerinage de vie humaine*[2]

The anonymous 'she' who climbs on to the pilgrim's bed at the end of the *Pèlerinage de vie humaine*, the manuscript in which Remiet's name appears, cannot be mistaken for anyone else (Fig. 89). Her visage is not that of the wrinkled old woman described in the text and visible in many miniatures depicting this moment in other manuscripts of the poem (Fig. 90). Hairless beneath her hood, she is eaten away to the white bone. Rather than the black, hollow eye-sockets we might expect, the tiny pupils of her glaring, globular pink eyes look down in haughty, delirious triumph over her helpless victim. A human being was believed to be not completely moribund until every scrap of flesh had disintegrated by the process of natural decay, making this face an ambiguous one, a dry skull holding the spherules of optical liquid sensation. Death, unlike Love, Fate or Fortune, cannot be blind. At the moment of death, the pilgrim sees his own future status in another's face, as in a mirror. It is a personal confrontation, a meeting of gazes, a moment of recognition. As a creator of tiny human dramas, Remiet hardly ever concentrated on faces in this way. Most of his figures have the same neutral, mask-like stares, pointed chins, downturned mouths and drawn-in cheeks. None of them has the complexity of character that Death has here. They tend to be bony in their bodies too, and no one is obese, that is, except for fat Death, who has no 'figure'. In her grossness she is unlike any other person he ever pictured, and filling her face is one of the rare smiles in his whole oeuvre. It is etched into the bone as if it were the holes cut in a mask, a *rictus*

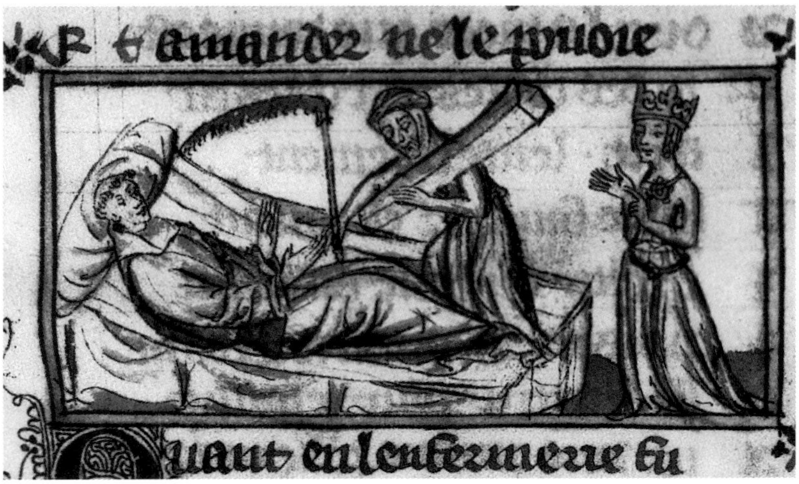

90. French or Flemish illuminator, late fourteenth century. Douai, Bibliothèque Municipale, MS 768, fol. 94. *Pèlerinage de vie humaine.* Death and the pilgrim; Grace Dieu stands by.

of uncomprehending horror with her teeth, the only parts of our skeletons that are visible throughout our lives, jutting up loose in the large jaw. This emphasis upon the mouth recalls Bartholomeus Anglicus's etymology whereby 'death (*mort*) is so called because it bites *(mord)* horribly', and the notion of death as a hungry devouring animal 'who would rather sink her teeth into a rich lady with a smooth white bosom than into a scrawny old woman', in the words of Gautier de Coincy, is here reversed so that the old woman is herself feeding and fattening herself on others.[3] Remiet created this glacial masterpiece using white paint for the glint of chalky bone and metallic scythe, but he left the rest of the image a tonal gradation of greys, except for the dense black on the bedclothes where the great visitor casts her ominous shadow. There is no other place in Remiet's work where a body, or anything else for that matter, casts a shadow. Only she is substantial enough as a body to obscure the constancy of illumination; only Death is so life-like as to make Remiet into a realist painter.

Remiet has left out of the scene altogether the figure of Grace Dieu, or Grace of God, who in miniatures in other manuscripts of Deguileville's narrative at this point, hovers around the deathbed to explain to and comfort the pilgrim (Fig. 90). It is she who reveals the identity of the person before him: 'See this is Death (*la Mort*),' she explains, 'the most terrible of things. She seeks to put an end to your life and to put all in decline and to place your body in her coffin and to take it to be food for stinking worms. This is the common experience of all men and women. Man in this world is exposed to Death as is the grass in the meadow to the scythe, for that which is green today is dry tomorrow.'[4] This metaphor was a common biblical one and is visible painted on the expansive wall of death in the Campo Santo in Pisa, where the old woman with bat-like wings swoops down upon her victims with a scythe (Fig. 91). But this fresco, painted nearly half a century before, is a totally different projection of life's end. Devils grasp the pudgy little souls of cardinals and queens from out of their obscenely open mouths. As opposed to this public mass death at the site of a cemetery, Remiet's is a more intimate and thoroughly individual experience in the space of a book.

The speechless and terrified expression on the face of the dying man, trapped in the heavy bedclothes like a baby tightly bound in its swaddling bands, his head swathed in a sweaty cloth, is also something that the illuminator has emphasized. We are able to 'read' his face only in these final moments, rather like the doomed physiognomy of plague victims described by a doctor, Simon of Corvino: 'Hardly is there one whose face does not pale; merely in the expression of women and men can the dire writing be read, and the imminent calamity of death on the way is betokened by pallid signs . . . death is seen seated in the face.'[5] Alexander Neckham had described how for three days before the death of a man the brightness of the pupil is already darkened so that 'the image of an observer does not appear in it', the eyes being thought to be the parts of the body which die first.[6] One of the means of verifying death was thus not just the candle or feather held before the mouth to register the exhalation of breath, but the apposition of mirrors and objects against the pupil to see if the eye has lost its capacity to represent, to take in and emit the visual rays upon which sight, cognition and the vital spirit depend. The sunken ghostliness that all medical sources describe as the very first signs of death's approach is clearly visible in the grey half-lidded glimmer lodged in the face of Remiet's bedridden pilgrim. The dead cannot see.

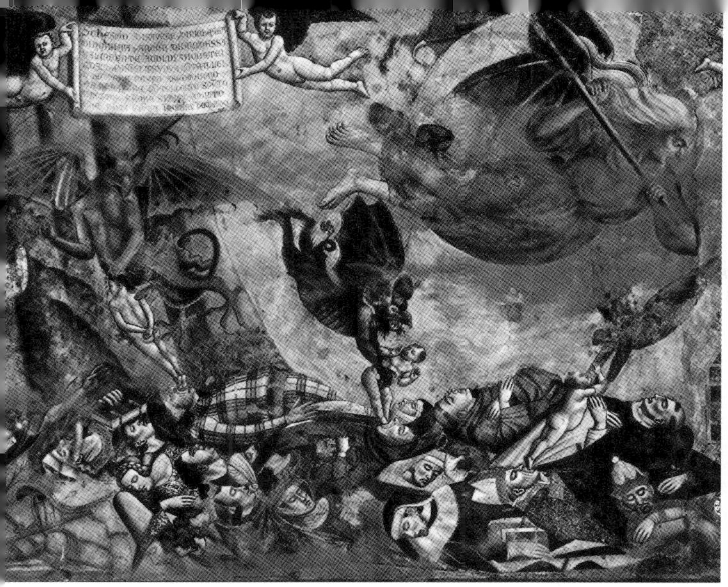

91. Buffalmacco, *The Triumph of Death*, fresco, south wall, Pisa, Campo Santo.

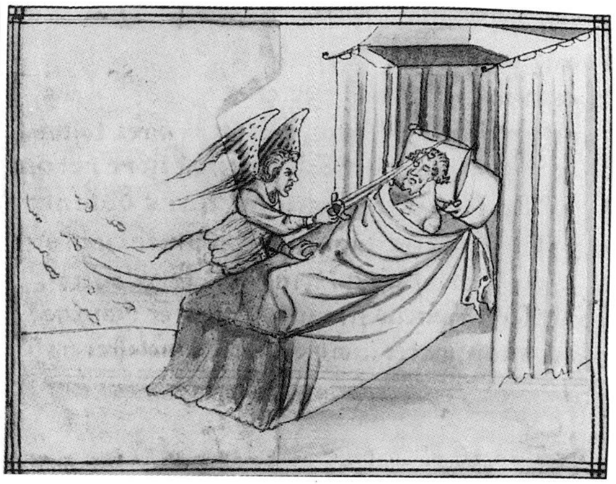

92. Remiet. New York, Pierpont Morgan Library, M.526, fol. 14v (detail). Hermann de Valenciennes, *Histoire de la Bible*. The angel of death visits the first-born of Egypt (right half damaged).

Sometimes Death came to her victims when their eyes were closed, when they were asleep, as does the angel of death to the first-born of Egypt in Hermann de Valenciennes's *Histoire de la Bible*, in which Remiet represents the other traditional weapon, the sword, rather than the scythe (Fig. 92). The idea of the sword or dart of death as a weapon was common in the fourteenth century, especially linked with the plague, and here it represents the retributary justice of the end come too soon as punishment.[7] The scythe is, by contrast with the sword, not a weapon but a tool used in the cyclic replenishment of the fields in continual generation and decay. Its cutting edge is not justice but time. Death's two attributes are crucial in the narrative of development/decay that we are to follow. The wooden coffin is described not as the pilgrim's future bed but merely as a means of transporting him to worms in the ground, which evokes the future of the body that we shall discuss in Chapter 5. The scythe is what splices the link between body and soul, allowing the latter to find the freedom we shall examine in Chapter 6.

The visual misogyny that was so evident in Remiet's illustrations to Deschamps's *Lay de la fragilité humaine*, and which there articulated the ambiguous role of women as the origins of life, is also clearly evident in his depiction of death. In the *Pèlerinage* miniature, far from being a floating and ethereal angel, Death steps up between her victim's legs on to the bed, the shaft of her scythe pointing at his genitals. The bed is not only the site of birth as well as dreams, and thus so often the site at which Remiet stages his miniatures, it is also the place of sex, of what the *Lay* describes as the vile conception that sets the sad sequence of life in squirming motion with the spilling of the spirit in man's seed. The pilgrim's fevered upward gaze also reminds us of the loss of man's natural innate heat that Aristotle believed came with orgasm and death.[8] Women, by contrast, were described as lacking warmth and were thus not only insatiably addicted to the act of coitus, which through friction and penetration transferred life-giving warmth from male to female, but were thus at the same time associated with the coldness of heat-devouring death. Even the colour against which Remiet articulates the end is cold, wet and feminine. Throughout the manuscript he has retained a fascinating alternating system of miniatures:

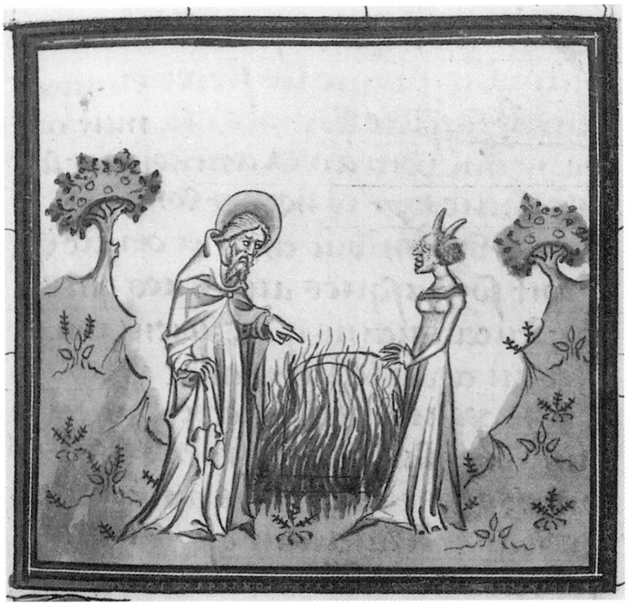

93. Remiet. London, British Library, MS Lansdowne 1179, fol. 268. *Miroir historial*. St Anthony tempted by the devil in the form of a woman.

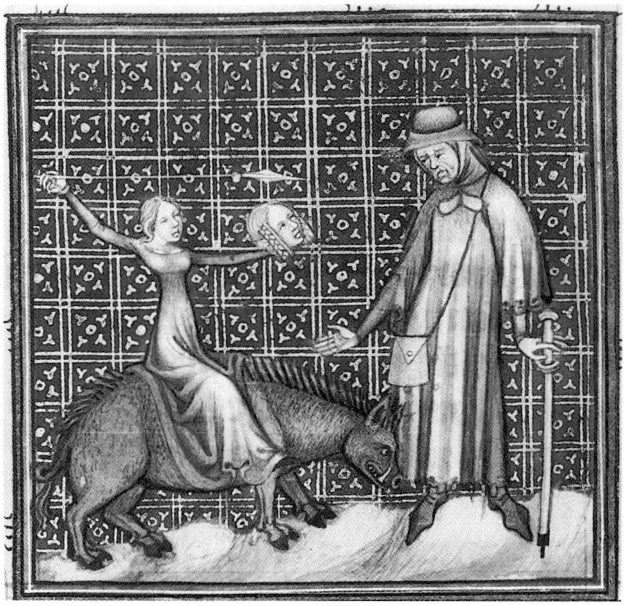

94. Remiet. Paris, Bibliothèque Nationale, fr. 823, fol. 71. *Pèlerinage de vie humaine*. The mask of Luxury/Venus.

a bright, warm-coloured miniature in which the figures are painted in full colour is followed by a cold, blue-background scene with figures painted in rich grey grisaille. This creates a dynamic of chromatic pulsations throughout the pilgrimage of life that is more evidence for its luxurious royal status. But occasionally it has meaning, as here, where at this, the coldest moment in human life, the miniature chills, with white and blue evoking even in the background pattern, sharp, glassy ice. Insatiable in her feminine desire, forever seeking the fire of union, every woman carried the scythe as Death does here. And every time the male had intercourse he suffered the 'little death'. The possible perversity of the deathbed scene in fourteenth-century terms is given a further gendered twist in that Death is 'on top' and man is at her mercy, passive and open to the thrust of her erect tool.

The association of death and woman was not only grammatical, *mors* and *la mort* being feminine, it was part of traditional exegesis. St Jerome had described death as *domina*, and she appears as a monstrous rider in the Apocalypse that Remiet would have seen carved on the west front of Notre Dame in Paris. In a different tradition she was a Fury-like female in the Roman image of *Atropos*, painted by Remiet's associates in illustrating classical texts and in the great frescoed graveyard at Pisa (Fig. 91).[9] The illuminator had painted many scenes of 'death entering through the eyes' in the form of the fascinating female body which was thought to lead men to sin. He had pictured St Anthony in his ascetic struggle of renunciation in the desert being tempted by the devil in the form of a beautiful woman (Fig. 93). The saint points to the flames of Hell between them as if to say, this is where you will lead me. Significantly too the face of the woman, which apart from its horns is that of a beautiful courtly lady, has been effaced by a later reader in the same way that the faces of demons and the evil eye are rubbed away in other manuscripts. For at least one reader of this book, to look at a woman's face was literally to behold the devil. Erasure of the 'evil eye' in manuscripts, this visible trace of fear on parchment, includes not only figures of devils and women but here also of the death they to some extent signified.[10]

Death's fascination in Remiet's portrayal (Fig. 89) was, however, somewhat different. No one later sought to erase her far more horrifying visage from Remiet's scene. For while the devil can be avoided, death cannot. It could be argued that Remiet makes her faceless: a skull is no longer a person but an idea of the inevitable. But against this it is clear that she is one of the most individual beings Remiet created, as he endowed this bony, noseless cranium with more character and expression than all of his other figures

95. Master of the Coronation of Charles VI. The Hague, Museo Mermanno-Westreenianum, MS 10.D.1, fol. 110. Aristotle, *Éthiques*. Science, Art, Prudence (with a death's head), Entendement and Sapience.

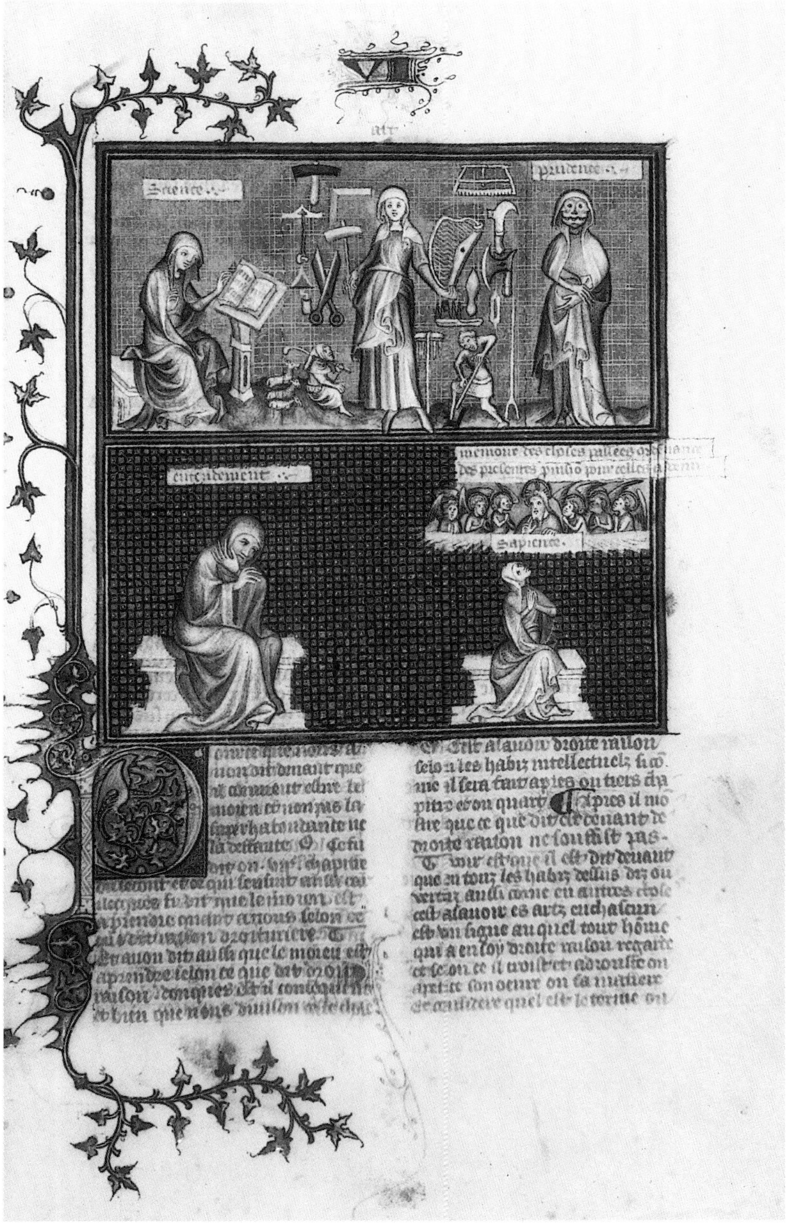

96. Remiet. Chantilly, Musée Condé, MS 277–1327, fol. 107. Aristotle, *Éthiques*. Science, Art, Prudence (without a death's head), Entendement and Sapience.

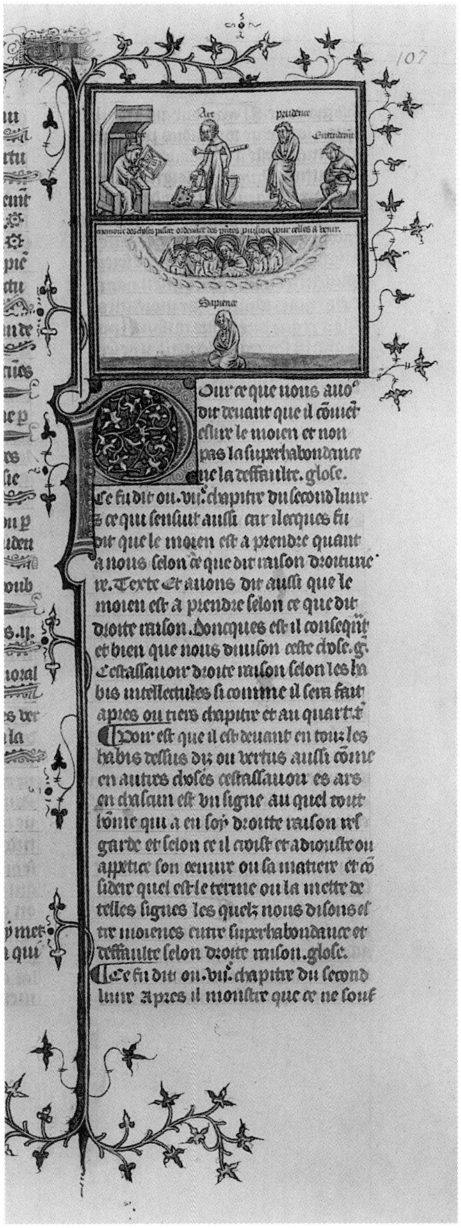

where we see, in T. S. Eliot's phrase, 'the skull beneath the skin'. For male churchmen like Jean Gerson and Pierre d'Ailly, the beautiful face of a girl was as horrifying and fascinating an object as that of a skull anyway. Earlier in the *Pèlerinage de vie humaine* the pilgrim encounters one of the Seven Deadly Sins, Luxury, who rides on a boar and who is described as having a mask of white beauty to cover her deadly face. Remiet makes both mask and face identically ideal (Fig. 94). This is a place where other illuminators depicted the skull or rot beneath the mask of appearances but Remiet, perhaps in divergence from his model, did not. Was it because he wanted to keep all the shock value of the skull for his climax?

What did the fleshless head mean to Remiet? It was by 1393 no longer a shocking subject. Illuminators had used it for over a century in depicting popular legends like that of 'The Three Living and the Three Dead' and in illustrating medical manuscripts.[11] It was visible not only in books but on walls of churches in similarly didactic images, in many carved tombs and even on street signs, like that of the 'sign of the Three Living and Three Dead' in Paris. Remiet used the skull very rarely and even avoided it in another important instance. In 1398 Louis d'Orléans ordered from Thevenin de l'Angevin a double volume set of Aristotle's works, and the latter provided Remiet with a model in the form of the small de luxe *livre de poche* set that had been copied in 1376 by Raoulet d'Orléans for Charles V and which is now in The Hague.[12] Here in Book VI of the *Ethics*, Remiet would have seen the three personifications of the Aristotelian intellectual virtues, Science, Art and Prudence (Fig. 95). Science, representing scholary inquiry, reads at a lectern, Art stands gracefully holding or surrounded by the floating tools and depictions of the various mechanical arts, while the third, Prudence, is motionless and without attributes. Her three faces – two in profile and a central frontal one – form a staring, grinning skull. Explained by an inscription, these refer to 'Memory of things past, ordering of things present and provision for things to come'.[13] Prudence does not simply look forward to death, her face becomes death.

Perhaps alerted to this strange reading, not only did Remiet *not* copy the skull into Louis d'Orléans manuscript, he reconfigured the whole scene (Fig. 96). Significant again in terms of his gender bias, he changed the sex of Science, who is now a male university scholar at his desk. Art is still a lady but she struggles with the heavy equipment of music and carpentry like a housewife carrying too much shopping. Moreover, Prudence is now a bearded male figure, his arms folded in a position similar to the mysterious old man in Remiet's Augustinian image of the Fall, also made for the same prince (see Fig. 30). Understanding, or Entendement, is a courtly gentleman rather than a shrouded sage, his arms folded, also squeezed into the top register. Only Wisdom, or Sapience, is close to the transcendental vision in the model, but rather than gazing up to heaven, she ignores it. Seated on the ground rather than a throne, she is surrounded by emptiness. While the earlier version of Book VI evoked the 'art of dying' alongside the arts of philosophy and the mechanical arts of making, Remiet sees knowledge in individual psychological terms rather than in personifications. Besides being the best example of his changing images to suit the intellectual introspection of his princely patron, it says something about the artist himself. It is his clearest avoidance of death in the form of a skull, which in his model was perhaps placed too close to the book (science) and the tools of image-making (art), the emblems of his own trade.

Old Age

I have become Total-Image, which is to say, Death in person. Roland Barthes[14]

Consider your birth the beginning, your life the middle, and your death the culmination. If you are handsome, if you are strong, if you are young, wait a little; ponder the end and draw the conclusion. Alas comes a little fever and your beauty pales. Comes a little illness and your strength drains away. Comes old age and your youth is gone forever. Pierre d'Ailly[15]

The impact of the moment of death that Remiet pictured at the end of the *Pèlerinage de vie humaine* must also be seen in terms of what people saw leading up to it and also the ways in which it was thought possible, temporarily at least, to defer it. There is no better way of sensing this than to examine what leads up to the climax of the allegorical journey of the pilgrimage of life as it is described in Deguileville's poem and visualized in Remiet's miniatures. A few pages before the deathbed scene, the pilgrim encounters Death's two messengers – an old woman with two crutches tied to her neck and with feet of lead and another carrying a bed on her head and who has her skirts tied up about her waist 'as if she were a wrestler' (Fig. 97). The latter represents Infirmity and she comes to grapple with rich and poor, weak and strong, telling the pilgrim that no medicines, plasters or ointments can stop her squeezing all the strength out of her victims and gaining the fall. She sometimes has to wrestle with Health and occasionally loses because of the interference of Medicine, although no ointments or plasters prevent her from gaining a fall when Death has sent her to attack. Eating the flesh and drinking the blood of her victims, Deguileville's Infirmity is in the tradition of all-devouring, gobbling Death, and yet she is friendly. Remiet represents her as a stout old woman and in the text she has a benign banter because her onslaught is not, like that of the vices, an outright attack, but a game which she can lose. Like Obedience, who in the opposite miniature of the first column rips out the pilgrim's tongue, they come to remind the body of its status and to prepare to face the end. Remiet has used the alternating warm and cold colour scheme again, in which bright vermillion in the first miniature of painful tongue-pulling, contrasts with sepulcral white for the wasted faces and bodies of the two harbingers of death, who hobble across a cold, blue background. The only continuity in the two miniatures is the earth, pale green and itself wasted, with dry shoots sticking out of a ground that, not only throughout this pilgrimage of human life, but throughout Remiet's own life from his earth-obsessed drawings in the *Lay de la fragilité humaine* to his very last works, defines the ground-line of bumpy and uneven human existence.

The other crone, who brings the pilgrim crutches, is Old Age herself, who, by contrast to Illness the lady wrestler, is more courteous. She beats her victims more slowly over a longer period of time but leaves them 'crippled and impotent', wracked with pain and either wise or, like children, without any wits at all. Deguileville, in choosing wizened old women to represent the vices in his poem, and even Death herself in his text, was following a long-held physiognomical and medical tradition which linked the old woman, or *vetula*, with the pernicious dry and cold qualities of mortification.[16] Allegory is often

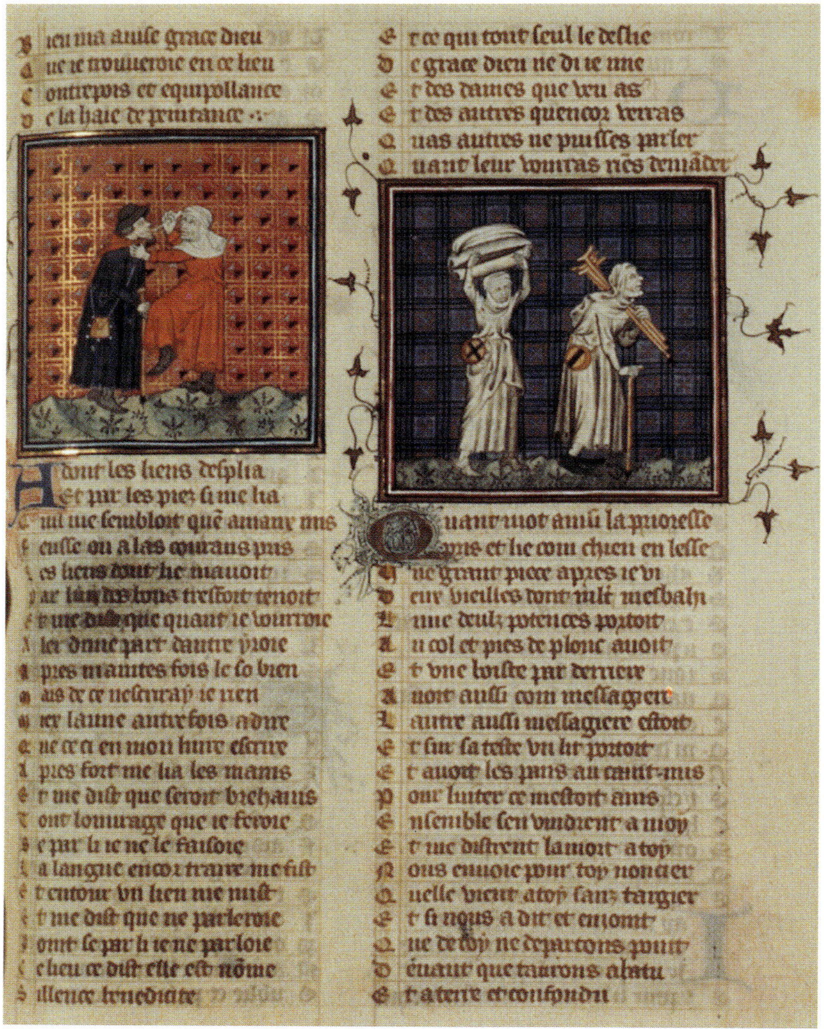

97. Remiet. Paris, Bibliothèque Nationale, fr. 823, fol. 91. *Pèlerinage de vie humaine.* Obedience binds the pilgrim's tongue; Old Age and Infirmity arrive.

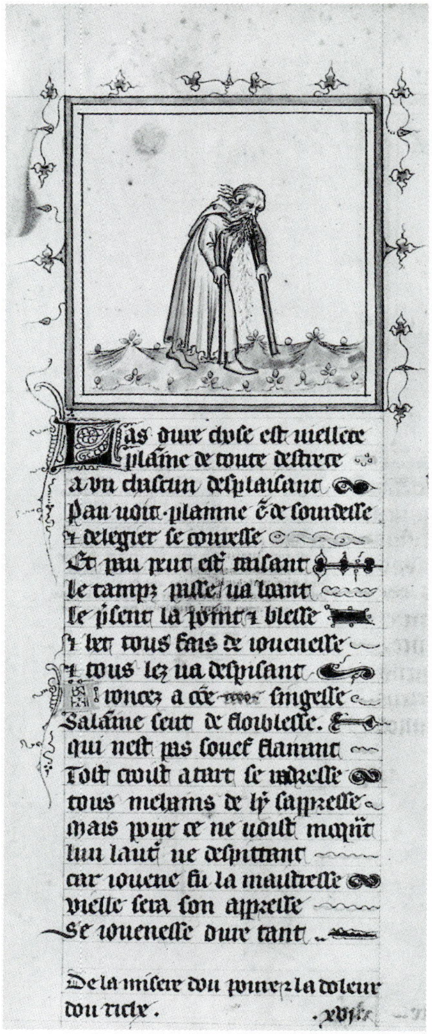

98. Remiet. Paris, Bibliothèque Nationale, fr. 20029, fol. 10. *Lay de la fragilité humaine.* The hard thing that is Old Age.

described as a disembodied and distant mode of discourse, but here Deguileville somatizes each allegorical act so that it registers more profoundly than any realism, the individual facing the inevitable decline, the dry rot as medievals understood it. Remiet's characters too are powerful embodiments of process, capturing in a single gesture or attribute the creeping continuity of life's conflict with forces of decay and decrepitude. The pilgrim, as a result of the violent ministrations of Infirmity and Old Age, is left prostrate and waiting only for the arrival of the final blow, from their sister with the scythe.

These allegorical images can be contrasted with another striking picture of senility that Remiet had produced in the *Lay* ten years earlier (Fig. 98). This describes that 'hard thing (*dure chose*)' that is old age, and relates how people used to live to great ages in the past, whereas today 'few now reach forty years, very few sixty. If, however, one does reach old age, his heart weakens straightaway and his head shakes, his spirit fails and his breath stinks, his face wrinkles and his back bends, his eyes dim and his joints falter, his nose runs and his hair falls out, his touch trembles and his competence fails, his teeth rot and his ears become dirty.'[17] The 'hard thing that is old age' is presented even more powerfully in verse by Deschamps, who, because of the feminine noun, creates a portrait of a withered old woman, wrinkled as a she-monkey ('fronciez est comme singesse'), following medical traditions of describing the marasmic or wasting face.[18] Interestingly, Remiet chose to represent this more sympathetic old figure not as an old woman, like those personifications in the *Pèlerinages*, but as a man. The old are described as 'stingy, greedy, dejected and complaining, quick to speak and slow to listen' – an imbecilic return to the cradle. Remiet's image is less cruel and embodies, rather than a grotesque second childhood, a weakening and failing of the body that demands a use of two crutches by the bent, bald figure. Phlegm spits from his mouth as he hobbles along across the same knobbled terrain that his personified essences will struggle over ten years later in the *Pèlerinage*. In this second infancy the processes of the grave have already begun.

In the *Pèlerinage* illustrations Remiet was careful to personalize the allegory so that the pilgrim ages in the course of his journey. After the onslaught of the vices and despairing that he will never find salvation, he loses his staff of faith and is shown prostrate, as if lifeless, his face marked by a beard and a distinctly older physiognomy than when he began (Fig. 99). From the clouds above, Grace Dieu comes to the rescue and restores his staff and his desire for salvation. He has another visitor to his bedside before the arrival of Death, a lady – Mercy – who comes to give him suck and who literally returns the feeble old man to an infant at the breast (Fig. 100). What leads up to the thread of his life being cut in Deguileville's poem makes the final image far more positive an experience for a person who has had his full threescore years and ten. These scenes of the old, bedridden pilgrim can be compared with a miniature in a

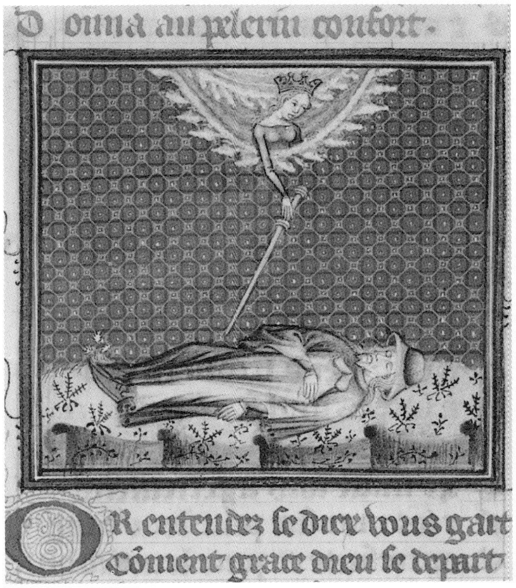

99. Remiet. Paris, Bibliothèque Nationale, fr. 823, fol. 74v. *Pèlerinage de vie humaine*. Grace Dieu returns the pilgrim's staff of hope.

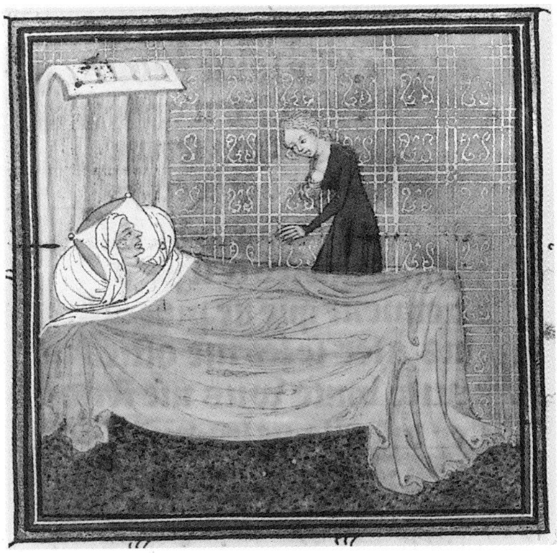

100. Remiet. Paris, Bibliothèque Nationale, fr. 823, fol. 93. *Pèlerinage de vie humaine*. Mercy offers the pilgrim her breast.

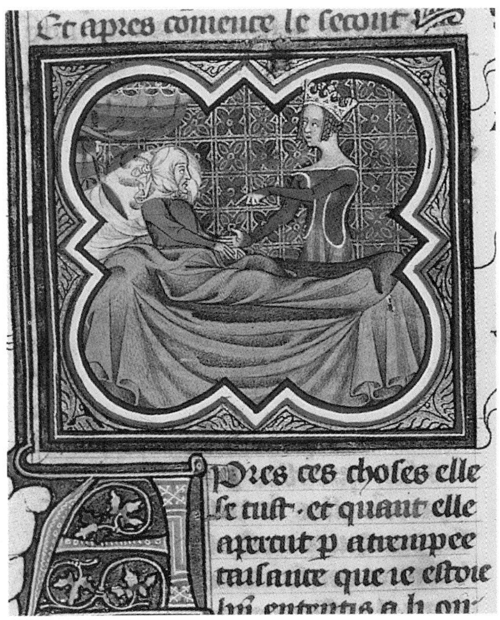

101. Remiet and others. Besançon, Bibliothèque Municipale, MS 434, fol. 300v. *Consolation de Philosophie*. Sick and old, Boethius sees Lady Philosophy at his bedside.

'mirror for princes' made for Charles V in 1372, heading Book II of one of the most influentual of all medieval texts, Boethius's *Consolation de Philosophie* (Fig. 101). The poet lies not in prison but in bed, his head swathed in the same sweatbands or nightcap worn by the pilgrim, trapped in his decrepit body and comforted only by the soothing words, the medicine, of Lady Philosophy. In making such images Remiet learned, as a twenty-year-old, to delineate what Boethius called 'the misery of my old age'.[19]

Because the fatal moment was more of a social process than an individual one, it was not easy to depict. There was no visible sign, like the elevation of the host or the ringing of bells, that so carefully separated various moments of the mass for onlookers. Remiet too was literally not able to draw the line between life and death, since his miniature shows the dying man's shock at seeing the arrival of Death and not the moment when she separates his soul from his body. The exact moment of death was difficult to pin down both pictorially and medically. Deguileville's description and Remiet's image of Death about to step on the chest of her victim, to crush and constrain him, suggest the stopping of the heart – the most vital of the organs, according to then-current medical views. For this was not just a pump but the centre of animation and, according to Aristotle, of sensation in the body. Medical theories of ageing and the causes of death also lay behind the metaphor of Deguileville's poem of the green grass becoming hay and needing to be cut down by the scythe. This is suggestive of the predominant theory of ageing which involved the loss of what was called radical moisture. According to one medical theorist, Bernard of Gordon, 'some have said that the cause of the natural death of the body . . . is the potential dissimilarity and contrariety of nutriment to that body, . . . which acts upon the living body and its heat, continually altering and weakening it'.[20] This had been maintained by many Parisian professors, including Albertus Magnus, who in his treatise on ageing, *De aetate*, describes the inevitability of decay being due to the fact that 'food is not wholly assimilable to the human body, life therefore cannot be perpetual' and 'dryness is the primary condition of senility. The whole body, like a land parched with drought, loses its watery vitality.' For Galen, from the moment of birth this innate heat and moisture was decreasing. Roger Bacon used the metaphor of a lamp: 'the heat drying up the substance, or moisture, it uses as fuel'.[21]

Was there anything that could halt this dry dessication, the inexorable onslaught of old age and death? The legends of the fountain of youth that were carved on ivory mirrorbacks and courtly coffers reveal a yearning for everlasting beauty that was also discussed by the doctors of the day. Roger Bacon's treatise on old age includes seven prescriptions against it. These youth potions include potable gold, the flesh of vipers, corals, pearls, rosemary, dragonsblood and the exuviae from young beautiful people. Drugs made from the fat or flesh of the recently dead, known as *mumia* or 'mummy', were especially popular.[22] Some of the unusual mineral and vegetable ingredients in this list explain the precious pearls, gems and other unusual objects which were collected in their hundreds by the Duke of Orléans and other members of the royal family, not because they were 'curiosities' for their nascent museums, but because they were effective amulets against ills and preventative medicine as the medievals understood it. The medicinal properties of various precious stones were recounted in Book XVI of Bartholomeus Anglicus's encyclopaedia on the properties of things, which the Valois princes and their entourage knew in the translation of Jean Corbechon. For the sickly and pathologically frail line of rulers, for the mother of Charles VI especially, Jeanne de Bourbon, death could be warded off by the strange white stones of St Margaret, which also protected his wife, Isabeau de Bavaria, in childbirth. As we take vitamins with the same belief in building up indomitable resistance, the medievals grasped at rubies, emeralds and lapis lazuli, the very stuff from which Remiet made parts of his immortal miniature worlds.[23] The relationship between manuscript illuminators and magic has not been fully researched, but medieval book painters along with metalworkers were often associated with alchemists because of the materials they used in their work.[24] The many blood-red dragons, monstrous beasts and birds that Remiet painted in the borders of manuscripts are not only apotropaic, like the gargoyles projecting in stone from his local church of Saint Séverin, they are also signs of the magical world of things that people from all walks of life believed could protect them against death.

The notion that old age was a rarity in the Middle Ages has recently come under some revision, and research on the ageing process, on actual demographics and on images of the 'Ages of Man' tradition in the period has revealed a more complex picture of a time in which many, if they lived beyond their twenties, could expect to reach what we still consider old age today.[25] For St Thomas old age began at fifty, for Dante, at forty-five, while Deschamps in the *Lay de la fragilité humaine* uses the usual sixty, which was when soldiers serving the king had to retire. Cicero, whose *De senectute* was in the libraries of Louis d'Orléans and many others at the time, saw old age as liberation from sensuous appetites and passions, a time of wisdom. There was indeed a tension between young and old in a society in which authority was based upon tradition and maintaining the hierarchy. The retirement forced upon the elderly by physical weakness came for most men when they could no longer ride a horse, but as the poet Jean Molinet confessed, 'I see harsh old age coming to torment me. I shall have to give up writing and dictation.'[26] When was it deemed advisable for an illuminator to put down his pen and colours?

In 1401 when Remiet was given the job of illuminating the prestigious copy of Bartholomeus Anglicus's *Propriétés des choses* for Philippe le Hardi, he was already past middle age. Here he painted one of the most magnificent variations on his beloved corpse, which we shall examine in the next chapter (see Fig. 124), so it is clear that his powers of creative re-combination were not dimmed. However, his lavish four-part frontispiece of the Creation in this manuscript, which we examined in Chapter 1, looks as though it could have been created decades before, the very format harking back to the golden age of Charles V with its quatrefoil frames and flatly luminous figures (see Fig. 4). In the lower

102. Remiet. Brussels, Bibliothèque Royale, MS 9094, fol. 12. *Livre des propriétés des choses*. Frontispiece (detail): youth and old men in the lower margin.

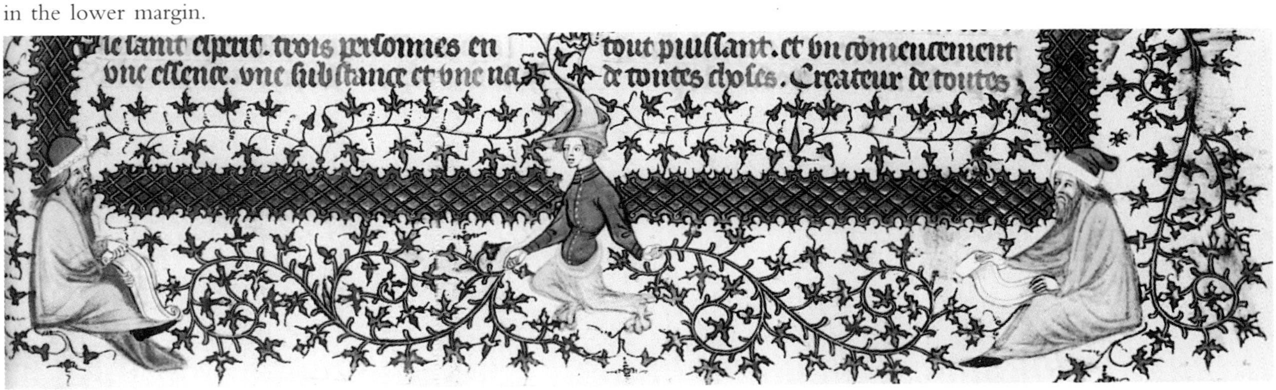

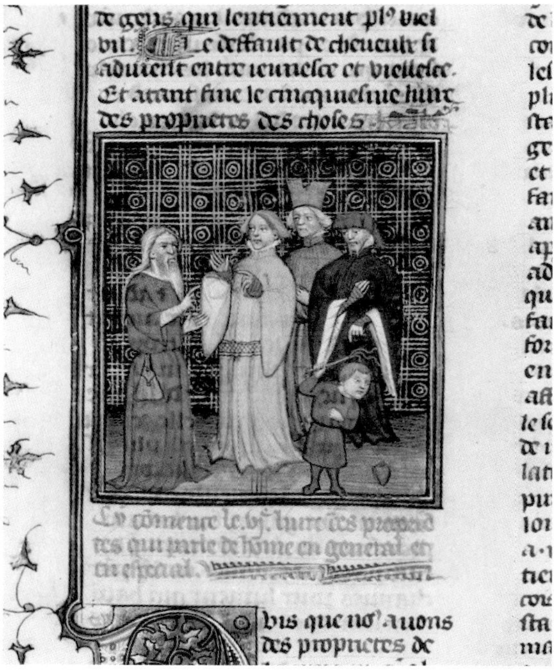

103. Virgil Master. Brussels, Bibliothèque Royale, MS 9094, fol. 94v. *Livre des propriétés des choses*. The ages of man.

margins two old prophets with long beards hold scrolls and flank the figure of a sprightly youth with a pointed cap and the lower quarters of an animal, who holds the flowering tendrils together at the centre (Fig. 102). This image presages the conflict between youth and age, common in fourteenth-century society, that plays itself out in this very manuscript. In addition to the frontispiece, six of the miniatures in the manuscript are by Remiet, but others are by younger illuminators, Jean de Nizières and the Virgil Master, both of whom appeared in the 1393 *Pèlerinages* when one of them was perhaps apprenticed to Remiet, though now, ten years later, both are his competitors. The Virgil Master especially was very prolific at this time and he was given the job of illustrating the chapter 'de homme en general et en especial' (Fig. 103). This shows five 'ages of man', a child whipping a top, a young dandy in pink, and two middle-aged gentleman behind, one clean-shaven, the other bearded. The fifth age, seen in the bearded old man on the left, seems to admonish them all. Contrasting the carefree pleasures of childhood, the responsibilities of middle age and the stern, woeful accusations of decrepitude, this miniature is part of a tradition of illustrating this chapter which has been described as emphasizing 'the themes of the transience of youth and the vanity of things in the world'.[27] What this image does not show is death itself as a phase in human life – the dead as 'an age group'.[28] This younger man's image of the ages of man has many of the stylistic features that a new generation of illuminators were adopting in the years around 1400, notably a wider colouristic range with fuller, fleshier features in face and figure. Remiet, who was supervising the production of this royal commission of the *Propriétés des choses*, would have been, to this younger painter, the greybeard, the admonishing master, working in an 'old' manner.

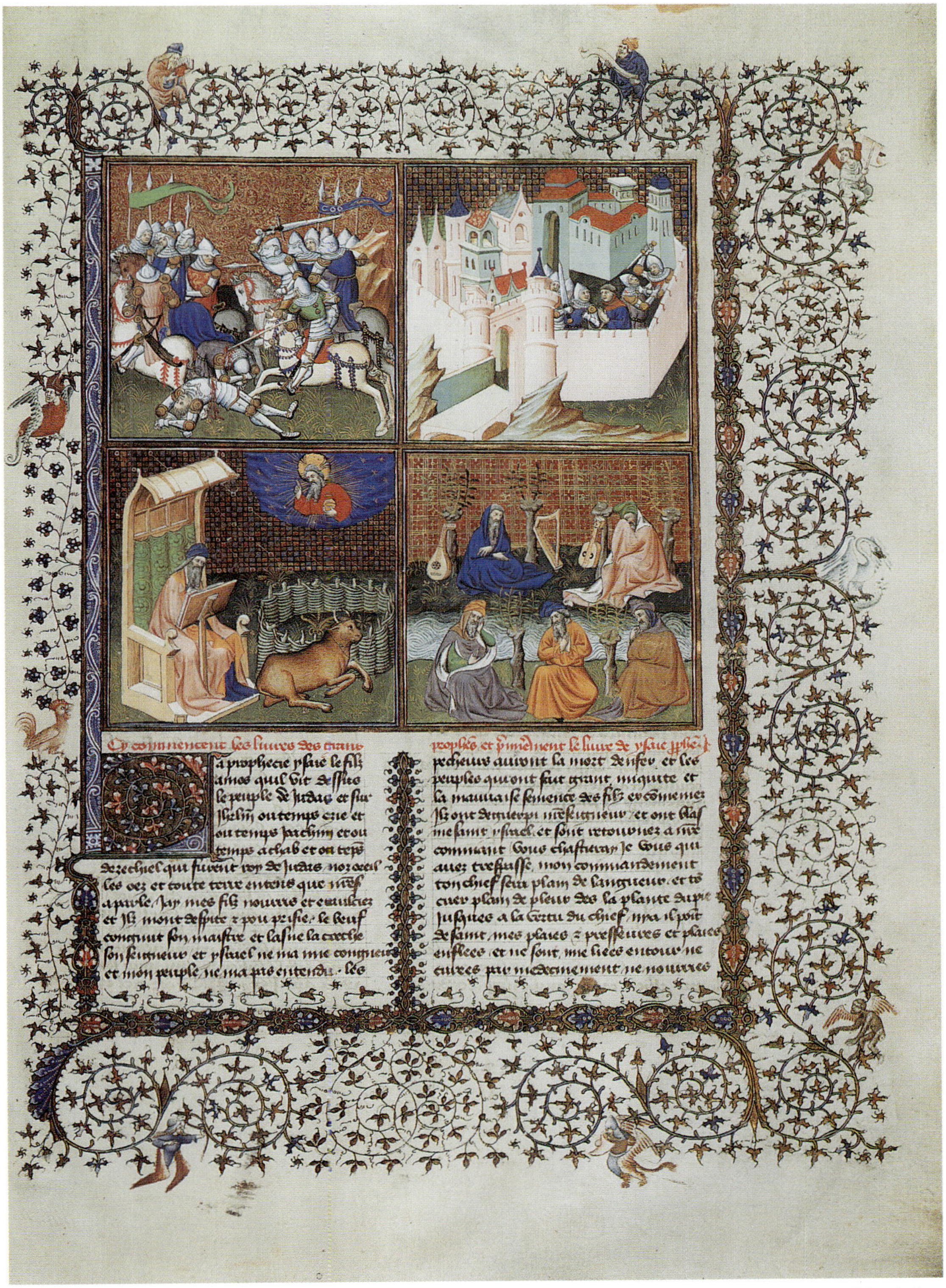

104. Frontispiece by the Master of Berry's Cleres Femmes, borders by Petrus Gilberti, monsters and birds by Remiet. Brussels, Bibliothèque Royale, MS 9002, fol. 61. *Bible historiale.*

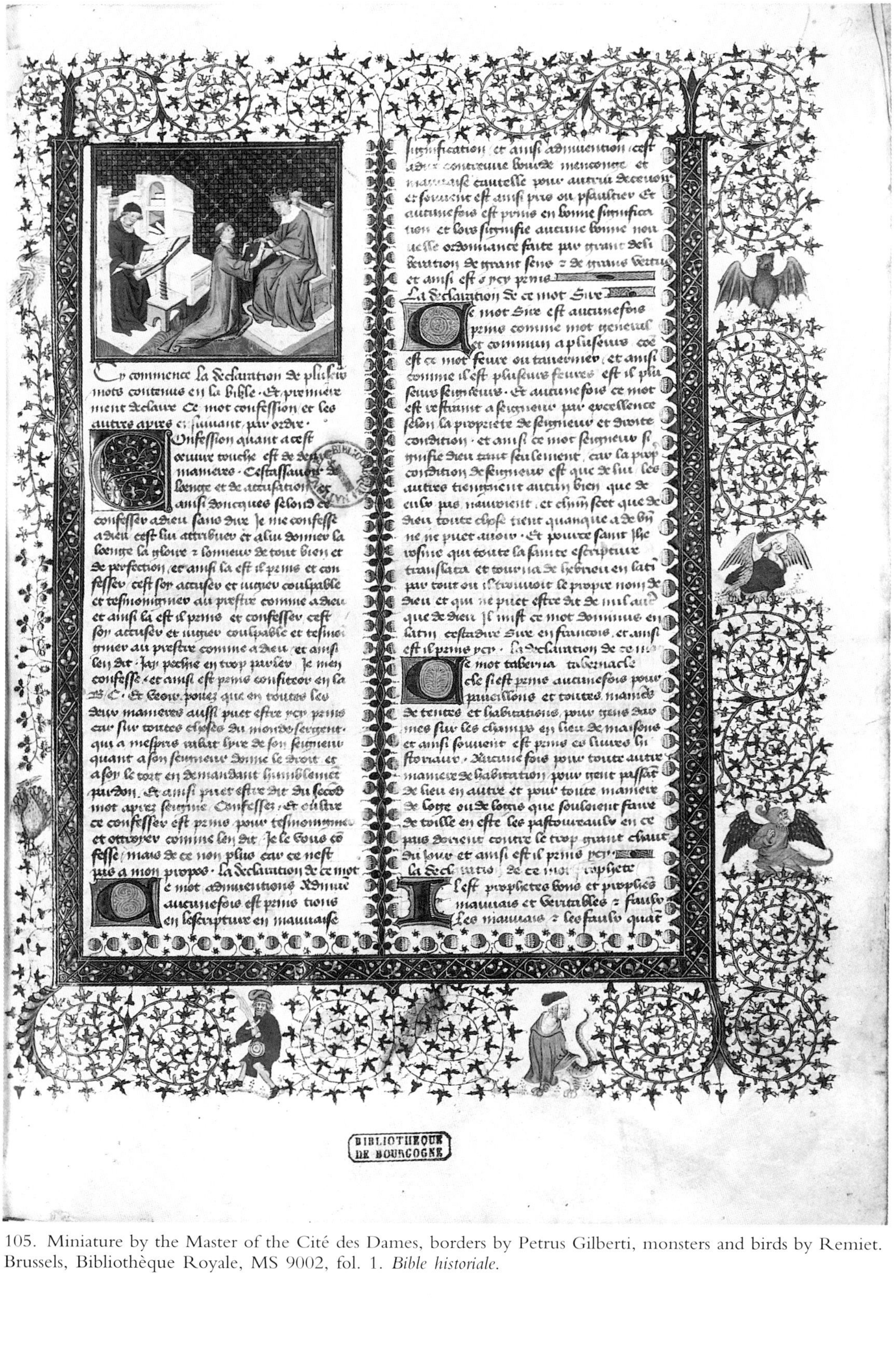

105. Miniature by the Master of the Cité des Dames, borders by Petrus Gilberti, monsters and birds by Remiet. Brussels, Bibliothèque Royale, MS 9002, fol. 1. *Bible historiale*.

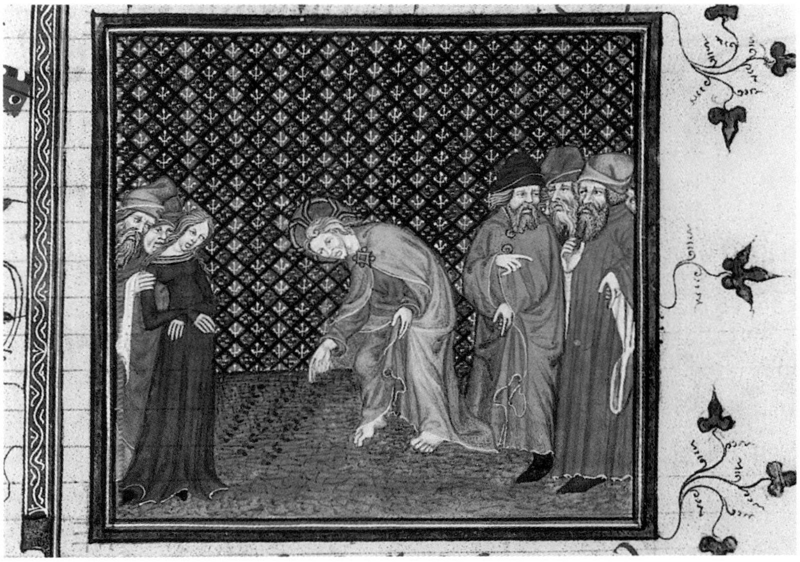

106. Remiet. Brussels. Bibliothèque Royale, MS 9002, fol. 288. *Bible historiale*. Christ and the woman taken in adultery.

Remembering the patrons for whom these illuminators were making images, it is not that surprising that their agents sought out the older, more conservative master for this commission. The man for whom this lavish volume was produced was himself in his early sixties. Philippe's favourite Book of Hours had been made for him thirty years earlier by the Boqueteaux Master and would have still seemed the very acme of refinement. Myopic but able to afford the new optical inventions of the glassmakers, the duke would have examined the tricolour quatrefoils and minute 'little trees' of Remiet's magnificent frontispiece in the Brussels encyclopaedia (see Fig. 5) with the help of a special silver lorgnon fashioned by the court goldsmith. It is exactly at this time too that illuminators depict scribes and evangelists with spectacles, suggesting their introduction for those making as well as viewing such art.[29] What seems to us *retardataire* by 1400, might not have seemed so to this patron. In imposing an external chronology of stylistic development on the history of art, we often forget the individual life trajectories that make developments far less linear and more complex than our smooth narratives suggest. As patrons grew old they could gaze with nostalgia at their old things. For artists, who survived by making and remaking, that luxury of return was not possible. There are works that show Remiet in his dotage, making a few extra derniers, perhaps at the indulgence of a friendly *libraire*. These include the highly schematized and roughly painted illustrations to a Livy in Paris (see Fig. 67) and the miniatures he completed in a romance, *Guiron le courtois*, where as a result of either haste or faltering sight, the background reticulations do not follow the straight ruled lines made for the script and often crudely overlap the dirty-green ground (see Fig. 39). Are these miniatures to be interpreted as his feeble attempts to 'keep up' with the fashion for pastel shades and more modelled surfaces after the turn of the century or, more probably, his lack of funds to buy better quality colours?

Remiet makes his last appearance in an important manuscript listed in the inventories of the dukes of Burgundy. It was made for Jean sans Peur, the murderer of Remiet's illustrious patron Louis d'Orléans, just before his own murder. This two-volume copy of the *Bible historiale* in Brussels was dated to *c.*1415 by Millard Meiss, who distinguished the work of four of its numerous illuminators but did not notice the old man whose work appears mostly in the margins (Figs. 104 and 105).[30] These folios prove that Remiet continued working to what his contemporaries would have considered a ripe old age of nearly seventy. Remiet's final efforts as an illuminator appear on the very first folio, though not in the miniature showing the royal presentation of the book, which is by a much younger artist, but in the marginal birds and monsters (Fig. 105). These alone, not the elaborate vine borders in which they are embedded, are the work of his hand. These rich, vine-swollen bar-borders were by Petrus Gilberti, who audaciously signed his name in Latin in many of the line-endings throughout the two volumes.[31] Remiet's usual birds perhaps allude to his role in the margins, for by now he is no longer the leader of a group but a minor figure in the making of this book, the delineator of the ugly, of serpent-tailed ladies and scowling half-human creatures on the edge. In the second volume, the four framed *histoires* to the Book of Prophets are the work of a talented younger artist who originated, like many of the innovators of the era, from the Low Countries, and who worked for the Duke of Berry (Fig. 104). This painter is adept at displaying both the complex spatial architecture of Babylon and the scintillating chromatic surface *varietas* of the 'International style'. Remiet's figures, by contrast, are still set in that spaceless flow of vines and 'nothing' where his art was first nurtured. Just as he had begun his career making such marginal creatures (see Fig. 21), he here ends it in a playful, foolish second childhood of winged monkeys and monsters, the dotage described so well by the poet Deschamps. In fact most of these marginal motifs were signs of old age; in addition to the bearded prophets, the whiskered ape was a common image of simian senility.[32] Remiet did not even have the keeness of eye or the steadiness of hand to make the scintillating golden-leafed borders or the line-endings on these pages. Yet someone involved in the project remembered that Remiet's forte was the ugly rather than the beautiful and made him the master of these minute, monstrous elements in the book.

The old man did, however, complete four small miniatures in the two volumes, which if seen in isolation could easily be dated half a century earlier. They are full of the confusion of someone no longer secure in the pictorial system in which he was trained, struggling to introduce depth into a system that had never used it. Such is the picture of Christ and the woman taken in adultery on fol. 288r, where he gets the feet of the Pharisees mixed up with Christ's robe, errors that result from copying without understanding (Fig. 106). His clumsy hobbling figures have swollen, arthritic feet, signs of approaching death, according to the contemporary doctor Bernard of Gordon, as though the bending figure of Christ here was an extension of the old man's own aching body. Instead of focusing on these vestiges of his now-outmoded performance, it is more charitable to think of Remiet in his still-inventive capacity as a marginal master, where the new trends encroached far less and where he could, at the end as he had at the beginning, make all sorts of references and puns. At the top of the prophets page he painted a hoary old prophet, who holds not the usual scroll but a book which he peers at short-sightedly (Fig. 105). In a more romantic age than ours and in a system that would see value in minor masters and not just major works, this would surely be taken to be Remiet's 'self-portrait'.

Illness

In former times doctors communicated with death by means of the great myth of immortality or at least of the gradually receding limits of existence. Now, these men who watch over men's lives communicate with their death in the fine, rigorous form of the gaze. Michel Foucault[33]

The confessor saves only the soul of the penitent; the surgeons, by a local remedy or even by a single word, save a finger, a hand, sometimes an arm, and therefore the livelihood of the poor sick artisan, for if he dies, his wife and children who subsist on his 'métier', die also. Henri de Mondeville, surgeon[34]

Saints Cosmas and Damian seem more like two confessors with penitents kneeling at their feet than doctors with wounded and sick folk imploring help from their healing hands in Remiet's scene in the *Miroir historial* (Fig. 107). The person who today we expect

107. Remiet. Paris, Bibliothèque Nationale, fr. 313, fol. 221. *Miroir historial.* Sts Cosmas and Damien heal the sick.

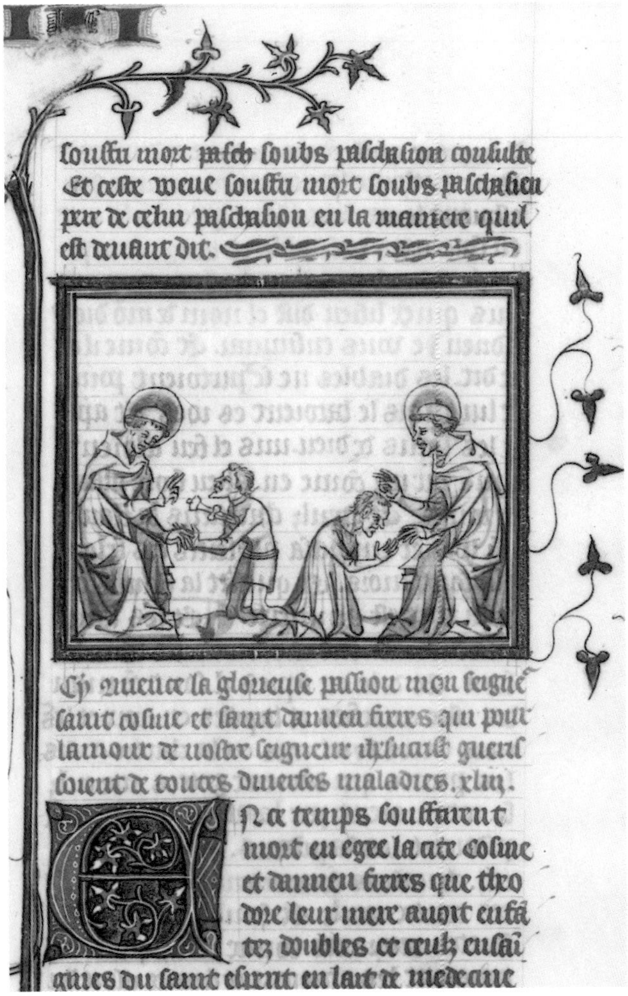

108. Remiet. New York, Pierpont Morgan Library, M.526, fol. 31v. Hermann de Valenciennes, *Histoire de la Bible.* Two doctors treat King Herod.

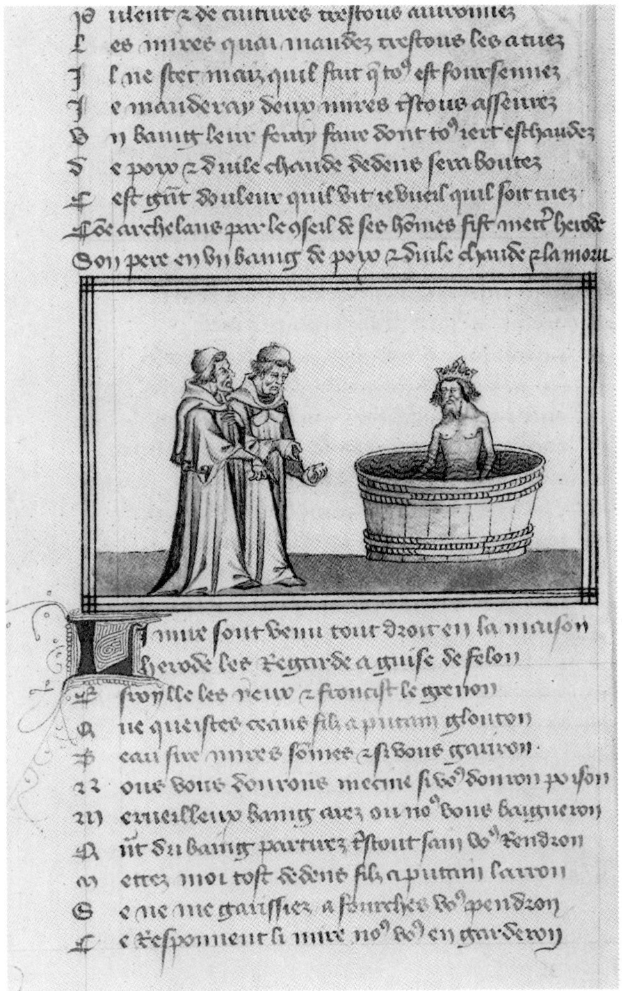

will preside over our death and who will actually proclaim us dead was most often not present at all during the demise of a person in the fourteenth century. Nobody comes between the pilgrim and the grinning skull in Remiet's picture, and certainly not a doctor. The problem of defining death of the body, still controversial today for those seeking organ transplants and those on life-support machines, was just as anxiety-provoking in the Middle Ages, but not so much because it rendered ambiguous the end of life but because it seemed to cloud the more important process beyond it. In this subtle negotiation between the realms of the living and the dead, the true specialists were not doctors but confessors. The sick were sinners and illness was punishment sent by God, which meant that medical treatment had only a secondary importance to spiritual care given those struck down by illness. The largest of the Parisian hospitals was the Hôtel Dieu next to the cathedral, which had 279 large communal beds in four large rooms and looked after 400–500 people on a day to day basis, most of whom left only for the cemetery.[35] Gerson, in his *Science de bien mourir*, remarks that only those who had received confession on the first day were admitted. The Parlement of Paris later ordered physicians to deny all treatments to those who refused to receive a confessor, interesting since it implies there were those who did! Saving souls was thus always deemed more important than saving bodies.[36]

The doctor was often feared and resented not because he cost money but because his art was still seen by many to be cheating or fiddling with the inevitable. The saintly doctors Cosmas and Damian, before whom kneels a man with a dagger stuck in his chest (Fig. 107), could of course perform miracles, but this was different. Although it was in Paris in the fourteenth century that the professionalization of medical practice developed most rapidly, the man with a medical degree from the university was far from being the general practitioner.[37] Like the two medical men dressed in their university robes who squabble among themselves while advising King Herod to take a bath in hot oil in the *Histoire de la Bible* (Fig. 108), and in which he will perish in agony, they are seen as theorists rather than as practitioners, learned quacks closer to magicians than to healers. Only the wealthy could afford to hire such expertise. Remiet's image of the quack doctors advising the inflamed Herod reminds us that, even for the ruler, proper medical help was hard to find. After his first attack of madness while riding in a forest near Le Mans in 1392, the king had been tended by the renowned and successful physician Guillaume de Harcigny, who, on his own death at the age of ninety-three a year later, would be buried in one of the first *transi* tombs (see Fig. 123). But no doctor was able to help Charles in the subsequent visitations of mania. He forgot who he was, hallucinating that he was made of glass and that he was being pricked by a thousand lead needles, and significantly (in art-historical terms), he threw things at images and tapestries, the visual ideology of Valois kingship that his father had so built up. He had a special aversion for the fleur-de-lis and the arms of France, that symbol of his own body and its interwined connections with the state.

In illustrating Psalm 52, 'Dixit inscipiens' – 'The fool said in his heart there is no God' – illuminators had often juxtaposed the wise King David and the court fool or jester. Remiet's initial to this psalm in the Manchester breviary presents nothing like this but shows instead an isolated scrawny fool waving his human-headed bauble like a parodic sceptre and running mad, holding not a ball or a loaf, as was usual, but an ambiguous

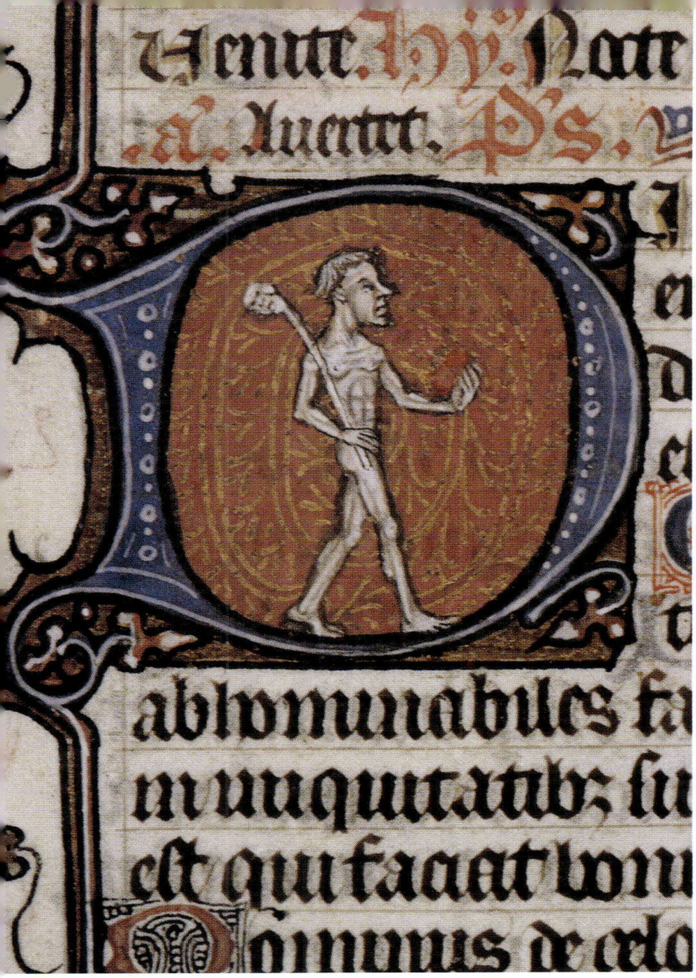

109. Remiet. Manchester, John Rylands Library, lat. 136, fol. 32v. Breviary. The naked fool of Psalm 52.

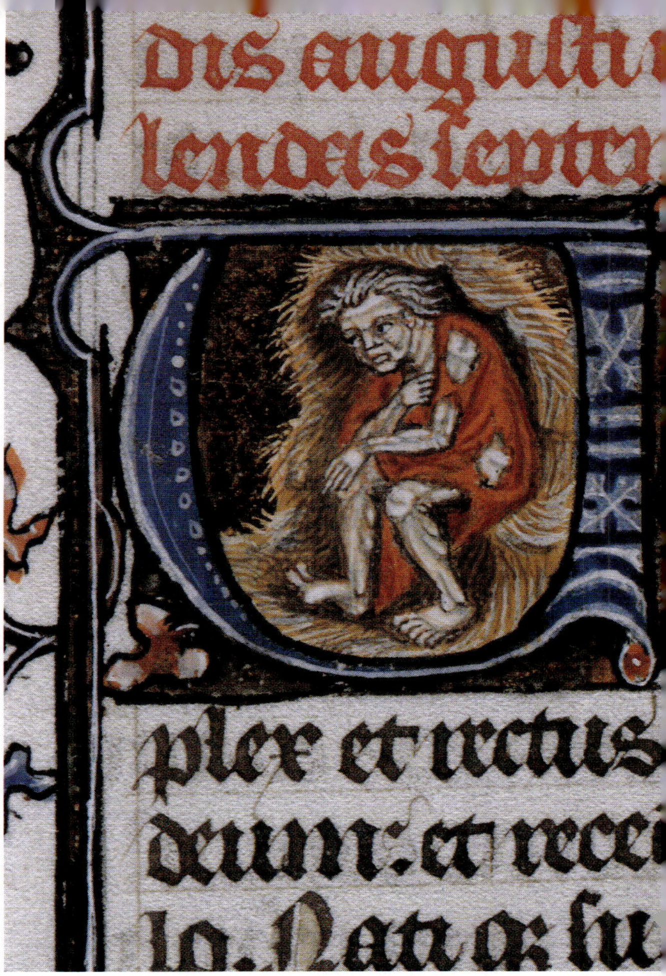

110. Remiet. Manchester, John Rylands Library, lat. 136, fol. 136. Breviary. Job.

blood-red object (Fig. 109). For Remiet and his contemporaries, the irony could not have been lost that the king and the fool were at this time indistinguishable and that the Hôtel Saint Pol was filled with the manic laughter not of the paid idiot but of the royal one. The nakedness of this lonely fool which Remiet depicted in the king-fool's brother's breviary linked his pale flesh to the lunacy of the moon and the beggarly destitution of the mentally ill in medieval society. It also evoked the nudity of the corpse, through the Book of Proverbs' description of the man who has lost his wisdom being placed 'among the dead'. There are indeed accounts of Charles VI which treat him as a living corpse, cowering in a corner unwashed and ragged like a figure of Job, his verminous clothes melding with his foetid flesh, and crying, 'if there is any one of you who is an accomplice in this evil I suffer, I beg him to torture me no longer but let me die!'[38]

Death actually came more quickly to those would-be medics who tried to relieve the king's suffering. On 30 October 1398 two Augustinian hermits, after a long day of ritual public degradation during which they were paraded in the streets of Paris wearing paper mitres, their bodies covered with strips of parchment on which their crimes were inscribed, after being stripped of their ecclesiastical office before ten bishops and a cheering crowd, were finally beheaded and their bodies quartered and hung out for display. Their crime was having attempted to cure the king's madness using powdered pearls and incantations that had been ridiculed by the apothecaries of Paris. Before their demise they made the mistake of accusing the Duke of Orléans of causing the king's illness through 'maleficia extrinseca.' Pierre Salmon, the king's biographer, had been told that the royal madness was being caused by a certain magic silver image that was made at the request of the Duke of Milan. Two more sorcerer-healers were also burnt in Paris for using diabolic invocations of the devil to the same purpose. One healer even brought the king a magic book called *Smagorad*, which, he claimed, had been given to Adam.[39]

For people of Remiet's class, the doctor was more often the local apothecary or barber-surgeon who pulled teeth, lanced boils and bled. These men were given the authority to tend wounds 'that were not mortal' by an ordinance of Charles V in 1372.[40] The court physician, like the Italian Guido da Vigevano, who was doctor to Philippe VI and also a designer of war-machines, was a theorist of death, not its preventer, probing bodies in ways that the Church found dangerous. Opening up the corpse like a book, he sought to reveal the flesh as a diagram of diseases, a practice that was still illegal in many places. The unfolding illustrations in a Chantilly manuscript of this doctor's *Anathomia* reveal a corpse that is the very opposite of Remiet's cadaver type (Fig. 111) – upright not horizontal, frontal not profile, and opened not closed. That this was something of a taboo in France compared to other centres in Europe is indicated by the fact that the first legal dissection of a corpse was permitted at the Faculty of Medicine at the University of Paris only in 1407 and then in order to perform an autopsy to verify the cause of death. While not a 'medical' image in the modern sense, Vigevano's is still a corpse under the gaze of the doctor who lays it upon the dissecting table and looks down on it.[41] This is the new anatomized body that Remiet did not touch and which was still feared and illicit in the general culture. It is death taken outside society and analyzed, unlike all of Remiet's corpses, which lay firmly within it.

Remiet depicted terrible scenes of violence wrought upon the human body by other human bodies, but like most artists of the fourteenth century, the visible pall of sickness and the body vulnerable to disease were things he avoided. Herod's skin (Fig. 108) shows no marks of disease just as Remiet's lepers are lesionless. It is not just that disease was too detailed and part of a rejected 'realistic' approach to representation. In other areas of somatic experience, mostly after death and dealing with the corpse, he filled his surfaces with much of the minutiae of decomposition. This erasure of disease may be owing to the association of sickness with the visible itself and to the impact of the Black Death of 1348–9 upon a whole generation of artists. According to one French physician, the epidemic was spread most effectively not through the air by breathing but through the eyes by looking. Basing his argument on what he calls 'Euclid's Book on Mirrors' about burning and concave mirrors, he describes a similar power of reflection whereby the toxic and venomous spirit passes with a look. 'But the greater strength of this epidemic and, as it were, instantaneous death is when the aerial spirit going out of the eyes of the sick person strikes the eyes of the well person standing near and looking at the sick, especially when they are in agony.'[42] If this strikes today's reader as too psychological an interpretation, it is worth remembering that among the many official and for the most part feeble responses of those at the University of Paris to the epidemic, most of whom saw it as a malign

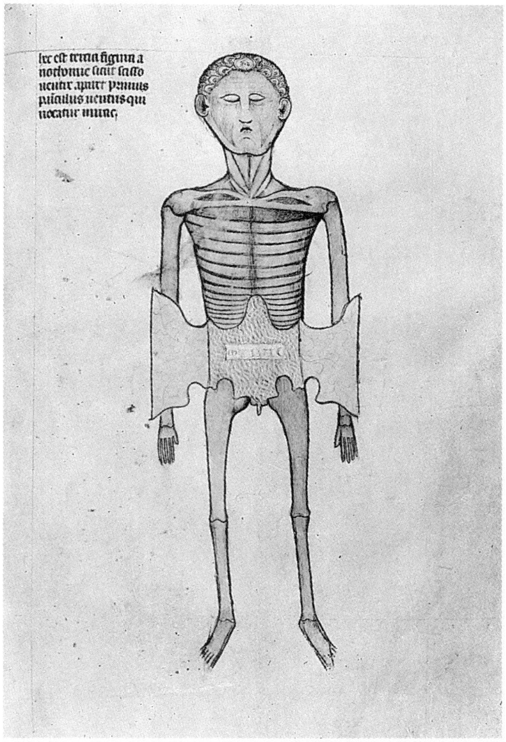

111. Chantilly, Musée Condé, MS 569, fol. 261. Guido da Vigevano, *Anathomia.* The third figure of the dissected corpse.

conjunction of the stars, is the observation that diseases of the body often arise from accidents of the soul. Fear, worry and weeping were all seen as causes, as was an overactive imagination, which explains why, according to doctors, the intellectually gifted are the worst at avoiding it and idiots the best. A prescription by an anonymous cleric for warding off the *grand mortalité* that struck Paris in 1433 is reminiscent of recipes Remiet would have used for pigments. Its unctious and dream-like prescription of efficacy recalls a world of correspondences, the magical attraction of 'like by like' which makes all 'likenesses' into powerful means of exorcism. This revolting mixture works as much through representation as any combination put together by an artist.

> First, take the bile and entrails of a magnet, and the lungs of a piece of marble, the nose of a stone pillar, the brain from a wedge head, the head of a iron barrel, blood from sand, tong's breasts . . . all ground together in a glass mortar with a pestle of very strong steel, and then stir in milk from a nurse who has never broken wind and boil it in a clay pot on a grumbling fire . . . and at vespers when you are in bed . . . drink it at one breath and know that if you do this you will find yourself, if you are not lost, healthy.[43]

Art historians have always sought to see the effects of the Black Death of 1348 in the visual arts and representations that registered its horrific impact. But are not the most horrific events of our own century those we have erased from art?[44] One might argue that Remiet's whole output is possible only because of his urge to submerge the mass death that followed his birth and that his subsequent obsession with corpses is a response to a repressed experience that he is none the less forced to repeat endlessly. But even that would be to place too much emphasis upon a founding moment of traumatic origin. Rather than the first outbreak of the pestilence which came to Paris in late spring 1348, Remiet experienced the plague as a constant threat, a continuum, not as a single event, with major outbreaks affecting the city eighteen times again before 1400 and with serious effects in 1360–2, 1374, 1400–1, 1403 and 1419.[45]

A few of Remiet's images show his awareness of the body in pain, a body we might associate with the plague, as in his tiny image of Job huddled in the womb-like dung-heap, who was the exemplar of the suffering self in medieval culture, in an initial in the Manchester breviary (Fig. 110). It follows the rubric 'Incipit liber Job qui legendus est de k[alendis] augusti us[que] ad k[alendus] septembris (Here begins the book of Job which is to be read from the first of August to the first of September)' and opens with the text of Job 1: 'There was a man in the land of Hus whose name was Job, and that man was simple and upright and fearing God and avoiding evil.' Exactly the opposite of upright, this bent emaciated figure represents the suffering subject of God's tribulations in the later chapters. The bones of the huddled figure seem to poke out of the flesh, which is stretched taut over the frame, glistening like an X-ray and evoking the lines of Job 10:8–12: 'Thou hast clothed me with skin and flesh: thou hast put me together with bones and sinews.' Such phrases in Latin were known even to the illiterate because of their incorporation into the liturgical offices, including the often-experienced Office of the Dead, where this passage formed part of the Third Lesson.[46] Job is represented inside rather than upon the dung-heap because he curses the day of his birth and the womb from whence he came (Job 3:3), but he is also in this place an exemplar of submission before God's justice, which all the sick, especially those afflicted with leprosy and the newer scourge of syphillis, called 'le mal de monsiegneur Job', were encouraged to feel, since illness was seen as God's punishment. The embryo-like image of Job as suffering trapped within the flesh, which Remiet repeated on a number of occasions, is distinctly different from the image of Job seated as a Christ-like Man of Sorrows on the dung-heap, which developed in the fourteenth century.[47] Rather than making the parallel between Job and Christ, it reinforces the reader's own association with the figure, and later in the century François Villon would write a poem addressed to his friends, assimilating himself with this ravaged body:

> Have pity, do have pity upon me,
> You at least, if you please, who are my friends.
> I lie in a pit, not beneath holly nor may,
> In this prison to which I am consigned.[48]

If such overlaps between the verbal laments of Job and individual poetic identity are not uncommon in the fourteenth and fifteenth centuries, what of the overlaps between the image of Job and the self-image of the artist? During periods of illness, when the body begins to speak for itself, this image of inward-turning hibernation, with its one dangling hand and the other placed in one's breast as a sign of sloth, useless and not working, perhaps provided a model with which he could identify. There must have been times when Remiet put his hand under his vest like this and did not, or could not, lift the brush.

While the history of medicine and attitudes and representations of medical practice can be written, who can write or for that matter depict the history of suffering? There is a description in the journal of a 'bourgeois de Paris' of a cough called the *tac* that shook all of the city, a cough that we can only hear through the onomatapoeic sound of its name but whose somatic effects must have been heard above countless writings and paintings, interrupting not only prayers but the making of images. Instead of looking for a depiction of a sick person in Remiet's art, we can sometimes see sickness in the fractured lines, the limp washes of colour in which Remiet does not represent but rather embodies illness itself. Once we accept that images like Remiet's were made by a body as well as a mind, the possibility of illness being made visible go beyond mirrors of iconography which can describe only as the following does:

> There was a song at that time that the little children used very often to sing as they went to fetch wine or mustard in the evening; it ran: 'What a cough you've caught in the cunt old girl, What a cough, what a cough, in the cunt!' And it pleased God that a foul corrupt air should fall upon the world, an air which reduced more than a hundred thousand people in Paris to such a state that they could neither eat, drink, nor sleep. They had very sharp attacks of fever two or three times each day, especially whenever they ate anything. Everything seemed very bitter to them, very rotten and stinking, and all the time, wherever they were, they shook and trembled. Even worse, besides all this, they lost all bodily strength so that no one who had this disease could bear to touch any part of his body, so wrechedly ill did he feel . . . Yet no one died of it.[49]

When art historians divide up hands in manuscripts and make distinctions between superior and inferior artistry based on the colouristic refinement and delicacy of detail in individual miniatures, they forget that artists, like other people, have bodies and that images too are part of the somatic struggle to survive. Historians of medicine have drawn attention to the fact that for fourteenth-century town-dwellers, some form of low grade sickness was the norm, just as in underdeveloped countries today. The 'off-day', as we euphemistically call it, can be seen in many of Remiet's miniatures, where lack of concentration was not perhaps caused by anything as severe as the *tac* but by the manifold aches and pains of everyday life and has resulted in blotches, smeared lines and wavering definitions.

Another striking description by the Parisian diarist is of a recurrence of the plague that struck Paris in 1418. The scene is not, however, one of horror or panic, but one of people's awe at the immanence of Christ's body, in the form of the Eucharist, which was so eminently visible at this time being carried everywhere to those about to die, and how it aided their perception, their ability to see their maker at the end.

> The death rate in and around Paris this September was higher than it had been for three hundred years, so old men said. No one who was struck by the epidemic escaped, particularly young people and children. So many people died so fast that towards the end of the month they had to dig great pits in the cemeteries of Paris and lay thirty or forty in at once, in rows, like sides of bacon, and then a bit of earth scattered over them. You could not go out into the street day or night without encountering Our Lord being carried to the sick, and all the dying had the clearest perception of Our Lord God at the end that any Christian ever had.[50]

Dying Well

But in producing an image of the dying man . . . I am participating in the illusion that localizes death elsewhere, in the hospital or in the last moments. I am transmogrifying it into an image of the other; by identifying this image with the dying person, I make it *the place where I am not*. Through representation, I exorcise death, which is shut up next door, relegated to a moment that I assume is not mine. I protect my place. The dying person whom I speak about remains obscene if he is not myself. Michel de Certeau[51]

When she will be in the agony of death, the priests who are assisting will not stop reading the Passion of Our Lord Saviour Jesus Christ in the Gospels, the recommendations of the soul and other prayers that they are accustomed to read, right up until she has expired. Will of a widow[52]

In the *Miroir historial* Remiet illustrated the tale often recited by preachers of 'the poor widow whom the Virgin Mary honoured at her end' (Fig. 112). A priest is summoned to the house of a dying rich man, whose bed is of furs and soft feathers, and neglects an earlier call to go to the *maisonette* of a poor widow who is gasping her last breath on the hard ground. Refusing to go to such a miserable place, he has sent his deacon instead. The deacon comes to the hovel to find the dying woman attended by the Virgin Mary herself and her angelic retinue and on returning to his master sees, by contrast, the rich man's luxurious deathbed surrounded by panderers and flatterers in the form of devilish cats. The story ends with the souls of the rich man and the priest both being ripped out by devils. This tale reveals the fear of dying without a priest's intervention, 'sans confession et sans recevoit les sacrements'. Besides castigating ecclesiastical greed and the money that could be made from the wealthy dead, it elevates the death of a poor but pious person above that of a rich man who can afford all the lavish liturgical rituals to attend his demise. Remiet's two-tiered miniature, in which things are reversed as they often are in death – the lower being the more elevated – is full of telling details like the elaborate pyx held by the corrupt priest containing the host for the rich man's final communion, the ominous paws of the demonic creatures clawing on his pillow, the rushes strewn on the floor of the old widow's hovel below, where the Queen of Heaven pays honour to the stiff, lifeless corpse by covering it with a winding-sheet.

The fear faced in this miniature is that of dying alone, one's body uncleansed, unshriven and uncovered. Yet this is how the pilgrim in Remiet's *Pèlerinage de vie humaine* faces his end. It depicts as a lonely event what was, usually, a social one. The deathbed would normally have been surrounded by many onlookers, servants, friends and family, all taking part in an elaborate ritualized process of leave-taking. Clambering around the deathbed too were a thousand possible spiritual intercessors as well as devils and angels waiting for the separation of the soul from the body and for the fight over the soul to begin. All these comprise not an earthly society but an extra-terrestrial one that Remiet excluded from his death scene. It was also not so much 'the hour of our death' but the hours and even days of long drawn out waiting, during which the sick person would be the focus of prayers

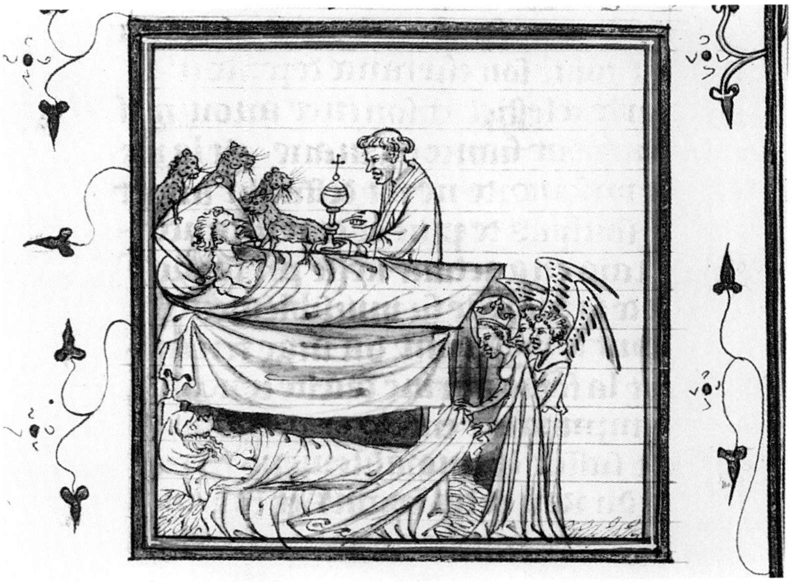

112. Remiet. Paris, Bibliothèque Nationale, fr. 312, fol. 334v. *Miroir historial.* The deaths of the rich man and the poor widow.

and readings from the Gospel. For the wealthy there was also the matter of getting one's household in order and saying farewell. Ultimately a priest took the last confession and administered the final communion of Extreme Unction, reciting the words of James 5:14: 'Is any sick among you? Let him call for the elders of the church; and let them pray over him, anointing him with oil in the name of the Lord.' The sufferer was anointed at both head and feet, and the final communion introduced the body of Christ into the body of one about to die. If the mortally ill were to recover after receiving the last sacraments, as sometimes happened, he was thought to exist in a liminal space, halfway between this world and the next, and was urged to absolve from sexual activity and live the rest of his life leper-like as a marked category.

A notary might also be present at the bedside making a will dictated by the dying man, as depicted in legal manuscripts of the period.[53] For the wealthy, the will was the all-important script for the staging of the funeral and all its obligations and gifts to the poor of the parish and various churches, so it was usually made long before. Besides outlining these public self-presentations and posthumous acts of charity, contemporary wills show men and women leaving to their heirs their books, sometimes the very manuscripts that contain Remiet's images. On 8 September 1417 the procurer of the Parlement of Paris made his will as follows: 'I, Guillaume de Vaux, considering that there is nothing more certain than death, nor less certain than the hour of its arrival, wish to dispose of the goods that God has given me.' To his father he left his Book of Hours, his little psalter and 'the book called *Pèlerinage de l'âme*', which would have provided him with a preview of what he hoped would come as well as salutory lessons in preparing for it.[54] In that poem the pilgrim sees those who are chained to money chests in Hell who are the victims of faithless executors of wills, executors who did not follow the wishes of their dear departed friends. The last will and testament of Louis d'Orléans was made four years before his murder, when, in October 1403, he was on the eve of a battle in the wars of papal succession. The document stresses that the duke, if killed, would have died 'in the service of God against the enemies of the Faith and in defence of the realm'. Like a bourgeois testator, his priorities are familial, remembering his father, Charles V, his mother, Jeanne de Bourbon, his 'wife and companion', Valentina Visconti, and his children, whom he blesses 'as Abraham blessed Isaac'. Oddly, there is no mention of his brother, the mad king. There is emphasis placed on the funeral, where his arms should be displayed, and how the men of his *hôtel* should not wear the usual black, but 'out of love for me will dress themselves in grey-brown *tenné*'.[55] The duke thus sought to project into the future rites around his death the same grisaille tones that Remiet provided him with in miniature.

Remiet's will has not survived, but we know that one of his associates in the book trade who appears in the 1368 university list of those exempt from the watch was a donator to the local parish church of Saint Séverin. Up until the revolution a small plaque in red leather hung on the second pillar of the nave, inscribed with these words: 'The executors of the deceased Antoine de Compiègne, 'enlumineur de pincel', and of Oudette his wife, had this pillar made from the residue of the goods of the said deceased, in the year 1414. Pray to God for their souls. Amen.'[56]

Another aspect of Deguileville's poem following the soul after death that must have worried the shivering body in its last frightful hours was the increasingly legal image of death. The soul is brought before a heavenly court and a mock trial begins in which St Michael pleads on behalf of the accused and the prosecutors call upon Sinderesis, the worm of conscience, to list all the soul's misdemeanours during life. This newly litigious afterlife, a response to the increasing bureaucracy and legal pressures emergent in urban life at the time, also affected how people viewed their own mortality. For example, Jean Le Fèvre, procurer of the Parlement of Paris, wrote his poem *Le Respit de la mort* after recovering from a serious illness which struck him on 9 October 1376 when he was over fifty. The word *respit* in the title refers to a letter of *respit* or deferral which could be obtained from the royal chancellery and which excused the applicant from payment of a debt until an extended due date. Jean saw his recovery in terms of his own legal world – God had literally given him a further loan on life – and the poem ends with the knowledge that the debt is still outstanding to 'mon puissant crediteur'.[57] This long poem is further evidence for the self-conscious attitude to one's own mortality that was widespread at the time, and significantly it is here too that the first reference occurs to the famous 'Danse macabre'. Le Fèvre says, 'Je fis de Macabre la danse (I have done the Dance of Macabre)', a phrase whose meaning is obscure, but which scholars have interpreted as a way of describing his having come close to joining the skeletal processions that became so popular in paintings of the subsequent century (Fig. 113). The famous but long-since-vanished mural that accompanied the poem was not painted at the Holy Innocents cemetery in Paris until 1424, but the theme was obviously known before this date.[58] Those living in the city could here face their rotting alter-egos, in which 'the dead leads forward the live man', in a series of fifteen pairs of figures, alternating cleric and layman from pope and emperor down to friar and child. Even more striking is that each social actor meets his own personal *mort* as a skeleton, in a series of thirty potential self-portraits, providing the onlooker with a range of identities and professions. 'See yourself in us, dead,

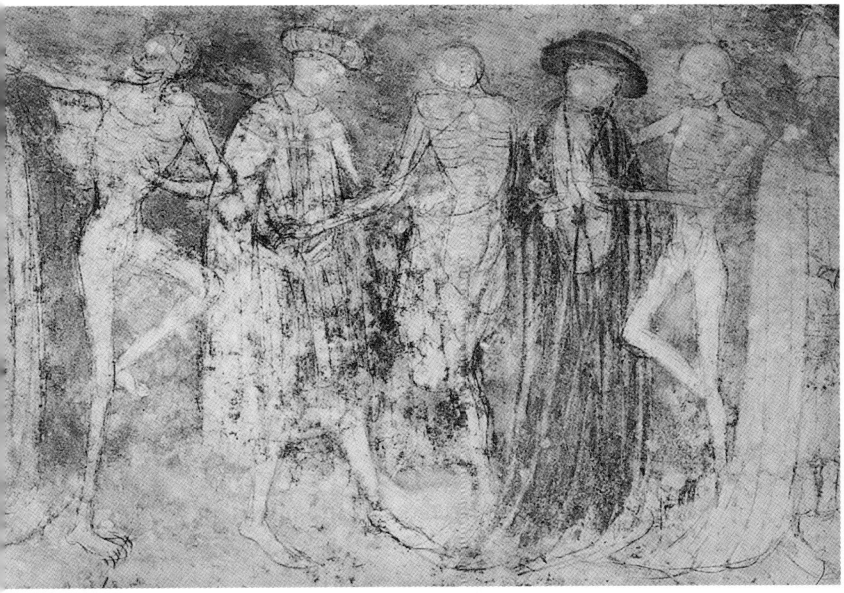

113. *The Dance of Death*, outer choir enclosure wall painting, Abbey of La Chaise Dieu.

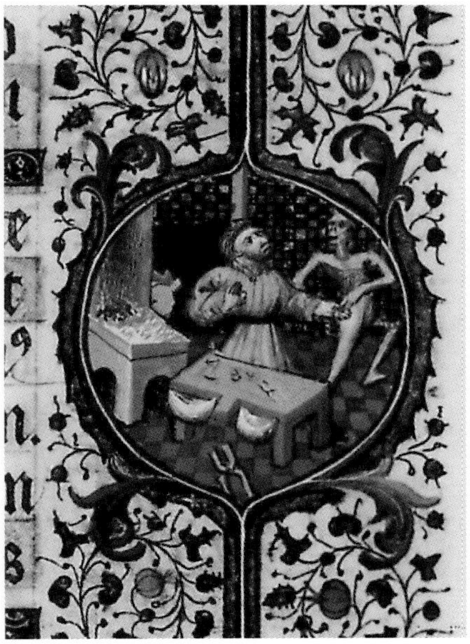

114. Bedford Master. New York, Pierpont Morgan Library, M.359, fol. 145. Book of Hours. Death carries off a goldsmith.

rotten and stinking', they cry. The death in life closest to Remiet's was the 'citizen' who is goaded by his other to 'Hurry up! Quickly! You have no wealth or possession to save you from death' and who laments how 'I am deeply grieved to leave so soon my revenues, houses, rents and livestock, but you, Death, humble poor and rich; that is your nature'.

What seems odd to us today is that in many ways these paintings were entertaining and even funny to their original audience. Cemeteries like the Innocents were places of public peddling, chatting, soliciting and courting. Dancing in churchyards has a long and mysterious history, but it is clear that the paintings of the dancing dead replayed a traditional association between the body's liberated movement in dance and its degradation in death. The viewer identifies, in this respect, not only with the unprepared living, but in Natalie Davis's words, 'with the grinning and powerful dead, who deflate all wordly pretentions and plans and overturn all worldly hierarchies and bear off king, pope and peasant'.[59] The preliminary verses refer to the mural as a 'mirror' in which everyone can see and read why they must, in the end, dance like this.[60] Thus at a very public site and not in the private spaces of the devotional prayerbook, death stalked and laughed at the imaginary and found its reflection in each citizen who chanced upon this procession. People often defined themselves and expressed their identity according to their work or trade, and it is no surprise that death begins to invade the workplace in the early fifteenth century. Numerous accidents are recorded, especially in those Parisian trades involving hazardous materials, which included metal and paint. In a Book of Hours made for the Englishman John, Duke of Bedford, while regent of Paris in the 1420s, a dance of death is separated out into the margins of the Office of the Dead with skeletons coming to drag off their victims in the midst of their various labours, where, for example, a goldsmith is

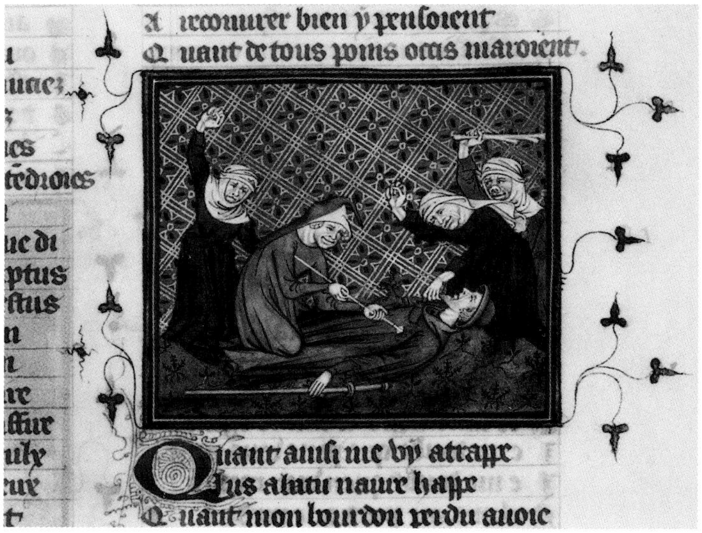

115. Remiet. Paris, Bibliothèque Nationale, fr. 823, fol. 74. *Pèlerinage de vie humaine.* The all-out attack of the deadly sins.

grabbed in his shop (Fig. 114). We do not know whether Remiet was struck down so suddenly, but we can be sure that by contemplating such images, he was always prepared for that inevitability.

A crucial aspect of fourteenth-century dying alluded to in the individual death of the pilgrim is the art of 'dying well', which meant being prepared for the arrival of death throughout one's life and having confessed all one's sins before God. The miniatures of the *Pèlerinage de vie humaine* follow the trajectory and reveal the sequence of a common life, not everyman's of course, since no one is everyone, but a life that the individual reader, and Remiet himself, could at times identify with. Remiet would have experienced the important ritual stages in life that he pictured, a life that, as moralists were fond of saying, was from the beginning a preparation for dying. He would have been baptized and confirmed, sacraments crucial during childhood. Remiet made two miniatures of the next important sacrament, marriage, first in the allegorical journey of life in the *Pèlerinage de vie humaine* and then as a law in an illustrated gloss on the Decretals in his only manuscript preserved in Oxford.[61] It is probable that Remiet experienced the sacrament of marriage, since we know that he left heirs owning property on the Rue de la Parcheminerie.

A major sacrament experienced throughout a Christian's life was confession, which parishioners were supposed to undergo at least once a year and of course at the end of life as part of Extreme Unction.[62] Every day and on that last day, people were faced with deciding between various actions that the Church encouraged them to think of as the choices between virtue and vice, good and evil, and to articulate their sins in language before a confessor. Since the early thirteenth century when the citizens of Paris had the whole panoply of their vices presented on the west front of Notre Dame, there had been a tradition of visualizing these infamous acts that could damn the soul forever.[63] In that last gasping confession the dying person would have admitted misdeeds and guilty secrets in terms of the seven deadly sins that were the forces of death for the soul. These could pull

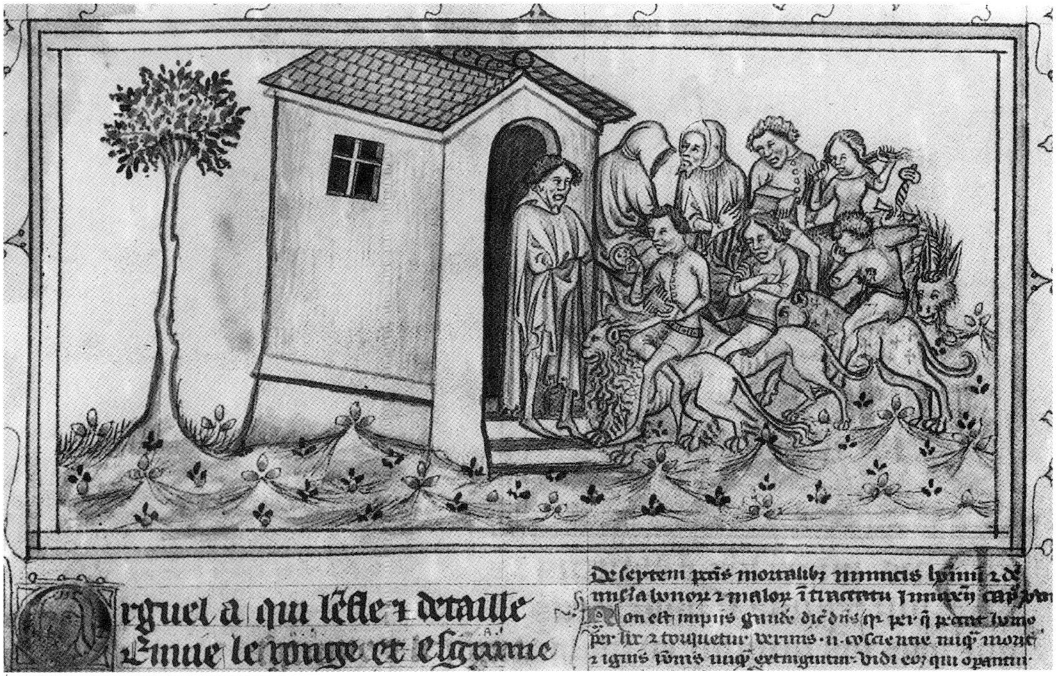

116. Remiet. Paris, Bibliothèque Nationale, fr. 20029, fol. 11v. *Lay de la fragilité humaine.* Man assailed by the seven deadly sins.

117. Remiet. Paris, Bibliothèque Naticnale, fr. 312, fol. 1. *Miroir historial.* The author Vincent of Beauvais addresses the court.

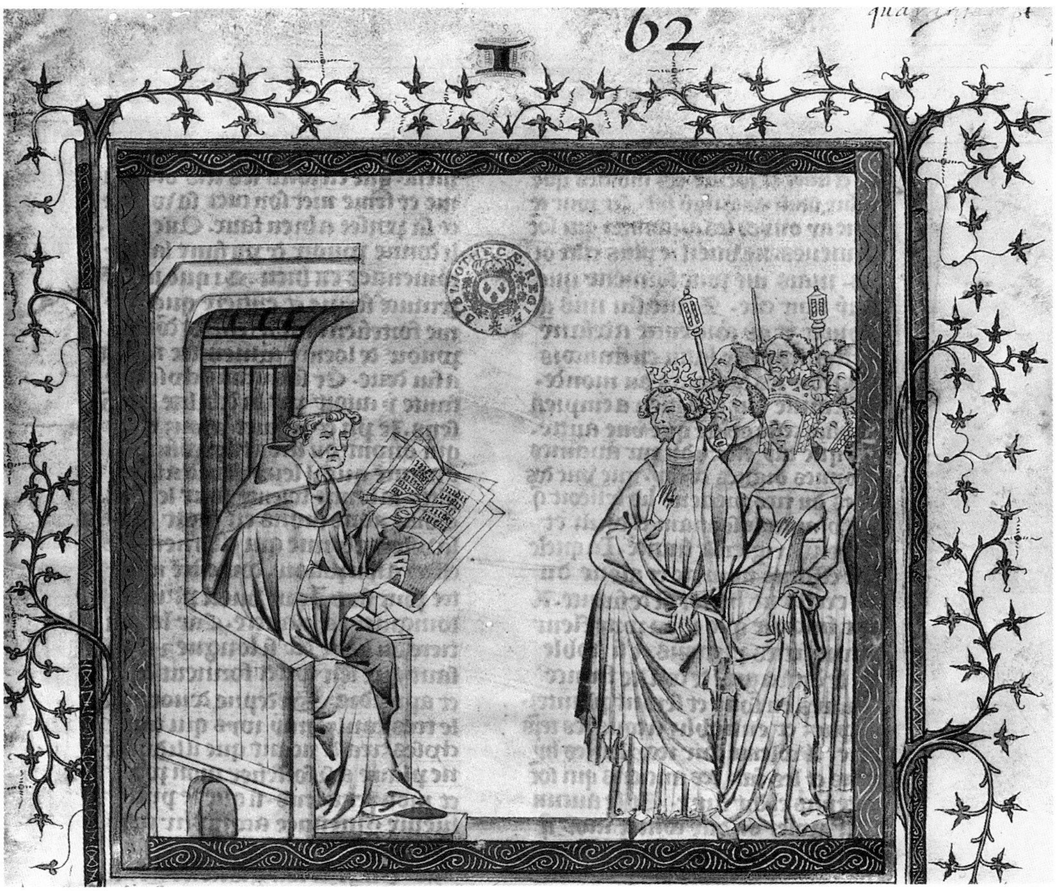

the Christian away from his proper contemplation of that moment through the lure of his bodily appetites. In the *Pèlerinage de vie humaine*, Pride, Anger, Envy, Sloth and Gluttony are represented as hideous old women who in turn attack the pilgrim on his life's journey before they pull him to the ground *en masse* (Fig. 115).

Ten years before in the *Lay de la fragilité humaine* Remiet created a unique illustration of 'How man is assailed each day by the seven mortal enemies in this sad and doleful world' (Fig. 116).[64] The vices, based again on Innocent III's treatise, are shown as allegorical figures riding animals, an unusual tradition that is not specified in the text. More interesting still is their association with a specific social group. The prominent male figures in the front have the pinched waists, low-slung belts and vast chests that not only conform to Remiet's usual male figure type with bloated upper body and thin appendages, but represent the ideal bodily type of the period, visible in extant examples of these buttoned and tight padded vests or pourpoints.[65] The aristocratic vices here are associated with aristocratic luxurious living in contrast to the cloaked figure of the man standing in the doorway of his house and facing the seven deadly sins on his doorstep. Their order in the text is Orgueil (Pride), Envie, Avarice, Glotonnie, Luxure, Homicide and Mensonge (Lying), but it is hard to differentiate them in any order as they crowd around the little house. For example, the figure of the handsome youth on the lion looking into a mirror, is this a male Luxury or a vain Pride? The only woman in the group, pulling her hair at the back, is also ambiguous. Ira is missing in the French verse but not in Innocent III's Latin, which thus lists not seven but eight vices. The 'lost profile' of the figure stabbing himself (the usual personification of the vice of Despair) here might actually be meant to signify homicide as suicide, an additional sin to the usual panoply. The elderly monk-like figure at the back has a gloved hand, perhaps indicating Avarice. But who then is the youthful figure bearing a box next to him, a slim Gluttony? The bearded figure, the 'I' of the perceiving subject, his arms folded, like one of the very vices he faces, perhaps representing his inaction and passivity before sin, stands before his house and idly watches this cavalcade approach.

The texts we read structure our lives. We do not know if Remiet 'read' the texts that came to his desk. It would have been difficult for him to follow the narrative anyway, since the books arrived in pieces, divided into gatherings that perhaps never allowed him to see the coherence of beginning, middle and end. In this case he either misread or was given poor directions in depicting the text. But rather than see this as mistake it can be understood as Freud understood errors, slips of the tongue, as revealing desire and its deflection. The fact that the vices are confused serves only to reinforce their ever-changing falseness, always out to lead the pilgrim into sin and a miserable death. The most haunting of the faces that Remiet gave the sins in this miniature is not a face at all but a missing visage. The faceless Mensonge, or Lying, who of course forever hides his/her face, looks like a hooded and shapeless *pleurant* such as those carved in white marble on contemporary tombs.[66] Is this one of the places where we have to accept that Remiet was naive or rather that he wanted to suggest some hypocrisy in the overinflated value of mourning by giving this personification such a funereal aspect?

In the *Pèlerinage de vie humaine*, the great enemy to be shunned is the World. It is a sea in which the pilgrim nearly drowns until he finds the ship of religion. Remiet also represented the six fountains of the Vanity of the World as described in the *Lay de la*

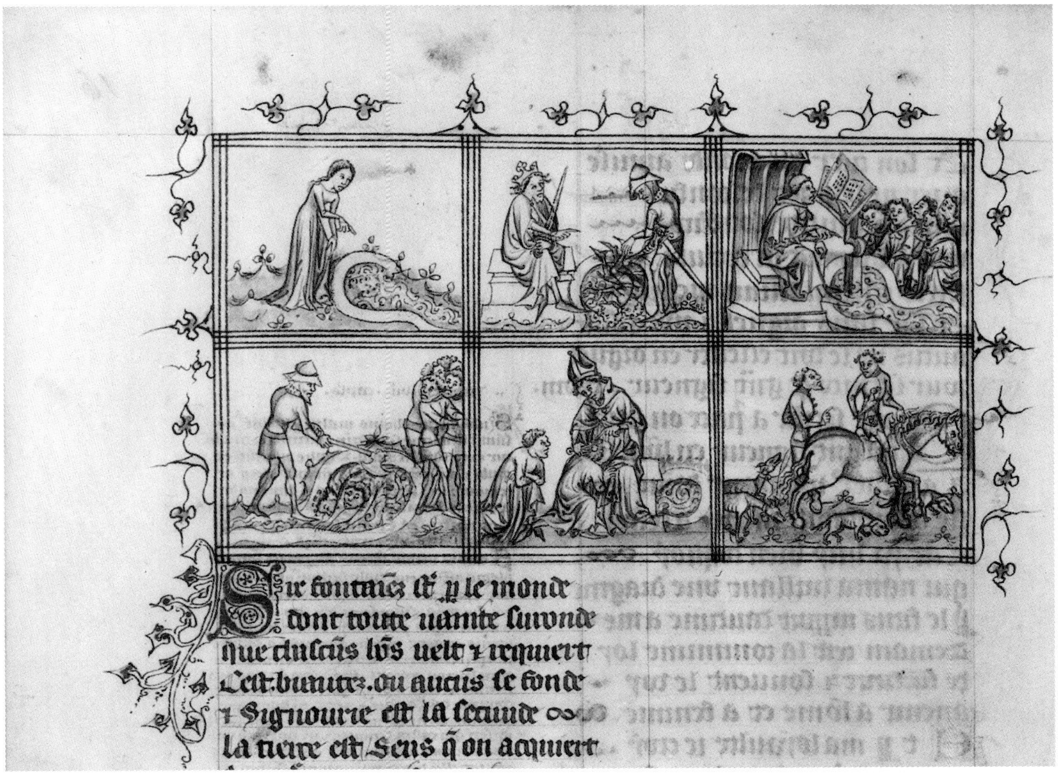

118. Remiet. Paris, Bibliothèque Naticnale, lat. 1024, fol. 126. *Lay de la fragilité humaine.* The six fountains of worldly vanity.

fragilité humaine, beauty, seigniory, knowlege, prowess, clergy and nobility (Fig. 118). These verses of the twenty-ninth chapter are the only part of the poem that are not taken directly from Innocent III or another Latin source and represent an original addition by the poet, being Deschamps's personal critique of the court of Charles VI. 'Vainglory is the abundant water' in which the estates of society revel, their beautiful bodies exterior hiding the putrid ordure within ('Car beau corps et belle faconde / Par dehors dedans remplis yert / De toute ordure ou il s'afonde').[67] Deschamps transforms the fountain, that symbol of youth and joy in medieval love poetry, into an empty mirror, a spectacle of sinners. This includes all estates, tonsured priests as well as university lecturers, nobles as well as kings. It is significantly another object of reflection, like a mirror, yet opposed to the virtuous mirror of self-knowledge represented in Deguileville's allegory of human life. What is reflected in the running waters of the fountain is the ever-changing flux and reflux of human desire.

This is where the moral force of these illustrated allegories, made after all for the wealthiest members of the French court, and in the case of the *Lay* for the king himself, seem to be at odds. The petty intrigues and backbiting of the court blew up into scandal surrounding the duke's wife, Valentina Visconti, who in 1398 was accused of attempting to poison the king when one of her children died supposedly from eating an apple. Because she had tried to aid the mad king's relapsed condition with advice from her own

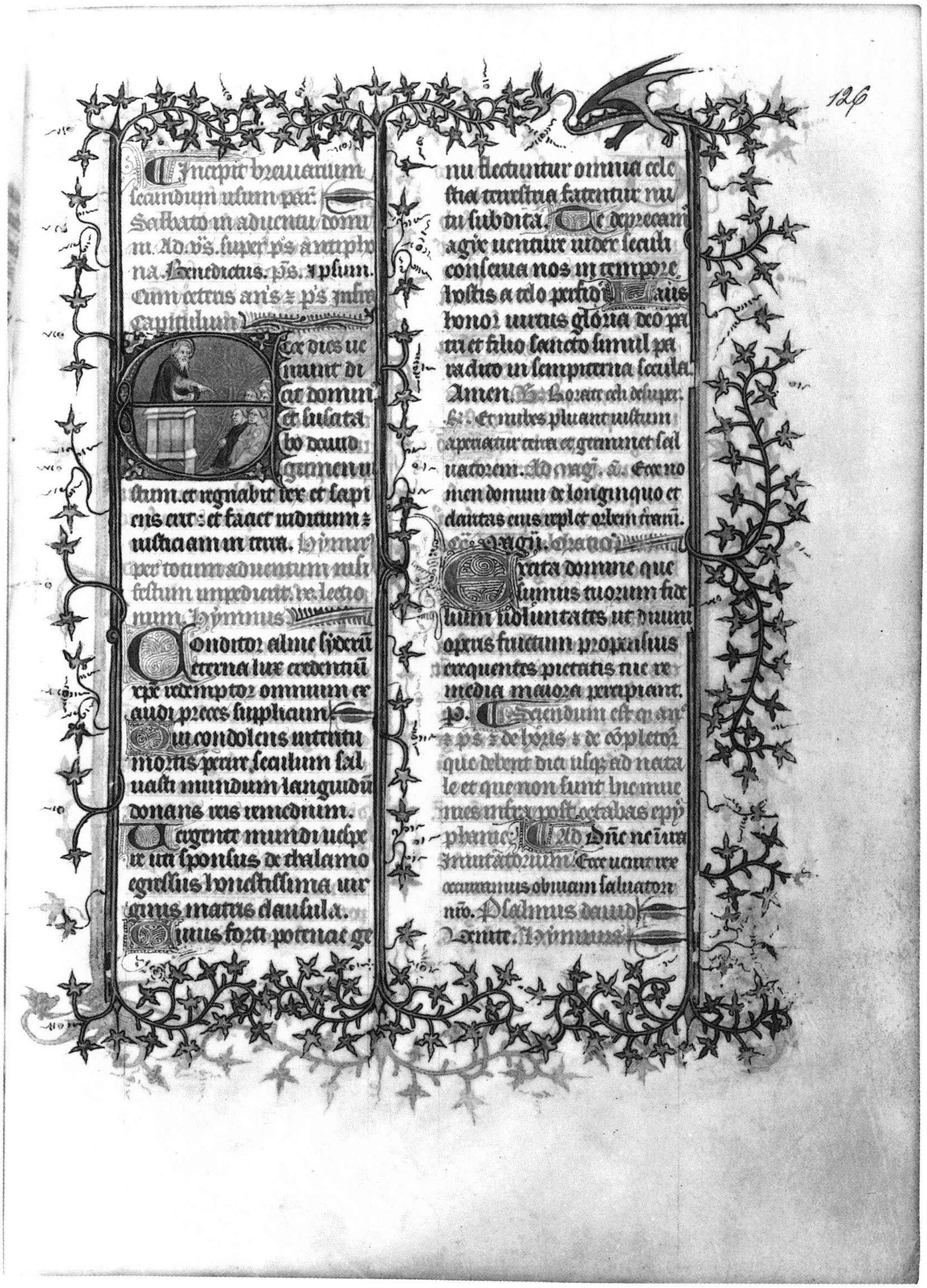

119. Remiet. Paris, Bibliothèque Nationale, lat. 1024, fol. 126. Breviary. St Benedict preaches on the first Sunday in Advent.

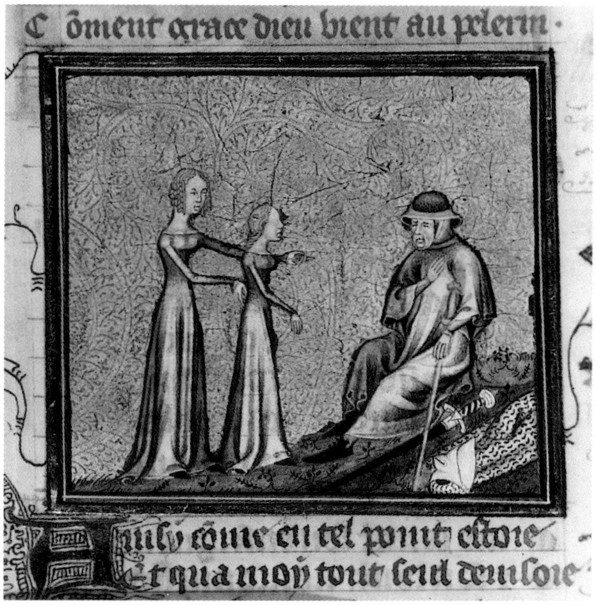

120. Remiet. Paris, Bibliothèque Nationale, fr. 823, fol. 34v. *Pèlerinage de vie humaine.* Grace Dieu introduces Memory, who has eyes in the back of her head, and who will carry the pilgrim's armour of faith.

doctors, his worsening condition was blamed by the Parisians on her 'witchcraft'.[68] The stiff, attentive court of Philippe VI and his queen (original patrons of the text), who stand admonished by the author Vincent of Beauvais in the frontispiece to Louis d'Orléans's *Miroir historial*, ordered in 1396, are also mirrors of Louis's own retinue, which found itself increasingly isolated in Paris during these years (Fig. 117). In fact it fills a gap, since Louis's own consort was not at his side, as in the image, but had been forced to leave Paris because of the rumours. The tight-knit cluster of nobles protected by armed men look towards the cleric for moral guidance in a time of crisis.

What they heard from the learned did not always please them. On Ascension Day 1405 the Augustinian monk Jacques Legrand preached a sermon before the court, then focused around Louis d'Orléans, calling it the orgiastic haunt of Venus in which ladies wore outrageous and lewd costumes. In urging them to renounce their luxury, he urged them to think of death.[69] Louis could see images of preachers booming from their pulpits in the minute letters of his breviary, images of an age when men like Jean Gerson captivated thousands with his weekly sermons, many of them on the theme of the *ars moriendi* (Fig. 119). For most Parisians, unlike the aristocratic owners of books with Remiet's pictorial preaching, and perhaps for Remiet himself, most doctrinal and theological knowledge came not via the written word but by way of mass spectacles of rhetorical fervour that kept audiences rapt for hours and even days. The 1390s saw the rise of a new ascetic rather than aesthetic attitude at the French court, in which an evangelical faction sought to burn and censor what they considered illicit, especially sexual themes in art and poetry, and to ban all except religious verse. There was growing censorship under which no one could mention the pope or the great schism. A highly formalized aristocratic culture and Charles VI's 'Court of Love' co-existed alongside a reactionary religious hysteria in which every desire was implicated, every look interpreted as witchcraft or treachery. When Christine

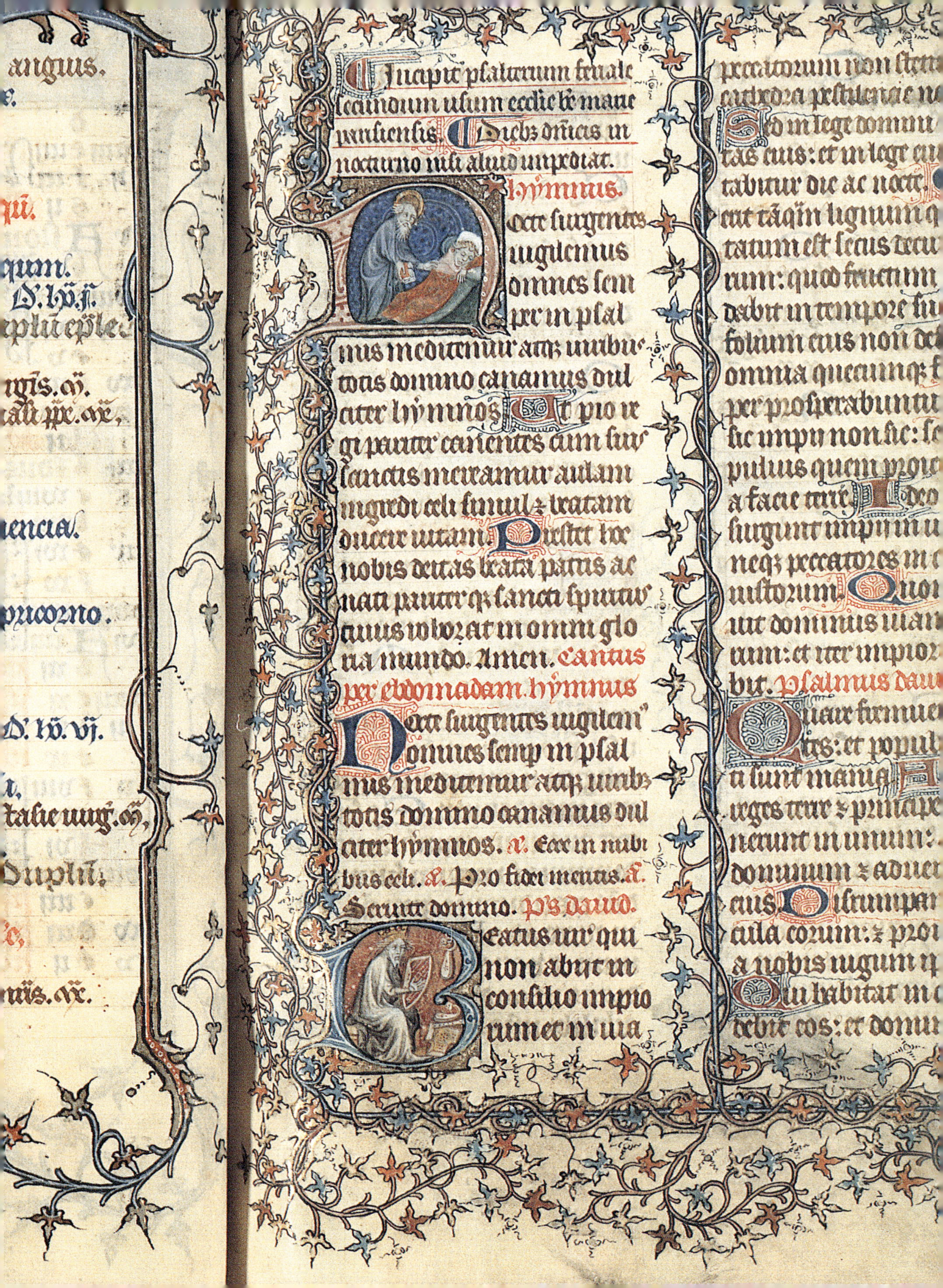
Incipit psalterium feriale
secundum usum ecclesie beate marie
parisiensis. Diebus dominicis in
nocturno nisi aliud impediat.
Hymnus.
Nocte surgentes
vigilemus
omnes sem
per in psal
mis meditemur atque viribus
totis domino canamus dul
citer hymnos. Ut pio re
gi pariter canentes cum suis
sanctis mereamur aulam
ingredi celi simul et beatam
ducere vitam. Prestet hoc
nobis deitas beata patris ac
nati pariterque sancti spiritus
cuius reboat in omni glo
ria mundo. Amen. Cantus
per ebdomadam. hymnus
Nocte surgentes vigilemus
omnes semper in psal
mis meditemur atque viribus
totis domino canamus dul
citer hymnos. a. Ecce in nubi
bus celi. a. Pro fidei meritis. a.
Servite domino. Ps. david.
Beatus vir qui
non abiit in
consilio impio
rum et in via

de Pizan attacked the court for its excesses and vain luxuries, it was against artists that she railed most strongly, for they provided the very basis of delight and desire.[70] Remiet's art might in this sense be regarded as a reaction against luxury; its etiolated surfaces and the intentional 'ugliness' of its drab colours, manifested above all in the *Lay de la fragilité humaine*, designate it as anti-courtly art of the highest order. It is significant that no copy of the *Roman de la Rose* from Remiet's hand survives, only the clerical 'answer' to the *Rose* in the Cistercian Deguileville's dark pilgrimage of life. Remiet may have been sought after by certain patrons precisely because he was a prudish painter of austere histories, a trusted and old-fashioned limner of the lugubrious, nothing too fancy, the only obscenities being those of death.

Remiet's own sins would not have been those stimulated by fantasies in ivories and jewels enjoyed by Louis and his retinue, although they might have involved the 'luxury' of the stews and brothels, many of which were in his neighbourhood. The street before the church of Saint Séverin was always listed among the disreputable streets of the city. Most people's sins were the minute accumulations of everyday angers and envies that lacked the opulent shows of vice that only the court could afford. Jean Le Fèvre thought of his literary productions and his scribal duties in the office of the Parlement as part of the expiations for his guilt, as work against sin that would save him from Hell: 'Parchment is the cure for you who have made this writing.' So too Remiet must have integrated his everyday work with his world-view and his hopes not just for a future life but for a future death. Like all semi-literate people, he depended upon his memory (the figure of which has eyes in the back of her head in Deguileville's *Pèlerinage*) in order to follow the true path (Fig. 120). It is this lady who carries the pilgrim's armour of faith, hope and strength throughout his life. There has been a great deal of interest in the subject of memory and medieval image-making recently, but one must remember that pictures were not only commemorative – they also looked forward as constructive tools for future preparation and projection, recalling a future that had always to be kept in mind.[71]

Each day one remembered, prepared for and practised one's future death in that most death-like state – sleep. Opening the winter portion of his breviary in what for us is still the middle of the night, Louis d'Orléans would have seen in the first initial a sleeping figure being awakened by a nimbed saint (Fig. 121). This is the matins hymn 'Nocte surgentes vigilemus omnes, Semper in psalmis meditemur, atque (Now that we have risen while it is still night, let us all keep watch, fixing our attention always on the psalms)'. Rising in the early hours to recite these prayers, the user of this book was meant to be aware of the constant imminence of death. Inscribed into the pattern of their vigilance, monks, priests and devout layfolk like Louis would wake in the middle of the night from their half-death sleep in order to kneel and shiver in insatiable contemplation of the longest night that was yet to come. Opening this breviary today, we should perform our own *ars moriendi* in the sense that it is all too easy to forget that we are holding in our hands the traces of a look of death, of a face, many faces, which have been where ours are today. Medieval manuscripts are not the crystal clear 'mirrors' that we want them to be. Otherwise we would see not only the visage of the patron, Louis d'Orléans, reflected here but that of the artist, Remiet, who in order to paint the soft pillow and heavy-lidded eyes of this slumberer must also have pressed his face up very close, breathing on and almost touching the flesh.

121. Remiet. Paris, Bibliothèque Nationale, lat. 1024, fol. 21. Breviary. 'Nocte Surgentes' (Now that we have risen while it is still night, let us all keep watch).

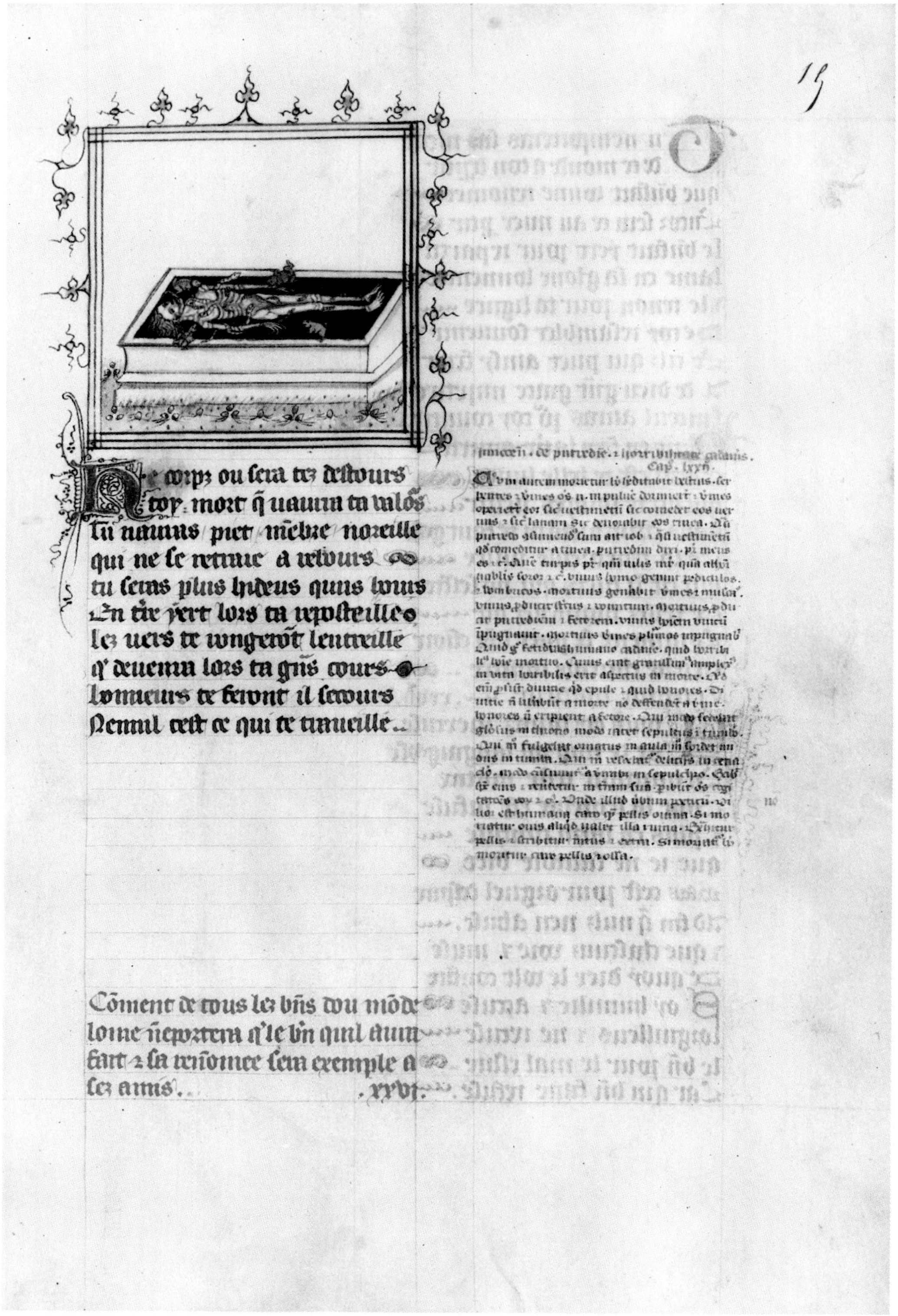

122. Remiet? Paris, Bibliothèque Nationale, fr. 20029, fol. 15. *Lay de la fragilité humaine.* The most hideous sight.

5. THE BODY OF DEATH

The great never had to suffer like this, Remiet thought bitterly, like worn-out beasts of burden left to rot by the roadside, bereft of comfort and alone. They had retinues and followers, long lines of healthy sons and daughters whispering in anticipation and kneeling expectant at the velvet bed-curtains, ranks of servants whose tears were already flowing long before the departure of their lord. The death of kings was a spectacle that people even queued up to see, thronging to be admitted into that chamber where the body politic, something that was a part of them, visibly ebbed way. But his long illness had taxed the patience of even his closest friends and relatives, who could not wait forever by his bed. Remiet knew that he would have to wait until the funeral to regain any sense of the respect owed him by his peers. He had spent many hours planning and preparing it, imagining the ceremony and the solemn procession (which would be a short one – to the graveyard in Saint Séverin, just across the street). Who would come? Would the highest dignitaries of the corporation of sculptors and painters be there? He knew which four men would carry his shrouded corpse. Not old Colart de Laon and the others, who were long dead themselves. He could not even count on the university 'libraires' and the other professional bodies with whom he had dealt all his career. That was the trouble with living to be so old. Everyone forgot.

He had some solace, however. He had made his will and testament out to a notary in the presence of witnesses some years ago, long before this last illness, when he was still clear-headed and his eyes worked. His meagre treasure, the gold pieces given him by that gracious lord of

123. Laon, Musée. Tomb of Guillaume de Harcigny (d. 1393), physician to Charles VI.

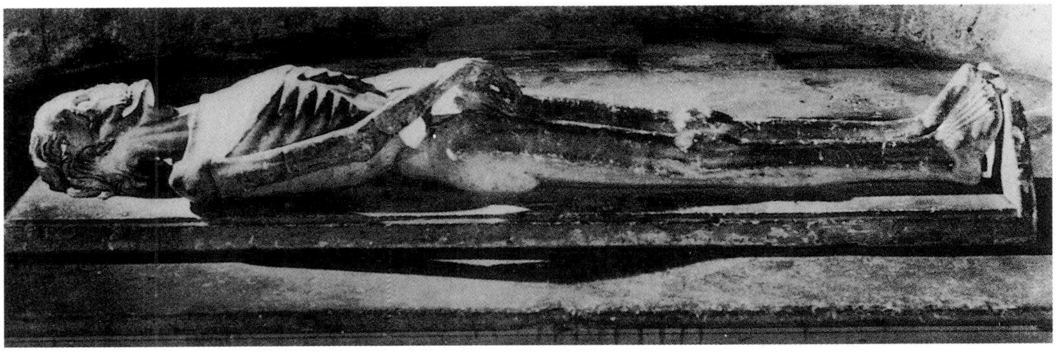

blessed memory, Louis, Duke of Orléans, would serve its purpose if his rascally sons had not already filched them to spend in the stews. Not trusting Remiet the younger, the old man had asked his good friend Regnault François the scribe to be his executor. Not that there was much to leave. No rich tapestries or embroideries, no jewels or painted panels, not even any illuminated books were to be bequeathed to Remiet's heirs, only the stuff that such wonderful things are made of. 'Boites' full of parchment in pieces and rolls, a thousand blunted and broken goose-feather quills, dozens of shimmery-surfaced seashells encrusted with the dried up remnants of size and glair or filled with pungent fish glues and oriental unguents whose names he had forgotten, vinegar vapours, tan bark and dung for making white lead, long-since congealed, and treacly deposits of gesso and gum arabic that had once laid the ground for God's golden rays. Most valuable were his actual colours – the pure ultramarine blue of lapis lazuli from far across the blue sea, ground in a fine powder that he had been saving for the mantle of the greatest Mother of God he would paint, until that great commission – which never came. It still sat like a crystal reliquary in the saracen jar in which he had bought it from the merchant at the Lendit fair. White made from calcined bones was the most common pigment, even more relic-like since he always suspected that these bones that made the flesh of his tiny folk were themselves from men and not beasts. That was all pigments were anyway – expensive dust, many of them made from the process of fire, from ashes. Remnants of the rainbow lay in tiny vials and jars, his greens, celadonite and malachite, his yellows, bile of tortoise, orpiment and saffron from the crocus, his red vermillion and minium and cinnabar, which was red sulphate of mercury. Only gold was lacking, since that was too expensive of late and he only bought it when he had been paid in advance. There was a single book, more a ragged folder of loose sheets than a proper volume, falling apart after so much use and stained with decades of workshop spills – a little treatise on the art of illumination. His son sadly had no use for it. Would he sell all its secrets?

Most important in his will had been the provision for masses to be sung in the churches. He didn't have the money of that notorious magician-'escrivain' Nicolas Flamel who had found by chance the magic book with the secret of the Great Elixir in it, enabling him to make silver from lead! With all their gains, fat Flamel and his wife Pernelle, mere public-scriveners working in a tiny booth on the Right Bank among the butchers near Saint Jacques de la Boucherie, had become rich burghers, and had had themselves commemorated all over the city and even as far as Boulogne – building fourteen hospitals, three chapels, paying for years of anniversary masses, pilgrimages and hundreds of pounds of candles. In the Innocents graveyard, that rascal Flamel had even erected in 1399 a sculpted arch filled with mysterious signs that many tried to read as depicting the cosmic concoction of vile matter into spirit, or the Philosopher's stone. Lacking Flamel's ill-gotten gold, he could not afford any golden embroideries for his obsequies nor a tomb to mark his grave but only his 'suaire' of white cotton that would wrap him up in a handy linen bag so that Abraham could carry his soul up into his bosom. He was relieved to think that he had already made that little plaque painted in gold letters on red leather that was to be hung in his memory on a pillar in the nave of his parish church of Saint Séverin, reminding parishioners to pray for his soul. It was only a small thing and would probably not last for long. Only the great could afford indestructible materials like bronze and stone to simulate themselves in eternal sleep. They even tried to make their flesh immortal, paying butchers and doctors to take out their innards and fill their rotten carcasses with sweet-smelling spices. It only served to make them tastier for worms. None of that for him, just the simple winding-sheet and a hole in the soil of Saint Séverin, the rich soil in which his wife and many of the fruit of their union had been planted. Beneath that shady flowering tree that he loved in the centre of the garden, a tree that was like the tree of good and evil and the tree under which he had painted the old man longing for death. He will rot below its branches. Why spend all that money on embalming and lead coffins when bodies were worthless, the flesh gone so soon. It only drew death out longer. The only reason was to cover up that terrible sight, a sight he remembered vividly from his childhood when he chanced upon it, crossing a field on the outskirts of the city. Remembering only vague sensations at its edges, the stench, the caw of carrion crows, a ragged bit of cloth covering a white dead leg, something moving in the waxy stillness of flesh, something unspeakable that should only happen in the darkness of the earth.

Rot

The image does not, at first glance, resemble the corpse, but the cadaver's strangeness is perhaps also that of the image. Maurice Blanchot[1]

'Man is rottenness and his son a worm.' How foul the father, how vile the mother, how abominable the sister! For man is conceived of blood made rotten by the fire of lust; in the end worms stand by his body like mourners. Alive, he brings forth lice and tapeworms; dead he will beget worms and flies. Alive, he produces dung and vomit; dead he produces rottenness and stench. Alive, he fattens one man, dead he will fatten many worms. What, then, is more foul smelling than a human corpse? What more horrible than a dead man? Lotario dei Segni (Innocent III)[2]

Innocent III describes the inevitable consequences of death for the flesh with the relish of a gourmand describing tasty delicacies, except that those eating are of course worms, and it is we who are on the menu. His mouth-watering imaginings were translated into vernacular verse by Deschamps in the *Lay de la fragilité humaine* in 1383 where they are capped by an attempt to put into a picture this notion of extremity – what can be more repugnant than this *chose horrible* (Fig. 122). That which is disgusting is etymologically linked to that which forces one to vomit, to expel the object in order not to incorporate, to mourn it. That which is disgusting thus becomes 'that which one cannot resign oneself to mourn', which is why the corpse has to be represented and displayed as a beautiful aesthetic object in the late fourteenth century.[3] But not here. What is described in the text of the *Lay* as 'beyond imagining' was somehow also beyond Remiet picturing, since its gorgeous horribleness was painted on one of his 'off days'. This corpse lacks his subtle handling of tones, standing out crudely against a flat, black field. Instead of being his cadaverous masterpiece, it seems a rushed job perhaps given to an apprentice.

Another reason for disappointment is that whereas other depictions of the dead in this manuscript are animated and seething with that ambiguity of life itself still somehow present in the corpse, this one seems more literally dead. The historian of medicine Katherine Park has recently argued that in Northern Europe, as opposed to the South, the corpse had to be protected and contained far more carefully, since it was not believed to be fully dead, but potentially sensitive and active. Still continuous with the community it had left, individuality adhered to its flesh up until this 'self' dissolved away into skeletal anonymity.[4] Anthropologists have shown how in most cultures the human corpse provides a site where a multitude of contradictory fantasies, from fascination to repugnance, are played out, often involving a complex negotiation between the 'first death' (the extinction of living breath) and 'second death' (the mineralization of the corpse to its hard remains – teeth and bones).[5] In the late fourteenth century there existed simultaneously an intense effort to deny decay, in miracles of bodily incorruption and the display of relics for example, and at the same time an urge to celebrate it, in the show of tombs and in Remiet's own art. In this particular miniature display of 'first death' (Fig. 122), the thing that is dead is actually alive with vermin, crawling with worms and toads. Still to be cleaned of its flesh and in the process of becoming a skeleton, it is laid out with its head, almost a skull, thrust back atop a tomb, ostentatiously, almost theatrically, revealing itself to the onlooker. Picturing the decomposition that normally goes on hidden within the sepulchre or under the earth, the artist was here bringing into the open something that deeply horrified his contemporaries. But he was not alone in doing this. By placing his cadaver on top rather than underneath the tomb slab, Remiet is associating the display of the corpse and fashionable funerary memorials carved in stone known as *transi* tombs, which exhibited the appearance of the corpse after death, usually accompanied by a suitable admonition to the onlooker to the effect that 'As I am so shall you be'. This small picture and the cadaver type found throughout the *Lay* by Remiet's own hand in fact predates by a decade the earliest extant French example of this tomb type, the *transi* of Guillaume de Harcigny, physician to King Charles VI, who died in his early nineties on 10 June 1393 and whose limestone tomb slab, originally part of his elaborate tomb in the cemetery of the Cordeliers at Laon, is still extant (Fig. 123).[6]

That Remiet used the *transi* image in order to stabilize death, to make its hollowness signify life, can be shown in his strange use of it to illustrate the chapter of the encyclopaedia by the Franciscan Bartholomeus Anglicus, the *Livre de propriétés des choses* that concerns 'les qualites des elements et des iiii humeurs' (Fig. 124). Here he places man's body in the midst of the four elements, which are the materials of change and decay in the sublunary world. Most images that illustrate this chapter of the encyclopaedia show man standing upright and resplendent in the world of the elements, but here Remiet uses the discussion of the elements and humours to show man embedded in the pale green of the earth, another horizontal stratum, like the aqueous and white-blue swirl of water and the deep blue cool of air, rather than the vertical aspirations of red fire, although it is this element that was thought to give man his animating *spiritus*. Looking at this miniature, Remiet would have thought of the significance of colour in his pictorial universe, how red has the vertical force of fire and blue the tranquil serenity of the sky and as well was the colour of the robe of the Mother of Heaven and Earth, the Virgin Mary. Gold leaf, which hangs like a strange fifth element, an aether between earth and air, was the most spiritual 'colour' in the illuminator's arsenal. It is significant then that in setting out his colour theory not on a wheel but in the horizontal strata of the mundane, it is earth in which his figure is embedded. The tendency of all of Remiet's lines towards this undulating horizontal is significant. Just as we still tend to associate the flowing pulse of life with the always moving zig-zagging of the encephalograph or other visual monitors

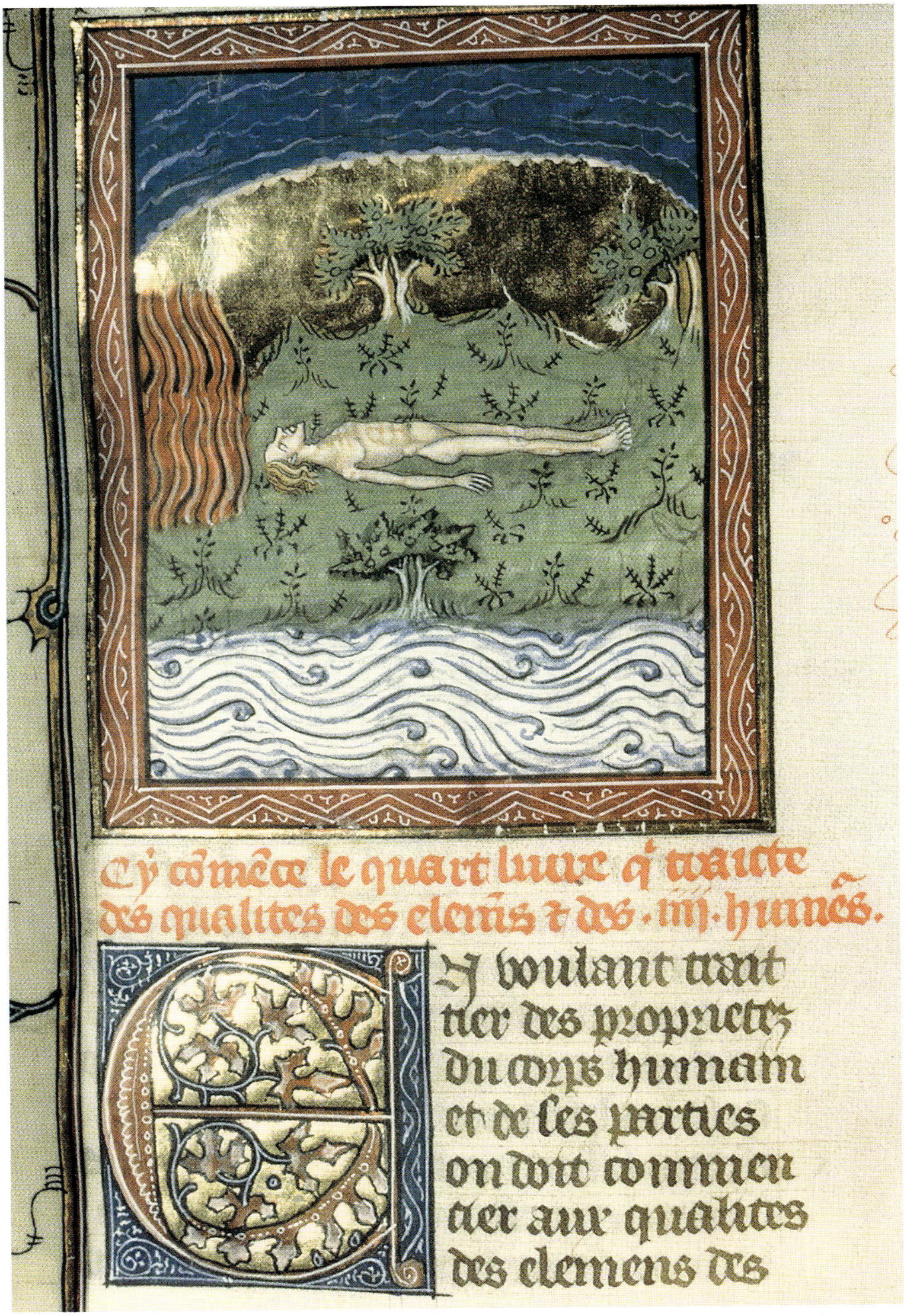

124. Remiet. Brussels, Bibliothèque Royale, MS 9094, fol. 45. *Livre des propriétés des choses.* The four elements and the corpse.

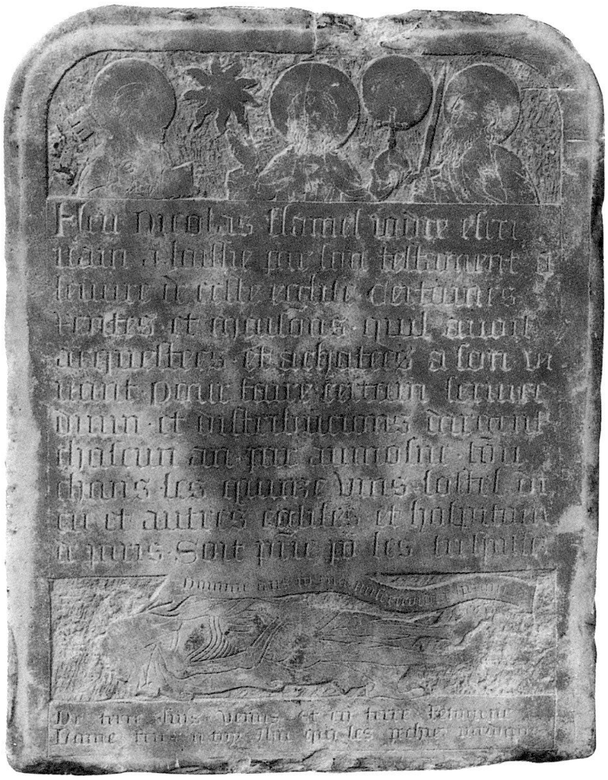

125. Paris, Musée de Cluny. Tomb of Nicolas Flamel (d. 1418).

of bodily rhythms in use in hospitals today, the wavering horizontal line was even then emblematic of a pulsing life, and its flatlining, the horizontal nullity of extinction – no reading – death. Remiet's lines are always moving and wavering, their ceaseless pulsing literally dependent on his own blood pumping into his arm, to his hand and fingers.

This corpse lying amidst the flux of the elements is a combination of all of them and yet its natural resting place, its 'end' in Aristotelian terms, is the earth to which all flesh returns. It is interesting in this respect that the tomb of Guillaume de Harcigny at Laon originally bore a long inscription, part of which read: 'Deo et Nature reddo simplicia. Acta compossititi sint Deo Grata (To God and nature I give back in simple form what was composite by the grace of God)'.[7] Also significant at this point is the extant tombstone of the Parisian scribe and alchemist Nicolas Flamel, which his will tells us he kept in his house before his death in 1418 (Fig. 125). Below the blessing Christ and a long list of his numerous pious bequests given in return for prayers, is Flamel's naked *transi* lying stretched out on its shroud. This has been linked to the symbolism of the alchemical *negrido*, the black corpse emblematic of the corruption that, according to the alchemists, is necessary for all generation and which allows for the transcedence of the dissolution that is called death.[8]

The spectacle of death was all important. Between the skulls grinning over the other famous *transi* of this type, that of Cardinal Jean de la Grange at Avignon, who died in 1402, ran the usual inscription about foetid rot, worms, etc., but its beginning,

'Spectaculum facti sumus mundo', is derived from I Corinthians 4:9: 'For we are made a spectacle unto the world.'[9] As John Chrysostom explained in his discussion of relics, the crucial aspect of death was that men should see within their own lives their future end.

> God allowed Abel to die first, so that Adam, the transgressor, could learn what death really is from its appearance . . . Had Adam died first he would never have seen any dead bodies. Adam though, remained alive, and saw in another body – that of his son – the triumph of death. Thus he could recognize more clearly and exactly just how huge his punishment was . . . God showed that death was bitter and hostile. Adam learned this not only through the first sight of death, but also through all that happened after: through the foul smell of the corpse, through the pus which oozed from it, through the ashes into which it was transformed, and through all the circumstances which followed the burial.[10]

The *transi* tomb is an effort to make the earth transparent and to reveal what goes on in the ground – to make the fact of death a continuing spectacle to the living. The ability of artists to depict the facts of decay had long been admired. Aristotle had described how 'Things which in themselves we view with distress, we enjoy contemplating when they are represented with very great accuracy – the forms of the lowest animals, for instance, and also of dead bodies', and Augustine described the visual *curiositas* ellicited by corpses, asking 'what pleasure hath it, to see in a mangled carcass, what will make you shudder, and yet if it be lying near, they flock hither to be made sad, and to turn pale?'[11] The corpse is in a sense a unique kind of image, and its own double, neither in this world nor totally absent from it, with no relation to anything except itself, occupying a suspended position in time and space, but a position that is also constantly diminishing, always changing under the pressure of increasing fragmentation. Such instability made the corpse the antithesis of the aesthetic object, which in the Middle Ages tended to be seen in terms of stillness, permanence and wholeness. The chaos of the squirming and collapsing cavities only assumed such a permanent status when it became bones. What Remiet's own spectral double represented is a picture of a corpse, a representation of something becoming representation.

The first thing that made this a horrible sight to behold is that it was, contrary to what we might think today with our lurid plague-filled visions of the Middle Ages, quite rare actually to see a corpse in this advanced state of decay. Records suggest that interment usually followed very quickly after death. Another Avignonese cardinal, Pierre Blau, stipulated in his will that on his death his body should be interred without pomp 'two or three hours after' his decease.[12] The time a corpse went without burial was extended if, for example, the death occurred in the late afternoon, when it was forbidden to celebrate mass; wills order that testators wait until the following day. Although it has been argued that medieval funerals were long drawn out affairs because of the uncertainty surrounding the moment of death and the always present fear of live burials, miraculous resuscitations were rare.[13] The rapidity of burial was partly a result of the still deep rooted fear of contagion by the corpse, partly for practical reasons during the foetid summer months. But it also indicates a fear of witnessing exactly the spectacle of decomposition that Remiet depicts.

Another shock for the contemporary viewer of this image would have been the nakedness of the corpse. Naked one came into the world and naked one left it was a cliché of the preachers, but this lack of clothing evinced a deeper shame, going back to the invention of death at the Fall. For it had been only at the moment of sin that Adam and Eve 'saw that they were naked' and felt shame at the sight of their sexual organs, henceforth called *pudenda*.[14] The late fourteenth century saw the efflorescence of what we would call modern urban commercial pornography, which the chancellor of the University of Paris, Jean Gerson, saw daily, complaining of 'the filthy corruption of boys and adolescents by shameful and nude pictures offered for sale at the very temples and sacred places'.[15] Although a corpse can feel no shame, people obviously looked forward with dread to this exposure of their members, just as they feared sleeping naked lest this be mistaken for their final slumber. Traditionally the naked corpse, before and during the funeral ceremonies, was covered with a *sudaria* of the finest cloth, depending upon the wealth of the deceased. Sometimes this textile was offered to the poor after interment, but sometimes the will stipulated that it be buried with the body, its only protection against the worm-filled earth. Only priests and persons of the highest rank were allowed to be interred in their vestments and insignia of rank. One reason it was so popular for wealthy layfolk who were reaching their end to join the mendicant orders was that they could then be buried in the frock of a Franciscan or Dominican and thus not go naked into the next world.

As the word *transi* itself suggests, another disturbing aspect of the cadaver type was its transformation and disintegration. Just as death was not an end but a transition, the *transi* embodied in a static image the process of becoming nothing. It was not until all the flesh had been stripped away by a natural process of decay that a person was thought to be fully dead. In many societies it is only after the flesh is dissolved and reduced to bones or ashes that the spirit is freed, an attitude implicit in many of the taboos and strictures about the corpse that continued well into the fourteenth century. The process of decay is thus a necessary but unpleasant one. Only the very wealthy, in their elaborate rituals of perfuming and embalming, sought to bypass it. The difficulty of transporting their illustrious corpses over long distances for burial (with accompanying stories of them giving off murderous odours) and the practice of royalty bequeathing different parts of their body to be enshrined by different religious institutions had led to the practice of the division of the corpse. This meant that the bodies of French and English notables were often dismembered immediately after death and boiled in a mixture of wine and water. Their flesh and entrails could be buried locally and only their clean white bones would proceed to the chosen place of eternal rest. This practice of the division of the corpse had so disgusted Pope Boniface VIII that, in his 1299 bull *Detestande feritas*, he had prohibited the practice 'so that the ferocity of the said abuse will no longer tear apart the human body and move the mind of the faithful with horror'.[16] Division still continued to be popular, however, and in Remiet's time it was de rigueur for his princely patrons. The fashion for *transi* sculptures might be seen partly as a response to the increasing fragmentation of the corpse, holding the whole together in the unity of a still-individual body, representing in stone what had often been ripped apart in flesh. For those wealthy enough to afford such a tomb, rot could be represented and putrefaction portrayed in loving personal detail.

Most people did not have the luxury of an individual grave, let alone a *transi* carved above it. They went through a lengthy process of disintegration, going immediately and complete into the earth in unmarked graves, where they would rot amidst a crowd of other bodies in various states of decomposition. After a time, usually a year, they were exhumed. Then their bones would be piled up amongst the rest in the charnel houses, forming a fantastic calcified exhibition of anonymous fibula, tibia and skulls. That was part of the natural cycle of things. What was not natural was to see this process before one's eyes. Just as today's jaded audiences are simultaneously disturbed by and yet drawn to be voyeurs of images of the body as a sexual object, fourteenth-century people were troubled and yet at the same time obviously titillated by peeks at the putrid object of their anxiety. Hamlet's question 'How long will a man lie i' the earth ere he rot?' asked of the gravedigger, was often voiced in the fourteenth century. Theories of decomposition varied. I have been unable to verify Huizinga's statement that 'it was believed that a human body took only nine days to decompose'. The many stories of exhumation of saints' bodies in the Middle Ages suggest that there was no clear rule, and the period of a year pronounced as the time it took for flesh to divide from bone in Pope Boniface's legislation on the division of the corpse provided a safe margin.[17] What people knew from everyday experience, and what doctors and other learned men told them from their reading of Aristotle's *De generatione et corruptione*, was that soon after the spirit leaves the body, it changes its composition and begins to decay and return to the elements from which it was composed, in a kind of anti-creation, the opposite of Remiet's image of God forming man out of clay. This de-composition had no parallels with myths of artistic creation, but was simply a return.

What we see in pictured corpses, here and on other pages of the *Lay de la fragilité humaine*, are the external medical signs of putrefaction which follow soon after death. These include a spreading greenish colour extending from the abdomen, discoloration and swelling of the face as well as of the scrotum or vulva, distension of the belly with gasses, a brownish coloration of the surface veins giving an arborescent pattern on the skin, escape of blood-stained fluid from the mouth and nostrils, liquefaction of the eyeballs, shedding of nails and loosening of the hair, blistering of the flesh causing an eventual shedding of the epidermis, conversion of the tissues into a semi-fluid mass, and the presence of maggots. The bloating is caused by micro-organisms of decomposition producing methane gas, which collects in the tissues. Within twelve to eighteen hours it is not uncommon for facial features to be unrecognizable, the hair having slipped away from the scalp and the entire body swollen to two or three times its normal size.[18] Many of these traits are visible in Remiet's cadavers in *portraits d'encre*, suggesting that these signs, even if they were taken from modelbook drawings, ultimately depended upon his and his audience's knowledge of the actual processes of death.

One convention clearly at work in Remiet's image and in many texts, like Innocent III's, was the topos of the body as 'food for worms'. In some texts and images of the period, the worms have voices and enter into a *disputatio* with their fleshy food.[19] A way to avoid the worm and get down to the bare bones as quickly as possible was to separate the bones and flesh immediately after death by boiling the corpse, and, as we have seen, this had become accepted practice for the nobility and royalty of Northern Europe in the thirteenth century. The fear and fascination with worms and other vermin were wide-

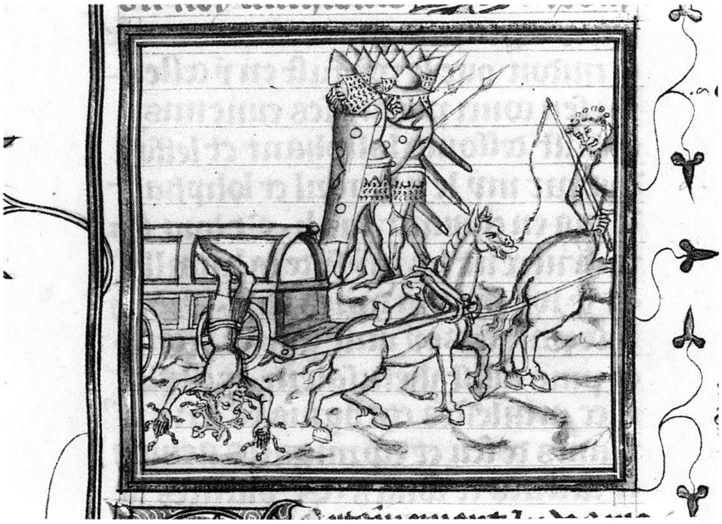

126. Remiet. Paris, Bibliothèque Nationale, fr. 312, fol. 215. *Miroir historial.* The ugly death of King Antiochus.

spread in Europe at this time and were partly in response to fears of contagion and disease but also reflective of a new interest in the processes of nature. For it was believed that these creatures were born in decomposition from corruption rather than semen and that, in the words of Bernard of Gordon, 'worms, serpents and beetles are generated by putrefaction in the human body, just as worms and flies are born of the earth'. The serpent itself is born in the marrow of a dead man, according to the popular *Etymologiae* of Isidore of Seville, who cites Ovid as saying that 'some believe that when the spine rots in the sealed tomb, human marrow turns into snakes'.[20] For Thomas Aquinas, 'the production of a new being requires only the pneuma, heat and humidity: that is why we see living animals born of fermenting or putrefying bodies'. Recipes made use of cadaverous products: according to a popular treatise called the *Liber vaccae*, worms are generated in the human head soon after death; called *sinciput* by the philosophers, they make especially powerful candles. After seven days the worms become flies and after fourteen days they are great dragons whose bite is instantaneously fatal. When made into a candle with a wick of crape, 'you will thereby behold with great fear a great thing and indescribable forms'.[21] Not only birth and death but creation and death are again combined in the cadaver.

Such rot was a signal of the soul's having fled. Sometimes the worms of decay appear miraculously before death or at the moment of death in order to show the evil nature of the deceased. This is the case with the *laide morte*, or 'ugly death', of Antiochus of the Book of Maccabees, a ruler whose pride commanded everything, but who died 'eaten by worms and in stench', according to the *Miroir historial* (Fig. 126). Here as the evil tyrant falls from his chariot, slithery things crawl out of his body ('les verse issurent de la char'), the moral of which is that man should be subservient to God ('home mortel estre sugiet a dieu'). It was precisely this premature rot suffered by lepers that led to their exclusion from society, not only as dead but as evil. By contrast, the 'special dead' often forestalled rot. In numerous saints' legends their divine corpses remain sweet-smelling and undecayed. But besides exhibiting these signs of either good or evil, the corpse was believed to be able to communicate even more actively with the living. The best evidence for this are records of how the corpse of a murder victim could be called upon to witness or identify the guilty party. Northern European law admitted the principle of 'bier-right', which held that the corpse could bleed or make some other physical sign in the presence of its murderer.[22]

The stretched-out position of Remiet's corpse, its head thrust back and mouth gaping upwards, is also a traditional one. Jewish burial customs, by contrast, prescribed the corpse, to be buried face downward, and various cultures laid out the corpse quite differently. The liturgist Bishop Durandus, at the end of the thirteenth century, decreed that 'the dead person should lie on his back so that his face always looks towards heaven'.[23] The corpse was laid in the earth facing east, ready to regard the Redeemer on the great awakening at the Last Judgement. The complex of anxieties surrounding the processes of decomposition and dissolution of the flesh were perhaps so prevalent in the 1390s because the end of time was expected at any moment, and all that flesh, whether in the stomachs of worms, slowly disintegrated or quickly boiled to naught, would be at that moment returned, the rot reversed.

Requiem

Not having been taken back inside the self, digested, assimilated as in all 'normal' mourning, the dead object remains like a living dead abcessed in a specific spot on the ego. It has its place, just like a crypt in a cemetery or temple, surrounded by walls and all the rest. The dead object is incorporated in this crypt – the term 'incorporated' signalling precisely that one has failed to digest or assimilate it totally, so that it remains there, forming a pocket in the mourning body. Jacques Derrida[24]

We have recourse to burial for the sake of both the living and the dead. For the sake of the living, lest their eyes be revolted by the disfigurement of the corpse, and their bodies be infected by the stench, and this as regards the body. But it profits the living also spiritually inasmuch as our belief in the resurrection is confirmed thereby. It profits the dead insofar as one bears the dead in mind and prays for them through looking on their burial place, wherefore a *monument* takes its name from remembrance, for a monument is something that recalls the mind (monens mentem), as Augustine observes. Thomas Aquinas[25]

In his images of the actual funeral rites, Remiet obscures the horror of decay with layers of elaborate cloth and of complex rituals that efface the still-lively corpse and keep it at its proper distance (Figs. 127–9). Here we cannot see the dead, only remember them. Remembrance of the dead played a fundamental role in medieval social and individual consciousness in rituals that were experienced at the funeral of an individual and whose repetition permeated the whole culture. Mourning is a form of aestheticization, a distancing that detaches all interest from the lost object. Catholicism at the end of the Middle

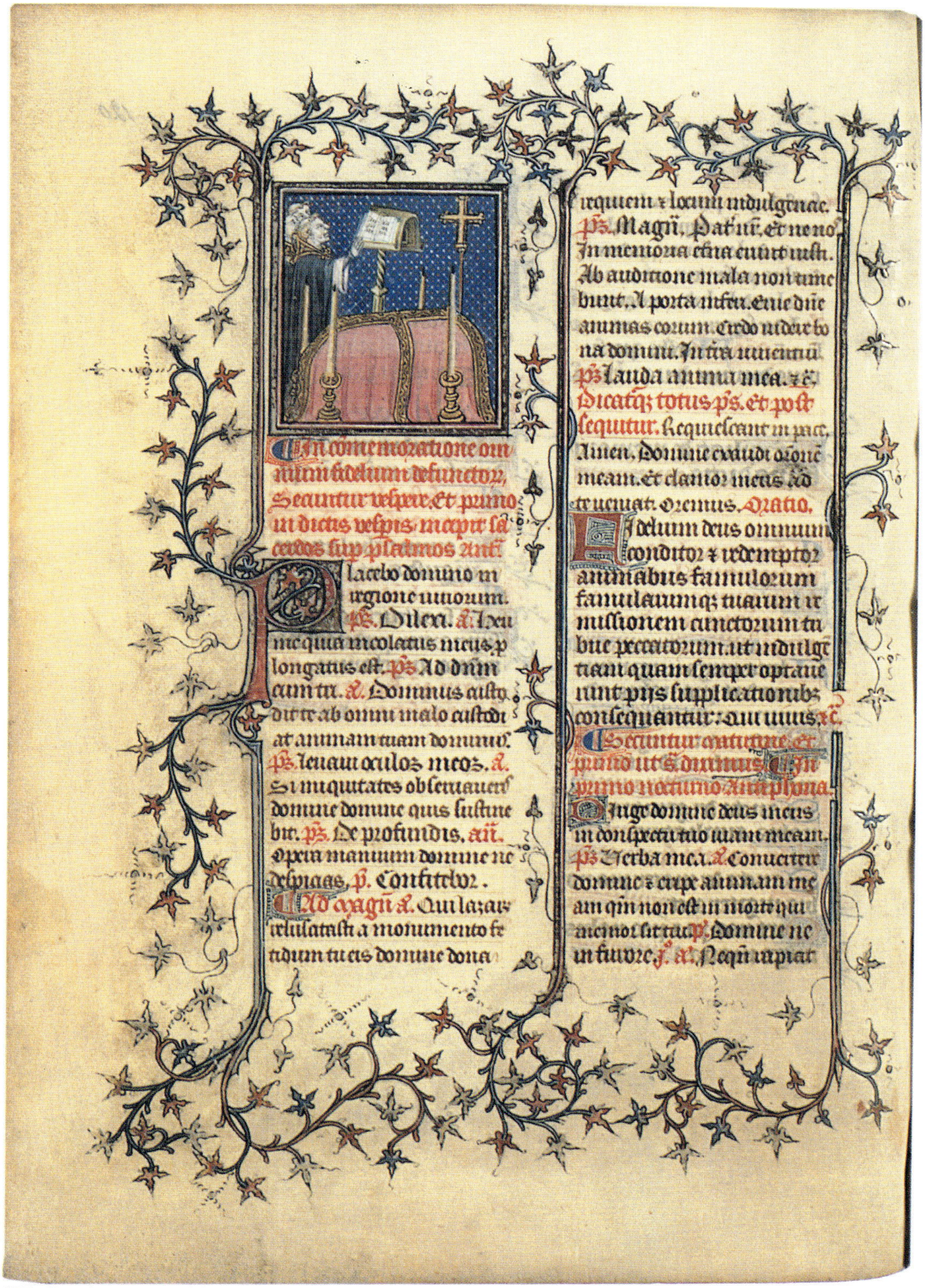

127. Remiet. Paris, Bibliothèque Nationale, lat. 1024, fol. 13. Breviary. Office of the Dead with priests around the bier.

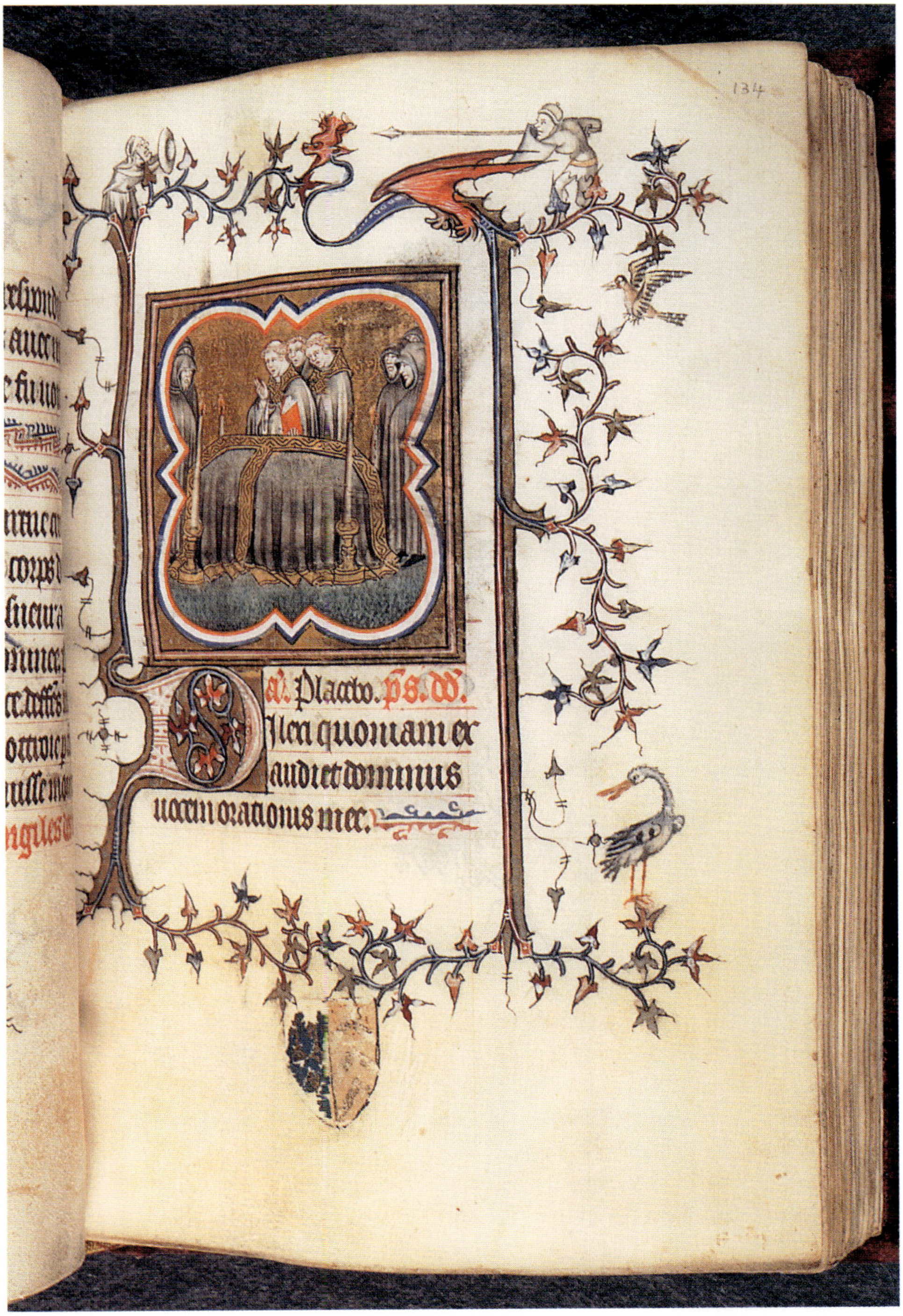

128. Remiet. London, British Library, MS Yates Thompson 45, fol. 134. Book of Hours. Office of the Dead with priests and monks around the bier.

Ages was 'a cult of the living in the service of the dead', and its two major celebrations, the Requiem Mass and the recitation of the Office of the Dead, were the major means of social cohesion among those still living and the beginnings of a massive urge towards aesthetic pleasure.[26] Burial took place only after a formal series of obsequies performed by the clergy and varying enormously in length and elaboration depending upon the status of the deceased. The minimum necessary was probably the most common type of low mass, *de mortuis*, which required only a single priest and was ten times cheaper than the elaborate sung service of the Requiem Mass, which was celebrated by the priest for the repose of one or more souls and was increasingly associated not just with funerals but with performance in private on a daily basis as a means of obtaining special grace for the souls of the departed. The series of psalms and antiphons that constituted the other major liturgical service, the Office of the Dead, developed out of the practice of adding special prayers for the dead to the Divine Office and was part of the Roman Breviary. In the medieval funeral, this office preceded the requiem or funeral mass and was performed through the night before the burial in the morning. This association with darkness not only links this performance with sleep but explains the importance of candles in the service, visible in all of Remiet's depictions of the subject.

When Remiet represents the Office of the Dead, he is illuminating a scene of darkness. The two-volume breviary that corresponds to that described in the inventories of Louis d'Orléans opens with the Vespers of the Dead, the first part of the office and that which the young prince would have recited (Fig. 127). The red rubric below the miniature announces that this is the service 'in commemoration of all the faithful dead (omnium fidelium defunctorum)' and opens with the antiphon 'Placebo domino in regione vivorum', which sometimes gave this part of the service its name. At the bottom of the first column, the text reads: 'Qui lazorarum resuscitasti a monumento fetidum (He who raised Lazarus from the stinking tomb)', and in the course of the fifteenth century illuminators sometimes represented the biblical scene at this point. But for Remiet and his contemporaries, the image that should go here was that depicting the ritual itself in the ongoing present. The word 'monument' in this phrase would have evoked not only the actual tomb of Lazarus but the medieval etymology of the word 'monument' from *monere* and *mentem* – to hold in the mind.[27] For such images are not representations of actual funerals. These representational 'vigils' being sung over the corpse as it lay in the church were an elaborate effort in memorialization, in which the splendid silk and gold cloths, candles and number of attending priests all signified the status and importance of the individual being buried, not only in his past life but in future memory. In one of the first rhetorical treatises written in French, *Archiloge sophie*, the Augustinian Jacques Legrand describes the role played by manuscript illuminations in the cultivation of mnemonic techniques. 'The first rule for remembering something, and especially for incorporating it by heart, consists of putting into the heart and the imagination the figure and the form of the thing to be remembered. Wherefore one best learns from illuminated books, for the difference between the colours bestows remembrance on the different lines, and therefore the thing itself.'[28] According to the medieval liturgist Durandus, the office is to be interpreted as a totally mournful experience in which all canticles of exultation and joy are omitted in order to emphasize the penal nature of death, its nature as punishment that must always be kept in mind.[29]

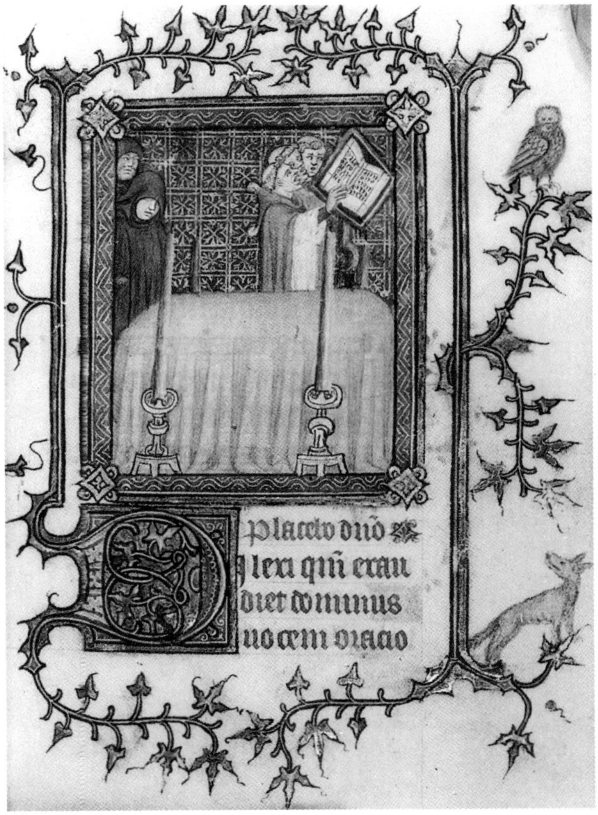

129. Whereabouts unknown: Sotheby's sale, 13 July 1977, fol. 41. Book of Hours. Office of the Dead with priests and monks around the bier.

Chanted on behalf of all the deceased by the priest, the office was also an integral part of every Book of Hours and thus was not a special process but something recited daily by the devout for whom the first person voice of the prayers must have resonated with special urgency. The office continues with five psalms beginning with Psalm 114, 'Dilexi quoniam', which implores the Lord to 'deliver my soul from death'. In one Book of Hours, Remiet painted a large version of the breviary composition, with the funeral rites being sung over a grey bier covered in a sumptuous grey cloth but likewise embroidered with a gold cross (Fig. 128). Once again Remiet is showing his sensitivity to the significance of colour, the tonality here being totally grey but sumptuous in its effects. These obsequies are obviously for the death of a wealthy man, since the pall over the deceased is the type of rich *pannum*, of taffeta, silk or brocade of Lucca, that only notables refer to in their wills.[30] The importance of this covering is that it obliterates the fact of the death – a traditional anxiety that led to the covering of the upturned face of the deceased – veiling the rot that Remiet had so lovingly delineated in other contexts. In another version of the subject, the visible teeth of the open-mouthed chanting priest add a macabre skeletal note to the ritual (Fig. 129). What Remiet is representing in these three images of public death ceremony is not a covered coffin but a covered body, a corpse separated from the living by the slightest tissue or veil. Without individuality, these are anonymous future deaths of a group or class – those who could afford such signs. Another index of wealth is the placing of four large tapers at the corners of the bier. Wax was a major expenditure at funerals, and lighting the body during the Vigils of the Dead and the hours until burial was carefully stipulated in wills. Aimery de Montragoux, a notary who was murdered on the Pont Saint Michel on 7 August 1405, stipulated in his will that four torches, each of three pounds of wax, should surround his body at the church of Saint Séverin.[31]

In Remiet's most splendid Office of the Dead miniature (Fig. 128), three priests at the centre chant the office from a big red book. Thus, although this text and its image were used in private devotional space, the medieval reader was projected through memories of sight and sound into a full liturgical setting. On either side there are groups of hooded men in grey. These represent the professional mourners, or *pleurants*, who were often monks hired by the wealthy to moan ostentatiously and weep resplendently over their corpses, along with widows, mendicants and members of special burial confraternities that were specially set up to aid the clergy in funeral rites. Their hooded anonymity reveals exactly this status as paid performers in a theatre of death.[32] The same hooded mourners appear in the *Lay de la fragilité humaine* and evoke the wailing liturgy of the dead in contrast with the joyful sounds of horns and drums that lead the young courtiers in dancing and enjoying 'les delis du monde' (Fig. 130). Remiet was especially good at making these sharp contrasts between youth and age, joy and sorrow, so typical of his time. Below on the same page is another such contrast, a chivalric joust of four knights and two corpses being carried off the field on stretchers. Here too we see the hidden face, like that of Mensonge in the same manuscript, covered by a hood as a sign of sorrow. Thus cloth not only served, in Elizabeth Brown's words, 'to protect observers from the strange force which the dead, through their visages, could exert over the living' but also became a sign of mourning itself.[33]

The Roman Histories of Valerius Maximus were transformed, as we saw in Chapter 3, into a treatise on the 'fragility of human life' by their translator Simon de Hesdin. In the Troyes manuscript of this text, juxtaposing gorgeous gold borders with miniatures in a grim, grey wash tinged with blue and rose, Remiet produced one of his most playful images of death, an image that undid or reversed the expectations of these carefully coded rituals (Fig. 132). This miniature introducing Book III bears no relation to the introductory remarks by the translator at this point. In the text we read that this first chapter is about the 'yndole' or 'image of virtue yet to come', which can be discerned in the man of good character from his infancy in his 'bonne physiognomie' and 'bonne manière'. In the image, however, courtly manners are associated with coffins and the rituals of infancy with mourning. On the left is the strange spectacle of two elegant and youthful couples dancing around a bier, while on the right four hooded mourners lament around the baptism of a baby! Such a reversal of ritual protocols at the beginning and ending of life seems especially poignant in an age when many infants died before they could be baptized (and were thus excluded from church graveyards) and when the fascination with the funerary did indeed become a courtly dance.[34] This is one of those places where text and image come apart, where Remiet seems to be resisting the text, playing rather at juxtaposing and contrasting his own visual ideas about the rituals surrounding birth and death, beginning and ending.

Following the Requiem Mass, which was usually performed in the morning, the

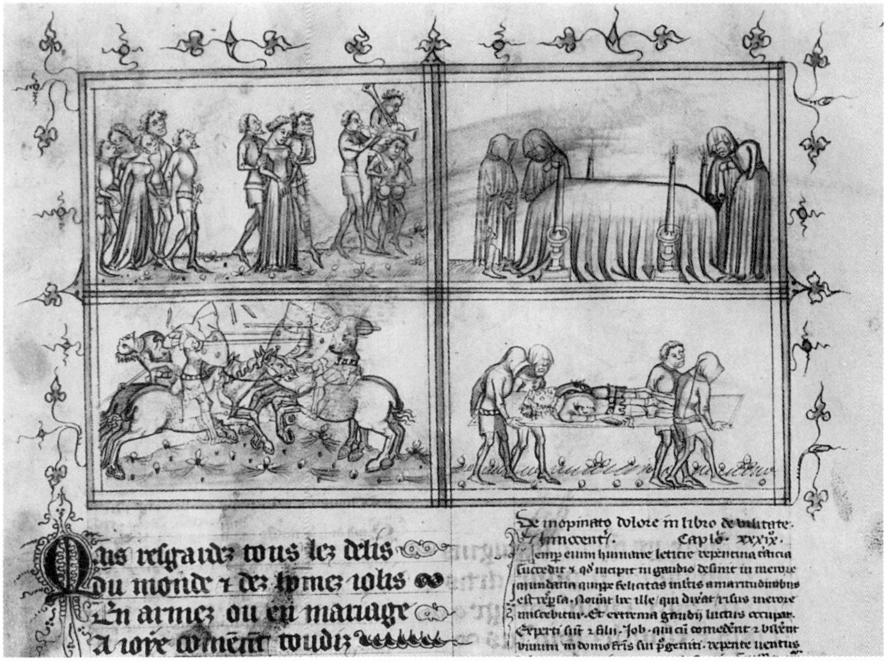

130. Remiet. Paris, Bibliothèque Nationale, fr. 20029, fol. 13. *Lay de la fragilité humaine.* Festivals and funerals.

131. Remiet. Paris, Bibliothèque Nationale, fr. 268, fol. 247. Livy, *Histoire romaine.* The funeral of an emperor.

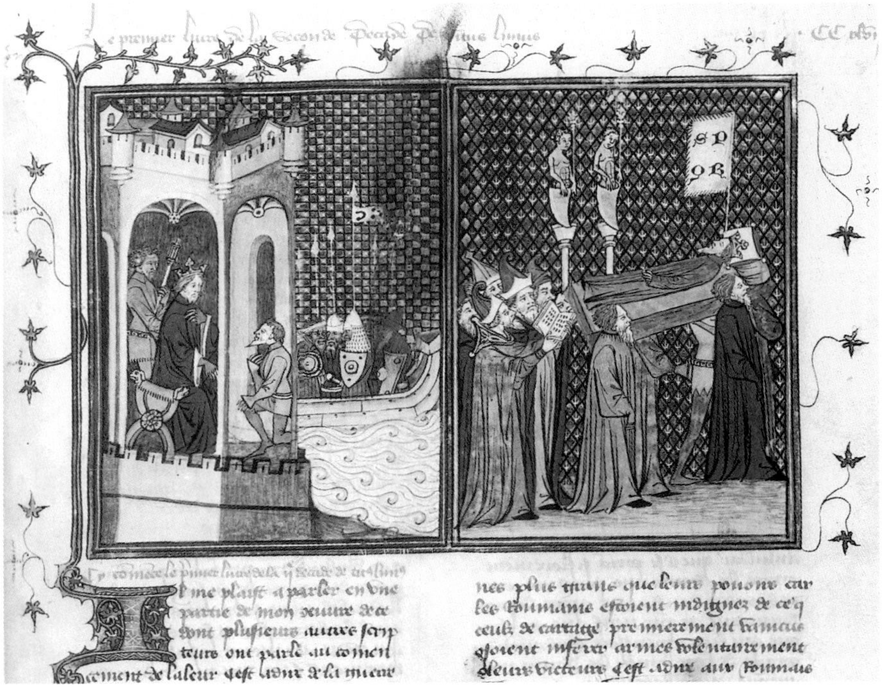

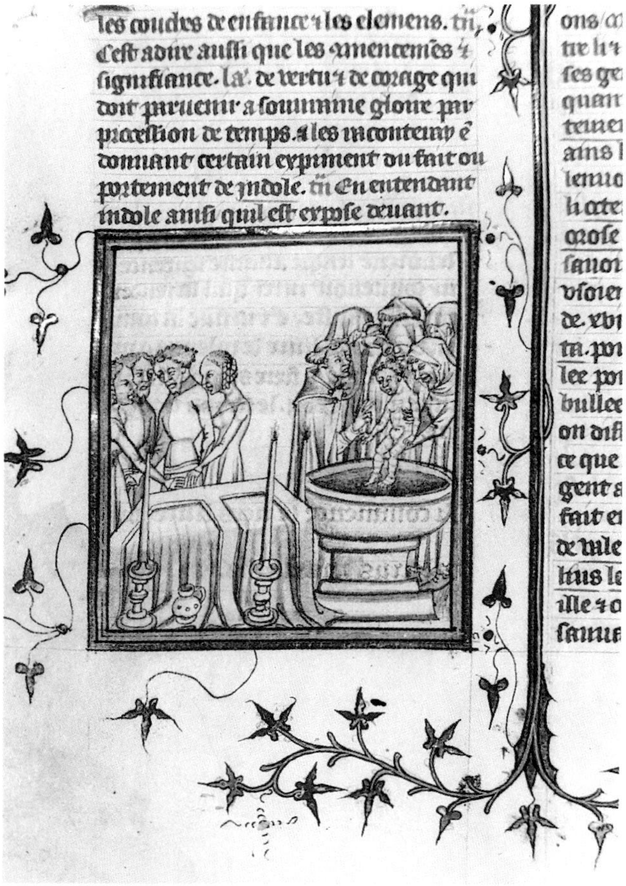

132. Remiet. Troyes, Bibliothèque Municipale, MS 261, fol. 124v. Valerius Maximus, *Faits et dits mémorables*. Dancing at a funeral, mourning at a baptism.

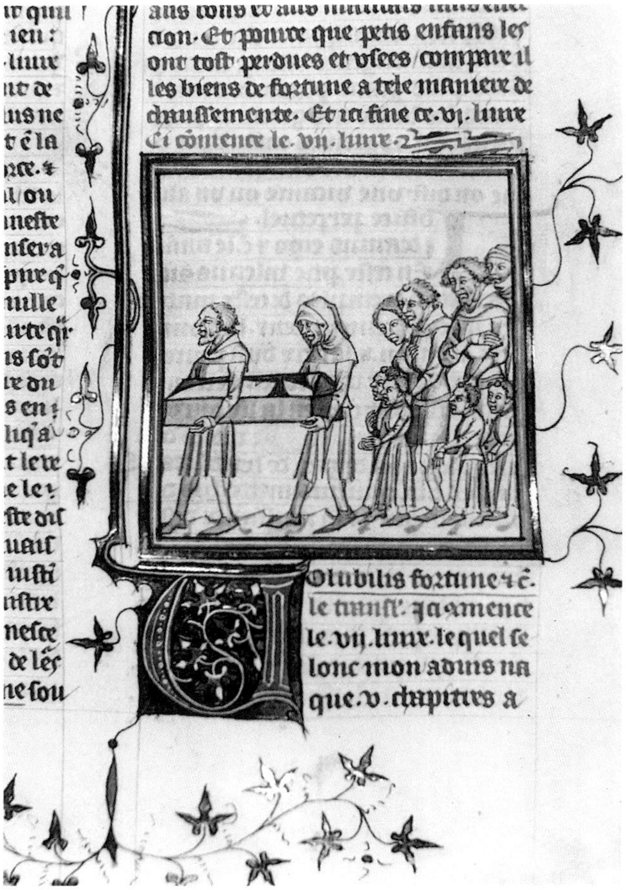

133. Remiet. Troyes, Bibliothèque Municipale, MS 261, fol. 261. Valerius Maximus, *Faits et dits mémorables*. The funeral of Metellus.

blessing of the bier with holy water, and the Absolution, there followed the procession to the burial site. This performance traversing the spaces of the living was represented by Remiet for the funeral of the mighty (Fig. 131) and the more humble (Fig. 133). Those who bear the bier from church to grave should be of equal status and rank to the deceased, according to Durandus, and women were excluded from this crucial act of leave-taking. In the copy of Livy's History, Hannibal's funeral is attended by the leaders of the community in their long robes and, by contrast to images of the Vigils of the Dead, the corpse is displayed openly on the bier. The face of the deceased is exposed, not covered. But perhaps this is not a corpse at all. The stiffness of the body suggests another aspect of the interpenetration of representations and rituals in Remiet's time – the use of wax or wooden effigies for the deceased. In royal funerals in the fourteenth century, the emphasis upon seeing the body of the monarch led to the use of effigies which were carried before the eyes of the crowds. It was exactly this period that saw the increased use of these simulacral cadavers, as one recorded in the will made by Louis d'Orléans in 1403, which describes the need to make 'une representation'.[35] These representations were complex portraits, the head constructed from a mortuary mask painted to be as life-like as possible and the body a wooden or wax core dressed in the magnificent robes of rank.

The physician to the French court Henri de Mondeville assumed that the faces of kings, queens, popes and important figures would be exposed to the gaze of the crowd after death.[36] While it might seem that such a display of face, hands and feet of a deceased person suggests an increasing acceptance of human mortality, this use of representational substitutes, along with the veiling of the face of the deceased attested at earlier royal funerals, suggests the increasing unease and fear of the living with facing even the most powerful, the royal, dead, even in rituals. Representing is here a form of veiling and obfuscating the terror of the flesh rather than, as is usually thought, the revelling in it. While the display of the earthly rank of the dead person became increasingly important, the finality of the body's temporal death was something that could exist publicly only in the spectral realm of simulacra. We are dealing here, not with representation *of* mourning but with representation *as* mourning, in that artists like Remiet were the ones who produced these elaborate simulations. In 1388 Remiet's associate the court painter Colart de Laon was paid for his work on the funeral or 'obséques du comte d'Eu', specifically for painting three golden draperies and making the fake fur for the count's effigy, or what is referred to as 'the representation of the said deceased (la representacioun du dit defunct)'.[37]

Funeral processions usually halted three times on the way to the church. Indeed the death of a great person was something of a boon to business in the city, especially in the trades that provided the candles and cloths and organized the great spectacle of the procession. To judge from contemporary descriptions, the funeral of Charles VI in 1422 was something between a fair and a theatrical show, with countless changes of costume in the form of rich cloths for the doll-deceased. The nearest Remiet came to depicting a royal funeral was in a copy of Livy showing the funeral of an emperor attended by pallbearers and watched over by the idols of the city (Fig. 131). What is being carried here looks like a representation rather than an actual corpse. The ruler's represented body represents his dignity as a God-given status and thus is eternal, while his other body, not present before the eyes of the crowd but what is of course interred, represents his individuality as a human being, a mortal.[38]

For the poor parishioner of Remiet's district, a coffin would have been a luxury, for although occasionally biers made by the Menusiers were lent for the solemn procession to the cemetery, once the rites were over they were not interred with the dead. In the funeral of Q. Metellus that Remiet pictures in the Troyes Valerius Maximus manuscript, the two pallbearers and the crowd that follow could easily be imagined winding through the narrow streets of the Right Bank to the Innocents and have very little 'antique' about them (Fig. 133). Ancient culture preferred cremation, as many do today, which horrified the medievals. The diverse groups of people in Remiet's little scene contrast to the serried ranks that followed the funerals of the Parisian great in the period – with sometimes hundreds of poor men dressed in new white tunics through the charity of the deceased, widows and orphans in separate phallanxes, confraternities and different religious groups, all cashing in on the corpse's pre-purchase of paradise. The men, women and children closely following the bier in Remiet's scene represent the family of the deceased, who help define social status along with co-workers. The guilds of Paris stipulated that the bier of a deceased member be carried by his confrères.[39] In 1388 when the Count of Foix, a relative of the Count of Foix-Bearn who owned this manuscript of Valerius Maximus, heard of the death of his son Gaston, he summoned his barber for a close shave and dressed himself in black, showing the proper physical transformation of the body in the act of mourning.[40] The procession has been called the most fundamental part of the funeral ritual, separating the dead and the living, but at the same time it was an incorporation of the spectators in the spectacle of death that, over the course of one's life, inscribed the path to the cemetery, a path that all would one day take on the shoulders of others rather than with their own feet. Everyone had experience of sharing in such rites. How many funerals did Remiet attend, solemnly marching behind the bier with his head slightly sunken like the little figures in this funeral scene?

This liminal status of death as a transition between zones that were much less clearly defined than today can be seen in the treatment of a group in society who were considered already dead yet still alive. As the popular riddle put it: 'Without my eyes I saw a dead man die; after his death he was not dead; still he lives and yet he is dead; all this after death I see.' Answer: 'A person condemned as a leper, whom one can see living, walking and talking.'[41] Lepers were excluded from society, even from its margins, since the fear of infection demanded the strictest isolation. Prevented from entering towns, their mobility was prohibited and they were entrusted to the leprosaria, the largest in Paris being Saint Lazare, named after the man whom Christ allowed to live to die a second death. Although the disease of leprosy was itself diminishing throughout the fourteenth century, the fears that it stirred were not.[42] The liturgy of the *Separatio leprosorum* pronounced the Office of the Dead over those afflicted. In some dioceses the ceremony was literally like a funeral. The priest led the leper, whose face was covered just like that of the ordinary corpse, to church, chanting the seven penitential psalms. Kneeling between a black cloth set between two trestles simulating the bier, the leper confessed his or her sins.[43] Friends and family would file past the body and then a solemn procession would follow the leper to where he was to be 'interred' alive. The ceremony reached its climax with the sick person kneeling before the priest to accept the *cliquettes* (clappers which announced his coming), gloves and *panetière*, while those assembled sang the *De profundis*. Outside the house or place where the leper was to spend the rest of his days, the priest threw a piece of earth taken from a cemetery on to its roof and shouted to the leper within, 'Sis mortuus mundo, vivens iterum Deo'. Then he announced a series of rules which the leper had to obey. He had to promise never to enter churches, flour mills or markets, never to wash in rivers or go barefoot, never to have sex with any other woman but his wife and never to touch children. When he was dead his body was to be buried in his house and not in the cemetery. Finally the priest planted a cross of wood at the door of the hut as a sign to all. This incarceration of those who began to rot away and whose flesh gave birth to worms while they were alive shows how much death was considered not so much as an end but as another state.

Remiet did not depict this living death as it was lived but in its double negation. As part of the ideology of royal power, which increasingly demonized the 'other' by association with death, he pictured lepers in the *Grandes Chroniques* being burned alive in 1321 at the orders of Philippe V, who accused them, along with the Jews, of having poisoned wells (Fig. 134). The skin's eruption in any kind of mottling or patterning brought terrible dread; it was literally thought of as the externalization of inward corruption and God's punishment. Lepers were the children of those who had engaged in

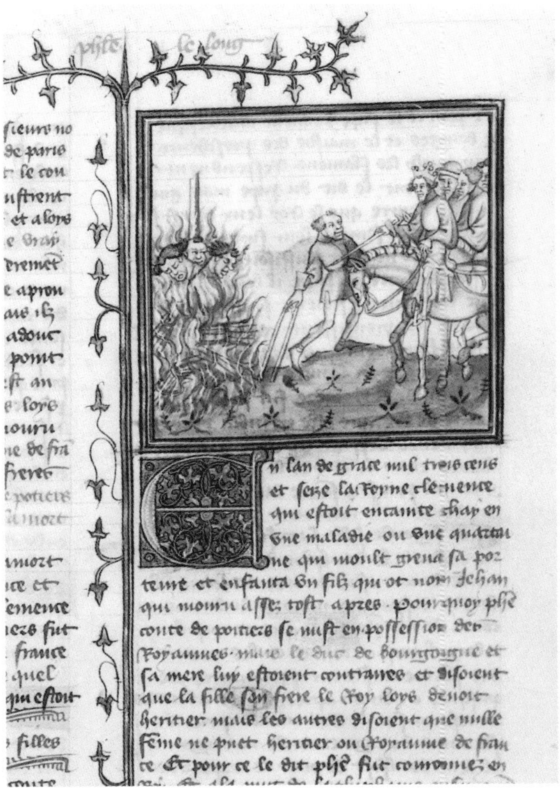

134. Remiet. Paris, Bibliothèque Nationale, fr. 2606, fol. 363. *Grandes Chroniques de France*. Burning lepers alive.

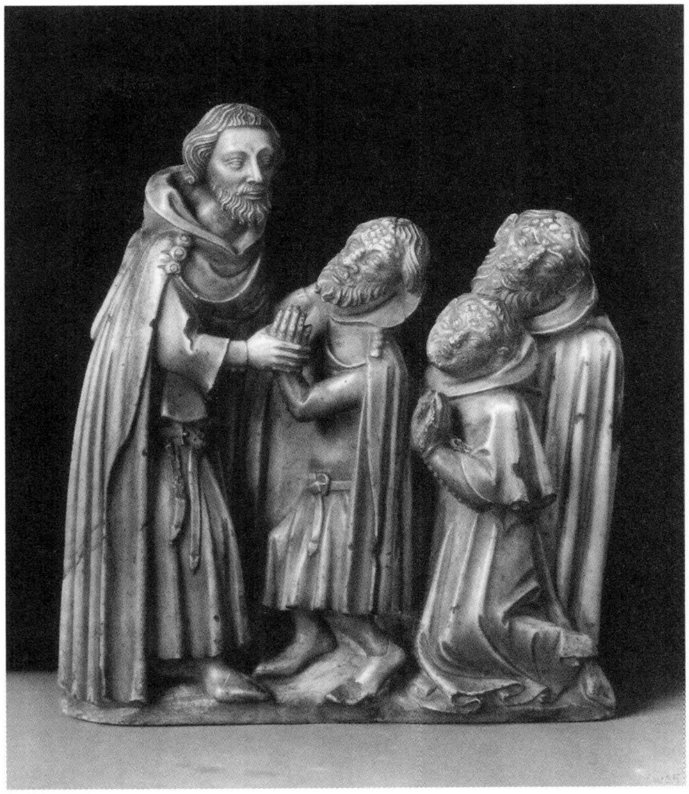

135. Baltimore, Walters Art Gallery. Marble relief of St Elzear of Sabran curing lepers.

unlawful sexual positions during intercourse or those who had been coitally created during a woman's menstruation. If Remiet's minute art is not up to the delineation of such stigmatized skin conditions, sculptors of the period were able to use the surface effects of swelling, blistering and flaking of the epidermis to great effect (Fig. 135).

But to return to the rites surrounding those who were more than metaphorically dead, Remiet never depicted the funeral of a French king, though he took part in the illumination of manuscripts like the *Grandes Chroniques* of Charles V which included lavish funerals of kings and queens. More intimate obsequies were reserved for his portrayal of the Virgin's death and funeral in Hermann de Valenciennes's *Histoire de la Bible* (Fig. 136). Immediately after her demise the Virgin's face or at least her eyes were covered and she was asperged with holy water. One angel holds this in a cup while two others transport her diminutive naked soul to heaven in a sheet. The dormition of the Virgin, especially as celebrated as a liturgical feast, became a positive 'type' or model for Christian death. Although, as the text states here, this soul is not like any other but is clearer than the sun and is not 'disfigured', its ritual obsequies represent those yearned for by any Christian.[44] At her funeral, in the second miniature on the page, an enormously long coffin, its lid marked with a great cross just like that in the pagan funeral of Metellus (Fig. 133), is carried by her holy co-workers, the apostles. The ambiguity of death in Christianity even reached the very highest dead. Why, after the Virgin's soul has been carried up to heaven in a little sheet by two angels in the previous picture, directly into heaven and thus not

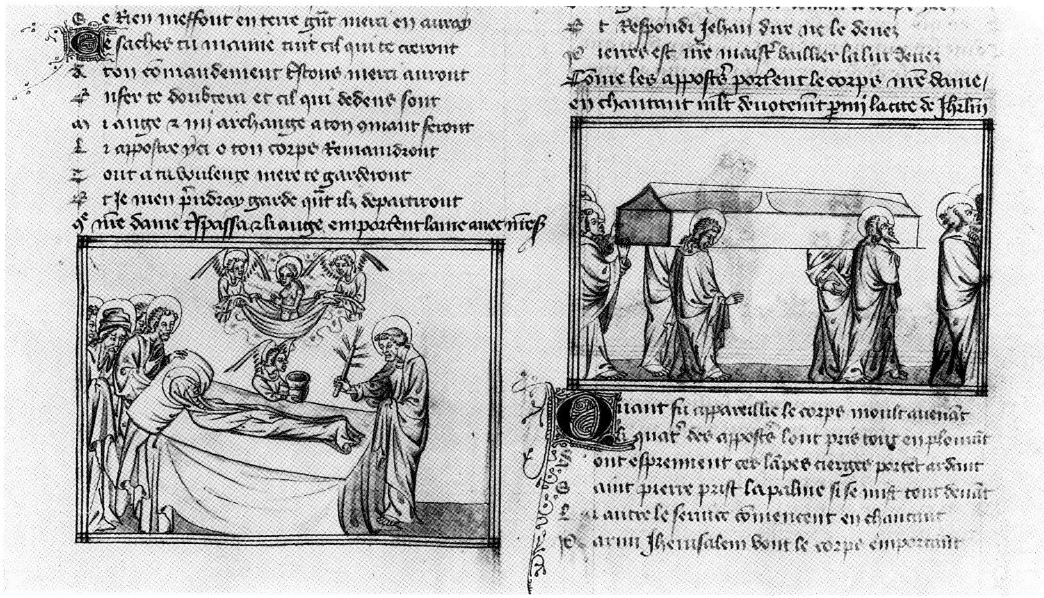

into the liminal zone of Purgatory, is it necessary for her corpse to be carried by apostles in a solemn procession with singing? What dues are being paid to this empty sign of an empty sign? For the Virgin's body, more than in any mere mortal passing, is not in a phase of transition, laid aside until the Final Reckoning, but is already ascended to join her son in celestial eternity. The reason for the continued importance of mortuary ritual even for a soul already rejoined to its body and in bliss is underlined here in relation to the Virgin as herself representing ecclesia – the church.

Her last rites are also here staged to enforce certain ideologies about the power of Christianity over other religions, and specifically its power over death. In the next picture in the sequence, Remiet pictures the legend of the unbelieving Jew who, mocking the elaborate funeral procession, attacks the Virgin's bier only to find his hands sticking to it and being ripped off, to be later miraculously restored by St Peter (Fig. 137). In Hermann de Valenciennes's retelling, the Jew is converted by the miracle, making this a spectacular show of power. All Parisians, even those without access to Remiet's picture, knew this story from a carved quatrefoil on the north transept of the cathedral of Notre Dame. But Remiet is as usual more fascinated by the moment of fragmentation and bodily dismemberment: the Jew's hands are shown separated from his arms by the horizontal bier. This visual isolation articulates the fear of defilement by the 'dirty' hands of unbelief and reinforces the culture's policing of boundaries, untouchable areas, especially around death. It was usually around the body of Christ in his sacrificial death, in the form of the Host, that stories of Jewish defilement were most often propagated, but here in the ancient narrative the process of punished pollution has already begun. In Remiet's lifetime the small Jewish community that existed in Paris, which was delimited by royal jurisdiction to two *juiveries* on the Right Bank and to certain moneylending practices, was viciously attacked by Parisians in 1380 and 1382. Jewish babies were stolen and many persons

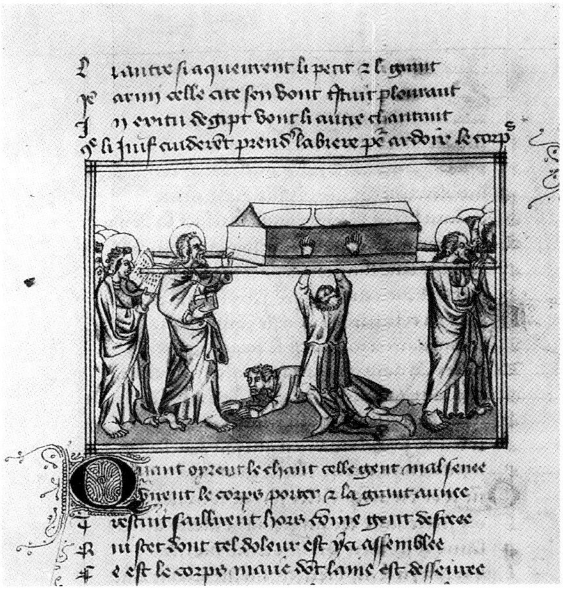

136. Remiet. New York, Pierpont Morgan Library, M.526, fol. 43. Hermann de Valenciennes, *Histoire de la Bible.* The death of the Virgin and her funeral.

137. Remiet. New York, Pierpont Morgan Library, M.526, fol. 43v. Hermann de Valenciennes, *Histoire de la Bible.* The miracle of the Jew who attacked the Virgin's bier.

138. (*below*) Remiet. Paris, Bibliothèque Nationale, fr. 313, fol. 382v. *Miroir historial.* The obsequies of St Mary of Egypt.

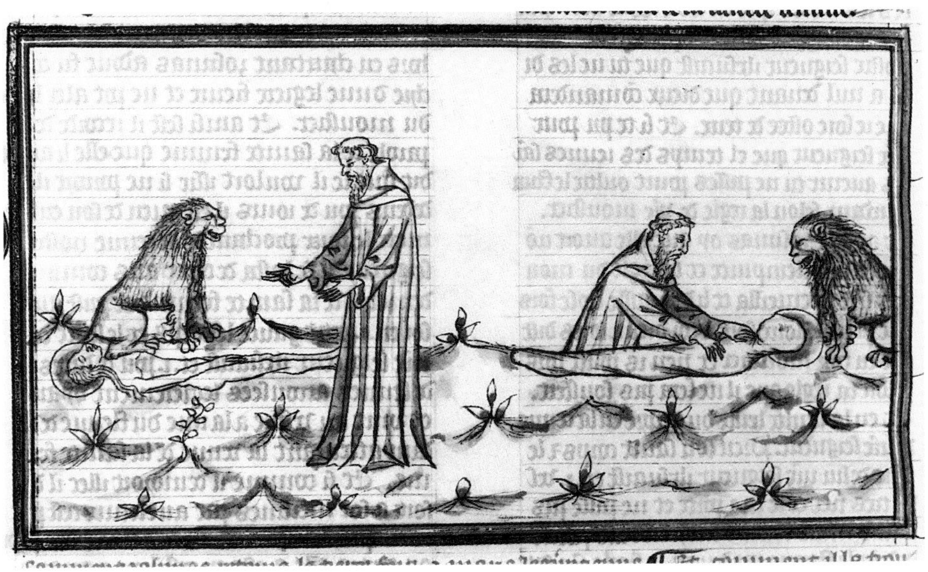

forcibly converted. A provost of the city was executed for seeming to side with the Jews, and pogroms continued until finally in 1394 the Jews were expelled from the country by ordinance of Charles VI.[45] The hands left by the arrogant unbeliever in this image are traces of repeated terrible violence and the erasure not just of an individual in a mythic story but of a whole community in the city of letters. However, for Remiet, as for most fourteenth-century Parisians, this disappearance was celebrated rather than lamented and its memory, the marks of countless contructed defilements of the holy corpse, was visible both at Notre Dame and in Remiet's minute rendering.

In the *Miroir historial*, Remiet presents us with more post-mortem rituals, undertaken in the desert by Zosimas the hermit upon the body of a female saint, Mary of Egypt (Fig. 138). First he comes upon what the text describes as 'the body of the holy woman lying without a soul'. The totally naked corpse, its flesh miraculously preserved in the dry desert heat, was facing east, a sign of how much she had been prepared and how gladly she had embraced her own end after years of self-mortification. Reversing this orientation in the second scene, Remiet shows the hermit, and his lion assistant, dutifully performing the rituals of respect and honour that are due this saintly body. He is described as singing canticles and making 'oraisons sollonelles', although in the picture his half-length form leaning over her now more sensuous, shroud-wrapped body, seems more intimate. This minimal funeral is still a more prestigious one than any pictured in the *Grandes Chroniques* or ancient histories, because of the status of the deceased. The honour shown to the dead saint is also suggestive of the way in which Christian culture became increasingly necrophilic, in its commemoration of and devotion to its most special dead.

Tombs, Idols and Relics

Each time we find a skeleton, we call it human if it is in a sepulchre. Jacques Lacan[46]

For, if such things as a father's clothes, and his ring, are dear to their children in proportion to their affection for their parents, then the actual bodies are certainly not to be treated with contempt, since we wear them in a much closer and intimate way than any clothing. A man's body is no mere adornment, or external convenience; it belongs to his very nature as a man. Hence the burials of the righteous men of antiquity were performed as acts of loyal devotion. St Augustine[47]

One of the reasons why images became so important in late medieval culture was not because they were seen as representations of life but because they worked as powerful reminders of death. Their status was not that of the living, but was just like funeral effigies themselves, mineral matter, artificial, stone phantoms of lost objects, meant to keep the pleasure of the deceased alive in the imaginary. Many fourteenth-century anti-image tracts, especially by the English Lollards but also in poems by the Parisian Deschamps, stress that images rather than being 'life-like' are death-like. Nevertheless, great respect was paid to them and through them the dead person – no longer present but in a way still residual – continued to be represented. All this pomp is in contrast to the *Lay de la fragilité humaine*, which stresses that there is only 'une fins et une mors' – 'one end and one death' – and that 'it is one for man and beast' (Fig. 139). Remiet's picture shows a man eating, following Genesis 3:19 ('In the sweat of thy face shalt thou eat bread till thou return to the earth out of which thou wast taken'), and then being quickly dispatched to it by two gravediggers. This is juxtaposed with the adjacent scene of cattle and horses feeding alongside their corpses lying like equine *transi* on the ground, their legs stuck in the air. Again there is an emphasis upon the mouth in relation to death, of the ceaseless incorporation and engorgement of matter that must always be expelled, vomitted or in its

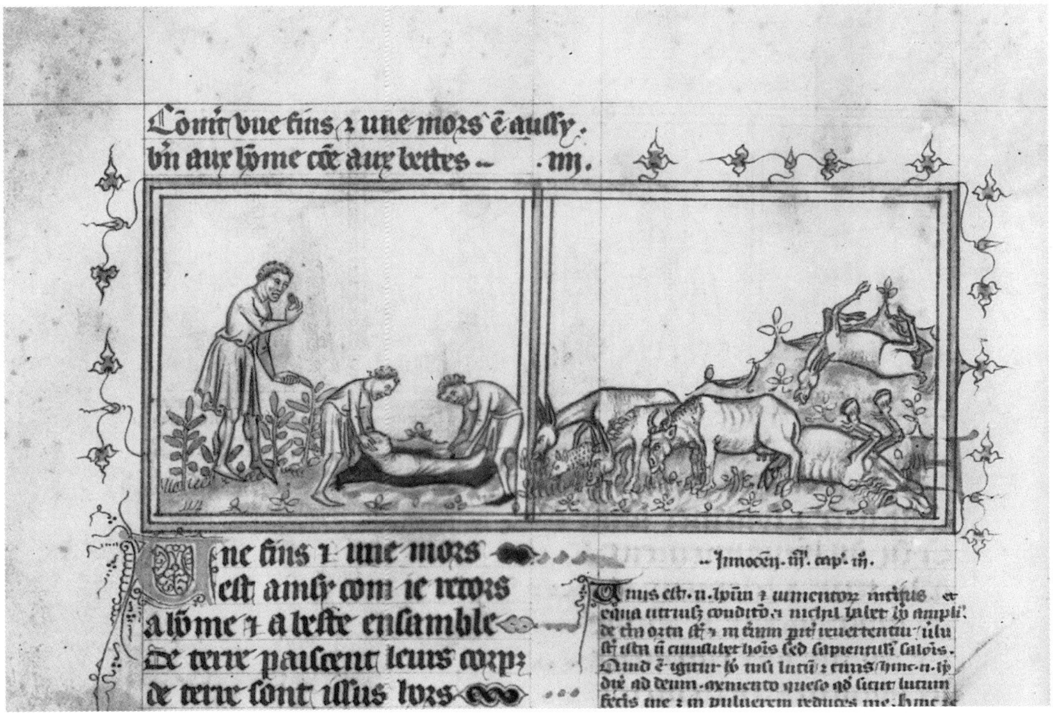

139. Paris, Bibliothèque Nationale, fr. 20029, fol. 6v. *Lay de la fragilité humaine*. The same end for man and beast.

turn eaten by the worm. There is not a priest or a mourner in sight. This is the anonymous death of the pauper, not so much in an unmarked grave, which was normal for most people, but in an unmarked social event, simply consigned like the body of a beast, to the earth.

That the bodily remains of the dead still 'represented' the deceased, no matter how denuded, can be seen in the common medieval process of reinterment. This is illustrated by Remiet in the *Histoire de la Bible* with the elaborate funeral ritual of Jacob, whose remains were embalmed and carried to Hebron by his son Joseph in order that he might be buried with his ancestors (Genesis 50:7) with great pomp and by 'a very great company' (Fig. 140). Carried by horses, an ark-like bier includes the disembodied head of the patriarch, looking like a medieval reliquary bust. Below in the next miniature is Joseph's own tomb, represented as a traditional thirteenth-century type used for rulers, a slab surmounted by a carved three-dimensional *gisant*. Instead of the staff of office, however, he bears the traditional scroll of a prophet, as though Remiet just imagined an Old Testament jamb figure from the cathedral of Notre Dame lying down (*gisant*) as his model. In this manuscript Remiet repeated this Gothic tomb type no fewer than four times, to represent the deaths of Old Testament kings, Joseph (5v), Moses (18v), David (21r) and Solomon (23r). On fol. 15r Joseph's tomb is forgotten as his bones are shown being dug up and taken for reburial in Israel (Exodus 13:19). Later men and woman are also shown gathering the bones of John the Baptist, whose relics were very common in fourteenth-century France (Fig 141). According to Pope Boniface VIII, the ancient

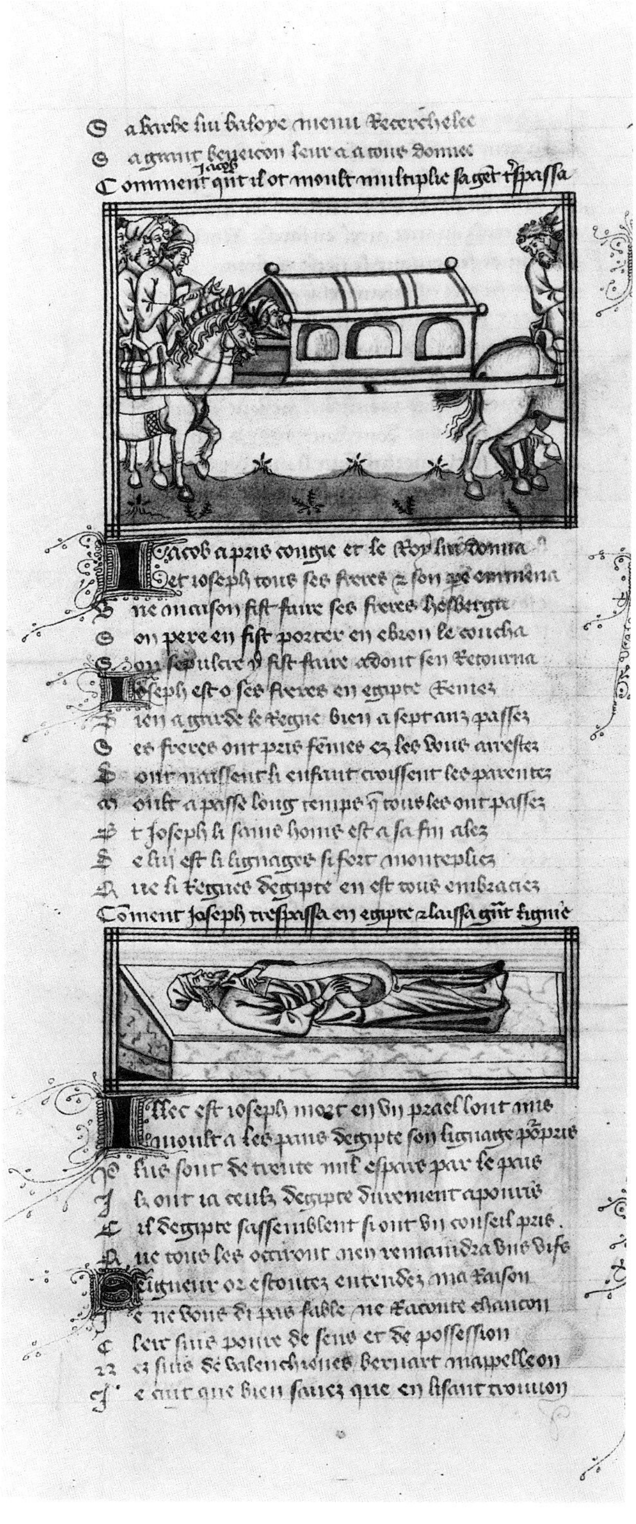

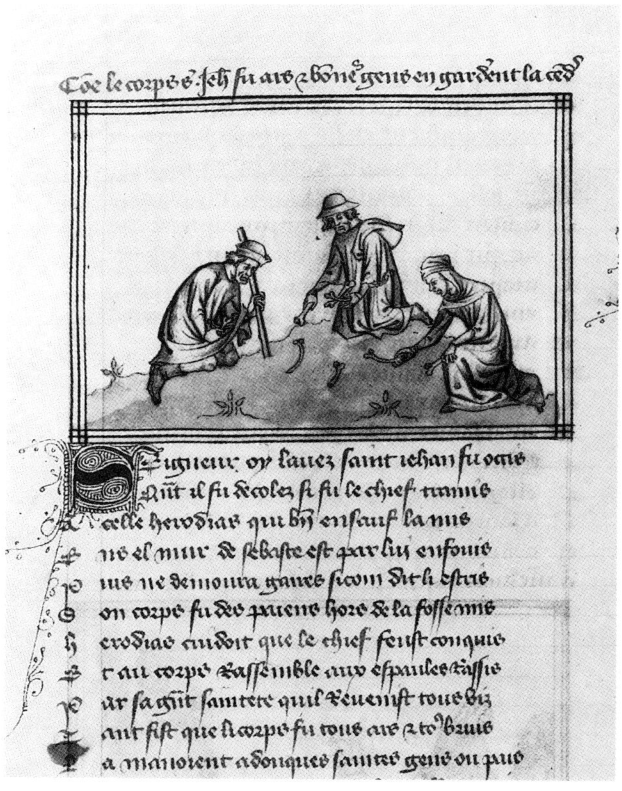

141. Remiet. New York, Pierpont Morgan Library, M.526, fol. 34v. Hermann de Valenciennes, *Histoire de la Bible*. Two men and a woman dig up John the Baptist's bones.

140. Remiet. New York, Pierpont Morgan Library, M.526, fol. 5v. Hermann de Valenciennes, *Histoire de la Bible*. Jacob's funeral and Joseph's tomb.

Jewish custom of inhumanization, or translation of the body after the flesh had been consumed, was considered licit for Christians, and the period of dissolution was defined as a year. Urban V, for example, who died in 1370, ordered that his body first be buried at Avignon and then, after its disintegration, that his bones be taken to Marseilles for burial in the church of Saint Victor, before the main altar.[48] There were obvious advantages in being moved, but for most of the deceased the sorting out of who was whom among the piles of dust and bones made reinterment an impossibility.

Nothing was more equalizing than the medieval graveyard. This space that occupies a marginal position in modern culture, a derelict landscape setting for horror films and the drive-through at the occasional funeral, was, by contrast, the lively heart and centre of medieval urban social life, 'the noisiest, busiest, and most animated, most commercial place in the rural or urban centre'.[49] A place for real dancing, and not only with death, the graveyard was the space where the sacred aura of the church met the profane world beyond. It was a place of communion with the community of the dead. To be buried in the *cimiterium*, which by canon law was integrally part of the church, was to rest within the consecrated precincts of the sacred place. The local parish church was not just a place for the community of the living but, in its cemetery, a site where the living could meet and remember the dead as well as pray for their own souls, which would eventually join their ancestors in the same place. Walled in like gardens, filled with magnificent memorials, sculptures and painted arcades, often with trees to offer shade, urban cemeteries were leisure centres, their cool shade in the summer providing the perfect strolling place for amorous young couples and ideal spots for family picnics. Things had got to such a state in Avignon in 1394 that Pope Clement IV was forced to prohibit dancing, prostitution and boules-playing from the cemetery of Champfleury. Unlike the rest of the city, which was delimited by numerous local jurisdictions and prohibitions, the many cemeteries were open places where a diverse group met in life as well as death.

They were also important places where one could look at art. This was certainly the case with the largest and most frequented cemetery in Paris, the Cemetery of the Holy Innocents on the Right Bank. From its origins until its destruction in 1786, this was a warehouse of death, displaying, in addition to the heaped-up piles of gleaming white bones and skulls under the arcades of the bounding walls, called *charniers* (from *carnis* – flesh), shops and stalls selling various items from rosary beads, to count out one's last days, to foodstuffs. The Innocents was described as 'un grant cimetière moult grant enclos de maisons appelées charniers, la ou les morts sont entasses'. Here were piled up the gleaming white tibia, ribs and skulls of countless corpses. In the social function of the *charnier* we can see the important cultural distinction between flesh and bone that existed in the fourteenth century. If the flesh, especially in its decay, was viewed with horror, the bones were deemed clean and pure. Here one could also listen to preachers, like Brother Richard the Franciscan, who kept crowds of thousands rapt from five in the morning till ten or eleven.[50] Obviously people did not separate, as we do, the realms of rot and repast, decomposition and recreation. According to a fifteenth-century account, the spectacular images that one could see there, even before the famous wall painting showing the Dance of the Dead, included a carved tympanum of the Three Living and the Three Dead commissioned by the Duke of Berry, who also wished to be buried there, and a stone statue of the Virgin, surmounting someone's tomb and 'so life-like that dogs would not piss against his sepulchre'.[51] There was also an entire Holy Innocent, encased in gold and silver, kept in the church. This was the martyrdom of infants that Remiet had depicted in the Paris portion of a breviary, the babies literally trampled underfoot and into the ground by Herod's soldier, perhaps because there was not enough room in the tiny 'B' for him to swing a cat, let alone a baby (Fig. 142). But it also speaks to the particular devotion to the Innocents on the part of the Parisians, who not only observed this feast day on 28 December each year, but also viewed it as a 'black letter day' (a notion linked to the colours and rubrication of calendars like those illuminated by Remiet). All year long, the day of the week on which the preceding Innocents' Day fell was considered unlucky and was particularly ill-omened for setting out on journeys or fighting battles.

Huizinga in his highly influential chapter on Death imagery in *The Waning of the Middle Ages* called this type of cult a 'curious example of spontaneous accretion of religious usage', and in the section of his book called 'Religious Thought Crystallizing into Images', in sympathy with some of the religious thinkers of the later Middle Ages like Pierre d'Ailly, protested against the 'multitude of images' as 'an evil of superfluity'.[52] His criticism of the 'mechanical' multiplication of feasts and festivals is, however, a modernist, rationalist attitude that equates large quantity with emptiness and considers uniqueness to be the only expression of true feeling. What he saw as superfluity and excess has to be considered, not from the viewpoint of narrow doctrinal theology on the one hand or as the equivalent of today's mass delusional *National Enquirer* on the other, but rather as 'religious practice'.[53] Instead of being just a proliferation of superficial images, the widening range of rituals, feasts and festivals, and their visual manifestation, made for more intersubjective spaces, increasing dynamic interplay between persons and things and creating a far richer interplay of feelings and experiences in both sacred and secular spheres of life than had previously been possible. This was nowhere as evident as in the spectacular culture of death, which must be understood as part of the lived experience of the everyday and not just as the history of an idea. If Remiet's depiction of the Massacre of the Innocents is to be seen as a manic intensification of traditional iconography or as its routine repetition, we must view both its making and its reception as more than the cheapening of spirituality by some medieval version of mass-market appeal.

The dead were a community that lived close by and shared space with the living. Remiet's shop on the Rue de la Parcheminerie looked out directly on to the south side of the walled-in cemetery of his own local parish church of Saint Séverin, which itself later developed into one of the most renowned charnel houses in Paris and whose Gothic arcades for the display of bones still stand. This is where his body was probably laid to rest. Another local illuminator whose name appears on the 1368 document alongside Remiet's, Antoine de Compiègne, who died between 1411 and 1414, was certainly interred at Saint Séverin. The parish had eighteen burial chapels in the church as well as two unequal sections outside divided by a path, the larger sector called 'the cemetery of the poor' and the smaller area 'the cemetery of the rich'. It was important to establish such social marks of distinction, since the bones were mixed up and displayed under the *charnier*. An exemplum of the day described a man who, every time he passed by his local cemetery, always took care to recite a *de profundis* for the departed. He was beset upon by robbers and was saved by the dead who 'rose up and each held in his hand a tool that he had used during his lifetime, and defended him vigorously'. The moral of this story was that people

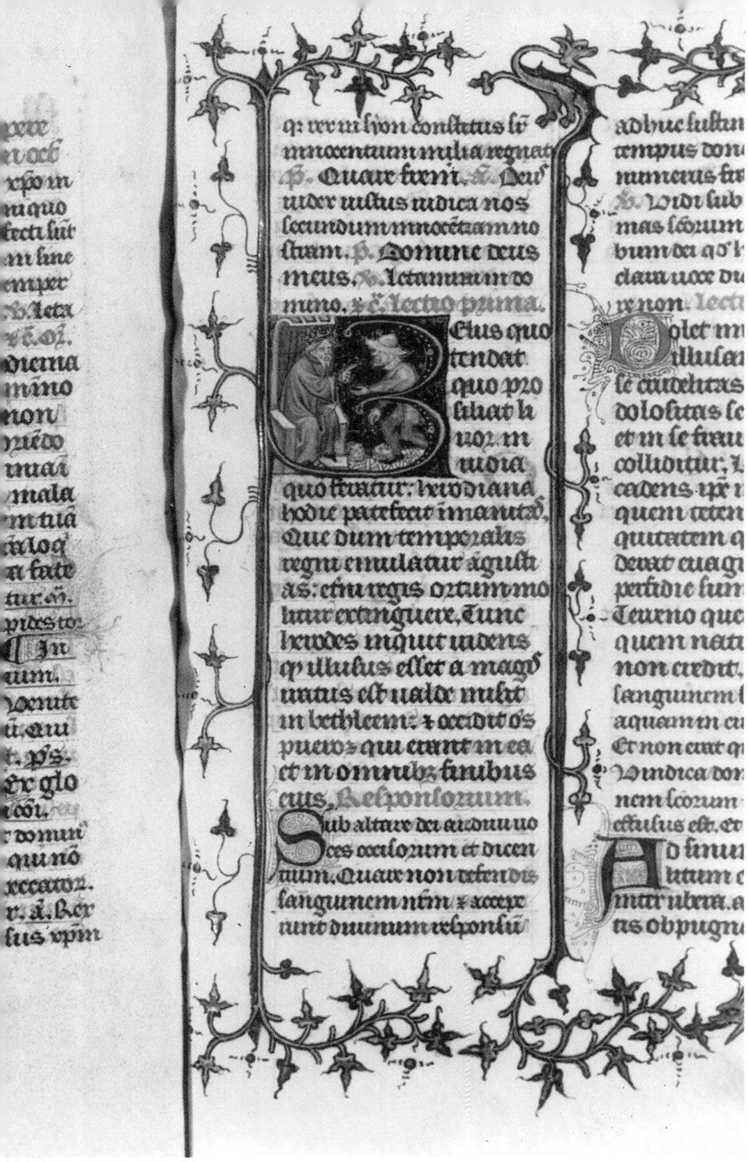

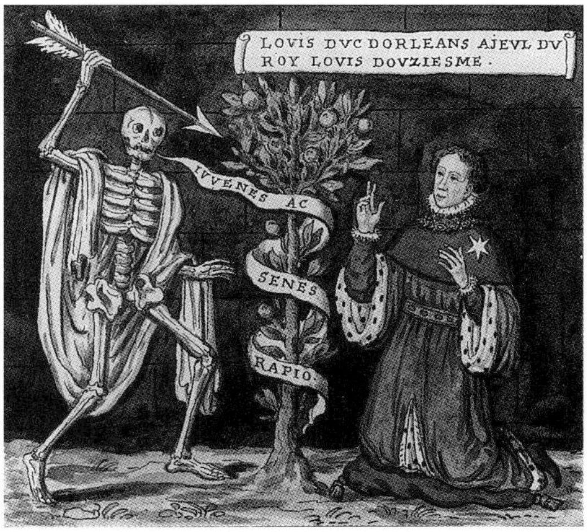

143. Drawing of the lost wall painting in Louis d'Orleans's chapel at the church of the Célestins. Oxford, Bodleian Library, MS Gough Gaignières 2, fol. 1.

142. Remiet. Paris, Bibliothèque Nationale, lat. 1024, fol. 29. Breviary. The Feast of the Holy Innocents.

should aid the souls suffering in Purgatory through prayers, alms and the holy mass.[54] An even more disturbing graveyard story, which enjoyed renewed popularity in Remiet's time and was illustrated by the Limbourgs in the *Belles Heures* of the Duke of Berry, was that of Raymond Diocres, tutor to St Bruno, who lifted the lid and spoke out from his coffin to assembled mourners during the night obsequies and again at the burial in the graveyard, where his voice boomed, 'I am damned!'[55]

The woman and two men grubbing for the bones of the Baptist in Remiet's miniature represent part of that underworld of rag-and-bone scavenging that was a basic of his visual world (Fig. 141). The grave was not considered a place of eternal rest in the fourteenth century but a waiting-place for rotting. This immediately suggests a psychological difference for medieval viewers that distinguishes the iconography of death most clearly from our own perceptions – the distinction between flesh and bones. The latter were everywhere visible and 'clean' in the sense of being totally dead. Among the category of the

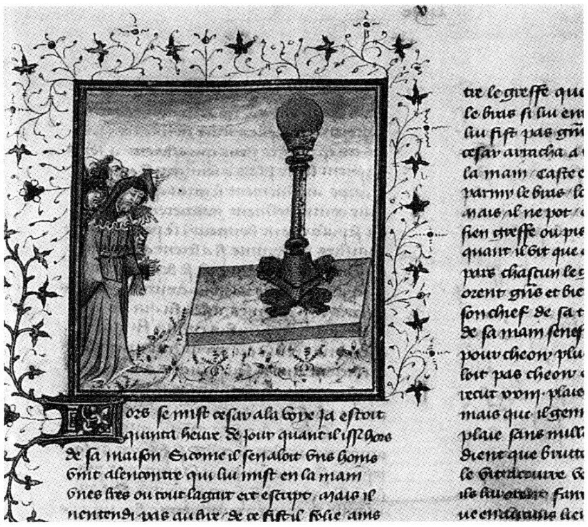

144. Remiet. Paris, Bibliothèque Nationale, fr. 250, fol. 411. *Faits des romains*. The tomb of Julius Caesar.

'special dead' whose remains were often re-interred were the kings of France, and miniatures contemporary with those of Remiet's show prelates and subsequent kings handling the skulls of their ancestors in ceremonious displays of reburial. Such was the case of Philippe IV, who wanted to remove the remains of his grandfather St Louis from the abbey of Saint Denis to the royal Sainte Chapelle, but after a squabble with the monks, received papal clearance only for parts of the head, teeth, chin and lower jawbone, which were removed and placed in a sumptuous new reliquary *châsse*.[56] To these monuments hobbled all manner of near-dead folk, the lame, blind, sufferers from eye and skin diseases and paralyzed, all flocking in the hope of a cure. The tomb of St Louis at Saint Denis was an orchestrated arrangement of statues, windows, lights and masses that utilized the power of the tomb to reinforce the power structure of the living. The continued efficacy of these royal burial places is best evidenced by their destruction during the revolution, when the royal tombs at Saint Denis were opened and the royal remains thrown to the winds or carried off for souvenirs.

The tomb – for those who could afford it, the last resting place for their body – was another liminal zone of ambiguity in the later Middle Ages, and Remiet seems to have been fascinated by representing monuments in various forms in his miniatures. They occur in the sacred context of divine history and in representations of pagan history as well as in the depictions of the everyday life of death in the *Lay de la fragilité humaine*. Their status was not without problems in the contentious theology of the fourteenth century. While kings and popes continued to demand them, and Remiet's friends the *tailleurs d'ymages* continued to carve them for the royal necropolis at Saint Denis, they were denounced as vainglorious and a waste of money by the mendicants and other orders. Louis d'Orléans's tomb, which was in his private chapel at the Convent of the Célestins, was an elaborate affair showing him and his wife as tranquil and definitely not decomposing *gisants* attended by mournful lapdogs. Nearby, a wall painting by Remiet's associate Colart de Laon showed another allegorical representation of Louis's murder. The chapel and its wall painting, which were renowned throughout the city in the fifteenth century, are long destroyed, but the latter was recorded by Gaignières in the eighteenth century (Fig. 143).

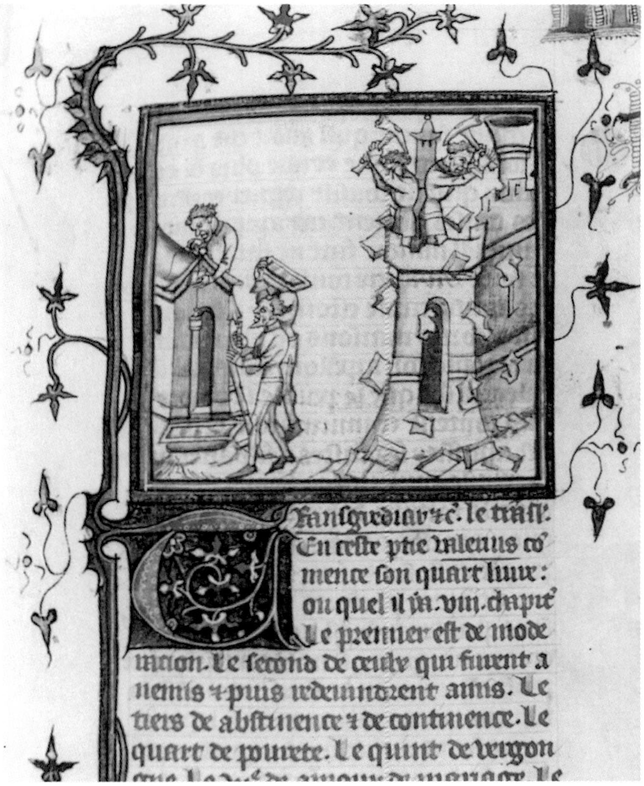

145. Remiet. Troyes, Bibliothèque Municipale, MS 261, fol. 173. Valerius Maximus, *Faits et dits mémorables*. Builders destroy a large castle and build a smaller one.

146. Remiet. Troyes, Bibliothèque Municipale, MS 261, fol. 124v. Valerius Maximus, *Faits et dits mémorables*. Religious rites of the Romans.

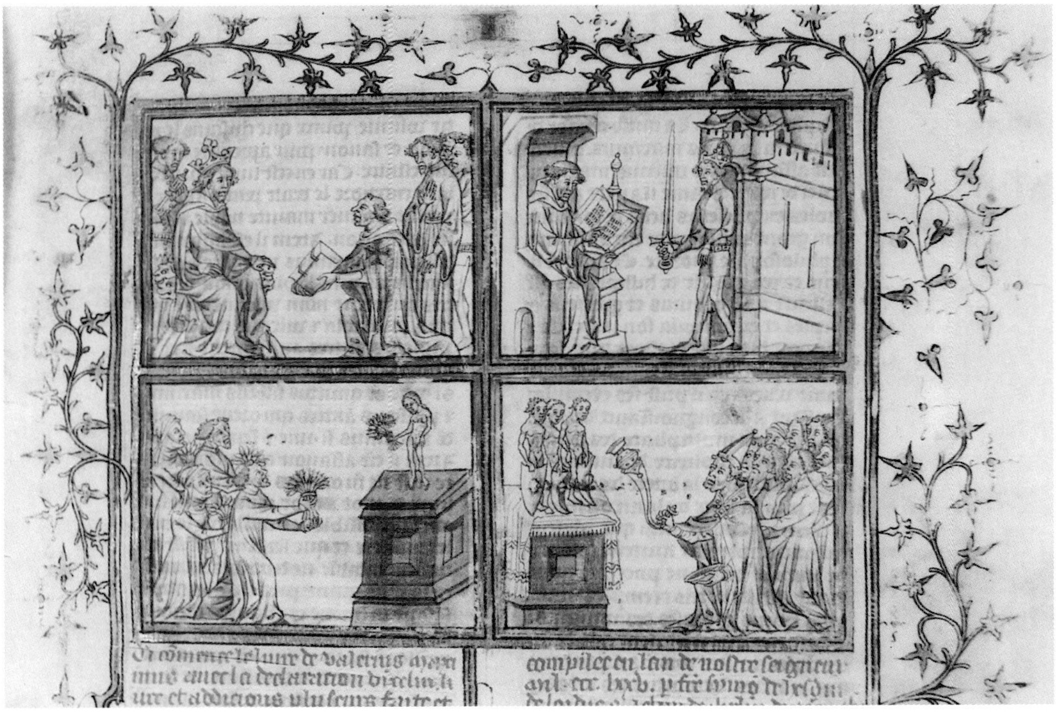

It shows the young prince assailed by Death wielding a dart.[57] Most medieval tombs incorporated, as did Louis's, a portrait or image of the deceased. But this too was viewed as vanity in some quarters. In his *Pèlerinage de l'âme*, the Cistercian author Deguileville provides a scathing satire on the vanity of such worldly self-perpetuation that was all the fashion in fourteenth-century France, by having the pilgrim presented with a field of asses' tombs, each monument inscribed with an image of the asinine deceased. This warning against self-representation in death was not heeded by the patrons of such manuscripts.

At the end of one of Remiet's ancient histories, where the text describes how the senators of Rome murdered Julius Caesar, Remiet pictured not this violent act but his magnificent tomb on the Champ des Mars, a golden ball surmounting a marble table with four lions – a monument to pagan idolatry of the self but, unusually, without an effigy or representation of the defunct (Fig. 144). This dramatic denial of self-representation is not an act of humility but a symbol of power. Another image of this taste for noble austerity, evoking the anxiety about patronage of art and architecture that was too overtly exhibitionistic, is evidenced in another classical text, Remiet's miniature to Book IV of Valerius Maximus's *Faits et dits mémorables*, which shows Valerius having his grandiose citadel demolished in order to build a more modest edifice in its stead (Fig. 145). Men knock down a great castle on the right while other masons with plumb-lines and tools create a smaller but more elegant *hôtel* on the left. One of a number of images Remiet made of builders at work, it is a miniature about miniaturization, which will be a major aristocratic taste for the next four centuries and which simultaneously avoided the Tower of Babel syndrome while satisfying the desire for a more intimate bodily possession of things.[58]

Idolatry was not only a matter of ancient history from the time of Caesar, it was still a major issue in the late fourteenth century. It was what the irate monks of Saint Denis accused the Parisians of when they had their dispute over who had the 'real' head of the saint. Jean Gerson preached against new kinds of image types, like the 'Vierge Ouvrant' he saw at the Carmelite church in Paris. So as an image-maker Remiet had to be careful. He depicted many 'standard' idols of the 'other', the Jews and pagans in his illustrations of ancient history, but often these are ambiguous. In his frontispiece to Valerius Maximus are two scenes of pagan idolatry: in the first a crowd bring corn offerings to the naked statue of Ceres, and in the next a bishop censes a vested altar surmounted by three more naked statues (Fig. 146). In the text the high priest Supicius is described as having an 'ornament de tête' and as ministering at various 'autels'. For the devisors of the standard iconography of this scene in the late fourteenth century, however, these pagan attributes have become a bishop's mitre and the sacrifice, an ecclesiastical censing.[59] This is a visual analogy to the denunciation of idols on Christian altars made by Remiet's contemporary, the poet Deschamps, who wrote in one of his *ballades*:

> Do not make gods of silver, of gold, of wood, of stone or of bronze, that lead people to idolatry . . . Because the work has a pleasant shape; Their colouring of which I complain, The beauty of shining gold, Makes many ignorant people believe That these are God for certain And they serve by foolish thoughts Such images as stand about In churches they place too many of them. That is very ill done; in short Let us not adore

such counterfeits (telz simulacres n'aourons). Prince, let us only believe in one God And let us adore him to perfection In the fields, everywhere, for this is right. No false gods, of iron or of stone, Stones which have no understanding: Let us not adore such counterfeits.[60]

In the *Miroir* that belonged to that collector of luxurious images Louis d'Orléans, one of the many depictions of idols is that of Potiphar's daughter Asseneth, who, following the advice of Joseph, destroys all the idols in her parents' house as though she were doing the spring cleaning (Fig. 147). These two supposedly lifeless simulacra being chucked out of the window of a tower, bending their legs as they fall, are represented by Remiet with a deft and economical series of swift pen-strokes that to our modern eyes express exactly that animated 'life-likeness' they are supposed to deny. To the fourteenth-century artist and viewer, however, the sketchiness of these images of images signalled not only their uncanny animation as the habitation of devils but also their being on a lower scale in the pictorial register, half-done, unfinished things made by human hands.[61] Thus Remiet inscribes this very made-ness within the scale of linear values at his disposal, which valued the solidity of the finished and the veracity of the heavily inscribed above the light and fluid forms of evanescent nature. Statues were already loaded with intimations of mortality in the late fourteenth century. According to the French philosopher of today Michel Serres, statues have always been the major means of visible mediation between the living and the dead.[62] Standing for the vulnerable and always dying human body, the statue

147. Remiet. Paris, Bibliothèque Nationale, fr. 312, fol. 66v. *Miroir historial.* Potiphar's daughter throws idols out of the window.

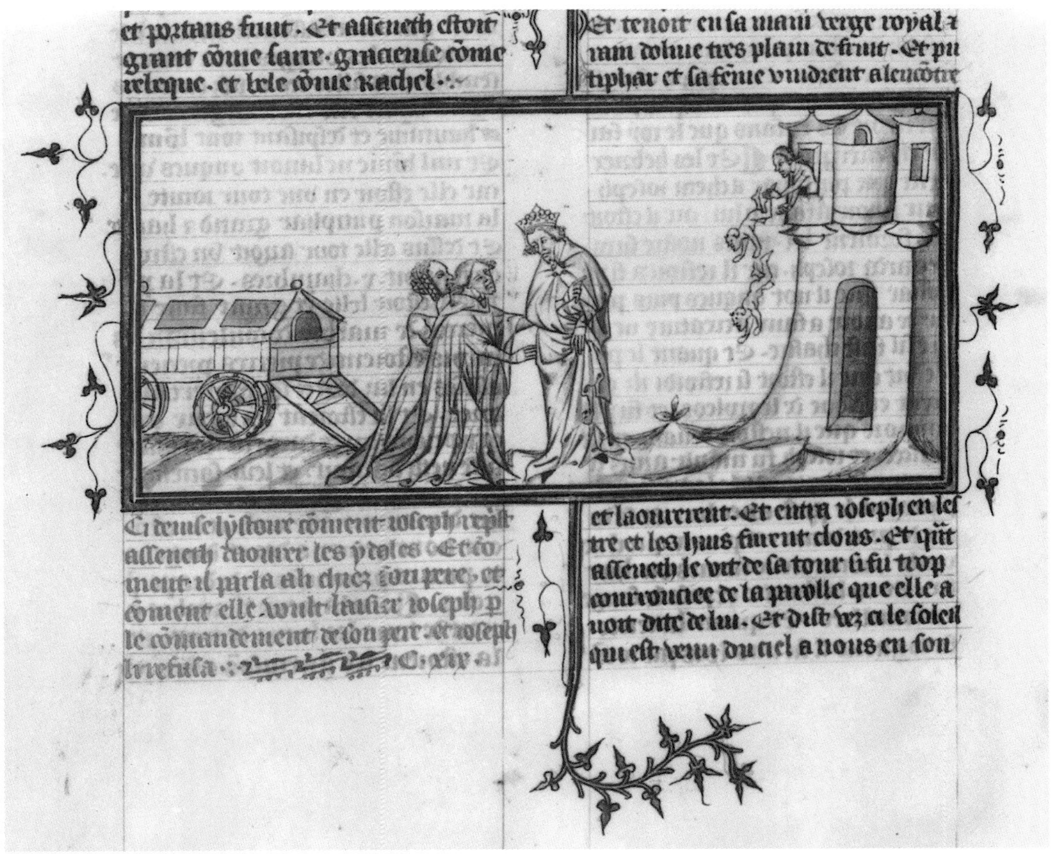

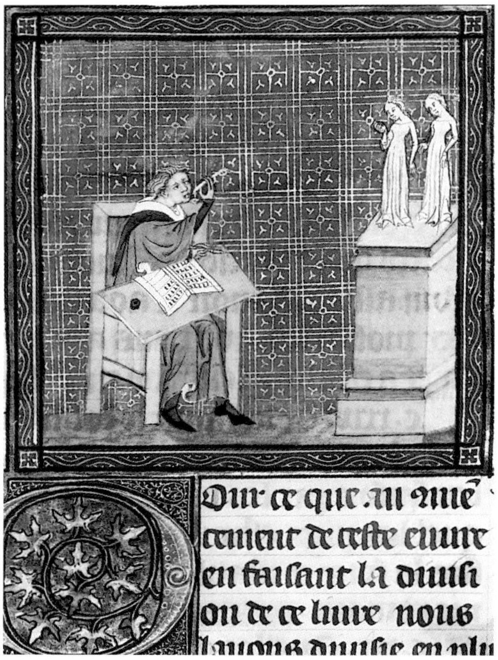

148. Remiet. Paris, Bibliothèque Nationale, fr. 170, fol. 174v. Augustine, *La Cité de Dieu*. How the pagans dissimulate knowledge through their simulacra.

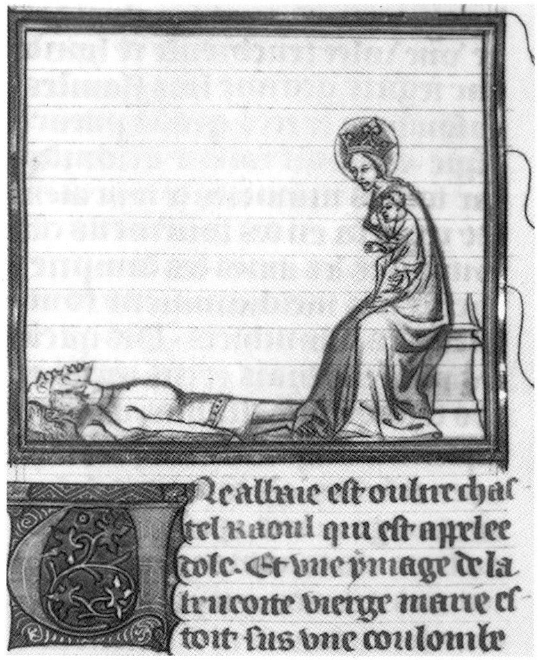

149. Remiet. Paris, Bibliothèque Nationale, fr. 312, fol. 342. *Miroir historial*. Thieves killed by a statue of the Virgin and Child.

persists, stabilizing our relationship with the corpse, since it often makes present what is absent, fixing memory and anchoring desire around a body that will never decompose. Not only the many three-dimensional sculptures of *gisants* and *transi* carved on tombs, but also their minute simulacra made by Remiet's pen are efforts at this negation.

One of Remiet's most twisted images directly juxtaposes the living word and the dead image, the text and the idol in Augustine's influential discussion of pagan idolatry in Book IV of the *Cité de Dieu* (Fig. 148). The pagans spread their knowledge, which is called 'dissimulation', through their books ('par les livres') which Remiet represents by an animated scribe seated at the left at a lectern. He could be any of the many writers that Remiet represented except that his pen points in reference to two female statues on an altar. The perversity of this image would have been immediate to Remiet's viewers. For the pagans the word is focused upon the image – writing follows representation – whereas for the Christian artist, like Remiet himself, representation must always be secondary. To put the image first, like this writer does in gazing upon and writing upon idols, is to make writing itself an empty simulation, a form of death.

Christian images, that is, statues of Christ, his mother and the saints, are, by contrast to these ambiguous idols, secure, grounded and fully realized, representing plenitude rather than loss, precisely because they follow the text of Logos. Remiet purposefully depicts in the same *Miroir historial* many scenes of Christian image-worship, especially focused around statues of the Virgin, when for example a boy leaves his friends playing ball to wed himself to her statue. Sometimes, however, the image serves a more ominous function, as when

150. Remiet. Paris, Bibliothèque Nationale, fr. 176, fol. 1. *Rational des divins offices*. Synagogue and Ecclesia, and the High Priest at the altar.

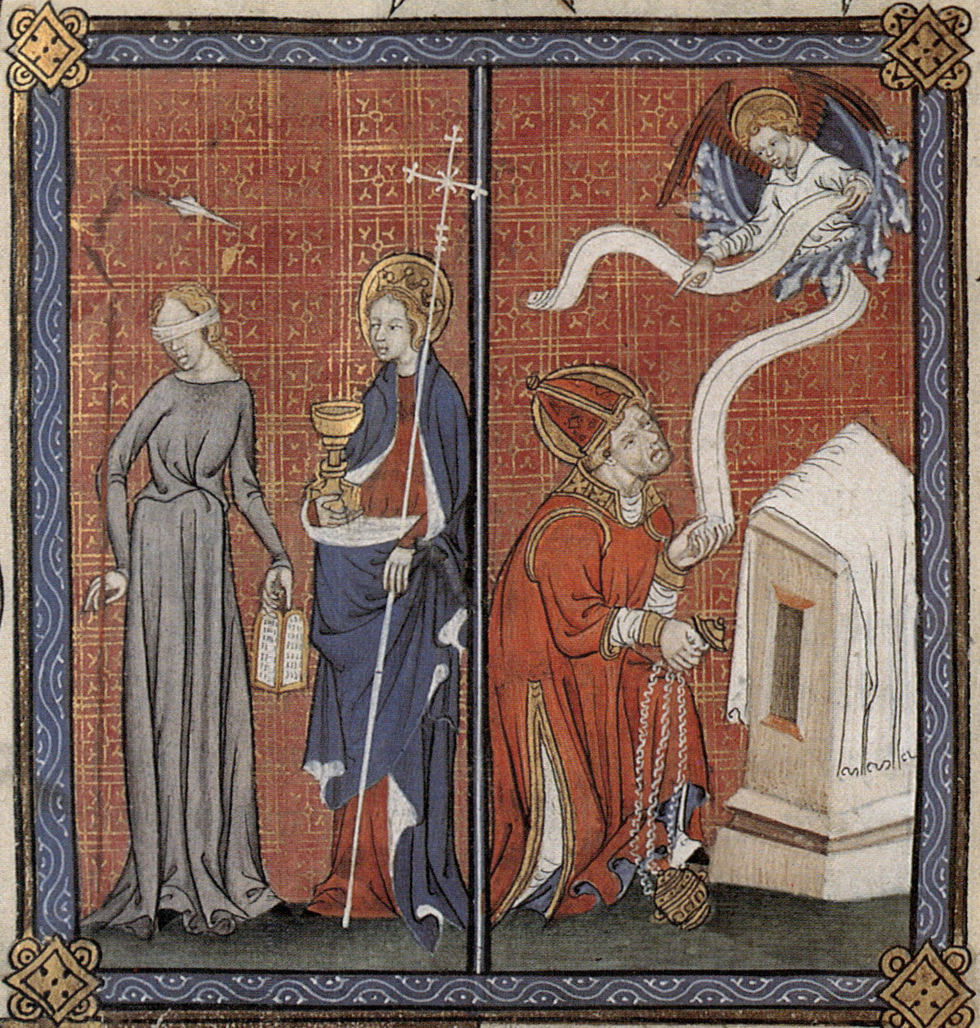

Toutes les choses qui sont apparte nantes au devin offi ce tant en aornemens cõme autres choses q̄l conq̄s se elles sont re gardees et cerchees de cuer devot par diligente inquisicion / sont plaines de misteres et de douces significaci those who throw stones at her statue are themselves struck stone dead (Fig. 149). As an image-maker, Remiet also had to be on the side of representation, which here is an instrument of vengeance, punishing with the horizontal sign of lifelessness those who had assumed that the static, upright image of the mother of God was only lifeless matter. In this mostly empty image there is nothing to tell the viewer that this is meant to be a statue, indeed here the pictorial roles seem reversed; the Virgin and child are divine and animated actors compared to the statue-like *gisants* of the two human and defunct reprehensibles stretched out before them.

Remiet never illuminated to my knowledge an anti-image tract, but he did supply historiated initials to one of the most 'orthodox' medieval manuals concerning images, Jean Golein's French translation of Durandus's *Rational des divins offices*, which princes sought to have to order the services in their lavish private chapels. This copy was acquired by the Duke of Berry before 1402 and is described in his 1416 inventory as 'historiated at the beginning with a pope, the Church and the Synagogue' (Fig. 150).[63] This is a mistake, since the figure on the right represents the Old Testament High Priest. On this altar of course there are no idols, only a white cloth, and the two halves of this picture depict, on one side, the symbolic figures and, on the other, the liturgical actions which are the subject of the treatise. Durandus begins by telling us that 'ecclesiastical offices and furnishings' are 'divine signs or figures, not in themselves virtues'. While Synagogue is blind and dressed in cold violet, Ecclesia, like the Virgin Mary, is sumptuously robed in finest most saturated blue. Here Remiet also makes manifest the power of colour, which makes the Church into a chromatic sanctuary of signification with its moments, rituals and times of changing hue. While historical texts could be illuminated without it, the rituals and objects of Christian worship were perforce constructed out of chromatic difference. Durandus spends much of his third book on vestments dealing with the complex symbolism of various colours in which red is associated with the cross, violet with times of Penitence, and blue almost exclusively with the Virgin.[64] The importance of images in the liturgy is shown by the fact that the crucial section, 'Des paintures des courtines et des adornemens de l'eglise', is the third chapter of the very first book, occurring in this manuscript in the same gathering as the frontispiece miniature. Paintings and ornaments are here described as 'lessons and scriptures of the laity', citing the famous passage of Gregory the Great, although there is also the statement, important to consider if one is an *enlumineur* like Remiet and not an *ymagier*, that 'in churches we pay less reverence to books than to images and paintings'.[65]

Durandus deals with cemeteries in the fifth chapter of the first book, decribing how the latter are sacred places 'where the entire body of a man, or at least the head, is buried, because no man can have two sepulchres', and goes on to give them diverse appelations: 'cemetery, polyandrum, andropolis, sepulchrum, mausoleum, dormitorium, tumulus, monumentum, ergastulum, pyramid, sarcophagus, bustum, urna, spelunca'. He also notes that 'no body ought to be buried in a church or near an altar, where the Body and Blood of our Lord are made, except the bodies of holy fathers, who be called patrons . . . bishops and abbots, and worthy presbyters and laymen of eminent sanctity'. Most of his prohibitions focus around the pollution of the cemetery with blood or the burial of Jews or unbaptized Christians or those 'returning from any place of fornication' who, if they are slain along the way, would taint the holy place if they were interred there, although he

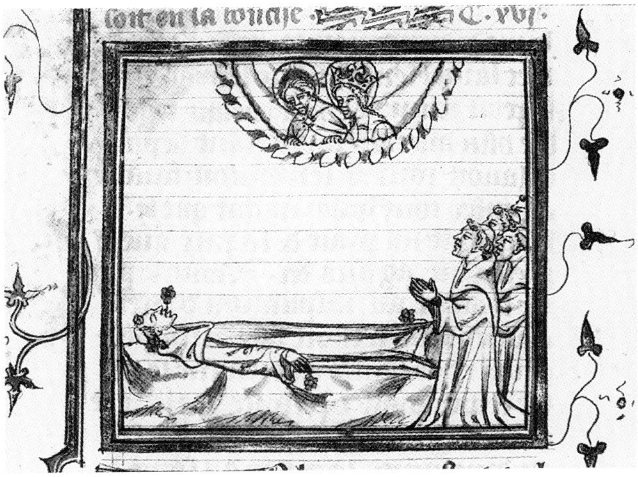

151. Remiet. Paris, Bibliothèque Nationale, fr. 312, fol. 345. *Miroir historial.* The miracle of roses growing from the corpse of a monk who devoted himself to the Virgin.

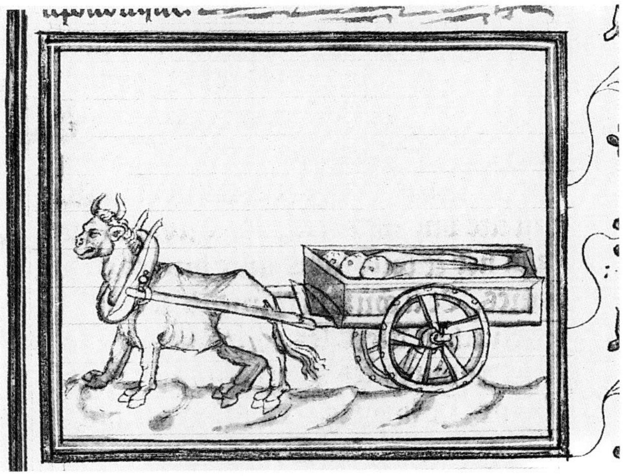

152. Remiet. Paris, Bibliothèque Nationale, fr. 312, fol. 219v. *Miroir historial.* The corpses of St Vincent and his companions too heavy for oxen to pull.

shows leniency in his attitude to women who die in childbirth, who 'some say should not be carried into the church'.[66]

In arguing that 'those who come to a violent death are not borne into the church, lest the pavement be polluted with blood', Durandus was overlooking a category of the special dead whose presence in cemeteries and churches was crucial and whose ends had been almost theatrically violent. If the tombs of the wealthy were compared to the idols of the ancients, there was a class of tombs that were, by contrast, the focus of intense medieval 'idolatry' and propitiary observance – those of the saints. These contained the relics of the special dead. Much medieval art, not only funerary art, was a kind of embalming, a framing in gold and other precious materials of these fragments of long-dead ancestors. Remiet pictured people digging in mounds of earth to collect the bones of John the Baptist as part of biblical history. Relics were bones for the most part or bits of cloth soaked in the blood of a martyr. They were not flesh. The saints whose relics were revered were precisely those men and women who had triumphed over the flesh and its normal processes of decay, whose corpses had, by contrast, smelled of roses or even sprouted sweet-smelling flowers (Fig. 151) and whose opened tombs revealed them as fresh as the day they were buried – signalling the fact that they had never properly died. Remiet pictured this in the Manchester breviary in his tiny but brilliantly coloured miniature of the invention of the relics of St Stephen, which took place outside Jerusalem whence they began a long journey to Constantinople, to Rome and then to France. These two gravediggers are not putting bodies in the earth but digging them up, and they discover St Stephen and his companions to be as clean and white as the day they were interred, their haloes shining (Fig. 153). It was their historical victory over death that we saw Remiet picturing earlier that gave these bodies special resiliance and power over decay. Often Remiet portrayed the glamour of the saintly corpse, such as in his haunting image of a great ox unable to pull the shrouded corpses of St Vincent and his companions, reminiscent of descriptions of the carts filled up at plague time, but actually signalling the power over death contained by the cadavers of the saints (Fig. 152).

Relics were sometimes displayed on altars in churches, as we see in Remiet's miniature

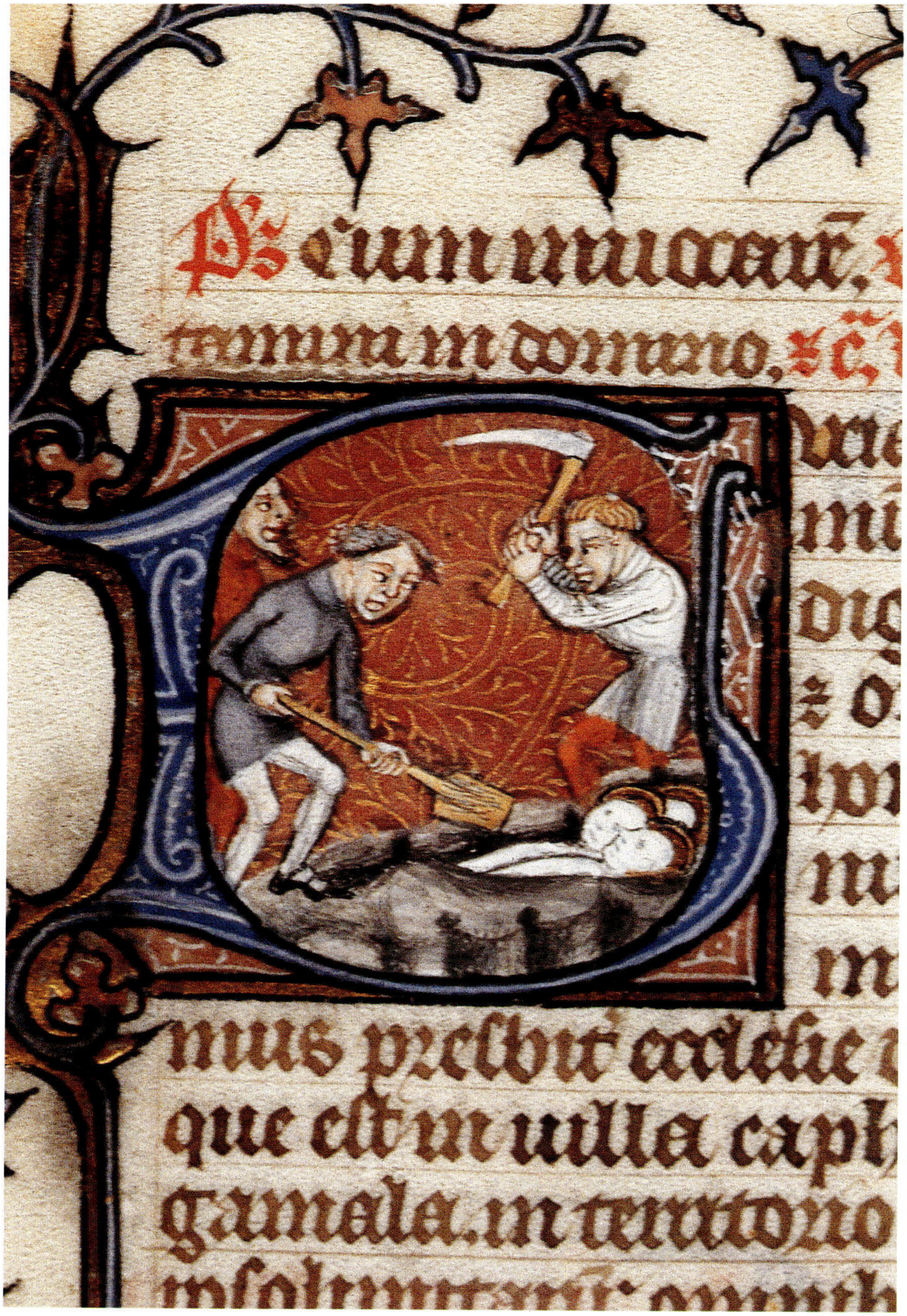

153. Remiet. Manchester, John Rylands Library, lat. 136, fol. 48. Breviary. The invention of the body of St Stephen.

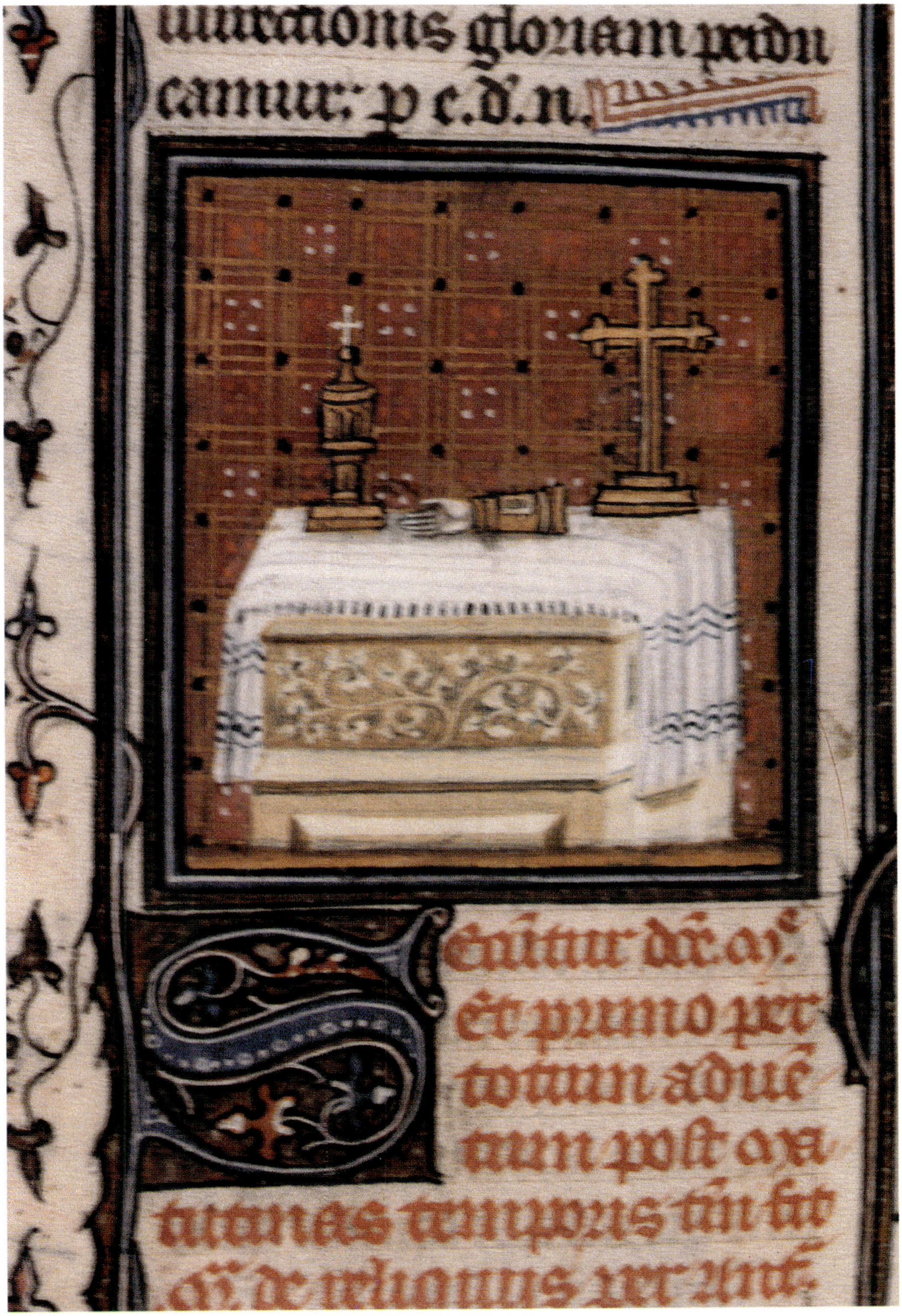

154. Remiet. Manchester, John Rylands Library, lat. 136, fol. 87. Breviary. Memoira of relics.

illustrating the Memoria of relics in the Manchester breviary, which include an arm reliquary and a cyclindrical ostensory, an object which allowed the bits of bone to be viewed through transparent glass or crystal (Fig. 154). Just as the *charniers* displayed the calcified bones of the masses in large-scale architectural complexes, the bones of the 'special dead' were visible in miniaturized Gothic vitrines in the golden and silver reliquaries that were made for their display. Even small foundations like Remiet's own parish church owned such splendid objects as he pictured in the breviary volume. Saint Séverin housed three fragments of the True Cross embedded in an antique crystal, a variety of tiny bones thought to be of the hands and feet of St Martin, all 'authenticated' by parchment strips bearing inscriptions. A large silver arm reliquary labelled 'le bras de Monseigneur saint Séverin', the titular saint of the church, was displayed on the altar on feast days.[67] Such relics were also privately owned commodities collected by Remiet's patrons, especially Charles VI, who hoarded them in his vain effort to relieve his madness, and among which was a reliquary of John the Baptist's tooth in crystal along with other parts of St John the Evangelist and St Bartholomew. The very saints whose bodies these royal bibliophiles saw being torn apart and ravaged in manuscripts like the *Miroir historial* were vividly presented to them in their fragmentary remains. Louis d'Orléans had them encased in tiny jewelled fittings so he could wear them as talismanic jewellery. Most prized, despite its being not a human body part but a mute object, were relics, unearthed by St Helena, of the True Cross (Fig. 155), pieces of which were owned by most of Remiet's clients. He pictured the unearthing of the whole cross in a large missal that was itself later cut into pieces so to as to make more money from the pieces rather than the whole, a trick long practised in the trade in relics.

The relic would seem to be at the opposite end of the spectrum of death from the decaying corpse. Even though it was often just a fragment of a body or its trace, a bone, a tooth, or a bit of wood clotted with blood, it was more powerfully present than any human figure could ever be. It was metonymic, standing in for the once great wholeness of a person – the opposite of death, which dissolved and destroyed the whole body. It was this metonymic wholeness that the monks of Saint Denis sought to preserve when they argued against the authenticity of the cranium fragment preserved at Notre Dame in the trial of 1410, partly because they owned what they knew to be a bigger piece.[68] Relics were the only signs in medieval culture which assured people that, although the flesh might decay, something powerful might still remain.[69] In the mountains far south at Montaillou in the fourteenth century, locks of hair and fingernail clippings were taken from the dead 'to prevent the dead person carrying away with him the good fortune of the house', suggesting that, on the more popular level, the fragments of the corpse could retain power.

Most relics of Christ's body were objects that had come into contact with his own – the shroud, the crown of thorns, the cross – since he left behind nothing of his fleshly nature at the ascension. One bit that was left, however, and which increasingly obsessed people, was his prepuce, cut off at the circumcision, a moment that Remiet relished representing in the *Pèlerinage de Jésus-Christ* (Fig. 157). Here the Virgin, her hand to her chin signalling her grief, holds her numinous but squirming offspring steady by his little nimbus as though it were a cardboard hat, so that the Old Law can perform her duty, the duty of the High Priest. Of course to any contemporary viewer this shedding of a small

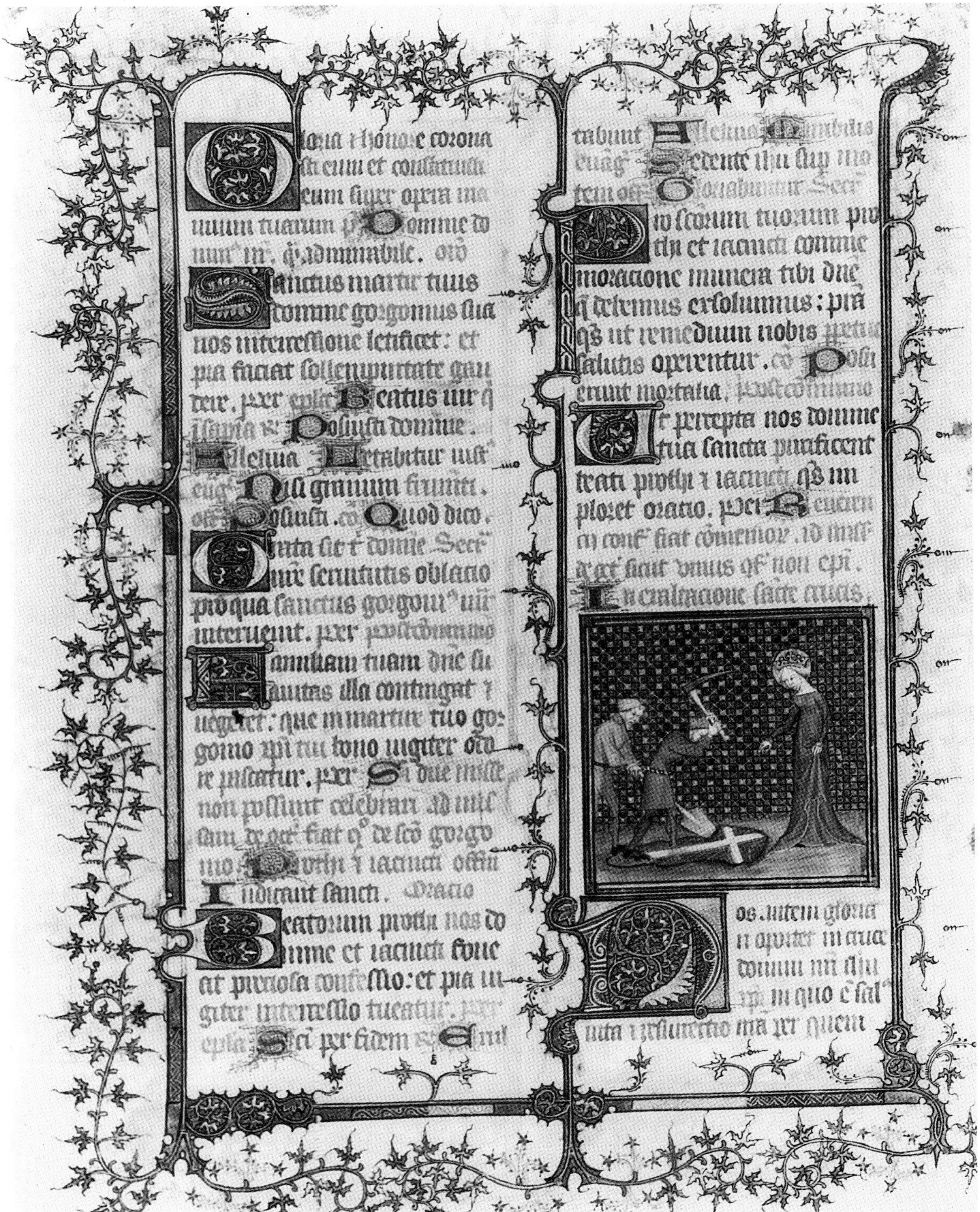

155. Remiet. Bloomington, Indiana, Lilly Library, Ricketts MS (65). Leaf from a Missal. The finding of the True Cross.

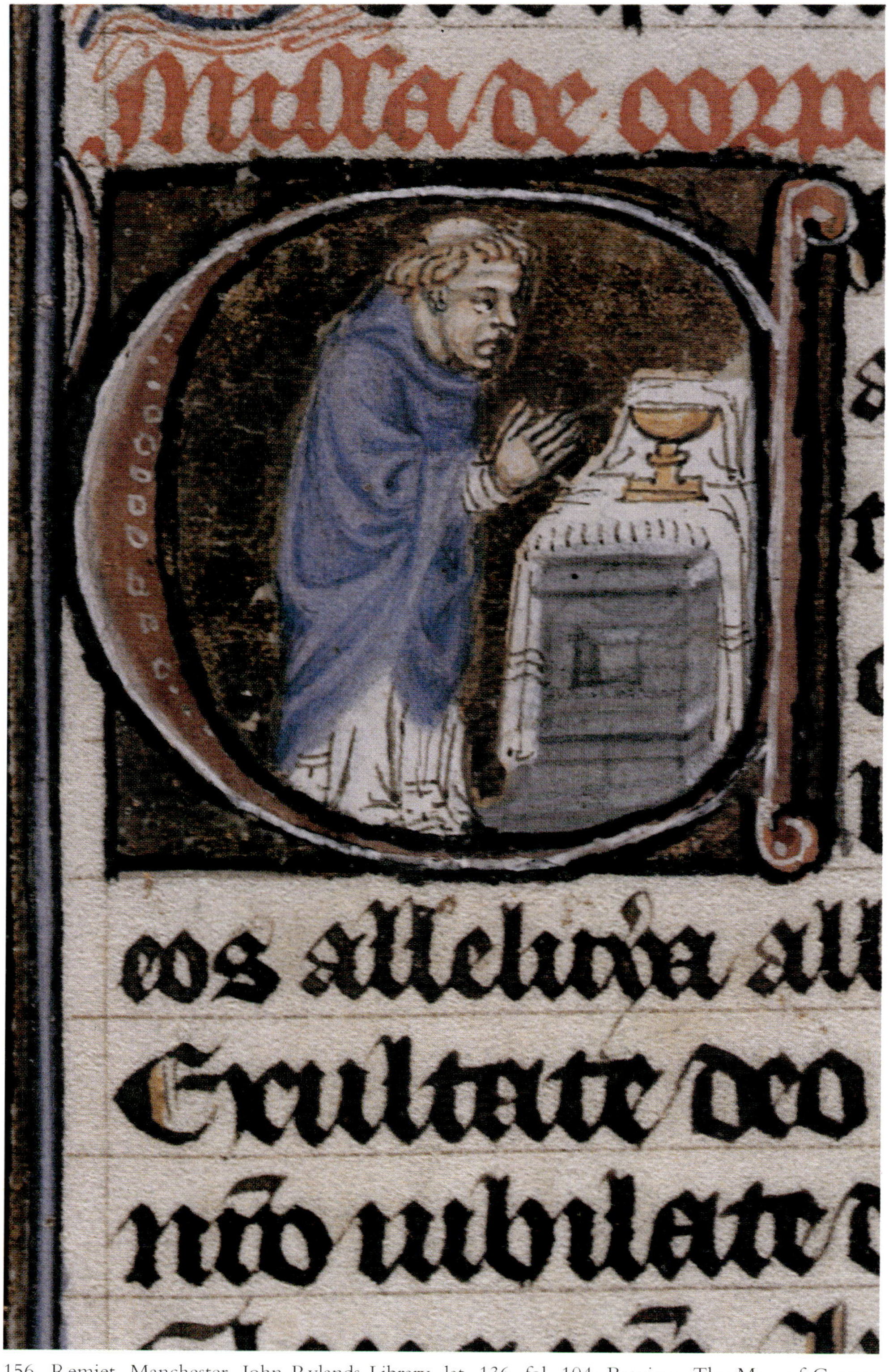

156. Remiet. Manchester, John Rylands Library, lat. 136, fol. 104. Breviary. The Mass of Corpus Christi.

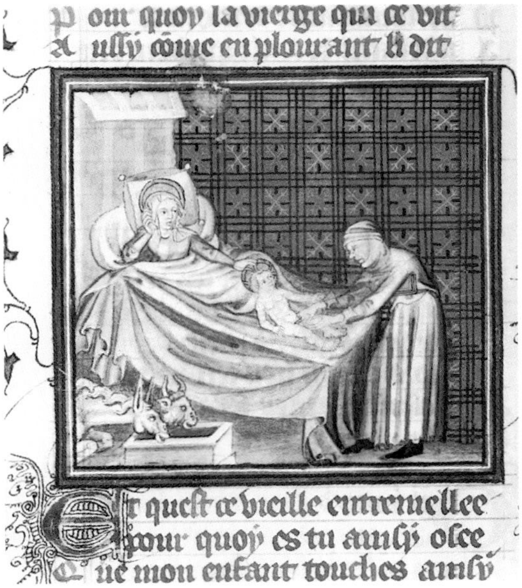

157. Remiet. Paris, Bibliothèque Nationale, fr. 823, fol. 185v. *Pèlerinage de Jésus-Christ.* The Old Law circumcizes Christ.

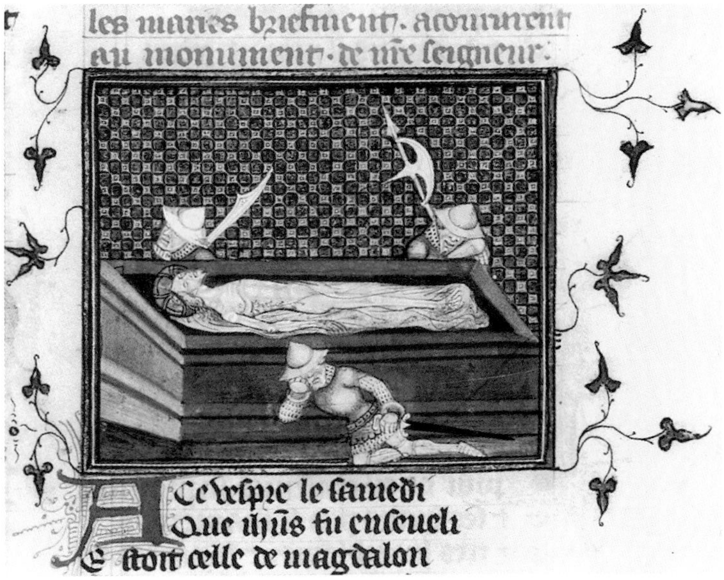

158. Remiet. Paris, Bibliothèque Nationale, fr. 823, fol. 235. *Pèlerinage de Jésus-Christ.* Christ dead in the tomb.

amount of the saviour's blood was a prefiguration of the larger amount later spilled when he was crucified, and was more than a distant Old Testament ritual. The journal of the 'bourgeois de Paris' records the excitement that was stirred in the city when 'Our Lord's foreskin was brought to Paris'. It came with letters of indulgence from the pope that, he complains, could only be bought at a very dear price, but indulgences could be purchased on a sliding scale according to one's wages. This document promised absolution from 'all sin and guilt at the hour of death'.[70] As often with relics, it was the combination of bodily fragment and authenticating text that made it efficacious. Whereas during the mass Christ's flesh came back to be witnessed by the congregation (Fig. 156), the theatrically displayed foreskin needed no such transubstantiation. This relic caused such a stir precisely because it presented to the human gaze that most human part of the Saviour's body. Nothing in this overtly phallocentric culture was more potent than a penis-particle.

The Death of God

The unadorned representation of human death, the well-nigh anatomical stripping of the corpse conveys to viewers an unbearable anguish before the death of God, which is here mingled with our own death because there isn't the slightest suggestion of transcendence. Julia Kristeva[71]

'Death to God' is the worst blasphemy. Eustache Deschamps[72]

The most startling and unique *transi* that Remiet ever painted is stretched out on a dark tomb slab that encases it like a frame, its head thrust back, its limbs stiffening in the beginning of decomposition; just flesh exposed to the elements and to decay like any other cadaver – except that this 'it' is not any old body. It is the body of God (Fig. 158). Around his tomb are three soldiers whose recumbent forms usually accompany the glorious moment of the resurrection in late medieval iconography, but this is too early for the guards to 'shake and become as dead men' (Matthew 28:4). The only dead man here lies on the tomb. This stiffening corpse, like the famous predella panel of the same theme by Holbein in the Basel Museum, calls for the total implication of the subject in Christ's suffering which 'allows him to experience death and resurrection even in his physical body, thanks to the imaginary identification – and of its actual effects – with the absolute Subject (Christ)'.[73] Unlike a single panel, however, Remiet's image is part of Deguileville's allegorical narrative, the *Pèlerinage de Jésus-Christ*. It is the third poem, in which Christ becomes a pilgrim upon the earth, a wanderer in the world he has created and has come to save, that is most radical in theological terms and least known today.[74] It is unique among the illustrative cycles of this poem, focusing not upon the glorious resurrection described in the rubric above the image here, where the Marys come to the 'monument' and find only the discarded cloths, but the three days before this; the terrible space when Christ shared in what, since the Fall, had made humanity human. Following miniatures of the crucifixion and the three Marys and John, this one stands as the still centre of the allegorical narrative, and yet is totally unallegorical in its presentation of flesh as dead matter. The next miniature in the sequence does not show the saviour rising up in the same place but instead exposing his wounds to the apostles. Looked at in the process of reading the poem, this image of physical death is part of the movement necessary, the transition that even God's body has to go through, in order to reach eternity that he has created. Whereas the most usual image of Christ's necessary death was his hanging on the cross, for Remiet it had to be his being a corpse and lying horizontal on the tomb. Part of the problem of representation in modernity has been the loss of this narrative association, the break in the flow of this possibility which meant that the isolated painted image can become the paradigm only for artistic practice, not for living itself, framed in a place of illusionary coherence, the museum, and disconnected from the Word.

Another narrative into which this image of unbearable loss fitted both allegorically and performatively was that of the mass, which was experienced by the congregation and described by liturgists like Durandus as a re-enactment of Christ's Passion. Masses were often performed in commemoration of the dead. Rubrics in missals directed the priest to say, while holding the host over the chalice, 'gracias agimus tibi', offering thanks for the beatified and for those in Purgatory. But it was new feasts like that of Corpus Christi, confirmed in 1264, which only became an organic part of the French Missal by the mid-fourteenth century, that saw the installation of Christ's body at the centre of things. In the Manchester portion of the two-volume portable breviary, Remiet illustrated the Feast of Corpus Christi, which occurred on the Thursday after Trinity Sunday in June, under the rubric 'Missa de corpore Christi' in the initial 'C' of the introit of the mass, 'Cibavit eos ex adipe frumenti' (see Fig. 156). In most breviaries of the period the moment chosen for illumination was the elevation of the host, the spiritual and emotional climax of the rite for the laity, who could observe the officiating priest only from afar.[75] In Remiet's initial, not only are we closer to the celebrating priest in his blue chasuble, but only the chalice with corporal stands on the altar. Within the corporal, hidden, or rather shrouded, are the small wheaten discs which embody the saving Christ. After the elevation, the consecrated wine in the chalice and the host hidden in the cloth come to stand for Christ's blood and body, and the corporal, the cloth sudarium that covered it. The altar table becomes the tomb in which Christ's body was placed by Joseph of Arimathea. The three prayers said while the oblation remains on the altar (prologue, paternoster, embolism) represent the three days Christ 'rested' in the tomb. Even in his liturgical images there is an emphasis upon the dark interim, the time of death before the resurrection, as experienced by every Christian taking part in the mass, and depicted as a historical image in the *Pèlerinage de Jésus-Christ*.[76]

Controversy had raged since the twelfth century in the Parisian schools as to the nature of Christ's body in the tomb and its implications for the cult of the dead. New theories of Aristotelian hylomorphism emphasized the notion of the material continuity of the resurrected body. Some theologians, like Thomas Aquinas, resisted this idea of continuity between the living body and the corpse, arguing that the rotting cadaver was something *other* than the body. For others, especially Parisian scholastics imbued with the northern culture of the still-living corpse, denying continuity had the disturbing implication that 'if the cadaver is not the body, then Christ's body did not lie in the tomb for the three days between Crucifixion and Resurrection'.[77] Remiet's image seems a direct answer to these debates by making Christ nothing more than a body.

By having the tomb display his corpse, Remiet also recalls the contemporary craze for *transi* figures in sepulcral monuments. Like these, it makes the body vulnerable, even for the short time before the resurrection, to the first stages of decay. Recent studies have suggested that in the late Middle Ages Christ revealed his humanity through his body and its sexuality. But this is only half the story. It was not that little bit of flesh, the possibly erect penis or the lost foreskin that was the only relic of the Lord on earth, that signalled Christ's partaking in humanity so much as his willingness to accept death in order to save mankind.[78] But Remiet's illustration is unusual in the sense that very few texts and images of the period allow this most holy body to change in any way. While much meditation and devotional emphasis was placed on its broken, vulnerable openness and its multiple lacerations before death in the flagellation and crucifixion, Christ's subsequent post-mortem state is never defined. Like the sweet-smelling and incorruptible bodies of the saints, it is covered by the aura of gold rays and the perfume of flowers, after the embalming by the Marys, even in the tomb. In Remiet's radical miniature, by contrast, the most positive and, for most fourteenth-century viewers, life-enhancing in his whole pictorial panoply of death, Christ's carcass decomposes as the model for their own, in order that rot can be transcended and rebirth made possible.

6. THE DEATH OF DEATH

Something was ebbing from him, unravelling his empty bowels and bubbling up through his throat as he lay flat in the darkness. His rasping breath grew drier and shorter but he did not want to let it go just yet. His wiry body, though frail, was fighting for authority, holding back that incorporeal little beggar as it had done for these near-eighty years. The scholars said the soul, 'anima', was 'the form of the body', but it was easier to think of it as one's breath, what he was struggling with now, his 'spiritus'. Was it his soul that Remiet could feel shaking and squirming in his gullet like a human-shaped gob of white slime, its tiny arms flailing and its legs kicking against his heart. Some people spoke of the immortal soul as a butterfly, but the beating he felt was not of wings but of a pounding fist. Man is composed of matter and form and when these separate, man dies. Flying from his mouth like a wingless angel once death had cut the thread holding together the two parts that made up his person, his soul would return to the God that created it and the matter of his body to the earth from which it was made.

Body and soul. The images, less distinct now, their crisp lines blurred by pain, were still floating somewhere in his head whereas what he felt was elsewhere, deeper inside, lower down towards his heart, where many said the soul was seated. The faculties in his head had begun to mix up; memory images, opening the flap of the cerebral worm, flooded forward into his 'fantasia' mingling with his common sense, making strange ghostly shapes, blurring echoes of images. But what use were images now? Vain fleeting things that were just dancing shadows, nothings. Those painted pictures of the hour of death which showed the soul, a luminous babe exhaled like a breath with the angel and devil playing a tug of war for possession of it. Was it the theologians and scholars who came up with these things? Who made the rules for pictures and moreover how did they know – those who had never been there – what death was like?

Would beyond be like here, carefully demarcated and separate, with different places for the high and the low? Or would all be the same? Equal? That was the hardest to fathom. But they would all be naked, so who could tell a prince from a poor man like himself? On the west front of Notre Dame the dead jump out of their graves at the sound of the trumpet wearing their bishops' mitres and their matrons' wimples. He expected there would still be fashion in Heaven and certainly of course in Hell. Perhaps the next world would be like one of his illuminated pictures, with bright sunlit colours and gold shimmering behind everyone's smiles, like in a beautiful garden, or would everything be as ethereal as his 'portraits d'encre'? Would there be colours, or were these too material? But would it be so still as a picture? It was so vague, so vague, what the preachers described and what the texts told him and even what the pictures pictured. The modelbooks he had copied in his youth, the upturned faces and the carefully shaded folds that his master had praised him for – they were just tricks, bits of the world, not explanations of it. But it was not the pictures of the soul flying out of the mouth to freedom that were confusing. The problem was neither this end – death – nor the end beyond that – the Final Reckoning – but what came in between. Where would he be in the interim? How long would he have to wait in Purgatory? Would all those alms and prayers, pounds of candles and pious pictures given as benefactions to the Célestins, would they work for him now? Would he be able to see again in Heaven? How could he collect all his bones in time to see his God? It was no good being impatient in eternity. But how long would he have to wait until, like Lazarus risen from the dead, smelling of rot and conscious of the cold tomb in which he had lain, he would see his Redeemer standing at the last day upon the earth or seated on a glorious rainbow? A picture is meant to be an answer. But now they all seemed to be questions.

Expiration: Soul Departing

The death of the other, this death of the other in 'me,' is fundamentally the only death that is named in the syntagm 'my death.' Jacques Derrida[1]

I can't see anything come out of men or women when they die. For if I saw their soul, or anything at all, coming out, I'd know that the soul existed. But as I see nothing, I can't make out what it is, the soul . . . When men die, one only sees them expire, and their last breath is nothing but wind. Guillemette Benet of Montaillou[2]

Death is always only an image. Though represented, it can never be known or felt by an individual, returned from or described as such. The story of Lazarus, as pictured by Remiet in Hermann de Valenciennes's *Histoire de la Bible*, provided an uncanny exception and an ideal opportunity for grasping that always deferred experience through its miraculous negation (Fig. 159). In the biblical account the stiffening corpse of Lazarus, 'four days already in the grave', emerges from the rocky tomb at Christ's command ('Lazarus, come forth!') as part of a complex family narrative of mourning and ritual in which Jesus says to Martha, 'I am the resurrection and the life: he that believeth in me, although he be dead, shall live' (John 11:25). But in Remiet's desolate half-empty ink image just as in the confrontation between Death and the pilgrim in the *Pèlerinage de vie humaine*, we see only the meeting of two gazes, a confrontation between the passive subject of life and death and Him who gives life and death. Lazarus, who starts up stiffly, like a child waking up from a bad dream, was something of an equivocal, if not disturbing, figure for late fourteenth-century viewers. If the fear of death's inevitability was assuaged somewhat by the fact that it was not an end, exactly what happened afterwards seems to have caused anxiety. This was only reitterated in the doctrinal and theological controversy over the exact nature of the immortality of the soul, the resurrection of the body and the relationship between Purgatory and Hell – debates that were not confined to the Latin Quarter. Images of the afterlife have always had to be constructed out of this one. There is no radical difference, no real otherness beyond the grave, since Purgatory and Hell were increasingly constructed as 'mirrors' of earthly hierarchies and punishments. Today those

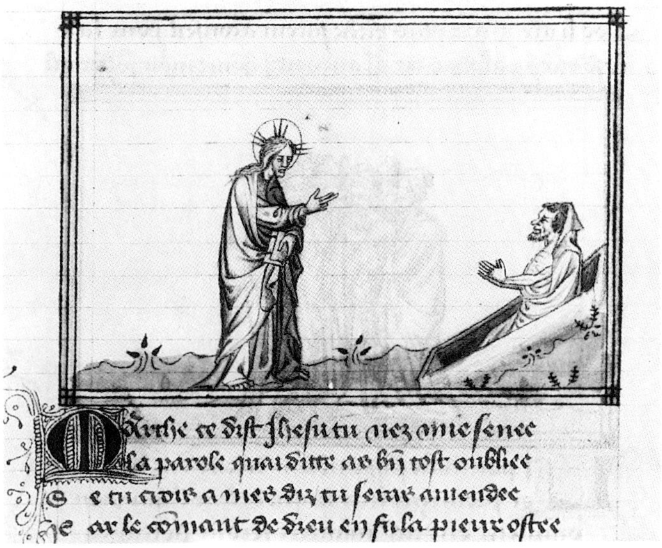

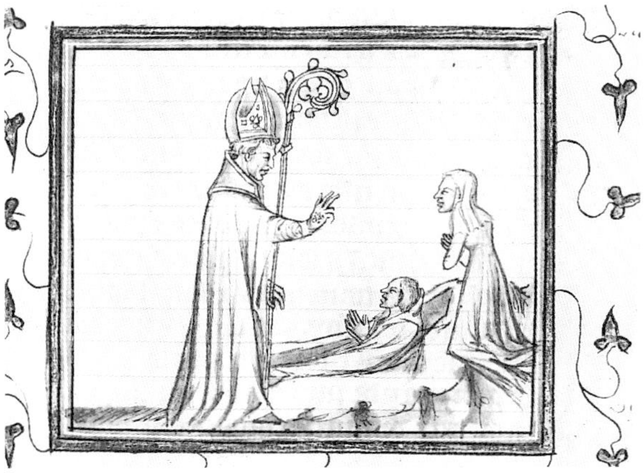

160. Remiet. Paris, Bibliothèque Nationale, fr. 313, fol. 313. *Miroir historial.* St Hilary of Poitiers raises the dead.

159. (*left*) Remiet. New York, Pierpont Morgan Library, M.526, fol. 40. Hermann de Valenciennes, *Histoire de la Bible.* The raising of Lazarus.

161. Remiet. Paris, Bibliothèque Nationale, fr. 250, fol. 327. *Faits des romains.* Pompey dreams of his wife emerging from a tomb.

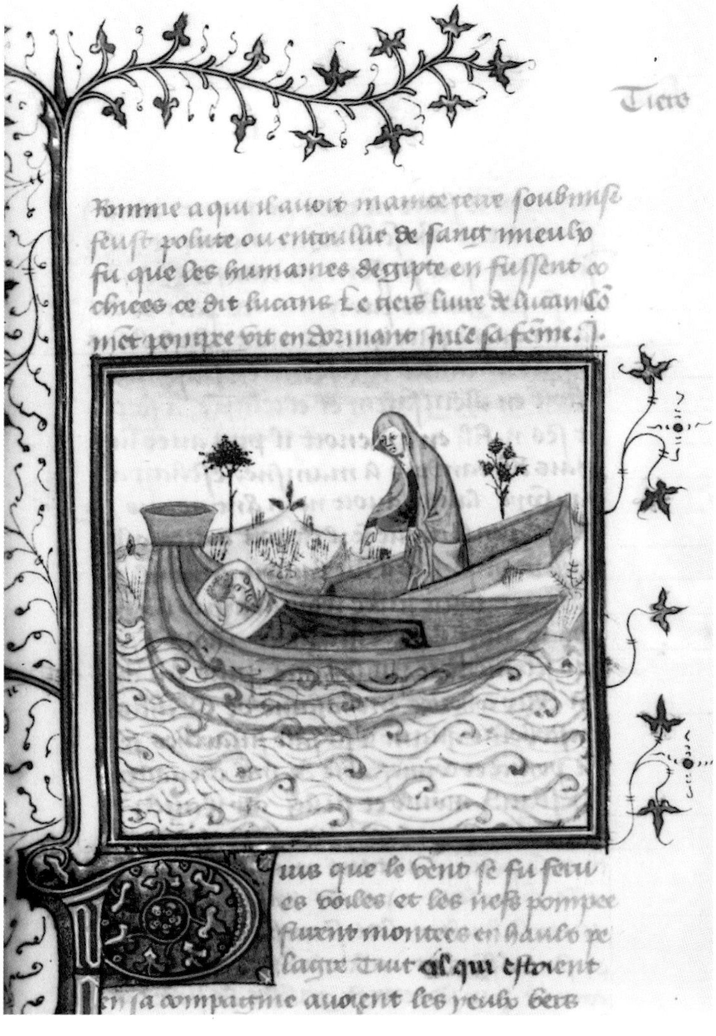

who return from and recount 'near-death experiences' describe Hollywood visions of enticing white light at the end of tunnels, filling the screen of our imaginary with vaguely cinematic expectations. By contrast medieval authors recount how Lazarus returned from a far more concrete, mapped-out and known unknown, as did most medieval visitors to the afterlife, with only horror stories to tell, living out the rest of his miserable second life in fear of having to go through the gates of death yet again.[3]

The image of Lazarus's escape from mortality would have struck viewers as strange and wonderful – as a miracle and thus not as an event happening in accordance with the rules of nature. Although some early Christian saints such as Bishop Hilary of Poitiers performed the same feat (Fig. 160), raising people from the dead was prohibited in Remiet's time, by a decree of Pope John XXII in 1331, so no one put much hope in seeing such miracles again.[4] The image of Lazarus would also have stirred fears of being buried alive, which, according to contemporary accounts, was not uncommon and which gave the recovered corpse, if he or she were lucky enough to wake up before interment, a Lazarine liminal status.[5] As we have seen, the line between life and death was not as strictly marked as it would become in subsequent periods. Only the steady flame of a candle held before the mouth signalled the loss of breath, the vital *spiritus*, and thus the demise of the subject. Medieval literature is full of visions of *spiritus* in the form of revenants, vampires and ghosts, those who return from the dead to haunt the living with warnings, messages or admonitions. The dead rose again usually only in dreams, as in the vision of Pompey, illustrated by Remiet in the *Faits des romains*, who, asleep on his ship, has a dream in which his dead wife Julie rises up from a coffin to address him (Fig. 161).[6] Precisely because the borders between life and death were less accurately drawn than they are today, this realm of the wandering dead was a powerful cultural force, not only among country folk who were told to keep their elbows well in or they might knock a ghost over. In the Latin Quarter the favourite ghost story told most eloquently by Jacques de Vitry described how a student appeared a day after his death to his former master wearing a cope made entirely of parchment and covered with tiny writing. 'These words, that weigh more than if I carried on my head the tower of that church,' he said, pointing to the massive Romanesque tower of Saint Germain des Prés, 'are the sophisms and curiosities on which I spent my days.' Scalded by a drop of sweat from this academic shade's hand, the master departed the schools of logic quoting the verse, 'I leave croaking to frogs, the morning to ravens, and empty things to the vain. / I am awakened from logic which does not fear death.'[7] This notion that one's action and labours upon earth, such as that of a scholar here, were all adding up in the afterlife to inscribe punishment on one's soul in the hereafter, charged every waking desire and thought with an inescapable implication for one's post-mortem experience. What would have been the visual equivalents of the vanities of the logicians that Remiet might have feared he was wasting his time upon? Perhaps the marginal monsters that animated the edges of manuscripts or the fictive surfaces of scenes in romances? Whatever the answer, these were two genres of image-making that Remiet generally avoided, in favour of sacred or historical narrative.

But what made Lazarus's sudden awakening even more disquieting was that most Christians fully expected to experience this very moment for themselves at the general resurrection. Mortality was not the end of death. It would, or could, happen again and this

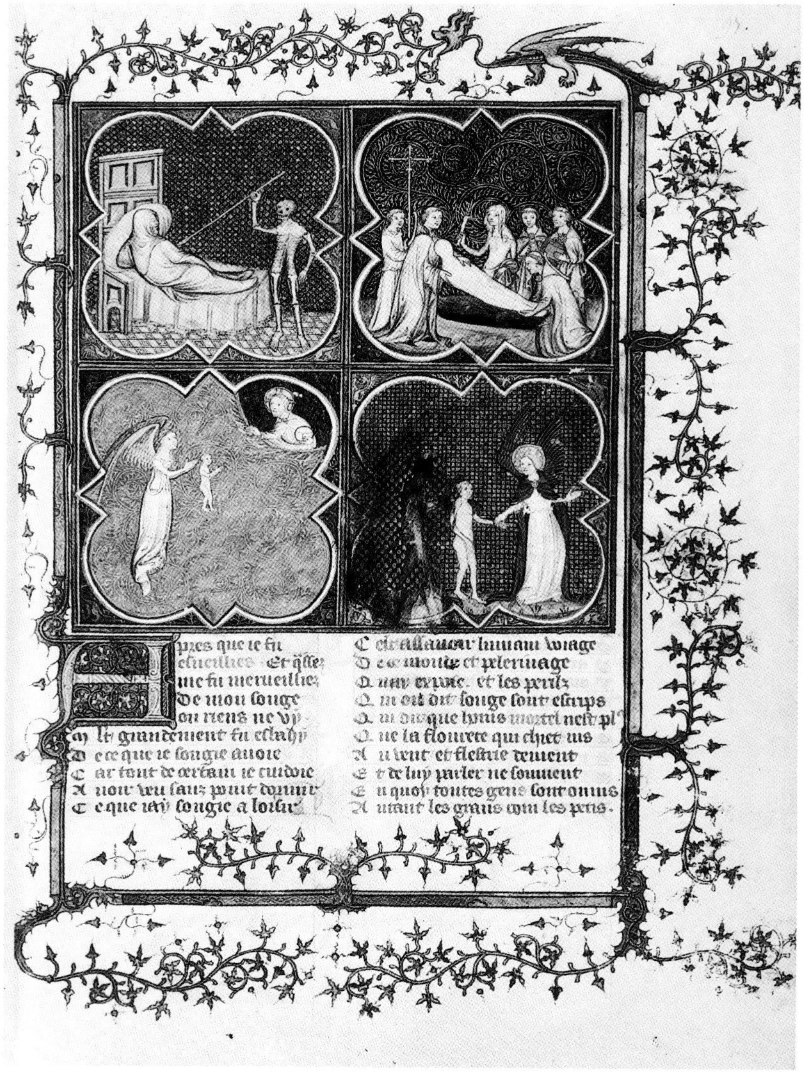

162. Jean de Nizières. Paris, Bibliothèque Nationale, fr. 823, fol. 95. *Pèlerinage de lâme.* Frontispiece: death and burial of the body; Prayer taking the soul to the heavenly court; the soul between the devil and the angel.

time not to the body but to the soul. In Remiet's picture Lazarus jerks upright in his winding-sheet, his hands in an attitude of prayer and submission to God's will. This is the identical gesture to the dead who are resurrected *en masse* in carved and painted representations of the Last Judgement. Lazarus was thus a prototype for all who looked forward to eventual resurrection in their own flesh, after staying much longer in the earth than stinking old Lazarus had done. People stipulated in their wills not only that their corpses, usually without the coffin seen in this picture, be buried with their feet towards the east in anticipation of eventually facing their maker directly, but that they retain their shoes, to be prepared for the long trek, they hoped, heavenward.[8] The 'second death' of the damned at the Last Judgement, referred to in wills as 'timor, metus, anxietas' of the awaited 'Jugement terrible', or God's 'fureur terrible', inspired as much dread as the painful reality of the first. Human history, which began with the Fall, must end, so that all souls can be judged independent of the vagaries of the temporal world and, after the long night, there would be a general awakening, for some to the eternal light of Heaven, and for others to the everlasting darkness of Hell.

An earlier focus of fear, however, was the *pericula* or peril which awaited the soul at the moment of death, often referred to in last testaments.[9] This refers to the first judgement by a devil and an angel that were thought to lurk around the deathbed. In images of the period they often play a tug of war with the diminutive soul when it exits the body. This is the struggle that begins the narrative of the continuation of Guillaume de Deguileville's *Pèlerinage de vie humaine*, the *Pèlerinage de l'âme*, which, again in a dream-allegory, tells the story of the soul's fate after death. In the Paris manuscript of 1393 that bears Remiet's name, this poem was probably completed last, and another younger illuminator, pehaps Jean de Nizières, painted the large, four-part frontispiece (Fig. 162).[10] It was in another, much less luxurious copy of the *Pèlerinages* that at least a decade later Remiet himself painted the image of the soul released from the flesh (Fig. 163). Here 'la mort' is a bald, grinning skull, without the feminine attributes pictured at the end of the previous pilgrimage, and with a more neutral, emaciated body she strikes the pilgrim's heart, splitting his body and soul asunder with her 'venemous dart'. The prostrate body with its youthful face and long golden curls is a variation on Remiet's usual corpse-cliché. Out of its mouth emerges the frail-looking form of the soul, who glances sheepishly towards its guardian angel at the head of the bed. The body is described in the text here as an object of horror for the soul for whom it 'seemed vile to me, smelly and dirty, without movement, lying (*gisant*) quite dead. I had never seens a more vile pile of rot.'[11] The central position in the miniature is taken up by the smudged figure of the angel's other, a blackened amorphous creature, more horrifying even than Death – the demon who will claim the soul. Neither this devil nor the angel seems very extra-terrestrial, however; they stand at the bedside like mundane morticians, their eager eyes focused on their vulnerable prey.

The artist of the Paris frontispiece had the space to expand this opening narrative, which Remiet compressed into a single, one-column miniature, into four scenes (Fig. 162). The first is very like Remiet's, with the spear-wielding figure of Death looming over the bed. In the second, the pilgrim's body is buried by a group of clerics and attended by the asperging female personification of 'misericorde'. The soul appears when we get to the third scene, where it flies heavenward assisted by Prayer, and in the fourth where it stands between the devil and angel guardians who will lead it to St Michael, 'prévôt du ciel', procurator of Heaven. Here too, just as in Remiet's smaller version, the black form of the demon has been smudged away, beyond recognition, a sign of the fear evoked by such seemingly schematic and miniscule representations for contemporary and subsequent readers. Today our terror surely makes us keen to excise Death in the image, whereas medieval readers erased what was, for them, the far more frightening form of the dark spirit, the evil that could damn their souls forever. No scraping or rubbing away, an attempt to neutralize the demonic evil eye or the power in the image, could take away that inevitable and absolutely necessary representation. To try to erase the image of Death would be like trying to rub out oneself.

The soul in both these illustrations of the *Pèlerinage de l'âme* is like a child, an unformed, asexual little body, and not really a person, since it has lost its body and will only be rejoined with its 'other half' at the very end of time. If Deguileville's narrative is, as usual, quite vague about such bodily details, Remiet's image clarifies that this is the soul *in expiratione*. The notion of breathing out was literally linked to the word 'expire' and meant that the last breath and the exit of the soul were synonymous. Remiet had pictured the traditional separation of the soul from the body before, at the opening of Book XIV of Louis d'Orléans's copy of the *Cité de Dieu*. In a strangely pastoral scene, two elegantly dressed philosophers come upon a similarly richly clothed corpse in a forest, whose tiny naked soul leaps out of his mouth (Fig. 164). Looking closely, we notice that this is no conventional expiration scene. The diminutive soul snatches in its tiny hand a red apple from a tree, literally illustrating what the translator Raoul de Presles calls the 'second death of the soul'. Re-enacting the Fall of its first parents, this soul has rejected the grace of God through its choice of sin. According to the stoic philosophers, the text says, 'the vices are born not only in the flesh but in the soul as well'. This idea of a corporeal soul, capable of lusts of the flesh, has been brilliantly conceptualized by Remiet, repeating gestures of the primal sin, but after death, reconfiguring the corpse and the apple tree that he had represented more conventionally years earlier (see Fig. 23). For, whereas traditionally the Fall was seen as leading to the birth of death, here that physical death gives birth to a second far more terrifying and eternal fall – 'la mort seconde de la grace de Dieu'.

This soul, however, is represented in the form of the body. Medieval artists had long struggled to represent the soul – an incorporeal thing – in a corporeal image. From the thirteenth century it was argued that the soul was to be confused not with the *spiritus*, a principle that enlivened the body, but with a higher incorporeal attribute or *anima*. For some medical writers this force was associated with the *pneuma* and was, like the breath, invisible. It is this association with breathing and the last gasp, so to speak, that makes Remiet put its exit at the mouth. Usually visualized on its entering the body to animate it during conception/creation, the soul must have seemed a strange and ambiguous representation. In some contemporary manuscripts God imbues Adam with a soul in the form of a homunculus that emerges from the Creator's mouth and flies towards the lifeless body.[12] In the thirteenth century the newly translated Latin text of Aristotle's *De anima* had been illustrated by the soul exiting the mouth in the same way. As the Aristotelian 'form of the body', it was represented as a body yet it was supposed to be the body's antithesis. We always look at medieval images as though they were clarifications of high theological doctrine, when in fact their variety and complexity were often confusing to contemporaries. The thirteenth-century Oxford theologian Thomas Docking described as theologically and philosophically erroneous the way artists depicted the soul as a baby leaving the mouth of the deceased.[13] But discussions in Oxford and Paris about the soul's actual status and controversy about the stages of the soul's journey after death do not seem to have affected the urge towards illustration, which had to conceive it corporeally. Like its origins when implanted by God in the mother's womb, the soul's eventual union with its creator was clouded with ambiguity in representations precisely because artists were compelled to create images of the spirit out of matter, the soul out of the body.

The point is that the soul is not only the anonymous entity suggested by the cor-

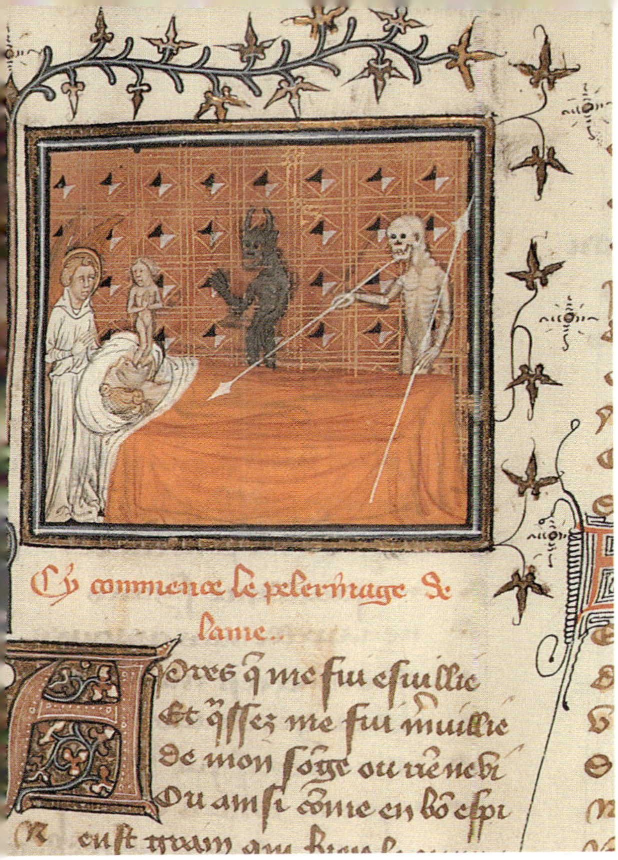

163. Remiet. Leiden, University Library, MS BPL 74, fol. 92. *Pèlerinage de l'âme*. The death of the body, the expiration of the soul, and the two attendents.

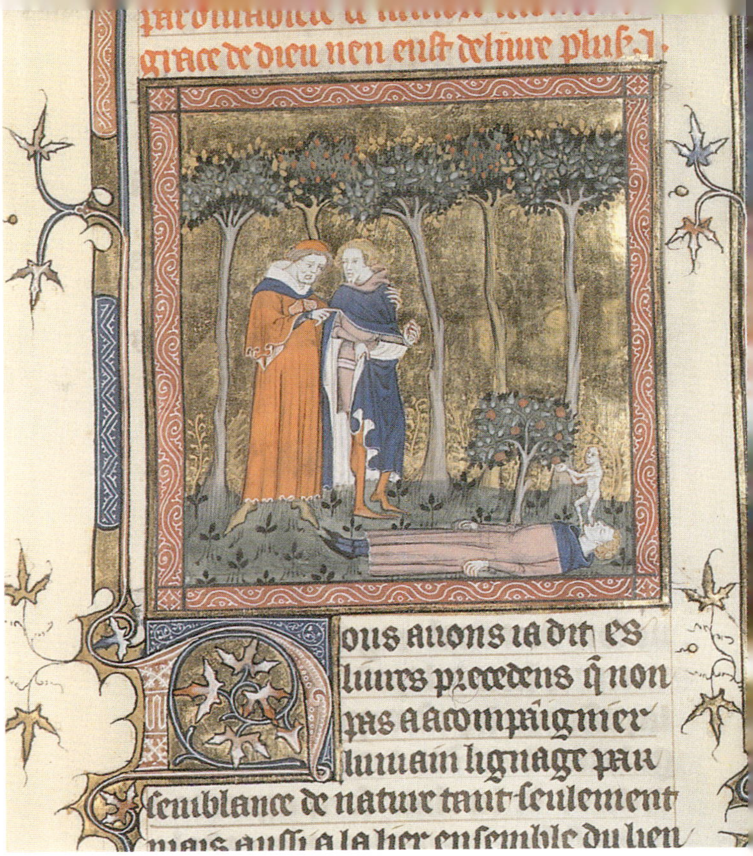

164. Remiet. Paris, Bibliothèque Nationale, fr. 171, fol. 62. Augustine, *La Cité de Dieu*. The death of the soul, and two men observing the expiration of the soul, which re-enacts the Fall.

165. Remiet. Bayeux, Bibliothèque du Chapitre, MS 61, fol. 15v. Missal-Pontifical. The Bishop raises his soul to God.

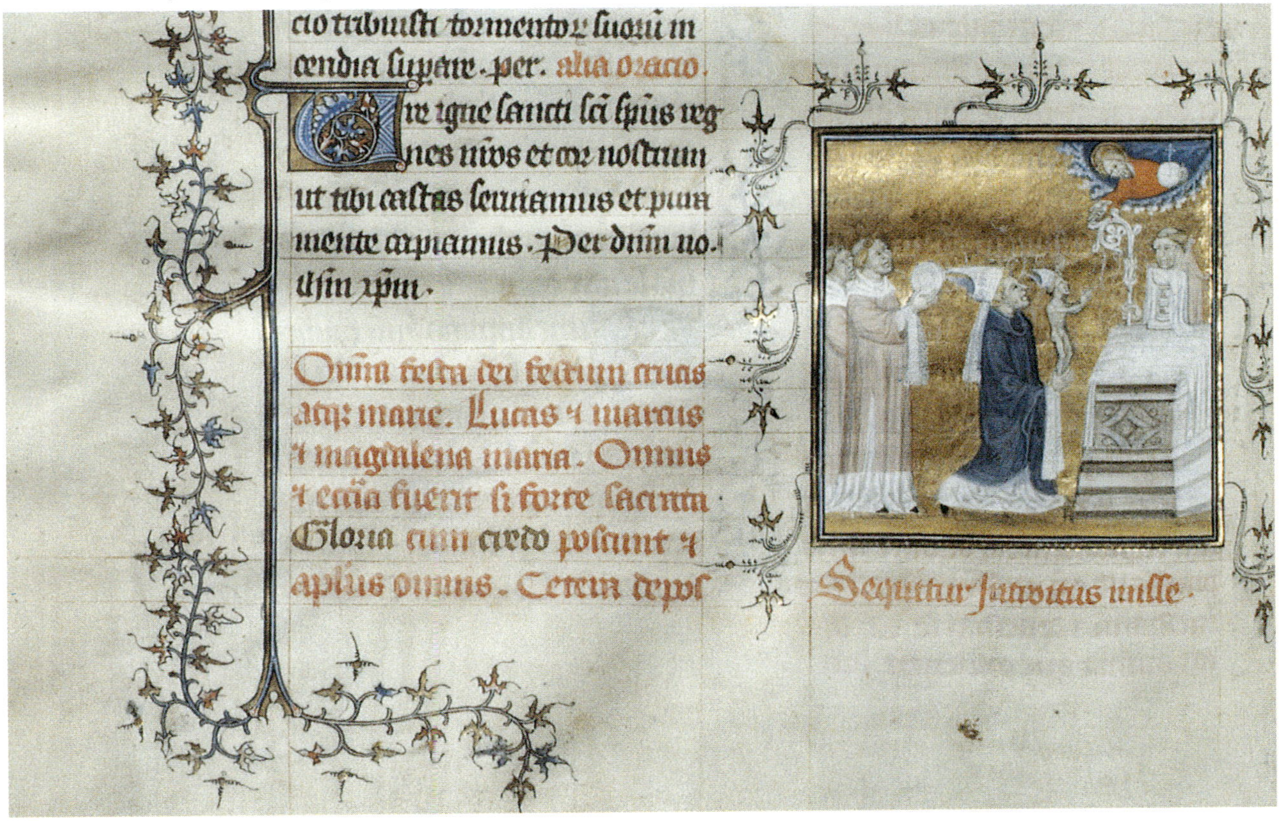

puscular waif in Remiet's scenes of death, but the real form of the individual which is carried into the next world. In the missal-pontifical made for the Bishop of Luçon, Remiet shows the bishop at the Introit of the mass holding up his soul toward God as he says the words 'Ad te levavi animam meam (Unto you I lift my soul)'. This little soul has a bishop's mitre too (Fig. 165), stressing that it is *his* particular soul. The nakedness of the soul, meant to express the Christian ideology of equality of all persons before God, is here undermined by the necessity of social distinction. Only in such liturgical scenes is the soul of a self visible during life. There is one other important instance, however, early in the narrative of the *Pèlerinage de vie humaine*, when Reason, in order to show the pilgrim how his flesh is the source of his weakness, separates his soul from his body (Fig. 166).

This is in response to a searching question of self-identity that the pilgrim asks her, 'Tell me, Lady, who am I, if I am not my body?' 'You are the portrait, image and figure of God your Father,' she tells him, 'not the son of Thomas Deguileville.' This is a moment of authorial self-identification too, where the Cistercian author inserts his own father's name into this debate about selfhood between the pilgrim and Reason. In the miniature Remiet too gives this moment an intense physicality and an intimacy that is not seen in any of the other versions of the scene, and suggests that another supplementary self – that of the artist – is not merely interpreting the text in an image, or copying a model. Reason leans over the muscular, not totally recumbent, form of the pilgrim, suddenly naked as though to emphasize his fleshliness. In the text her 'pulling out' of his soul is described in almost visceral terms and there is a definite suggestion of erotic contact between the elegantly sleeved and crowned female figure and the body beneath her. This is, in many respects, another version of death's visit, a little death, or a rehearsal of that ultimate orgasm. The language here too is sensuous. For a few exciting moments the pilgrim feels himself liberated, ravished up into the air with a feeling of weightlessness and incredible relief. From this vantage point he is able to see everything. 'It is as if nothing in the world were hidden from me.' His omnipotent gaze looks down upon his lifeless 'vile' body, which is described as 'a simulacra made of dung, a statue of clay, a scarecrow. By itself it cannot move, or work or do anything, for it is powerless and paralyzed, deaf, blind and counterfeit.' This last term *contrefait* and the other terms like *simulacre* all suggest the lifeless body's secondary status as an empty representation.[14] If his soul is made in the portrait of God, not his fleshly father, his body, produced in the carnal act of copulation, is a useless statue. This anti-three-dimensional language, promoting a fleshless immaterial image of man's assimilation to God in portraiture or likeness, goes a long way to explaining Remiet's own reduced and spare aesthetic practice, the fear of three-dimensionality that would make the naturalistic image all too easily and immediately into a corpse.

Remiet focuses upon this moment of what we would call an out-of-body experience, as the soul imperiously looks down on his more substantial but empty alter ego, his arms folded as if to signal the soul's relaxed transcendence over the merely muscular flesh below. The body is described as looking as though it were asleep, which explains why Remiet gives it a pillow. This also points to a weakness that Reason underlines, which is the body's tendency to seek its own pleasure in soft beds and other luxuries. 'You see now your enemy!' she tells him. But whom does she tell? Remiet is also illuminating a split in the subject, a fissure that Reason opens up between two competing viewpoints – between the lifeless/sleeping prostrate subject, now become object, and its soul, which has become the new subject, surveying all below. Remiet's problem is that he is unable to depict the body from the soul's point of view, to locate his scene within a subject position. He does not know how to utilize the new 'trick' of the painters, the bird's-eye view, which would have allowed him to look down upon the pilgrim's corporeal flesh from the vantage point of the soul floating above. Like all medieval artists, he knows representation only from the body's point of view. The idea of viewpoint, which is clearly articulated in Deguileville's text, is not yet fully developed. Reason has already told the pilgrim that the bodily senses and especially the lust of the eyes will be replaced in the soul with spiritual sight, the sight that allows him to see far and wide. But Remiet's vision is as bound to the body as the monkey to its ball and chain – a metaphor the pilgrim uses when he is finally 'brought to earth' in his body again. Feeling himself suddenly trussed and imprisoned in his flesh, he weeps bitterly at his return; having glimpsed but briefly the bliss of freedom from the flesh, he now realizes its horror all the more. Yet he thanks Reason for having shown him how his body is 'always contrary to me' – how his identity is bound up not in that vile bag of veins and skin but in a perception that had floated above it. Of all Remiet's images, this one shows his struggle to make distinctions between categories of perception using his inherited and ultimately limited repertoire of images. But it also shows how much we have to revise our understanding of medieval iconography as 'clarification' or, even worse, 'illustration' of a text. Instead, the image is bound, like the body, to schematic envelopes of fleshly signs, pieces of parchment, unable to gain the vantage point of the soul – and thus, in medieval terms, the self.

Another such moment of the self-splitting occurs after death, in the *Pèlerinage de l'âme*, where as part of his tour of Purgatory the soul is introduced to his own corpse rotting in the cemetery (Fig. 167). 'Horrible spectacle,

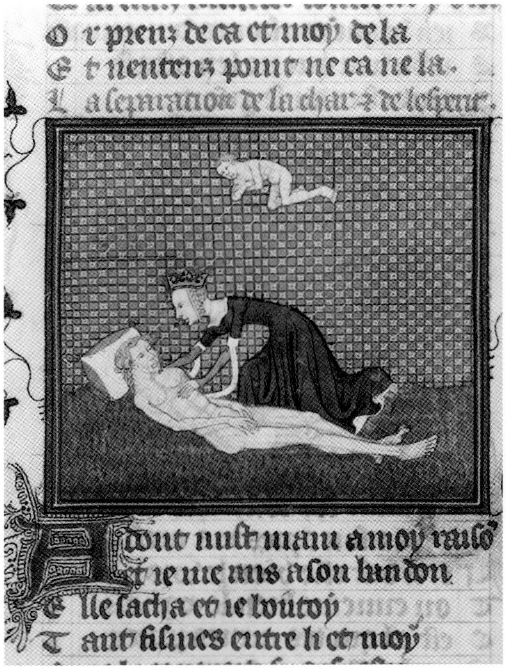

166. Remiet. Paris, Bibiothèque Nationale, fr. 823, fol. 44. *Pèlerinage de vie humaine*. Grace Dieu separates the pilgrim's soul from his body.

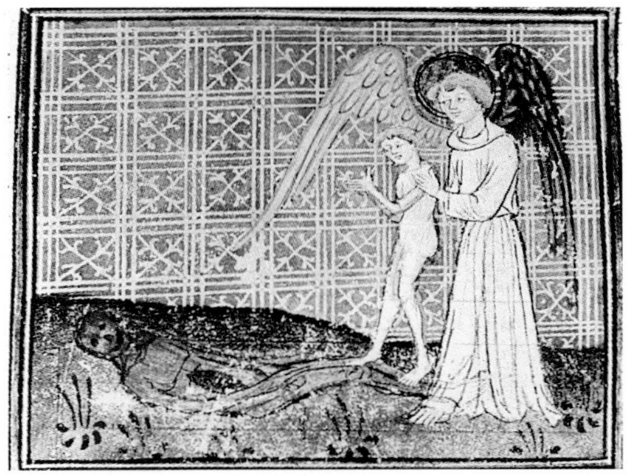

167. Parisian illuminator, *c*.1390. Paris, Bibliothèque Sainte Geneviève, MS 130, fol. 118. *Pèlerinage de lâme*. The pilgrim meets his own rotting corpse.

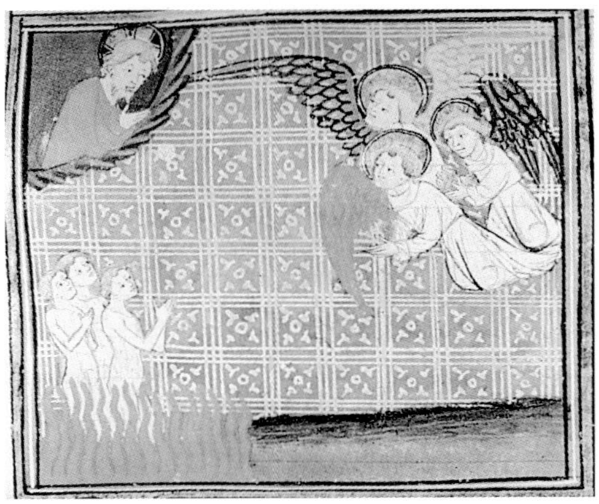

168. Parisian illuminator, *c*.1390. Paris, Bibliothèque Sainte Geneviève, MS 1130, fol. 112. *Pèlerinage de l'âme*. Angels bring comforting ointment to souls waiting in Purgatory.

are you the body – vile, dirty and smelly, meat for worms?' the soul spits out in anger. 'You are there punished for all the evil you made me do. You were always against me. You always led me down the paths of evil . . . and it is because of you that I am damned!' The cadaver raises its neck a little and replies, 'Don't blame me! . . . Was I not made part of yourself? Is it not in your bones and your flesh that you will come to judgement, as it is written? If I am deformed and hideous it is because of you.' As part of their lengthy disputation, an early example of a popular genre of the period, the body argues that he is a sack of matter which can only be moved by the animating soul, who is the real perpetrator of sin.[15] The dichotomy we are apt to make today between the corruptible body and the pure incorruptible soul did not exist for Remiet and his contemporaries, for whom the soul could be just as distorted and disfigured as its rotting receptacle. Moreover, these two halves of the split self, the more loquacious corpse tells his soul mate, will eventually be joined together again after a period of languishing in the newly invented waiting-room of the afterlife.

Purgatory: Soul Waiting

Consciousness, therefore, is consciousness only in having *been* born, dead, and having awakened itself from this double indifference. (But to what extent is it double? To what extent is death already determined as the negative moment of [re]birth?) Jean-Luc Nancy[16]

Alas! Hard Farewell! Painful end! Pitiful conclusion! Your soul will go to hell or at least to the fire of purgatory, to receive pain and punishment for its sins. Pierre d'Ailly[17]

A dramatic theological and doctrinal development, which had confusing repercussions for artists and viewers alike and which had enormous impact on Remiet's art of death, was the idea of Purgatory. Whereas the Scriptures and Church Fathers like Augustine pronounced that Judgement would come only at the end of time, offering eternal life or eternal death, the construction of Purgatory, in the course of the twelfth and thirteenth centuries, had interjected something in between – not only an individual judgement immediately after death, imagined as the struggle for the soul between angels and demons, but in addition a temporal *place* of purification where the soul could be cleansed of its burden of sin. This new space in the afterlife was partly a response to increasingly powerful judicial procedures and developments in lay and seigneurial power in this life, but it also fulfilled a need to concretize individual experience beyond the grave. The 'greater' Judgement at the end of time was too long to wait for people newly conscious of clock-time, and so the 'lesser' judgement, imaginable as nearer and immediately following death, raised people's hopes for a more speedy receipt of their just rewards.

It was also a time and a space that could be altered and measured from the here and now, and most fourteenth-century devotional strategies were concerned with shortening one's own or a dead relative's time in the purgatorial fires by special prayers, indulgences, pardons and pilgrimages. The time of Purgatory no longer extended the whole interval

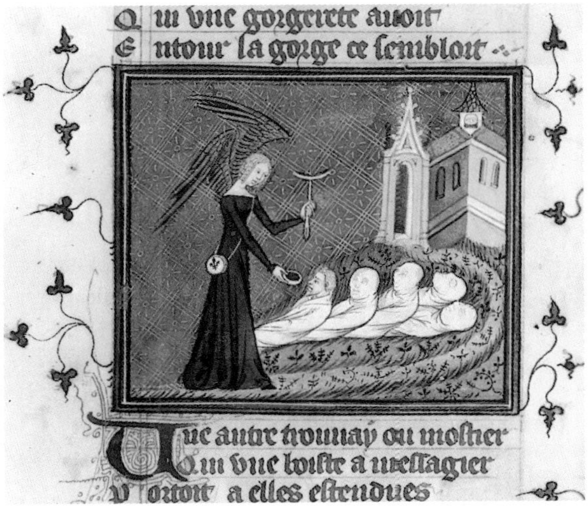

169. Remiet. Paris, Bibliothèque Nationale, fr. 823, fol. 88v. *Pèlerinage de vie humaine.* Prayer feeding the dead.

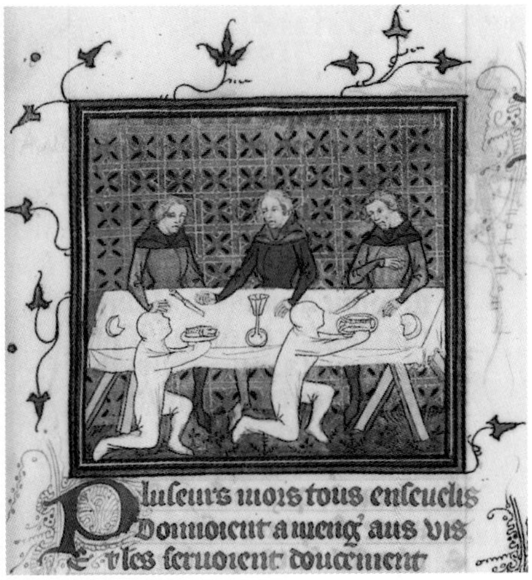

170. Remiet. Paris, Bibliothèque Nationale, fr. 823, fol. 89. *Pèlerinage de vie humaine.* The dead feeding the living.

between death and resurrection but was on a variable, measurable and moreover manipulable time-scale, like a prison sentence.[18] Whereas the Final Reckoning was out of one's individual control, the purgatorial sentence was infinitely more flexible. Deguileville's *Pèlerinage de l'âme* describes how souls in Purgatory are literally refreshed by ointments, brought by prayer to the angels, who take them to soothe the pains of those in the flames (Fig. 168). The pilgrim sees some souls writhing in constant torment, the ointment boxes that are brought to them being empty. His angel guardian tells him that this is because, although they are being prayed for by relatives on earth, these efforts are useless because they died without repenting their sins. Others, however, have their ointment boxes refilled again and again because they have frequent masses celebrated for their souls. Angels also bring special comfort in oils containing the prayers of friends and parents, which are most efficacious. The metaphor of medicinal ointment is another somatic insistence upon continuities between physical and post-physical experience. In these bridges between this world and the next, rather than anticipating things to come, emphasis was redirected towards what one could do in this life to make it easier for oneself and one's relatives in the next. The whole culture of death that I have been describing in this book and that Remiet was involved in as representer, from birth to baptism, making wills, buying indulgences, seeking out relics, preparing to die, the 'dramatization of the moment of death' – all these were stimulated by the new conception of time and space afforded by Purgatory. Its most elaborate representation in a literary text, the *Pèlerinage de l'âme*, is an important testimony of new mental outlook, described by Jacques Le Goff as 'the complex system of bookkeeping associated with the world to come' – the increasingly bureaucratic vision of the afterlife.[19]

Remiet had already depicted a number of purgatorial themes towards the end of the earthly pilgrimage, the *Pèlerinage de vie humaine*. Here the pilgrim comes, at the end of his life's journey, to a monastery, a ship which saves him from drowning in the sea of the world and where he finds the theological virtues, ladies representing the monastic and

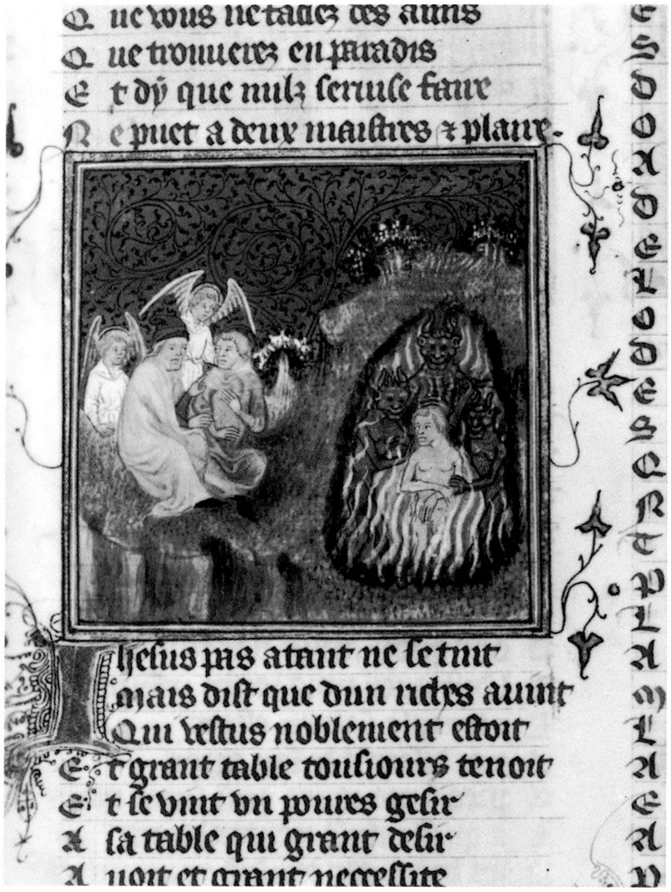

172. Remiet. Paris, Bibliothèque Nationale, fr. 823, fol. 217. *Pèlerinage de Jésus-Christ*. Dives in Hell and Lazarus in Abraham's bosom.

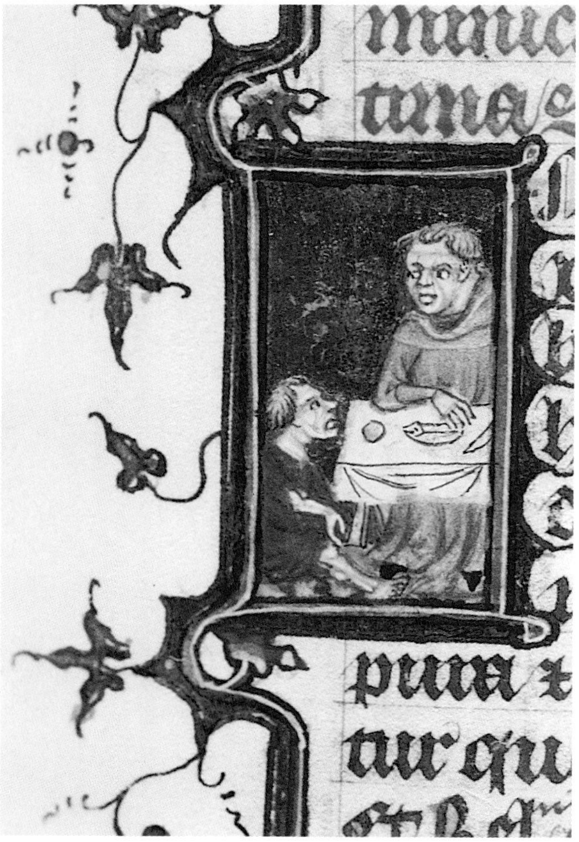

171. Remiet. Manchester, John Rylands Library, lat. 136, fol. 150. Breviary. Dives and Lazarus.

173. Parisian illuminator, c.1390. Paris, Bibliothèque Sainte Geneviève, MS 130, fol. 113v. *Pèlerinage de l'âme*. The leper Lazarus sits on the edge of Hell.

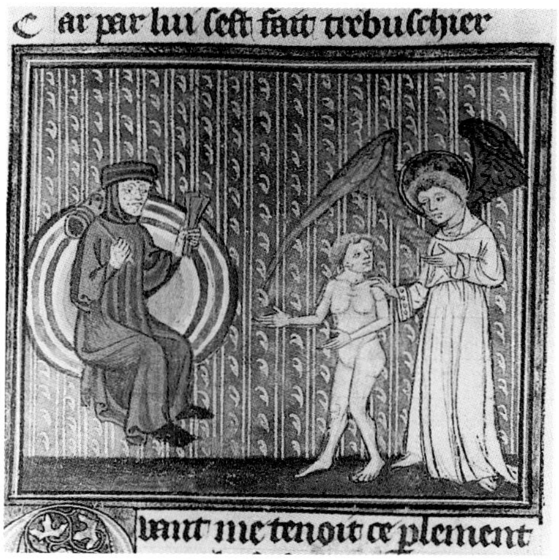

spiritual life as opposed to the hideous vices encountered earlier. One of these is Prayer whom he sees feeding the dead, as they lie in their winding-sheets in a churchyard cemetery, a literal embodiment of the idea of earthly prayers for the deceased continuing to aid them in Purgatory (Fig. 169). The idea is not of easing pain but of providing sustenance, keeping the dead alive and feeding them during their second earthly womb-time before their eventual rebirth, through the continuing devotion and worship of the community. Lady Prayer is an envoy to the next world and has her messenger's pouch at her waist, and she holds out an auger with which to bore a hole in the clouds to reach heaven. But Remiet, unlike most illuminators, emphasizes her more mundane, sepulchral ministrations. The dead are not shown here in Purgatory, some other place, but as sitting waiting in the very places of their rotting – the cemetery – kept in kind of foetid half-life in the wet, cold soil. Anonymous, apart from the first hungry face that sits up to drink from Prayer's cup, the physical experience of these zombie-like figures is strangely ambiguous.

In this domestic economy between the zones of life and death, the dead reciprocate. Only a few lines later in Deguileville's poem, they feed the living, kneeling and serving them at table (Fig. 170). The shrouded male corpses in Remiet's miniature are a kind of anti-'Three Living and Three Dead'. Instead of greeting the living as the horrific portent of their future decay, here in the monastery they provide succour as ghoulish servants at a Founders' Feast. Only in the vain, courtly world of princes are the dead to be feared. In the monastery and for the devout, the dead are those friends whom one feeds with prayer and who in return provide spiritual and of course, through their monetary bequests, literal sustenance. This interplay between the living and the dead was visible at Remiet's local parish church of Saint Séverin, where most of the rituals performed were memorial masses for founders who had left large sums of money for the purpose. Indeed the very refurbishment of the church, as recorded on many of its pillars, was paid for by families and benefactors whose names were entered on the obituary rolls as paying for the perpetual prayers for their souls.[20] Many of the things we now call works of art, altarpieces, votive statues and chapel decorations, were part of this economy of death, expenditure that served those who had spent everything already, that mitigated suffering in the afterlife by giving glory to God visibly in this one. This newly created space in the afterlife helped stimulate the building of vast new spaces in this one. One might even describe much medieval art in terms of the 'dead feeding the living'.

The living had a duty to feed the less fortunate, as in the story of that other Lazarus illustrated by Remiet who did not overcome death in life but instead suffered a horrible lingering end from poverty. Illustrating a Sunday sermon in a breviary, Remiet paints Dives and Lazarus in their earthly inequality, the scraggy little beggar pointing to the sores on his bony legs placed directly below the rich man's feast. Disdainfully, Dives places his expensive, blue-covered elbows on his well-stocked table, in a gesture of withdrawal (Fig. 171). What everyone knew as the outcome of the story and the reversal of their positions appears in the *Pèlerinage de Jésus-Christ* (Fig. 172). Here Lazarus sits clothed in the green meadows of heaven with Abraham and two angels while, below, Dives sits naked in the belly of the earth, Hell, surrounded by three hideous grinning demons. He begs for water and cries 'Abraham have mercy', but in a similar self-satisfied gesture of disinterest as Dives himself had shown at table, Lazarus sits quite unaffected by the horrible

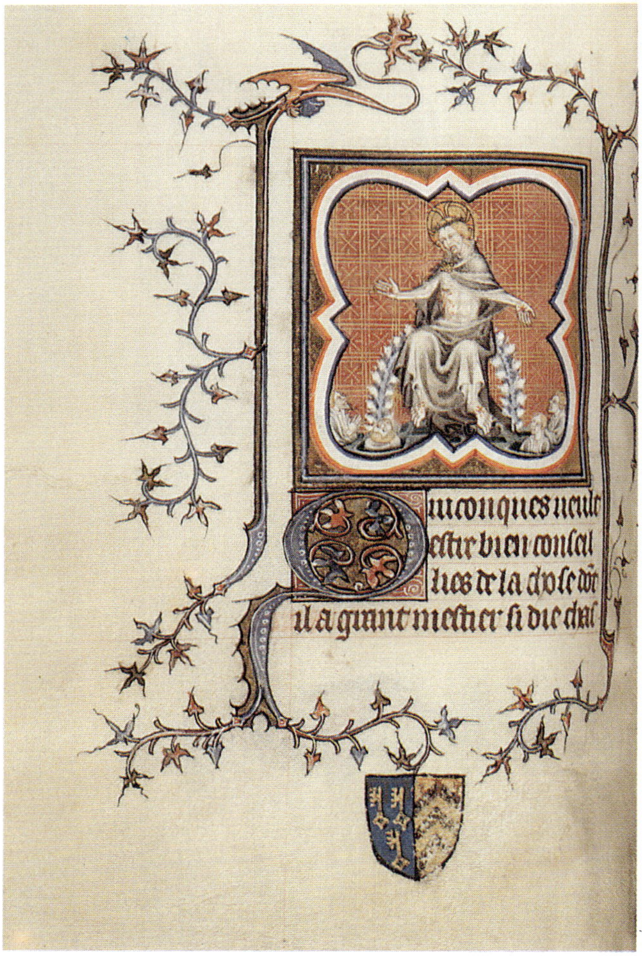

174. Remiet. London, British Library, MS Yates Thompson 45, fol. 124v. Book of Hours. Prayer to the Five Wounds of Christ, and the Last Judgement.

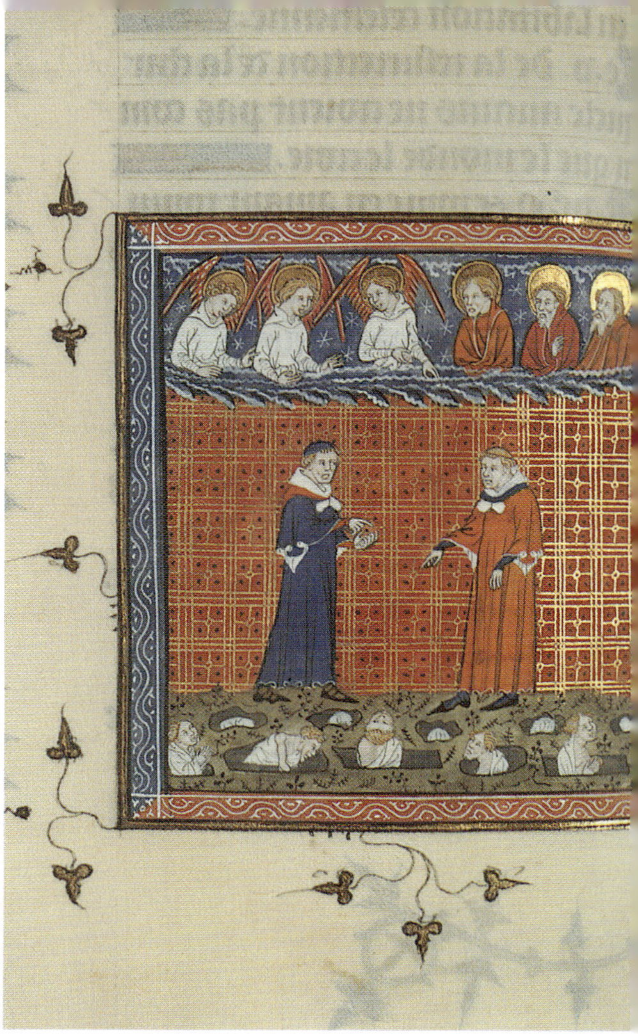

175. Remiet. Paris, Bibliothèque Nationale, fr. 171, fol. 383v. Augustine, *La Cité de Dieu*. Two philosophers discuss the resurrection of the dead at the Last Judgement.

screams coming from below. One of the greatest torments of Hell was that the damned would be able to see the saved basking in heavenly light, but it is not clear whether the blessed had the reverse view. In this miniature, Heaven and Hell seem rather too close for comfort.

The leper Lazarus appears again as part of the otherworldly vision of the *Pèlerinage de l'âme* painted by another illuminator close to Remiet. Here he continues to carry his leper's clappers and is as pock-marked in the next world as he was in his earthly existence (Fig. 173). He sits on the edge of Purgatory, which in Deguileville's topography is the outer shell of a concentric nut-like form whose central kernel is Hell. Remiet was never one for complex diagrammatic representations or spatial experiment. In his own miniature of Dives and Lazarus, Lazarus sits and chats on a grassy bank with the Old Testament Patriarch (Fig. 172). In the liturgy of the dead, the soul of the deserving deceased is described as carried to Abraham's bosom immediately after death, not at the end of time, and so this delightful meadow with a front-seat view of Hell is only temporary. Lazarus waits, like all the souls of the departed, for the Final Day.[21]

Judgement: Body Rising

To counter the dazzling sight of earthly communities, the Church imposes a *political economy of individual salvation*. First through faith (which became the soul's *personal* relation to God instead of the effervescent community), then through the accumulation of works and merits, that is, an economy in the strict sense of the term, with its final account and its equivalences. It is then, as always since the appearance of processes of accumulation, that death really arose on the horizon of life. It is then that the Kingdom really passes to the other side of death, before which everyone finds themselves *alone* once again. Jean Baudrillard[22]

Deliver me, O Lord, from eternal death in that great day when the heavens and the earth are moved, that day, that day of wrath, ruin and misery, that great and bitterest of days. Response in the Office of the Dead[23]

The event that people looked forward to at the hour of their death is pictured alongside a vernacular prayer, found in many Books of Hours, which sometimes forms part of a meditation on the five wounds, 'les V plaies notre Christ' (Fig. 174). This opens with a prologue 'Quiconques veult estre bien conseillier (Whoever would be well counselled)', which makes the plea that if the reader should not die on that day 'vilainement' – that is, without proper confession – by having said a paternoster, an Ave Maria and this prayer on the five wounds, his soul would still be saved.[24] This text and image of last resort, of panic insurance in case of being run over by a cart or falling down a well, points far forward from the accidental moment of unshriven death to the very borders of eternity. In the little Book of Hours in the British Library, this urgent prayer is illustrated by Remiet with Christ's Second Coming upon the rainbow, showing his wounds to four astonished and diminutive dead folk who rise from their graves below. These figures, freshly embodied in their flesh, but oddly dressed in little white surplices, to represent perhaps their being reunited with the spiritual raiment of their souls, pop up their heads as though out of rabbit holes, craning their necks to get a better view of their saviour whose blood drips down from above. It is because of this sacrificial liquid, and the five wounds marking the gigantic body that looms above them, that their own bodies and souls can now, at the end of time, be reunited. In the decade before 1400, fuelled by the Great Schism and its relation to prophecies of the reign of Antichrist described in the Book of Revelation and calculations by mystics like Joachim of Fiore, apocalyptic fears of the world's end were rife. Churchmen were giving sermons on the doom, Eustache Deschamps was writing poems about its impending arrival and Nicolas of Clamanges, a pupil of Pierre D'Ailly, wrote, 'I estimate scarcely three years to be left until the time of that day most greatly to be feared'. In 1399, at the age of forty-nine, Pierre d'Ailly himself, chancellor of the University of Paris, ordered his tomb to be built in the cathedral of Cambrai in earnest expectation of what was to come.[25] This *fin du monde*, or end-of-time, image was in this respect far more timely, more contemporary, than many of Remiet's *histoires*.

The status of the newly resurrected body at the Last Judgement had been a hotly disputed question during the previous century, between Aristotelian scholastics like Thomas Aquinas, who denied the continuity of form between the living and the dead body, and the Paris Augustinians like Henry of Ghent, who argued for the body's material continuity. St Paul had stated, not unequivocally, that 'the dead shall rise incorruptible and we shall be changed. For this corruptible body must put on incorruption and this mortal being must put on immortality' (I Corinthians 15:52–3). As Caroline Bynum has shown, these theological arguments focused around one key issue – that of identity, the notion that the *caro radicalis*, the core of flesh passed on from parents to child and through food, was at the end of time reassembled by God, no matter how diffuse and separated its parts. But if it is not *re-surrectio* unless the same person rises again, 'what does it mean for a person to be the same?'[26] One argument taken from Augustine and repeated by Peter Lombard used the analogy of the statue that, once melted down, can be recast as the same statue again.[27] Such analogies taken from the mechanical arts suggest that there was not a vast chasm separating the scholastic arguments of Parisian doctors of theology and the notions of an unlearned man like Remiet, who was not a passive illiterate merely manipulated by images of hell-fires as was Villon's mother. In his thoughtful illustrations to the *Cité de Dieu*, Remiet later depicted two contemporary Parisian philosophers debating the resurrection of the dead and the significance of the *fin du monde*, standing between the heavenly firmament above and the earth below, which has already opened as though giving them a preview of the unimaginable end of time (Fig. 175). One of them points down to where the souls clamber out of their graves. Raoul de Presles's version of Augustine's work is full of additional commentary citing more current and contradictory authorities on the issue, like Aristotle and Aquinas. It also announces that it is aimed at lay readers, those 'qui sont purs lays', making available to them, in the vernacular form of 'paroles', the 'theologie' of the Doctors of the Church. Debates about the resurrection were aimed at everyone, since all stood, like these philosophers, between the two, heaven and earth, waiting.

There were inconsistencies and odd gaps in the triumphant Augustinian vision of the resurrection of the flesh, however, that must have made many people's flesh creep and raised unsettling questions. Did all the food that one had eaten and digested and that in medieval terms had become part of one's body, did all that reappear and thus bloat the risen dead beyond recognition? Did all one's hair and nails return to be twenty feet long? What of cannibalism where the same matter had been in two or more bodies. Would the deformed get their deformed bodies back? What would happen to aborted foetuses, the stillborn and those born as monsters with two heads? What about those whose bones had been burned and scattered into infinite dust particles? One hardly looked forward to seeing the flayed shade of Bartholomew or the blood-speckled flesh of Julien in heaven, but Augustine assured his devout readers that the glorious scars of the martyrs would shine resplendent. He had argued that, in contrast to this fearful vision of the resurrection as a freak show, everything would be beautiful in 'those pure, youthful, eternally resplendent bodies'.[28] Faced with these fears, artists had for centuries striven to represent the resurrected bodies as physically perfect human beings, standing glorified and illuminated by a subtle light as they could never have stood in their previous mundane flesh. Remiet could see these glorious bodies standing in painted stone on the façade of nearby Notre Dame.[29]

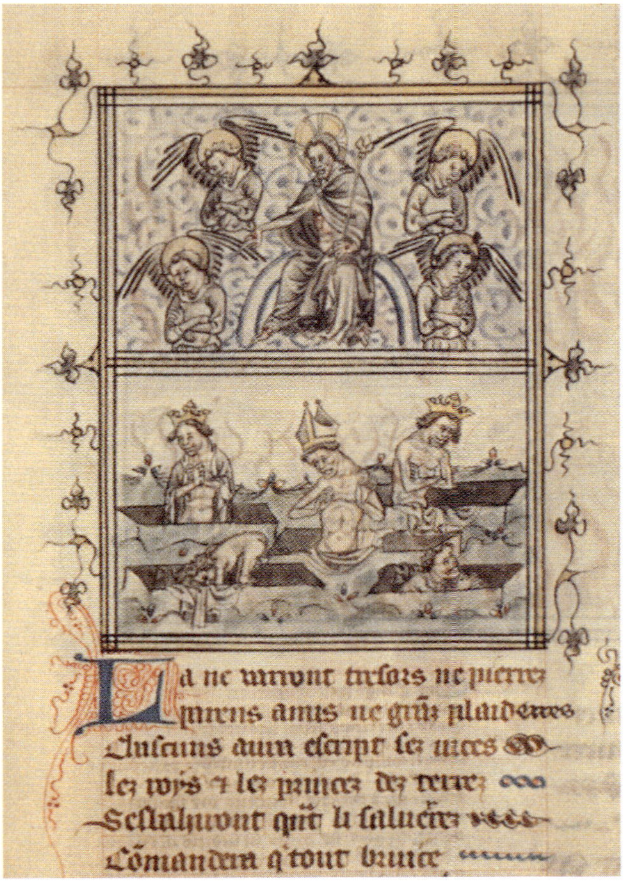

176. Remiet. Paris, Bibliothèque Nationale, fr. 20029, fol. 18. *Lay de la fragilité humaine.* Kings and bishops rise from their graves at the Last Judgement.

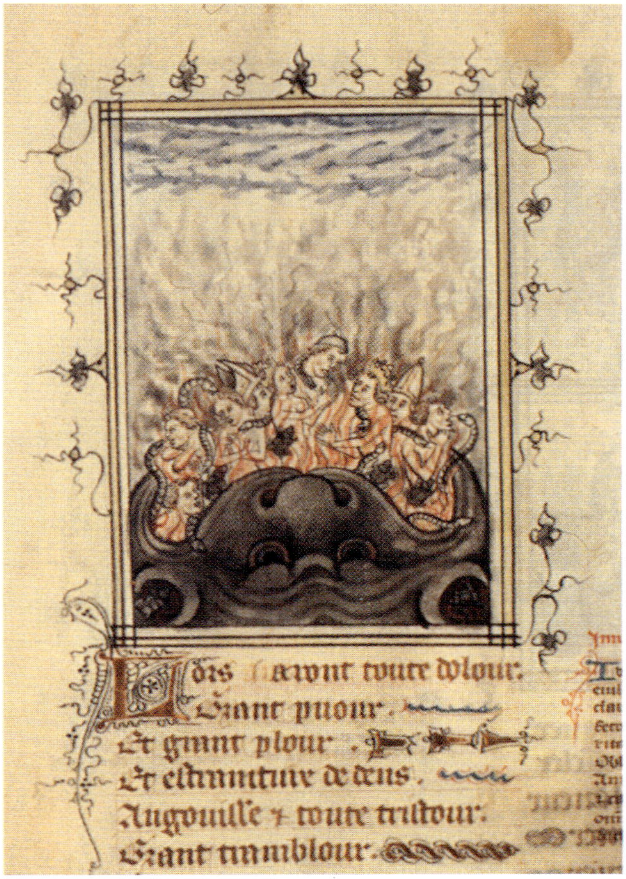

177. Remiet. Paris, Bibliothèque National, fr. 20029, fol. 19v. *Lay de la fragilité humaine.* The Mouth of Hell.

The anodyne aesthetics of Heaven were always harder to imagine and depict than the sensational torments of Hell. Whereas in other religions the beyond was a place which mirrored this one, in which the deceased required all the equipment for continued pleasure provided by funerary objects, Christianity made this the greatest gap, the emptiest space. This was true for Remiet in completing the last few pages of Deschamps's *Lay de la fragilité humaine*, which ends with the end of time. Innocent's original Latin treatise had been clear on the issue of bodily reformulation: 'All that are in their graves shall hear the voice of the Son of God, and they that have done good things shall come forth unto the resurrection of life, but they that have done evil things, unto the resurrection of judgement . . . Death and Hell shall give up their dead that were in them' and 'every eye shall see and also they that pierced him . . . the Son of Man coming in the clouds of heaven with great power and majesty'. Remiet managed to include these delicate clouds in his image of the Last Judgement in the Book of Hours (Fig. 174). In the *Lay* he had a more complex sequence of judgement images to make. On Judgement Day the corpses are shown rising from their graves (fol. 17v) and on the following page, illustrating chapter XXXII, the 'kings and princes of the world' are shown rising up naked except for their headgear, which identifies their social position (Fig. 176). Two kings flank a bishop in the

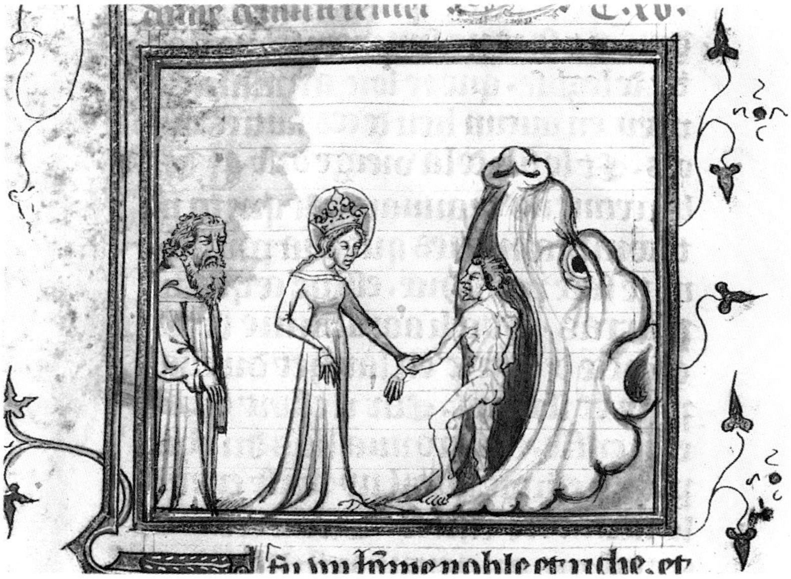

178. Remiet. Paris, Bibliothèque Nationale, fr. 312, fol. 344v. *Miroir historial*. The Virgin saves from Hell a boy who was promised to the devil at birth.

centre, and a man looking as though he is frantically searching for something he has lost, bends over as if wanting to return to his previously disembodied state. On the right another man looks tentatively out of his grave, surprised that it has actually happened. These bodies are brilliantly conceived as newly, shockingly sensate; shivering with the cold, still feeling the damp must of the earth to which they had been consigned, they are reconstituted in their frail flesh. There are no glowing resurrected forms here but people still weighed down by their earthly headgear and worldly paraphernalia of crowns and tiaras. The next scene of the terrible conflagration and the end of heaven and earth in which all becomes nothing is again one of those moments in the manuscript where the hermeneutic and the material aspects of the book seem to conjoin, and the chaos of nothing is a splattered, ugly mess of elements engulfing a castle. As one would expect, the treatise lingers over the fires of eternal punishment far longer than over the peace of Heaven. Hell is described as the place where the ungodly 'as if consumed by death will revive to death so that they are forever dying'.

> Then will death be undying; then will the dead live who are dead to life. They who have had and lost life will seek and not find death. Hear John in the Apocalypse saying 'In those days men shall seek death and shall not find it, and they shall desire to die, and death shall fly from them.' O death, how sweet you would be to those to whom you were so bitter; they who violently hated you alone will eagerly desire you alone.[30]

Death and desire meet in the flames of Hell in this ironic reversal for the human subject, now eternally imprisoned without the hope of death. For as the Response to the third Nocturn in the Office of the Dead, repeated in this treatise, but which echoed throughout people's daily lives, says, 'quoniam in inferno nulla est redempcio (in Hell there is no redemption)'. Remiet illustrated Deschamps's reworking of the Judgement and Hell sequence of the *Lay* with a series of highly conventional images, images of souls writhing in the flames, but also with striking details from Innocent's account, like the souls being bound up and thrown into the fire like bundles of kindling (fol. 19r). Innocent III had relegated all sinners to the same torment, but Deschamps's French verse adds more specific sinners who have been thrown into Hell for their demerits: 'larrons, murdriers et sodomites'. The next scene of the pains of Hell presents a conventional inverted Hellmouth (Fig. 177). Here the verses' sharp, short lines rhythmically evoke the same endlessly repeated spurts of agony that are registered in Remiet's squirming, tormented figures, packed into the smouldering maw.

Then [the damned] will suffer great pain
Great stench
And great tears
And they will clench their teeth
And suffer anguish and sadness
And great trembling
And heat
And many groans,
Wails
Hunger, thirst, and all kinds of languor . . .
Vermin and serpents shall assail them,
All torments
Will dwell with them
And ne'er depart again.
In fear
Will come God's judgement.[31]

In the *Miroir historial* Remiet had pictured a young boy being rescued from the jaws of Hell by the Virgin (Fig. 178). His mother had devoted him at birth to the devil, but because she had conceived him during Christ's passion on Easter Eve, he is saved by the patriarch of Jerusalem, who stands on the left, and by the Virgin herself. Like an alternative Lazarus rescued from the dark pit of the open grave, this scene depicts the far more urgent need for resurrection into eternal and not just human life. Although Hell had a far more complex and hierarchical set-up in the detailed representations of fourteenth-century Mystery plays, frescoes and narrative poems, where each sin had its place and form of punishment, a powerful primal image like the Hellmouth, visible on countless carved tympana, announced the all-encompassing idea of devouring death.[32]

At the end of the *Lay de la fragilité humaine* Deschamps dares not leave his royal reader in Hell but adds two wholly new chapters, mostly taken from a description by St Augustine of the joys that the blessed can expect in Paradise. Suddenly the mood changes to an account of the good news of salvation that awaits those men and women, 'ceuls et celles', who have followed God's laws. However, Remiet's illustration shows nothing of this eternal state of bliss. As always, transcendence is deferred, and instead we see humanity seeking solace and hope of future bliss through the ministrations of the Church. Three representatives of the different types of clergy are shown from top to bottom, reading to the blind, providing alms to the sick and giving food to the hungry, while another priest

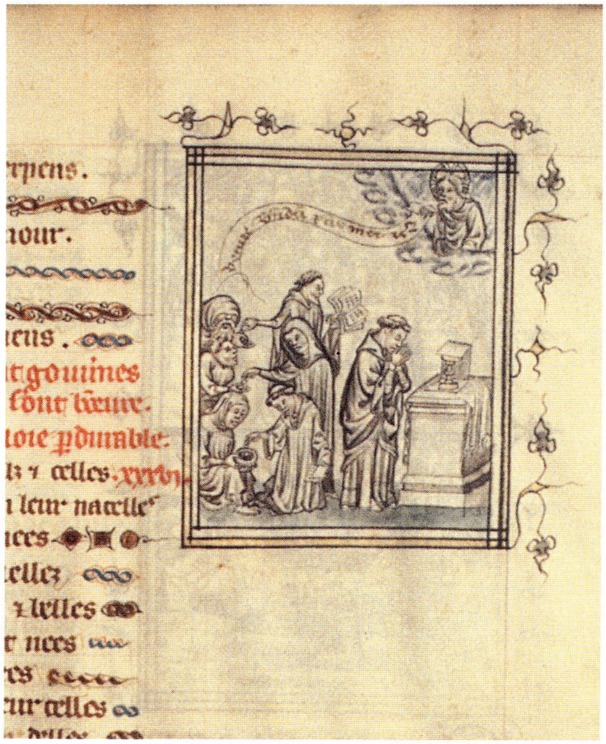

179. Remiet. Paris, Bibliothèque Nationale, fr. 20029, fol. 20. *Lay de la fragilité humaine*. A happy ending for the good.

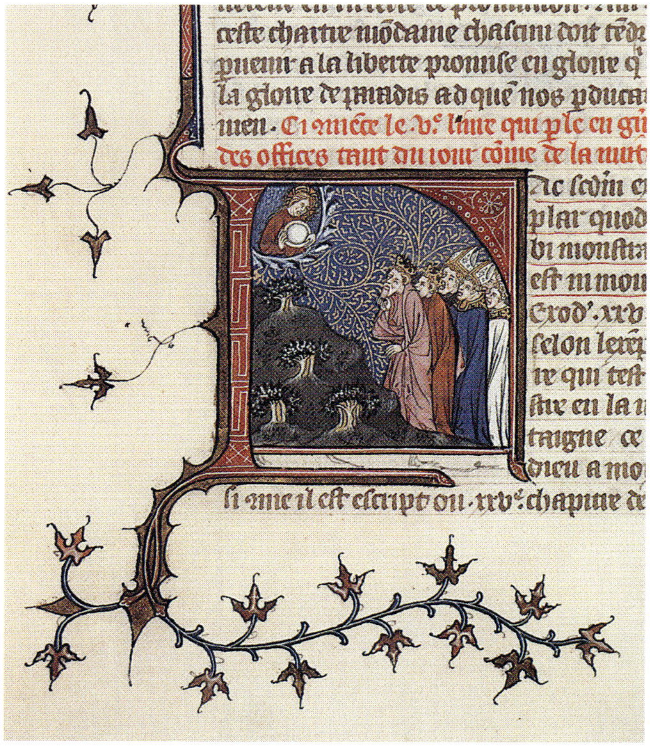

180. Remiet. Paris, Bibliothèque Nationale, fr. 176, fol. 110v. *Rational des divins offices*. God holds the moon/mirror before kings and clergy.

celebrates a High Mass (Fig. 179). Although the text describes the 'perpetual joy' that awaits the blessed, the image shows only the sufferings of the flesh and the sacraments as the means to salvation, leaving the reader in the dark as to the visibility of that promise.

God cannot be seen 'face to face'. He must be reflected or deflected, as in the mirror he holds up in a miniature of the *Rational des divins offices* (Fig. 180). Here the night offices are compared to the shadowy form in which Moses saw God on the mountain and the glass through which one now sees only darkly. Two kings, two bishops and a priest stare up to God's moon-like mirror in the night. All image-making is on this dark side of the glass and doomed to phantasmic decay compared to the face-to-face contact on the other side of death. This metaphor of the mirror was used by the preacher Jean Gerson in his vernacular sermons. The soul he describes is so charged with the cinders of humility and the fiery furnace of charity that it becomes a beautiful clear glass that is polished to reflect (*representer*) the Deity. The soul must feel the oblivion or forgetfulness, like the dead on the other side of the mirror, in order to experience the shadowy darkness and obscurity in which God can be seen.[33]

The final image in the little book made for Charles VI shows the *acteur*, the author of the poem, Deschamps, kneeling before 'la souveraine Vierge' above the final verse of the poem in which Deschamps implores the help of 'la mere d'humilite', who through her pity will lead us 'to the doors of salvation and protect us from sin' (Fig. 181). There was no surer way of overcoming death than by begging the intercession of the mother of God.

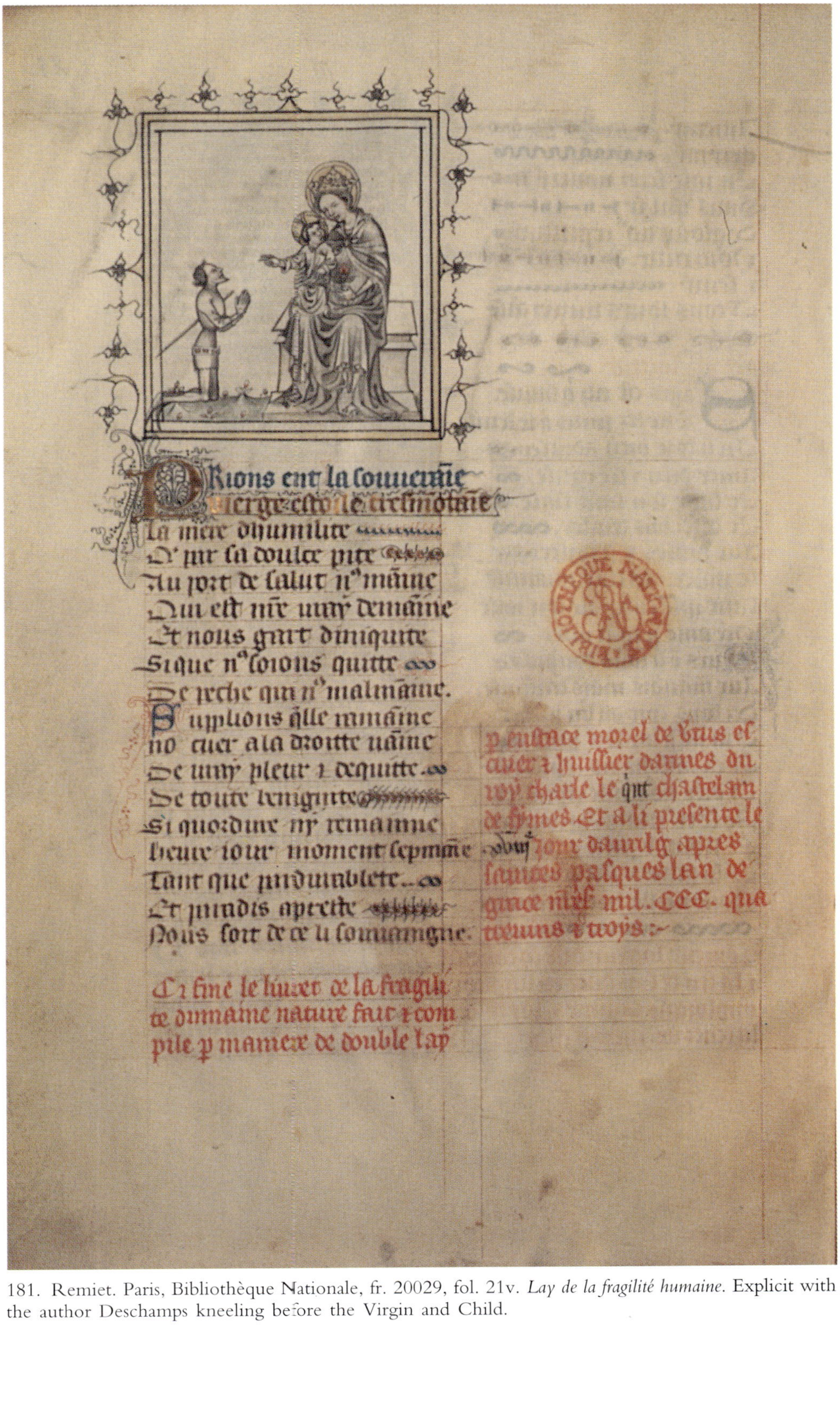

181. Remiet. Paris, Bibliothèque Nationale, fr. 20029, fol. 21v. *Lay de la fragilité humaine*. Explicit with the author Deschamps kneeling before the Virgin and Child.

Remiet pictured this virgin mother as a giantess twice the size of the poet, seated on the throne with the Christ-child, who extends his hand in blessing. Deschamps does not call for Christ's mercy at all, only hers. This is partly because in medieval culture Mary was far more available and approachable and was able to rescue even the damned. For the kneeling poet Deschamps, this image locates him within the economy of salvation, making his work a gift to the Virgin herself, as well as to its royal recipient. For the scribe who wrote the first line in brilliant blue or for Remiet who portrayed its author so carefully here, no such self-signification was possible. But image-makers are also beholders. Although Deschamps and his patron, Charles VI, are the signalled and represented 'subjects' within this morbid mirror for princes, Remiet, who illustrated it, must surely be another.

The Virgin represented here at the climax of the *Lay* might also have represented a melancholy station of identification for the man who made her. According to André Green, 'behind the blank mourning for the mother, one catches a glimpse of the mad passion of which she is, and remains, the object, that renders mourning for her an impossible experience. The subject's entire structure aims at a fundamental fantasy: to nourish the dead mother, to maintain her perpetually embalmed.'[34] Remiet's miniatures, like the beautiful seated Virgin here, are more than lost objects in the sense described in contemporary psychological terms by Nicolas Abraham and Maria Torok as 'works of mourning'.[35] Their capacity to keep alive the image of a person, to hold it before one, has to be seen against the literal and irrevocable loss of each image, soon after it was made. Remiet was constantly being separated from the objects he produced, which, as soon as he finished them, were carried off by the *libraire* to be bound, perhaps alongside some other practitioner's work, and sent off to the patron. The only means of reparation was repetition.

The End – Return

In this terror before mass-produced death there is the sadness of the artist who honors well-wrought things, who wants to make a work and make of death his work. Death is thus from the start linked to the movement, so difficult to bring to light, of the artistic experience. Maurice Blanchot.[36]

Hence it is, as the twelfth chapter of Ecclesiastes notably says: 'Of making many books there is no end.' For as the bodies of books, made by a mixture of their contraries, must experience a continuous wasting of their elements, so by the wisdom of clerks there ought to be found a remedy by which a sacred book, after paying the debt of nature, may obtain a substitute by inheritance and thus like a seed be raised up to the dead brother, and that saying in the thirtieth chapter of Ecclesiasticus is proved true; 'The father is dead, and he is as if he were not dead, for he hath left one behind him who is like himself.' So then the transcribers of old books are, as it were, begetters of new sons. Richard de Bury, Bishop of Durham[37]

In the end only one death was worth repeating, an image that Remiet and his contemporaries saw and were affected by more often and more intensely than by any other – that of Christ on the cross. This was not just an object of contemplation but an actual event and a body which viewers were encouraged not just to observe but to *become*. This was true of the image only a few inches high that Remiet painted in the Book of Hours in the British Library which, although spare and seemingly simple in its three composite figures and cross, provides the book's owner with a multiplicity of self-definitions and determinations especially around the five wounds spattered with blood-red vermillion (Fig. 182). Late medieval theology emphasized the crucifixion even above the resurrection, and Christ's hanging body developed from being a symbol of unity for the Christian community as a whole, to being a point of contact between the individual and the society.[38] The individual responses of viewers of Christ's body, their erotic fantasies and dreams of incorporation, have been discussed a great deal lately, without much awareness of the problems that appertained to the production of such images.[39] Whereas mystics like Margery Kempe could construct elaborate somatic fantasies around contemplated images of the crucifixion that allowed them to enter Christ's body via his wounds, to drink at the fountain of his ejaculated liquids, delighting in the hybridity of a lacerated but open body that they embraced as flesh, artists could not play so evocatively with the signs. They had to follow certain rules in providing orthodox representations which could only ever be points of departure. Although there are stories of monastic artists carving images of the crucifix only on Fridays and fasting so as to create the proper state of humility and grace for someone who was shaping out God's body, such stories decrease as the arena of image-making moves to the urban workshops of lay professionals. Crucifixes were still, however, the most legislated of medieval images precisely because they were so powerfully sites of projection. In 1306 a German sculptor working in London had been reprimanded for carving a *crux horribilis* that was not 'the true form of the cross' (it was an iconographic variant known as the Y-shaped cross), and other cases attest to the dangers of diverging from the norm.[40] The rules of the guild of crucifix and knifehandle-makers in bone and ivory, those 'ymagiers' who 'taillent cruchefis è Paris' are interesting in that they show how much economic and devotional concerns could be combined in the mass-production of holy merchandize and in one particular image-type. Besides the usual rules about nightwork and apprentices for these craftsmen who produce objects as different in use as handles that help knifes cut into flesh at the dinner table and objects venerating Christ's triumph over the flesh at the *mensa* of the altar, there are statutes describing the carving of the 'body' which is 'not good and true if it is made of many pieces'. A method of making crucifixes of three pieces, with separately carved arms, is seen as inferior, as 'cheating' and a danger to the guild, not only because of considerations about quality of materials and craftsmanship but also perhaps owing to consternation that it is Christ's corpus that is being fragmented in this fashion. Concern as to the status of things produced by manufacturers for religious use stretches to include the stipulation that images which turn out badly or are *fausse* should not be burned, 'out of reverence to the saints in whose memory they were made'.[41] This last warning also refers to painters. The crucifix-makers of Paris, and this included Remiet's two-dimensional as well as these more legislated three-dimensional versions, were in this respect the last artists working in a system in which the material and the sacral were interconnected, in which

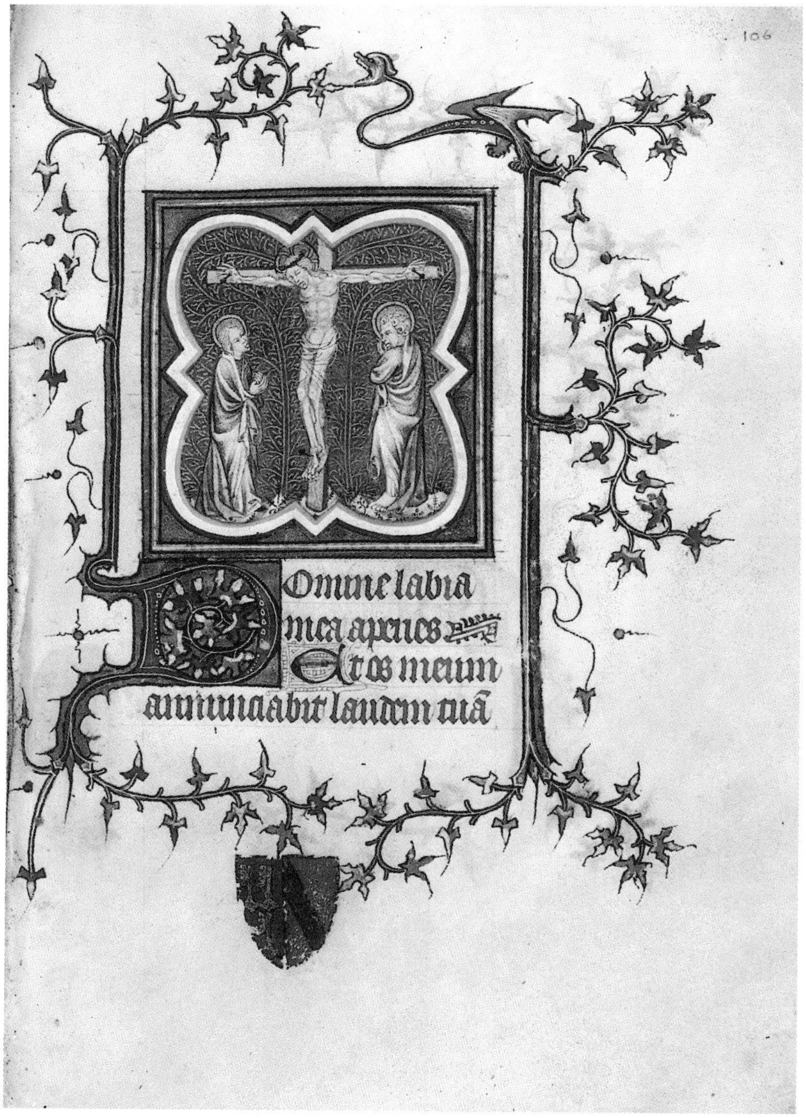

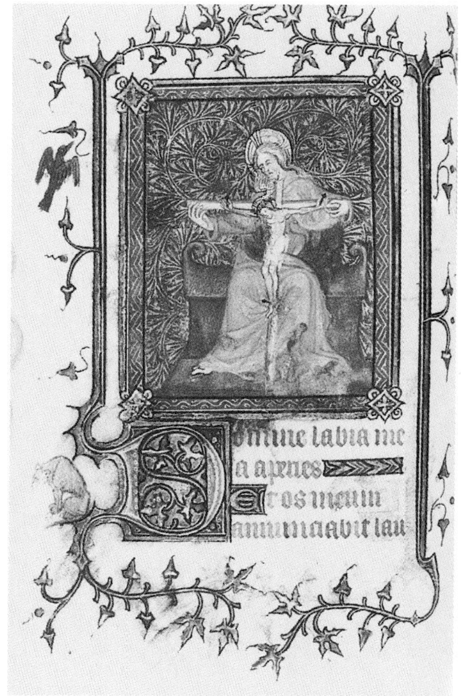

183. Remiet. Whereabouts unknown: Sotheby's sale, 13 July 1977. Book of Hours. Hours of the Holy Spirit with the Throne of Mercy.

182. (*left*) Remiet. London, British Library, MS Yates Thompson 45, fol. 106. Book of Hours. Crucifixion at the Hours of the Cross.

184. (*below left*) Rohan Master. Cambridge, Fitzwilliam Museum, MS 62, fol. 116v. Book of Hours with marginal images from the *Pèlerinages*. The pilgrim meets Mortification of the Flesh.

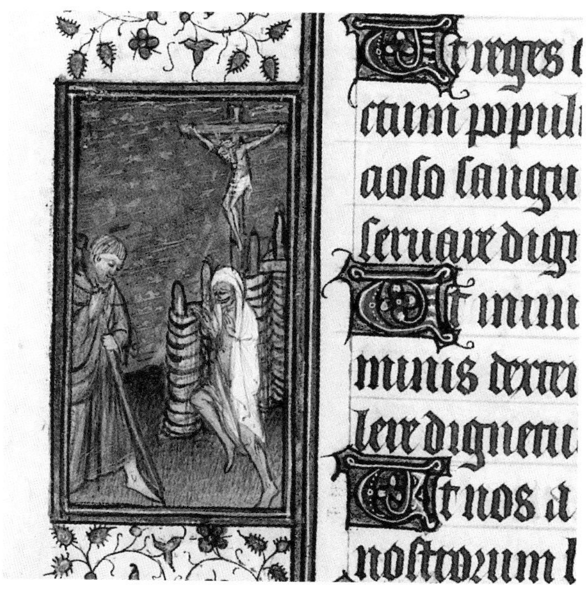

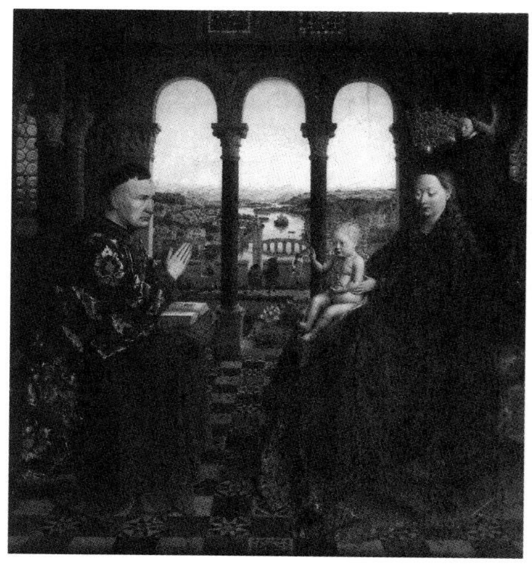

185. Jan Van Eyck, *Madonna and Chancellor Rolin*. Paris, Musée du Louvre.

the power of what the object represented was more important than the power of who made it.[42]

This brings me back to the questions of the dynamics of creation and performance with which this book began. What was Remiet actually making here? Certainly it was nothing new. He repeated it as part of other programmes like the *Cité de Dieu* (see Fig. 32) and numerous times in the *Miroir historial*. It was also combined with other images, as in the Trinity type known today as the Throne of Mercy, where the Father presents the Son, but which Remiet used in a miniature illustrating the Hours of the Holy Spirit in which his God the Father seems to be seated on a sarcophogus rather than a throne (Fig. 183).[43] If the crucifix was the most legislated of signs, guarded as carefully as any heraldic crest or family coat of arms, it was also the most replicated. This infinity of repetition ensured the permeability and power of the image to cross boundaries. In luminous colours it was painted in the newly fashionable altar retables in the richest churches, in carved wood and metal it stood on the numerous altars, in stone and marble it projected from the walls of churches and abbeys, soaring over doorways, filling the skyline, topping every spire. In the streets below, it appeared at nearly every crossroads, like that of the Place Maubert near Remiet's shop. Miniaturized, the body of Christ was carved by a special guild of ivory crucifix-makers, already discussed; it was painted in every Book of Hours and also in liturgical books like missals, where a second crucifix had to be painted below that opened at the mass text, since the main image was literally kissed away by the officiating priest in repeated mouth to flesh contact. The same image, in metal, was kissed daily by the congregation at the end of the mass in the kissing-board or *osculatorium*, which replaced the kiss of peace passed among the people. Cast in silver and gold as well as in less-precious metals, the crucifix was also worn on the body, round the neck, pinned to the cloak in badges and medallions, embroidered on clothes and vestments; it was even stamped upon the tarts of bakers – making the number of digestible and indigestible crucifixes visible in fourteenth-century Paris literally uncountable. It also crossed over from the sacred to the profane. At the heart of the city's political structure, the Grande Chambre of the Palais Royale on the Ile de la Cité, in which the king presided over the Parlement from his *lit de justice*, was a crucifixion panel on the north wall, commissioned in 1405 from 'Jean Virelay, illuminator, living in Paris'.[44] Every street corner had a small and often crudely carved crucifix, and they were also set up at wells and outside stopping-points like inns, making Christ's tortured body, of all the multifarious street signs and house signs in the capital, the most ubiquitous. Often the crucifix was carried in processions, leading all funerals and ostentations of relics, embroidered on the shimmering copes of the clergy. That the crucifixion was placed and processed in the public intersections of space and power in the city is important, since this was a society in which the boundaries of the sacred and profane were under constant negotiation and sacerdotal authority was constantly reinscribing its boundaries not only in the streets but in the imaginary, where the openings and closings of Christ's body took on a profound metaphorical significance in terms of the body politic.[45] For this image so permeated late medieval urban culture that it came to be inscribed upon the bodies of people, especially the clerical and lay devout, in innumerable gestures of genuflection made every day, whether in church or over a dropped prayerbook. Moreover, it was meant to be inscribed on the imaginary, or what the medievals termed 'the heart'. This is what the gruesome skeletal character called Mortification of the Flesh tells the pilgrim in the second recension of Deguileville's *Pèlerinage de vie humaine*, as he brandishes what he calls his 'banner of the cross'. The *corpus* of Christ is here carried by a figure that looks like a shrouded corpse (Fig. 188).

Below the sign of the cross in Remiet's Book of Hours (Fig. 184) are the very different signs of worldly power of the family who owned it. These are the arms of Nicolas Rolin, Chancellor of Burgundy (1376–1462).[46] Born at Autun, he had first entered the service of Philippe le Hardi and became chancellor of Burgundy under Philippe le Bon. It is in this office that he kneels at his prie-dieu over an open Book of Hours in the famous panel by Jan Van Eyck, which hung next to the altar in his private chapel in the church of Notre Dame du Chastel in Autun (Fig. 185). Painted around 1430, it includes a portrait not only of a person but of a book, open at the Matins of the Virgin, 'Domine, labia mea aperies'. Here, however, painting has left words behind, and itself becomes miracle, a transubstantiation of matter, a mystical mirror that literally is able to confront the patron with his own vision of the Mother of God. While this little prayerbook is but one small prop in the microcosmic detail of this hyper-detailed world, it would be wrong to see panel painting here triumphing over manuscript illumination. According to Panofsky's argument, the book was where Early Netherlandish painting began. Visual strategies do not come and go, wane and triumph, in this way like theatrical venues; rather, they overlap and interact on multiple and conflicting stages. Van Eyck's magnificent panel has recently been shown to be based upon the Canonical Office of the Virgin, the text of which is written on the hem of the Virgin's embroidered mantle.[47] Remiet's manuscript is technically and conceptually vastly different from these oil-based spaces and veristic vistas, although it exists as part of the same world. Whereas Remiet's art provided only a starting point for contemplating a subject like the Virgin Mary, as in the last page of the *Lay* (Fig. 179), Van Eyck provided their finished and finite goal, their end, in glistening, almost magical hyper-veritas.

A radically new alternative to Remiet's visual language had already been developed in manuscripts illuminated by the Limbourg brothers, who were still described as *enfants* in 1400 but whose works for the Duke of Berry already announced what Jonathan Alexander has called the 'extreme negative of Death' – a new signifier based upon Italian and utimately ancient sources in which the dying figure is shown falling, breaking into space and 'thus denying the normal horizontal alignment parallel to the picture plane'.[48] Whereas Remiet's signifier of death was nearly always this horizontal line, as straight as that ruled for writing (Fig. 186), the sign used for the representation of plague victims being suddenly struck down in the *Belles Heures,* painted eight years before the brothers and their patron themselves all succumbed to an outbreak of the plague in 1416, makes death a deep diagonal thrusting into space (Fig. 187). The diagonal embodies negation; in examples as diverse as heraldry's bend sinister signifying bastardy to the tilted angles in horror films, it represents 'the primary visual signifier of moral transgression against pious equilibrium and perpendicular hierarchies of God and Nature'.[49] In Remiet's singular image of dying as a process rather than an already completed event at the climax of the *Pèlerinage de vie humaine*, it is not the horizontal flatliner but the diagonal that marks this liminal moment, although it does not waver from the picture plane (see Fig. 192). If the Limbourgs made death into a pose, for Remiet it was always more a performance, a sign

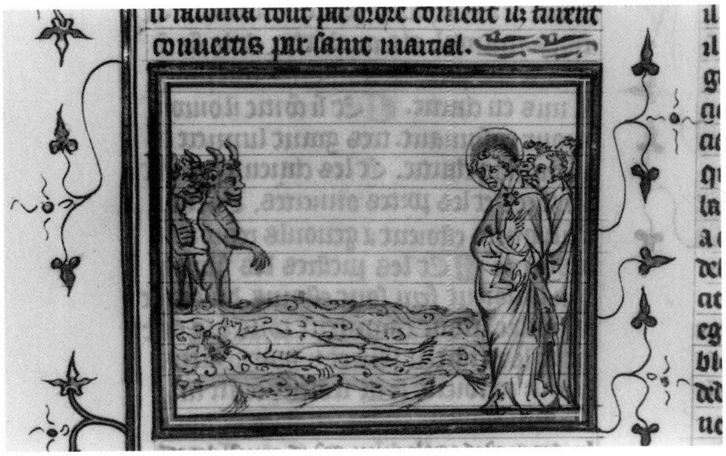

186. Remiet. Paris, Bibliothèque Nationale, fr. 313, fol. 74v. *Miroir historial.* Corpse of a drowned youth saved by St Martial of Limoges.

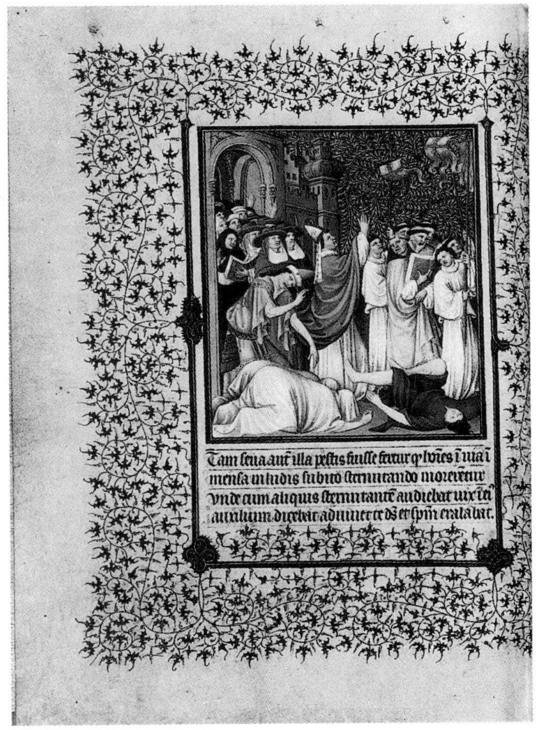

187. Limbourg Brothers. New York, Cloisters Museum, *Belles Heures*, fol. 73v. St Gregory the Great intercedes for the plague to cease.

that, like the crucifixion, the *ur* death, had to be repeated and re-enacted without change or novelty over and over and over again.

Remiet's laid-out corpse-type had something of an after-life in the work of other illuminators, although they tended to construct absolute boundaries around an image that he had always left open. Another great innovator of the second decade of the new century, who worked for Duchess Yolande of Aragon in Paris and at Angers, used what at first seems a very similar image in what is the most famous Office of the Dead miniature in medieval art (Fig. 188). Adelheid Heimann suggested that this vision of death was directly inspired by Remiet's miniatures in the *Pèlerinages*.[50] Has Remiet's cadaver type here 'come to life'? Though it might owe something to Remiet's example, or, more probably, to the writings of Guillaume de Deguileville, this image strikes me as very different in both its meaning and its effects. Racked in the last spasmodic death throes, hands stiffening in rigor mortis, this is a man not a corpse, spread on the great dead diagonal in the bone-strewn graveyard, who is still in the process of communicating to his God. Although his tiny blond soul has been snatched by the devil who fights with St Michael for final possession, there is a sense of urgency, of a moment that this painter has focused upon, as though with a camera shutter he might click and record the ectoplasmic release of the spirit simultaneously with the final split second of human consciousness. It is this sense of time that makes the Rohan Master's death far more comprehensible to us than Remiet's. In addition, whereas Remiet's concern was always more with God's mother as intercessor at death, the Rohan Master was obsessed with white-haired old fathers, and here it is the father's voice, who speaks in French. The dying man mumbles his own Latin plea for salvation in another long speech scroll.[51] Remiet never made such

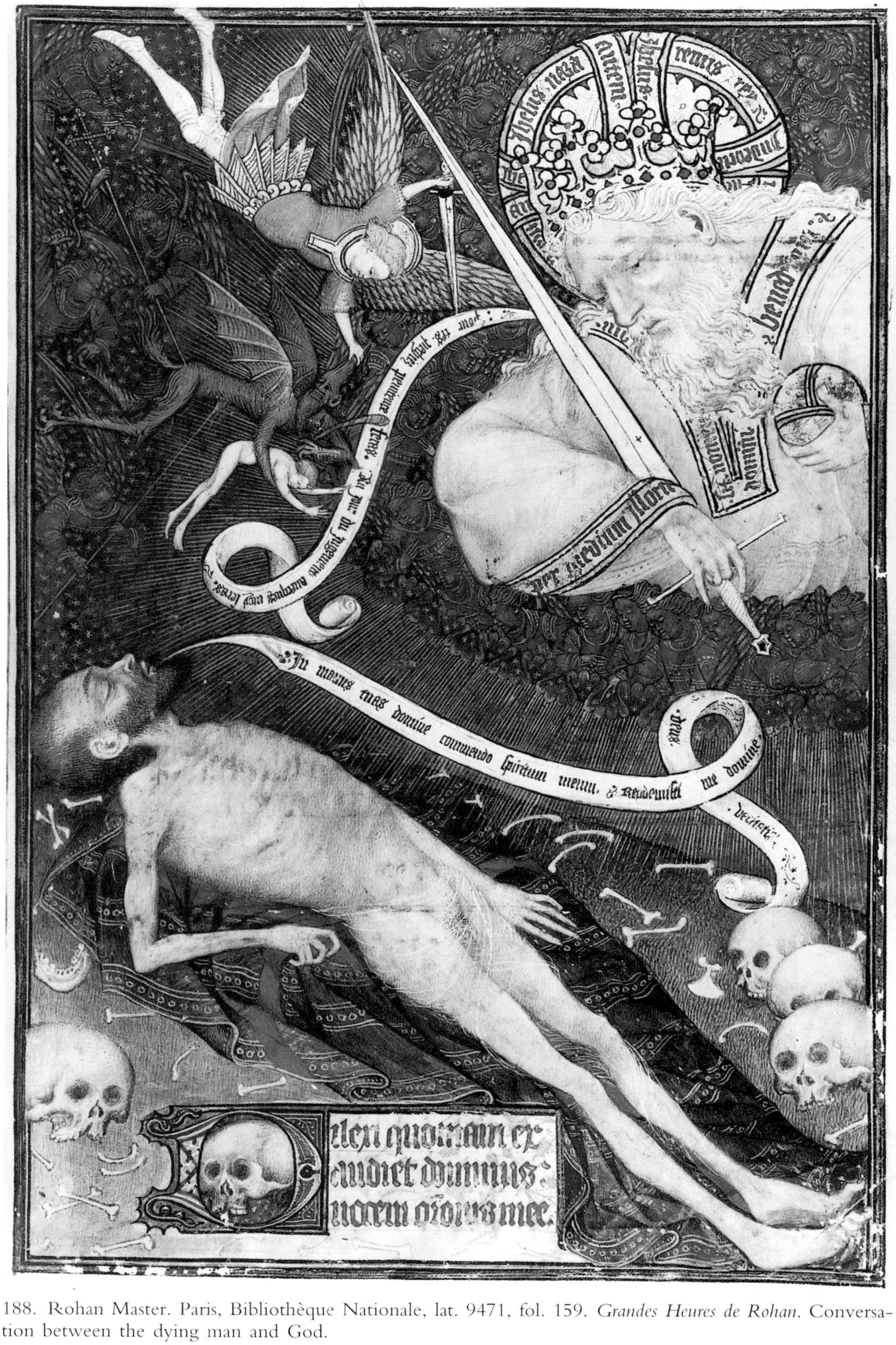

188. Rohan Master. Paris, Bibliothèque Nationale, lat. 9471, fol. 159. *Grandes Heures de Rohan*. Conversation between the dying man and God.

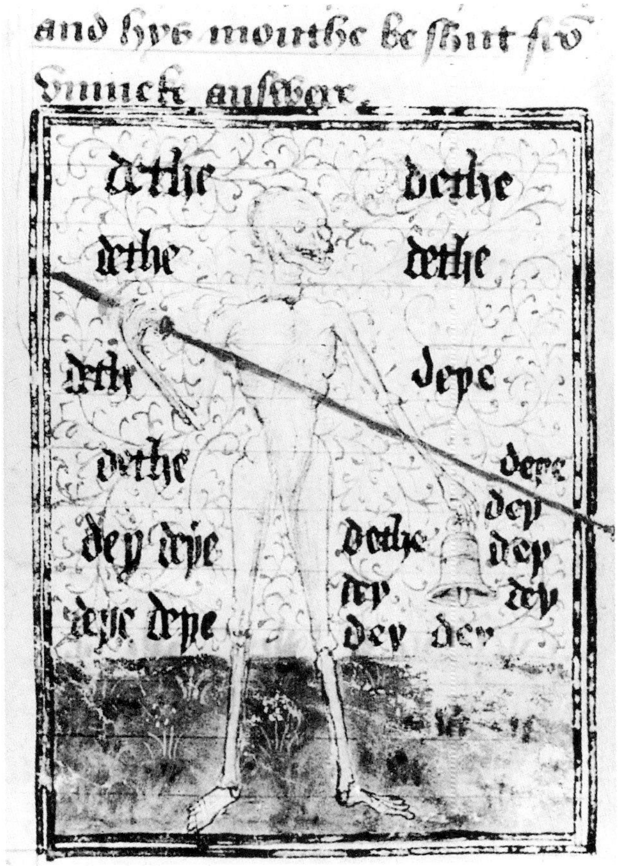

189. English illuminator, early fifteenth century. Oxford, Bodleian Library, Douce MS 322, fol. 19v. John Lydgate, 'Death's Warning to the World'. Death reitterated in language.

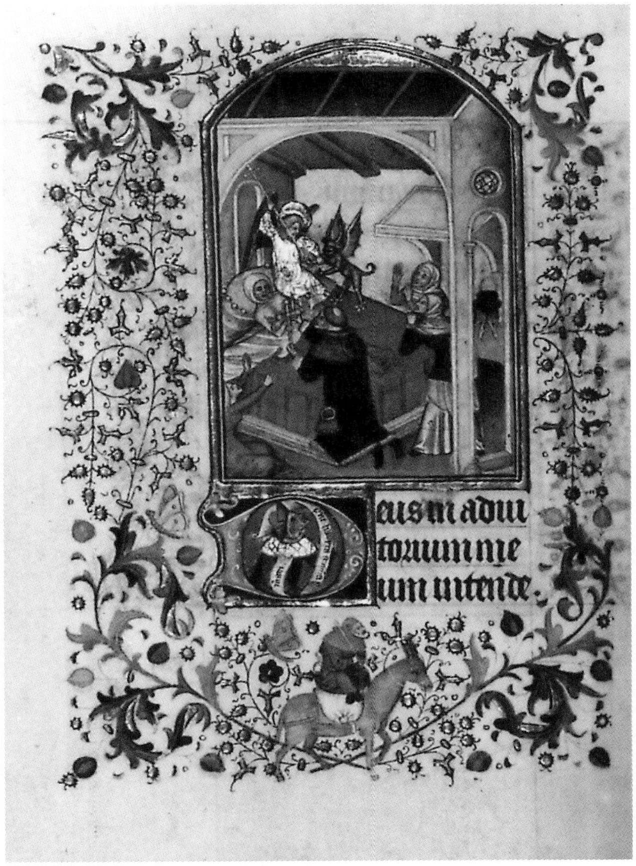

190. Illuminator working *c.*1420. Baltimore, Walters Art Gallery, MS 219, fol. 80v. Book of Hours. Office of the Dead with scene of dying man.

a speaking image, but neither did he make such a powerfully independent one that stands alone and arrogantly transcends its place in the text.

My work has always hinged on the relationship between words and pictures and the power of images, which I hope emerges in these pages too. As Martin Jay has argued, it was only after the Enlightenment that French thinkers came to mistrust that power.[52] It was not so in the Late Middle Ages, when it was the Lollard iconoclasts and proto-Reformation preachers across the Channel who first started to question visual signs and move towards the destruction of the Catholic image-world that Remiet lived within. For one English illuminator, depicting Lydgate's poem 'Death's Warning to the World', the horror of the skeleton was not enough and the word had to supplement the image (Fig. 189). The bell that the skeleton holds is another aural indicator of an anglophone textuality that in French culture was always more spatial, more visual. The repeated sounds of the word, varying as if to stress its multivocality, sometimes a verb *deye*, sometimes a noun *deth*, fill this etheral and intangible image with language that begins and ends. Words, sounds that literally die away, and not the image of the grinning skeleton, are the real in this image. For contemporary illuminators in France the culture of death was less contained by language. Remiet never needed to write or speak death – la mort – in his own tongue because that would be to set limits on it, to have it begin and end.

By the late 1420s, the time when Remiet himself reached his end, the deathbed had become an even more finite space, hollowed out of the page in a tiny Parisian Book of Hours in Baltimore (Fig. 190). But it was an arena in which St Michael and the devil still continued to battle for possession of the soul. It is far easier to imagine the man Remiet's 'real' deathbed from this deep and crowded doll's house interior with all its rich details of everyday life, the priest thrusting the wooden crucifix into the face of the dying man, the wailing wife, and the pot still cooking in the fireplace, than from his own starkly confrontational image of the end. But in giving us less to go on, I think Remiet actually gave us more of himself. His depthless deathbed scene in the *Pèlerinage de vie humaine* is less specific and detailed, and cannot be taken out of the textual matrix in which it is embedded. Part of the flow of a poem, it is powerful precisely because, like all 'good ends', it refuses to see death as the end, the limit and, like the book of which it is a part, opens up to infinite returns and recurrences.

Making my own good end, I want to conclude with some remarks that I hope will also refuse that absolute boundary. My primary aim all along has been to view this artist's life (and death) from within his own work. 'Life' and 'work' were often simplistically synonymous in the 'Old' Art History, but in the 'New' they are all too often totally separated. This has been part of a larger trend in the humanities, to dismantle individual subjectivity. But now we are putting the pieces back together again aware that 'the death of the author' is just another oppressive form of textuality that always seeks to keep 'life' at bay.[53] The miniatures discussed in these pages comprise a body of work that can be attributed to a single person, but to see them as the expression of a coherent self in the modern sense would be to misunderstand what Remiet and his contemporaries were doing. These are not products of a lone psychic agency but things in the world, and for that reason I have used them to explain not so much a self as a society. This was my second aim: to confound a number of still-current clichés about late medieval culture. First, that this was a visual culture in decline from an earlier, spiritual 'high point'; second, that it was 'popular', serving a less intellectual, more jaded audience; and third, that stylistically its practitioners were increasingly obsessed with 'the real'. Remiet's art is dense with a prurient moral intensity, fraught with anxious and convoluted meanings that were not for the *simples gens*. Moreover it seems resistant to 'individualism', forestalling or denying the birth of the Renaissance self in a late medieval no one, as well as refusing the ruse of realism with a vengeance. It was the early twentieth-century cultural historian Johan Huizinga's *Waning of the Middle Ages*, mentioned in my Introduction and still a useful source of reference, which propounded these myths. Huizinga called Eustache Deschamps 'a superficial poet and a commonplace mind'.[54] He would likely have said the same thing of Remiet. In his nineteenth-century obsession with sentiment, he lamented the lack of an 'elegiac note' and exclaimed that the Middle Ages did not know the 'divine depth of sorrow . . . [I]n all these sombre lamentations about death the accents of true tenderness are extremely rare.'[55] Such criticism seems alien to us today, since we now have much more in common, I would argue, with the late fourteenth century than with the late nineteenth.

The increased interest in the cultural construction of death in the humanities and social sciences as well as among contemporary artists, suggests there is a postmodern culture of the macabre. From Dilthey to Derrida, death has of course always fascinated modern philosophers who have described it as the foundation of human identity and selfhood.[56] But the idea that death alone imposes unity on a person is peculiar to modern thinkers and quite different from the beliefs of medieval philosophers, who saw death and identity linked far more in terms of material continuity and the body rather than ontological 'being'. Much has been written about how increasingly in this century we have made death unrepresentable, nuclear death, for example, being a kind of annihilation that is invisible. In the words of Heinz Weinmann, 'At the end of the Middle Ages, death invoked images of death . . . Dances of Death . . . A rather joyous and idyllic affair, as compared to our idea of it. What makes death by atomic vaporization so horrible is that it leaves us nothing, no images to contemplate. It is thus unimaginable, unrepresentable death.'[57] It is in response to the AIDS crisis, which forces us to look again at countless individual deaths and not the abstract genocide of war, that, in the words of Monique Brunet-Weinmann, there has been a 'resurgence of the Middle Ages in our memory, our conscience, and our imagination'.[58] Douglas Crimp has criticized the arguments, once put forward by many in the art world, that 'Art against AIDS' initiatives were important because 'Art lives on forever' and will ultimately 'transcend the epidemic', as being hopelessly divorced from the negotiations inherent in real social life.[59] In much the same vein, I am wary of seeking eternal values in medieval art, either to resurrect a desired past or to suggest patterns of representation for our future. For a host of reasons – not only AIDS but also new and rapidly advancing medical technologies, cybernetic pseudo-bodies, computer-intelligence systems and organ transplants – we face radically new and fundamental questions about our notions of self, body and thus mortality. The visual arts, which have always been seen as building their theoretical stability upon the idea of presence, narrative, animation, and 'life' (such as in the term 'still life', although the French call the same genre 'nature morte'), are now more often expressions of absence, simulation and not the life-like but the life-less.[60] In calling Remiet's art 'lifeless' in the title of this book, I was in no way denigrating his work by comparison with a verisimilitude that can only play at being 'like' life, as happens in the thousands of horrifyingly superficial, simulated deaths we see every day on television, but rather celebrating what I see as its reality traced within and from the body of a historical subject.

Do ends matter more than beginnings? With books I am not so sure, since we can so easily turn back the pages to the opening *incipit* and start all over again. As Georges Duby describes the death of William Marshall – which ends the thirteenth-century life but begins his twentieth-century book, this second birth – death – always mattered more than the first one. It is *obits* not births that were more often recorded in the calendars that Remiet illuminated; it was the points of exit from and not entry into life that defined a person for posterity.[61] The artist called Remiet, who if we did not have that name we might well call 'The Master of Death', worked in a world in which death was no less difficult to negotiate than in our own, but during a time when it was far more available to representation. Because God was not dead, every image, no matter how lifeless it looked, pointed towards the possibility of an eternal life elsewhere. What made life worth living was that Christ himself had also lived it, taking part in this fleshly pilgrimage and walking the same road between birth and death. This is how Remiet depicted him in the

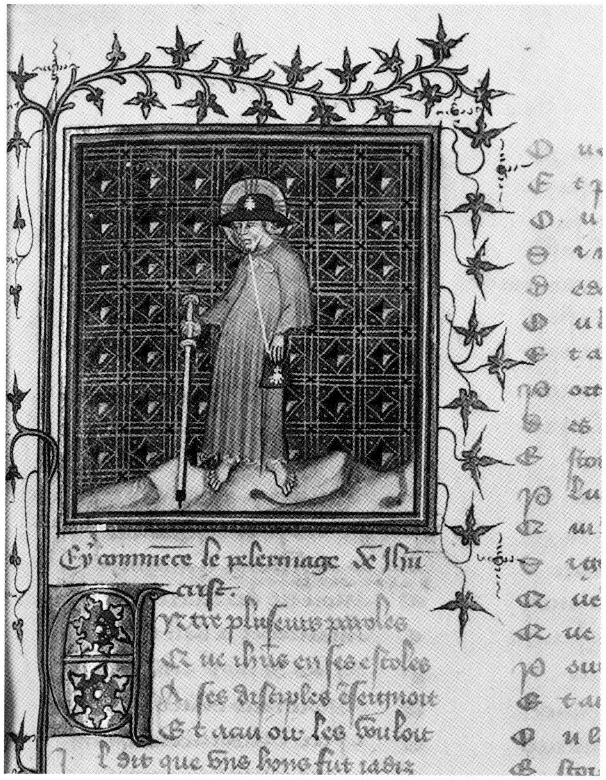

191. Remiet. Leiden, University Library, MS BPL 74, fol. 170. *Pèlerinage de Jésus-Christ.* Christ as a pilgrim to Santiago.

allegorical pilgrimage poem that follows that of human life and that of the soul, the *Pèlerinage de Jésus-Christ* (Fig. 191). Painted towards the end of his own life, Remiet made his Saviour into just another pilgrim to the shrine of St James at Compostella, trudging along on his fat, flat feet, scrip and staff in hand. It is this brilliant banality, the mundane audacity of the commonplace, that gives this system of representation its power to move. Of course this is not a self-portrait in the modern sense, but it is an image with which Remiet would surely have identified, as a fellow-traveller. To use a current term, this was his subject position.

This has been a hard book to finish, partly because the temptations of the pilgrim and wanderer are to keep on searching, even after fifteen years, and partly because indentification with my subject means I do not want to give up his ghost. More miniatures that can be attributed to him must exist hidden away in obscure libraries, like the Christ as pilgrim in Leiden, which I only discovered at the very last minute before this book went to press (Fig. 191). I am sure there are more works out there waiting to be discovered, images that might totally change our view of this artist and tell quite a different story, one that need not begin with, or focus so much on, his end (Fig. 192). This miniature of Death coming to the pilgrim's bedside to which I keep returning is the one that has always fascinated me most. It was the one that first drew me to this enigmatic artist, a subject who has drawn me in more ways than I have been able to draw him.

He was done with waiting. He would ask her to come. Make a good end, he told himself. He tried to remember some of the words of the Office of the Dead from the many quires from Books of Hours he had fingered in his long life, 'Quiconques veult estre bien conseiller' . . . how did the rest of it go? It was so frustrating, all he could remember were the beautiful criss-cross colours of the vermillion backgrounds or the snapping dragon-mouths he had made in the margins and not the texts within. But he had never been a scribe, not one of that self-opinionated lot. It was just as good, he thought, to contemplate the image of Our Lord on the Cross – that most piteous of all scenes which moved all who saw it to tears. But no sooner had he focused on the crucifixion of the Lord and seen the stretched-out limbs in their agony, just as his own limbs were stiffening and shaking now, he thought he saw, in the corner of his mind's eye, a skull somewhere at the corner of the page, but moving closer to the centre. It was at the place of the skull, Golgotha, that the Lord had been crucified, but now these tiny white globes and their dark-socketted eyes seemed to loom larger than anything else in the picture. The pictures in his head were changing more rapidly now, as if they had all to be got through, repeated one last time. He could not possess them once they came before him in his mind, just as he had never been able to keep them long during his life. They had always been images meant for other people. But in another way they were still his. Pictures of pilgrims struggling, saints drowning, soldiers dying, and a figure laid flat out, just as he was now on his deathbed.

Suddenly out of the corner of his eye, as if appearing on the very margins of his consciousness, he saw Death, just as he had pictured her at the end of the great pilgrimage of life. She was no longer wielding the sharp curling scythe but something that looked more like the smooth curved end of a finely cut quill, a pen that could inscribe and delineate anything, drawing him unto her. Her large empty coffin with its black centre was nothing but a pool of deepest and most permanent pigment. Ah, yes, he knew it, she was a painter all along! As she drew him, he felt a marvellous turning over of his faded flesh, remaking what had become as brittle and crackled as old parchment. She was unravelling it and illuminating it with a soft brush that swept down on his chest, stopping his breath with finest ultramarine, covering his face with chalky bone-white, filling the margins of his skin with gold leaf. And as he started to choke against a blackness darker than any ink he had ever used, a paralysis of paint solidified in every muscle and bone of his now bright body. The master maker had come to do her work at last, and as suddenly and as mysteriously as they had begun, the pictures that had unfolded for so long in the turning pages of his head closed shut. Remiet was finished.

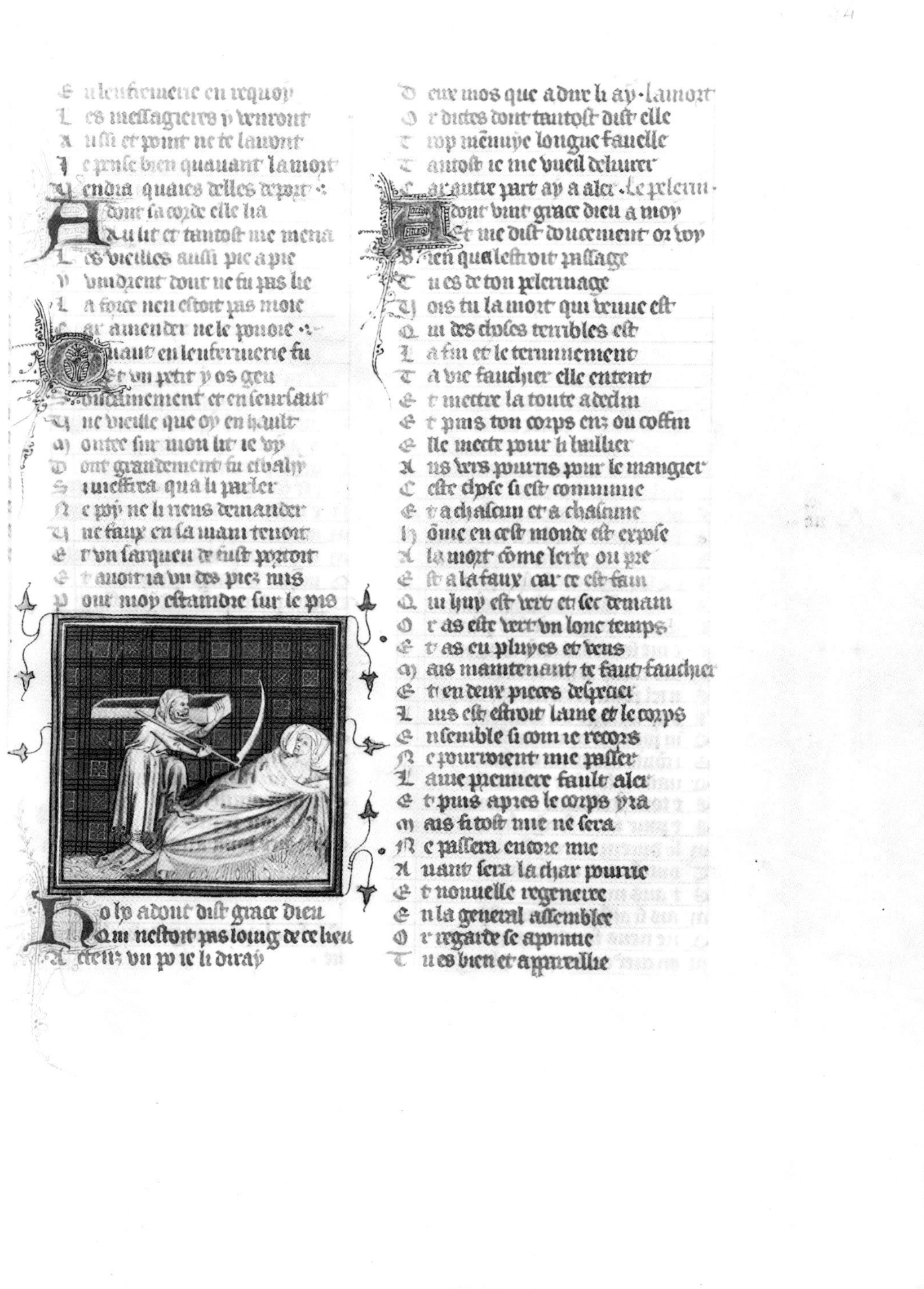

192. Remiet. Paris, Bibliothèque Nationale, fr. 823, fol. 94. *Pèlerinage de vie humaine.* The end of the pilgrimage.

Appendix
MANUSCRIPTS CONTAINING MINIATURES BY PIERRE REMIET

This list does not contain those manuscripts with miniatures that have subsidiary or part-decoration by Remiet made when he was an apprentice in the 'Boqueteaux Shop' discussed in the text, i.e., Besançon MS 434 and London MS Royal 16.G.vii.

Bayeux, Bibliothèque Municipale, Fonds du Chapitre, MS 61

Missal-Pontifical of Étienne de Loypeau
15, 227 and 93 fols. 355 × 260 mm
18 miniatures, 5 by Remiet and the rest by the 'Master of Luçon' with borders by the 'A Master'. For four leaves once cut from this MS, see Bloomington.
SEE: Figs. 73, 165
PROVENANCE: Étienne de Loypeau, Bishop of Luçon (1388–1407); left to the Cathedral of Bayeux by Bishop Louis d'Harcourt in 1474. .
BIBLIOGRAPHY: L. Delisle, 'Le Missel et pontifical d'Étienne de Loypeau, évêque de Luçon', *Bibliothèque de l'École des chartes* 48 (1887), pp. 527–34; V. Leroquais, *Les Pontificaux Manuscrits des bibliothèques de France* (Paris, 1937), I, pp. 69–75, pls. LXXIX–LXXXII; *Rêve de livres: Abbaye aux Dames, Caen* (Caen, 1991), p. 62, no. 37; A. S. Farber, 'Considering the Work of a Marginal Master: The Work of an Early Fifteenth-Century Parisian Manuscript Decorator', *Gesta* 32 (1993), p. 23, fig. 13.

Berlin, Kupferstichkabinett, MS 78.C.2, 1380s

Guillaume de Machaut, *Dit du Lion*
16 fols. 302 × 196 mm
9 miniatures by Remiet? Instructions to illuminator on fol. 11v.
PROVENANCE: From the Duke of Hamilton Collection, no. 214
BIBLIOGRAPHY: P. Durrieu, 'Notes sur quelques manuscrits français des bibliothèques d'Allemagne', *Bibliothèque de l'École des chartes* 53 (1892), p. 124; J. Kirchner, *Beschreibendes Verzeichnis der Miniaturen und des Initialschmuckes in den Phillips-handschriften* (Leipzig, 1926), p. 40.

Bloomington, Indiana, The Lilly Library, Indiana University

4 leaves from a Missal. 350 × 260 mm
The Birth of the Virgin (numbered XLV), Finding of the True Cross (LXV), St Michael (LXIX), St Andrew (LVII).
SEE: Figs. 52, 155
PROVENANCE: Cut out from the Bayeux Missal-Pontifical; Caen Collection Mansell; Lemallier sale (1907); Chicago, Coella Lindsay Ricketts Library.
BIBLIOGRAPHY: S. de Ricci, *Census of Medieval and Renaissance Manuscripts in the United States and Canada* (New York, 1935), I, p. 627, no. 65.

Bordeaux, Bibliothèque de Bordeaux, MS 730, 1370s

Livy, *Histoire romaine*, Decades I–IV, trs. Pierre Bersüire.
478 fols. 475 × 315 mm
Frontispieces and borders on fols. 6 and 192 by Remiet.
SEE: Figs. 20–2
BIBLIOGRAPHY: A. Mason, 'Le "Tite-Live" de Bordeaux l'atelier du "maître aux boqueteaux"', *Tresors des bibliothèques de France* 31 (1936), pp. 11–33.

Brussels, Bibliothèque Royale Albert I[e], MSS 9001–2, *c.*1415

Guyart Desmoulins, *Bible historiale* (from Petrus Comestor)
435 and 385 fols. 456 × 330 mm
In MS 9001 marginal figures on fol. 1, miniatures on fols. 212r, 214v, 374r, and in MS 9002 marginal figures on fol. 61r and miniatures on fols. 288r and 319v by Remiet. Other miniatures by Master of Berry's Cleres Femmes, Master of the Cité des Dames and Virgil Master. Petrus Gilberti executed the line-endings.
SEE: Figs. 104–6
BIBLIOGRAPHY: C. Gaspar and F. Lyna, *Les Principaux Manuscrits à peintures de la Bibliothèque royale de Belgique* (Paris, 1937–47), I, pp. 445–59, no. 189; Meiss, *French Painting*, III, pp. 375, 408, fig. 633.

Brussels, Bibliothèque Royale Albert I[e], MS 9094, *c.*1401

Bartholomeus Anglicus, *Le Livre des propriétés des choses* (for Philippe le Hardi)
381 fols. 408 × 285 mm
Miniatures by Remiet fols. 12, 18, 30v, 45, 144, 167, 177v, plus minatures by 3 other hands including the Virgil Master.
SEE: Figs. 5, 37, 102, 124
PROVENANCE: Library of Philippe le Hardi (inventory of 1420); Margaret of Bavaria (1427).
BIBLIOGRAPHY: L. Delisle, *Mélanges de paléographie et de bibliographie* (Paris, 1880), pp. 228–9; L. Delisle, *Recherches sur la librairie de Charles V* (Paris, 1907), I, pp. 91–2; C. Gaspar and F. Lyna, *Les Principaux Manuscrits à peintures de la Bibliothèque royale de Belgique* (Paris, 1937–47), I, pp. 359–61, no. 151; D. Byrne, 'Rex imago Dei: Charles V of France and the *Livre des propriétés des choses*', *Journal of Medieval History* 7 (1981), p. 103; Winter, *Bibliothèque*, pp. 195–7, no. 4, figs. 180–3.

Chantilly, Musée Condé, MS 277 (formerly MS 1327), 1397–8

Aristotle, *Le Livre d'Éthiques*, tr. Nicole Oresme (for Louis d'Orléans; companion volume to BN fr. 9106)
196 fols. 336 × 240 mm
10 miniatures in *portraits d'encre* by Remiet.
SEE: Fig. 96
PROVENANCE: Louis d'Orléans; given to Jean de Berry; Marie de Bourbon; *ex libris* L. J. Raussin, Rheims; acquired by Duc d'Aumale, 1856.
BIBLIOGRAPHY: J. Meurgey, *Les Principaux Manuscrits à peintures du Musée Condé à Chantilly* (Paris, 1930), pp. 46–50, pl. 32; A. D. Menut, *Le Livre de Éthiques d'Aristote* (New York, 1940), p. 48 (where the number is given erroneously as 227); Meiss, *French Painting*, I, p. 314; Sherman, *Imaging Aristotle*, p. 71.

Leiden, University Library, MS BPL 74

Guillaume de Deguileville, *Pèlerinage de vie humaine*, *Pèlerinage de l'âme*, *Pèlerinage de Jésus-Christ*
249 fols. 270 × 188 mm
3 miniatures by Remiet on fols. 1, 92, 170.
SEE: Figs. 163, 191
BIBLIOGRAPHY: J. P. Gumbert, 'Medieval Manuscripts in French in the Leiden University Library: A Handlist', in *Medieval Codicology, Iconography, Literature, and Translation: Studies for Keith Val Sinclair*, ed. Peter Rolfe Monks and D. D. R. Owen (Leiden, 1994), p. 30, fig. 6.

London, British Library, Add. MS 21143

Grandes Chroniques de France (from origins to 1380)
505 fols. 410 × 305 mm
13 miniatures by Remiet.
BIBLIOGRAPHY: Hedeman, *Royal Image*, p. 210.

London, British Library, MS Lansdowne 1179, *c.*1400

Vincent of Beauvais, *Miroir historial*, Books IX–XVI, tr. Jean de Vignay companion volume to BN fr. 52
358 fols. 410 × 300 mm
78 miniatures by Remiet.
SEE: Figs. 13, 72, 74–6, 78, 83, 88, 93
BIBLIOGRAPHY: P. Paris, *Manuscrits françois de la bibliothèque du roi* (Paris, 1836–46), I, p. 57.

London, British Library, MS Yates Thompson 45

Book of Hours (for use of Paris)
237 fols. 177 × 123 mm
38 miniatures by Remiet.
SEE: Figs. 128, 174, 182
PROVENANCE: Nicolas Rolin (1376–1462).
BIBLIOGRAPHY: British Museum, *Reproductions from Illuminated Manuscripts, Fifty Plates*, Series V (London, 1965), no. XXX, p. 18.

Lyons, Bibliothèque Municipale, MS 880

Grandes Chroniques de France (from origins to 1350)
418 fols. 365 × 360 mm
Some miniatures by Remiet.
BIBLIOGRAPHY: F. Cotton, 'Les Manuscrits à peintures de la Bibliothèque de Lyon', *Gazette des Beaux-Arts* 55 (1965), no. 44; Hedeman, *Royal Image*, pp. 228–30.

Manchester, John Rylands University Library, MS lat. 136

Breviary (for use of Paris, Notre Dame), Summer portion (pendant to Paris BN lat. 1024)
45 fols. 185 × 133 mm
69 miniatures by Remiet.
SEE: Figs. 14, 109, 110, 153, 154, 156, 171
BIBLIOGRAPHY: M. R. James, *A Descriptive Catalogue of the Latin Manuscripts in the John Rylands Library at Manchester* (Manchester, 1921 rpt. H. M. Taylor, Munich, 1980), pp. 238–42, no. 136; J. Pierce, 'Liturgy and Image: The Advent Miniature in the Salisbury Breviary', in *Medieval Texts and Images: Studies of Manuscripts from the Middle Ages*, ed. M. M. Manion and B. J. Muir (Sydney, 1991), p. 28, fig. 14.

New York, Pierpont Morgan Library, M.526

Hermann de Valenciennes, *Histoire de la Bible et de l'assomption Notre Dame*
43 fols. 360 × 265 mm
233 miniatures by Remiet in *portraits a'encre*.
SEE: Figs. 92, 108, 136–7, 140, 141, 159
PROVENANCE: Barrois Collection before 1849; Ashburnham sale, London, 1901, cat. no. 263; purchased by J. P. Morgan from Quaritch, 1902.
BIBLIOGRAPHY: M. M. Gilles, *Religious Life in the High Middle Ages* (1946), pp. 27, 29, 39, 40, 64, 66; E. Rickert, *Chaucer's World* (New York, 1948), p. 298.

New York, Pierpont Morgan Library, M.907

Honoré Bouvet, *Arbre des batailles*
152 fols. 245 × 169 mm
Full-page prefatory miniature by Remiet.
SEE: Fig. 61
BIBLIOGRAPHY: *12th Report to the Fellows of the Pierpont Morgan Library* (1962), pp. 11–13; H. P. Kraus, *In Retrospect: 100 Outstanding Manuscripts sold in the last four decades by H. P. Kraus* (New York, 1978), pl. 44; Hindman, *Christine de Pizan*, p. 161, fig. 63.

Oxford, New College, MSS 197–8

Questiones on the Decretals, Books III–V
435 fols. 395 × 265 mm
One historiated initial by Remiet, three others cut out.
PROVENANCE: Given by Richard Andrew, fellow, Dean of York (d. 1477).
BIBLIOGRAPHY: J. J. G. Alexander and E. Temple, *Illuminated Manuscripts in Oxford Libraries* (Oxford, 1986), p. 73, no. 746, pl. XLII.

Paris, Bibliothèque de l'Arsenal, MS 5223

Grandes Chroniques de France (from origins to 1380)
534 fols. 350 × 240 mm
32 miniatures by Remiet.
SEE: Fig. 57
PROVENANCE: Philippe le Bon (inventory of 1420).
BIBLIOGRAPHY: G. Doutrepont, *Inventaire de la 'librairie' de Philippe le Bon (1420)* (Brussels, 1906), pp. 161–2, no. 239; H. Martin, *Catalogue des manuscrits de la Bibliothèque de l'Arsenal* (Paris, 1889), V, p. 165; *Les Principaux Manuscrits à peintures de la Bibliothèque de l'Arsenal à Paris ouvrage posthume de H. Martin, terminé par Ph. Lauer* (Paris, 1929), pl. 76; Winter *Bibliothèque*, pp. 166–7; Hedeman, *Royal Image*, pp. 233–4.

Paris, Bibliothèque Nationale, MS fr. 52

Vincent of Beauvais, *Miroir historial*, Books XXV–XXXII, tr. Jean de Vignay
266 fols. 440 × 310 mm
33 miniatures by Remiet.
SEE: Fig. 62
PROVENANCE: Prigent de Coëtivy.
BIBLIOGRAPHY: E. Langlois, 'Le Miroir historial: exemplaie de Prégent de Coetivy', *Romania* 14 (1885), pp. 131–2; C. A. Chavannes-Mazel, 'Problems in Translation, Transcription and Iconography', in *Vincent de Beauvais: intentions et receptions d'une oeuvre encyclopédique au moyen âge* (Montreal, 1980), p. 363.

Paris, Bibliothèque Nationale, MS fr. 158

Guyart Desmoulins, *Bible historiale*, Book II (from Petrus Comestor)
350 fols. 423 × 305 mm
One miniature by Remiet on fol. 26v.

Paris, Bibliothèque Nationale, MSS fr. 170–1, 1396–8

Augustine, *La Cité de Dieu*, tr. Raoul de Presles (for Louis d'Orléans)
431 and 419 fols. 430 × 300 mm
21 miniatures by Remiet; fr. 170, fol. 1, by 'Pseudo Jacquemart'.
SEE: Figs. 4, 30, 32, 85, 148, 164, 175
PROVENANCE: Louis d'Orléans; Visconti Library in Pavia.
BIBLIOGRAPHY: A. de Laborde, *Les Manuscrits à peintures de la Cité de Dieu de Saint Augustin* (Paris, 1909); S. D. Smith, 'Illustrations of Raoul de Praelles' Translation of St. Augustine's City of God, 1375–1420' (Ph.D. New York University, 1974).

Paris, Bibliothèque Nationale, MS fr. 176

Durandus, *Rationale des divins offices*, tr. Jean Golein
340 fols. 415 × 315 mm
7 miniatures by Remiet.
SEE: Figs. 150, 180
PROVENANCE: Duc de Berry.
BIBLIOGRAPHY: J. Guiffrey, *Inventaires de Jean Duc de Berry, 1401–1416* (Paris, 1894), p. 226, no. 858; L. Delisle, *La Librairie de Charles V* (Paris, 1907), II, p. 229, no. 43; Meiss, *French Painting*, I, p. 312.

Paris, Bibliothèque Nationale, MS fr. 250

Orosius, *Histoire ancienne jusqu'à César* and *Les Faits des romains*
412 fols. 415 × 315 mm
28 miniatures by Remiet.
SEE: Figs. 35, 63, 144, 161
BIBLIOGRAPHY: L. F. Flutre, *Les Manuscrits des Faits des romains* (Paris, 1932), pp. 56–7; D. Oltrogge, *Die Illustrationszyklen zur 'Histoire Ancienne jusqu'à César', 1250–1400* (Frankfurt, 1989), pp. 34–5, figs. 71, 72, 105.

Paris, Bibliothèque Nationale, MS fr. 268

Livy, *Histoire romaine*, Decades III–IV, tr. Pierre Bersuire.
579 fols. 415 × 310 mm
9 miniatures by Remiet.
SEE: Figs. 67, 131
PROVENANCE: Jacques, grandson of Louis de Bourbon, Comte de la Marche, King of Hungary, Sicily and Jerusalem; Jacques d'Armagnac, Duc de Nemours.
BIBLIOGRAPHY: Delisle, *Cabinet des manuscrits*, p. 86; C. Samaran, 'Pierre Bersuire', in *Histoire littéraire de France*, xxxix (Paris, 1962), p. 406.

Paris, Bibliothèque Nationale, MSS fr. 269–72

Livy, *Histoire romaine*, Decades I–IV, tr. Pierre Bersuire. *c.* 408 × 305 mm
All miniatures by Remiet.
SEE: Fig. 66
PROVENANCE: Jeanne de Navarre, daughter of Charles VI who married Henry IV of England; Jacques d'Armagnac, Duc de Nemours.
BIBLIOGRAPHY: C. Samaran, 'Pierre Bersuire', in *Histoire littéraire de France*, XXXIX (Paris, 1962), p. 406; M. Manion and V. Vines, *Medieval and Renaissance Illuminated Manuscripts in Australian Collections* (London, 1984), pp. 178–9, figs. 183–6.

Paris, Bibliothèque Nationale, MSS fr. 312–14, dated June 1396 (by scribe Raoulet d'Orléans in vol. I, fol. 354v)

Vincent of Beauvais, *Miroir historial*, tr. Jean de Vignay
3 vols., 354, 392 and 438 fols. 400 × 280 mm
552 miniatures in *portraits d'encre* by Remiet.
SEE: Figs. 38, 53, 68–9, 71, 77, 84, 107, 112, 117, 126, 138, 147, 149, 151, 152, 160, 178, 186
PROVENANCE: Louis d'Orléans.
BIBLIOGRAPHY: Delisle, *Cabinet des manuscrits*, pl. xlvi, no. 6; H. Martin, *La Miniature française du XIIIe au XVe siècle* (Paris, 1923), p. 99; C. A. Chavannes-Mazel, 'Problems in Translation, Transcription and Iconography', in *Vincent de Beauvais: intentions et receptions d'une oeuvre encyclopédique au moyen âge* (Montreal, 1980), p. 363; Jenny Stratford, *The Bedford Inventories: The Worldly Goods of John, Duke of Bedford, Regent of France, 1389–1435* (London, 1993), pl. LXIII.

Paris, Bibliothèque Nationale, MS fr. 338

Guiron le courtois
481 fols. 395 × 285 mm
1 miniature by Remiet on fol. 39v; 72 other miniatures by the Master of the Roi Modus (BN fr. 12399) and the Master of BN fr. 810.
SEE: Fig. 39
BIBLIOGRAPHY: P. Paris, *Les Manuscrits françois de la bibliothèque du roi* (Paris, 1836–46), II, pp. 345–53; R. Lathuillère, *Guiron le courtois: étude de la tradition manuscrite et analyse critique* (Geneva, 1966), pp. 58–9.

Paris, Bibliothèque Nationale, MS fr. 823

Guillaume de Deguileville, *Pèlerinage de vie humaine, Pèlerinage de Jésus-Christ, Pèlerinage de l'âme*, dated 1393 (on fol. 168v)
249 fols. 305 × 210 mm
All miniatures in first and third poem by Remiet; those in second by Jean de Nizières and the Virgil Master.
SEE: Figs. 1, 6, 34, 46, 50, 89, 94, 97, 99, 100, 115, 120, 144, 157–8, 166, 169–70, 172, 192
PROVENANCE: Jean Bourré, treasurer of France under Louis XI; Charles VIII.
BIBLIOGRAPHY: Delisle, *Cabinet des manuscrits*, p. 37; P. Durrieu, 'Notes sur quelques manuscrits française conservés en Allemagne', *Bibliothèque de l'École des chartes* (1892), p. 122; *Exposition des Primitifs français au palais du Louvre et à la Bibliothèque nationale* (Paris, 1904); É. Mâle, 'La Miniature à l'exposition des primitifs', *Gazette des Beaux-Arts* 32 (1904), p. 47, no. 76; F. de Mely, *Les Primitifs et leurs signatures: Les miniaturistes* (Paris, 1913), p. 70; Paris, Bibliotheque Nationale, *Les manuscrits a peintures en France du XIIIe au XVe siècles* (Paris, 1955), p. 72, no. 143; *Fastes du gothique*, n. 294; Avril, 'Trois manuscrits', pp. 307–8; Meiss, *French Painting* III, p. 411; V. L. Kolve, *Chaucer and the Imagery of Narrative* (Berkeley, 1984), pp. 57–9, figs. 24–9; S. K. Hagen, *Allegorical Remembrance: A Study of 'The*

Pilgrimage of the Life of Man' as a Medieval Treatise on Seeing and Remembering (Athens, Ga., 1990), fig. 37; H. Toubert, 'Fabrication d'un manuscrit, l'intervention de l'enlumineur', in *Mise en page et mise en texte du livre manuscrit*, ed. H. J. Martin and J. Vezin in (Paris, 1990), pp. 417–20; Alexander, *Medieval Illuminators*, p. 62, n. 50.

Paris, Bibliothèque Nationale, MS fr. 2813

Grandes Chroniques de France (from origins to 1350, continued to 1379; for Charles V)
543 fols. 350 × 240 mm
14 miniatures by Remiet in fols. 149–230r.
SEE: Figs. 58–9
PROVENANCE: Library of Charles V (colophon on fol. 263v).
BIBLIOGRAPHY: Avril, *Librairie de Charles V*, pp. 112–13; Hedeman, *Royal Image*, pp. 244–6.

Paris, Bibliothèque Nationale, MS fr. 9106, 1396–8

Aristotle, *Politiques* and *Économiques*, tr. Nicole Oresme
390 fols. 336 × 240 mm
6 miniatures by Remiet (first gathering missing).
SEE: Figs. 15, 49, 64–5
PROVENANCE: Louis d'Orléans.

Paris, Bibliothèque Nationale, MS fr. 20029, dated 1383 (no fol. 21v)

Eustache Deschamps, *Lay de la fragilité humaine*
24 fols. 270 × 182 mm
30 miniatures by Remiet, some frames blank.
SEE: Figs. 23–7, 40, 45, 47–8, 79, 80 86, 98, 116, 122, 130, 139, 176–7, 179, 181
PROVENANCE: Nicolas de Herberay, 1536.
BIBLIOGRAPHY: Deschamps, *Oeuvres*, II. G. Hasenohr, 'Discours vernaculaire et autorités latines', in *Mise en page et mise en texte du livre manuscrit*, ed. H. J. Martin and J. Vezin (Paris, 1990), pp. 288–291.

Paris, Bibliothèque Nationale, MS lat. 1024

Breviary (for use of Paris, Notre Dame), Winter portion (pendant to Manchester MS 136)
445 fols. 194 × 445 mm
58 miniatures by Remiet.
SEE: Figs. 118–19, 121, 127, 142
BIBLIOGRAPHY: V. Leroquais, *Les Breviares manuscrits* (Paris, 1939), II, p. 475.

Paris, Bibliothèque Nationale, MS lat. 14247

Nicolas de Lyra, *Postilla litteralis super Biblia*
182 fols. 450 × 320 mm
3 frontispiece miniatures by Remiet.
SEE: Figs. 11, 19, 36
PROVENANCE: Library of Saint Victor, Paris, 1514.
BIBLIOGRAPHY: *Le catalogue de la bibliothèque de l'abbaye de Saint-Victor de Paris de Claude de Grandrue, 1514* (Paris, 1983), p. 12.

Private Collection

Aristotle, *Politiques* and *Économiques*, tr. Nicole Oresme
396 fols. 315 × 210 mm
1 miniature by Remiet (fol. 1r); others by the Master of the Bible of Jean de Sy, Master of the Coronation of Charles V and Master of the Livre du Sacre.
PROVENANCE: Charles V before 1380; Louis d'Anjou; Duc de Bourgogne.
BIBLIOGRAPHY: L. Delisle, *Recherches sur la librairie de Charles V* (Paris, 1907), I, p. 256; *Avril, Librairie de Charles V*, no. 203, p. 118; C. R. Sherman, 'Some Visual Definitions in the Illustration of Aristotle's *Nicomachean Ethics* and *Politics* in the French Translations of Nicole Oresme', *Art Bulletin* 59 (1977), pp. 320–35; Sherman, *Imaging Aristotle*, fig. 44.

Soissons, Bibliothèque Municipale, MSS 210–12

Guyart Desmoulins, *Bible historiale* (from Petrus Comestor)
3 vols., 217, 211 and 111 fols. 440 × 330 mm
4 minatures by Remiet in vol. I; 3 miniatures in vol. II; and numerous others by at least four other illuminators, including the Virgil Master, the Medallion Master and the Master of BN fr. 810.
SEE: Figs. 17, 29, 56, 81
BIBLIOGRAPHY: M. de Laprairie, *Bulletin de la Société archéologique de Soissons* 14 (1860), pp. 128–9; Meiss, *French Painting*, III, p. 411; *Le Plume et le plomb: tresors des bibliothèques de Picardie* (Amiens, 1991), pp. 22–3.

Troyes, Bibliothèque Municipale, MS 261

Valerius Maximus, *Faits et dits mémorables*, tr. Simon de Hesdin
379 fols. 320 × 230 mm
7 miniatures by Remiet.
SEE: Figs. 70, 82, 132–3, 145–6
PROVENANCE: Jean I de Foix.
BIBLIOGRAPHY: L. Morel-Payen, *Les Plus Belles Manuscrits et reliures de la bibliothèques municipale de Troyes* (Troyes, 1935), pp. 139–42, pl. XXVII, fig. 92; Christiane Raynaud, 'Les Transpositions iconographiques médiévales des actes faits mémorables de Valere Maxime dans le ms. 261 de la bibliothèque municipale de Troyes', in *Images et pouvoirs*, pp. 87–99.

Vienna, Österreichisches Nationalbibliothek, cod. 1969

Book of Hours (for use of Paris)
215 fols. 142 × 103 mm
12 miniatures by Remiet.
SEE: Fig. 51
PROVENANCE: Alexander Lubomirsky.
BIBLIOGRAPHY: H. J. Hermann, *Beschreibendes Verzeichnis der Illuminierten Handschriften in Osterreich*, VII/2 (Leipzig, 1936), pp. 87–90; D. Thoss, *Französiche Gotik und Renaissance in Meisterwerken der Buchmalerei* (Graz, 1978), p. 87, no. 11, fig. 4.

Whereabouts Unknown, Sotheby's sale, 13 July 1977, lot 71

Book of Hours (for use of Paris)
115 fols. 140 × 95 mm
4 miniatures by Remiet (attributed to a follower of Jacquemart de Hesdin in the sale cat.).
SEE: Figs. 129, 183

List of Abbreviations

Libraries

Bibl. Mun.	Bibliothèque Municipale
Brussels BR	Brussels, Bibliothèque Royale Albert I[e]
London BL	London, British Library
Oxford, Bodl.	Oxford, Bodleian Library
Paris BN	Paris, Bibliothèque Nationale
Paris BSteG	Paris, Bibliothèque Sainte-Geneviève
Vienna ONB	Vienna, Österreichische Nationalbibliothek

Frequently Cited Sources

Alexander, *Medieval Illuminators*	J. J. G. Alexander, *Medieval Illuminators and Their Methods of Work* (New Haven and London, 1992).
Ariès, *Hour of Our Death*	P. Ariès, *The Hour of Our Death* (London, 1982).
Artistes, I–III	*Artistes, artisans et production artistique au moyen âge*: I. *Les Hommes*; II. *Commande et travail*; III. *Fabrication et consommation de l'oeuvre*, ed. X. Barral i Altet (Paris, 1986–90).
Avril, *Librairie de Charles V*	François Avril, *La Librairie de Charles V* (Paris, 1968).
Avril, 'Trois manuscrits'	François Avril, 'Trois manuscrits napolitains des collections de Charles V et de Jean de Berry', *Bibliothèque de l'École des chartes* 127 (1969), pp. 291–328.
Brown, 'Death and the Human Body'	E. A. R. Brown, 'Death and the Human Body in the Later Middle Ages: The Legislation of Boniface VIII on the Division of the Corpse', *Viator* 12 (1981), pp. 221–70.
Camille, *Gothic Idol*	M. Camille, *The Gothic Idol: Ideology and Image-Making in Medieval Art* (Cambridge, 1989).
Camille, *Image*	M. Camille, *Image on the Edge: The Margins of Medieval Art* (London, 1992; Cambridge, Mass., 1992).
Chiffoleau, *Comptabilité*	J. Chiffoleau, *La Comptabilité de l'au delà: les hommes, la mort et la religion dans la région d'Avignon à la fin du moyen âge* (Rome, 1980).
Delalain, *Librairie parisien*	Paul Delalain, *Étude sur le librairie parisien du XIIIe au XVe siècle* (Paris, 1891).
Delisle, *Cabinet des manuscrits*	L. Delisle, *Le Cabinet des manuscrits* (Paris, 1868), vol. I.
Deschamps, *Oeuvres*	E. Deschamps, *Oeuvres complètes de Eustache Deschamps*, ed. Marquis de Queux de Saint-Hilaire, 11 vols. (Paris, 1878–1903), vol. II (1880).
Fastes du gothique	*Les Fastes du gothique: le siècle de Charles V*, catalogue by F. Baron et al. (Paris, 1981).
Finucane, 'Sacred Corpse'	R. C. Finucane, 'Sacred Corpse, Profane Carrion: Social Ideals and Death Rituals in the Later Middle Ages', in *Mirrors of Morality: Studies in the Social History of Death*, ed. J. Whaley (London, 1981), pp. 40–60.

Foucault, *Language*	Michel Foucault, *Language, Counter-Memory, Practice: Selected Essays and Interviews*, ed. D. Bouchard (Oxford, 1977).
Geremek, *Margins of Society*	B. Geremek, *The Margins of Society in Late Medieval Paris* (Cambridge, 1987).
Guenée, *Between Church and State*	B. Guenée, *Between Church and State: The Lives of Four French Prelates in the Late Middle Ages* (Chicago, 1991).
Hedeman, *Royal Image*	A. D. Hedeman, *The Royal Image: Illustrations of the 'Grandes Chroniques de France', 1274–1422* (Berkeley, 1991).
Hindman, *Christine de Pizan*	S. Hindman, *Christine de Pizan's 'Épistre Othéa': Paintings and Politics at the Court of Charles VI* (Toronto, 1986).
Huizinga, *Waning*	Johan Huizinga, *The Waning of the Middle Ages: A Study of the Forms of Life, Thought, and Art in France and the Netherlands in the Fourteenth and Fifteenth Centuries*, tr. F. Hopman (London and New York, 1976; 1st Eng. ed. 1924).
Laborde, *Ducs de Bourgogne*	L. de Laborde, *Les Ducs de Bourgogne: études sur les lettres, les arts et l'industrie pendant le XVe siècle* (Paris, 1852), vol. III.
Le Roux de Lincy and Tisserand, *Paris*	A. Le Roux de Lincy and L. M. Tisserand, *Paris et ses historiens aux XIVe et XVe siècles* (Paris, 1867).
Lotario dei Segni, *De miseria*	Lotario dei Segni (later Pope Innocent III), *De miseria condicionis humane*, ed. R. E. Lewis (Athens, Ga., 1978).
Meiss, *French Painting*, I-III	M. Meiss, *French Painting in the Time of Jean de Berry*: I. *The Late Fourteenth Century and the Patronage of the Duke* (London, 1967); II. *The Boucicaut Master* (London, 1968); III. *The Limbourgs and Their Contemporaries* (London, 1974).
Pouchelle, *Body and Surgery*	Marie-Christine Pouchelle, *The Body and Surgery in the Middle Ages* (New Brunswick, N.J., 1990).
Raynaud, *Images et pouvoirs*	Christiane Raynaud, *Images et pouvoirs au moyen âge* (Paris, 1993).
Sherman, *Imaging Aristotle*	Claire Richter Sherman, *Imaging Aristotle: Verbal and Visual Representation in Fourteenth-Century France* (Berkeley, 1995).
Shirley, *Parisian Journal*	Janet Shirley, tr., *A Parisian Journal, 1405–1449*, translated from the anonymous *Journal d'un Bourgeois de Paris* (Oxford, 1968).
Stürzinger, *Pèlerinage*	J. J. Stürzinger, ed., *Le Pèlerinage de vie humaine de Guillaume de Deguileville* (London, 1893).
Winter, 'Copistes'	Patrick de Winter, 'Copistes, éditeurs et enlumineurs de la fin du XIVe siècle: la production à Paris de manuscrits à miniatures', in *Actes du 100e Congrès national des Sociétés savantes (1975)* (Paris, 1978), pp. 233–56.
Winter, *Bibliothèque*	Patrick de Winter, *La Bibliothèque de Philippe le Hardi, duc de Bourgogne, 1364–1404: étude sur les manuscrits à peintures d'une collection princière à l'époque du style gothique internationale* (Paris, 1985).

Notes to the Text

Notes to the Introduction

1. Huizinga, *Waning*, pp. 232–3. The cheap Peregrine edition (London, 1976) has no illustrations except Van Eyck's *The Madonna and Chancellor Rolin*, reproduced in vivid colour on its cover, and was the first serious book about the Middle Ages I ever owned and read. I shall refer to this edition throughout, although there are many subsequent reprintings.
2. First published in Haarlem in 1919, the original title of Huizinga's book was *Herfsttij der Middeleeuwen: Studie over levens-en gedachtenvormen der veertiende en vijftiende eeuw in Frankrijk en de Nederlanden*. From its first publication in English in 1924, the translation lacked the footnotes and references in the original text and for these one must consult either the Dutch edition or the German: *Herbst des Mittelalters* (Munich, 1931). A valuable essay about the reception and influence of the book is M. Aston, 'Huizinga's Harvest: England and the Waning of the Middle Ages', *Medievalia et Humanistica* 9 (1979), pp. 1–25, and its art-historical impact has recently been explored by F. Haskell, 'Huizinga and the Flemish Renaissance', in *History and its Images: Art and the Interpretation of the Past* (New Haven and London, 1993), pp. 431–95.
3. Huizinga, *Waning*, p. 146; the chapter on the tendency of thought to embody itself in images directly follows the chapter on death. For Huizinga's views on the rise of photographic reproduction resulting in intellectual laziness, see his *Homo ludens* (London, 1970), pp. 228–9, and H. Gerson, 'Huizinga und die Kunstgeschichte', in *Johann Huizinga, 1872–1972*, ed. W. R. H. Koops E. H. Kosman and G. van der Plaat (The Hague, 1973), p. 221. It is also worth noting that Millard Meiss bewailed the 'long shadow' of Huizinga, which, in his view, cast a pall over the study of late fourteenth-century manuscript illumination; Meiss, *French Painting*, III, p. 5.
4. F. Braudel, *Civilization materiélle, économie et capitalisme, 16e–18e siècles*, 3 vols. (Paris, 1979). The series, published by Gallimard, includes such studies as M. Volvelle's *La Mort en Occident de 1300 à nos jours* (Paris, 1983). For this trend among recent French historians to incorporate visual material, see M. de Certeau, 'Images', in *Dictionnaire des sciences historiques*, ed. A. Burguière (Paris, 1986), pp. 345–7, and P. Carrard, *Poetics of the New History: French Historical Discourse from Braudel to Chartier* (Baltimore and London, 1992), pp. 153–5.
5. The original French edition of volume II of the *Histoire de vie privée: de l'Europe feodale à la Renaissance*, ed. G. Duby (Paris, 1985), went as far as to ape the appearance of a fourteenth-century manuscript, with red rubrics in the outer margins as captions to the hundreds of richly reproduced illustrations, which appeared under the auspices not of an author but of two people listed on the back flyleaf as being responsible for 'Iconographie'. That this notion of writing an illustrated history of the private sphere is not especially new is suggested by the twenty-three volumes by Alfred Franklin, *La Vie privée d'autrefois*, published in Paris between 1887 and 1901, which treat everday life in the medieval capital.
6. J. Favier's volume in the Nouvelle Histoire de Paris series, *Paris au XVe siècle, 1380–1500* (Paris, 1974), reproduces on p. 255 the six framed images of 'peasants, clergy, knights, councillors, craftsmen and merchants' from Remiet's *Politiques* (BN fr. 9106), totally altering their order and arrangement in the manuscript (see here Figs. 64 and 65). A study with many examples of how French medieval historians have misused manuscript images in this way is F. Garnier, *L'Âne a la lyre: sottiser d'iconographie médiévale* (Paris, 1988).
7. A page illuminated by Remiet in Deschamps's *Lay de la fragilité humaine* (BN fr. 20029, fol. 6v) is reproduced in a book by R. S. Loomis entitled *A Mirror of Chaucer's World* (Princeton, 1965), no. 119. For a colour reproduction of Remiet's picture of the presentation of the book to Charles V, cut out from its surrounding text in the Chantilly *Éthiques*, see J. Cequiglini-Toulet, *La Couleur de mélancolie: la fréquentation des livres au XIVe siècle, 1300–1415* (Paris, 1993), pl. V.
8. For the biography as a genre in this period, see Guenée, *Between Church and State*, pp. 3–6: 'Over the last ten or twenty years, however, history and biography have once again drawn closer together. History is tired of being faceless and flavourless. It is turning back to the qualitative and singular.' Jacques Le Goff has described this 'return to the individual' in 'The Whys and Ways of Writing a Biography: The Case of Saint Louis', *Exemplaria* 1 (1989), pp. 207–25.
9. J. Le Goff, 'Les mentalités une histoire ambiguë', in *Faire de l'histoire* (Paris, 1974), III, p. 89, described the importance not only of working on the 'great' figures of history but of 'the odd word here and there'. Major works of this tradition, one exploring a society and the other an individual in society, are E. Le Roy Ladurie, *Montaillou, village occitan*

de 1294 à 1324 (Paris, 1975), trans. as *Montaillou* (London, 1978); and Natalie Zemon-Davies, *The Return of Martin Guerre* (Cambridge, Mass., 1993). See also C. Ginzburg, The Cheese and the Worms: Cosmos of a Sixteenth-Century Miller. For the revival of biography in history, see Peter Burke, *The French Historical Revolution: The 'Annales' School, 1929–1989* (London, 1990), p. 89.

10 M. Foucault, 'La Vie des hommes infâmes', *Cahiers du chemin* 29 (1977), p. 12. Other exceptional cases of medieval self-absorption occur in the mentally ill; see A. Gourevitch, 'L'Individualité an moyen âge: le cas d'Opicinus de Canistris', *Annales E.S.C.* 48 (1993), pp. 1263–81.

11. Meiss in all three volumes of his *French Painting* cites manuscripts by Remiet as 'Boqueteaux trend' or 'Late Boqueteaux' (III, p. 420), referring to an earlier artist so-named because of his 'little trees' or *boqueteaux*. Charles Sterling, *La Peinture médiévale à Paris, 1300–1500* (Paris, 1987), I, gives great space to associated illuminators like the 'Maître de la Bible de Jean de Sy' but mentions Remiet (not by name but as the 'peintre anonyme du *Pèlerinage de vie humaine*) only on p. 19, where he is grouped, erroneously in my opinion, with foreign artists working in Paris 'originaires des Pays-Bas'. An exception to the appearance of Remiet in general surveys of art is the mention by one of his great early promoters, Comte Paul Durrieu, in André Michel, *Histoire de l'art* (Paris, 1907), III, part 1, p. 158. Winter described 'Perrin Remy' in rather negative terms in 'Copistes', but more recently in his *Bibliothèque*, p. 92, he is more positive, describing how, 'even though his work has a commercial hardness', it shows a talent for rapid sketching *con brio*.

12. F. Avril called this artist 'profilique mais monotone' in his entry on BN fr. 823 in the exhibition catalogue, *Fastes du gothique*, pp. 338–9, cat. no. 294.

13. É. Mâle, 'La Miniature à l'exposition des primitifs', *Gazette des Beaux-Arts* 32 (1904), p. 47; *Exposition des primitifs français au palais du Louvre et à la Bibliothèque nationale* (Paris, 1904), cat. no. 76.

14. A full bibliography of the scholarship on later medieval manuscript illumination can be found in Alexander, *Medieval Illuminators*, pp. 121–49. For the ubiquitous dependence on models, see Douglas Farquhar, *Creation and Imitation: The Work of a Fifteenth-Century Manuscript Illuminator* (Ft Lauderdale, 1976), and see here Chapter 1. The argument for the need to explore the more 'ordinary' products of manuscript illumination was first made more than twenty years ago by L. M. J. Delaissé in his review of Meiss, *French Painting* I, in *Art Bulletin* 52 (1970), pp. 206–12.

15. Sotheby's sale cat., 5 Dec. 1994, lot 21, a leaf from Livy, *Histoire romaine*, attributed to 'Perrin Remiet illuminator'. This cutting along with another recently for sale in Paris (*Les Enlumineurs*, sale cat. 1 (1992), no. 21), also identified by Sandra Hindman as 'Remiet', is not by Remiet but by another much younger illuminator whose work sometimes appears alongside miniatures by Remiet. I see this hand as closer to Jean de Nizières, who signed his name in Paris BSteG MS 1028; see P. d'Ancona and E. Aeshliman, *Dictionnaire des miniaturistes* (Milan, 1949), p. 119, pl. LXV, and see here Chapter 1, note 16.

16. P. Durrieu, 'Notes sur quelques manuscrits français des bibliothèques d'Allemagne', *Bibliothèque de l'École des chartes* 53 (1892), p. 124.

17. Philippe Ariès, *Essais sur l'histoire cle la mort en occident du moyen âge à nos jours* (Paris, 1975) and *L'Homme devant la mort* (Paris, 1977), translated as *The Hour of Our Death* (London, 1982). A richly illustrated account of funerary art by the same author has recently appeared in English as *Images of Man and Death* (Cambridge, Mass., 1985).

18. M. Volvelle, 'Encore la mort: un peu plus qu'une mode?' *Annales, E.S.C.* 37, no. 2 (1982), and the same author's 'The History of Mankind in the History of Death', *Proceedings of the Annual Meeting of the Western Society for French History* 6 (1978), pp. 91–108. This scholar's own approach to the issue was published in two books, *Mourir autrefois: attitudes collectives devant la mort au XVIIe et XVIIIe siècles* (Paris, 1974), and op. cit. n. 4. A useful overview of French historical research and its obsession with this theme is John McManners, 'Death and the French Historians', in *Mirrors of Mortality: Studies in the Social History of Death*, ed. J. Whaley (London, 1981), pp. 106–30. Recent scholarship is not restricted to France, however; see *Death in the Middle Ages*, ed. H. Braet and W. Verbeke (Louvain, 1983), and for German reactions and scholarship, Arno Borst, 'Three Studies of Death in the Middle Ages', in *Medieval Worlds: Barbarians, Heretics and Artists in the Middle Ages* (Chicago, 1992), pp. 230–43; N. Ohler, *Sterben und Tod im Mittelalter* (Munich, 1990); and *Tod im Mittelalter*, ed. A. Borst, G. V. Graevenitz, A. Ptschovsky and K. Stierle (Constance, 1993). Anglo-American interest is best surveyed in *Mirrors of Mortality*, ed. Whaley.

19. Art-historical studies of the theme are numerous and will be found here in notes to the chapters, but major general surveys include: É. Mâle, *L'Art religieux de la fin du moyen âge en France* (Paris, 1908); translated as *Religious Art in France: The Late Middle Ages*, ed. H. Bober (Princeton, 1987); A. Tenenti, *La Vie et la mort à travers l'art du XVe siècle* (Paris, 1952); T. S. R. Boase, *Death in the Middle Ages: Mortality, Judgement, Remembrance* (London, 1972); and most recently, N. Llewellyn, *The Art of Death: Visual Culture in English Death Ritual, c.1500–c.1800* (London, 1991).

20. J. Derrida, *Aporias* (Stanford, 1993), p. 43, and *Specters of Marx* (London, 1994), pp. xviii-xix. For Georges Bataille's 'eroticism is assenting to life even in death', see *Eroticism, Death and Sensuality* (San Francisco, 1986), p. 11, and for Maurice Blanchot's attraction 'to the ordeal . . . where the power to die is wagered', see *The Space of Literature* (Lincoln, Neb., 1982), p. 107. The notion of 'death as limit' in all these writers is taken from the work of M. Heidegger; see especially his *An Introduction to Metaphysics* (New York, 1961), p. 133. For the way death as both 'power and limit' also structured the life and work of Michel Foucault, see J. Miller, *The Passion of Michel Foucault* (New York and London, 1993), pp. 241–4; for Roland Barthes, see J. Derrida, 'The Deaths of Roland Barthes', in *Philosophy and Non-Philosophy since Merleau-Ponty*, ed. H. J. Silverman (New York, 1988), pp. 270–5.

21. P. Ricoeur, *Time and Narrative*, III (Chicago, 1988), pp. 118–19.

22. For the impact of new technologies in the humanities, see the penetrating essays in R. Lanham, *The Electronic Word* (Chicago, 1994), and for the expanding role of images in this process, see J. Hillis-Miller, *Illustration* (Cambridge, Mass., 1992), pp. 37–60.

23. Walter Benjamin, 'The Storyteller', in *Illuminations* (New York, 1969), p. 94.

Notes to Chapter 1

1. Foucault, 'Fantasia of the Library', in *Language*, p. 109.
2. Theophilus, *De diversis artibus*, ed. C. R. Dodwell (London, 1961), p. 63: 'Through the spirit of fear of the Lord, you remember that you can do nothing of yourself; you reflect that you have or intend nothing, unless accorded by God.'
3. The note is somewhat famous among specialists of manuscript illumination, having been cited first by Delisle, *Cabinet des manuscrits*, I, p. 37. As Alexander notes in *Medieval Illuminators*, p. 62, n. 50, there have been a variety of interpretations as to who wrote the note, and to whom. Henry Martin assumed that the space was meant to be filled with a simple geometric figure, but argued that an assistant wrote the note to a *chef d'atelier*. The reverse notion, that the note is from the head illuminator to his assistant, has been put forward by Avril, 'Trois manuscrits', pp. 307–8, and followed by H. Toubert, 'Fabrication d'un manuscrit: l'intervention de l'enlumineur', in *Mise en page et mise en texte du livre manuscrit*, ed. H. J. Martin and J. Vezin (Paris, 1990), pp. 417–20. As will become clear in what follows, I am in agreement with Paul Durrieu, who long ago saw these words as written by the scribe Oudin de Cavarnay telling the illuminator to reserve the space for a diagram. See also S. Berger and P. Durrieu, 'Les Notes pour l'enlumineur dans les manuscrits du moyen âge', *Mémoires de la Société des antiquaires de France* 53 (1893), p. 26. Notes to the illuminator also remain in another manuscript attributed to Remiet, once in the Hamilton Collection and now Berlin, Kupferstichkabinet MS 78. D. 2, *Le Dit du Lion*, as noted by P. Durrieu, 'Notes sur quelques manuscrits française conservés en Allemagne', *Bibliothèque de l'École des chartes* 53 (1892), p. 122.
4. The explicit is illustrated in F. de Mély *Les Primitifs et leurs signatures – les miniaturistes* (Paris, 1913), p. 70. For Oudin de Cavarnay or Carvanay, see H. Martin, *Les Miniaturistes français* (Paris, 1906), p. 84, n. 3, and Winter, 'Copistes', p. 190.
5. For the university's control over the book trade, which did not preclude their producing and selling books to the court or to wealthy laymen of the capital, see M. A. Rouse and R. H. Rouse, 'The Book Trade at the University of Paris, *c*.1250–*c*.1359', in *La Production du livre universitaire au moyen âge: exemplar et pecia*, ed. J. Bataillon, B. G. Guyot and R. H. Rouse (Paris, 1988), pp. 41–123, reprinted in *Authentic Witness: Approaches to Medieval Texts and Manuscripts* (South Bend, Ind., 1991), esp. pp. 268–9; and Alexander, *Medieval Illuminators*, pp. 22–3.
6. For different methods of transmitting directions to illuminators in addition to Alexander, *Medieval Illuminators*, pp. 52–72, and the same author's 'Preliminary Marginal Drawings in Medieval Manuscripts', in *Artistes*, III, pp. 307–9, see the founding work by Berger and Durrieu, op. cit. n. 3, pp. 1–30, and Henry Martin, 'Les Esquisses des miniatures', *Revue archéologiques*, 4th ser., 4 (1904), pp. 17–45. Recently, marks have been discovered that are neither writing nor drawing but which use signs to indicate colour and pattern as well as subject matter. See P. Stirnemann and M. T. Gousset, 'Marques, mots, pratiques: leur signification et leur liens dans le travail des enlumineurs', in O. Weijers, ed., *Vocabulaire du livre et de l'écriture au moyen âge* (Tournhout, 1989), pp. 34–5, and P. Stirnemann, 'Réflexions sur les instructions non iconographiques dans les manuscrits gothiques', in *Artistes*, III, pp. 351–6.
7. For the 'L-square', see Susan K. Hagen, *Allegorical Remembrance: A Study of 'The Pilgrimage of the Life of Man' as a Medieval Treatise on Seeing and Remembering*, (Athens, Ga., and London, 1990), pp. 59–60.
8. See F. de Mely, 'Familles d'artistes au moyen âge', *Bulletin de la Société nationale des antiquaires de France* (1928–9), p. 181. I came across this article in an invaluable publication listing all the important documents and secondary sources for this period by C. Lord, *Royal French Patronage of Art in the Fourteenth Century: An Annotated Bibliography* (Boston, 1985).
9. See Brian Rotman, *Signifying Nothing: The Semiotics of Zero* (New York, 1987).
10. Christine de Pizan, *The Book of the City of Ladies*, tr. E. J. Richards (New York, 1982), p. 85, best discussed by Hindman, *Christine de Pizan*, pp. 69–71.
11. A. S. Farber, 'Considering a Marginal Master: The Work of an Early Fifteenth-Century Parisian Manuscript Decorator', *Gesta* 32 (1993), pp. 21–39. Study of the relationship between decorative and pictorial elements in Western manuscripts lags behind studies of Byzantine illuminators. See the comments of my colleague Robert Nelson, *Theodore Hagiopetredes: A Late Byzantine Scribe and Illuminator* (Vienna, 1991), who writes (p. 128): 'And still the medieval context of this material remains buried in an intricate maze of craft traditions, personal practices, artisinal associations, and patronage opportunities that can only be dimly perceived in the late twentieth century.'
12. Richard de Bury, *Philobiblon* ed. M. Maclagan (Oxford, 1960), p. 101. For a fascinating discussion of these metaphors of harvesting the fruits of the page, see I. Illich, *In the Vineyard of the Text: A Commentary to Hugh's* 'Didascalicon' (Chicago, 1993), p. 57.
13. See Winter, *Bibliothèque*, p. 195, cat. no. 4, and Brigitte Buettner, 'Jacques Raponde, 'marchand' des manuscrits enluminés', *Médiévales* 14 (1988), pp. 23–32.
14. The tradition of illustrating this text was treated fully by Donal Byrne in 'The Illustrations to the early manuscripts of Jean Corbechon's French Translation of Bartholomeus Anglicus's "De Proprietatibus Rerum", 1372–1420' (Ph.D. Cambridge University, 1981). The Genesis scene from London BL Add. MS 11612, which follows the same model as Remiet's, is reproduced in his article 'Rex imago Dei: Charles V of France and the *Livre des propriétés des choses*', *Journal of Medieval History* 7 (1981), p. 105, and by Alexander, *Medieval Illuminators*, fig. 243. For creation iconography, see J. Zahlten, *Creatio Mundi: darstellungen der sechs Schöpfungstage und naturwissenschaftliches Welbild im Mittelalter* (Stuttgart, 1979), who reproduces Remiet's creation in fig. 183.
15. For 'nobody', see G. Calmann, 'The Picture of Nobody: An Iconographical Study', *Journal of the Warburg and Courtauld Institutes* 23 (1960), pp. 60–75. and for *nemo*, see M. Bakhtin, *Rabelais and His World* (Bloomington, Ind., 1984), pp. 413–14. For the late-medieval mastersinger literally naming himself as No One, Nuls Homs, see G. B. Stone, *The Death of the Troubadour: The Late Medieval Resistance to the Renaissance* (Philadelphia, 1994), p. 17.
16. The artist of the second frontispiece can be identified with the illuminator who completed a Book of Hours (London BL Add. MS 23145) and a *Livre des propriétés des choses* (Paris BSteG MS 1028) which bears the name of Jean

de Nizières; Byrne, op. cit. n. 14, p. 119. For a list of works attributed to the Virgil Master, including certain miniatures in the *Pèlerinage de l'âme*, see Meiss, *French Painting*, III, p. 411. The much shorter cycle of miniatures for the second poem of the trilogy in BN fr. 823 and the unique iconography compared to other fuller cycles suggest that there was a problem obtaining an exemplar; see M. Camille, 'The Illustrated Manuscripts of Guillaume de Deguileville's "Pèlerinages", 1330–1420' (Ph.D. Cambridge University, 1985), pp. 106–13.

17. Épitaphiers manuscrits de la Bibliothèque de l'Arsenal, no. 4619, fol. 47, and no. 5402, pp. 272–4; see Martin, op. cit. n. 4, p. 84.

18. Sotheby's, Phillips Collection sale, Wednesday, 26 Nov. 1975, lot 830, p. 43. Cachelart started quite a business later in the same year selling, for forty gold pieces, two copies of the Golden Legend to Louis d'Orléans; see Delisle, *Cabinet des manuscrits*, I, p. 102.

19. Émile Mâle, *Religious Art in France: The Thirteenth Century*, ed. H. Bober (Princeton, 1984), p. 400. For the changing attitudes to the medieval artist in general, see M. Warnke, *The Court Artist: On the Ancestry of the Modern Artist* (Cambridge, 1994); Camille, *Gothic Idol*, pp. 27–49; A. Martindale, *The Rise of the Artist in the Middle Ages and Early Renaissance* (London, 1972); and V. W. Egbert, *The Medieval Artist at Work* (Princeton, 1967).

20. The differences between monuments and documents as repositories of memory are discussed in P. Ricoeur, *Time and Narrative*, III (Chicago, 1989), pp. 118–19.

21. Michel de Certeau, *The Practice of Everyday Life* (Berkeley, 1988), p. 140.

22. L. Delisle, *Rouleaux des morts du IX au XVe siècle recueils et publiés pour la Société de l'histoire de France* (Paris, 1866), p. 390. For the use of the Latin quatrain in preaching, see S. Wenzel, *Fasciculus morum: A Fourteenth-Century Preacher's Handbook* (University Park, Pa., and London, 1989), p. 98.

23. R. de Lespinasse and F. Bonnardot, *Les Métiers et corporations de la ville de Paris, XIIIe siècle: le 'Livre de métiers' d'Étienne Boileau* (Paris, 1879), LXI, is transcribed from a later manuscript (BN fr. 24069) and contains rules laid down, probably in 1268, for painter-sculptors, goldsmiths, textile workers and other trades. For fourteenth-century ordinances, see R. de Lespinasse, *Les Métiers et corporations de la ville de Paris, XIV–XVIIIe siècles*, 3 vols. (Paris, 1886–97). Streets and shops are discussed in Jean-Pierre Leguay, *La Rue au moyen âge* (Rennes, 1992).

24. The study of the effects of colour in illuminated manuscripts beyond its merely technical analysis is as yet little researched, but see for now the important studies of M. Pastoureau, *Figures et couleurs: études sur la symbolique et la sensibilité médiévales* (Paris, 1986), and *Couleurs, images, symboles: études d'histoire et d'anthropologie* (Paris, 1989), and J. Gage, 'Color in Western Art: An Issue', *Art Bulletin* 72, no. 4 (1990), pp. 518–41. Brigitte Buettner's forthcoming study of the miniatures in the Duke of Berry's copy of Boccaccio's *De cleres et nobles femmes* (Paris BN fr. 12420) will provide the first clear application of colour theory to manuscript illumination.

25. Delalain, *Librairie parisien*, pp. xxxi, 8, 33. For the rules against selling foreign goods, see J. Guiffrey, *Inventaires de Jean duc de Berry, 1401–1416* (Paris, 1894–6), I, p. 147.

26. This area has been studied by R. H. Rouse and M. A. Rouse, 'The Commercial Production of Manuscript Books in Late Thirteenth-Century and Early Fourteenth-Century Paris', in *Medieval Book Production: Assessing the Evidence*, ed. L. L. Brownrigg (Los Altos Hills, 1990), pp. 103–17.

27. Basic and crucial for the topography of the city in this period are R. Cazelles, *De la fin du regne de Philippe Auguste à la mort de Charles V, 1223–1380*, and Jean Favier, *Paris au XVe siècle, 1380–1500*, both in the series Nouvelle Histoire de Paris (Paris, 1974).

28. Dante, *Purgatorio*, XI, vv. 79–81, 'di quell'arte ch'alluminar chiamata e in parisi'. See P. Durrieu, 'Oderisi da Gubio et ce que l'on appelait à Paris au témoignage de Dante 'L'Art d'enluminer', *Mémoires de la Société de l'histoire de Paris et de l'Île-de-France* 42 (1915), pp. 154–70; R. Branner, *Manuscript Painting in Paris during the Reign of Saint Louis: A Study of Styles* (Berkeley, 1977); and Alexander, *Medieval Illuminators*, p. 22.

29. W. Sauerländer, 'Medieval Paris, Center of European Taste: Fame and Realities', in *Paris: Center of Artistic Enlightenment*, Papers in Art History from The Pennsylvania State University, vol. IV (1989), pp. 13–24; C. Lacaze, 'Parisius-Paradisus: An Aspect of the Vie de St. Denis Manuscript of 1317', *Marsyas* 16 (1972–3), pp. 60–6. Both Jean de Jandun's *Éloge de la cité de Paris* composed in 1323 and the poem by Guillbert of Metz, *Description de la ville de Paris sous Charles VI* written in 1434 are printed in Le Roux de Lincy and Tisserand, *Paris*, pp. 3–75.

30. Paris, Archives Nationales, KK 402: 'La Rue de la Parcheminerie: De Pierre Remyet, pour sa maison assise en ladite rue, qui fait front à ladite rue dudit Erembourth de Brye, 4 l. p. par an, à paier auxdits termes, pour ce, ycy pour lesdits termes. 4 l. p. Somme par soy. 4 l. p.', published in *Comptes du domaine de la ville de Paris: I. 1424–1457*, ed. A. Vidier, L. Le Grand and P. Dupieux (Paris, 1948), col. 5, and also cited by Henry Martin, *La Miniature française du XIIIe au XVe siècle* (Paris, 1923), p. 67. For the street and its history, see A. Berty, *Topographie historique du vieux Paris: VI. Region Centrale de la Université*, ed. L. M. Tisserand and C. Platon (Paris, 1897), pp. 16–17, 176–7; and Jacques Hillaret, *Dictionnaire historique des rues de Paris* (Paris, 1985), I, p. 236.

31. For the number of scribes and illuminators living on the Rue Boutebrie in 1292, see F. Baron, 'Enlumineurs, peintres et sculpteurs parisiens des XIIIe et XIVe siècles d'après les rôles de la taille', *Bulletin archéologique du Comité des travaux historiques et scientifiques*, N.S., 4 (1969), pp. 40–3.

32. An excellent study of parchment, including a list of documents from fourteenth-century Paris, is M. Gullick, 'From Parchment to Scribe: Some Observations on the Manufacture and Preparation of Medieval Parchment Based upon a Review of the Literary Evidence', in *Pergament: Geschichte. Struktur. Restaurierung Herstellung*, ed. P. Rück (Simaringen, 1991), pp. 145–57. M. T. Gousset, 'Parcheminiers et libraires rouennais à la fin du quatorzième siècle d'après un document judicaire', *Viator* 24 (1993), pp. 234–45, collects interesting evidence for the book trade in nearby Rouen. The best general discussion of material aspects of medieval manuscript production, with a special emphasis on parchment, is C. de Hamel, *Scribes and Illuminators* (London, 1993).

33. For the names of houses on Remiet's street, see the *Comptes du domaine* (see n. 30), col. 7. For signs in general, see J. J. Dufour and F. Boucher, *Les Enseignes de Paris* (Paris, 1924), and Y. D. Papin, 'Les Enseignes médiévales: un langage pittoresque et universel', *Archéologia* 69 (1974), pp. 37–42. A. Berty and L. M. Tisserand, *Topographie historique de vieux Paris* (Paris, 1866), I, p. 160, cite a 'House of the

Three Living and the Three Dead', which had been a theme popular in manuscript illumination since the beginning of the century.

34. These are the words of Molly Nesbit, whose *Atget's Seven Albums* (New Haven and London, 1992), pp. 16–17, stimulated me to think of the two Parisian masters in these terms.

35. *Comptes du domaine* (see n. 30), col. 186: 'Rue de la Parcheminerie: De Pierre Remiot, et depuis sire Jehan Luillier, pour un maison où demeure Regnault François, escriptvain.' Besides this scribe, tenants include a parchment-maker, suggesting the continued association of the building with book-making. According to another document, no taxes were collected at this time and the building lay vacant: 'ladicte maison est demouré vuide, vague et la viz fondue' (p. 243). In 1457 when it is described as 'once belonging to Pierre Rennot [*sic*]', it belonged to a spice-merchant, *Comptes du domaine de la ville de Paris*: II. 1457–1489, ed. J. Monicat (Paris, 1958), col. 7.

36. Geremek, *Margins of Society*, p. 69, lists variations in taxes paid by various social groups, as much as 48 livres in 1297 and as little as from 2 to 5 sous. He also notes that in this quarter there were 'few rich burgesses'. Neither Remiet nor any of his heirs are mentioned in the three tax rolls of 1421, 1423 and 1438 published by J. Favier, *Les Contribuables parisiens à la fin de la guerre de cent ans* (Geneva and Paris, 1970), but these documents do not include all parishes, and the last numbers only 578 household heads.

37. Geremek, *Margins of Society*, p. 78, who also discusses the way Nicolas Flamel the scribe and alchemist made his notorious gold more through his being a landlord than through magic (pp. 80–1). Our knowledge of urban housing is still patchy, but see the study of the poor quality of housing on the Left Bank by S. Roux, 'L'Habitat urbain au moyen âge: le quartier de l'Université de Paris', *Annales E.S.C.* 24 (1969), pp. 1196–1219.

38. Rouse and Rouse, op. cit. n. 26.

39. Student life and college buildings on the Left Bank are evoked by Simone Roux, *La Rive gauche des escholiers, XVe siècle* (Paris, 1992), p. 33. This was also an area where high prelates had their *hôtels*; see J. P. Willesme, 'Quelques témoinages archéologiques de l'habitat des hauts prélat de province sur la rive gauche de la Seine à la fin du moyen âge', in *Archéologie urbaine: actes du 100e Congrès national des Sociétés savantes* (Paris, 1978), pp. 157–9.

40. The document is printed in H. Denifle and E. Chatelain, eds., *Chartularium universitatis parisiensis* (Paris, 1894), III, pp. 178–9, and in Delalain, *Librairie parisien*, pp. 43–8. For the *guet*, or night watch, which lasted from curfew till sunrise, see F. B. Millett, 'Craft-Gilds of the Thirteenth Century in Paris', *Bulletin of the Departments of History and Political and Economic Science in Queen's University, Kingston, Ontario, Canada* 17 (1915), p. 18, who makes the point that it was the guilds serving the aristocracy – the goldsmiths, plumed-hat makers and painters – that were usually exempt from this irksome 'duty of the watch'.

41. See A. Dauzat, *Dictionnaire étymologique des noms de famille et prénoms de France* (Paris, 1956), 'Perin', p. 475, and 'Remy', p. 515.

42. For this note, see G. Warner and E. Gilson, *Catalogue of Western Manuscripts in the Old Royal and King's Collections* (London, 1921), II, pp. 375–7, and the more recent analysis by Avril, 'Trois manuscrits', pp. 300–10.

43. For Regnault's career, see Winter, 'Copistes', pp. 194–5, and for his trial, L. Mirot, 'Le Procès de maitre Jean Fusoris Chanoine de Notre-Dame de Paris, 1415–1416: episode des négotiations franco-anglaises durant la guerre de cent ans', *Mémoires de la Société de l'histoire de Paris et de l'Île-de-France*, 27 (1900), pp. 147–8, and p. 186 for his deposition in which he gives his age as 'XL ans ou environ' and testifies to having worked in the Parisian book trade for twenty-seven years. I have profited from conversations with Richard and Mary Rouse about Regnault. Their Lyell Lectures in Oxford, which I was unable to hear, included 'The Decline of Courtly Patronage in Paris: Regnault du Montet and the Organization of Book Production, 1399–1418', delivered on 12 May 1992.

44. Avril, 'Trois manuscrits', pp. 308–10, argues that this second artist of BN fr. 301 who is also the second artist of BN fr. 823, is to be identified as Remiet! Lillian Randall, *Medieval and Renaissance Manuscripts in the Walters Art Gallery*: I. *France, 875–1420* (Baltimore, 1989), p. 201, figs. 148–9, follows Avril in identifying the main hand in Walters 125–6, a *Bible historiale* (the second hand in BN fr. 823), as 'Perrin Remiet'. The clearest refutation of Avril's position was made by Sharon Dunlap Smith in what remains the only survey of Remiet's work to date: 'Remiet occurs in the first Pèlerinage which is painted throughout by the illuminator we wish to designate as Remiet. Avril's identification of Remiet as the author of fols. 95 and 102v in the second Pèlerinage therefore seems improbable'; see Sharon Dunlap Smith, 'Illustrations of Raoul de Praelles' Translation of St. Augustine's City of God, 1375–1420' (Ph.D. New York University, 1974), p. 71. Meiss, also in disagreement with Avril on this attribution, gave the miniatures in BN fr. 301 to the Orosius Workshop; see *French Painting*, III, p. 420.

45. Alexander, *Medieval Illuminators*, Figs. 230 and 231 reproduce the full-page frontispieces from both the Angevin model and the Parisian copy.

46. J. le Goff, *Intellectuals in the Middle Ages* (Cambridge, 1993), pp. 82–3. For the original Latin text and discussion of scholarly furniture in general, see W. Wattenbach, *Das Schriftwesen im Mittelalter* (Leipzig, 1896), p. 272, and Jean Vezin, 'Un curieux meuble médiéval, le fauteuil à bras mobiles des scribes', in *Mélanges de la Bibliothèque de la Sorbonne offerts à Andre Tuilier* (Paris, 1988), pp. 87–92.

47. Carla Bozzolo and Ezio Ornato, *Pour une histoire du livre manuscrit au moyen âge: trois essais de codicologie quantitative* (Paris, 1983), pp. 46–8.

48. R. de Lespinasse, *Les Métiers et corporations de Paris* (Paris, 1866), p. 52. For labour time, see also B. Geremek, *Le Salariat dans l'artisanat parisien aux XIIIe–XVe siècles: ètude sur le marché de la main-d'oeuvre au moyen âge* (Paris, 1968), pp. 78–83; A. Franklin, *La Vie priveé d'autrefois: la mesure de temps* (Paris, 1888); J. Le Goff, 'Labor Time in the "Crisis" of the Fourteenth Century: From Medieval Time to Modern Time', in *Time, Work and Culture in the Middle Ages* (Chicago, 1980), pp. 43–58; and in general A. Borst, *The Ordering of Time: From the Ancient Computus to the Modern Computer* (Chicago, 1990).

49. *Le Menagier de Paris*, ed. G. E. Brereton and J. M. Ferrier (Oxford, 1981), p. 1, translated by E. Power as *The Goodman of Paris: A Treatise on Moral and Domestic Economy by a Citizen of Paris, c.1393* (London, 1928), p. 47.

50. 'Nostre mestre enlumineor / Qui pour enluminer le monde, / Qù toute iniquitez habonde / Et tous malz, deüssent au mains / Porter double lumiere aus main.' *Ovid moralisé*, Book XIV, vv. 3362–6, discussed by C. Lord,

'Three Manuscripts of the *Ovide moralisé*', *Art Bulletin* 57 (1975), pp. 163–4.

51. The text is by Michael de Massa, Vienna ONB MS. lat. 1512, fol. 180v, cited in the useful account of medieval time in W. J. Courtenay, *Schools and Scholars in Fourteenth-Century England* (Princeton, 1987), p. 4.

52. Millett, op. cit. n. 40, p. 13.

53. This is in a poem to the Virgin Mary translated from Deguileville's *Pèlerinage de vie humaine* (Stürzinger, *Pèlerinage*, ll. 11,001–3): 'Kalendier sont enlumine / Et autre livre enterine / Quant ton non les enlumine'; see B. Boyd, *Chaucer and the Liturgy* (Philadelphia, 1967), p. 23.

54. J. Gerson, *Tractatus de laude scriptorum ad cartusiensis et coelestinos* (Cologne, n.d.), discussed in Winter, 'Copistes', p. 173; and for Henry of Langerstein, see N. H. Steneck, 'A Late-Medieval *Arbor Scientarium*', *Speculum* 50 (1975), p. 266.

55. This document is discussed in E. Pellegrin, 'La Bibliothèque de l'ancien collège de Dormans-Beauvais à Paris', *Bulletin philologique et historique* (1944–5), p. 146, and see also Winter 'Copistes', p. 196.

56. R. D. M. Chapotin, *Le Collège de Dormans-Beauvais* (Paris, 1870). Masons' wages are dicussed in P. Spufford, *Money and Its Use in Medieval Europe* (Cambridge, 1988), p. 324. For the problem of shifting values in fourteenth-century currency, see A. Van Nieuwenhuysen, *Les Finances du duc de Bourgogne, Philippe le Hardi, 1384–1404* (Brussels, 1990), pp. 177–9.

57. *Menagier de Paris* (see n. 49), p. 185, l. 23.

58. Pellegrin, op. cit. n. 55. For more discussion of contracts, see Alexander, *Medieval Illuminators*, pp. 36–8, and his publication of late fourteenth-century Dijon documents which show an individual, 'Master Jehan Demolin', contracting to make an Hours of the Virgin and a Missal (p. 180).

59. Pellegrin, op. cit. n. 55, pp. 133, 151–2. For the borders of Bayeux MS 61, by the decorator who later worked on the Duke of Berry's *Belles Heures*, see Farber, op. cit. n. 11.

60. Laborde, *Ducs de Bourgogne*, p. 168, no. 5864.

61. For the decreasing value of the sums given to Thevenin to pay book workers, recorded in Laborde, *Ducs de Bourgogne*, nos. 5678, 5703, 5762, 5820 and 5829, see H. A. Miskimin, *Money and Power in Fifteenth-Century France* (New Haven and London, 1984), p. 77.

62. See Gustav Fagniez, 'Essai sur l'organization de l'industrie à Paris au XIIe et XIVe siècles', *Bibliothèque de l'École des chartes*, 29 (1868), p. 30.

63. Le Roux de Lincy and Tisserand, *Paris*, refers to the chapel on p. 539 and to contemporary accounts describing it as having a profusion 'd'or et d'argent' and painted figures. See also Fig. 143 here for a drawing recording a lost wall painting from the chapel. For royal interest in the Célestins, see W. Cahn, 'The Angelic Pope and the Portal of the Paris Célestins', *Wiener Jahrbuch für Kunstgeschichte* 46 (1993–4), pp. 131–9.

64. 'Quittance par Pierre Remiot, enlumineur, à Jean Gilon payeur des oeuvres de la chapelle du duc d'Orléans près les Célestins à Paris, de cent sols parisis pour avoir enluminé et laoelé à images d'or et fines couleurs un tableau ouquel est transcrit la bulle du pape, pardons et indulgences accordés aux oyans messe en ladicte chappelle. Le 22 juin 1396', published in Laborde, *Ducs de Bourgogne*, p. 119, no. 5710. L. Delisle, in *Recherches sur la librairie de Charles V* (Paris, 1907), reads the word after 'enluminé' as 'cadelé', or gilding.

65. Laborde, *Ducs de Bourgogne*, p. 151, no. 5805.

66. As Brigitte Buettner has remarked in 'Profane Illuminations, Secular Illusions: Manuscripts in Late Medieval Courtly Society', *Art Bulletin* 74 (1992), p. 75, the role of the wives of the great Valois collectors has received far less attention; but see A. Vallet de Vireville, 'La Bibliothèque d'Isabeau de Bavière', *Bulletin du bibliophile* 36 (1858), pp. 663–87; S. L. Hindman, 'The Iconography of Queen Isabeau de Bavière, 1410–1415: An Essay in Method', *Gazette des Beaux-Arts* 102 (1983), pp. 102–10, and more generally S. G. Bell, 'Medieval Women Book Owners: Arbiters of Lay Piety and Ambassadors of Culture', *Signs* 7 (1982), pp. 742–68.

67. H. O. Lancaster, *Expectations of Life: A Study of the Demography, Statistics and History of World Mortality* (New York, etc., 1990), pp. 8–10. Guenée, *Between Church and State*, pp. 30–2, argues that in setting the human life span at seventy years, following Psalm 90, medieval people were 'reporting on their own experience'.

68. J. Derrida, *The Ear of the Other: Otobiography, Transference, Translation*, ed. C. MacDonald (Lincoln, Neb., and London, 1985), p. 22.

69. *Self and Society in Medieval France: The Memoirs of Abbot Guibert of Nogent*, ed. John F. Benton (Toronto, 1984), p. 48.

70. The reversal of this trope in a thirteenth-century drawing by Matthew Paris reproduced in a postcard at the Bodleian Library stimulated J. Derrida to write a whole book on the issue of philosophical origins, *The Postcard* (Chicago, 1990), discussed in M. Camille, 'The Dissenting Image: A Postcard from Matthew Paris', in *Criticism and Dissent in the Middle Ages*, ed. R. Copeland (Cambridge 1996), pp. 115–50.

71. For women in the booktrade, see D. Miner, *Anastasie and Her Sisters* (Baltimore, 1974). For Jeanne de Montbaston, see Delalain, *Librairie Parisien*, pp. 38–42, and Rouse and Rouse, op. cit. n. 5, p. 54, and Alexander, *Medieval Illuminators*, p. 23. A marginal image of them both at work, probably by Jeanne herself, is reproduced in Camille, *Image*, p. 147. Christine de Pizan's famous description of Anastasie describes her as an 'experte' in *vignette* borders and the 'champainges d'ystoires'. The famous series of women artists depicted in the Duke of Berry's copy of Boccaccio's *De cleres et nobles femmes* are studied in depth in a forthcoming book by Brigitte Buettner.

72. The production of a *chef-d'oeuvre* is the first item on the 1391 statutes of the image-makers, published in *Collection des meilleurs dissertations notices et traités particuliers relatifs a l'histoire de France*, XXIX (Paris, 1837), p. 451. See also J. Guiffrey, 'La Communauté des peintres et sculpteurs parisiens, dite Académie de Saint-Luc, 1391–1766', *Journal des savants* 13 (1915), pp. 146–7, and the useful analysis by W. Cahn, *Masterpieces Chapters on the History of an Idea* (Princeton, 1979), pp. 5–22.

73. This point is made by H. A. Miskimin, *Money and Power in Fifteenth-Century France* (New Haven and London, 1984), p. 7.

74. Published in *Sources d'histoire médiévales*, ed. G. Brunel and E. Laclou (Paris, 1992), pp. 604–6; Denifle and Chatelain, eds., op. cit. n. 40, pp. 51–2.

75. For the illiteracy of Parisian glassworkers, see M. Parsons Lillich, 'Gothic Glaziers: Monks, Jews, Taxpayers,

Bretons, Women', *Journal of Glass Studies* 27 (1985), p. 75.

76. See G. Ovitt, Jr., *The Restoration of Perfection: Labor and Technology in Medieval Culture* (New Brunswick, N.J., 1987), p. 136, and the discussion of the theoretical distinction between *ars* and *scientia* in Warnke, op. cit. n. 19, pp. 34–5. For Remiet's image of 'art' with tools we associate more with labour, in the companion volume of Aristotle's *Éthiques*, see here Fig. 96.

77. Gustav Fagniez, *Documents relatifs à l'histoire de l'industrie et du commerce en France* (Paris, 1900), p. 170, no. 73. This severe pedagogical approach also applied to medieval schools, where language was inscribed on to children's bodies and memories with Grammar's birch. See the discussion of pain as a sign of love in K. F. Morrison, 'Incentives for Studying the Liberal Arts', in *The Seven Liberal Arts in the Middle Ages*, ed. D. L. Wagner (Bloomington, Ind., 1986), pp. 46–7.

78. Foucault, 'The Father's No', in *Language*, p. 72. The Giotto legend, repeated by Vasari and others, is first recorded in Ghiberti's *Commentarii*; see *Lorenzo Ghibertis Denkwürdigkeiten*, ed. J. von Schlosser (Berlin, 1912), I, p. 35.

79. Meiss, *French Painting*, I, p. 9, and for the 'would-be illuminator', II, fig. 410.

80. For this exemplum, see E. Kris and O. Kurz, *Legend, Myth, and Magic in the Image of the Artist* (New Haven and London, 1979), p. 115.

81. Brussels BR MS 9001, fol. 382v: 'Finis adest operi quem scriptor gaudet haberi.' Another example would be these words by a well-known scribe of the period: 'Or est ci fini nostre livre, / Benoit soit Dieu, je en suis delivré, / Et l'a escript Henri du Trevou'; Brussels BR MS 9507, fol. 125. Elaine Scarry notes in her book on the body and pain the association in history made by Marx between labour of the back and labour of the hand; *The Body in Pain: The Making and Unmaking of the World* (Oxford, 1985), p. 284.

82. Document published by Pellegrin, op. cit. n. 55, pp. 151–2, and for Hervi's career, see Winter, 'Copistes', p. 187.

83. Philippe Ariès, *Centuries of Childhood* (New York, 1962). For critiques of his arguments, see Shulamith Shahar, *Childhood in the Middle Ages* (London, 1990), pp. 1–7.

84. The name was coined by Martin, op. cit. n. 30, p. 44. A discussion of the problems associated with this group can be found in P. de Winter, 'The *Grandes Heures* of Phillip the Bold, Duke of Burgundy: The Copyist Jean L'Avenant and His Patrons at the French Court', *Speculum* 57, no. 4 (1982), pp. 793–7. As Avril points out in *Librairie de Charles V*, p. 195, Remiet's earliest work appears alongside the 'Master of the Bible of Jean de Sy' (another name for the Boqueteaux Master) and the Master of the Coronation Book of Charles V, which suggests a formation under either of these figures.

85. F. Avril, 'A quand remonent les premiers ateliers d'enlumineurs laïcs à Paris', *Enlumineur gothique: les dossiers d'archéologie* (1976), pp. 40–1.

86. Cahn, op. cit. n. 72, p. 9. The figures are from Favier, op. cit. n. 36. N. Raynaud, 'Les Maîtres à noms de convention', *Revue de l'art* 42 (1978), pp. 41–52, deals with the later designations of 'master of the' by art historians.

87. For this theme, see Wolfgang Stechow, 'Shooting at Father's Corpse', *Art Bulletin* 24 (1942), pp. 213–24.

88. For the Bible of Jean de Sy, see *Fastes du gothique*, pp. 325–6, no. 280, and Jenny Stratford, *The Bedford Inventories: The Worldly Goods of John, Duke of Bedford, Regent of France, 1389–1435* (London, 1993), pp. 91–2.

89. The author-portrait is on fol. 1r (my thanks to François Avril for first showing me a photograph of this miniature). For a description, see Avril, *Librairie de Charles V*, p. 118, no. 203, and Sherman, *Imaging Aristotle*, pp. 317–19, who reproduces the portrait as fig. 44.

90. For Lyra's notion of the author, see J. Coleman, *English Literature in History, 1350–1400: Medieval Readers and Writers* (London, 1981), pp. 203–4; A. J. Minnis, 'Discussions of 'Authorial Role' and 'Literary Form' in Late Medieval Scriptural Exegesis', *Beiträge zur Geschichte der deutschen Sprache und Literatur* 99 (1977), p. 46; and the same author's *Medieval Theory of Authorship* (Philadelphia, 1988).

91. N. Hathaway, 'Compilatio: From Plagiarism to Compiling', *Viator* 20 (1989), pp. 19–42, discusses these issues as well as Bonaventure's hierarchy of text producers – scribe, compiler, commentator and author.

92. Michel Foucault, 'What is an Author?' in *Textual Strategies: Perspectives in Post-Structuralist Criticism*, ed. Josué V. Harari (London, 1979), p. 143.

93. 'Les uns aprendent à escrire / de greffes et en tables de cire. / Les autrez sievent la coustume / de former lettres à la plume, / et paignent par dessus lez piaux / et des moutons et des viaux, / et a coulourer se doctrinent; / ils flourettent, il eluminent.' Jean Le Fèvre, *Le Respit de la mort*, ed. G. Hasenohr-Esnos (Paris, 1969), p. 89.

94. Richard de Bury, op. cit. n. 12, p. 19.

95. Deschamps makes his plea for immortality in his *Miroir de Mariage*, in *Oeuvres*, IX, vv. 795–805, discussed in a fascinating section, 'Entre les tombes, entre les pages', in Jacqueline Cerquiglini-Toulet, *La Couleur de la mélancolie: la fréquentation des livres au XIVe siècle, 1300–1415* (Paris, 1993), p. 142.

96. I have been helped in formulating these ideas about naming by Anne Middleton, 'William Langland's "Kynde Name": Authorial Signature and Social Identity in Late-Fourteenth-Century England', in *Literary Practice and Social Change in Britain, 1380–1530*, ed. Lee Patterson (Berkeley, 1990), pp. 15–82. For Christian names and surnames in Paris, see K. Michaëlson, *Études sur les noms de personne français d'après les rôles de taille parisiens* (Uppsala, 1927), I, pp. 60–1.

97. Delisle, *Cabinet des manuscrits*, I, pp. 12–13.

98. For Petrus Gilberti, see P. d'Ancona and E. Aeshliman, *Dictyionaire des miniaturistes du moyen âge et de la Renaissance* (Milan, 1949), p. 169, and G. Dogaer, 'Petrus Gilberti, een vroeg-vijftiende-eeuws Frans verluchter', *Archives et bibliothèques de Belgiques* 38 (1967), pp. 117–19.

99. *La Vielle ou les derniers amours d'ovide: poeme français du XIVe siècle*, ed. H. Cocheris (Paris, 1861), p. 43, ll. 750–2.

100. For the depiction of particular birds signalling that the artist was now capable of 'seeing for himself', see O. Pächt, 'Early Italian Nature Studies and the Early Calendar Landscape', *Journal of the Warburg and Courtauld Institutes* 13 (1950), pp. 18–19, and for a more naive argument which describes the 'impressionistic' and 'unnatural attitudes' of birds in French manuscript illumination, see B. Yapp, *Birds in Medieval Manuscripts* (London, 1981), pp. 102–4.

101. A. Blanchet, 'Sceaux de marchands et artistes parisiens (fin du XIVe–commencement du XVe siècle)', *Bulletin de la Société de l'histoire de Paris et de l'Île-de-France* 59 (1932), pp. 64–5.

102. Jacques Derrida, *Glas* (Lincoln, Neb., 1986), p. 11,

and see also his discussion of the problem of the proper name in *Signéponge/Singsponge* (New York, 1984).
103. A. Masson, 'Le "Tite-Live" de Bordeaux et l'atelier du 'Maitre aux Boqueteaux', *Tresors des bibliothèques de France* 21 (1936), pp. 11–35.
104. For earlier self-inscriptions at the edges of books and buildings, see Camille, *Image*, pp. 147–52. For manuscript illumination, see S. Hindman, 'The Roles of Author and Artist in the Procedure of Illustrating Late Medieval Texts', in *Text and Image*, *Acta*, vol. X, ed. D. W. Burchmore (Binghamton, N.Y., 1986), pp. 27–62, and for the Middle Ages in general, the writings of P. C. Claussen, notably 'Nachrichten von der Antipoden oder der mittelalterliche Künstler über sich selbst', in *Der Künstler über sich in seinem Werk*, ed. M. Winner (Weinheim, 1992), pp. 19–54, with further bibliography.
105. Pächt, op. cit. n. 100, pp. 13–19.
106. J. D. Farquhar, 'Identity in an Anonymous Age: Bruges Manuscript Illuminators and their Signs', *Viator* 11 (1980), pp. 371–8. The author hopes at the end of this article that 'after all these years of paying hommage to patrons, library numbers and stylistic peculiarities, it is foreseeable that we can identify the hitherto anonymous works with their creators'.
107. M. Blanchot, *The Space of Literature* (Lincoln, Neb., and London, 1982), p. 258.

Notes to Chapter 2

1. Georges Bataille, *The Accursed Share: An Essay on General Economy*: II. *The History of Eroticism* (New York, 1991), p. 92.
2. 'Sur toute chose mondaine / Est nostre nature humaine / De trop grant fragilité, / D'ordure et de vilité, / De toute misere plaine; / Vils conceus, nez a paine, / Nourriz d'orribilité / Ou ventre ains nativité / Est homs: c'est chose certainne.' Deschamps, *Oeuvres*, II, p. 242.
3. The best introduction to this subject is the Introduction to the Latin text and English translation, Lotario dei Segni, *De miseria*, pp. 3–12. J. Delumeau, *Sin and Fear: The Emergence of a Western Guilt Culture, 13th–18th Centuries* (New York, 1990), pp. 44–7, discusses the Latin text, making the point that, according to numbers of extant manuscripts, the heyday of its popularity was the thirteenth century.
4. The whole poem is edited but only two of its miniatures reproduced by Saint-Hilaire in Deschamps, *Oeuvres*, II, pp. 239–305. For the complex layout, see Geneviève Hasenohr, 'Discours vernaculaire et autorités latins', in *Mise en page et mis en texte du livre manuscrit*, ed. H. Martin and J. Vezin (Paris, 1990), pp. 289–91.
5. Deschamps, *Oeuvres*, VII, *ballade* 190, v. 13. The best biographical information on the poet is the introduction by G. Raynaud to volume XI of the *Oeuvres*, but see also the extended discussion in D. Poirion, *Le Poète et le prince: l'évolution du lyricisme courtois de Guillaume de Machaut à Charles d'Orléans* (Paris, 1965), pp. 218–22.
6. For Christine's involvement with illustrations of her own work, see Hindman, *Christine de Pizan*.
7. The 'livre de la misere de l'omme' is the final work in Besançon, Bibl. Mun. MS 434, a sumptuously illuminated volume containing various treatises for the education of princes, written for Charles V in 1372 by Henri de Tevou; see Fig. 101 here and Avril, *Librairie de Charles V*, pp. 106–7, no. 184. The prose text in two columns is preceded by a miniature showing the pope receiving the work from Cardinal Lotario, later Pope Innocent III. For the more emotive poetics in Deschamps's version, see Poirion, op. cit. n. 5, p. 86, and C. Martineau-Génieys, *Le Thème de la mort dans la poésie française de 1450 à 1550* (Paris, 1978), pp. 126–33.
8. Charles V's death is described in A. Brachet, *Pathologie mentale des rois de France: Louis XI et ses ascendants: une vie humaine étudiée à travers six siècles d'hérédité, 852–1483* (Paris, 1903), pp. 560–2.
9. Deschamps, *Oeuvres*, II, p. 362; L. Kendrick, 'The Monument and the Margin', *South Atlantic Quarterly* 91, no. 4 (1992), pp. 653–6, posits that the presentation occurred 'after the onset of the mental illness that unbalanced him and demonstrated so dramatically the frailty of the human condition'.
10. H. Kelly, 'The Metamorphosis of the Eden Serpent During the Middle Ages and Renaissance', *Viator* 2 (1971) pp. 301–29; and Camille, 'The Fallen Body', in *Gothic Idol*, pp. 87–9.
11. R. Koehler, 'Die Erde als jungfräuliche Mutter Adams', *Germania* 7 (1862), pp. 476–80. For the metaphor of the 'body–cave', see Jean-Luc Nancy, 'Corpus', in *The Birth to Presence* (Stanford, 1993), p. 192.
12. This is Innocent's Latin text: 'Quare de vulva matris mee egressus sum' (BN fr. 20029, fol 4v, *Double Lay de la fragilité humaine*), in Deschamps, *Oeuvres*, II, p. 245.
13. R. Potz McGerr discusses the 'Petit Job' and cites this part of the text in 'Guyart Desmoulins, the Vernacular Master of Histories, and the Bible Historiale', *Viator* 14 (1983), p. 22.
14. Foucault, 'Preface to a Transgression', in *Language*, p. 29.
15. Augustine, *The City of God*, Book XIII, ch. 12, tr. H. Bettenson (London, 1984), p. 522.
16. The 'Bible' here refers to the now lost 11-volume French translation of the Bible begun under Charles V; see Jenny Stratford, *The Bedford Inventories: The Worldy Goods of John, Duke of Bedford, Regent of France, 1389–1435* (London, 1993), p. 92. Many of the documents from the Orléans archive were destroyed by the fire at the Bibliothèque du Louvre during the 1871 Commune but had been thankfully published in Laborde, *Ducs de Bourgogne*, p. 116, no. 5703; A Le Roux de Lincy, 'La Bibliothèque de Charles d'Orléans à son Château de Blois en 1427', *Bibliothèque de l'École des chartes* (1843), pp. 35–8.
17. Laborde, *Ducs de Bourgogne*, p. 166, no. 5859.
18. This is also the thesis of S. D. Smith, 'Illustrations of Raoul de Praelles' Translation of St. Augustine's City of God, 1375 and 1420' (Ph.D. New York University, 1974), p. 71. In the same author's 'New Themes for the City of God around 1400: The Illustrations of Raoul de Presles' Translation', *Scriptorum* 36 (1982), pp. 68–82, focuses upon another unusual cycle produced for this text by the Virgil Master.
19. Christine de Pizan, *Le Livre des fais et bonnes meurs du sage roy Charles V*, ed. S. Solente (Paris, 1936–40), I, pp. 169–76. For the Amiens cathedral buttress statues, commissioned as a gift by Cardinal La Grange, the tutor to Louis, and whose later tomb at Avignon is so crucial in the history of death iconography, see C. R. Sherman, *The Portraits of Charles V of France, 1338–1380* (New York, 1969), pp. 58–60. For the life and character of Louis, see E.

Jarry, *La Vie politique de Louis de France, Duc d'Orléans, 1372–1407* (Paris, 1889); F. D. S. Darwin, *Louis d'Orléans, 1372–1407: A Necessary Prologue to the Tragedy of La Pucelle d'Orleans* (London, 1936); and more recently B. Guenée, *Un meutre, une société l'assassinat du duc d'Orléans, 23 novembre 1407* (Paris, 1992), pp. 143–50. I was unable to consult C. R. Shultz, 'The Artistic Patronage of Louis of Orleans and his Wife Valentine Visconti' (Ph.D. Emory University, 1977).

20. For the Duke's collections of jewels, see Darwin, op. cit. n. 19, p. 100, and for his houses and palaces, see J. Mesqui and C. Ribéra Pervillé, 'Les Châteaux de Louis d'Orléans et leurs architectes, 1391–1407', *Bulletin Monumentale* 138 (1980), and C. Ribéra Pervillé, 'Les Hôtels parisiens de Louis Ier d'Orléans, 1372–1407', *Bulletin de la Société de l'histoire de Paris et de l'Île-de-France* 107 (1981), pp. 23–70. F. M. Graves, *Deux inventaires de la maison d'Orléans (1389 et 1408)* (Paris, 1926), is also useful.

21. For the 'bal des ardents', see B. Tuchman, *A Distant Mirror: The Calamitous 14th Century* (London, 1979), pp. 507–8, and for a late fifteenth-century miniature picturing the event in a copy of Froissart's *Chronicles*, see R. H. de Villefose, *Nouvelle Histoire de Paris: solennités, fêtes et rejoussances parisiennes* (Paris, 1980), p. 64.

22. Jarry, op. cit. n. 19, p. 102.

23. For the possibility of Remiet being involved in decorating the library, see here Chapter 1. In addition to the *Cité de Dieu* (BN fr. 171), the Aristotle translations by Oresme (BN fr. 9106, and Chantilly, Museé Condé MS 277) and the three-volume *Miroir historial* (BN fr. 312–14), I would link four more extant manuscripts illuminated by Remiet with books mentioned in the Orléans inventories. First, the two-volume breviary, Manchester, John Rylands Library MS 136, and BN lat. 1024, which may be identified with 'a breviary in two volumes obtained from master Andre Dessous l'Orme in 1398 for 200 "francs d'or"' (Delisle, *Cabinet des manuscrits*, p. 103; Le Roux de Lincy, op. cit. n. 16, p. 41, no. 31). Second, BN fr. 250, an *Histoire ancienne* which may be identified with that obtained by Robert Escuier for 160 écus in 1397 (Delisle, p. 103; Le Roux de Lincy, p. 39, n. 26; Laborde, *Ducs de Bourgogne*, p. 141, no. 5785). Third, BN lat. 1447, the *Postille* of Nicolas de Lyra bought in 1398 from the priest Guillaume Daniel, for 300 francs (Le Roux de Lincy, p. 42, n. 34). Fourth, the three-volume *Histoires escolastres* in Soissons, Bibl. Mun. MSS 210–12, which may be identified with that bought from Thevenin de l'Angevin in 1395 (Le Roux de Lincy, p. 34, n. 9; Laborde, p. 99, n. 5651). Louis's wife, Valentina Visconti, may have owned the rare romance illuminated by Remiet, BN fr. 338, *Guiron le courtois*, and had its binding restored by Jean d'Arras in 1398 (Le Roux de Lincy, p. 43; Laborde, p. 171, no. 5871).

24. Philippe Henwood, 'Raymond du Temple: maître d'oeuvre des rois Charles V et Charles VI', *Bulletin de la Société de l'histoire de Paris et de l'Île-de-France* 105 (1979), p. 67.

25. Laborde, *Ducs de Bourgogne*, p. 151, no. 5805, gives the document concerning the payment for decorating the library, including a 'Peirin de Dijon'. See also Graves, op. cit. n. 20, p. 50, and Denise Bloch, 'Les Collections des Orléans', *Histoire des bibliothèques françaises: les bibliothèques médiévales*, ed. A. Vernet (Paris, 1989), p. 319. Recent studies of the library are by Pascale Thibault, *La Bibliothèque de Charles d'Orléans et de Louis XII au Château de Blois* (Blois, 1989), pp. 5–8, and Ursula Bauermeister and Marie-Pierre Laffite, *Des Livres et des rois: la bibliothèque de Blois* (Paris, 1992), pp. 35–6.

26. Delisle, *Cabinet des manuscrits*, p. 99, and for the breviary, now divided between Manchester and Paris and lacking its sumptuous coverings, see Graves, op. cit. n. 20, p. 53 and app. 1.

27. For this gift, see J. Guiffrey, *Inventaires de Jean duc de Berry, 1401–1416* (Paris, 1984), I, p. 265. For the lavish cloth bindings of the period, see J. S. Van Leeuwen, 'The Well-shirted Bookbinding: On Chemise Bindings and Hülleneinbande', in *Theatrum orbis librorum amicorum Presented to Nico Israel on His 70th Birthday*, ed. T. Croiset van Ucheln (Utrecht, 1989), pp. 277–305.

28. From A. Le Roux de Lincy, 'Description de Paris sous Charles VI, *c.*1407–1432', in Le Roux de Lincy and Tisserand, *Paris*, pp. 199–201. I am grateful to Martha MacFarlane for bringing this text to my attention.

29. D. Byrne, 'An Early French Humanist and Sallust: Jean Lebègue and the Iconographical Programme for the *Catiline* and *Jugurtha*', *Journal of the Warburg and Courtauld Institutes* 49 (1986), pp. 41–65, discusses the carefully coded miniatures and their written interpretations in a manuscript made for Louis, now Paris BN lat. 9684. For Christine de Pizan's *Epître d'Othéa* (Paris BN fr. 606), see Hindman, *Christine de Pizan*.

30. R. Bechmann, *Trees and Man: The Forest in the Middle Ages* (New York, 1990), pp. 290–1.

31. See Smith, 'New Themes', op. cit. n. 18, pp. 68–82.

32. Augustine, op. cit. n. 15, Book XIII, ch. 2, pp. 510–46.

33. For the text, see J. J. Stürzinger, ed., *Le Pèlerinage de Jésus-Christ de Guillaume de Deguileville* (London, 1897).

34. See Doris Oltrogge, *Die Illustrationenzyklen zur 'Histoire ancienne jusqu'à César', 1250–1400* (Frankfurt, 1987), pp. 34–5, figs. 105–6.

35. Meiss, *French Painting*, I, p. 226.

36. Luce Irigaray, *Speculum of the Other Woman*, tr. G. C. Gill (Ithaca, 1985), p. 225.

37. *Miroir historial*, Paris BN fr. 312, fol. 36v: 'dame et non pas d'ymage de dieu creé à la coste de l'ome'.

38. 'L'Appostile de maistre Nicole de Lire, en rois grans volumes tous neufs, historié et enluminé d'or et d'azur, en lettre de forme toute neufve'; Le Roux de Lincy, op. cit. n. 16, p. 73, and P. Champion, *La Librairie de Charles d'Orléans* (Paris, 1910), p. xii. Before entering the royal library, BN lat. 14247 was in the library of Saint-Victor; see *La Catalogue de la bibliothèque de l'abbaye de Saint-Victor de Paris de Claude Grandrue, 1514* (Paris, 1983), no. C1, p. 12.

39. Nicolas de Lyre, *Postilla litteralis* (Venice, 1588), I, 28D–F, discussed in H. Hailperin, *Rashi and the Christian Scholars* (Pittsburgh, 1963), pp. 148–51.

40. A. Henry, *Biblia pauperum* (Ithaca, 1987) p. 99.

41. R. Lathuillère, *Guiron le courtois: étude de la tradition manuscrite et analyse critique* (Geneva, 1966), no. 338. This continuation of the Arthurian cycle was very popular with the Valois princes, and also in Italy.

42. I use these visual and artisanal metaphors found in Lyra's text here, but for an interesting textual analysis of the subject in which Eve's perversity is linked to the 'lateral: as the outgrowth of Adam's flank, his *latus*, she retains the status of *translatio*, of translation, transfer, metapor, trope', see H. R. Bloch, 'Medieval Misogyny', *Representations* 20 (1987), p. 11, but see also the responses to Bloch in the *Medieval Feminist Newsletter* 6 (Fall 1988) and 7 (Spring 1989).

43. P. Ruelle, *L'Ornement des dames (Ornatus mulierum: texte anglo-normande du XIIIe siècle* (Brussels, 1967).
44. BN fr. 20029, fol. 7r; Deschamps, *Oeuvres*, II, p. 250, ll. 85–95.
45. Book VI, ch. 14; see M. Goodich, 'Bartholomeus Anglicus on Child-Rearing', *History of Childhood Quarterly* 3, no. 1 (1975), pp. 81–3.
46. Ibid.; see also Lotario dei Segni, *De miseria*, pp. 98–9.
47. Aristotle, *Problemata*, Book IV, 1, *The Complete Works of Aristotle*, ed. J. Barnes (Princeton, 1984), p. 1350. Louis d'Orléans's commission is described in Champion, op. cit. n. 38, p. xii.
48. For the diagram defining the moment of the conception of the clerk of Pavia, Opicinis, see R. Salomon, *Opicinis de Canistris* (London, 1936), I, pp. 204–21, and M. Camille, 'The Image and the Self: Unwriting Late Medieval Bodies', in *Framing Medieval Bodies*, ed. S. Kay and M. Rubin (Manchester, 1994), pp. 87–95. A visual introduction to the rise of astrology at this period is provided by H. Bober, 'The Zodiacal Miniature of the "Très Riches Heures" of the Duke of Berry: Its Sources and Meaning', *Journal of the Warburg and Courtauld Institutes* 11 (1948), pp. 1–34.
49. For this Oxford manuscript exhibited in *Fastes du gothique*, p. 355, no. 289, see M. E. Poulle, 'Horoscopes princiers des XIVe et XVe siècles', *Bulletin de la Société nationale des antiquaires de France* (1969), pp. 62–77, and L. Delisle, *Recherches sur la librairie de Charles V* (Paris, 1907), p. 266.
50. Deschamps, *Oeuvres*, II, p. 257, ll. 173–8. See also L. Kendrick, 'Transgression, Contamination, and Woman in Eustache Deschamps's *Miroir de Mariage*', *Stanford French Review* 14 (1990), pp. 220–1.
51. Deschamps, *Oeuvres*, II, p. 262.
52. M. P. Merrifield, *Original Treatises on the Arts of Painting* (London, 1849), 2nd ed., 2 vols. (New York, 1967), II, p. 80.
53. *Chronique du religieux de Saint-Denys*, ed. M. L. Bellaguet (Paris, 1841), p. 349. See G. Dodie, 'La Folie de Charles V', *Revue historique* (1926), p. 179.
54. Pouchelle, *Body and Surgery*, pp. 168–71, discusses the bodily production of vermin.
55. G. Vigarello, *Concepts of Cleanliness: Changing Attitudes in France since the Middle Ages* (Cambridge, 1989), pp. 28–9.
56. *Ordonnances des roys de France de la troisième race, recueilles par ordre chronologique*: VIII. *Contenant les ordonnances de Charles VI, donées depuis le commencement de l'année 1395 jusqu'à la fin de l'année 1403*, ed. D. F. Secousse (Paris, 1750), p. 43. A. Franklin, *La Vie privée d'autrefois: hygiène* (Paris, 1890), app. 1, p. 6, for the lavish loos of Charles VI and Louis d'Orléans.
57. Deschamps, *Oeuvres*, II, p. 263. For discussion of this tradition that a tree was a reversed human being, see A. J. Grieco, 'The Social Order of Nature and the Natural Order of Society in Late 13th–Early 14th Century Italy', *Mensch und Natur im Mittelalter*, Miscellanea Mediaevalia, 21.2 (Berlin, 1992), II, pp. 902–3. Pouchelle's reproduction of 'A man born of an elm tree' in *Body and Surgery*, fig. 7 (Paris BSteG MS 2000, fol. 172), is not in this tradition but is rather a visual pun on the name of the author of the text, Robert d'Ulm, or 'Robert of the Elm'.
58. A magisterial account of this change in the human body's position in the universe is F. Saxl, 'Microcosm and Macrocosm', in *Selected Lectures* (London, 1957), pp. 58–72. I have briefly explored this neurotic displacement of the centrally placed microcosmic man by late medieval models of the body in Camille, op. cit. n. 48, pp. 62–100.
59. Pouchelle, *Body and Surgery*, pp. 164–7.
60. C. Klapisch Zuber, 'The Genesis of the Family Tree', *I Tatti Studies* 4 (1991), pp. 105–29, points out that the family tree was 'inverted' in this period, having its roots at the top in order to respect the idea that the family descended from a common ancestor. See also her essay 'Le Corps de la parenté', in *Micrologus: Nature, Sciences and Medieval Societies*: I. *Discourses of the Body* (Brepols, 1993), pp. 43–60.
61. J. Kristeva, 'Holbein's Dead Christ', in *Fragments for a History of the Human Body, Part One* (New York, 1989), p. 243.
62. Lotario dei Segni, *De miseria*, pp. 104–5.
63. For the iconography of birth, see L. MacKinney, 'Childbirth in the Middle Ages as seen in Manuscript Illustrations', *Ciba Symposium* 8, nos. 5/6 (1960), pp. 230–6; V. Lehmann, *Die Geburt in der Kunst: Geburtshilfliche Motive in der darstellenden Kunst in Europa von der Antike dis zur Gegenwart* (Brunswick, 1978); D. Alexandre-Bidon and M. Closson, *L'Enfant à l'ombre des cathédrales* (Lyons, 1985); and S. Laurent, *Naître au moyen âge: de la conception à la naissance: la grossesse et l'accouchement, XIIe–XVe siècles* (Paris, 1989).
64. A. Pardailhé-Galabrun, *The Birth of Intimacy: Privacy and Domestic Life in Early Modern Paris* (Oxford, 1991), p. 75, gives a full account of the bed as 'the temple of life' and notes that beds were generally placed near a window, according to inventories made after death. A useful pictorial survey with many medieval examples is H. Juin, *Le Lit* (Paris, 1980).
65. For midwives, see M. Green, 'Women's Medical Practice and Health Care in Medieval Europe', *Signs: Journal of Women in Culture and Society* 14, no. 2 (1989), pp. 434–73.
66. Deschamps, *Oeuvres*, II, p. 259: 'de la douleur de l'enfantement et du cry et brait de l'enfant'.
67. A. J. Schulte, 'Churching of Women', *New Catholic Encyclopedia* (New York, 1908), III, p. 761; F. Lebrun, *La Vie conjugale sous l'ancien régime* (Paris, 1975), p. 123.
68. Bartholomeus Anglicus, *Liber de proprietatibus rerum* (Strasbourg, 1505), Book VI, ch. 5; *On the Properties of Things: John of Trevisa's Translation of Bartholomeus Anglicus* (Oxford, 1975), pp. 300–1. M. Goodich, 'Bartholomeus Anglicus on Childrearing', *History of Childhood Quarterly* 3, no. 1 (1975), p. 77.
69. S. Shahar, *Childhood in the Middle Ages* (London, 1990), pp. 85–7. M. W. Gleason, 'The Semiotics of Gender: Physiognomy and Self-Fashioning in the Second Century C.E.', in *Before Sexuality: The Construction of Erotic Experience in the Ancient Greek World*, ed. D. Halperin, J. J. Winkler and F. I. Zeitlin (Princeton, 1990), pp. 402–6, describes the 'moulding of men'.
70. See the scene of two women wrapping a corpse in a graveyard in London BL MS Add. 25695, fol. 165, reproduced in P. R. Monks, 'The Rolin Master's Hand in London BL MS Additional 25695', in *Medieval Texts and Images: Studies of Manuscripts from the Middle Ages*, ed. M. M. Manion and B. J. Muir (Sydney, 1991), fig. 26.
71. Cited in Huizinga, *Waning*, p. 35.
72. For the Juan of Monzon affair at the University of Paris, see Guenée, *Between Church and State*, pp. 159–69.
73. M. Miles, 'The Virgin's Bare Breast: Female Nudity and Religious Meaning in Tuscan Early Renaissance Culture', in *The Female Body in Western Culture: Contemporary*

Perspectives, ed. S. R. Suleiman (Cambridge, 1986), pp. 196–208.

74. Jacobus de Voragine, *Legend Dorée*, ed. J. B. M. Roze (Paris, 1967), I, p. 423. This story is discussed in detail in Pouchelle, *Body and Surgery*, pp. 80–1.

75. Cited in Kieran Nolan, *The Immortality of the Soul and the Resurrection of the Body According to Giles of Rome* (Rome, 1967), p. 44. See also A. Hewson, *Giles of Rome and the Medieval Theory of Conception* (London, 1975).

76. The theme of Caesarian birth is extensively treated in R. Blumenfeld-Kosinski, *Not of Woman Born: Representations of Caesarian Birth in Medieval and Renaissance Culture* (Ithaca, 1991), where this image is Fig. 7, on p. 66.

Notes to Chapter 3

1. Jean-François Lyotard, 'Lessons in Paganism', in *The Lyotard Reader*, ed. A. Benjamin (Oxford, 1989), p. 126.

2. C. Segre, *Li bestaires d'amours di maistre Richart de Fornival et li response du bestaire* (Milan, 1957).

3. See most recently, R. Potz McGerr, 'Guyat Desmoulins, the Vernacular Master of Histories and his Bible Historiale', *Viator* 14 (1983), pp. 211–45, but see also S. Beger, *La Bible française au moyen âge* (Paris, 1884), pp. 157–99, and S. R. Daly, 'Petrus Comestor: Master of Histories', *Speculum* 32 (1957), p. 71.

4. The terminological distinctions between *histoire* and *enluminure* are discussed in P. Durrieu, 'L'Enlumineur et le miniaturiste', *Comptes rendus Académies des inscriptions et belles-lettres* (1910), pp. 330–46, and J. Gage, 'Lumen, Alluminar, Riant: Three Related Concepts in Gothic Aesthetics', in *Europäische Kunst um 1300: Akten des XXV. Internationalen Kongresses für Kunstgeschichte* 6 (Vienna, 1986), pp. 31–8. See also J. Cerquiglini, 'Histoire, image: accord et discord des sens à la fin du moyen âge', *Littérature* 74 (1989), pp. 110–25.

5. I am relying here on B. Buettner, 'Profane Illuminations, Secular Illusions: Manuscripts in Late Medieval Courtly Society', *Art Bulletin* 74 (1992), p. 82. It was Panofsky, in *Renaissance and Renascences in Western Art* (Uppsala, 1965), who drew attention to what he called 'the principle of disjunction' between past appearances and present ones in representations of classical subjects, which in his view was only overcome in the Renaissance.

6. The best introduction to the genres of history writing in the period is B. Guenée, *Histoire et culture historique dans l'occident médiévale* (Paris, 1980). A major new study by Hedeman, *Royal Image*, provides a framework for understanding this text. The term 'political', as I use it, is also suggested for these illustrations by G. Spiegel, 'Moral Imagination and the Rise of the Bureaucratic State: Images of Government in the Chroniques des Rois de France, Chantilly MS 869', *Journal of Medieval and Renaissance Studies* 18 (1988), pp. 157–73. See also R. Morse, *Truth and Convention in the Middle Ages: Rhetoric, Representation and Reality* (Cambridge, 1991).

7. See R. H. Lucas, 'Medieval French Translations of the Latin Classics to 1500', *Speculum* 45 (1970), pp. 225–33, and J. Monfrin, 'La Connaisance de l'antiquité et le problème de l'humanisme en langue vulgaire dans la France du XVe siècle', *The Late Middle Ages and the Dawn of Humanism Outside Italy*, ed. G. Verbeke (Louvain, 1972), pp. 131–70. For Livy, translated by Pierre Bersuire in 1355 and dedicated to King Jean le Bon, see J. Monfrin, 'La Première Traduction française de Tite-Live', *Bulletin de la Société nationale des antiquaires de France* (1958), pp. 82–5, and the useful study by K. V. Sinclair, *The Melbourne Livy: A Study of Bersuire's Translation Based on the Manuscript in the National Gallery of Victoria* (Melbourne, 1961). For the 'Histoire ancienne', see, for the textual tradition, L. F. Flutre, *Les Manuscrits des faits des romains* (Paris, 1932), and L. F. Flutre and K. Sneyders de Vogel, *Li Fet di romains* (Paris, 1938); and for a study of the illustrative tradition, see D. Oltrogge, *Die Illustrationenzyklen zur 'Histoire ancienne jusqu'à César', 1250–1400* (Frankfurt, 1987), p. 34, and p. 167 for BN fr. 250. For Valerius Maximus, translated by Simon de Hesdin for Charles V (and completed by Nicolas de Gonesse for Jean de Berry in 1404), see D. M. Schullian, 'A Preliminary List of Manuscripts of Valerius Maximus', *Scriptorium* (1966), pp. 81–112.

8. For the circumstances of the translation for Jeanne de Bourgogne, wife of Philippe IV, see L. Delisle, 'Exemplaires royaux et princiers du miroir historial (XIV siècle)', *Gazette archéologique* 11 (1886), pp. 87–101. For the textual tradition, see *Vincent de Beauvais: intentions et réceptions d'une oeuvre encyclopédique au moyen âge*, ed. M. Paulmier-Foucart, S. Lusigan and A. Nadeau (Montreal and Paris, 1990); and for manuscripts, M. C. Duchenne, G. Guzman and J. B. Voorbij, 'Une liste de manuscrits du *Speculum historiale* de Vincent de Beauvais', *Scriptorium* 41 (1987), pp. 286–94. For the tradition of illustrations in the vernacular translation, see C. A. Chavannes-Mazel, 'Expanding Rubrics for the Sake of Layout: Mise-en-page as Evidence for a Particular Scribe', in *Medieval Book Production: Assessing the Evidence*, ed. L. L. Brownrigg (Los Altos Hills, 1990), pp. 117–29.

9. For the text and translation, see R. Potz McGerr, 'Guyart Desmoulins, the Vernacular Master of Histories and the Bible Historiale', *Viator* 14 (1983), esp. pp. 219–20. Paris BN fr. 158, is the second volume of a *Bible historiale*, or *Histoire escolastres* as it was referred to in some inventories, beginning with the Parables of Solomon containing only a single miniature by Remiet, a seated Virgin and Child illustrating the Song of Songs on fol. 26v. The rest of the illuminations are by the Master of the *Livre de Roi Modus et Reine Ratio* (Paris BN fr. 12399). A complete three-volume copy of the text (Soissons, Bib. Mun. MSS 210–12) is illuminated by Remiet and three other artists (see Appendix).

10. A work erroneously known as the *Roman de Sapience* from a scribal error in the first line writing 'Romans' for 'Comens de Sapience, ce est le cremors de Dieu' was partly edited in 1914 at the University of Griefswald; *La Bible von Hermann de Valenciennes*, ed. O. Moldenhauer, H. Burkowitz, E. Kremers, E. Martin and C. A. Strate (the latter listing 29 manuscripts, pp. xviii–xix, none of which bears resemblance to the Morgan copy).

11. For non-royal patrons of history in this period, see F. Autrand, 'Culture et mentalité: les librairies des gens du Parlement au temps de Charles VI', *Annales E.S.C.* 28, no. 5 (1973), pp. 1219–44; D. B. Tyson, 'French Vernacular History Writers and Their Patrons in the Fourteenth Century', *Medievalia et humanistica* 14 (1986), pp. 103–24, and M. H. Tesnière, 'Les Manuscrits copiés par Raoul Tainguy: un aspect de la culture des grands officiers royaux au début du XVe siècle', *Romaria* 107 (1986), pp. 282–323.

12. In some commissions, such as the *Miroir historial*, which has hundreds of miniatures, colour is reduced to a few

yellow and green washes added with a brush. In other cases, such as the *Histoire ancienne*, more money was available for richer golds, blues and reds to be used in the details.

13. These thoughts were stimulated by the important article by P. Saenger, 'Silent Reading: Its Impact on Late-Medieval Script and Society', *Viator* 13 (1982), pp. 385–403, who sees new modes of reading in this period and also links these changes to an increasingly internalized sense of personal identity and authorship.

14. D. Byrne, 'Manuscript Ruling and Pictorial Design in the Work of the Limbourgs, and the Bedford Master', *Art Bulletin* 66 (1984), pp. 118–36, is crucial. He quotes the words of D. V. Thompson at the head of his essay: 'Illumination was built in, with all the forces of *Ingenium*, *Intellectus*, and *Ratio*, not sprinkled on top like candied violets hundreds and thousands on a dish of trifle.'

15. N. F. Regalado, '*Effet de réel, effet du réel:* Representation and Reference in Villon's *Testament*', *Yale French Studies* 70 (1986), p. 74.

16. P. Lacoue-Labarthe, *Typography: Mimesis, Philosophy, Politics* (Cambridge, Mass., 1989), p. 117.

17. Guillaume de Nangis, *Vita Sancti Ludovici*, ed. M. Daunou, *Recueil des historiens des Gaules et de la France*, XX (Paris, 1845), p. 310.

18. Winter, *Bibliothèque*, p. 167. The volume was described as 'couvert de drap de soye damas noir'.

19. For the text, see *Les Grandes Chroniques de France*, ed. J. Viard (Paris, 1920), I, pp. 9–10, and for the Trojan myth of origins, see G. Spiegel, 'Genealogy: Form and Function in Medieval Historical Narrative', *History and Theory* 22 (1983), pp. 43–53.

20. A. Hedeman, 'Valois Legitimacy and Editorial Changes in Charles V's *Grandes Chroniques de France*', *Art Bulletin* 66 (1984), pp. 97–118. C. Raynaud, 'Le Langage et violence dans les enlumineurs des *Grandes Chroniques de France*', *Journal of Medieval History* 17 (1991), pp. 149–70, tells us that of the two hundred chapters of the text, 53 per cent directly treat violence.

21. Hedeman, *Royal Image*, pp. 224–7, attributes fourteen of the miniatures to a sixth hand in the manuscript: 'Perhaps principal artist of BN fr. 823'. Avril, *Librairie de Charles V*, p. 112, no. 195, first drew attention to this artist as 'perhaps identifiable with Remiet'.

22. M. Drogin, *Anathema! Medieval Scribes and the History of Book Curses* (Totowa, N.J., 1983), p. 106.

23. Geremek, *Margins of Society*, p. 53.

24. Shirley, *Parisian Journal*, p. 81.

25. For the relation between public execution and art, see S. Y. Edgerton, *Pictures and Punishment: Art and Criminal Prosecution during the Florentine Renaissance* (Ithaca, 1985), and for humanist interest in corpses, see M. Baxandall, 'Guarino, Pisanello and Crysoloras', *Journal of the Warburg and Courtauld Institutes* 28 (1965), p. 190.

26. Huizinga, *Waning*, p. 23. A valuable discussion of taboos around hanging is Finucane, 'Sacred Corpse', pp. 49–51, who notes that in 1406 the relatives of an executed traitor petitioned the Paris Parlement for permission to bury him in a chapel he had founded and were allowed to collect the pieces of his quartered and decapitated body.

27. Banishment rites are discussed in Geremek, *Margins of Society*, p. 19. For Montaigu's execution, see Tesnière, op. cit. n. 11, p. 321, and for his books, Delisle, *Cabinet des manuscrits*, pp. 59–60.

28. G. W. Coopland, *The Tree of Battles of Honoré Bonet* (Liverpool, 1949), is a useful edition with an introduction.

29. Ibid., p. 79.

30. Remiet's diagram and its political context is reproduced and discussed in Hindman, *Christine de Pizan*, p. 161, fig. 53.

31. The theme of the 'just war' is discussed by N. A. R. Wright, 'The *Tree of Battles* of Honoré Bouvet and the Laws of War', in *War, Literature and Politics in the Late Middle Ages*, ed. C. T. Allman (Liverpool, 1976), pp. 14–16. Until G. Ouy published 'Honoré Bouvet (appelé à tort Bonet)', *Romania* 85 (1959), pp. 255–9, the surname was thought to have been Bonet.

32. Coopland, op. cit. n. 28, Book IV, ch. 1.

33. An overview of the turbulent history of these decades is best presented in English in ch. 12, 'France: Armagnacs and Burgundians, 1380–1422', in *The Cambridge Medieval History*, VII (Cambridge, 1968), pp. 368–92, and in the highly readable account of B. Tuchman, *A Distant Mirror: The Calamitous 14th Century* (London, 1979), especially for the disaster at Nicopolis, pp. 534–81. But see also L. Mirot, *Les Insurrections urbaines du début du règne de Charles VI* (Paris, 1905), and M. Norberg, *Les Ducs et la royauté: études sur le rivalité des ducs d'Orléans et de Bourgogne, 1392–1407* (Stockholm, 1964).

34. This copy of Oresme's translation of Aristotle's *Politiques* (BN fr. 9106) and its companion volume of the *Éthiques* (Chantilly MS 1327) was ordered from Thevenin de l'Angevin along with the *Cité de Dieu* that Remiet illuminated; see Laborde *Ducs de Bourgogne*, p. 116, no. 5703. For the history of the tripartite model, see G. Duby, *The Three Orders: Feudal Society Imagined* (Chicago, 1986); and for iconography, see O. Niccoli, *I sacerdoti, i guerrieri, i contadini: storia di un'immagine della società* (Turin, 1979). For the text of the French translation, see A. D. Menut, *Maistre Nicole Oresme: le livre de politiques d'Aristote*, Transactions of the American Philosophical Society, 60 (1970), p. 302; and for an interpretation of its importance in the history of political thought, see S. M. Babbitt, *Oresme's 'Livre de Politiques' and the France of Charles V*, Transactions of the American Philosophical Society, 75 (1985). The best introduction to the issues around Oresme's translations is, however, C. R. Sherman, 'Some Visual Definitions in the Illustrations of Aristotle's Nicomachean Ethics and Politics in the French Translations of Nicole Oresme', *Art Bulletin* 59 (1977), pp. 320–30, and Sherman, *Imaging Aristotle*, although on pp. 70–71 she attributes the Chantilly MS to 'the Master of the Coronation of Charles V'.

35. The sexpartite Aristotelian scheme in Brussels BR MSS 11201–2, fol. 263r, where the six groups appear compartmentalized in the same order but on a single page is reproduced in L. M. J. Delaissé, *Miniatures médiévales de la librairie de Bourgogne* (Brussels, 1959). As Avril points out in *Librairie de Charles V*, p. 119, no. 204, these volumes provided Remiet with his visual models. This princely prioritization of order and rank is lost in the reproduction of these miniatures in J. Favier, *Paris au XVe siècle, 1380–1500*, Nouvelle Histoire de Paris (Paris, 1974), p. 255, where the two largest groups are placed in the middle of the page with the four smaller ones around them.

36. Foucault, 'Theatrum Philosophicum', in *Language*, p. 172.

37. This is my translation of part of the prologue to Bersuire's translation of Livy made for Jean le Bon before his capture at Poitiers in 1356 and cited in Sinclair, op. cit. n. 7, p. 16.

38. Autrand, op. cit. n. 11. Some of the 'discordance'

between the two cultures, classical and medieval, is noted by Christiane Raynaud, discussing a copy of Livy made for Charles V and now Paris BSteG MS 777: 'Entre texte antique et image médiévale', in *Images et pouvoirs*, pp. 74–86.

39. A. Tuetey, *Journal de Nicolas de Baye, greffier du Parlement in Paris, 1400–1417* (Paris, 1885), p. lxxxj, no. 34.

40. For the ownership of BN fr. 268, recorded in an inscription on fol. 567v, see Delisle, *Cabinet des manuscrits*, I, p. 86, and C. Samaran, 'Pierre Bersuire', *Histoire littéraire de France*, XXXIX (Paris, 1962), p. 406. It contains only Decades III and IV. Remiet's earliest independent work was in the Livy (Bordeaux MS 730); see here Figs. 20–2, and André Masson, 'Le "Tite-Live" de Bordeaux et l'atelier du 'maître aux Boqueteaux', *Tresors des bibliothèques de France* 21 (1936), pp. 11–33. Another complete set of the Decades, illuminated by Remiet in the 1390s, is Paris BN fr. 269–72, which was also in the hands of an important royal patron, Jeanne de Navarre, daughter of Charles VI who married Henry IV of England (Samaran, p. 406). This MS is discussed in relation to a later copy, now in Melbourne, made for Philippe le Hardi's son in 1400, by M. Manion and V. Vines, *Medieval and Renaissance Illuminated Manuscripts in Australian Collections* (London, 1984), pp. 178–9, figs. 183–6.

41. This aspect of the Trajan story is discussed by A. J. Minnis, *Chaucer and Pagan Antiquity* (Cambridge, 1983), pp. 53–5.

42. These thoughts are based upon the important article by L. O. Fradenburg, 'Voice Memorial: Loss and Reparation in Chaucer's Poetry', *Exemplaria* 2 (1990), p. 185, and on M. Bloch, 'Death, Women and Power', in *Death and the Regeneration of Life*, ed. M. Bloch and J. Parry (Cambridge, 1982), pp. 211–30.

43. For suicide, see J.-C. Schmitt, 'Le Suicide au moyen âge', in *La Mort au moyen âge* (Strasbourg, 1977), pp. 49–52, and for the figure of Cleopatra, see B. Taylor, 'The Medieval Cleopatra: The Classical and Medieval Tradition of Chaucer's *Legend of Cleopatra*', *Journal of Medieval and Renaissance Studies* 7 (1977), p. 255.

44. The images in the beautiful manuscript at Troyes have been poorly reproduced and briefly discussed by Raynaud, 'Les Transpositions iconographiques médiévales des actes et faits mémorables de Valere Maxime dans le ms. 261 de la bibliothèque municipale de Troyes', in *Images et pouvoirs*, pp. 87–99.

45. For BN fr. 250, see L. F Flutre, *Les Manuscrits des Faits des romains* (Paris, 1932), pp. 56–7, and Oltrogge, op. cit. n. 7, pp. 34–5. See also B. Guenée,' La Culture historique des nobles: le succès des *Faits des romains*, XIIIe–XVe siècles', in *La Noblesse au moyen âge, XIe–XVe siècles*, ed. P. Contamine (Paris, 1976), p. 268.

46. A. J. Droge, *A Noble Death: Suicide and Martyrdom among Christians and Jews in Antiquity* (San Francisco, 1992).

47. G. Bataille, *The Trial of Gilles de Rais* (Los Angeles, 1991), p. 12.

48. Augustine, *The City of God*, Book XIII, ch. 8, tr. H. Betterson (London, 1984), p. 516.

49. For this fascinating trial, see the documents published by H. F. Delaborde, 'Le Process du chef de saint Denis en 1410', *Mémoires de la Société de l'histoire de Paris et de l'Île-de-France* 11 (1884), pp. 297–409. The Duke of Orléans kissing the entire head of St Denis is described in the Chronicles of the monk of the abbey; see p. 303.

50. The arguments of this paragraph are taken from the important study of the trial by I. Bahr, 'Aussagen zur Funktion und zum Stellenwart von Kunstwerken in einem pariser Reliquien Prozess des Jahres 1410', *Wallraf-Richartz-Jahrbuch* 45 (1984), pp. 41–56, who reproduces the manuscripts of the *Vie de St Denis* from the thirteenth and fourteenth centuries which were used in evidence.

51. These are Maureen Quilligan's words, referring to a lecture by Stephen J. Nichols, in her essay 'Allegory and the Textual Body: Female Authority in Christine de Pizan's *Livre de la Cité des Dames*', in *The New Medievalism*, ed. M. S. Brownlee, K. Brownlee and S. J. Nichols (Baltimore, 1991), pp. 286–91, the only discussion I have found of the powerful images of saints being martyred in BN fr. 313. She also illustrates the scene of St Christine before the idols from the *Miroir historial* in 'The Name of the Author: Self-Representation in Christine de Pizan's *Livre de la Cité des Dames*', *Exemplaria* 4 (1992), pp. 218–19.

52. Two of the three extant volumes of this set, Paris BN fr. 52 and London Lansdowne 1179, are illuminated throughout by Remiet, but the first volume, Rome, Vatican Library, Reg. lat. 538, is illuminated by Jean de Nizières (Fig. 33). See the table of 'Manuscripts of the *Miroir historial*' in the important study by Chavannes-Mazel, op. cit. n. 8, pp. 363–4. In the same volume Serge Lusignan discusses the princely patronage of the text on p. 499.

53. The sexless status of these represented saints in the *Miroir* was pointed out by Quilligan, op. cit. n. 51, p. 287. The voyeuristic private sexuality emergent in early fifteenth-century manuscripts was first noted by Saenger, op. cit. n. 13, p. 413, but has been brilliantly explored for the Valois princes by B. Buettner, 'Dressing and Undressing Bodies in Late Medieval Images', in *Artistic Exchange, XXVIII International Congress of the History of Art* (Berlin, 1994), II, pp. 383–93. My claim about the sexuality of the Duke of Berry, as yet unexplored by scholars, is based not only on Froissart's claims that he kept boy favourites, but on the anal-erotic line-endings of the *Grandes Heures*, which were first brought to my attention by Jean Wirth.

54. Bataille, op. cit. n. 47, p. 36.

55. A brilliant survey of changing attitudes is M. Mollat, *The Poor in the Middle Ages: An Essay in Social History* (New Haven and London, 1986), esp. pt 4: 'Paupers and Beggars: Alarming Presences'. For beggars in manuscripts, see Camille, *Image*, pp. 131–6.

56. For the history of this gesture, also used to depict Idleness in Deguileville's *Pèlerinage de vie humaine*, see S. Koslow, 'Frans Hal's Fisherboys: Exemplars of Idleness', *Art Bulletin* 57 (1975), pp. 418–32. Deschamps incorporated this later passage on the sin of Avarice from *De miseria* (Book II, ch. 6); see *Oeuvres*, II, pp. 267–8.

57. Deschamps, *Oeuvres*, II, p. 268.

58. Mollat, op. cit. n. 55, p. 264.

59. For convenient reference I cite the story as told in Innocent III's treatise; see Lotario dei Segni, *De miseria*, p. 138. The Boucicaut Master sets another version of the story, in which a Jewess is the perpetrator, in a domestic setting; see Meiss, *French Painting*, II, p. 50, figs. 384–6.

60. Muchembled, *Popular Culture and Elite Culture in France, 1400–1750* (Baton Rouge and London, 1985), p. 17. For a study of famine and its effects, see M. Berthe, 'La Famine et la mort dans les campagnes du Royaume de Navarre au XIVe siècle', in *La Mort au moyen âge* (Strasbourg, 1977), pp. 67–80.

61. Deschamps, *Oeuvres*, II, p. 227.

62. P. Guérin, *Archives historiques du Poitou*, XXIV (Poitiers 1893), pp. 299–301.

63. *Chronique du religieux de Saint-Denys*, III, ed. M. L. Bellaguet (Paris, 1841), pp. 730–45. P. Raymond, 'Enquête du prévôt de Paris sur l'assassinat de Louis, duc d'Orléans (1407)', *Bibliothèque de l'École des chartes* 26 (1965), pp. 215–49. The best modern account is now B. Guenée, *Un meutre, une société: l'assassinat du duc d'Orléans, 23 Novembre 1407* (Paris, 1992), pp. 7–8. He reproduces a later fifteenth-century miniature, Paris BN nouv. acq. fr. 4811, fol. 17, which depicts the murder. The statue of Louis at Amiens has also lost its hand (see here Fig. 31).

64. For Jean's propaganda effort to justify his act, which he first claimed was inspired by the devil, but then resulted in four lavish copies of the allegory of the assassination, see Carl Nordenfalk, 'Hatred, Hunting and Love: Three Themes Relative to Some Manuscripts of Jean sans Peur', in *Studies in Late Medieval and Renaissance Painting in Honor of Millard Meiss*, ed. I. Lavin and J. Plummer (New York, 1977), pp. 324–41.

Notes to Chapter 4

1. "Dialogue with Emmanuel Levinas' conducted by Richard Kearney in *Face to Face with Levinas*, ed. R. Cohen (Albany, N.Y., 1986), pp. 23–4.

2. Soutainement et en seursaut
Une veille qui estoit haut
Montee sur mon lit je vi
Dont grandement fu esbahi.
Si m'effrea qi'a li parler
Ne peu ne li riens demander.
Une faus en sa main tenoit
Et i sarclis de fust portoit
Et avoit ja i des pies mis
Pour moi estaindre sur le pis.
Stürzinger, *Pèlerinage*, p. 411, ll. 13, 418–27.

3. These associations of death and the mouth are developed from Pouchelle, *Body and Surgery*, p. 172, and are discussed in more detail in her article 'Une parole médicale prise dans l'imaginaire: alimentation et digestion chez un maître chirurgien du XIVe siècle', in *Actes du colloque 'Pratiques et discours alimentaires au XVIe siecle'* (Paris, 1982), pp. 179–92.

4. 'Voiz ci la Mort qui venue est / Qui des choses terribles est. / La fin et l'aterminement / Ta vie faucher ell'entent / Et metre la tout a declin / Et puis ton cors en son cofin.' Stürzinger, *Pèlerinage*, ll. 13, 432–5.

5. Cited in A. M. Campbell, *The Black Death and Men of Learning* (New York, 1931), p. 60.

6. From the excerpt of Neckham's *De proprietibus rerum* in E. Grant, ed., *A Source Book of Medieval Science* (Cambridge, Mass., 1974), p. 60. The belief is described as one of the 'critical tests of death' by Thomas Browne in *Urne Burial: The Works of Sir Thomas Browne* (Chicago, 1964), p. 160.

7. A wall painting at Rampillon shows death holding the darts of the plague, as does a panel painting in Hanover repoduced in H. H. Mollaret and J. Brossollet, 'La Peste: source méconnue d'inspiration artistique', in *Koninklijk Museum voor Schone Kunsten Jaarboek* (Antwerp, 1965), p. 61.

8. Aristotle, *Problemata*, Book IV, 1, *The Complete Works of Aristotle*, ed. J. Barnes (Princeton, 1984), p. 1350. These issues are discussed in D. Jacquart and C. Thomasset, *Sexuality and Medicine in the Middle Ages* (Princeton, 1988); see also Michel Foucault, *The Use of Pleasure: The History of Sexuality*, II (New York, 1985), pp. 133–5.

9. For death as a female Apocalyptic rider at Notre Dame and in the poem by Helinand de Froidement, *Vers de la mort*, see the dissertation by L. E. Jordan, 'The Iconography of Death in Western Medieval Art to 1350' (Ph.D. University of Notre Dame, 1980). The figure of Atropos, one of the three fates from Italian tradition, was used by Christine de Pisan in her *Épître d'Othéa*; see M. Meiss, 'Atropos-Mors: Observations on a Rare Early Humanist Image', in *Florilegium Historiale: Essays Presented to Wallace K. Ferguson*, ed. J. G. Rowe and W. H. Stockdale (Toronto, 1971), pp. 152–9, and Hindman, *Christine de Pizan*, pp. 114–15. For the Pisa fresco, recently redated to before the Black Death of 1348, see L. Bellosi, *Buffalmacco e il Trionfo della Morte* (Turin, 1974).

10. Erasure of specific themes in manuscript illumination is discussed by Camille, *Gothic Idol*, pp. 21–3, and J. Yarcza Luaces, '*Fascinum*: Reflets de la croyance au mauvais oeil dans l'art médiévale hispanique', *Razo. Cahiers du Centre d'études médiévales de Nice* 8 (1988), pp. 113–27. In another issue of this journal (6, 1986), see J.-C. Schmitt, 'Les Masques, le diable, les morts dans l'Occident médiévale', pp. 87–119.

11. Still fundamental for the development of this whole realm of imagery is É. Mâle, *L'Art religieux de la fin du moyen âge en France*, 5th ed. (Paris, 1949), pp. 347–89, and R. van Marle, *Iconographie de l'art profane au moyen âge et à la Renaissance* (The Hague, 1932), II, pp. 361–414. Much of the vast literature on the Dance of Death, to be discussed later, deals with the appearance of the Three Living and the Three Dead theme. Most useful are H. Rosenfeld, *Der mittelalterliche Totentanz*, 3rd ed. (Cologne, 1974), and P. Chihaia, 'Le Roman de Barlaam et Joasaph et l'origine de "la rencontre des trois vifs et des trois morts"', in *Immortalite et decomposition dans l'art du moyen âge* (Madrid, 1988), pp. 40–69. C. Blum, 'Recherches sur les fonctions épistémologiques d'une représentation allégorique: l'exemple de l'apparition en occident de l'allégorie de la mort en squelette', *Journal of Medieval and Renaissance Studies* 15 (1985), pp. 13–27.

12. According to Avril, *Librairie de Charles V*, p. 119, no. 205.

13. D. Menut, ed., *Le Livre de éthiques d'Aristote* (New York, 1940), Book VI, ch. 5, p. 337, and Sherman, *Imaging Aristotle*, pp. 124–8, for a superb account of Prudence.

14. R. Barthes, *Camera Lucida: Reflections on Photography* (New York, 1981), p. 15.

15. Cited in the biography of Pierre D'Ailly (1351–1420) by Guenée, *Between Church and State*, p. 141.

16. J. Agrimi and C. Crisciani, 'Savoir médical et anthropologie religieuse: les représentations et les fonctions de la *vetula* (XIIIe–XVe siècle)', *Annales E.S.C.* 48 (1993), pp. 1281–1309.

17. Deschamps, *Oeuvres*, II, pp. 264–5.

18. Bernard of Gordon's treatise from early fourteenth-century Montpellier describes the face of the old person 'looking like the face of a monkey'; see L. Demaitre, 'The Medical Notion of "Withering" from Galen to the Fourteenth Century: The Treatise on Marasmu by Bernard of Gordon', *Traditio* 47 (1992), p. 280.

19. For this important royal manuscript, now in Besançon, which also contains a prose version of Innocent III's *De miseria condicionis humane*, see here Chapter 2, note 7, and P.

Courcelle, *La Consolation de philosophie dans la tradition littéraire* (Paris, 1967), p. 83, fig. 31.

20. M. McVaugh, 'The Humidum Radicale in Thirteenth-Century Medicine', *Traditio* 30 (1974), p. 281.

21. These sources are discussed in a valuable article by T. S. Hall, 'Life, Death and the Radical Moisture: A Study of Thematic in Medieval Medical Theory', *Clio Medica* 6 (1971), pp. 3–23. For old age in general, see M. M. Sheehan, ed., *Aging and the Aged in Medieval Europe* (Toronto, 1990), with articles by L. Demaitre, 'The Care and Extension of Old Age in Medieval Medicine', pp. 3–23, and P. Osmund Lewry, 'Study of Aging in the Arts Faculty of the Universities of Paris and Oxford', pp. 23–39, and the larger picture presented by G. Minois, in *History of Old Age: From Antiquity to the Renaissance* (Chicago, 1989). See also S. Shahar, 'The Old Body in Medieval Culture', in *Framing Medieval Bodies*, ed. S. Kay and M. Rubin (Manchester, 1994), pp. 160–87.

22. See A. G. Little and E. Withington, *Rogeri Baconi De retardatione incidentium senectutis* (Oxford, 1928), pp. xxxix–xlii. See also A. Paravicini Bagliani, 'Rajeunir au moyen âge: Roger Bacon et le mythe de la prolongation de la vie', *Revue médicale de la suisse romande* 106 (1986), pp. 9–23.

23. L. Hansmann and L. Kris Rettenbeck, *Amulet und Talisman: Erscheinungsform und Geschichte* (Munich, 1961), and J. Riddle, 'Lithotherapy in the Middle Ages', *Pharmacy in History* 12 (1970), pp. 39–50. For some of the stones used by Jeanne de Bourbon, see A. Brachet, *Pathologie mentale des rois de France* (Paris, 1903), pp. 594–7.

24. A start has been made by A. Wallert, 'Alchemy and Medieval Art Technology', in *Alchemy Revisited: Proceedings of the International Conference on the History of Alchemy at the University of Groningen*, ed. Z. R. W. M. von Martels (Leiden, 1990), pp. 154–9, and M. M. Gauthier, 'Iris, le peintre et l'alchimiste du savoir-faire au style', in *Pigments et colorants de l'antiquité et du moyen âge: teinture, peinture, enlumineure études historiques et physico-chimiques* (Paris, 1990), pp. 59–65.

25. The best iconographic study is E. Sears, *The Ages of Man: Medieval Interpretations of the Life Cycle* (Princeton, 1986). That the old played an essential role in late medieval political society is argued by Guenée, *Between Church and State*, pp. 30–5.

26. *Les Faictz et dictz de Jean Molinet*, ed. N. Dupire (Paris, 1936), I, ll. 337–40.

27. Sears, op. cit. n. 25, p. 131, n. 49, and figs. 67–70.

28. A. Varagnac, *Civilization traditionelle et genres de vie* (Paris, 1948), p. 244, and N. Zemon-Davis, 'Some Tasks and Themes in the Study of Popular Religion', in *The Pursuit of Holiness in Late Medieval and Renaissance Religion*, ed. C. Trinkaus (Leiden, 1974), p. 327.

29. See G. Piegnot, *Catalogue d'une partie des livres composant la bibliothèque des ducs de Bourgogne* (Dijon, 1341), p. 32, and P. de Winter, 'The *Grandes Heures* of Phillip the Bold', *Speculum* 57 (1982), p. 813. This is also the only scholarly discussion I know of the effects of old age upon the output of a medieval illuminator, in this case the Coronation Master, still at work in the 1370s, pp. 796–7. For eyeglasses in manuscript illuminations, see Meiss, *French Painting*, I, figs. 296–7, and for an earlier example, see J. S. Neaman, 'The Mystery of the Ghent Bird and the Invention of Spectacles', *Viator* 24 (1993), pp. 189–203.

30. Meiss, *French Painting*, III, lists the Brussels manuscript under three illuminators: the Master of Berry's Cleres Femmes (p. 374), the Master of the Cité des Dames (p. 378) and the Virgil Master (p. 408). The manuscript is fully described in C. Gaspar and F. Lyna, *Les Principaux Manuscrits à peintures de la Bibliothèque royale de Belgique* (Paris, 1937–47), pp. 446–8, no. 189, where it is noted that the borders and grotesques are particularly magnificent.

31. For the illuminator Petrus Gilberti, who signed his name in another manuscript, London BL Royal 15.D.III, fol. 15v, see G. Dogaer, 'Petrus Gilberti, een vroeg-vijftiende-eeuws Frans verluchter', *Archives et Bibliothèques de Belgiques* 38 (1967), pp. 117–19. It was L. M. J. Delaissé, *Medieval Illuminations from the Library of Burgundy in the Department of Manuscripts of the Royal Library of Belgium* (Geneva, 1959), pp. 96–9, who made the point that blanks were left in the borders for the painting of the monsters, a new workshop practice that can be seen in later fifteenth-century manucripts like the Hours of Catherine of Cleves; see R. G. Calkins, 'Stages of Execution: Procedures of Illumination as Revealed in an Unfinished Book of Hours', *Gesta* 17 (1978), pp. 61–70.

32. For the ape and old age, see Demaitre, op. cit. n. 18, p. 280.

33. M. Foucault, *Birth of the Clinic: An Archeology of Medical Perception* (New York, 1975), p. 166.

34. *Chirurgie de maître Henri de Mondeville, 1306–1320*, ed. E. Nicaise (Paris, 1893), p. 199.

35. Geremek, *Margins of Society*, p. 175.

36. I am indebted in this whole section to the work of Marie-Christine Pouchelle, especially her book *Body and Surgery*, which examines attitudes to the body through the writings of Henri de Mondeville; but see also her article directly touching on the issue of the status of doctors relative to priests, 'La Prise en charge de la mort: médecine, médecins et chirurgiens devant les problèmes liés à la mort à la fin du moyen âge, XIIIe–XVe siècles', *Archives européennes de sociologie* 17 (1976), pp. 249–78.

37. P. Kibre, 'The Faculty of Medicine at Paris: Charlatanism and Unlicensed Medical Practices in the Later Middle Ages', *Bulletin of the History of Medicine* 27 (1953), pp. 1–20; T. G. Sistrunk, 'The Function of Praise in the Contract of a Medieval Public Physician', *Journal of the History of Medicine* 48 (1993), pp. 320–33.

38. For a contemporary's account of Charles VI's madness, see *Chronique du religieux de Saint-Denys*, ed. M. L. Bellaguet (Paris, 1840), II, pp. 87–91. The association between the fool in Psalm 52 and the madman is made in D. J. Gifford, 'Iconographical Notes Towards the Definition of the Medieval Fool', *Journal of the Warburg and Courtauld Institutes* 37 (1974), pp. 330–9.

39. These remedies are discussed in G. Dodu, 'La Folie de Charles V', *Revue historique* (1926), pp. 184–7. The execution of the two Augustinian hermits is described in *Chronique du religieux de Saint-Denys* (see n. 38), p. 664; and for Salmon's accusations of witchcraft, see P. Salmon, *Les Demandes faites par le roi Charles VI touchant son état et le gouvernement de sa personne*, ed. G. A. Crapelet (Paris, 1833), p. 55. Yet another theory of Charles's madness links it to magic and alchemy at the court; D. Ravel, *L'Oeuvre royale de Charles VI: symbolique alchimique et mystère royal* (Paris, 1984).

40. *Ordonnances des rois de France*, 5, ed. L. Secousse (Paris, 1736), p. 530.

41. The Chantilly manuscript's eighteen full-page illustrations are reproduced in full in E. Wirkersheimer, *Anatomies de Mondino dei Luzzi et de Guido de Vigevano* (Paris, 1926), but see also his 'Les Premières Dissections à la

Faculté de médicine de Paris', *Bulletin de la Société de l'histoire de Paris et de l'Île-de-France* 37 (1910). For early dissection, see N. G. Siraisi, *Medieval and Early Renaissance Medicine: An Introduction to Knowledge and Practice* (Chicago, 1990), pp. 86–90. I disagree with Robert D. Romanyshyn's analysis of Vigevano's dissected corpse, which he argues is a depiction of a 'dead body' and not yet a depiction of 'corpse', which will appear only in Renaissance anatomical illustrations; see *Technology as Symptom and Dream* (London, 1989), pp. 120–7. However, his discussion of how 'the corpse, in hiding death from us, is our grim image of life' is pertinent to themes I shall explore here in Chapter 5.

42. See A. M. Campbell, *The Black Death and Men of Learning* (New York, 1931), p. 61. The most exhaustive study is J. N. Biraben, *Les Hommes et la peste*, 2 vols. (Paris, 1975–6).

43. This text is discussed in R. Muchembled, *Popular Culture and Elite Culture in France, 1400–1750* (Baton Rouge and London, 1985), pp. 156–7.

44. M. Meiss, *Painting in Florence and Sienna after the Black Death* (Princeton, 1951), is the best example of this urge to find post-traumatic stress in art, and a work that has recently been reassessed in the light of wills and practices of the period by S. K. Cohn, Jr., *The Cult of Remembrance and the Black Death: Six Renaissance Cities in Central Italy* (Baltimore, 1992), pp. 271–80. R. S. Gottfried makes the strange claim that the Black Death killed off so many English illuminators that 'the English could not maintain their standards in this special art form'; *The Black Death: Natural and Human Disaster in Medieval Europe* (New York, 1983), p. 91. D. Williams, 'Fourteeth-Century Iconography of Death and the Plague', in *The Black Death: The Impact of the Fourteenth-Century Plague*, ed. D. Williman (Binghamton, N.Y., 1982), challenges the assumption of 'an essential link' between art and the epidemic. The best study in English of the epidemic itself is still P. Zeigler, *The Black Death* (New York, 1969), which treats Paris on pp. 77–9. The only near-contemporary depictions of the Black Death in manuscript illumination occur in the Annals of Giles de Muisit of Tournai, of 1353 (Brussels BR MSS 13076–7); see *Die Parler und der Schöne Stil, 1350–1400* (Cologne, 1978), III, pp. 73–5.

45. P. Chaunu, *La Mort à Paris, 16e, 17e, 18e siècles* (Paris, 1978), p. 36. See also M. Mollat, 'Notes sur la mortalité à Paris au temps de la peste noire d'après les comptes de l'oeuvre de Saint-Germain-l'Auxerrois', *Le Moyen Age* 69 (1963), pp. 506–14.

46. I am indebted here to the study of Job in late medieval culture by B. N. Sarent-Baur, *Brothers of Dragons: 'Job dolens' and François Villon* (New York, 1990), pp. 35–41.

47. See G. van der Osten, 'Job and Christ: The Development of a Devotional Image', *Journal of the Warburg and Courtauld Institutes* 16 (1953), pp. 153–8, and C. D. Cuttler, 'Job–Music–Christ: An Aspect of the Iconography of Job', in *Miscellanea in Memoriam Paul Coremans (1908–1965)*, in *Bulletin de l'Institut royal du patrimoine artistique* 15 (1975), pp. 87–94. Remiet completed at least four related depictions of Job: first in 1382 in the *Lay de la fragilité humaine* (Fig. 26), twice in the Soissons *Bible historiale*, MS 211, fol. ccxxvi (rubbed) (Fig. 29) and fol. cxxxvi (Fig. 81), and in the Manchester breviary (Fig. 110).

48. Aiez pictié, aiez pictié de moy,
A tout le moins, s'i vous plaist, mes amis!
En fosse gis, non pas soubz houz ne may,
En cest exil ouquel je suis transmis.

See B. Sargent-Baur, pp. 72–6, for a complete analysis of Villon's poem, written while in prison in 1461, in terms of its echoes of Job.

49. Shirley, *Parisian Journal*, p. 85.

50. Ibid., p. 131.

51. M. de Certeau, *The Practice of Everyday Life* (Berkeley, 1984), p. 194.

52. This is one of the documents discussed by J. Chiffoleau, *Comptabilité*, p. 119, n. 109.

53. See the Italian miniature of a dying man making his will in a Justinian manuscript, Turin, Biblioteca Nazionale MS E I 8, in G. Bologna, *Illuminated Manuscripts: The Book Before Gutenberg* (New York, 1988), p. 113.

54. A. Tuetey, *Testaments enregistrés au Parlement de Paris sous le règne de Charles VI* (Paris, 1880), p. 347.

55. For the testament, see F. Autrand, *Charles VI: la folie du roi* (Paris, 1986), pp. 378–9.

56. A. Boinet, *Les Églises parisiennes: moyen âge et Renaissance* (Paris, 1958), p. 219. Antoine is named as one of fourteen *libraires* in the 1368 document; see Delalain, *Librarie parisien*, p. 44.

57. *Le Respit de la mort par Jean Le Fèvre*, ed. G. Hasenohr-Esnos (Paris, 1969).

58. Ibid., pp. 195–7, l. 3078. The 'bourgeois de Paris' records that 'in this year 1424 the Danse macabre was made at the Innocents. It was begun about August and finished in the following Lent.' Le Roux de Lincy and Tisserand, *Paris*, use printed images from Guyot Marchant's 1486 edition, but for the text, see E. F. Chaney, *La Danse macabré des charniers des Innocents à Paris* (Manchester, 1945), discussed in J. M. Clark, *The Dance of Death* (Glasgow, 1953); and P. Vaillant, 'La Danse macabre de 1485 et les fresques du charnier des Innocents', in *La Mort au moyen âge: colloque de l'Association des historiens médiévistes français réunis à Strasbourg* (Strasbourg, 1977). The vast general literature on this theme includes S. Cosacchi, *Makabertanz: der Totentanz in Kunst, Poesie und Brauchtum des Mittelalters* (Meisenheim am Glan, 1965), and Rosenfeld, op. cit. n. 11, but I have profited most from two articles by Jane Taylor, 'Un Miroir salutaire', in *Dies Illa: Death in the Middle Ages: Proceedings of the 1983 Manchester Colloquium*, ed. J. H. M. Taylor (Manchester, 1984), pp. 29–43, and 'Danse Macabré and Bande Dessinée: A Question of Reading', *Forum for Modern Language Studies* 25 (1992), pp. 356–69.

59. Zemon-Davis, op. cit. n. 28, p. 331.

60. Chaney, op. cit. n. 58, pp. 46, 52. Jean Batany has emphasized the rigid social hierarchy of the dance as an alternative image of 'social order' in 'Les "Danses macabres": une image en negatif du fonctionalisme social', in *Dies Illa* (see n. 58), pp. 15–26. Women, excluded from the public dance eventually had their own manuscript version in *The Danse Macabre of Women*, ed. A. T. Harrison and S. Hindman (Kent, Ohio, 1994).

61. The marriage in the *Pèlerinages*, Paris BN fr. 823, fol. 6v, is reproduced in *Fastes du gothique*, p. 339, no. 294. The 'Anonymous Questiones on the Decretals' in Oxford, St John's College MSS 197–8 has only one remaining initial (the rest having been cut out), which shows a tiny marriage scene in an 'O' initial; J. J. G. Alexander and E. Temple, *Illuminated Manuscripts in Oxford College Libraries* (Oxford, 1986), no. 746.

62. C. Caspers, 'The Role Played by the People in the Liturgy According to the Synodal Statutes of the Ancient Dioceses of Cambrai, Liège and Utrecht, *c.*1300–*c.*1500', in *Omnes Circumstantes: Contributions towards a History of the Role of the People in the Liturgy*, ed. C. Caspers and M.

Schneiders (Kampen, 1990), pp. 155–69.

63. M. W. Bloomfield, *The Seven Deadly Sins* (Ann Arbor, 1952). For the individual's conscience become an agent of social control in the Paris reliefs, see Camille, *Gothic Idol*, pp. 12–14.

64. Deschamps, *Oeuvres*, II, pp. 271–2, ch. XIX.

65. There is a superb example in the Musée Historiques des Tissus, Lyons, which belonged to Charles de Blois. The best discussion of the radical changes in late fourteenth-century costume is S. M. Newton, *Fashion in the Age of the Black Prince: A Study of the Years 1340–1365* (Woodbridge, Suffolk, 1990).

66. See *Les Pleurants dans l'art du moyen âge en Europe* (Musee des Beaux-Arts de Dijon, 1971).

67. Deschamps, *Oeuvres*, II, pp. 288–9.

68. R. C. Famiglietti, *Royal Intrigue: Crisis at the Court of Charles VI, 1392–1420* (New York, 1986). Sandra Hindman argues that the miniature of Bouvet presenting his *L'Apparition maistre Jehan de Meun* to Valentine of Orléans (Paris BN fr. 811, fol. 1v), is a direct response to and a representational repudiation of these sorcery charges, in its focus on the wrongly accused biblical Susanna. For this miniature and one in the same manuscript showing her standing with a physician, see Hindman, *Christine de Pizan*, pp. 164–9, figs. 66–7.

69. For the importance of preaching at court and in Paris generally, see D. C. Brown, *Pastor and Laity in the Theology of Jean Gerson* (Cambridge, 1987), pp. 11–55.

70. Censorship at the court is discussed in an interesting article by S. Delaney, 'Mothers to Think Back Through: Who are They? The Ambiguous Example of Christine de Pizan', in *Medieval Texts and Contemporary Readers*, ed. L. A. Finke and M. B. Schictman (Ithaca, 1987), pp. 177–201. For the text of Christine's *Livre du corps de policie*, see Meiss, *French Painting*, I, p. 3.

71. On memory and its relation to images, see M. Carruthers, *The Book of Memory: A Study of Memory in Medieval Cullture* (Cambridge, 1990), and for the allegorical figure as she appears in Deguileville's poem, see S. K. Hagen, *Allegorical Remembrance* (Athens, Ga., and London, 1990), pp. 86–105. The 'ars moriendi' and the 'ars memorativa' are closely linked; see the full bibliography in N. F. Palmer, 'Ars moriendi und Totentanz: Zur Verbildlichung des Todes im Spätmittelalter', in *Tod im Mittelalter* (Constance, 1993), pp. 330–4.

NOTES TO CHAPTER 5

1. M. Blanchot, *The Space of Literature* (Lincoln, Neb., and London, 1989), p. 256.

2. Lotario dei Segni, *De miseria*, p. 204. For the French version in Deschamps's *Lay de la fragilité humaine* (BN fr. 20029, fol. 15v), see Deschamps, *Oeuvres*, II, pp. 282–3.

3. J. Derrida, 'Economimesis', *Diacritics* 11 (1981), p. 23, discusses the tension between aesthetics and disgust. In another poem Deschamps describes Hell as something that is too disgusting for even the most melancholy artist to depict; *Oeuvres*, IV, no. 810: 'Li cruex d'enfer n'est mie, plus hideux; De le veir seroit on hors du sens, Car peintre n'est tant melencolieux.'

4. K. Park, 'The Sensitive Corpse: Body and Self in Renaissance Medicine', in *Fenway Court, 1990–1991* (Boston, 1992), pp. 77–87, and her 'The Life of the Corpse: Division and Dissection in Late Medieval Europe', *Journal of the History of Medicine* 50, no. 1 (1994), pp. 111–32.

5. L. Vincent Thomas, *Le Cadavre: de la biologie à l'anthropologie* (Brussels, 1980), and P. Camporesi, *The Incorruptable Flesh* (Cambridge, 1988).

6. E. Wickersheimer, *Dictionnaire biographique des médecins en France au moyen âge* (Paris, 1936), I, pp. 246–7. For the tomb of Harcigny, see É. Mâle, *Religious Art in France: The Late Middle Ages* (Princeton, 1987), p. 356. For the text of his testament, see M. Thillois, 'Étude biographique de Guillaume de Harcigny', *Bulletin de la Société académique de Laon* 6 (1856), and *L'Homme et la mort autrefois à Laon* (Musée de Laon, 1995), pp. 31–2. The best work on the *transi* tomb is K. Cohen, *Metamorphosis of a Death Symbol: The Transi Tomb in the Late Middle Ages and the Renaissance* (Berkeley, 1983), but see also A. Tenenti, *Il senso della morte e l'amore della vita nel Rinascimento* (Turin, 1957), pp. 139–84, and P. M. King, 'The Cadaver Tomb in England: Novel Manifestations of an Old Idea', *Church Monuments: Journal of the Church Monuments Society* 5 (1990), pp. 26–37. Ariès, *Hour of Our Death*, p. 118, states enigmatically that the geographic distribution of *transi* tombs to Northern Europe 'coincides almost perfectly with the practice of covering the dead. Macabre iconography exists in those places where the face was concealed.' Good general histories of the subject are E. Panofsky, *Tomb Sculpture: Four Lectures on its Changing Aspects from Ancient Egypt to Bernini* (New York, 1964), and K. Bauch, *Das mittelalterliche Grabbild: Figürliche Grabmäler des 11. bis 15. Jahrhunderts in Europa* (Berlin and New York, 1976).

7. I am following the translation of Cohen, op. cit. n. 6, p. 104, who suggests that the reference to 'simple form' for the body and the soul is like the 'simple substance' of alchemical terminology: 'For what consists of pure and simple substance remains incorruptable in eternity.' As the same author points out, Harcigny was familiar with alchemy, having written a treatise on the properties of precious stones.

8. This is Cohen's argument, op. cit. n. 6, pp. 101–2. The problem of discussing Flamel is that so much of the evidence of his writings, including his *Hieroglyphical Figures* used by this author to argue for alchemical interpretations, dates from the period of his mythic recreation in the seventeenth and eighteenth centuries.

9. A. M. Morgenstern, 'The La Grange Tomb and Choir: A Monument of the Great Schism in the West', *Speculum* 48 (1973), p. 62.

10. St John Chrysostom, 'Homily on the Transferral of Martyrs' Relics', in *Texte der Kirchenväter*, ed. Alfons Heilman (Munich, 1964), III, p. 426, is cited and translated in the stunning exposition of death and subjectivity in Northern Renaissance art, which stimulated so much of my own thought: Joseph Leo Koerner, 'The Mortification of the Image: Death as Hermeneutic in Hans Baldung Grien', *Representations* 10 (1985), p. 53.

11. Aristotle, *Poetics: The Complete Works of Aristotle*, ed. J. Barnes (Princeton, 1984), p. 2318. St Augustine, *Confessions*, tr. H. Chadwick (Oxford, 1991), Book X, ch. 35, p. 211.

12. This was in 1407. For this fascinating will, see M. L. H. Labande, 'Testament du cardinal P. Blau', *Annales du Midi* 7 (1895), p. 19. For more examples of testators urging speedy burial, see the indispensable study of Avignon deaths in Chiffoleau, *Comptabilité*, p. 123.

13. H. Phillipeau, 'Textes et rubriques des *Agenda Mortuorum*', *Archiv für Liturg* 4 (1955), p. 63. This and other useful references to the fear of burial alive can be found in Finucane, 'Sacred Corpse', pp. 41–3.
14. See Camille, *Gothic Idol*, pp. 87–101.
15. Cited in D. Catherine Brown, *Pastor and Laity in the Theology of Jean Gerson* (Cambridge, 1987), p. 241. Gerson was significant in the controversy surrounding the *Roman de la Rose*, manuscripts of which contain many nude figures; see Camille, *Gothic Idol*, pp. 320–5.
16. Boniface VIII, Bull of 27 September 1200, in G. Digard, ed., *Les Registres de Boniface VIII: receuil des bulles de ce pape publiées ou analysées d'après les manuscrits originaux des archives du Vatican* (Paris, 1884–1939), II, cols. 576–7, no. 3409. Medieval embalming processes are described in E. von Rudloff, *Über das Konservieren von Leichen im Mittelalter: ein Beitrag zur Geschichte der Anatomie und der Bestattungswesens* (Freiburg, 1921). Fundamental to this issue is the deservedly famous article by Brown, 'Death and the Human Body', pp. 229–72. See also the response by F. Santi, 'Il cadavre e Bonifacio VIII, tra Stefano Tempier e Avicenna: Intorno a un saggio di Elizabeth Brown', *Studi medievali* 28, no. 2 (1987), pp. 861–78. Park, op. cit. n. 4, has argued that the Pope's abhorrence represents an Italian expression of discomfort with what were specifically Northern funerary customs.
17. Huizinga, *Waning*, p. 144; Brown, 'Death and the Human Body', p. 251.
18. Details discussed in P. Barker, *Vampires, Burial and Death: Folklore and Reality* (New Haven and London, 1988), p. 106.
19. See M. M. Malvern, 'An Earnest "Monyscyon" and "thinge Delectabyll" Realized Verbally and Visually in "A Disputacion Betwyxt the Body and Wormes": A Middle English Poem Inspired by Tomb Art and Northern Spirituality', *Viator* 13 (1982), pp. 415–43, and F. Wormald, 'Some Popular Miniatures and Their Rich Relations', *Miscellanea pro arte: Festschrift für Hermann Schnitzler* (Düsseldorf, 1975), pp. 279–85.
20. These examples are cited in Pouchelle, *Body and Surgery*, p. 170, nn. 52, 55.
21. L. Thorndike, *A History of Magic and Experimental Science* (New York, 1923–58), II, p. 737.
22. H. Platelle, 'La Voix du sang: le cadavre qui saigne en présence de son meutrier,' in *La Piété populaire au moyen âge: actes du 99e congrès national des Sociétés savantes* (Paris, 1977), pp. 161–79.
23. Durandus, *Rationale divinorum officiorum*, Book VII.xxxv (Naples, 1859), pp. 705–7. Philippe Ariès, *Essais sur l'histoire de la mort en occident du moyen âge à nos jours* (Paris, 1975), p. 25.
24. J. Derrida, 'Roundtable on Autobiography', in *The Ear of the Other: Otobiography, Transference, Translation* (Lincoln, Neb., and London, 1985), p. 57.
25. *The Summa Theologica of St Thomas Aquinas: Third Part (Supplement)*, qq. 69–86, art. 20 (London, 1921), pp. 39–73.
26. The point about late medieval culture was made by A. N. Galpern, 'Late Medieval Piety in Sixteenth-Century Champagne', in *The Pursuit of Holiness in Late Medieval and Renaissance Religion* (Leiden, 1974), p. 149. In this section I have depended heavily upon a series of useful studies of death ritual, mostly focused on Books of Hours; R. S. Wieck, *Time Sanctified: The Book of Hours in Medieval Art and Life* (Baltimore, 1988), pp. 124–36, is the best general introduction. M. Meiss, 'La Mort et l'office des morts à l'époque du Maitre de Boucicault', *Revue de l'art* 1 (1968), pp. 17–25; F. Arne, 'Les Images de la mort dans les livres d'heures, 13ème–15ème siècles', *La Maison Dieu* 145 (1981), pp. 127–48; G. C. Fiero, 'Death Ritual in Fifteenth-Century Manuscript Illumination', *Journal of Medieval History* 10 (1984), pp. 271–94; and most recently G. Bartz and E. König, 'Die Illustration des Totenoffiziums in Studenbüchern', in *Im Angesicht des Todes: Ein interdisziplinäres Kompendium* (St Ottilien, 1987), I, pp. 487–528.
27. This etymology discussed by Thomas Aquinas in his *Summa*, qq. 69–74, art. 11 (see n. 25), is explored in the context of Portraiture by R. Recht, 'Le Portrait et le principe de réalité dans la sculpture: Phillipe le Bel et l'image royale', in *Europäische Kunst um 1300: 25th International Congresses für Kunstgeschichte*, VI (Vienna, 1986), pp. 189–201.
28. J. Legrand, *Archiloge Sophie: livre des bones moeurs*, ed. E. Beltran (Paris, 1986), ch. 24. The translation is B. Buettner's, from 'Profane Illuminations, Secular Illusions: Manuscripts in Late Medieval Courtly Society', *Art Bulletin* 74 (1992), p. 79.
29. Durandus, *Rationale*, VII.xxxv, discussed in G. Rowell, *The Liturgy of Christian Burial: An Introductory Survey of the Historical Development of Christian Burial Rites* (London, 1977), p. 67.
30. For the *pannum* and its importance in wills, see Chiffoleau, *Comptabilité*, pp. 132–3.
31. A. Tuetey, *Testaments enregistrés au parlement de Paris sous le règne de Charles VI* (Paris, 1880), p. 374.
32. For these figures and their importance, especially in funerary sculpture, see *Les Pleurants dans l'art du moyen âge en Europe* (Musée des Beaux-Arts de Dijon, 1971), and Raynaud, 'Quelques remarques sur les cérémonies funéraires à la fin du moyen âge', in *Images et Pouvoirs*, p. 45.
33. E. A. R. Brown, 'The Ceremonial of Royal Succession in Capetian France: The Funeral of Philip V', *Speculum* 55 (1980), pp. 286–7. For a royal funeral more contemporary with Remiet himself, see Y. Grandeau, 'La Mort et les obséques de Charles VI', *Bulletin philologique et historique* (1970), pp. 157–8.
34. Christiane Raynaud's interpretation of this scene as a literal contrast between a low birth and elevated end seems far too literal; see 'Les Transpositions iconographiques médiévales des actes et faits mémorables de Valere Maxime dans le ms. 261 de la bibliothèque municipale de Troyes', in *Images et pouvoirs*, p. 91.
35. Paris BN nouv. acq. fr. 7112, fol. 260r, discussed in C. Beaune, 'Mourir noblement à la fin du moyen âge', in *La Mort au moyen âge* (Strasbourg, 1977), p. 129. Beaune describes the effigy proper as appearing between 1403 and 1422, but it seems to have been used much earlier in England, for example at the funeral of Edward II in 1327, where there were practical reasons for avoiding the display of the very messed up real thing. For more analysis of royal ceremonies and effigies, see R. A. Giesey, *The Royal Funeral in Renaissance France* (Geneva, 1960), pp. 19–21, and A. Erlande-Brandenburg, *Le Roi est mort: étude sur les funérailles, les sépultres et les tombeaux des rois de rance jusqu'à la fin du XIIIe siècle* (Geneva, 1975).
36. This source and much more on these issues of veiling and revealing the royal corpse can be found in Brown, 'Death and the Human Body', p. 268. For a miniature showing Jean le Bon's funeral with a death mask, see Bauch, op. cit. n. 6, p. 271.

37. Documents published by M. Vallet de Vireville, 'Jean d'Orléans et Colart de Laon, Peintres, 1385–1408', *Archives de l'art français* 9 (1857–8), p. 181.
38. E. H. Kantorowicz, *The Kings Two Bodies: A Study in Medieval Political Theology* (Princeton, 1957), pp. 383–450, which E. Panofsky uses to describe the 'double' effigies showing rotting corpse and ideal status in fifteenth-century tombs in *Tomb Sculpture* (New York, 1964), pp. 64–5. For a miniature of the funeral procession of Charles V's wife, Jeanne de Bourbon, painted in the *Grandes Chroniques* which Remiet also put his hand to in the 1370s, see C. R. Sherman, *The Portraits of Charles V of France, 1338–1380* (New York, 1969), pl. 36, and the same author's discussion 'The Queen in Charles V's "Coronation Book": Jeanne de Bourbon and the "Ordo ad Reginam Benedicendam"', *Viator* 8 (1977), pp. 288–9.
39. Chiffoleau, *Comptabilité*, pp. 134–5.
40. For this and other examples of mourning dress, see A. Franklin, *La Vie privée d'autrefois: les magasins de nouveautés* (Paris, 1895), p. 31, as well as L. Taylor, *Mourning Dress: A Costume and Social History* (London, 1983), p. 65.
41. Cited in Pouchelle, *Body and Surgery*, p. 253.
42. Geremek, *Margins of Society*, pp. 173–4, discusses the leper-houses in Paris, but see also F. Beriac, *Histoire des lépreux au moyen âge* (Paris, 1988).
43. E. Martène, *De antiquis ecclesiae ritibus* (Antwerp, 1788), I, p. 361, *ordo* IV, and examined by Finucane, 'Sacred Corpse', p. 55.
44. For the text, see the edition by K. A. Strate, *De l'Assomption Nostre Dame von Hermann de Valenciennes* (Greifswald, 1913), p. 39. C. Andronikof, 'La Dormition comme type de mort chrétienne', in *La Malade et la mort du chrétien dans la liturgie* (Rome, 1975), pp. 9–13, describes how the mother of God's 'triumph' over death and her immediate reception into heaven were crucial to the ecclesiastical notion of death as 'issue, exoce, passage, transit'. For the pictorial tradition, see K. Schreiner, 'Der Tod Marias Inbegriff christlichen Sterbens', in *Tod im Mittelalter* (Constance, 1993), pp. 261–312.
45. For Jews in fourteenth-century Paris, see J. Favier, *Paris au XVe siècle, 1380–1500*, Nouvelle Histoire de Paris (Paris, 1974), p. 80, and M. Roblin, *Les Juifs de Paris: démographie, économie, culture* (Paris, 1952). For the ascription of ritual acts of host desecration and cannibalism to Jews in the later Middle Ages, see G. I. Langmuir, *History, Religion and Antisemitism* (Berkeley, 1990), and A. Dundes, ed., *The Blood Libel Legend: A Casebook of Anti-Semitic Folklore* (Madison, 1991), and the useful remarks and much more extensive bibliography given in K. Biddick 'Genders, Bodies, Borders: Technologies of the Visible', *Speculum* 68 (1993), pp. 402–9.
46. J. Lacan, *Le Sémainaire:* III: *Le Psychoses, 1955–6* (Paris, 1981), p. 111. One might also think here of Andre Bazin's remark in 'The Ontology of the Photographic Image', in *What is Cinema?* (Berkeley, 1967), p. 12, that 'if the plastic arts were put under psychoanalysis, the practice of embalming the dead might turn out to be a fundamental factor in their creation'.
47. St Augustine, *The City of God*, Book I, ch. 13, tr. H. Bettenson (London, 1984), p. 22.
48. Cited in Brown, 'Death and the Human Body', p. 251, n. 118.
49. Ariès, *Hour of Our Death*, p. 113. See also M. Ragon, *The Space of Death: A Study of Funerary Architecture, Decoration, and Urbanism* (Charlottesville, Va., 1983), p. 137, 'Death as Urban Spectacle'. The best discussion of cemeteries is Chiffoleau, *Comptabilité*, pp. 154–77.
50. For the Paris cemetery, see Le Roux de Lincy and Tisserand, *Paris*, p. 183. Friar Richard's preaching is described by the eyewitness account of the 'bourgeois de Paris'; Shirley, *Parisian Journal*, p. 230. Another useful source with pictures is M. Fleury and G.-M. Leproux, *Les Saints Innocents* (Paris, 1990), pp. 37–54.
51. See *Description de la ville de Paris au XVe siècle par Guillebert de Metz*, ed. A. Le Roux de Lincy (Paris, 1855), p. 61.
52. Huizinga, *Waning*, p. 149.
53. Part of this change in attitude was owing to work undertaken by historians, not of medieval, but of Early Modern and Reformation thought, notably R. Scribner, 'Interpreting Religion in Early Modern Europe', *European Studies Review* 13 (1983), pp. 89–105, and the whole revival in the study of 'popular religion': J.-C. Schmitt, 'Religion populaire et culture folklorique', *Annales E.S.C.* 31, no. 5 (1976); A. Gurevich, *Medieval Popular Culture* (Cambridge, 1988).
54. For the cemetery of Saint Séverin, see the short but penetrating analysis by R. E. Etlin, *The Architecture of Death: The Transformation of the Cemetery in Eighteenth-Century Paris* (Cambridge, Mass., 1984), pp. 10–11, fig. 6. For the story of the dead coming to the aid of the living, recorded by a fifteenth-century monk, see R. Muchembled, *Popular Culture and Elite Culture in France, 1400–1750* (Baton Rouge and London, 1985), pp. 63–4.
55. Meiss, *French Painting*, III, pp. 125–6, figs. 467–8.
56. Here the work of Elizabeth R. Brown proves invaluable: see her 'Phillipe le Bel and the Remains of St. Louis', *Gazette des Beaux-Arts*, 6th ser., 95 (1980), pt 1, pp. 175–82, which reproduces a miniature showing the disinterment on p. 177, and more generally, 'Burying and Unburying the Kings of France', in *Persons in Groups: Social Behaviour and Identity Formation in Medieval and Renaissance Europe*, ed. R. C. Trexler (Binghamton, N.Y., 1985), pp. 241–66.
57. For the chapel of the Duke of Orléans at the Célestins, see Le Roux de Lincy and Tisserand, *Paris*, p. 539, and the reproduction of the tomb from a drawing facing p. 542. For animals associated with funerary art, see M. Pastoureau, 'Le Bestiare des morts: présence animale sur les monuments funéraires, Xe–XIXe siècles', in *La Figuration des morts dans la chrétienté médiévale jusqu'à la fin du premier quart du XIVe siècle*, Cahiers du Fontevraud, I (1988), pp. 124–37.
58. For another miniature showing a building, this time at the orders of a king, see the *Miroir historiale* (Paris BN fr. 312, fol. 338v), which is wrongly attributed to Raolet d'Orléans (who was a scribe not an illuminator) in M. Warnke, *Bau und Uberbau: Sociologie der mittelalterliche Architektur nach den Schriftquellen* (Frankfurt, 1982), p. 212, fig. 10. For another mislabelled miniature of the archetypal vain building, the Tower of Babel in Remiet's *Cité de Dieu* (Paris BN fr. 171, fol. 135), see H. Minkowski, *Vermütungen über den Turm zu Babel* (Freren, 1991), fig. 87. Miniaturization is brilliantly discussed in S. Stewart, *On Longing: Narratives of the Miniature, the Gigantic, the Souvenir, the Collection* (Baltimore, 1984), pp. 37–50.
59. See B. Drake Boehm, 'Valerius Maximus in a Fourteenth-Century French Translation: An Illuminated Leaf', *Metropolitan Museum Journal* 18 (1983), p. 57.
60. Deschamps, *Oeuvres*, VIII, p. 201; translation from Huizinga, *Waning*, p. 169.

61. For other examples of illuminators stressing 'the inferior formulicity of the manufactured object' in representations of statues, see Camille, *Gothic Idol*, pp. 67–8. For Jean Gerson's attacks on idolatrous new image-types, see M. Glorieux, *Oeuvres complètes* (Paris, 1968), VII, p. 963.

62. Michel Serres, *Statues: le second livre des fondations* (Paris, 1987), and *L'Hermaphrodite: Sarasine sculpteur* (Paris, 1987), pp. 106–7, articulates a profound exploration of the association between three-dimensionality and death. I have also found useful the discussion by Kenneth Gross, 'The Death of Sculpture', in his *The Dream of the Moving Statue* (Ithaca, 1992), pp. 20–4.

63. J. Guiffrey, *Inventaires de Jean Duc de Berry, 1401–1416* (Paris, 1894), I, p. clxix, no. 18, p. 226, no. 858: 'Item, un autre livre en françois, appellé *Ranconnal* historié au commencement d'un pape, de l'église et de la synagogue; couvert de cuir rouge empraint.' See also the List of Berry's Extant Manuscripts in Meiss, *French Painting*, I, p. 312. The frontispiece was copied by Remiet from that in an earlier exemplar, Paris, Bibl. de l'Arsenal MS 2002; see H. Martin and P. Lauer, *Les Principaux Manuscrits à peintures de Bibliothèque de l'Arsenal* (Paris, 1929), p. 29, pl. XXV.

64. Durandus's text and ecclesiastical colours are discussed by M. Pastoureau, 'L'Église et la couleur des origines à la réforme', *Bibliothèque de l'École des chartes* 147 (1989), pp. 220–3.

65. BN fr. 176, fol. 7v. An edition of the Latin text is under way by P. Gy and P. Avril. J. M. Neale and B. Webb, *The Symbolism of Churches and Church Ornaments: A Translation of the Rationale Divinorum Officiorum Written by William Durandus* (New York, 1893), is still the only English translation of this crucial text available apart from excerpts. See pp. 42–5 for these passages. Good introductions to the author's exegetical strategies are in the *Dictionnaire de droit canonique*, V (Paris, 1953), cols. 1014–45, and J. F. White, 'Durandus and the Interpretation of Christian Worship', in *Contemporary Reflections on the Medieval Christian Tradition*, ed. G. H. Shiver (Durham, N.C., 1974), pp. 41–52. Another interesting reference in this section is where Durandus compares 'painters and practitioners of the mechanical arts' to professors of the liberal arts who seek in their work to understand the causes and laws behind the world of things. But here theory and practice would seem to diverge, since in this manuscript as in most others Remiet was not devising or analyzing anything, but simply copying from an earlier model. Although he provides small historiated initials of liturgical scenes for the second book, dealing with ministers of the church, and the third, which deals with vestments, in this vernacular version, made for a wordly prince, most of his effort goes into two elaborate miniatures representing the consecration with holy oils, not of bishops, but of a king and queen, special additions made by the French translator, on fol. 28r: Coronation of a king by bishop; fol. 31v: Coronation of a queen. This emphasis upon the royal liturgy follows the presentation copy made for the Duke of Berry's brother, Charles V, in 1374, BN fr. 437; see Sherman, op. cit. n. 38, p. 14.

66. See Neale and Webb, op. cit. n. 65, pp. 83–6.

67. Abbé Lebeuf, *Histoire de la ville et de tout le diocèse de Paris* (Paris, 1883), I, p. 107.

68. See I. Bahr, 'Aussagen zur Funktion und zum Stellenwart von Kunstwerken in einem Pariser Reliquienprozess des Jahres 1410', *Wallraff-Richartz-Jahrbuch* 45 (1984), pp. 41–56; discussed here in Chapter 2.

69. E. Le Roy Ladurie, *Montaillou: The Promised Land of Error* (New York, 1979), p. 32. On the increasing transparency of relics in 'display containers', see H. Belting, *The Image and its Public in the Middle Ages: Form and Function of Early Paintings of the Passion* (New York, 1990), pp. 82–3. For relics in general, see, in addition to Ariès, *Hour of Our Death*, pp. 29–35, the useful survey by N. Hermann-Mascard, *Les Reliques des saints: formation coutumière d'un droit* (Paris, 1975).

70. Shirley, *Parisian Journal*, p. 356. This relic, much revered, especially by women in childbirth, was later kept at the Sainte Chapelle. See H. Denifle, *La Désolation des églises en France* (Paris, 1897–1900), I, p. 167. In the twelfth century Guibert of Nogent attacked as distasteful the veneration of the holy prepuce, then treasured at St John Lateran in Rome and at the abbey of Charroux near Poitiers; *Patrologia Latina* 156, col. 659.

71. J. Kristeva, 'Holbein's Dead Christ', in *Fragments for a History of the Human Body*, Part I (New York, 1989), p. 241.

72. Deschamps, *Oeuvres*, I, p. 271, *ballade* 'Contre ceux qui jurent Dieu'.

73. Kristeva, op. cit. n. 71, p. 262, discussing the 1522 painting by Hans Holbein the Younger of the body of the dead Christ in the tomb, which is wrongly described as a 'rare, if not unique achievement'. Gilles Deleuze also describes 'the death of God' as the dissolution of the self: 'God's tomb is also the tomb of the self'; *The Logic of Sense* (New York, 1990), p. 294. The tradition of showing Christ dead in the tomb was not uncommon, especially in the North in the late Middle Ages where there are carved life-size representations used in Easter services; see Easter Sepulchre effigy of Christ from the Church of Weinhausen reproduced in Ulla Haastrup, 'Medieval Props in the Liturgical Drama', *Hafnia: Copenhagen Papers in the History of Art*, no. 11 (1987), p. 141, fig. 9.

74. J. J. Stürzinger, ed. *Le Pèlerinage de Jésus-Christ de Guillaume de Deguileville* (London, 1987), p. 381.

75. The iconography of the feast and its entry into liturgical books are covered in M. Rubin, *Corpus Christi: The Eucharist in Late Medieval Culture* (Oxford, 1991), pp. 196–8, who notes that 'the elevation of the mass, already the favourite choice for the canon of the mass', was 'the most widespread choice' for breviaries, citing that made for Charles V in 1380, BN lat. 1052, fol. 157.

76. See J. A. Jungmann, *The Mass of the Roman Rite: Its Origins and Development* (New York, 1950), II, pp. 266–7, and O. B. Hardison, *Christian Rite and Christian Drama in the Middle Ages* (Baltimore, 1965), p. 70. For the rite, see P. Batifol, *History of the Roman Breviary* (London, 1912), p. 166. For the iconography of altar/tomb, see B. Lane, *The Altar and the Altarpiece: Sacramental Themes in Early Netherlandish Painting* (New York, 1984), pp. 50–9.

77. There is an excellent analysis of these complex theological debates in C. Walker Bynum, 'Material Continuity, Personal Survival and the Resurrection of the Body: A Scholastic Discussion in its Medieval and Modern Contexts', in *Fragmentation and Redemption: Essays on Gender and the Human Body in Medieval Religion* (New York, 1991), pp. 253–65, and Elizabeth E. R. Brown, 'Authority, the Family, and the Dead in Late Medieval France', *French Historical Studies* 16 (1990), pp. 803–32.

78. Here I am in agreement with Bynum, who in her critique of Leo Steinberg's book *The Sexuality of Christ in Renaissance Art and in Modern Oblivion* (New York, 1983) describes how, rather than seeing the resurrection as 'triumph over body', she sees instead 'life coming from

death, of significance located in body, of pain and suffering as the opportunity – even the cause – of salvation'; C. Bynum, 'The Body of Christ in the Later Middle Ages: A Reply to Leo Steinberg', in *Fragmentation and Redemption* (see n. 77).

Notes to Chapter 6

1. J. Derrida, *Aporias* (Stanford, 1993), p. 76.
2. J. Duvernoy, ed. *Le Registre d'Inquisition de Jacques Fournier*, I (Toulouse, 1965), p. 261.
3. For Lazarus's fear, see Chastellain, *Le Pas de la mort*, VI, in *Oeuvres de Georges Chastellain*, ed. M. Le baron Kervyn de Letterhove, VI (Brussels, 1864), pp. 49–65, and for a text popular in the later fifteenth century recounting his experiences between death and resurrection, see T. Kren, 'Some Illuminated Manuscripts of the *Vision of Lazarus* from the Time of Margaret of York', in *Margaret of York, Simon Marmion and 'The Visions of Tondal'*, ed. T. Kren (Malibu, 1992), pp. 141–56.
4. For the papal prohibition of raising the dead, see Chiffoleau, *Comptabilité*, p. 399.
5. Finucane, 'Sacred Corpse', p. 41.
6. Chiffoleau reminds us in an interesting section on 'revenants' that 'they are one of the essential phenomena for understanding death in the Middle Ages'; *Comptabilité*, p. 399. See the full study by J.-C. Schmitt, *Les Revenants: les vivants et les morts dans la société médiévale* (Paris, 1994).
7. T. F. Crane, *The Exempla; or, Illustrative Stories from the Sermones Vulgares of Jacques de Vitry* (London, 1890), p. 12.
8. W. Durand, *Expicatio divinorum officiorum*, cap. CLXI (Naples, 1859), pp. 844–6, and Finucane, 'Sacred Corpse', p. 43.
9. Chiffoleau, *Comptabilité*, p. 109, gives examples of fear, citing the fourteenth-century Dominican Jean Gobi's pronouncement, in his article *Mors* that 'we should fear death for multiple reasons'.
10. In BN fr. 823 Remiet painted seventy-one miniatures for the story of the pilgrimage of life and fifty-seven for that of Christ's pilgrimage; this last part of the trilogy to be written and decorated was given over to another shop, and Oudin de Cavarnay left only nine spaces for miniatures which were completed by the Virgil Master. The rubric on the first page of BN fr. 823, illuminated by Remiet, tells us 'Cy comence le livre du pèlerinage de vie humaine, de jhesuchrist et de l'âme', which changes the usual order of the trilogy, which puts Christ's pilgrimage last. Also the date of completion of the work, 29 April 1393, occurs at the end of the *Ame* on fol. 168v, suggesting that the original order was later changed in binding.
11. J. J. Stürzinger, ed., *Le Pèlerinage de l'âme de Guillaume de Deguileville* (London, 1895), ll. 23–4.
12. Notions of *spiritus* are explored in an international colloqnium, *Spiritus*, ed. M. Fattore and M. Bianchi (Rome, 1984). The art-historical aspect of the idea of the soul has received very little attention, but see for now J. Baschet, 'Anima', in *Encyclopedia dell'arte medievale*, I (Rome, 1991), pp. 804–15. For the tiny soul flying down to the Virgin at the conception/Annunciation, see J. B. Friedman, 'Nicolas's "Angelus ad Virginem" and the Mocking of Noah', *Yearbook of English Studies* 22 (1992), pp. 162–80.
13. See M. Camille, 'Illustrations in Harley MS 3487 and the Perceptions of Aristotle's *Libri naturales* in Thirteenth-Century England', in *England in the Thirteenth Century: Proceedings of the 1984 Harlaxton Symposium*, ed. M. W. Ormrod (Harlaxton, 1985), p. 39.
14. Stürzinger, *Pèlerinage*, ll. 5814–20.
15. For this tradition, see R. W. Ackerman, 'The Debate of the Body and Soul and Parochial Christianity', *Speculum* 37 (1962), pp. 541–65. Jean Beleth, *Summa de ecclesiasticis officiis*, ed. H. Duteil, *Corpus Christianorum continuatio medievalis* 41 A (Turnhout, 1971), p. 317: 'Before the body is washed or wrapped in a winding sheet, the priest or his vicar should go to the place where it lies, and, with holy water and an outpouring of prayers, invoke the saints and pray to them to receive [the body's] soul and transport it to a place of joy. There are, in fact, some souls that are perfect, which, as soon as they leave the body, fly at once to the heavens. There are others entirely wicked, which fall immediately to hell. There are others, in the middle, for which a recommendation of this sort must be made.'
16. Jean-Luc Nancy, *The Birth to Presence* (Stanford, 1993), p. 15.
17. E. Brayer, 'Notice du manuscrit 574 de la Bibliothèque municipale de Cambrai, suivie d'une édition des sermons français de Pierre d'Ailly', in *Notices et extraits des manuscrits de la Bibliothèque nationale et autres bibliothèques*, XLIII (Paris, 1965), pp. 280–1.
18. Le Goff, *The Birth of Purgatory* (Chicago, 1981), p. 292. Many of these remarks have also benefited from A. J. Gurevich, 'Popular and Scholarly Medieval Cultural Traditions: Notes in the Margins of Jacques Le Goff's Book', *Journal of Medieval History* 9 (1983), pp. 71–89. A wonderful new resource for the iconography of Purgatory is the exhibition catalogue *Himmel Hölle Fegefeuer: Das Jenseits im Mittelalter*, ed. P. Jezler (Zurich, 1994), especially the essay by Jezler himself, 'Jenseitsmodelle und Jenseitsvorsorge – Eine Einführung', pp. 13–27.
19. See Le Goff, op. cit. n. 18, p. 28. The text of the poem can be found in the edition by Stürzinger, op. cit. n. 11, ll. 1–17, and conveniently in a new edition of the Middle English prose version edited by R. Potz McGerr, *The Pilgrimage of the Soul: A Critical Edition of the Middle English Dream Vision* (New York and London, 1990), I.
20. A list of obituary masses and other donations of individuals in Remiet's parish is given in M. A. Molinier, *Obituaires de la province de Sens*, I (Paris, 1902), 862–9. The church is also discussed by J. Avril, 'La Paroisse médiévale et la prière pour les morts', in *L'Église et la mémoire des morts dans la France médiévale*, ed. J. L. Lemaitre (Paris, 1986), p. 6203. For England there is an excellent study by J. T. Rosenthal, *The Purchase of Paradise: The Social Function of Aristocratic Benevolence, 1305–1485* (London, 1972).
21. D. Sicard, *La Liturgie de la mort dans l'église latine des origines à la reforme carolingienne: Liturgiewissenschaftliche Quellen und Forschungen* (Munster, 1978), p. 217; P. Sheingorn, 'The Bosom of Abraham Trinity: A Late Medieval All Saints Image', in *England in the Fifteenth Century: Proceedings of the 1986 Harlaxton Conference*, ed. D. Williams (Woodridge, Suffolk, 1987); J. Baschet, 'Medieval Abraham: Between Fleshly Patriarch and Divine Father', *Modern Language Notes* 108 (1993), pp. 738–58.
22. Jean Baudrillard, *Symbolic Exchange and Death* (London, 1993), p. 145.
23. For this response, 'Libera me domine de morte aeterna in die illa tremenda', etc., see R. J. Herbert, *Corpus*

antiphonarum officii (Rome, 1965–8), II, p. 718, and for its history and development, see G. Rowell, *The Liturgy of Christian Burial: An Introductory Survey of the Historical Development of Christian Burial Rites* (London, 1977), p. 67.

24. For this prayer, see V. Leroqais, *Les Livres d'heures: manuscrits de la Bibliothèque nationale* (Paris, 1927), I, p. xxvii, and R. Wieck, *Time Sanctified: The Book of Hours in Medieval Art and Life* (Baltimore, 1988), pp. 103–4.

25. See the discussion of the Great Schism and the Apocalypse in L. Ackerman Smoller, *History, Prophecy and the Stars: The Christian Astrology of Pierre d'Ailly, 1350–1420* (Princeton, 1994), pp. 92–5.

26. Best covered in C. Walker Bynum, 'Material Continuity, Personal Survival and the Resurrection of the Body: A Scholastic Discussion in its Medieval and Modern Contexts', in *Fragmentation and Redemption: Essays on Gender and the Human Body in Medieval Religion* (New York, 1991), pp. 253–97, and her book, *The Resurrection of the Body* (New York, 1994). These issues are also discussed in R. Grant, 'The Resurrection of the Body', *Journal of Religion* 28 (1948), pp. 120–30; K. Nolan, *The Immortality of the Soul and the Resurrection of the Body According to Gilles of Rome* (Rome, 1967); and P. Camporesi, *The Incorruptible Flesh* (Cambridge, 1988).

27. The statue metaphor is from Augustine, *Enchiridion*, ch. 23, par. 89, Corpus Christianorum: Series latina 46, ed. E. Evans (Turnhout, 1969), p. 97. But as C. Bynum points out (*The Resurrection of the Body* (New York, 1994), p. 404), those who adopted the new Aristotelian identity theory tended to reject the statue analogy, arguing that the reforged statue has a totally new form.

28. These arguments are discussed in H. I. Marrou, *The Resurrection and Saint Augustine's Theology of Human Values* (Villanova, 1966), pp. 25–9.

29. For a full and fascinating account of Last Judgement imagery, see the new study by J. Baschet, *Les Justices de l'au-delà: les représentations de l'enfer en France et en Italie, XIIe–XVe siècles* (Rome, 1993).

30. Lotario dei Segni, *De miseria*, p. 214.

31. Deschamps, *Oeuvres*, II, pp. 297–8, ll. 573–90.

Lors aront toute dolour,
Grant puour
Et grant plour
Et estrainture de dens,
Angoisse et toute tristour,
Grant temblour
Et ardour
Et divers gemissemens,
Hullemens,
Faim, soif et toute langour;
Des ce jour
Sans sejour
Seront tristes et dolens.
Trop horible yert leur clamour
En ce four;
Tenebrour
Sera toudis la dedenz
Ou ils sentiront chalour
Et froideur
A leur tour;
Aront vermine et serpens;
Tout tourmens
Feront avec eulx demour
Sans retour,
En paour:
C'est de Dieu li jugemens.

32. For the iconography of Hell, see D. D. R. Owen, *The Vision of Hell: Infernal Journeys in Medieval French Literature* (Edinburgh, 1970), and for the mouth in particular, see M. Camille, 'Mouths and Meanings: Towards an Anti-Iconography of Medieval Art', in *Iconography at the Crossroads*, ed. B. Cassidy (Princeton, 1993), pp. 98–107, and P. Sheingorn, 'Who can open the doors of his face?': The Iconography of the Hell Mouth', in *The Iconography of Hell*, ed. C. Davidson and T. H. Seiler (Kalamazoo, Mich., 1993). Another essay I have found useful in emphasizing 'a basic allegorical principle: the individual's actions and their significance are inscribed on his body and become legible there (Hell)', is R. M. Durling, 'Deceit and Digestion in the Belly of Hell', in *Allegory and Representation* (Baltimore, 1981), pp. 72–3; and see also Maureen Kupstas, 'The Monster, Death, Becomes Pregnant': Images of Hell and the Virgin in the Hours of Catherine of Cleves', *Chicago Art Journal* 3, no. 1 (1993), pp. 1–8.

33. D. Catherine Brown, *Pastor and Laity in the Theology of Jean Gerson* (Cambridge, 1987), p. 193.

34. A. Green, 'The Dead Mother', in *On Private Madness* (London, 1986), p. 162.

35. See N. Abraham and M. Torok, 'The Pain of Mourning and the Fantasy of the Exquisite Corpse', in *The Shell and the Kernel: Renewals of Psychoanalysis*, ed. N. T. Rand (Chicago, 1994), p. 121.

36. M. Blanchot, *The Space of Literature* (Lincoln, Neb., and London, 1982), p. 124.

37. Richard de Bury, *Philobiblon*, ed. M. Maclagan (Oxford, 1960), p. 147.

38. These words are taken from S. Beckwith, *Christ's Body: Identity, Culture and Society in Late Medieval Writings* (London and New York, 1993), pp. 40–1, which has been invaluable in thinking through this image, along with her article on a particular female subject, 'A Very Material Mysticism: The Medieval Mysticism of Margery Kempe', in *Medieval Literature, Ideology and History*, ed. D. Aers (Brighton, 1986), pp. 34–57. The theological supremacy of the crucifixion in this period is also underlined by C. Walker Bynum, ' The Body of Christ in the Later Middle Ages: A Reply to Leo Steinberg', in *Fragmentation and Redemption* (see n. 26), p. 343, n. 83, and discussed in V. Gillespie, 'Strange Images of Death: The Passion in Later Medieval English Devotional Writing', in *Zeit, Tod und Ewigkeit in der Renaissance Literatur*, Analecta Cartusiana, CXVII (1987), pp. 111–57.

39. The book that started the controversy was L. Steinberg, *The Sexuality of Christ in Renaissance Art and in Modern Oblivion* (New York, 1983), and see also the response by Bynum, op. cit. n. 38, pp. 79–119. Other important discussions include J. Wirth, 'Sur l'evolution du crucifix à la fin du moyen âge', *Les Ateliers des intereprètes: revue européene pour étudiants en histoire de l'art* 2 (1989), p. 177, who argues that Jesus hanging on the cross without genitalia referred to the virginal clergy and that the generative organs were considered 'ridiculous and ugly'. For a view arguing for a distinctly differentiated male and female response to the subject, see R. C. Trexler, 'Gendering Jesus Crucified', in *Iconography at the Crossroads*, ed. B. Cassidy (Princeton, 1993), pp. 107–19.

40. These cases are discussed in Camille, *Gothic Idol*, pp. 212–13.

41. R. de Lespinasse and F. Bonnardot, *Les Métiers et corporations de la ville de Paris, XIIIe siècle: le 'Livre des métiers' d'Étienne Boileau* (Paris, 1879), LXI, pp. 127–8. The reference to not destroying images refers to 'Peintres et Tailleurs d'ymages' in general, LXII, p. 130: 'Nule fause ouevre del mestier devant dit estre arse pour les reverances des Sains et des Saintes en qui ramenbrances elles sont faites.'

42. Camille, *Gothic Idol*, p. 213, and R. Howard Bloch, *The Scandal of the Fabliaux* (Chicago, 1986), p. 61, discuss a *fabliau* about a crucifix-maker.

43. In a Book of Hours, Vienna ONB cod. 1969, Remiet represented the crucifixion as part of the Throne of Mercy Trinity type but not separately; see H. J. Hermann, *Franzözischen und iberische Handschriften der erste Hälfte des XV. Jahrhunderts* (Leipzig, 1938), p. 87, pl. XXVII, and D. Thoss, *Französische Gotik und Renaissance in Meisterweken der Buchmalerei* (Graz, 1978), pp. 87–8, no. 11.

44. See J. H. Shennan, *The Parlement of Paris* (Ithaca, 1968), p. 106.

45. Beckwith, op. cit. n. 38, p. 56, describes how images of the crucifixion 'in late medieval reproductions and imitations *are* the very origin of sacrality; they are also, however, the place where divinity is systematically debased, humiliated and degraded, where the sacred, by lending itself to the humanity that degrades it, traduces its own nature in profanation'.

46. British Museum, *Reproductions from Illuminated Manuscripts: Fifty Plates*, Series V (London, 1965) p. 18, no. xxx. The arms of Rolin appear impaled by those of Marie des Landes, who was his second wife, not his first, as stated in this publication. For further details on Rolin's life and books, see *Le Livre au siècle des Rolin* (Autun, 1985), where the London Hours go unmentioned. Although he could have obtained the book later, it is entirely possible, since he worked for patrons of Remiet like Philippe le Hardi, that Rolin was the book's original owner.

47. A. Hagopian van Buren, 'The Canonical Office in Renaissance Painting, Part II: More About the Rolin *Madonna*', *Art Bulletin* 60 (1978), pp. 617–33. Panofsky's exposition of the relations between manuscript painting and panel painting in this period, *Early Netherlandish Painting: Its Origins and Character* (Cambridge, Mass., 1953), is still fundamental, although see p. 51 for his assessment of Remiet's generation as second rate.

48. J. J. G. Alexander, 'The Limbourg Brothers and Italian Art: A New Source', *Zeitschrift für Kunstgeschichte* 46 (1983), p. 434.

49. L. Lumpkin, 'The Sheriff of Not: A Short History of the Diagonal', *Art Issues* (Sept./Oct. 1994), p. 20. I am grateful to Lisa Pincus for this reference.

50. A. Heimann, 'Der Meister der 'Grandes Heures de Rohan' und seine Werkstatt,' *Städel Jahrbuch*, 7–8, (1932), pp 57–8, draws many comparisons between the miniatures in BN fr. 823 and the Rohan master's work.

51. Meiss, *French Painting*, III, pp. 271–2.

52. M. Jay, *Downcast Eyes: The Denigration of Vision in Twentieth-Century French Thought* (Berkeley, 1993), with an interesting discussion of the Middle Ages, pp. 31–41. He cites the anti-visual writings of the modern Catholic writer Jacques Ellul, *The Humiliation of the Word* (Grand Rapids, 1985), who argues that the negative effects of ocularcentrism came about as a response to the Great Schism and other crises in the fourteenth century (p. 41).

53. This is the argument of S. Burke, *The Death and Return of the Author: Criticism and Subjectivity in Barthes, Foucault and Derrida* (Edinburgh, 1992), p. 170.

54. Huizinga, *Waning*, p. 169.

55. Ibid., pp. 146–9.

56. For Wilhelm Dilthey, death alone imposes unity on a person; see his *Das Erlebnis und die Dichtung: Lessing, Goethe, Novalis, Hölderlin* (Leipzig, 1922), p. 230. Philippe Ariès, *Hour of Our Death*, followed Edgar Morin's Freudian argument that death and individuality are inextricably linked, in *L'Homme et la mort* (Paris, 1951). The most recent French philosopher to tackle the problem, though with a great deal of reference to Heidegger, is Jacques Derrida, who in op. cit. n. 1 has some interesting criticisms of the historians of death. He argues that 'because Ariès did not ground his research in an ontological elucidation of what death is and signifies, he knows neither what he is talking about nor how to determine the problematic closure of his domain' (p. 46).

57. H. Weinmann, 'Mort du genre, genre de mort', in *La Mort du genre* 2 (Montreal, 1989), p. 157.

58. M. Brunet-Weinmann, 'The Scythe, The Scales, and the Palette: AIDS and the Rupture of Representational Strategies', in *Fluid Exchanges: Artists and Critics in the AIDS Crisis*, ed. J. Miller (Toronto, 1992), pp. 146–62. Robert Farber is one contemporary artist living with AIDS who has used medieval visual forms and parallels with the Black Death to make important political statements; see M. Camille, 'Death and the Mirror in the Western Blot Series', in Robert Farber, *If I Only Had Time*, exh. cat., Artist's Space (New York, 1992).

59. Douglas Crimp, ed., 'AIDS: Cultural Analysis / Cultural Activism', *October* 43 (1987), p. 5.

60. In addition to works by Derrida and Crimp just cited, recent explorations of death in critical theory are J. Baudrillard, *Symbolic Exchange and Death* (London, 1993), originally published in French in 1976; S. Koffman, *Mélancolie de l'art* (Paris, 1985); S. Pfohl, *Death at the Parasite Cafe: Social Science (Fictions) and the Postmodern* (New York, 1992); E. Bronfen, *Over Her Dead Body: Death, Femininity and the Aesthetic* (Manchester, 1992); *Death and Representation*, ed. S. Webster Goodwin and E. Bronfen (Baltimore, 1993), pp. 10–12. Historians too have been unable to resist these issues – notably S. Schama, *Dead Certainties: Unwarranted Speculations* (New York, 1991), which examines two bodies, 'one embalmed in eulogy, the other grusomely dismembered'. Art historians who have made contributions to the iconography of death seem less willing to explore philosophical issues, with the exception of J. L. Koerner, 'The Mortification of the Image: Death as a Hermeneutic in Hans Baldung Grien', *Representations* 10 (1985), pp. 51–101; M. Bal, *Death and Dissymmetry: The Politics of Coherence in the Book of Judges* (Chicago, 1990); and Georges Didi-Huberman, 'Ce que nous voyons, ce qui nous regarde', *Cahiers du Musée national d'art moderne* 37 (1991), pp. 53–84.

61. G. Duby, *William Marshall: The Flower of Chivalry* (New York, 1985), p. 7. Duby had at his disposal a long thirteenth-century *chanson* about his subject of 'one hundred and twenty-seven parchment leaves', later published in three volumes by P. Meyer, *Histoire de Guillaume le Maréchal* (Paris, 1891–1901). Stephen Greenblatt begins his *Shakespearean Negotiation: The Circulation of Social Energy in Renaissance England* (Berkeley, 1986), p. 1, with the words, 'I began with a desire to speak with the dead'. By contrast, in the end, I would rather see them.

INDEX

Figure numbers are in Italic

'A' Master, the, 249
Abraham, 170, 228
Adam, 66–7, 75, 175; *39*; and Abel, 175; and Eve, 58, 62, 78–80, 101, 176; *23, 36–8*
ages of man, 144; *102–3*
AIDS, 245
Ailly, Pierre d' (churchman), 6, 139, 196, 224, 229
Alexander, Magister, 44
Amiens cathedral, 69; *31*
Anastasie (scribe), 12, 17, 42
Andrew, Richard, Dean of York, 251
Andrew, St, 249
Angevin, Thevenin de l' (*libraire*), 68–9, 74, 111 138
Anglicus, Bartholomeus, 134; *Le Livre des propriétés des choses*, 5, 18, 90, 142, 143, 172, 250; *5, 8, 37, 102–3, 124*
Annales School, 2, 3
Anthony, St, 136; *93*
Antichrist, 229
Antiochus, 178; *126*
apothecaries/apothecary shops, 25, 26, 152
apprenticeships, 31, 41–50
Aquinas, Thomas, 178, 179, 213, 230
Aragon, Pierre d', 69
Ariès, Philippe, 6, 44
Aristotle, 230; *De anima*, 220; *De generatione et corruptione*, 80, 177; *Économiques*, 253; *49*; *Éthiques*, 68, 138, 250; *95–6*; *Politiques*, 41, 48, 68, 110–11, 112, 253; *15, 64–5*; *Problemata*, 82
Armagnac, Jacques d', Duc de Nemours, 252
Armagnacs/Orléanists, 12, 109
artes liberales/artes mechanicae, 43, 230
Ashburnham (sale 1901), 251
Asseneth (Potiphar's daughter), 201; *147*
astrology/horoscopes/zodiac, 37, 83, 84, 87; *44*
Atget, Eugène, 29; *10*
Augustine, St, 230; *La Cité de Dieu*, 17, 68, 70, 75, 117, 118, 126, 192, 202, 219, 230, 251; *4, 30, 32, 85, 148, 164, 175*
Aumale, Duc d', 250
Autun, Notre Dame du Chastel, 240
Avignon, cemetery of Champfleury, 193

Babylon, 106
Bacon, Roger, 142
Bal des Ardents, 70
banishment, 105
baptism, 91; *50*
Barrois Collection, 251
Bartholomew, St, 121, 122, 208; *75*
Bataille, Georges, 6, 58, 117
baths, public (*estuves*), 86
Baye, Nicolas de (councillor of Parlement), 40, 112, 114
Bayeux missal-pontifical, 17, 119, 120, 222; *73, 165*. *See also* Appendix
Beauvais, Jehan de (parchment-maker), 11
Becket, Thomas, 103
Bedford, John, Duke of, 12, 159
Bedford Master, *114*
beds, 88, 135, 156, 244
Begue, Jean le, 73, 86
Benedict, St, *119*
Benedict XIII, antipope (Pedro de Lune), 106
Benet, Guillemette, of Montaillou, 215
Berlin MS. *See* Appendix; Machaut
Bernard of Gordon (medical theorist), 142, 148, 178
Berry, Duke of. *See* Jean
Bersuire, Pierre (translator), 99, 112, 249, 252; *66*
Besançon, 'Mirror of Princes', 60
Bible historiale. *See* Desmoulins. *See also* Comestor
bifolia, 14
birds, 54, 56
birth/parturition, 83, 84, 88–95; *48*
Black Death. *See* plague
Bloomington, Ind., missal leaves, 91–3; *52, 155*. *See also* Appendix
Boethius, 142; *101*
Boethius Master, *8*
Boileau, Étienne, *Livre des métiers*, 42
Boniface, St, 121; *74*
Boniface VIII, Pope, 176, 177, 193
Boniface IX, Pope, 106
book trade, 4, 26
bookbinders (*reliures des livres*), 11, 26
Books of Hours, 36, 183, 229, 239
booksellers, 26
Boqueteaux Master (Master of the Little Trees), 45, 48, 55, 145; *16, 18*. *See also* Master of the Bible of Jean de Sy
Bordeaux MS. *See* Livy; Appendix
borders. *See* margins
Boucicaut Master, 43, 101
bouquin/book, 74
Bourgeois de Paris, Le, 104, 155, 211
Bourgot (scribe and illuminator, daughter of Jean le Noir), 12, 42
Bourré, Jean (treasurer of France), 252
Boutonne, Florence la (embroiderer), 72
Bouvet, Honoré, *Arbre des batailles*, 22, 106–8, 251; *61*
breast feeding, 93
Bruges, 56
Brussels MSS. *See* Anglicus; Desmoulins; Appendix
Buffalmacco, *91*
Burgundians, 12, 109
Burgundy, Duke of. *See* Jean sans Peur; Louis d'Anjou; Philippe le Hardi
burial, 91, 105, 176, 182
Bury, Richard de, Bishop, 17; *Philobiblon*, 51, 236

Caboche, Simon (skinner, leader of revolt), 109
Cachelart, Johannes (scribe), 22
Caen, Collection Mansell, 249
Caesar, Julius, 94–5, 200; *55, 144*
calendar, 36
Cambrai cathedral, 229
candles, funeral, 184
Canistris, Opicinis de (illuminator), 83; *43*
cannibalism, 125–6, 230; *83–4*
Capeluche (hangman), 109
carpenter's square, 14, 43; *2*
Castile and Leon, King of, 108
Cauchon, Jean (scribe), 12
Cavarnay, Oudin de (*libraire*), 13, 14, 22; his wife, Jeanne, 22
cemeteries/graveyards, 195, 196, 204. *See also* Avignon; Laon; Paris, Holy Innocents
Ceres, 200
champaignes d'histoires (chequered backgrounds), 131
Champs, Jean des (illuminator), 44
Chantilly MS. *See* Aristotle; Appendix
charity, 124
Charles V, King of France, 40, 60–1, 84, 105, 112, 252, 253
Charles VI, Emperor, 108
Charles VI, King of France, 40, 61–2, 69, 84, 86, 108, 151, 163, 187, 208, 236; *24*
Charles VIII, King of France, 252
Charles, Duke of Orléans, 70, 109
charnage (meat days), 35
charnel houses/*charniers*, 177, 195, 196
Chaucer, Geoffrey, 75
Chicago, Coella Lindsay Ricketts Library, 249
child-killing, 110, 117, 122, 125–6; *83–5*
chômages (prohibited work days), 35
Christ, 67, 79, 148, 155, 208, 212–13, 215, 229, 237; *158, 191*; Christ-child, 93, 208, 236; *157*. *See also* Virgin and Child
Chrysostom, St John, 175
Church Fathers, 50
Cicero, 143
Cimabue, 43
circumcision/prepuce of Christ, 208; *157*
Cité de Dieu, La. *See* Aristotle
Clement VII, Pope, 106
Cleopatra and Mark Anthony, 117; *69*
clocks/clock-time, 35
Coëtivy, Pregent de (royal councillor and bibliophile), 73, 120, 122, 251
coffins, 135, 187
Coincy, Gautier de, 134
colophons, 44, 61, 120
colour/colours, 25–6, 38–9, 45–6, 48, 65, 66, 78, 97, 101, 135–6, 139, 172, 183, 204; *8*
Comestor, Petrus, 78, 99, 250, 251, 253; *Historia scholastica*, 46, 65, 100. *See also* Desmoulins
Compiègne, Antoine de (illuminator), 158, 196; his wife, Oudette, 158
Compostella, Santiago di, 246; *191*
conception, 80, 83, 135, 220
confession/confessors, 150, 229
contemptus mundi tradition, 58, 60
copyists. *See stationnaires*
Corbechon, Jean (translator), 18, 142
Corbie, Arnaud de, 100
corpses, 56, 58, 62, 115, 143, 152, 171–2, 175, 179, 223–4; *111, 124, 167*
Corpus Christi, Feast of, 212; *156*
Cosmas, St, 149, 150; *107*
Council of Vienne, 105
'Court of Love', 78, 165
cremation, 187
Cross, the True, 208, 249; *155*
crucifixes/crucifixion, 237, 239; *182*
cultures: Frankish, Roman, Jewish, 99, 102
curfew, 35

Damian, St, 149, 150; *107*
Danse macabre (Dance of the Dead), 110, 132, 158, 195; *113*
Dante, 26, 115, 143
David, King, 150, 193
Davy, Pierre, mother of, 42
days: blue/red/black/gold letter, 37, 196
death/Death, 80, 112, 133–8, 141, 142, 150, 156–67, 172, 219; *89, 90, 114, 162–4*
decay/decomposition/rot, 65, 142, 171–9, 188, 195, 213, 224
Deguileville, Guillaume de, *Pèlerinages*, 13-17, 21, 22, 241, 250, 252; *184*; *Pèlerinage de l'âme*, 24, 158, 200, 219, 225; *7, 162–3, 167–8, 173, 192*; *Pèlerinage de Jésus-Christ*, 75, 212, 213, 227, 246; *34, 157–8, 172, 191*; *Pèlerinage de vie humaine*, 22, 23, 86, 91, 133, 138, 139–41, 160, 162, 219, 225, 240, 244; *1, 2, 6, 46, 50, 89, 90, 94, 97, 99, 100, 115, 120, 166, 169–70*
demon/devil, 219, 233, 241; *93*
Denis, St, 118–19, 198; *72–3*
Derrida, Jacques, 6, 41, 179, 215
Deschamps, Eustache, 6, 38, 51, 60, 244; *Lay de la fragilité humaine*, 3, 58, 60–2, 85, 86, 88, 101, 122–3, 126, 141, 143, 162–3, 171, 192, 211, 233, 234, 253; *23–7, 40, 45, 47–8, 79, 80, 86, 98, 116, 118, 122, 130, 139, 176–7, 179, 181*
Desmoulins, Guyart (translator), *Bible historiale*, 5, 22, 44, 45, 46, 47, 65, 98–9, 100, 123, 250, 251, 253; *16, 17, 29, 56, 81, 104–6*. *See also* Comester
Diocres, Raymond, 197
dismemberment, 121, 176
Dives and Lazarus the leper, 227–8; *171–2*
Doche, Jean (translator), 82
doctors, 150, 152; *108*
Domitian, Emperor, 129
'double lay', 62
Duchie, Jacques, 73
Durandus, G., Bishop, *Rational des divins offices*, 179, 182, 204, 252; *150, 180*
Durrieu, Paul, 5
dynasties: Merovingian, Carolingian, Capetian, 102

Elzear of Sabran, St, *135*
emptiness, medieval abhorance of, 15–17, 104
enlumineurs/historiateurs (illuminators), 11, 15, 26, 30, 37, 43, 45, 50, 54
escriptvains/escrivains (scribes), 11
Eucharist, 155
Eve, 93. *See also* Adam and Eve
evil eye, 137
executions, 104, 118, 151
exegesis, 50, 136
exemplars. *See* models

Faits des romains. *See* Orosius
Fall, the, 58, 52, 66, 68, 73, 75, 138, 220
famines, 124–5
female. *See* women
Fèvre, Godefroy le (duke's treasurer), 39
figures, 9, 14
filth/stink, 84–6
Flamel, Nicolas (scribe and alchemist), 170, 174; *125*; his wife, Pernelle, 170
Flanders, 109
Foix, Count of, 187; his son, Gaston, 188
Foucault, Michel, 13, 51, 68, 112, 149
Fournival, Richard de, 98
François, Regnault (scribe), 170
French Missal, 212
Froissart Chronicles, 108
frontispieces, 18, 21, 61; *6, 20–1, 32, 57, 66, 102, 104, 162*
funerals, 158, 186–7, 239; *130–1; 133*

Gaignières, Roger de, 198

Galen, 142
genealogy, 102
Gerson, Jean, preacher, Chancellor of University of Paris, 37, 105, 118, 165, 200, 234
Giac, Pierre de, Chancellor, 70
gibbets, 104, 105
Gilberti, Petrus, 54, 148, 250; *104–5*
Giles of Rome, 94
Giotto, 43
gisants (lying figures), 193, 198, 202
gold leaf, 45, 48, 172
Golden Legend, 93; *54*
goldsmiths, 26, 43
Golein, Jean (translator), 204, 252
Grace Dieu, 86, 134, 141; *90, 99, 120, 166*
Grandes Chroniques de France, 58, 99, 101, 102–3, 104, 105, 106–8, 118, 120, 188, 189; *57–60, 134. See also* Appendix: London; Lyons; Paris
Grange, Jean de la, Cardinal, Bishop of Amiens, 69, 174
Gregory the Great, Pope and St, 204; *187*
grisaille, 100, 136
Guelin, Robin (maker of *vignettes*), 38
Guerre, Martin, 3
Guibert of Nogent, 41
guide letters, 13
guilds, 25, 42, 56, 131, 187, 237, 239
Guiron le courtois, 72, 145; *39. See also* Appendix: Paris

Hamilton, Duke of, 249
Hamlet, 177
'hands', 4, 5, 22
Hannibal, 186
Harcigny, Guillaume de, 150, 172, 174; *123*
Harcourt, Louis d', Bishop, 249
Hasdrubal, 114; *66*
Heaven, 219, 228, 231
Helena, St, 208; *155*
Hell, 215, 219, 228, 231, 232; *177*
Henry of Gaunt, 230
Henry of Langestein (theologian), 37
heraldry, 51, 108
Herberay, Nicholas, de, 253
hermaphrodites, 78
Herod, King, 150, 196; *108*
Hesdin, Jacquemart de (painter and illuminator), 76, 128–9, 254
Hesdin, Simon de (translator), 100, 114, 117, 184, 253
Hilary of Poitiers, St and Bishop, 217; *160*
Histoire ancienne jusqu'à César. See Orosius
Histoire de la Bible. See Valenciennes
Histoire romaine. See Livy
histoires, 2, 9, 99, 101
historieurs, 14, 99
Holbein, Hans, 212
horizontal corpse, 62–3, 67, 95, 212
hours, liturgical, 34–5
Huizinga, Johan, 1, 196, 244
humoral dispositions, 5
Hundred Years War, 102, 108, 109

idols/idolatry, 192–211
illness, 149–55
illuminators. *See enlumineurs*
images. *See* simulacra
immaculate conception, 93
immortality of soul, 215
Innocent III, Pope. *See* Segni
intercourse/coitus/copulation, 82, 135–6, 189, 222; *41*
Isabeau de Bavaria (consort of Charles VI), 78, 84, 102, 143
Isidore of Seville, 178

Jacob, 193; *18, 140*
Jacques (grandson of Louis de Bourbon), 114, 252
James, St, 246
Jean I de Foix, 40, 253
Jean le Bon, King of France, 112
Jean of Garland (grammarian), 33
Jean sans Peur, Duke of Burgundy, 129, 145
Jean, Duke of Berry, 15, 40, 86, 118, 204, 250, 252; his wife, 70
Jeanne de Bourbon (consort of Charles V), 84, 143
Jeanne de Bourgogne (consort of Philippe VI of Valois), 100, 165
Jeanne de Navarre (consort of Henry IV of England), 112, 252
Jeremiah, Prophet, 63; *25*
Jerome, St, 77; *19*
Jerusalem, 205
Jesse, Tree of, 63
Jews, 104, 124, 188, 190–1, 195, 204
Joachim of Fiore, 229
Job, 65–6, 123, 154; *26, 29, 81, 110*
John of Holland, 76, 128
John of Jandun, 26
John the Baptist, St, 193, 197, 205, 208; *141*
John the Evangelist, St, 208, 232
John XXII, Pope, 217
Joseph, prophet, 193; *140*
Joseph of Arimathea, 213
Juan of Monzon, 93
Judith and Holofernes, 98–9; *56*
Julien, St, 122; *78*

La Chaise Dieu, Abbey of, *113*
Laius, King of Thebes, 75
Laon, cemetery of the Cordeliers, 172
Laon, Colart de (painter), 39, 54, 70, 131, 187, 198
Last Judgement, 179, 224–5, 229–36; *174–6*
Latin, 27, 31, 50, 60, 69, 70
Launay, Jean de (sculptor), *31*
Lawrence, St, 122
Lay de la fragilité humaine. See Deschamps
Lazare, St, 188
Lazarus, 182, 215, 217, 218; *159*
Lazarus the leper, *173. See also* Dives and Lazarus
Le Coq, Robert (royal secretary), 40
Le Fèvre, Jean (jurist and poet), 6, 51, 54, 158, 167
Legrand, Jacques (monk), 165, 182
Leiden MS. *See* Appendix; Deguileville
Lemallier (sale 1907), 249
Lendit fair, 13
lepers/leprosy, 188–9; *134–5*
lettre bâtarde (cursive script), 100
lettres, grandes and *petite*, 38, 44, 99
Lewis the Great, King of Hungary, 108
liber/livre, 74
libraires (MS coordinators), 12, 13, 14–15, 22, 26
libraires jurés (official booksellers), 12
libraries, 12, 26–7, 39, 70–2, 73
life expectancy, 40, 140, 143
Limbourg brothers (Paul, Jean and Herman Malouel), 4, 15, 73, 101, 197, 240; *187*
line-endings (*versets*), 38, 121
literacy, 43
liturgical books (pontificals, missals, psalters), 36, 119–20, 239
Livre des métiers. See Boileau
Livre des propriétés des choses. See Anglicus
Livy (Titus Livius), *Histoire romaine*, 4, 54, 55–6, 99, 112, 114, 186, 187, 249, 252; *20–2, 66–7, 131*
Logos, 202
Lollards, 192, 243
Lombard, Peter, 50, 230
London Book of Hours, 183, 229, 231, 237, 240; *128, 174, 182. See also* Appendix
London MSS. *See Grandes Chroniques de France*; London Book of Hours; Vincent of Beauvais; Appendix
Louis, Duke of Orléans (formerly of Touraine), 15, 27, 39, 40, 60, 68–70, 73, 75, 78, 84, 109, 111, 118, 129, 131, 158, 165, 167, 198, 208, 250, 251, 253; *31–2, 44, 87, 143*
Louis, St, King of France, 198

Louis I d'Anjou, Duke of Burgundy, 40, 108, 253
Louis VI, King of France, 103
Loypeau, Étienne de, Bishop of Luçon, 17, 40, 93, 249
Lubomirsky, Alexander, 254
Lucretia and Tarquin, 117; *70*
Lydgate, John, 243; *189*
Lyons *Miroir historial*, 16
Lyons MS. *See Grandes Chroniques de France*; Appendix
Lyra, Nicolas de, *Postilla litteralis super Biblia*, 31, 34, 50, 78, 253; *12, 19, 36*

Macarius, St, 83; *42*
Maccabees, Book of, 178
Macedonia, 106
Machaut, Guillaume de, *Dit du lion*, 5, 249
Magnus, Albertus, 142
Maillotins, 104
male. *See* men
Malet, Guillaume, 102
Mallet, Gilles (librarian), 70
Manchester breviary, 36, 154, 205–8, 212; *14, 109–10, 153–4, 156, 171*. *See also* Appendix
Marcel, Étienne, 102, 112
Marcienne, St, 121–2
Mares, Jean des, 104
Margaret, St, 143
margins, 5, 21, 31, 54, 148; *1, 4, 5, 11, 102, 104–5*
Marie de Bourbon, 250
'Marmousets', 69
Marseilles, church of Saint Victor, 195
Marshall, William (Guillaume le Maréchal), 245
Martha, 215
Martial of Limoges, St, *186*
Martin, St, 208
Martini, Simone, 67
Mary of Egypt, St, 192; *138*
Marys, the three, 212–13. *See also* Virgin Mary
mass. *See* sacraments
Massa, Michael de, Friar, 35
Massacre of the Innocents, 126, 196; *142*
Master Honoré, 45
Master of Berry's Cleres Femmes, 250; *104*
Master of BN fr. 810, 252, 253
Master of Luçon, 249
Master of the Bible of Jean de Sy, 102, 253; *16, 18*. *See also* Boqueteaux Master
Master of the Cité des Dames, 250; *105*
Master of the Coronation of Charles V, 253
Master of the Épître d'Othéa, 43
Master of the Little Trees. *See* Boqueteaux Master
Master of the Livre du Sacre, 48, 253
Master of the Roi Modus, 252
Master of the St George Codex, 67; *28*
master/*magister*/*maistre*, 44–5
Maximus, Valerius, *Faits et dits mémorables*, 100, 114, 117, 124, 184, 187, 200, 253; *70, 82, 132–3, 145–6*
Medallion Master, 253
medical books, 138
men/male, 78, 79, 87, 89, 90, 109, 117, 121; *49*
Menagier de Paris, Le, 34, 38
menstruation, 84, 189
Menusiers (carpenters' guild), 187
Metellus, Q., 187; *133*
Metz, Guillibert de (*libraire*), 73
Mezières, Philippe de (councillor), 105
Michael, St, 158, 219, 241, 249
midwives, 89, 90
Milan, Duke of, 69, 152
Miroir historial. *See* Vincent of Beauvais. *See also* Appendix: London; Paris
misogyny, 51, 84, 117, 135
modelbooks, 45, 76, 104
models/exemplars, 14, 15, 17, 38, 68, 70, 112, 138

Molinet, Jean (poet), 143
Mondeville, Henri de (physician), 149, 187
money, 38–9
Monstrelet (chronicler), 126
Montaigu, Jean de (king's financier), 100, 105, 112
Montaillou, France, 3, 208
Montbaston, Jeanne de (scribe and illuminator), 12, 42
Montbaston, Richard de (artisan), 42
Montet, Regnault du (*grand libraire* and bookseller), 29, 33
Montragoux, Aimery de (notary), 184
Morgan, J. P., 251
Moses, 193
mothers, 89, 90–5, 220
mourners/mourning, 115, 184, 187, 188

names, 13, 21, 51–5. *See also* 'hands'
Nangis, Guillaume de, 102
Nativity, 93; *51*
Nebuchadnezzar, 62
Neckham, Alexander, 134
Nero, Emperor, 93, 117; *54*
'New Historians', 2
New York MSS. *See* Bouvet; Valenciennes; Appendix
Nicolas of Clamanges, 229
Nicopolis, 108
nightwatch, 30, 35
nightwork, 35, 37
Nizières, Jean de (illuminator), 21, 33, 73, 144, 252
nobody/*nemo*, 21; *40*
Noir, Jean le (court artist), 31
nothing/*nihil*, 13–24, 56, 104; *1, 3*

Oedipus and Polybus, 75; *35*
Office of the Dead, 154, 159, 182, 184, 188, 229, 232, 241; *127–9, 190*
old age, 139–48
Oresme, Nicole (translator), 48, 90, 110, 250, 253
Orléans, Duke of. *See* Charles; Louis
Orléans, Raoulet d' (scribe), 102, 120, 138
Orliens, Agnes d' (parchment-maker), 11
Orosius, *Les Faits des romains*, 99, 252; *55, 144*; *Histoire ancienne jusqu'à César*, 31, 33, 99, 117, 252; *35, 63*; *Histoire universelle*, 99
Orosius Master (illuminator), 33
Ovid, 178
Oxford MS. *See Questiones on the Decretals*; Appendix

page (*pagina*), 17
parchment-makers (*parcheminiers*), 26, 29
parchment (*parchemin*), 29
Paris, map, *9*; Île de la Cité, 26; Latin Quarter, 29, 35; Left Bank, 26; *9*; Right Bank, 26
Boulevard Saint Germain (Rue du Foin), 29; Place Maubert, 239; Grand Pont, 26; Pont Saint Michel, 184; Rue Erembourth de Brie (Rue Boutebrie, Rue des Enlumineurs), 11, 27–9; *9*; Rue Neuve Notre Dame, 12, 26; Rue de la Parcheminerie (Rue aux Écrivains), 11, 27–9, 196; *9*; Rue de la Poterne, 70; Rue des Prêtres Saint Séverin, 29; *10*; Rue des Prouvelles, 73; Rue Vielle du Temple, 129
Cathedral of Notre Dame, 118, 136, 190, 208; Sainte Chapelle, 198; Saint Germain des Prés, 26; Saint Jacques de la Boucherie, 170; Saint Merry (Merri), 22; Saint Martin des Champs, 26; church and parish of Saint Séverin, 11, 26, 29, 158, 167, 170, 196, 208, 227; *9*; Saint Victor, 26; Library of Saint Victor, 253
Hôtel Dieu (hospital), 57, 150; Saint Lazare (leprosaria), 188; Cemetery of the Holy Innocents, 57, 124, 132, 158, 170, 195–6
Palais du Louvre, 12, 27, 105; Tour de la Faconnerie, 27; Palais Royale, 27, 35, 239; Chambre des Comptes, 27; Parlement, 27, 124, 239; Tour de l'Horloge, 35; Châtelet, 26, 104, 122; Hôtel Barbette, 129; Hôtel Saint Pol, 27, 70
University of Paris, 26, 43, 152; *9*; Sorbonne, 12, 26, 31;

College of Dormans-Beauvais, 37–8; College of Maître Gervais, 30; Collège de Presles, 68; Convent of the Célestins, 39, 69-70, 198; *143*; Convent of the Cordeliers, 31; Convent of the Mathurins, 11, 29, 30; Halles aux Parchemins, 11; Les Halles, 26
Paris, Bishop of, 39
Paris, Provost of, 26
Paris breviary, 36; *119, 121, 127, 142*. *See also* Appendix
Paris MSS. *See* Aristotle; Augustine; Paris breviary; Comestor; Deguileville; Deschamps; Durandus; *Grandes Chroniques de France*; *Guiron le courtois*; Livy; Lyra; Orosius; Vincent of Beauvais; Appendix
Paul, St, 117, 230; *71*
Pavia, Visconti Library, 251
Peirin de Dijon, 39
Pèlerinages. *See* Deguileville
Pergamum, 29
personifications, 123, 139–41, 162; *94–101, 120 150*
Peter, St, 190; *72*
Philip, St, 118
Philippe le Bon, Duke of Burgundy, 240, 251
Philippe le Hardi, Duke of Burgundy, 15, 40, 69, 102, 108, 109, 145, 240, 250
Philippe IV, King of France, 104, 198
Philippe V, King of France, 188
Philippe VI of Valois, King of France, 100, 152, 165
Pierre/Perrin, 30, 40
pigments. *See* colours
Pisa, Campo Santo, 134, 136; *91*
Pizan, Christine de, 3, 60, 167; *Épître d'Othéa*, 73
plague, 31, 57, 124, 132, 152–5; *187*
Poitiers, 128
Pompey and his wife, Julie, 217; *161*
portraits d'encre, 34, 100
Portugal, King of, 108
prefiguration/prototype, 211, 218
Presles, Raoul de (translator), 68, 74, 230, 252
Proverbs, Book of, 46, 123
Pseudo-Aristotle, *Livres d'économiques*, 48, 90
Pseudo-Jacquemart (illuminator), 68, 251
Pucelle, Jean, 4, 54, 97
Puiseux, Colinet de, 104
Purgatory, 215, 224–8; *168*

Questiones on the Decretals, 251

Rais, Gilles de (child-murderer), 122
Rapondi, Jacques (*libraire* and merchant), 15, 18
Rational des divins offices. *See* Durandus
Raussin, L. J., 250
reading stands/wheels, 50, 72, 112
rebuses, 54, 55, 56
Reformation, 243
reinterment, 193, 195, 197
relics/reliquaries, 118–19, 172, 192–211, 239; *154*
Remiet, Pierre, unrecorded birth and death dates, 8; named in MSS, 13–14, 30, 31–3, 39; *1, 11*; existence of family, 30; tax records establishing residence, 27; location of workshop, 30; apprenticeship, 44; 'master', 45; 'masterpiece', 55; most important patron, 70; final appearance, in margins, 5, 148; *105*
Remiet/*ramier*/*ramiet*, 54
Remiet/Remiot/Remy/Remigius, 30
Renaut. *See* Montet
requiem/requiem mass, 179–92
resurrection, 217–18, 230, 239
Rheims cathedral, 119
Richard the Franciscan, Brother, 195
rigor mortis, 104
Rohan Master, 241; *184, 188*
Rolin, Nicolas, Chancellor of Burgundy, 40, 240, 250; *185*
Roman Breviary, 182
Roman de la Rose, 23, 80, 167; *41*
Romans and Cimbrians, 110
Rome, 106; Champs des Mars, 200
Roosebeke, Battle of, 109

sacraments, 105, 225; last sacraments, 91, 105, 157
Saint Denis, Abbey of, 99, 102, 118–19, 198, 208
saints/martyrs, 117–22, 178–9, 205, 230
Salmon, Pierre (king's biographer), 152
Schism, Great, 106, 229
schools, 43
scribes. *See escriptvains; libraires*
scythes, 135, 136
Segni, Lotario dei (Pope Innocent III), *De miseria condicionis humane*, 60, 88, 162, 171, 233
Seneca, 117; *13*
Servius, Tullie, daughter of, 55; *22*
Séverin, St, 208
Sicambria, 102
signatures, 54
signs, house and street, 29, 119, 138, 239
Simon of Corvino (doctor), 134
simulacra/images, 186–7, 192, 200, 201–2, 222; *148*
Sinderesis (worm of conscience), 158
Sins, Seven Deadly. *See* Vices
social groups, 30, 108, 110–12, 162, 231–2; *64–5*
Socrates and Plato, 41, 43; *15*
Soissons MS. *See* Comestor; Desmoulins; Appendix
Solomon, King, 46, 193; *16*; and Roboam, 46
soul/*anima*, 214–23, 224, 229, 241; *162–6*
spectacles, 145
stationnaires (text copyists), 12
Stephen, St, 205; *153*
suicide, 117
Supicius (high priest), 200
Sy, Jean de (translator), 47, 102

taille. *See* taxes
tapestry weavers, 42
taxes, 27, 30, 40
Temple, Raymond du (architect), 70
temporale (church-time), 36
Theophilus, 13
Thomas, St, 143
Three Living and Three Dead, 29, 138, 195, 227
Throne of Mercy, 239; *183*
Tobias, 47; *17*
Tobit, Book of, 47; *17*
toilets, 86
Tourette, Elie de (president of Parlement), 124
Trajan, Emperor, 115; *68*
transi/*transi* tombs, 125, 150, 172, 174, 175, 202, 211–12, 213
trees, 63, 67, 68, 73, 75, 86–7, 106, 108, 220; *47, 61*; 'little trees', 44, 54; Tree of Good and Evil, 58, 88; Tree of Life, 68, 106; *30*; 'tree of mourning', 106–8, 109, 110. *See also* Jesse, Tree of
Trevou, Henri de (scribe), 102
Troislivres, Joachim (illuminator), 38
Trojan origins of France, 99, 102, 106, 112; *57*
Troyes MS. *See* Maximus; Appendix
Turks/Saracens, 108; *62*
typology, 101

Urban V, Pope, 195
Urban VI, Pope, 106

Valenciennes, Hermann de, *Histoire de la Bible*, 100, 135, 150, 189, 190, 193, 215, 251; *92, 108, 136–7, 140–1, 159*
Valentina Visconti (consort of Louis, Duke of Orléans), 69, 72, 163–5, 198
Van Eyck, Jan, 240; *185*
vanitas mundi, 114
Vaux, Guillaume de (procurer of Parlement), 157
veiling face of dead, 183, 187

vellum, 29, 63
vermin, 86, 172, 177–8
Vices, 93, 123, 138, 160–2, 227; *115–16*
Vienna MS, 93. *See also* Appendix
Vigevano, Guido da (doctor), 152
Vigils of the Dead, 184
vignettes, 12, 17, 18, 37, 38, 48, 100
Vignay, Jean de (translator), 100, 250, 251, 252
Villars, Guillaume de (bookbinder), 72
Villon, François, 154
Vincent, St, 205; *152*
Vincent of Beauvais, Friar, *Miroir historial*, 34, 50, 68, 78, 93, 100, 101, 115, 117, 118, 120, 125, 156, 165, 233; *3, 13, 33, 38, 42, 53, 62, 68–9, 71–2, 74–8, 83–4, 88, 93, 107, 112, 117, 126, 138, 147, 149, 151–2, 160, 178, 186*. *See also* Appendix: London; Paris
Virelay, Jean (illuminator), 239
Virgil Master, 21, 144, 250, 252, 253
Virgin Mary, 93, 156, 172, 189, 202–4, 208, 233, 249; *52, 136–7, 151, 178, 185*; and Child, 234–6, 240; *149, 181*; and Joseph, 101. *See also* Marys, the three
Virtues, 138, 225–7
Vital, St, 121, 122; *76*

wars, 106, 108, 109, 125
wills/testaments, 157–8
winding-sheets, 90
women/female, 42, 43, 62, 77, 78, 79, 80, 87, 90, 93, 109, 115, 121, 205; *49*
working practices, 4
workshops, 22, 30

Yolande of Aragon, Duchess, 241

zodiac. *See* astrology
Zosimas the hermit, 192